RAIN, MUD & SWAMPS

31st MISSOURI VOLUNTEER INFANTRY REGIMENT

MARCHING THROUGH THE SOUTH DURING THE
CIVIL WAR WITH GENERAL WILLIAM T. SHERMAN

BY GARY L. SCHEEL

1

COVER DESIGNED BY DANIEL MARTIN

FIRST PRINTING
3,000 COPIES, JULY 1998

PRINTED IN THE U. S. A.
BY:
PLUS COMMUNICATIONS
2828 BRANNON AVENUE
SAINT LOUIS, MISSOURI 63139

If you are interested in additional copies of this book, they are
available by writing to:
Gary L. Scheel
P.O. Box 312
Pacific, Missouri 63069

ACKNOWLEDGMENTS

I would like to take this opportunity to thank my wife, Mary for her patience while I spent countless hours typing and dragging her to the battlefields, cemeteries and resource areas to find materials that are found within. I also would like to thank my Mom for going along to the battlefields when my wife wouldn't or couldn't go.

I have been working on this book since April 26, 1992. It has been an enjoyable time for me. I would also like to thank my Mom's sisters who have shared information with me that got me started in the research of this book. Aunt Pat who gave Mom information on Fielding Jenkins Smith and his Civil War service. Aunt Jean for always looking for information and going with Mom and me to show us where to go in Jefferson City and Columbia, Missouri. And to Aunt Joan who has provided some interesting maps and written materials for my reading.

When Mom gave the information on my great-great-Grandfather I didn't know that I even had an ancestor who had served in the Civil War. In trying to find information on if he and the 31st Missouri Infantry had fought in any battles I became interested in writing a book. Another reason I wrote the book is because there is not that much information on Missouri Regiments in book form. Missouri furnished its share of regiments, both north and south, during the war. Most of the books that I have found dealt with the Southern side or were histories of the border wars or guerrilla war in Missouri.

I would also like to thank my daughter Stephanie Robinson who took my rough draft, and I mean rough, and corrected my punctuation, grammer and spelling. She informed me that I cannot write like I talk.

I would also like to thank my good friend, Anthony Gunn. He read the whole book and made some improvements and constructive criticism that made the reading easier. And I would like to thank another good friend, Ron Thiemann. He loaned me his Civil War Atlas and has let me keep it for a long time. I would also call him when I was confused about a term or an action and he could describe what it was. He has been a Civil War Re-enactor for almost twenty years and he has let me read some of his books.

I would also like to thank the staff at the Missouri Historical Society Library in Saint Louis who with their knowledge and willingness to help, was very much appreciated by a first timer who had never researched material for a book before. Everywhere I went the people at the archives, libraries and record centers from States like Georgia, Tennessee, Illinois, Mississippi, Oklahoma, Arkansas and Missouri were friendly and helpful.

But most of all I would like to thank God who has given me salvation by His grace through His Son, Jesus Christ and the Holy Spirit who has been with me on all my trips and protected me and those with me from harm.

TABLE OF CONTENTS

PICTURES

MAPS

CHAPTER ONE:
THE BIRTH AND INFANCY OF THE 31st MISSOURI VOLUNTEER INFANTRY REGIMENT

"On the 11th of July 1862, the Governor of Missouri responded to a call of the President for 300,000 more troops, in the tone and spirit of a patriot."(1) In the "Governor's Proclamation" of July 11, the Governor was "requested to raise as soon as practicable for the United States service, for three years or during the war, four regiments of infantry, being a part of the quota of the State under the call of the President."(2) From this call came the Blair Brigade (Brigadier General Francis P. Blair Jr.), which consisted of Colonel Thomas Fletcher's Excelsior Zouaves (the 31st Missouri Infantry) "already number more than 500 Strong, and are mustering at Benton Barracks."(3) In all, General Blair raised seven regiments. The 31st Missouri Infantry was recruited from the State of Missouri in different counties, though mostly from the eastern region. The counties, and number of soldiers enlisted from each of these counties were: "Butler furnished thirty-four men, Calloway furnished one man, Carter furnished twenty-six men, Crawford furnished eighteen men, Franklin furnished seventy-four men, Gasconade furnished eighty-six men, Iron furnished eleven men, Jefferson furnished one-hundred and thirty-one men, Knox furnished one man, Montgomery furnished twenty-seven men, Monroe furnished two men, Reynolds furnished two men, Ripley furnished eleven men, Saint Charles furnished two men, Saint Francois furnished eight men, Saint Louis furnished one-hundred and seventeen, Stoddard furnished two men, Warren furnished thirty men, Washington furnished two hundred and seven men, Wayne furnished one hundred and one men and there were sixteen men at large who joined the Regiment giving a total of nine hundred and seven men."(4) They came from farms, small communities and from big cities such as Saint Louis. Most often they were young men from farming areas throughout the eastern part of Missouri. Some of the towns the soldiers were recruited from were: Ironton, Moselle, Washington, Cuba, Dutzow, Caledonia, Desoto, Canaan, Greenville,

Potosi and other communities. On September 30,1862 General Order # 5 was issued in Saint Louis District it states,

"1. The regiments in this district serving south of Saint Louis are brigaded as follows, First Regiment Infantry Missouri State Militia (Gray's), Thirty-first Volunteers (Fletchers) Twenty-ninth Volunteers, (Cavender's) form the nucleus of the First Brigade. The Fifth Regiment Infantry Volunteers, Twenty-fourth Regiment (Boyds), Twenty-Third Iowa (Dewey's temporarily Harding's) Regiment form a nucleous for the Second Brigade.

3. The cavalry- First Wisconsin, Twelfth Missouri State Militia and Thirteenth Illinois-

By order of Brigadier-General Davidson:

James A Greason

Lieutenant and Acting Adjutant General"(5)

The 31st Missouri Infantry was organized in Saint Louis, Carondelet and Ironton, from August 11 to October 7, 1862. They were recruited, as stated above, as the Excelsior Zouaves. The Zouaves were fashioned after the elite French light infantry in the French Army. Units such as the 5th New York Zouaves or Duryee Zouaves were one of the better known Zouave units in the Union Army. Some of the Zouaves wore red baggy trousers, or pantaloons, tucked into high gaiters, or leggings, others wore light blue trousers with red trimming down the legs. Some like the 11th New York Zouaves wore a red kepi, blue Zouave jacket with yellow trimmings or a blue cutaway jacket with red trim some of the jackets having buttons and some without. Whatever their distinctive taste the Zouaves usually wore bright colored clothing. The 114th Pennsylvania Volunteer's wore their Zouaves uniform throughout the war with few changes. They wore the red kepi instead of the usual fez, which was the common headgear of the Zouaves. The fez was, as best as I can describe it, looked like a stocking cap with a tassle on the top and was usually red. For dress occasions they would wear a turban around the fez. The Confederates also had their Zouaves such as the Louisiana Tiger Zouaves and the 1st Battalion Louisiana Zouaves. I am uncertain whether the 31st Missouri Regiment was ever dressed in the Zouave uniform I have not seen anything to confirm this. During it's history, it had approximately one thousand men on its roll at one time or another. During it's approximate three years of service, the regiment lost four Officers and fifty-one Enlisted men who were killed or mortally wounded and 228 Enlisted men by disease for a total of 283.

The commanding officer of the 31st Missouri was Colonel Thomas Clement Fletcher. In the book "The Messages and Proclomations of the Govenors of the State of Missouri, Volume IV Pages 46 & 47" records the following information on Colonel Fletcher,

"In the summer of 1862, at the request of the President, he recruited the 31st Missouri Infantry and it is due to his personal character that most of the Union men of Jefferson County were on the roster of the 31st, and among them were his two brothers, William and Carrol. He was confined in Libby Prison until his exchange in May 1863. On the night preceeding the battle of Dallas, Georgia in the Atlanta Campaign, after a long march with his brigade in the rain, Colonel Fletcher contracted a severe cold, which settled in his back, so that he was unable to mount his horse. He was advised to return home, by the regimental surgeon, and did so, his first visit to his loved ones in nearly two years.

It was while commanding a brigade in the Army of the Tennessee, in the "March to the Sea," that he was nominated by the Republican party as the candidate for Governor and at the election in November 1864, he was elected by a large majority."(6)

He was a lawyer prior to the war and an early supporter of President Lincoln. He had also been involved in the formation of the Republican Party and attended the 1860 convention. Prior to becoming the commander of the 31st Missouri, he was the state's provost-marshal. He was wounded and captured at the Battle of Chickasaw Bayou, this was the regiments first battle, and was exchanged and returned to service in time to participate in the Vicksburg Campaign. He later would return to Missouri and form the 47th Missouri Infantry, which spent the remainder of the war in the Missouri with notable distinction at the Battle of Pilot Knob and in the 1864 invasion of General Sterling Price's army into Missouri. He received a brevet of Brigadier General of Volunteers for gallant services in this action. He resigned his commission on November 18, 1864 and was inaugurated on March 13, 1865 as Governor of Missouri, and became part of the radical Republican state government after the war. He was governor from 1865 through 1869.

10

He died in 1899 and is buried at Calvary Cemetery in Saint Louis, Missouri.

After the war Colonel Fletcher was in an organization called the Society of the Army of the Tennessee, which was an organization of officers of the Army of the Tennessee. The 31st Missouri Infantry Regiment was in this army throughout its military existence from its involvement in its first battle until it was mustered out in June 1865. While at the Reunion of the Society of the Army of the Tennessee, Colonel Fletcher made a speech in answer to a toast of "What we fought for." It is quoted in its entirety in the following paragraphs. He made this speech at Cleveland, Ohio on October 18th, 1883.

"Mr. Chairman:

To determine the question as to whether all the powers of government, not specifically conferred on the national government or on the states by the constitution, were reserved to the national or the state governments was what the war of the rebellion was about. We asserted that ours was a government by the people and of the people, and that all reserved powers—all powers not expressly conferred on the states could only be exercised by the people through the machinery of their national government. We claimed that the national authority was supreme, and so when the flag of the stars and stripes which symbolized the national authority was fired upon, we took arms to uphold that authority and did vindicate it by arms, and finally waved the emblem of that authority in victory over every political subdivision of the Republic, and made it the emblem of national supremacy forever.

But it was not merely to settle an abstract principle in government that called more than 1,000,000 men to arms—that 400,000 lives of loyal men was sacrificed and 300,000 patriotic soldiers and sailors were maimed and crippled for life, and 1,000,000 widows, mothers and orphans were left to mourn the loved ones who never returned, and more than 4,000,000,000 dollars were expended. It was for the preservation and perfecting of the form, and establishment of the necessary powers of government over a territory wherein providence had combined all the requiste conditions for the achievement of a grander and surer civilization; a higher and better

11

destiny than man had elsewhere attained in all the ages. It was to spread all over every one of the 4,000,000 square miles, over which the flag of the Republic waves, perfect security to every human being of life, liberty and prosperity; that broadest and highest liberty of the individual consistent with the safety and well being of the community. It was to found securely forever, here upon this continent, a government, by the people, of supreme authority over an area of extent of territory and with capabilities for sustaining and profitably maintaining a population sufficient to make it the most powerful nation on earth. It was to dedicate to Liberty and self-government a home extending from the Bay of Fundy to SanDiego; from the reefs of Florida to Cape Flattery. It was for this we fought.

Behold now this land of beauty and grandeur! Its ocean girt shores; its mountains and plains; its valleys and forests; its flocks and herds; its cities and villages reaching away from ocean to ocean; its grain fields of the North and cotton fields of the South; its varied, valuable and extensive resources; its 4,008,000 farms producing 2,300,000,000 bushels of grain; exporting annually 200,000,000 dollars worth of bread stuff; $225,000,000 worth of cotton, and over $700,000,000 of other exports; who can estimate its capacity for sustaining population? We fought to give this country to the untold millions of soldiers who shall come after us, as a bounty for their services in the cause of mankind. We fought to give them a country in which the yield of precious metals and the value of the products of manufactures exceeds that of any country in the world, and we made for them a nation of peace, and yet of power the per cent of whose income applied to the support of the army is less than that of any nation on earth.

We point to the Republic to-night as our trophy—its 110,000 miles of rail road, 22,000 miles of interior navigable rivers and canals, its water ways of great lakes, gulfs and sounds; its manufactures, which light up the shores of the great rivers, the smoke and fire of which ascend, a pillar of cloud by day and a pillar of fire by night, to lead on the 800,000 liberty-loving, enterprising people, who in a single year came to us from foreign

12

lands to find homes for themselves and their posterity. The victory of the national forces made us a nation, able to pay its debts and to pension its soldiers.

The victory was for all time and for all people; beneath the fostering care of the Republic, as made by our victory, the arts and sciences will know unprecedented progress. Here, in these great altitudes, and along the mighty river, surrounded by majestic scenery—the widespread book of nature—there will be developed, by the mingling of the races which cluster beneath our flag, the highest type of physical man that the world ever saw, and from the school house on every hill top will go forth into the field of practical life these strong men, crowned with the power of education, to enlist for life in the great advancing army of human progress, until the nation shall become the advance guard of that grand army to lead on mankind in the march to that higher and better civilization of which the philosopher dreamed, and for which the soul of man has yearned since the dawn of civilization.

It ought to make and did make this Republic to be the triumphal arch of Liberty, set up and keyed to span one-third of the land surface of the circumference of the globe, and to stand forever, like the rainbow of God's promise to the people of the whole world, that self government shall never be destroyed from the earth.

That is what we fought for, and that is what we won in the fight."(7)

The executive officer was Lieutenant Colonel Samuel Parsons Simpson, who later became the commander of the regiment after the return of Colonel Fletcher to Missouri to become Governor. Prior to the war he had many occupations which included merchant, postal worker and some city government positions. His service during the Civil War included First Lieutenant, Adjutant, 3rd U. S. Reserve Corps of Missouri; Lieutenant Colonel, 12th Missouri State Militia Cavalry; and Lieutenant Colonel 31st Missouri Infantry. When the 31st Missouri Infantry and the 32nd Missouri Infantry were consolidated into a six-company battalion in November 1864, he was made commander of the battalion. In January 1865, Lieutenant Colonel Simpson was appointed to the office of Adjutant General of Missouri by Governor Thomas C. Fletcher. He resigned his

PRIVATE ALFRED PATTON, COMPANY E, 31ST MO
His son Robert and wife Martha at their home in 1918.
The flag in the window was for another son William who was
fighting in France in World War One

command of the battalion to take this office. He was made Brevet Brigadier General, United States Volunteers, on March 13, 1865 for meritorious services. He was born in Saint Louis, Missouri in 1830 and died in Leavenworth, Kansas in 1905. He is buried at the Calvary Cemetery in Saint Louis.

The Civil War had been going on for approximately fifteen months prior to President Lincoln's call for 300,000 more volunteers in July of 1862. Major battle's such as Bull Run, Wilson's Creek in southwest Missouri and Lexington in northwest Missouri were fought and won by the Confederates. On July 31, 1861 there was a state convention held in Jefferson City, Missouri where they declared that the offices of governor and lieutenant governor were vacant, along with all the seats in the Missouri Legislature being declared vacant. Hamilton R. Gamble was appointed the new provisional governor of Missouri for the next four years. The legislature was also appointed without the vote of the people and this was the accepted government as far as the Federal government was concerned. The people living in Missouri at that time, as a whole, must have agreed with this action because there was no great outcry. I can't imagine what would be said and done today if something like this would happen. It was a time of war so this might explain why it appears to have been so readily accepted. I have wondered what we would do if a government that we had not voted for drafted you to fight for a government that really had no legal backing. Would we go or would we, like many Missourians, join the Confederacy? Missourian's fought on both sides in many battles throughout the Western theatre of the war. In the 31st Missouri Infantry two brothers in the unit, Private Alfred Alexander Patton and Private John D. Patton, both from the Moselle area, had two brothers in the 5th Missouri Infantry Regiment (Confederate), Private Dow Patton and William Patton. The units that the four brothers were in fought at the Battle of Vicksburg. I am not sure whether Dow and William were there or not, but since they both made it through the war I assume that they were. Mrs. Dorothy Votaw, the Grand-daughter of Alfred, told me that family tradition says all four brothers arrived home within twenty-four hours of each other at the end of the war. This is truly amazing considering that many families lost more than one son during the war. These four brothers fought in some of the major battles of the war in the western theatre.

15

COLONEL THOMAS CLEMENT FLETCHER
31st Missouri Regimental Commander 1862 - 1864.
Copied by Permission from Photograph and Print Division
Missouri Historical Society, St. Louis, Missouri.

LIEUTENANT-COLONEL SAMUEL PARSONS SIMPSON
31st Missouri Regimental Commander 1864 to 1865
Copied by Permission from Photograph and Print Division
Missouri Historical Society, St. Louis, Missouri

Missouri was represented by a star on the Confederate Flag, the Missouri Confederate Government spent most of its existence in exile. The legal governor of the State of Missouri, who had been elected was Governor Claiborne Fox Jackson with Thomas C. Reynolds as the Lieutenant Governor. Both of these men were pro-Southern and were determined that Missouri would support the Southern cause. The commander of the state militia was General Sterling Price who had also once been the governor of Missouri. These three men had taken the great seal of Missouri and fled to Boonville, Missouri, making good their escape from the forces of General Nathaniel Lyon. It was during this time that Governor Jackson went to Richmond, Virginia to let them know of his intention of bringing the state of Missouri into the Confederate States of America. Just a few weeks after the Confederate victory at Wilson's Creek Battle near Springfield, Missouri, On October 31, 1861 Governor Jackson called a special session of the 21st Missouri General Assembly, which met in the Masonic Hall in Neosha, Missouri where the government in exile established a temporary state government. There were enough legal representatives duly elected by Missouri citizens that were sympathetic to the Confederate cause when role was taken there was a quorum present. This meant they had enough representitives were present, that any bill or anything else they did was technically, a legal act or statement of the Legislature of the State of Missouri. They passed a bill known as "A Provisional Act of Secession" which ratified the Confederate constitution and Missouri then asked permission to join the Confederate States. This bill passed both houses and was signed by the Governor. November 28, 1861 the Confederate Congress officially admitted Missouri into the Confederacy. On December 6th Governor Jackson died at the provisional capital in Camden, Arkansas and Lieutenant Governor Thomas C. Reynolds then became the Governor. In 1863 with Federal forces close at hand Governor Reynolds moved the government of Missouri in exile to Marshall, Texas where it remained till the end of the war. On May 26, 1869 Thomas C. Reynolds returned Missouri's official seal to Governor John W. McClurg which had been out of the state almost eight years.

In 1862, there were major battles happening all over the country. On the 6th of February, Fort Henry fell to the forces of Brigadier General U. S. Grant and Fort Donelson soon fell to "Unconditional Surrender" Grant on the 16th, it was at the capture of Fort Donelson that General Grant received his nickname "Unconditional Surrender" because of the terms offered to the commanding officer of the fort. On March 6-8, the Union won a victory in Arkansas at a place called Pea Ridge or Elk Horn Tavern. New Madrid, Missouri on the Mississippi River, was taken by the Federals which gave them an important stretch of the river. Then the bloodiest battle of the war up to that time, was fought on April 6th and 7th at Shiloh Church in Tennessee which is about twenty miles north of Cornith, Mississippi. It was called Shiloh by the Federals and known to the Southern forces as Pittsburg Landing on the Tennessee River. Some other major battles followed such as Battle of Seven Pines or Fair Oaks, Seven Days Battle, Second Bull Run and in September the Battle of Antietam or Sharpsburg, which was the bloodiest of the war. It makes a person wonder why someone would want to enlist into the service of the Federal Government, they had lost more battles than they had won. Since Missouri was such a divided state why fight for something that may be doomed? Even the countries in Europe were leaning towards recognition of the Confederate States as a legitimate country. The enormous amount of casualties that were prevalent in the last year of the war were not even being considered yet as a possibility by most people. I believe that most of the men who joined the 31st Missouri Regiment did so for the preservation of the United States, and maybe a sense of adventure, to get into the fight, or even to get off of the farm. There was a bounty paid for enlisting, it would be called a signing bonus today, that may have induced the men to enlist. There was a call of patriotism from the Missourians by Governor Gamble who in "The Democrat" in Saint Louis, "Missourians, you need no other stimulant to patriotic effort and sacrifice than to know that your country needs your services, and to remember the gallant conduct of the troops of your State at Wilson's Creek, at Donelson, at Shiloh, and upon other fields." (8)

The 31st Missouri Infantry Regiment after being organized was attached to Cape Girardeau, District of Missouri, Department of Missouri, to December 1862. Company A was commanded by Captain Oscar Dover with a total enrollment, on file at the Missouri Archives in Jefferson City, of one hundred and six members. They were from towns such as Victoria, Hopewell, Hillsboro, Desoto, Valley Mines, Morse Mills, Herculaneum, Saint Louis and Steelville. Company B had in its ranks one-hundred and three officers and enlisted men. They enlisted from various towns such as Ironton, Saint Louis, Washington County, Jefferson County, Dundee, Franklin County, Pilot Knob, Carondelet, Patterson, New Haven, and Hemker. They were commanded by Captain Edward E. Allen. Company C consisted of ninety men and officers and was commanded by Captain William H. Judd. They were from Saint Francis County, Washington County, Potosi, Belleview, Saint Louis, Carter County, Butler County and Randolph County, Arkansas, with a large amount of the men coming from the town of Hopewell. More men died in this regiment of disease than all other forms of casualties such as wounded, killed and missing which is also true for almost all the units in the Union Army with few exceptions. Captain Andrew A. Harrison was the commander of Company D which consisted of one hundred and one officers and enlisted men during the war. The personnel of this company were from Greenville, Ardius, Patterson, Hillsboro, Carter County, Moselle, Wayne County, Saint Louis, Randolph County Arkansas, Popular Bluff, Butler County and Victoria. Company E was commanded by Captain Samuel R. McClay. Company E was tied with Company F with the lowest amount of men in the regiment, they only had eighty-four enlisted men and officers on roll. They were from Moselle, Cuba, Saint Louis, Franklin County, Saint Clair, Hillsboro, Gasconade County, Calvey, Leesburg, and Stanton. Quite a few of the men came from the Moselle area, a town in Franklin County. Company F had a roster of eighty-four officers and enlisted men. The men in this company came from towns and counties such as Canaan, New Haven, Sullivan, Stonyhill, Gasconade County, Warren County, Washington County, Hillsboro, Mineral Point, and Franklin County. The commanding officer of Company F was Captain Egbert O. Hill. Captain William Osterhorn was the commanding officer of Company G. There was eighty-eight men on the roll of Company G. They were from towns and counties such as Herman, Dutzow, Washington, Krakow, Saint Louis, Greenville, Ironton, Warren County, Montgomery County and Marthasville. Company H soldiers were almost all from Wayne County. No other group had so large a complement of Wayne countians as the 31st Missouri Infantry, one hundred one men. Company H stationed at Patterson in November 1862. Captain William Burch was the commanding officer. They were from towns and counties such as Patterson, Potosi, Mourer, Desoto, Van Buren, Arkansas, Washington County, Stoddard County, Butler County and Caledonia. The commanding officer of Company I was Captain Edward Hale Jr.. They had an enrollment of eighty-five throughout the war. The men were from towns of Saint Louis, Danville, Mineral Point, Patterson, Montgomery County, Carondelet, Desoto, Monroe County, Caledonia, Middleton, Calloway County, Washington County, Jefferson County, Sulpher Spring, Potosi, Victoria, Hillsboro, Adams County, and Saint Charles. Company K was commanded by Captain Francis Doherty and had ninety men and officers on its roll. They were all from different parts of Missouri: Ironton, Caledonia, Patterson, Carondelet, Saint Louis, Potosi, Maries County, Pilot Knob, Danville, Washington County, Desoto, Willsburg, and Canaan. The Field and Staff was made up of sixteen men and officers. Besides Colonel Fletcher and Lieutenant Colonel Simpson, they were, Regimental Surgeon Churchill G. Strother from Warrenton, Major Frederick Jaensch, 1st Lieutenant William H. Barlow Regimental Quartermaster from Saint Louis. This will give you an idea where the men from this regiment came from and how many there were.

The following is taken from the remarks section of the Morning Report book of Company C. It describes the route that the 31st Missouri Infantry Regiment took from Jefferson Barracks, Missouri till a few days before they were to enter their first major battle which is the subject of the next chapter.

"September 1862 14th- Marched Per Iron Mountain Rail Road to Camp Blair near Ironton. Distance 87 miles.

October 1862   20th- Marched from Archadia South to near Polks Spring. Distance 9 miles.

21st- Marched from Encampment near Polks Spring two miles South of Stoney Battery. Distance 2.3 miles.

22nd- Thence to Camp Hanes one mile north of Patterson, Wayne County, Missouri. Distance 3 miles.

28th- Marched from Camp Hanes to Camp Patterson at Pattersonville, Missouri. Distance 2 miles.

November 1862   24th- Left Camp Patterson at Eight O'clock marched 11 miles North on the

Ironton Road to Camp Janesch.

25th- Continued our march north on the Ironton Road 13 miles to Camp Davidson.

26th- Continued march to Pilot Knob. Distance 11miles.

27th- Marched from Camp at Pilot Knob to Camp Simpson on the road to Saint Genevieve. Distance 9 miles.

28th- Continued the march to Camp Strother. Distance 18 miles.

29th- Continued the march to Camp (?) Distance 17 miles.

30th- Laid all Day.

December 1862 1st- Took up march to St Genevieve. Distance 3 miles. Took Steamboat, Northerner, took Steamboat down the Mississippi to Saint Mary's, laid all night.

2nd- Went to Cape Girardo waited for Provisions and for the pay master to pay us.

3rd- Left at Day Break proceeded down the Mississippi to within 6 miles of Island #10 laid till day break.

4th- Continued down the River to Memphis, Tennessee.

5th- Evening started for Helena Arkansas. Arrived there on the morning of 6th.

6th- Crossed the Mississippi River to Mississippi and there camped (called Camp Steele).

21st- Struck tents at 3 p.m. o'clock and marced to the landing.

22nd- At Daylight started down to Friers Point. Laid all day and that knight on the Arkansas side of the Mississippi.

23rd-Proceeded down the River to Gains Landing and laid up for the Knight on the East side of the River (all well).

24th- About 11 o'clock Proceeded down River to (?)

25th- Started down River about 10 o'clock and laid over within 8 miles of

Vicksburg."(9)

Private Henry Kuck, who was a member of Company G, 31st Missouri Infantry Regiment, wrote letters to his wife, Metta, back in Saint Louis, Missouri. They had four children at the start of the war. He was a prolific letter writer and an artist, he used his talents to decorate the letter heads of some of the letters he sent home. His letters give you an idea of what it was like to be a private in the Federal army. He wrote his letters in German. What is recorded are translations of his letters. His first letter is given in its entirety so you have an idea of the way he wrote. Private Kuck is one of the few sources that I found that refers to the time when the 31st Missouri Infantry Regiment left Saint Louis and arrived in Patterson, Missouri.

"The 26th of October 1862

Dear Metta,

I received your letter yesterday on the 25th of October, and see from it that you are still active and healthy and that flour is expensive. For me, I'm still alert and healthy, and if I would always remain so healthy, I would never die. We're not at Ironton anymore, but have now marched 35 miles onward, thus we are about a mile from PATTERSON, a small country town. The nights from the 24th to the 26th of October approximately 300 infantry troops and artillary marched off from here support or help. I've heard the South has taken some of our troops captive. Also our REGIMENT had orders to march, but our COLONEL (leader) didn't want to fight before we received other weapons, and when we receive the weapons, we'll probably have to go into the field again. Don't worry about the flour, if flour comes to 3 Dollars a sack; buy yourself a whole barrel at once and buy yourself a small pig next winter, but also buy clothing for yourself and the children, for I think next week I will receive money, and then I'll send it immediately. But because we can't send it by mail, and that way it is risky.

Write again right away, right on the same day, whether my PORTRAIT and Claus Gerdel's arrived, and how you like it, whether it looks like me or not. Don't scrimp on food and drink and clothing, for when you have no more, I think, you will receive more again. Your letter was sent after us, and I received it here. So you should

23

write again quickly, for we will perhaps already be gone when I receive an answer to this letter, but the letters will be sent along to us. Don't neglect to write, and in fact right now. Last night there was snow, and it froze.

Greetings to you and everybody your loving,

Heinrich"(10)

The first Regimental color bearer was appointed by Regimental order number three. It follows in its entirety.

"Regimental Order # 3   Head Quarters

31st Regiment Mo. Volunteers

Patterson November 6th, 1862

At the recommendation of their respective Captains, the following Non-commissioned officers are hereby detailed as Color guard of the Regiment.

Sergeant Samuel H. Maddox	Company	F
Corporal Lewis Miller	Company	A
Corporal G. Y. Paterrson	Company	C
Corporal Andrew J. Shirley	Company	D
Corporal Jacob H. Brown	Company	E
Corporal Henry Houlthaus	Company	G
Corporal A. A. Lawrence	Company	H
Corporal Joseph Kalerhals	Company	I
Coporal Thomas Hicks	Company	K

By Order of
Thomas C. Fletcher
Colonel, Commanding

R. M. Swander
1st Lieutenant, Adjutant."(11)

24

CHAPTER TWO:
THE VALLEY OF DEATH

After spending about a month at Camp Patterson they were on the march as described in Chapter One. Private Henry Kuck, of Company G, in a letter, dated November 30, 1862, to his wife described what his expectations were for the coming few months.

"Dear Metta!

We are not in Camp Patterson anymore but have already been traveling now for more than 5 days, we went next to PILOT KNOB again and then from PILOT KNOB to St. Genevieve, which lies on the river and is not far from St. Louis, here we'll wait until we receive new weapons and more money, perhaps we'll receive money as soon as tomorrow, then I will send the money to RUDOLPH KETELKAMP, and you can get it there from him, or have friends bring it, and we will have received new weapons and munitions we'll probably travel down to HELENA, about 5 hundred miles under St. Louis, and I will perhaps stay the winter there, but it's still uncertain, because you don't know to write about where you are going.

When we receive money I'll write again right away. JOHANN GERDEL and HENRY AHRENS stayed behind sick and were probably sent to JEFFERSON BARRACKS, WILH. SCHWARZE, HENRY & CLAUS GERDEL and I are still healthy and active and, if it's possible, I'll visit you soon, but this is uncertain, anyway I can't complain, I have enough to eat and drink and our work is not unbearable, but even then I would rather be at home with you; we all believe that peace will be made next spring, and then we will all see each other in good health if Fate allows. Little Gerd Losmann sends many greetings to his mother, he is not yet well or up and around, he's a good soldier, he always served well, as well as the best soldier here or in the companies right now at camp or on the march; he carries his howitzer as well as the biggest man and is in my view healthy.

Yours,

Henry Kuck"(1)

By the time the 31st Missouri Infantry Regiment had marched from Patterson, Missouri on the 24th of November they had experienced a loss of man power for a variety of reasons. There were thirty-six men who deserted from the regiment, some of them before their company was mustered in. Ten of these men were from Company D, most of whom were from the Patterson area of Missouri. No one knows for sure why they did desert, maybe it is because they enlisted in this regiment to defend their home state. Once realizing that they were probably heading out of state, they may have decided to desert because they enlisted only to serve in Missouri. Some like Private William Hackworth of Company E, who deserted on November 27, 1862 was returned and sentenced to three years hard labor. Sergeant George McClue deserted on September 11, 1862 and was discharged from Missouri State Penitentiary on December 3, 1866. Some like Private Thomas Holman of Company A enlisted on August 11, 1862 and deserted on September 5, 1862; maybe he had enough of army life and no longer cared to participate in this man's army. Private Jesse Lane of Company D enlisted on November 15, 1862 and deserted on November 24, 1862. It took some soldiers less time to make up their mind than others. There were thirty-seven men who were discharged for various reasons ranging from failure to recruit a company or any part of a company to being discharged because of disability. The 31st Missouri Infantry had twelve men who died of disease and three men transferred to different units. Companies from the regiment lost men for different reasons, but the total of eighty-eight was difficult to justify as they got ready to proceed to Arkansas to participate in the Battle of Chickasaw Bayou.

The 31st Missouri Infantry Regiment left the Department of Missouri in December 1862. They were attached to the 1st Brigade, 11th Division, Right Wing, 13th Army Corps (old), Department of the Tennessee. From there they became part of the 1st Brigade, 4th Division, Sherman's Yazoo Expedition December 22, 1862 to January, 1863. They arrived in Helena, Arkansas on December 6, 1862, by river boat from Saint Genevieve, Missouri, on the mighty Mississippi River, they were placed in the 4th Division, who's commander was Major General Frederick Steele. Private Henry Kuck sent a letter to his wife on December 6, 1862 which follows:

"Dear Wife,

This morning on the 6th of December we arrived here in HELENA, and yesterday we were in MEMPHIS. I wrote a letter on the 30th of Nov. and mailed it at the post office as we came through ST. GENEVIEVE, in which I wrote you that we would soon be paid, and we were paid on the 2nd Decbr., that is, 2 days after I wrote the letter, but (were paid) on the Steamboat, and I have no opportunity to send away my money until Memphis, where the lot of us landed yesterday. We were paid up to the 1st of Novbr. and I received 30 dollars, of which I sent home 20 dollars, for I borrowed 2 dollars from CLAUS GERDEL and I wanted also to keep something for myself; I sent the money addressed to RUDOLPH KETELKAMP in St. Louis, it's 2 ten-dollar bills, UNITED STATES BILLS, brand-new money; as soon as you have this letter, R. KETELKAMP will also have the money and you can inquire about it there, about myself I'm still healthy and have not suffered, although there is a lot of grumbling in our regiment for the regiment which does not grumble enough does not exist, but even if I can bear it so well here, I would surely like best of all to be with my family-but what does it mean when one grumbles about his fate, we will hope that this unhappy war will soon end. We are now about 500 miles from home and are much closer to the enemy than we were until now, but they don't dare attack us here, for there are over 40 thousand soldiers here and word has it that the next move should be to Vicksburg to open up the river, but this is only a probability. Maybe next spring we'll be at St. Louis. Write back again as quickly as possible, the moment you receive this letter, on the very same day, for I'm anxious to hear if you received the money or not.

P.S. Good-bye, sweet wife and children! If fate will have it, we will meet again safe and sound, but if the future determines otherwise, we cannot oppose it, I cast over to you one more heart-felt kiss and greeting.

Your, Henry"(2)

By the time they left on the river boats enroute to

Chickasaw Bayou, they again were afflicted by desertion, death and sickness. The total of men who had left the regiment for one of the before mentioned reasons was thirty-three. This brought the total amount of men lost to one-hundred and thirty-two out of nine hundred and seven men lost prior to their first battle. Company A entered combat for the first time with ninety-five out of their original one hundred and six men. Company B had a total loss of fifteen which left them with eighty-eight. Company C's loss of three was the lowest in the regiment and entered into combat with eighty-eight. Company D took a real beating with the loss of twenty-six which reduced their number to seventy-five. Company E lost fourteen which reduced their effective strength to seventy. Company F loss of ten brought them down to seventy-four. Company G lost eight men and they were down to eighty men. Company H, like Company F, lost ten men, but they entered combat with ninety-one men which gave them twenty-one more men than Company F. Company I had eighty-five men when they started out but ended with eighty, a loss of five. Company K suffered fifteen losses which gave them a new enrollment of seventy-five. There is no Company J in any of the army regiments because of the possibility of confusing J with the letter I designation in Company I.

In a couple of more letters to his wife, Private Henry Kuck describes some of things that had happened to him. In a letter dated December 11, 1862, Private Kuck stated that he had not received a letter from his wife since November 6th. He was afraid that she had not received any of his letters for the past month so he let her know what he had been doing and how the pay was being done. He writes about some of the things that affected not only him but also other soldiers in any of the regiments in the army. Some exerpts from two letters follow:

"Since I have guard duty today, I have between times a nice opportunity to write you a few lines. On the 24th of Nov. we marched from Patterson and on 26th we arrived at PILOT KNOB and from there went toward St. Genevieve. We stopped three miles before St. Gen. on the 30th of Nov. and I used the opportunity to write, and I wrote you at that time that we probably would be paid the next day; the next day we pushed on in to St. Genevieve and received our new weapons and then boarded the Steamship Northern; and on the 3rd of Decbr. we received our payments, up to the 1st of Nov.

and I received 30 dollars. On Decbr. 5th we arrived at MEMPHIS and docked there for 24 hours.

Camp Steele Dec. 16, '62 — To be a soldier when one is healthy is not so hard, but being sick is entirely different. One can lie there and be very sick but no one comes to ask you if you want something. When you're sick here you have to pay if you want anything other than bacon, beans or crackers, and then three or four times the normal price will be demanded. He who has nothing is then in a sorry state, and he (Gerd) has no BOUNTY. At that time, those who didn't enlist before the 22nd of August were not to receive any bounty. Our names were written down for August 20 enlistment. Afterwards, as we received our bounty, Gerd along with lots of others received no bounty. Some were cheated out of a whole month, and Gerd was cheated out of 11 Days: He was written in for the first of September instead of the 20th of August. The ridiculous record keeping of our officers is solely responsible for this. Instead of 30 Dollars Gerd received only 26 Dollars. When one is at home and reads in the paper about such-and-such a regiment, one should believe, or normally it's so, that a regiment is a thousand men. But that's not so. Our regiment has more than, or at least, one thousand men in strength, but if one were to count it now it would be scarcely 500 able-bodied men. Same with the 30th Regiment next to us, numbering over a thousand, but there are only 450 men who serve, the others are either sick, dead or have deserted."(3)

Major General William T. Sherman had asked Brigadier General William A. Gorman for approximately ten thousand men in order to supplement his force during the attack of Vicksburg. General Gorman who was in command at Helena, Arkansas, had made ready to give General Sherman almost eleven thousand men. He had ordered General Frederick Steele to be ready with his division of three infantry brigades, two full batteries and six-hundred cavalrymen to be ready to load on transports and join General Sherman's force. He also threw in two regiments from General Frank P. Blair's brigade also. The two regiments were the 30th Missouri Infantry Regiment and the 31st Missouri Infantry Regiment. One of the regiments in General Blair's brigade was down with the measles and probably would not go. After all was said and done though General Sherman went ahead and took all of General Steele's brigade.

Major-General John A. McClernand of Illinois had spent his time since October 1862, he had went to Washington, D.C. and received permission from General Halleck and President Abraham Lincoln to recruit men for an independent force to attack Vicksburg. He would not be under the control of the commander of the department he was going to be operating in. That commander was General U. S. Grant. General Grant, who was in command of the Department of the Tennesse, found out about the raising of troops by Major-General McClernand and his plan to attack Vicksburg. General Grant, then made plans to speed up his attack on Vicksburg before General McClernand could arrive. General Grant issued orders on December 19, 1862, for Major-General William T. Sherman, in the absence of General McClernand, to take all troops at Memphis and General Frederick Steele's division at Helena, and to move with Porter's fleet by the river and cooperate in the attack. General Sherman's three divisions left Memphis on December 20th, just a few days before General McClernand arrived. December 21, 1862 General Steele's, 4th Division, loads on the boats at Helena, Arkansas. General Steele's division consisted of the 4th, 9th, 31st, 26th, 28th and the 34th Iowa Infantry Regiments, the 13th Illinois Infantry, 76th and 58th Ohio Infantry Regiments, 29th, 30th, 31st, 32nd, 3rd, 12th, 17th and 1st Missouri Infantry Regiments, plus Quartermasters stores and horses and the 1st Iowa Artillery. General Steele's division added twelve thousand men to General Sherman's force. December 26th found General Sherman's army on the Yazoo River about eight miles north of Vicksburg. They camped that evening on the plantation of General A. S. Johnston on the Yazoo River. He was killed at the Battle of Shiloh. General Blair's brigade, including the 31st Missouri Infantry Regiment, was ordered to make a reconnaissance out about two or three miles distance. Just a little ways out the 13th Illinois Infantry Regiment, who was acting as the advance skirmishers, drove in the Confederate skirmishers and captured two horses. They spent the night at the point where the reconnaissance was to end.

While General Sherman was preparing to attack Vicksburg, beginning his attack from Chickasaw Bayou General Grant was moving south from La Grange, Tennessee. He had made Holly Springs, Mississippi his secondary supply base which provided his army with the supplies needed to continue the defeat of Lieutenant General John C. Pemberton's army and the capture of Vicksburg. He had left a force of approximately fifteen hundred men under the command of a Colonel Murphy of the 8th Wisconsin Infantry. Confederate cavalry, under the command of Major General Earl Van Dorn, attacked the garrison at Holly Springs. Colonel Murphy surrendered his force without much of a defense. General Van Dorn's troops destroyed more than a million dollars worth of supplies that General Grant's army needed, on December 20th. This combined with Brigadier General Nathan Bedford Forrest raid into Western Tennessee in which sixty miles of railroad were destroyed, these two actions forced General Grant to retreat back to La Grange and Grand Junction. General Grant was unable to notify General Sherman of this set back, so General Sherman proceeded on as planned. At the same time General Pemberton was returning to Vicksburg to prepare for General Sherman's troops.

General Sherman had left Memphis, Tennessee with approximately twenty thousand men and with the twelve thousand from General Steele's division at Helena, Arkansas. This gave him the force of approximately a thirty-two thousand man army and sixty cannon's with which to attack Vicksburg. The convoy paused at Helena, Arkansas to take on wood and embark Steele's men.

"During Saturday the troops embarked on the boats. That night they were paid two months' pay, and on Sunday, December 21st, 1862, the Division left at 2 P. M. Memphis, where we had spent the last five months, was soon lost to view. The boat ran until 1 o'clock that night, then tied up at Friar's Point, twelve miles below Helena, Ark. Here the fleet of forty-five transports, loaded with troops and several gun-boats joined us. the whole fleet left on the following morning, stopping at sundown, twenty-five miles above Napoleon, Ark. — Leaving early the next day, we arrived at Milliken's Bend, La., early on Christmas morning, where we remained until the first brigade destroyed the Shreveport & Texas R. R." (4)

The 31st Missouri Infantry was loaded on the steamer "Isabella" while the 32nd Missouri Infantry, one of its sister regiments, was on the steamer Sucker State. At Christmas time men who are away from home think about what would be

MAJOR-GENERAL WILLIAM TECUMSEH SHERMAN
15th Army Corps, Army of the Tennessee,
District of Mississippi Army Commander
Used by Permission of the Print and Photograph Division,
Missouri Historical Socity, Saint Louis, Missouri

COLONEL ABRAHAM JEFFERSON SEAY
Consolidated Battalion, 31st and 32nd Missouri Infantry
Regiments Commander January 1865 - July 1865
Used by Permission of Chisholm Trail Museum
Governor Seay Mansion-Kingfisher Oklahoma

going on at home. In his diary, Major Abraham J. Seay of the 32nd Missouri Infantry, writes the following about his experiences on Christmas Eve, 1862.

"Wednesday Dec. 24.

We started at 11:30 A.M. come to or pass Greenville, Miss. at 2:30 P.M. a ville of 200 or 300 inhabitants. Here we see a pretty good gang of Guerillas. 5 on horse back and 25 afoot, the horse men rode away and one of the footmen leveled his gun twice to shoot. But I suppose he thought he was out of range besides the citizens may have restrained him by telling him it was Gen. Shermans order that a town be burnt if we are fired into. I looked at him thru a field glass which drew him in range and told the boys to load.

Ah it excites me to see the cut throats pointing their guns at us but I know many of our men have done very wrong for which I would seek revenge, if I were a rebel. We run till 2 in the morning – the first time we have run in the night since we left St. Louis. I fear some accident and sure enough the Kenneth (transporting a part of Fletchers 31st Regiment) ran into our stern injuring our stern and mashing their bow considerably. The fleet landed on the La. shore."(5)

The fleet spent the rest of the night at Miliken's Bend, Louisiana.

In his diary Major Abraham J. Seay wrote of an unusual event on Christmas day. General Sherman early in the war was against burning and pillaging of personal property. Later in the war he may have looked the other way, as various authors have stated, but here is Major Seay's diary entry that states how serious General Sherman, was that no acts of destruction of personal property would be tolerated in the latter part of 1862.

"Thursday Dec. 25th, 1862

This morning I rise and perform an entire ablution of my body (which by the way was needed) dress myself— come out and find breakfast over—greet the boys with Merry Christmas. I am unwell. It is very warm. We have had no fire in the cabin for 3 days. After breakfast Col. Warmoth and I took a ramble. We went out to a plantation where some skalawags had stuck the torch to some buildings. Gen. Sherman ordered them to the boats (his orders are for no property to be destroyed) which order some of them did not promptly obey. He sent out a guard to shoot and arrest which they did killing 5 or six – the others are to be shot.

This will teach thieves and incendiaries to obey orders. It is pretty severe but has to be done. To resume we rambled into a neighboring field and approach a green spot. Here we find a grave yard round about which has a variety of green growths. We took a limb from a species of cherry whose leaves are green and whose buds have begun to swell. This is La. and 25 miles above Vicksburg."(6)

The battle that was coming would be called Chickasaw Bayou near the Chickasaw Bluffs outside of Vicksburg, Mississippi. These bluffs run parallel to the Mississippi River on the Mississippi side of the river. Vicksburg was built on some of these bluffs and at this location they run right up to the river. The bluffs also run up to Memphis, Tennessee but not always as close to the river as at Vicksburg. The bluffs also are within easy marching of the Yazoo River which the bluffs follow for some distance. The Confederates were not surprised as they had ample defenses established. They were continually being reinforced by the same men who had left Vicksburg to defeat General Grant's forces. Since General Grant's retreat back to Tennessee, these forces were available to be thrown into the defenses against General Sherman's army. General Sherman's army disembarked from their steamers near the Johnson Plantation on the 26th and 27th of December. General Blair and his Brigade left the boats at Johnson's Plantation on the afternoon of December 26th. This brigade consisted of the 13th Illinois Infantry Regiment, 27th, 30th, 31st and 32nd Missouri Infantry Regiments, and the 58th Ohio Infantry Regiment, the 4th Ohio Battery and Company C of the 4th Missouri Cavalry Regiment. They proceeded forward on the Johnson road, the 13th Illinois Infantry Regiment were acting as skirmishers, where they were met by enemy pickets, who fired a few shots and withdrew. General Blair's brigade went into camp about two miles from the place where they landed. Major A.J. Seay, of the 32nd Missouri Infantry Regiment writes in his diary, "Friday, 26th dec. 1862. Moved continuously up the Yazoo 12 miles.

Disembarked. Went our two miles and camped on the low bottom. It rained on us that night."(7)

35

The area where they left the riverboats was a very wet area. With lakes, bayou's, swamps and low level land that could become wet with a lot of rain. These were some of the natural defenses that were available for use by the Confederate forces. The Confederates had used logs to strengthen their trenches and abatis that was caused by the cutting down of trees along the suspected path of march or charge, which really could slow down a charge. An abatis was a defensive measure used generally in front of trenches or other defensive positions. They were generally made of logs with stakes pointing straight out down the length of the log about eighteen to twenty-four inches apart. The stakes would line the log on four sides. Each stake was sharpened to a point to further make them dangerous to the charging enemy. Sometimes when in a hurry an abatis could be made by cutting trees down so that the tops of the trees were pointing in the direction of the path of the approaching enemy and if enough time was available the limbs could also be sharpened. These were usually cut down to obstruct a road to impede the progress of artillery and supply wagons. This type of abatis was very useful around entrenchment's when there were ample trees in the area. Imagine seeing one of these for the first time, it was probably considered inhumane and uncivilized, if there is such a thing in warfare.

On the morning of December 27th General Blair's Brigade again met resistance from the Confederates but in much larger numbers than from the previous day. When they passed through some timber at Mrs. Lake's plantation they were fired on by some of the Confederate artillery that was positioned at a white house on Chickasaw Bayou. The Federals returned fire with their artillery and the Confederate artillery soon withdrew to a safer place. Major A. J. Seay recorded in his diary, "Saturday, Dec. 27, 1862. Moved continuously up the bottom 2 or 3 miles. Most of the time in line of battle. A heavy cannonading in front of us – late in the eve musketry fires rapidly in front on the banks of the Bayou. Nothing decisive."(8) An hour or so after the Confederate artillery had withdrawn communications with General Morgan had been established as his troops were then disembarking his troops at Chickasaw Bayou. Company C, 4th Missouri Cavalry had been sent out on a reconnaissance to determine the size of the force they were facing. Company C's commander returned with his report that the Confederate's had a large force on the other side of the bayou. General M. L.

Smith ordered General Blair to send out a regiment as skirmishers. The 58th Ohio Infantry along with another regiment from the 2nd Division were sent out to find the Confederates, they found them and were soon involved in some fighting. They had confirmed the report that Company C, 4th Missouri Cavalry, had brought back earlier. General Blair's brigade then went into camp on the same ground where earlier his artillery had fired at and drove the Confederate artillery from earlier in the day.

Meanwhile, General Steele and the rest of the 4th Division was disembarked above the mouth of Chickasaw Bayou being separated from General George W. Morgan's 3rd Division by the Chickasaw Bayou which was reported to be to deep to ford and Thompson's Lake on the other side. General Morgan's division, after a reconnaissance, was found to be at one of the two feasible points that the main bayou could be bypassed. This was the point near the head of Chickasaw Bayou and the other was about a mile lower down in front of General M. L. Smith's 2nd Division. General Steele started to build roads through some thick timber to get to the levee. At this time Admiral Porter, whose boats were under fire by about four hundred Confederate sharpshooters, asked General Steele for some help. The 17th Missouri Infantry Regiment was sent to drive these ambushers from their position. The reason he sent this help was because the Confederate force was firing upon the gunboats which were to supply support for the attacking force headed by General Steele. General Hovey, whose brigade had the lead, had a sharp engagement with a Confederate outpost, with the outpost retreating leaving the field in Federal hands. They went into camp for the night on the ground that Captain Hoffman's 4th Ohio Battery fired at the Confederate earlier in the day, but had what was called a cold camp, which means without fire which made the night miserable for the soldiers.

December 28th, the march was resumed and the General Steele's skirmishers were almost immediately fired upon by the Confederate sharpshooters. The Federals were marching toward the levee where there was a curve about eight hundred yards away, the Chickasaw Creek was on one side and a wooded marsh was on the other side. The pioneers were sent forward to the levee to clear some of the Confederate obstructions. They were careful to stay within range of their artillery but the pioneers and the artillery were fired on by Confederate artillery. The Confederate artillery nearly wiped out the pioneers and inflicted severe damage on the Federal artillery. It became apparent to General Steele that his force had advanced as far as they could and reported to General Sherman that it was impossible to attack the Confederate forces on the bluffs in front of his position. General Sherman ordered him to leave a small force there to be observed by the enemy and to return to the west side of Chickasaw Bayou to support General Morgan's left. The 4th Division, except those left for the show of force, then boarded steamboats in the Yazoo River and proceeded to firm ground on the west side of Chickasaw Bayou to meet the orders given to support General Morgan's left.

Major A. J. Seay records in his diary his view of December 28, 1862.

"Sunday Dec. 28th 1862.

The ball opened very early this morning just where it ceased at nightfall on yesterday. The firing was terrific. A heavy fog enveloped us, which soon became so dense by mingling with the smoke of powder the glorious sun for a time refused to behold the storm. Here indeed were that days of war turned loose. During this fearful hour Gen. Sherman, walked his beat back and forth in the road as doth the sentinel on guard. His command short but earnest insentations.

Now having fought without cessation for 3 hours the sound of deadly missles became less frequent, but I hear the "clash of resounding arms" on the right. Attention 32nd, by the right flank we moved off on double quick. The boys are weak and weary. They throw off their knap sacks and right on. Now we arrive at the scene of action. 50 paces in the rear of 13th Ill. who pour it into the skulking rebels in ambush, i.e. behind logs in rifle pits concealed in cane breaks, etc. Here Col. Wyman fell shot thru the lungs – 3 of our boys got wounded by enemy bullets.

We occupy one bank of an impassible bayou and they the other. We can do nothing then we retrace our steps – move a mile and a half to the left – sleep on our arms without fire or anything to eat."(9)

General Blair's brigade was placed in reserve on the 28th of December as General Morgan advanced on the Confederates from his position at the white house and attacked the Confederates in their trenches past the bayou with such force that the attack caused the Confederates to withdraw. General M. L. Smith was severely wounded on this date. Later in the day before noon General Blair was ordered to take his brigade to the left of General Smith's division and to advance on the Confederates. Due to the terrain General Blair's artillery could not follow so they were ordered to proceed across the pontoon bridge, that had been set up, and join General Morgan's force. General Blair reports, "I pushed forward as fast as the nature of the ground would permit to the left of General M. L. Smith and engaged the enemy, with my entire brigade, in his rifle-pits and intrenchments in my front, beyond the bayou, and a sharp and brisk encounter silenced his sharpshooters."(10)

General Blair was then ordered to take his brigade to re-enforce General Morgan who was actively involved in fighting the Confederates to his front. While marching to their assigned position they soon came under fire from some of General Morgan's artillery and also Confederate artillery and withdrew. General Morgan told General Blair to place his brigade to the left across the bayou. Arriving at his assigned position with orders to perform a reconnaisance he failed to do this because of it being so late in the day. As a safety precaution General Blair ordered that the picket force be doubled for the night.

General Blair was about to make a reconnaisance on the morning of December 29th when he received orders from General Morgan to bring his brigade to the rear of General Morgan's force to help ward off an attack by the Confederates to his right flank. Before this maneuver could be completed however he received orders to return to the position he had just left. Once back in position he sent out a battalion from the 13th Illinois Infantry Regiment, whose colonel was killed in the fighting of the day before, Colonel John B. Wyman, to perform the reconniasance that had been canceled earlier, in order to find out the lay of the land to his front and determine the strength of the Confederates to his front. It proved to be very rough terrain in front of his force which he describes in a report reprinted below.

"The natural obstructions were certainly as great as from any other direction, and we had not the advantage of as thorough and complete a reconaissance of the ground, nor had we the facilities of a pontoon bridge to cross the bayou in our front, which was deep and the bottom of it nothing but a treacherous quicksand. The enemy had improved their naturally strong position with consummate skill. The bed of the bayou was perhaps 100 yards in width, covered with water for a distance of 15 feet. On the side of the bayou held by my troops (after emerging from the heavy timber and descending a bank of 8 or 10 feet in height) there was a growth of young cottonwoods, thickly set, which had been cut down by the enemy at the height of 3 or 4 feet and the tops of these saplings thrown down among these stumps so as to form a perfect net to entangle the feet of the assaulting party. Passing through this and coming to that part of the bayou containing water, it was deep and miry, and when this was crossed we encountered a steep bank on the side of the enemy at least 10 feet high, covered with a strong abatis and crowned with rifle-pits from end to end. Above them was still another range of rifle-pits, and still above a circle of batteries of heavy guns which afforded a direct and enfilading fire upon every part of the plateau, which rose gently from the first range of rifle-pits to the base of the embankment which formed the batteries. These formidable works defended by a strong force of desperate men such as held them on the 29th, would seem to require almost superhuman efforts to effect their capture."(11)

General Sherman gave the order for the attack to begin at 7:30 A.M. on the 29th of December. At this time the Union artillery started their bombardment that lasted most of the morning. At or near 12:00 P.M., the infantry began their attack. General Blair's brigade attacked between Chickasaw Bayou and Thompson's Lake, Colonel DeCourcy's Brigade went with General Blair's brigade and they went forward with a cheer and with confidence. The 4th Iowa Infantry of Brigadier-General John M. Thayer's brigade was the only one to follow Colonel DeCourcy's brigade and formed on its right. The reason they were the only regiment from their brigade is taken from a leaf from the diary of Captain Lyman Richardson who was Quartermaster of General Thayer's Brigade of General Steele's Division. "Soon after we started, an order came from General Sherman, who was conducting operations on our right, to send him a regiment at once. Morgan told Steele to fill order. He turned to the regiment that had just come up, which happened to be the Second Regiment of our brigade, and ordered it to the right. As the two other regiments of our brigade came up, of course they followed the one preceding. The consequence was that Thayer and the Fourth Iowa made the attack alone, as far as our brigade was concerned, supported only by Blair,"(12) They attacked the Confederate defensive lines, working their way through the abatis, and facing heavy fire and carried the advance rifle pits. They were later repulsed at the main Confederate defensive lines. The 4th Iowa Infantry made their way to the base of the Chickasaw Bluff but were being fired upon by the Confederates holding their rifles on the outside of the parapets and firing straight down into the 4th Iowa. The men in this regiment dug little cave like shelters and weathered the storm of shot and shell plus the cold rain that fell during most of the day. Finally their suffering was alleviated when darkness fell and they were able to return to their lines.

Brigadier-General Frank Blair's brigade, that included the 31st Missouri, lined up in the woods between Thompson's Lake and Chickasaw Bayou behind the bayou that connects the two other bodies of water. The regiments that were in the attack of General Blair's brigade were the 13th Illinois Infantry positioned on the right front and the 58th Ohio Infantry positioned about fifty yards behind them. The 31st Missouri Infantry went into position on the left front with the 29th Missouri Infantry being positioned about fifty yards behind them. The 29th Missouri Infantry's right company and the 58th Ohio Infantry's left company were acting as rear guard for the brigade. In the "History of the 13th Illnois Infantry Regiment" they described what they were facing.

"The works of the enemy on their right were more formidable than from any other approach. Almost every gun and rifle-pit bore upon us and many enfiladed our line of battle. The natural obstructions were certainly as great as from any other direction, and we had not the advantage of as thorough a reconnoissance of the ground, nor had we facilities of a pontoon-bridge to cross the bayou in our front, which was deep, and the bottom of it nothing but a treacherous quicksand. The enemy had improved their naturally strong position with consummate skill. The bed of the bayou was, perhaps, one hundred yards in width, covered with water for a distance fifteen feet. On the side of the bayou held by my troops (after emerging from the heavy timber and descending a bank eight or ten feet in height) there was a growth of young cotton woods, thickly set, which had been cut down by the enemy at the height of three or four feet and the tops of these saplings thrown down among these stumps so as to form a perfect net to entangle the feet of the assaulting party. Passing through this, and coming to that part of the bayou containing water, it was deep and miry, and when this was crossed we encountered a steep bank on the side of the enemy at least ten feet high, covered with a strong abatis and crowned with rifle-pits from end to end.   Above them was still another range of rifle-pits, and still above, a circle of batteries of heavy guns which afforded a direct and enfilading fire upon every part of the plateau, which rose gently from the first range of rifle-pits, to the base of the embankment which formed the batteries."(13)

Early in the morning, with General Blair's brigade formed in a line of battle, with fixed bayonets, was waiting for the signal to attack. The designated guns sounded the signal for the attack, the brigade lept forward rushing past all the before described obstacles carrying the first and second lines of Confederate rifle pits. A member of the 13th Illinois describes what he saw when the signal guns sounded. "The orders were 'Guide right, double-quick.' I looked at the line just before we came to the water, which many could not jump across, and I remarked that, though the wings traveled a little the fastest, and the line curved a little, both in the Thirteenth and the regiment that formed on our left (Thirty-first Missouri), the front was bold and magnificent, and the battle maintained with courage and splendor — if such things can be called splendor, that take men's lives."(14) Once across the bayou the brigade halted to regroup they saw General Morgan's troops coming up behind them, so they charged on, the whole time enduring fire from both the Confederate musket fire and cannister shot from the artillery. They were able to reach the Confederate rifle pits driving them back to the main line and continuing to charge till they reached the Confederate intrenchments from which they were forced to fall back the ones that were able. The bad thing about having to retreat back over the same ground that was just charged over is that the same people are shooting at you,

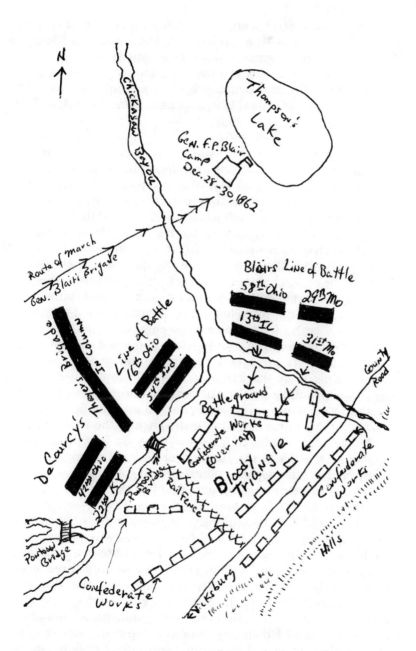

BATTLE OF CHICKASAW BAYOU, MISSISSIPPI
DECEMBER 29, 1862

they now have a second chance to kill you. This was the first battle that the 31st Missouri Infantry Regiment and the 29th Missouri Infantry Regiment had ever fought in.

The 30th Missouri and the 32nd Missouri Infantry Regiments, both in General Blair's brigade, were detached from the brigade to support General Morgan's batteries. Major A. J. Seay wrote the following in his diary.

"Monday Dec. 29th 1862.

We have no fire or breakfast. Recross a bayou. Are detached from our brigade and Col. Manter takes command of the 30 and 32 Mo. We are ordered to the center in the support of an Ohio battery. The big gun fight was terrible. The scis and whistle of shells and the crashing of the limbs of trees over our heads was fearful. We had but few men wounded but it was amusing to see the boys and officers dodge the bursting shell. All the while the cannon belced forth their deadly missles. Now the battle rages on the right and we are ordered thither. We go, fall on our faces to support a battery and a line of infantry, both of which are hotly engaged. Now Blairs Brigade charges the works on left – is repulsed with great slaughter. We are ordered to the center to support a charge made by the 21st Ky and the 9th Iowa. We advanced on double quick until our men many having been exhausted. On we went and charged into the field and over the fallen timber till just in range of the rifle pits. The we get an order to fall – which we do lying on our faces to the left of the battery till dark. The boys are entrenching themselves. Our regiment got into trenches and lie on their arms. It rains and fills the trench 6 in. with water. The boys are muddy hogs."(15)

The 32nd Missouri Infantry Regiment suffered two casualties during this battle both of them wounded enlisted men. This brigade suffered ninety-nine killed, three hundred and thirty-one wounded with one hundred and seventy-three missing, among them was Colonel Thomas Fletcher of the 31st Missouri Infantry. The casualties that were suffered by the four regiments of the brigade that were in the main attack are listed as follows. The 13th Illinois Infantry Regiment suffered the loss in killed, three officers and twenty-four enlisted men; wounded, eight officers and ninety-nine enlisted men; captured or missing, two officers and thirty-seven enlisted men for a total of one hundred and seventy-three. The 29th Missouri Infantry Regiment suffered the loss in killed, two officers and seventeen enlisted men; wounded, four officers and sixty-six enlisted men; captured or missing, four officers and fifty-seven enlisted men for a total of one hundred and fifty men. The 31st Missouri Infantry Regiment suffered the loss in killed, seventeen enlisted men; wounded, ten officers and sixty-two enlisted men; captured and missing, two officers and sixty enlisted men for a total of one hundred and fifty-one. One of these officers was Colonel Thomas C. Fletcher, he said in a speech during the Reunion of the Society of the Army of the Tennessee in Cleveland, Ohio on October 17, 1883;

"Somebody was saying but a few minutes ago that we were getting to be old. Now don't you know that it goes very hard with a man the first time he is called old Fletcher. A man will get old — he cannot help that — but he does not like to be told so. I remember the first time I was called old. To satisfy my curiosity I accidentally got too near to Vicksburg. I was captured by the Confederates and put in jail. I had an arm and a leg crippled and I had lain in the mud all night. I was dilapidated very much, and had nothing to eat and nothing to drink. I felt bad and looked bad. I have no doubt I looked as old as Methuselah. One man walked along with the mule, and another man with a gun guarded me. As I passed a house there were some ladies on the portico, and one said to me: You nasty old Abolitionist, what do you want down 'here?' That was the first time I was ever called old. I have forgiven the Southern Confederacy for all they have done, but that I cannot forgive."(16)

Colonel Fletcher after spending some time in Libby Prison in Richmond, Virginia was released on parole. From there he went home to Saint Louis, Missouri. While he was at home there was the celebration in DeSoto, Missouri of the anniversary of the capturing of the first stars and bars and the armed traitors that hoisted it over the city of DeSoto. While there Colonel Fletcher was asked to make a speech. The following is part of the speech that was printed on Wednesday May 20, 1863 in the "Daily Missouri Democrat" of Saint Louis, Missouri.

"There were rebel officers, brave and generous men,

who had fought battles of the war, who would have shown him every kindness if they had been permitted; but neither their rank nor their services could, without great trouble, procure them a pass to get into the prison. The fighting men and officers of the rebel army are generally disposed to treat a prisoner kindly; it is only the home guard officers about the towns and lounging around headquarters out of the smell of powder, who insult and mistreat a man who is defenceless and in their power. He was kindly treated on the battlefield and by all the officers until he was taken into Vicksburg on the morning after his capture; he was thrust into the common jail, a most loathsome apartment, with felons, negroes and worse than all, drunken secessionists; there he was kept a month, notwithstanding they exacted and he gave them his parole on the day after his capture. No human being was allowed to communicate with him in any manner; he was fed on corn bread made of unsifted meal, half cooked and without salt; a very little blue meat said to be beef was given them occasionally, some of his men died while there, one of them died soley for want of medicine, when he implored a rebel surgeon to give him medicine for the poor boy, the surgeon said, 'your master Abe Lincoln won't allow us any medicines,' he thought if rebels 'could not keep hotel they ought to sell out to some person who could. With twenty other officers he was taken to Jackson, Mobile, Montgomery, Atlanta, Knoxville, Lynchburgh and Richmond, at every place they were exhibited as a recent capture and thus they were paraded all over the Confederacy and the people were made to believe they had captured two thousand Yankee officers. The people at Knoxville little dreamed that we were the same officers of whose capture they had read accounts in the Jackson, Mobile and Atlanta papers. It was like everything else done by the rebel authorities – it was a fraud upon the people. At Jackson they were driven, like so many mules or cattle, into the ruins of an old bridge standing over the Pearl river, without blankets, straw or fire in the most inclement season of the year. They suffered there indescribable torture. A rebel officer, an old friend and clever fellow, brought him a blanket and gave him some medicine while he was sick. His fellow prisoners suffered greatly, and several died from the exposure. A Confederate General, one whose name is always seen in the accounts of their hardest fought battles, had the officers removed from the bridge to a house where where they were comparatively comfortable. The men, poor fellows, were left there and died in great numbers. He traveled in cattle or hog cars through the whole Confederacy. In the pineries of Alabama and Georgia the women, children and negroes came to look at them; the officer in charge told them we were Yankee officers, they remarked, we looked like people, he said we had a split hoof, when I ventured to suggest it was more than some of the animals fed to us had ever been possessed of."(17)

The 58th Ohio Infantry Regiment suffered the loss in killed, three officers and thirty-three enlisted men; wounded, seven officers and seventy-one enlisted men; captured or missing, two officers and nine enlisted men for a total of one hundred and twenty-five men. The other brigades losses were: DeCourcy had forty-eight killed, three hundred and twenty-one wounded and three hundred and fifty-five missing, with the 4th Iowa suffering seven killed and one hundred and five - wounded. The total casualties for the Union Army was one thousand nine hundred and twenty-nine with one hundred and ninety-one killed, nine hundred and eighty-two wounded and seven hundred and fifty-six missing.

While this was going on at General Morgan's front, General A. J. Smith's forces attacked the Confederate defenses. This occurred to the right of the attack of General Morgan's troops. On the previous night, General Smith's men had cleared away some of the abatis and made a path for them to attack through. The 6th Missouri Infantry, part of Brigadier General M. L. Smith's 2nd Division, charged across the stream and attempted to storm the enemy at what was called the Indian Mound section of the Confederate defensive line. They were stopped, and much like the 4th Iowa Infantry, had to dig into the steep bank to keep the Confederates from firing straight down at them. They experienced fourteen killed and forty-three wounded. They escaped this trap one by one that night. This part of General Sherman's army made five attempts to storm the defenses but could not carry them. Their casualties were not as high as those incurred on General Morgan's front, they had a total of twenty-one killed, one hundred and seventy-three wounded and two hundred and fifteen captured. It is reported that the Confederates loss was sixty-three killed, one hundred and thirty-four wounded and ten captured.

"In a report by Colonel Thomas C. Fletcher, he states that as Colonel Wyman of the 13th Illinois Infantry being killed, that he was the senior Colonel of the brigade. General Blair rode up and gave his orders that the 31st Missouri would be in the first line and the 29th Missouri would support them. The 13th Illinois Infantry would form in line to the right of the 31st Missouri and be supported by the 58th Ohio Infantry. Colonel Fletcher further states "I took my position in advance of my regiment and awaited the signal. When we heard it, we raised a shout, and started at a double-quick the 13th on my right. I saw no troops on my left. When we emerged from the woods, the enemy opened upon us; crossing the bayou under fire, and many of the men sinking in the mud and water, our line was very much disordered, but we pretty well restored it before reaching the abatis. Here we were greatly disordered, but somewhat restored the line on reaching the plateau or corn-field. The 29th Missouri came on gallantly supporting us. The 13th Illinois came out upon the corn-field, and the 58th Ohio followed close upon it. there was firing to my left, and as I afterward learned was from the 4th Iowa of Thayer's Brigade (and I believe of Steele's division). I was struck and fell, and my regiment went back in great disorder. The fire was terrific. I saw beyond the 13th Illinois, to my right, a disordered line, and learned afterward it was the 16th Ohio. When I was taken from the field by the enemy and taken into Vicksburg, I found among the wounded and prisoners men and officers of the 16th and 58th Ohio, and of the 29th and 31st Missouri, and 13th Illinois."(18)
Colonel Fletcher was later exchanged and rejoined his command during the siege of Vicksburg.

General John Clifford Pemberton's report of the Confederate defense of the Chickasaw Bluffs, is as follows;

"About 10 o'clock a furious cannonade was opened on General Stephen D. Lee's lines. This ceased about 11 o'clock, when a whole brigade about six thousand strong, understood to have been Brigadier General F.P. Blair's, though not led by him in person emerged from the woods in good order and moved gallantly forward under a heavy fire of our artillery. They advanced to within one hundred and fifty yards of the pits then broke and retreated, but soon rallied and dividing their forces sent a portion to their right, which was gallantly driven back by the 28th Louisana and 42nd Georgia regiments with heavy loss."(19)

An interesting story is told about both of the flags of the 31st Missouri Infantry Regiment in the history of the 13th Illinois Infantry.

"When Blair's brigade charged the enemy's works at Chickasaw Bayou, at noon on the 29th of December, 1862, the eight battle-flags of the four regiments in the brigade, in two lines of battle, were a most inspiring sight; and they were borne proudly on to the bloody field where some were lost, while others were trailed in the dust and trodden under foot by both friend and foe as the waves of battle ebbed and flowed in successes and reverses until our troops were driven from the field.

No flag was borne more proudly, defended more stoutly, or beckoned its brave followers nearer the last works of the enemy, than ours. The fortunes of war decreed its capture by the enemy. The brigade line of battle had been formed by placing our regiment Thirteenth Illinois, in the right front, and the Thirty-first Missouri in the left front; and it will be noticed that of those two regiments touching elbows in line of battle, the figures designating the number of one, are exactly transposed in that of the other. This will be shown to have been the cause of a most singular double mistake, after the repulse of our troops.

A strong personal friendship prompted Private Jack Kenyon, of Company K, Thirteenth Illinois, to crawl over on to the battle-field, after dark, to search for the wounded or dead lieutenants of his company, who were missing. In his search he came across a flag whose figures he thought were 'one' and a 'three.' While not knowing that our flag was missing, this seemed proof that it was so; and he determined to rescue it from eventually falling into the enemy's hands. He tore the flag from the staff and wound it about his body, and continued what proved an unavailing search. Just before daylight he had recrossed the bayou and reached camp only to find that the flag was the State flag belonging to the Thirty-first Missouri.

When driven off the field that same day, Private George W. Sutherland, of Company I, Thirteenth Illinois, was not so scared but that he noticed a flag partly rolled up, and nearly concealed under the body of a dead soldier and the other wreckage of a battle-field. Enough of the flag was exposed to show a figure 'three,' and he had no doubt that it was our flag; and making a mental memorandum of the locality, for that was all he could do then, as the bullets and shells of the rebs were 'speeding the parting guest,' and so Comrade Sutherland 'stood not upon the order of his going, but went at once.' After a tedious search, he found the flag, and dragged it, staff and all, to the first line of the rifle-pits, then ran for the bayou, across which he found a log which he used as a bridge, and triumphantly bore his trophy to Surgeon Plummer, who was taken down considerably by the revelation that it was the National colors of the Thirty-first Missouri, both of whose flags had been lost on the field, and both had been rescued and restored by soldiers of the Thirteenth Illinois, who both supposed that they were rescuing their own flag. An officer of the regiment to which the flags belonged, stood near and claimed the flag that Private Sutherland had delivered to Dr. Plummer, who too readily gave it up; and for the rescue of neither of these flags did any thanks come back."(20)

That night, December 29th, General Steele's division and one brigade of Stuart's were drawn out of line. This force, under the command of General Steele, was to look for a point below Haines's Bluff or Blake's plantation to attack from another point on the 31st of December. On the night of December 30th, they loaded up on the boats in the Yazoo River and proceeded up the Yazoo River just below Haines' Bluff. General Stephen D. Lee directed an attack against the transports as they were loading. One of his regiments did attack and caused the Union soldiers to hurry on board. In an extract to a letter home Captain S.J. Ridley, of Wither's artillery wrote, "The thrashing they got a Chickasaw was the most disgraceful one of the war. My opinion is that they could not rally their men to another attack. They were followed to their boats and fired into while getting into them. They departed precipitately, leaving many of their men who were guarding commissaries behind without letting them know, although they were but a little ways from them. They were competely demoralized."(21) Captain S. J. Ridley later was killed at Baker's Creek, Mississippi. After this attack the boats hurried away from shore while firing shells at the Confederates, causing them to withdraw from the boats. They were to disembark around daylight and charge the Confederates from the flanks in their positions on the hills. This attack was hoped to cause the Confederates to divert some of their men from the main attack from their front. At the most it was hoped that it would cause such a panic that the Confederate forces would then retreat to Vicksburg. While on the way up the river the fog became so thick that General Steele sent General Sherman a note notifying him that he felt that he could not succeed in the planned attack. This, with more rainfall convinced General Sherman that it was time to retreat from this engagement and he started making plans to that effect. Major A. J. Seay wrote in his diary his impressions for the rest of the year through January 4, 1863.

"TUESDAY DECEMBER 30, 1862.

Every thing is muddy and cheerless today. The men hungry wet cold and exhausted. Our total loss in killed and wounded and missing yesterday estimated at 2,000. In all the fighting before 500 to 2500. The battle is not renewed, all quiet. We went three times with a flag of truce to get our dead and wounded on the field it was fired on and driven back by the rebels every time.

WEDNESDAY DEC. 31, 1862

I came to the Sucker State last night pretty well used up, but not touched by a ball or shell, although some came unpleasantly near during the battle. Today the enemy permitted us to go to the field and remove the dead. Found them treated in the usual manner, i.e. stripped them of their clothes and robbed them of their money and all their valuables such is war. It is also a well established fact that many of our dead were once only wounded. Subsequently they were shot directly thru the head as they lay wounded and helpless on the field.

THURSDAY JAN 1ST, 1863.

I rise this morning rather lonely. Nobody greets me with a "Happy New Year". But I hear the groans and coughs of our sick men all around. It is a beautiful day – warm enough for lizzards to crawl. I am restless and lonesome as also weak and hungry. In the afternoon, I get on my horse and go up to the battle field. Find the 32d on board the steamer "Psamlet" with orders to proceed in company with Steele's division – Blair's regiment up the Yazoo to the upper batteries on Haynes Bluff. There we were to charge the enemies batteries, after our gun boats shelled for two hours – but soon the program was changed and we find ourselves moving down the Yazoo. At 8 p.m. we disembark and go aboard the "Sucker State" for the night.

FRIDAY JAN 2, 1863.

We move down the green waters of the Yazoo into the muddy waters of the Mississippi – land above the mouth. The rain pours down incessantly. A great many sick – I am.

SATURDAY JAN 3D, 1863

It rains furiously all day. We move up the river a mile and tie up at a fine farm on the La. side. Here is a very fine farm. 500 or 600 acres of land in the bottoms below high water mark. Here as fine corn as I ever saw grow. They planted but little cotton. The boys get any quanity of sweet potatoes turnips, beets, cabbage etc, just where they grow. I saw a beet 25 inches long this morning. Molasses in abundance. This is a fine mansion house facing to the river, which is beautifully set with shade and hedge trees and evergreens.

SUNDAY JAN 4TH, 1863.

A beautiful day the sun shines bright and nice as in spring. In the evening we start up the river. Run Nearly all night moon shines bright."(22)

When they arrived at Milliken's Bend it was still raining and the men had to wait for it to stop before they could start to unload. General A. J. Smith's division was to land up the river approximately one-half mile from the stores at Milliken's Bend, above him was to be General Morgan's division. General M. L. Smith's division would go into camp about two hundred yards below the stores with General Steele's division camped below him. The quartermaster was to take possession of all houses and sheds at Milliken's Bend for the storage of the stores. What happened to those who lived in these houses, if they had not already abandoned their homes, is not clearly stated but you can imagine they were kicked out without to much sympathy for their rights as home owners.

In the Daily Missouri Democrat for Monday January 19, 1863, a reporter sent an article of what he titled "The Battle of Vicksburg." From the article dated December 29, 1862 the writer states:

"Blair's division (Brigade) was drawn up preparatory to the charge in three lines, the 13th Illinois forming the right and 31st Missouri forming the left of the first of the advance line of battle, supported by the 30th Missouri on the right and 29th on the left, forming the second line, the 32nd Missouri on the right and 58th Ohio on the left forming the third line, in which order they were led to the charge, which was taken up gallantly by the advanced lines, closely followed by their supports. When they struck the double quick, the tremendous yells and cheers accompaning their brilliant dash, and the roar of deep-mouthed cannon, and the rattle of innumerable smaller arms, was the signal for the advance to the charge of Gen. Smith's division, which was immediately taken up and gallantly led by the 6th and 8th Missouri, supported by the balance of the division. The charge of Blair's division (Brigade) was made against a fortified battery, situated on Hall's Bluff, a little above the base of the bluff, surrounded by rifle pits and breast works, commanding an open field some seven or eight hundred yards in width, a bayou or ditch and an extensive abatis of fallen timber, even which the brigade had to advance under the incessant fire of the enemy. The 13th Ill., 31st Mo., and 29th Mo. continued to advance until they were close upon the muzzles of the enemies guns. The enemy having been driven from their rifle pits into their second breastwork, and nearly all the officers having been either wounded or killed by the storm of grape and canister and bursting shells, and innumerable Minie balls, and having lost a great many of their men, the forlorn hope was ordered to fall back, which they did, losing many in their retreat. Some who were so badly wounded they could not get off the field were taken prisoners. Among them were Col. Fletcher of the 31st Missouri, and Maj. Jaensch, of the 31st, Captain Dougharty and Captain McMurtry, all taken prisoners and nearly all the wounded officers, excepting those mentioned of the 31st were gotten off the field safely, Captain Edward E. Allen, Company B, 31st Missouri, in the advance, was on the extreme left of the regiment, kept the left up in the charge until arriving within one hundred yards of the enemy's battery, and although scarred three times by the enemy's riflemen, he continued gallantly, to lead until ordered to fall back. He had not fallen back with his men more than one hundred yards before he was struck with a rifle ball, piercing the right side of the back, passing through the vertebra, and came out on the left side near the shoulder. He was from that moment not only unable to command his men, but unable to stand upon his feet. Still, however, retaining his presence of mind, he preferred to risk every chance of death to captivity, and succeeded in crawling from the battlefield amid showers of shot and shell, through a deep mud ditch, and thus avoided being taken prisoner. His faithful little son was one of the first to discover him, and rendered that assistance which is always so grateful on such occasions."(23)

In a letter dated January 8, 1863, Private Henry Kuck gave his brief account of the Battle of Chickasaw Bayou or Vicksburg. In his letter he writes:

"I received your letter on the 7th of Jan, 1863, just as I, or we, came back from VICKSBURG. Just before Christmas our fleet, consisting of approximately 75 to 80 steamships and troops of approximately 35 thousand, went toward Vicksburg, namely we wanted to hunt the SECESHERS, but we had to be patient and retreat after we had plundered their packs. We drove them back over the mud to their former position but we couldn't draw them out of their fortifications.

On the 29th of Decbr. we had to attack a fortified position by Vicksburg, but here we were so hotly opposed that we turned back after a half hour, during which half of our soldiers were killed or wounded. There were about 3 thousand men in the attack, but I believe that more than half remained behind dead or wounded on the battlefield, and this all in a half hour, I thought it had lasted a whole hour, no one came back without a wound, I myself was somewhat wounded on my left leg, but it will soon be much better. WILHELM SCHWARZE and HENRY GERDEL had at the time mumps and were not in the battle. Claus Gerdel was there. I can tell you that in this battle you really call it slaughtering; it looked horrible. As soon as you shot off your rifle they were tearing at your back. A horrible memory. I'm now healthy and about, also Wilh. Schwarze and HENRY & CLAUS GERDEL. Good-bye, sweet wife and children, I wish the war would end and I would come back to you."(24)

Another letter sent to his wife dated January 10, 1863, Private Kuck sent home more details of the Battle of Chickasaw Bayou or as the Confederates refer to it as Vicksburg. As you will notice the letter ends abruptly because the rest of the letter is lost somewhere and not in the files.

"On Decbr. 27 we landed at the Yazoo River and on the very night we attacked the rebels, but later in the evening it became very dark and rained the whole night, and drove us back into the forest until morning; on the next day we went onward and gradually were able to drive the enemy to his fort, but this is all we could do, for their forts were on a high hill and very secure; and where we could, and had to, attack was a big cornfield with wood and bushes all cut down: that way they made it hard for us to attack the breast-works and the fort wall.

On the 29th, as I mentioned in this last part, we had to take a very unwise risk: attack one of the last forts on the Yazoo river not far from Vicksburg. F. Blair's Brigade, to which we belong, is the one which went to the Fort; I don't know exactly but I've heard it was about 3 thousand men. Anyway, on the 29 of Decbr. we were commanded to attack the fort. We lay there in the woods; as soon as "forward" was called, everyone went forwards, and we stormed a quarter mile through bushes where the whole front grew ragged, and then we emerged into a swamp and had to hop through an old creek where we got water and mud in our shoes and boots, and we had already tired ourselves out from running in the bushes where there was no danger. Now we climbed a 10-foot high sandbank. Before that we didn't notice how many cannons the rebels had, but just as we came out of the bushes onto the sandbank there came a fusillade upon us ......"(25)

This battle was referred to by the Federal army is "Battle of Chickasaw Bayou" while it was known to the Confederates as the first "Battle of Vicksburg." The title of this chapter "The Valley of Death" is taken from the following source, the 48th Ohio Volunteer Veteran History. In this book an unknown officers letter was reprinted that he sent home in August, 1863.

"Yesterday I concluded to pay a visit to the Yazoo Swamps, where our army was during the unsuccessful attack on Vicksburg last December. Accordingly, after breakfast, I mounted my charger, and in an hour's ride I passed through Vicksburg and by all the upper river batteries. From there I descended into the valley, which we occupied last winter. After a careful survey of the ground which the rebels occupied, and that which was held by us, I have come to the conclusion that their position was as near impregnable as art and nature could make it. The swamps are as silent and dismal-looking as ever. The valley is covered with a rank growth of timber, under-brush and creeping vines. The limbs of the trees are covered with spanish moss, that hangs in different lengths from every twig.

It is this that gives it the air of solemnity, more than anything else. Add to this the rattle of musketry, the booming of cannon, a heavy rain, and then under cover of darkness to out on double-quick, and leave on the boats for the Mississippi river, and last but not least it said that you are whipped, that Vicksburg can't be taken, then perhaps you can form a faint idea how we felt while going up the river, and why it was called 'The Valley of Death'."(26)

During the Civil War, the hospital facilities were not as clean as hospitals are reported to be today. A soldier would be sent to the hospital for treatment for a wound and while in the hospital become sick of disease which would cause his death, they could be listed as dying of their wounds. The hospital's were so bad that many men, especially later in the war, would almost do anything to keep from going to the hospital. They often turned to trying home remedies and other methods, such as strong drink, as a sure cure all. The Civil War hospitals were generally poorly ventilated and were nothing more than breeding ground for germs and disease. Medicine was still practiced much as it had been during the Middle Ages. It hadn't been that long since bleeding was a common practice, even in the early part of the nineteenth century. When the war began there were just sixteen hospitals in use by the army in the North. This more than met the needs of the military prior to the Civil War. At the start of the war both sides thought that it would not last very long, six months was figured as the longest, they were totally unprepared for the amount of wounded men that they treated during the war. For instance, in the East, the Army of the Potomac suffered twenty-six thousand and forty-seven wounded casualties from May 5th, 1864 through June 12th, 1864. These were in the battles of the Wilderness, Spottsylvania, North Anna, Totopotomoy and Cold Harbor. By the end of the war the Union army were sending their wounded to three hundred and fifty hospitals. Those in charge of the hospitals were not aware of how disease was transmitted or the need for good nutrition or sanitation. The men of the 31st Missouri Regiment were sent to the hospital's in Saint Louis, Missouri, Jefferson Barracks in Missouri, Paducah in Kentucky and in Memphis, Tennessee. Later in the war, the men were sent to the hospitals in Vicksburg, Mississippi and Nashville & Chattanooga, Tennessee.

The wounded man would walk or be carried to the surgeon's tent. He would then usually be carried into the tent by hospital stewards. If he was lucky one of the hospital stewards would be someone who might have been in his company or regiment and maybe he would receive special treatment. One of the most common cures for gunshot in an arm or leg, if the bones were broke or shattered or there appeared to be excessive muscle damage, was amputation. There was not much in the use of disinfectants. Most of the time when you were to be operated on, there was no use of masks, clean sheets or even clean utensils. Sometimes when the surgeon was done operating on one patient, he would immediately start operating on another patient. If the patient was lucky, the utensil would be washed off in water, clean or dirty, and wiped off on a cloth, an apron or pair of pants. Gangrene was a major cause of amputation. Once it set in, they would automatically amputate the limb. In many autobiographies or books that you read about this area of the war, one of the main things they stated that would make them sad, was the pile of amputated limbs that the surgeons would pile up outside of the tent until they could be taken and be disposed of later. Once you were treated you would be taken outside of the tent and placed with other men who had been treated. They would then await transportation to a rear area hospital for further treatment. This was accomplished by various methods. One of the most common methods used in the western army was to use a steam powered river boat. As described earlier when General Sherman's army moved to attack at the Battle of Chickasaw Bayou they traveled down the Mississippi River and up the Yazoo River. After the battle the wounded were loaded on the steamships and taken to Memphis, Saint Louis and Jefferson Barracks.

The 31st Missouri had many surgeon's and assistant surgeon's throughout the Civil War. The first one was Surgeon Churchill G. Strother. He was a leading physician prior to the war in Warrenton, Missouri in Warren County. He was mustered in on August 28, 1862. There is not much known about his service record but he died on November 1863 at Saint Louis, Missouri of disease. Can you imagine being a small community doctor and then being thrown into a situation where you have all these wounded being brought to you with violent serious wounds for you to treat. This had to be a very stressful situation to find yourself in. On September 6, 1862 Julius A. Ruge became the assistant surgeon. He mustered in at Saint Louis, Missouri. On August 11, 1863 he resigned. Maybe he had only enlisted for one year or maybe he had more than enough of bloodshed and war after Chickasaw Bayou, Arkansas Post and Vicksburg. Also on September 6th O. H. P. Stone was mustered in as an assistant surgeon, but the record also shows that he was mustered out on the same day. The next surgeon the regiment had was Surgeon Alexander W. Reese, he enlisted on May 30,1864 at New Hope, Georgia and mustered out on November 9, 1864 when the 31st Missouri Infantry Regiment and the 32nd Missouri Infantry Regiment were combined into a six company battalion. The assistant surgeon Addison Elston was mustered in on June 30,1864 and resigned on April 28, 1865 after the surrender of General Johnston's Army. These two men were involved in some of the major battles in the Atlanta Campaign. Assistant Surgeon Elston went on and made the March to the Sea and also the march through the Carolinas. Assistant Surgeon E. H. Hoffman was mustered in on September 5, 1863 but his commission was revoked effective December 18, 1863 by Special Order #231. Assistant Surgeon F. W. Wunderlich was mustered in on May 19,1864, his commission was likewise revoked on June 29, 1864 by a special order. Surgeons all held the rank of Major with the pay of a major in the cavalry until they went beyond the army corps level. The surgeon in chief of a department holds the rank of Lieutenant-Colonel and is on the staff of the Major-General commanding the department.

In a book that he published in 1870 Surgeon Alexander W. Reese describes what became known later in the war the operating corps. His description follows.

"The Surgeon in chief, or Medical Director, of a Corps, examines the records and, from these data, appoints a Surgeon, and assistants, to take charge of each Division Field Hospital and an 'Operating Corps', composed of the Senior Surgeons of the Division. The ranking regimental surgeon in the Division is, per se, the Surgeon in Chief of the Division—the highest, Medical officer in it—and all the medical officers in the Division are under his orders. The 'Operating Corps' is the chief surgical feature in the Division, and the position is eagerly coveted, by all Surgeons in the Army, who are anxious to improve in this special branch of the profession.

The duties of the Corps consisted solely in operating on the wounded men of the Division. No capital operation was allowed on the field which was not performed by this Corps. The Corps had its Headquarter with the Division Field Hospital, which was usually located about one mile in rear of the battlefield. During an action the duties of the Corps were very arduous. Wounded soldiers were brought in ambulances from the field, and operated upon, in turn, just as the necessities of each individual case seemed to require. I have seen an acre or two of ground covered with the wounded men—wrapped in their blankets—awaiting their turn for the surgeon's table.

And here I wish to correct a popular error—injurious to an arm of the service no less honorable and useful than any other portion of the army. There seems to have crept into the public mind an idea that 'army Surgeons', as a class, were a set of men totally reckless of limb and life, and, not infrequently, incompetent to the proper discharge of the grave and responsible duties imposed upon them. Some have even gone further than this, and declared them a useless appendage to the army. Such opinions could only originate in ignorance, prejudice, or willful misrepresentation of the facts in the case. That many lives and limbs are, necessarily, sacrificed in the army, which might be saved at home, a moment's reflection will enable any one to comprehend; but that there was any more want of care, skill, prudence, and principle among military surgeons, than with the same class of civilians, I do most emphatically and utterly deny. And I do so knowing what I say. The charge is unjust, unfounded, often malicious, and not supported by truth.

And I say here—with all due and proper respect to the great names I have quoted—that the science and the art of Surgery are, to day, a century in advance if what they would have been but for the experience of the late civil war; and that the advance, so claimed, is due—solely and entirely due—to the humble labors—the faithful and patient investigations—of the reviled 'Army Surgeons', whose opportunities of knowledge have been unequalled upon the face of the globe.

In addition to the general work of the operating corps my special duties consisted in noting down the name, rank, regiment, and Co, of the disabled soldier; keeping an accurate record of the situation, nature, and extent of his wound; what operation, if any, was required, and by whom the operation was performed. These duties were arduous and, combined with my regular work, in operating with Hudson, my colaborer, made me, during an action, a 'busy spectator' of the scene.

When on the march we had no Field Hospital, and then, during an engagement, the Operating Corps were ordered onto the field for the relief of the wounded officers and men. When a wounded soldier is brought in, he is put upon the table—a glass of whiskey given him—the men being usually exhausted from loss of blood.

Chloroform is then administered, and the nature and extent of his injuries ascertained. The board of Surgeons then determine what operation—if any—is needed. If an operation is decided upon the Surgeon in Chief assigns two Surgeons, or a Surgeon and one Assistant Surgeon, to take charge of him, and to perform the operation.

When a soldier—wounded in action—was placed upon my table, before giving him whiskey, or chloroform, I invariably talked to him in this way——'Well, my man, I see you are pretty severely injured! We want to give you chloroform—the better to enable us to examine your wounds—and also to decide upon what is the best line of conduct to pursue in your particular case. Now are You willing, if we find the injury so extensive as to require amputation, to allow us to remove the limb?' In ninety nine cases out of a hundred the reply would be 'Well, Doctor, I want you to save the limb, if you possibly can, but if you think it can't be done with safety, I am perfectly willing for you to do whatever you think best."(27)

One of the major sources of information that the United States public had during Desert Storm was television. We could, and most of the United States did, sit in front of the television and watch Iraq being bombed while they shot anti-aircraft rounds at the planes as it happened. In the Civil War the major source of information was the newspaper. The reporters of that era were no different than they appear now. They were trying to be the first to scoop their competition. Some of their methods, as today, were questionable. General Sherman was a victim of the press which he neither forgot nor forgave. Early in the war as the commander of the army in Kentucky he was reported by the press to be in a panic. The press quoted him as saying that in order for the Union to hold Kentucky, he would need over one hundred and fifty thousand men. In 1861 this was considered an impossibility and beyond comprehension. He was a very nervous person throughout the war and was under stress. He was later relieved because of the public outcry that was caused by these articles. He was given a short leave of absence and allowed to get his thoughts back together. His wife was a great comfort and helped him back on the road to recovery. Right or wrong, he blamed the press for his downfall and was very strict about their participation in any of his campaigns.

In the Chickasaw Bayou campaign he had forbidden the press to go on the steamboats to report on the campaign because of his strong dislike for them. Unknown to General Sherman, some crafty reporters did manage to sneak on board one of these steamships. Their names were Thomas W. Knox, correspondent of the New York Herald, Richard Colburn of the New York World, Junius Henri Browne of the Cincinnati Gazette, A. M. (Albert H.) Bodman of the Chicago Tribune and Albert D. Richardson of the New York Tribune. These men witnessed the Chickasaw Bayou attack. General Sherman was so mad about this disobedience that he was tempted to hang all of them. But cooler heads prevailed and he had them shipped north and confined for awhile. Throughout the war General Sherman was very strict about this subject, but with more and more reporters trying to be the first one to get the news to those left at home, and by direction of General Grant, he allowed them to accompany him on his later campaigns but his prejudice never changed.

After the Battle of Chickasaw Bayou, and prior to the capture of Arkansas Post Arkansas, there were more men lost to the regiment due to illness, desertion or death. In Company A, Private James A. Wideman of Victoria deserted at the mouth of the White River on January 8,1863, on the way to Arkansas Post, and was accompanied by Private Sampson Wiley . Private Samuel M. Mooney of Herculaneum died on January 5th, 1863 and Private Jesse Sutton of Victoria died at the Post Hospital in Helena, Arkansas of measles. Company B lost no men during this time for any reason. Company C lost to death Private Joe M. Marler from Washington County on January 1, 1863 in Memphis Tennessee. In Company D, Corporal George W. Swinea of Greenville was discharged on January 2, 1863 for disability. Company E lost Private Jesse Young of Moselle due to his death on January 8, 1863 at Helena Arkansas. Company F lost the following men due to reasons listed: Private John E. Smith of Canaan died on January 8, 1863 aboard the steamboat Isabella. Private John J. Carroll of Canaan died on January 1, 1863 inMemphis Tennessee: Corporal Pleasant F. Price of Canaan was discharged on January 9th. Company G lost no men at this time. Company H lost the following men: Private Joseph Hendriks of Wayne County was discharged due to disability on

January 6, 1863, also discharged for the same reason was Wagoner John M. Horton of Washington County on January 1, 1863 at Saint Louis Missouri; Corporal Henry White of Wayne County died at Helena Arkansas on January 5, 1863. Company I lost no men at this time. Company K's Private William Tesson from Danville was discharged on January 2, 1863 of disability at Jefferson Barracks Missouri.

CHAPTER THREE:
ARKANSAS POST, ARKANSAS

Fort Hindman at Arkansas Post, Arkansas is now in the Arkansas River, there are some Confederate entrenchments at the park that are still able to be seen. The park itself is in an out of the way place, but it has a very lovely body of water surrounding it and is a place where you can take your family and have a picnic, go fishing and enjoy the view. It is listed as a National Memorial Site which is part of the National Park Service. Arkansas Post has a history that dates back to the Spanish exploration and the French ownership of the fort. It is approximately one hundred and twenty miles northwest of Vicksburg. Arkansas Post was a small village, the county seat of Arkansas County and the Confederate force stationed there was commanded by Brigadier General Thomas Churchill. It was on a sharp turn in the river and on a bluff which made it a very defensible position. It was called Fort Hindman during the Civil War and was garrisoned by about four thousand eight hundred men. It was really not an important post and was not a strategic objective to get out of the way before they could proceed to Vicksburg however General Grant says in his Memoirs, "I was at first disposed to disapprove of this move as an unnecessary side movement having no especial bearing upon the work before us; but when the result was understood I regarded it as very important. Five thousand Confederate troops left in the rear might have caused us much trouble and loss of property while navigating the Mississippi."(1)   Fort Hindman was used by the Confederates mainly as a defensive position on the river to guard against an invading force headed for Little Rock, Arkansas on the river. General Churchill was not content just to sit there and wait for the war to come to him. He sent detachments to the mouth of the White River and Arkansas River to disrupt river traffic on the Mississipi River. They interfered with supply boats that were on their way from Memphis to the forces of General Sherman. General Sherman learned of the existence of Fort Hindman from a man who had been captured by the Confederates when the steamboat that he served on was captured. The boat, Blue Wing, was loaded with ammunition, mail and other supplies destined for General Sherman's army at Milliken's Bend.

Major General John A. McClernand finally arrived and took command from General Sherman on January 2nd, 1863. General McClernand was a politician from Illinois and was an acquaintance of the President of the United States. At the outbreak of the war, General McClernand resigned from Congress and offered his services to the government. He served in the Fort Donelson campaign and at the Battle of Shiloh. As a political general he was suspected of trying to gain glory only for fame sake with hopeful aspirations for the presidency. Shortly after the battle at Shiloh he took a leave of absence from the army and proceeded almost immediately to the capitol to tell President Lincoln that if he was given command of an independent army that he would raise, he could capture Vicksburg in short order. The President approved of the idea and General McClernand was ordered to proceed with his plans. He then proceeded home and started recruiting men for his force from Illinois, Ohio, Indiana and Missouri. Some of these men, once they enlisted, were immediately sent to the Army of the Tennessee. Some of these men arrived in time to participate in the Chickasaw Bayou campaign. General Grant was informed of General McClernand plans by a telegram from Major General Henry W. Halleck, who was now the General in Chief in Washington, D. C.. After the battle of Shiloh, General Halleck took over command of the Department of the Tennessee and made General Grant his second in command. It was at this time that General Grant considered resigning because he was basically put out to pasture. General Sherman convinced General Grant not to resign, because General Sherman had once been declared crazy and now he was again in the good graces of the government by again being given a command in General Grant's army. This is one of reasons that General Grant did not resign. Later in the war this decision was to prove to be of great benefit to the Union Army. General Sherman had done his country and his friend a great service. Once General Halleck received orders to go to Washington D. C., he returned General Grant to the command of the Department of the Tennessee, but not before he had dispersed his great army to different parts of the country.

General Sherman convinced General McClernand of the

importance of eliminating Arkansas Post, or Fort Hindman, as a threat to the Federal army by having an enemy position in their rear. General Sherman had received information that the fort could be difficult if not impossible to attack from the water, but could probably be easily taken from the rear. General McClernand agreed to the plan but some said he did so with great reservation. In a diary entry Lieutenant William H. Lynch, of Company I, 32nd Missouri Infantry Regiment, states that, "The Company embarked on the Steamer Sucker State the 1st day of January 1863, and proceeded slowly up the Mississippi River, thence through a Bayou into the Arkansas River and up that stream disembarking near 'Arkansas Post' Arkansas River, on the 10th January 1863."(2) On January 4, 1863 General McClernand issued his General Order #1, assuming command of the Army of the Mississippi. He divided the army into two corps; the first was to be commanded by Brigadier General George W. Morgan made up of his own division and Brigadier General A. J. Smith's. The second corps was made up of Brigadier General Frederick Steele's division and the division of Brigadier General David Stuart. This corps was commanded by General Sherman. General McClernand embarked his army of approximately thirty-two thousand men on the steamboats and transports and headed up the Mississippi River to the mouth of the White River, which they reached on the 8th of January. On January 9th they proceeded up the White River to the Arkansas River to the vicinity of Fort Hindman arriving there around dark. They had arrived at a position about three miles below their intended point of attack. It was to late that night to disembark from the boats so they decided to wait till the next morning. During the night it rained hard till around four a.m. when General Sherman began to arrange the boats in the order he wanted them to unload.

On the morning of January 10th, General Sherman's corps were the first ones to disembark off the boats. General Stuart's division moved up the river, along the bank soon coming into contact with the enemy who was entrenched behind earthworks. This line of earthworks stretched from the river to a swamp. General Steele's division, accompanied by General Sherman, was supposed to march by a road to get to firm ground in order to get to the rear of the fort. They moved out with General Hovey's brigade in the lead, General Thayer's brigade and General Blair's brigade bringing up the rear. General Steele's division marched through a swamp heading in a easterly direction for about two miles when they finally came to firm ground that had a cabin and a field. Asking the people who lived there plus some prisoners that surrendered at the sight of the Federal army, it was learned that in order to get to their destination that was desired they would have to march around seven miles in order to get behind Arkansas Post. If they could have marched in a straight line distance they would have gone only another two miles. General McClernand overtook them and informed General Sherman that the Confederates had abandoned their line of entrenchment's and taken positions in the fort. He then ordered General Sherman and General Steele's division to recross the swamp and hurried to catch up with General Stuart, who at the time was marching toward Fort Hindman. General Blair received orders to return to the mornings landing sight, then his brigade became the lead of the division. Around dark General Blair was ordered to advance up the road next to the river towards Arkansas Post, but because of the number of other troops on the road it was impossible to make much headway so around midnight he ordered his brigade to go into camp for the night. The Confederate first line of defense was about four miles from the fort. To get to the fort they had to go through some heavily wooded areas with very few open areas except close to the fort. During the night the Confederates were busy strengthening thier defensive positions. While the Federal infantry was moving into position for the night the Federal navy, under Admiral Porter, bombed the fort till well after dark.

On January 11th, a new line of entrenchment's were observed to their front. It stretched across a peninsula caused by the Arkansas River and the before mentioned swamp. General McClernand described what the Federal forces were facing.

"Below the fort occur the rifle pits and levee before mentioned. The levee exposed a convex line to our advance, was pierced for ten guns and lined on the inside by rifle-pits. The second line of rifle pits, with intervals left for six guns, extended across the high land from the river to the swamp, its rear approach being obstructed by an abattis of fallen timber. And still nearer the fort was a deep ravine, entering the river at right angles and extending inland, in different arms, in front of the left of our line. In front of the center of the line was an open field.

This strip of high land afforded the only available approach from our landing to the enemy's defenses, and above the second line of rifle-pits, expanded it to the dry plateau extending to the swamp on the east and northeast, and to the bayou and river on the west and south."(3)

General Sherman's corps, with General Stuart's division on the left and General Steele's division on the right having arrived in position after marching through the night, had the ground to the right and General Morgan's corps was on the ground to the left. General Blair was ordered at five a.m. to close up with General Thayer's brigade, which he accomplished at day break, which placed his brigade at the barracks on the Little Rock Road which the Confederates had abandoned the night before. General Blair's brigade was placed in reserve, but was to stay within supporting distance of the rest of the division, because of the terrible beating they had taken at Chickasaw Bayou. Their areas of operations were defined by a road that almost split this peninsula in half. Around one p.m. Admiral Porter's naval force started their bombardment. By one-thirty p.m. the troops on the Federal left began the charge having to cross about three-hundred yards of clearing under severe fire from the Confederates finally taking shelter in a line of woods behind some logs and brush. General Sherman issued the order for his artillery to begin firing about fifteen minutes after the barrage from the boats when General Sherman gave the go ahead for the infantry to charge. There was little cover for the infantrymen except for trees and logs that afforded very little if, any protection. The infantrymen began advancing under a heavy fire, periodically falling to the ground for cover and rest. General Sherman says in his Memoirs, "Every tree had its group of men, and behind each log was a crowd of sharp-shooters, who kept up so hot a fire that the rebel troops fired wild." (4) The fort's artillery was kept busy firing at the naval fleet and General Morgan's troops. The major source of fire confronting General Sherman's corps was the infantry and three sections of field-guns that were in the entrenchment's to which they were advancing. Once, the naval gunboats approached the fort so close that General Sherman could see their flags above the parapets of the fort. The battle continued to be hot and furious to General Sherman's front with the men steadily advancing in the face of infantry and cannon fire, when around four p.m. there was spotted a white flag.

There was almost immediately white flags appearing all along the fort to signify that the fort had enough. Soon after there were white flags appearing in different areas. General Sherman ordered cease fire and sent the word down the line to General Steele's force who had made about the same rate of progress on the right following the border of the swamp as General Stuart's men who was being accompanied by General Sherman. All firing had ceased except an occasional shot to General Steele's front. The new defenses that the Confederates had built were severely damaged in spots by the Union artillery, which caused many killed and wounded. Colonel Garland's Brigade occupied the trenches in front of General Sherman whom he ordered to form his brigade, stack arms and hang their belts on their muskets then to await further orders. General Steele was ordered to have the Confederates to his front to do the same thing. General Sherman, while in search of General Churchill, the commanding general of the fort, was approached by Major J. H. Hammond his adjutant-general with a report from General Deshler, who was in command of the Confederate brigade in front of General Steele's division. General Deshler had refused to stack arms and surrender because he had received no orders to this effect from his commander.

General Sherman then advised General Churchill that he had better issue these orders to General Deshler or he could not promise to control General Steele's division once an action started no matter what the cause or who was at fault. While accompanying General Churchill to General Deshler, General Sherman witnessed an angry exchange between General Churchill and Colonel Garland as to why Colonel had raised the white flag. They found General Deshler and asked why he had not surrendered . General Deshler responded," I have not received orders to do so." General Churchill then responded that it was very evident that they were in the hands of the enemy and to go ahead and surrender. He then issued the orders to stack arms and await further orders. General A. J. Smith was then ordered to take command of the fort because it was his troops who first entered the fort and General Sherman was ordered to proceed with the processing of the prisoners. General McClernand was ecstatic about the defeat of Arkansas Post and proclaimed that his star was on the rise. The Confederates were marched unarmed to a pocket formed by the river and two deep gullies just above the fort. After dark another Confederate regiment arrived from Pine Bluff, Arkansas and marched into captivity.

January 12, 1863 the prisoners were all loaded on the boats that were to transport them to Saint Louis as prisoners of war. There was four thousand seven hundred and ninety-one prisoners taken that day with all their arms and other military equipment that went with a military force stationed at a fort. On January 13th the victorious Union Army embarked on their boats and proceeded to Milliken's Bend to await General Grant's arrival. They laid over at Napoleon, Arkansas and held some conferences to discuss future plans with General McClernand hoping to move up the Arkansas River to capture Little Rock, Arkansas. The conferences lasted about two days with some severe personality conflicts between Admiral Porter and General McClernand. They re-embarked on the transports and left for Miliken's Bend, Louisiana. They arrived at Miliken's Bend on January 21st.

In a letter dated January 22nd, 1863 in which Private Kuck wrote a few lines of his impression of the battle at Arkansas Post.

".....again downriver, in that we didn't yet have our base there, and we came up the Arkansas River and landed there the 10th Jan. Our gunboats immediately launched a Cannonade against the Fort, but at first the Rebels didn't return the fire. The next morning, the Fortress and Breastworks were surrounded, and after a battle of 3 hours they hung out the white flag. Here in this battle we didn't even lose the 20th of our men, that is when you compare the number of participants to the time span of the attack ....but this last attack lasted 3 hrs. & 20 minutes. Perhaps just as in the Battle near Vicksburg, how many dead and wounded fell on both battlefields, so many to be compared for, and how many of those — at any rate hard to discover – that fell in Vicksburg that won't be noted in the newspaper, because Gen. Blair his Brigade ......"(5)

Another person who was at Arkansas Post, Arkansas, Major A. J. Seay of the 32nd Missouri Infantry Regiment, wrote in his diary his impression of the battle.

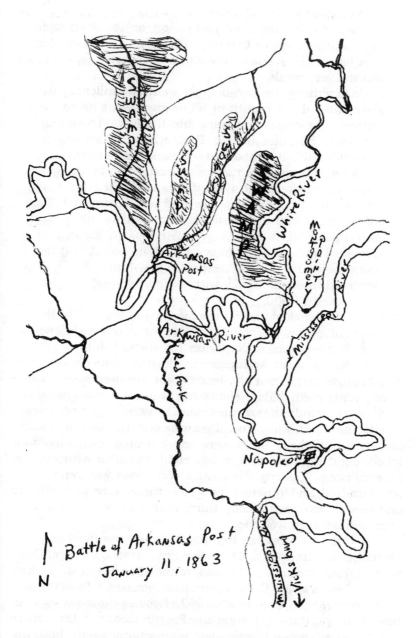

Battle of Arkansas Post
January 11, 1863

N

BATTLE OF ARKANSAS POST, ARKANSAS
JANUARY 13, 1863

"Wednesday Jan. 21st, 1863.

Since the 5th I have not had energy or ability enough to pick up the diary to write. I have now been on the sick list 20 days. Have this morning reported for duty, but am very weak.

Since writing the foregoing we went 200 miles up the river entered the mouth of White river went up to the cut off. Took that and went into the Ark. Thence up that river 50 miles to Ark. Post, where we arrived on Saturday 10th, disembarked – attack the Post by skirmishing. Sunday the right was brought on by the gun boats which kept up a terrific cannonading for four hours. In the meantime the land forces attacked the fort in front and on the flank with artillery and musketry. The fight was lively. The loss in killed and wounded on both sides heavy and about equal. But the game was ours, after a desperate resistance they surrendered unconditionally with all their stores, etc. No. of Prisoners 5,000.

We reembarked and on the morning of the 13th in the midst of a snow storm found ourselves on our way down the river – arrived at Napoleon 15th instant."(6)

The losses at Arkansas Post for the Confederate Army was approximately four thousand eight hundred men. There were twenty-eight killed, eighty-one wounded and four thousand seven hundred and ninety-one missing in action or captured. The Union Army casualties were one thousand and sixty-one men. Of these there were one hundred and thirty-four killed, eight hundred and ninety-eight wounded with twenty-nine missing. General Sherman's corps loss was reported at five hundred and nineteen of which there were four officers and seventy-five men killed, thirty-four officers and four hundred and six men wounded.

The 31st Missouri Infantry Regiment received only two casualties in this attack. They were Private Isaac Bruce of Company D from Greenville who was wounded and later died. Also wounded was Private Gideon Stump of Company K from Canaan who later died on January 26, 1863. Besides these two casualties, after the Battle of Arkansas Post in January 1863 there were quite a few desertions, deaths, discharges and those absent due to sickness. The following is a list of them by company and reason. Company A lost the following men to the accompanying reasons. Private John Graham of Hillsboro deserted on January 12th and on the same date Private James I. McCormik of Desoto accompanied him. Private Thomas H. Joplin of Desoto died on January 14th. Private George Rhevis of Steelville died on a hospital steamer on January 19th. Private John Williams of Victoria also died on a hospital steamer on Jannuary 14th. Company B's loss during this time was Private Leon A. Duclos of Washington County died on January 18th at Napoleon, Arkansas, an area they camped on their way to Milikens Bend after the Battle of Arkansas Post. Company C lost Private John Cobb of Hopewell who died on January 27th in Saint Louis Missouri. Private Benjamin Crumb of Hopewell died on January 19th on the steamer Isabelle. Private John J. Marler of Washington County died at Young's Point, Louisiana on January 23rd. Private Edward Simpson of Hopewell died on the steamer Isabelle on January 25th. Company D losses were Private Francis M. Dennison who died on January 21st and is buried at Jefferson Barracks in Missouri. Private Dale Copeland of Greenville died on January 13th. Private William B. Jackson of Butler County, Arkansas died at Miliken's Bend, Louisiana on January 11th. The following men, all from Greenville, Missouri, died at Arkansas Post, Arkansas. Private Alexander Cope died on January 14th, Private Marcus M. Deal, of Greenville, who died on January 11th, Corporal John W. Smith died on January 14th, Private William H. Southerlin died on January 13th and Private Andrew I. Williams who also died on January 13th. Private Joseph J. Newton of Greenville was discharged for disability on January 14th. Private John Ripley was also discharged he was also of Greenville. Private Francis M. Young of Victoria died on January 25th at Young's Point Louisiana. Company E losses were Private Esquire Young of Moselle died on January 12th and is buried at Jefferson Barracks. Private Thomas H. Brown of Moselle died on January 16th on a hospital boat. Private George M. Tater of Moselle deserted near Vicksburg Mississippi on January 29th. Private Harvey H. Kain of Saint Louis, Missouri died on January 23rd on a hospital boat. Private Jesse Phillips of Moselle died on hospital boat. Private Gain Skeggs of Moselle died on January 21st on a hospital boat. Company F lost the following men, all were discharged. Corporal Andrew J. Jenkins of Gasconade County at Jefferson Barracks, Missouri on January 19th, Sergeant Samuel H. Mattlock of Gasconade County on January 28th, Private

William R. Collier of Canaan on January 29th at Saint Louis, Missouri and Private Harrison Crower of Canaan because of disability on January 30th. Company G had no men lost at this time. Company H lost the use of the following men for the upcoming Vicksburg campaign. Private Augustine Clements of Wayne County died of disease at Arkansas Post, Arkansas on January 13th. Private John S. Crutchfield of Wayne County was discharged on January 16th at Saint Louis, Missouri. Private Francis M. Davis of Wayne County was also discharged on January 16th. Private Jesse W. Epley of Wayne County deserted at Arkansas Post, Arkansas, on January 13th. Private Joseph H. Raglan of Wayne County deserted on January 13th at Arkansas Post, Arkansas, he was fifty-two years old at this time. Private James H. Graves of Desoto died on January 18th. Private Lewis Hause of Wayne County died on the steamer Isabelle on January 23rd. Private Henry A. Lucy of Wayne County died on January 22nd at Memphis, Tennessee. Private Aldolpheus E. Perkins of Wayne County died on January 30th on the hospital boat Isabelle. Private James N. McConnell of Stoddard County was discharged on January 13th. Private George W. Miller of Wayne County was discharged for disability on January 14th. Private William P. White of Wayne County was discharged in Saint Louis, Missouri on January 20th. Company I lost Private Victor H. Hughes of Monroe County, who was discharged on January 13th. Company K losses were Private Philip G. Bryan of Potosi died of disease at Helena, Arkansas on January 15th. Private Nathan Alberty of Patterson deserted at Arkansas Post, Arkansas on January 13th, he was accompanied by Private James Spencer also of Patterson. Private George S. Owsly of Caledonia deserted at Napoleon, Arkansas on January 16th. Private John G. Farr of Patterson died on January 12th on a hospital boat. Private Francis M. Moore of Caledonia died on the hospital boat Isabelle on January 15th. Private Obediah Pruett of Ironton died on January 17th at Napoleon, Arkansas. All the before mentioned loss of manpower was given prior to the Battle of Chickasaw Bayou. Listed below are the companys in the 31st Missouri Regiment. Here is how they stood when they were getting ready to enter into the campaign for the conquest of Vicksburg.

At the National Archives the "Morning Reports" journals for Company C and Company G of the 31st Missouri Infantry Regiment can be found. The morning report for Company C states that at the end of January 1863 there was present and absent a total of "1 Officer and 58 men for a total of 59."(7) This was down from the high of one hundred and one in the November 1862 morning report. Company G, in the same time period, had present and absent, "3 Officers and 64 men for a total of 67."(8) This was down from the high of eighty-six in October 31, 1862.

CHAPTER FOUR :
YOUNG'S POINT, LOUISIANA

Major Abraham J. Seay of the 32nd Missouri Infantry Regiment writes in his diary the experiences that his regiment had which was probably much like the experiences of other regiments in the Federal army.

"SATURDAY JANUARY 17TH

Went up the Ark. 15 miles to wood. During our stay 20 men deserted. Sent two Companies A and B in pursuit. Captured 6 who (poor fellows) were stretched up by the wrists on the deck till their hands were black.

MONDAY 19TH

Returned to Napoleon and found that our fleet had gone down the river. We followed and soon overtook them. We are losing men every day more or less. When one has died his comrades go on shore with spade in hand and dig a rude hole in the sand bar in which his last remains are uncermoniously deposited. He dies far from home and friends like the beast of the field unwept and unsung.

THURSDAY 22d

We moved down the river and landed at a point on the La. shore from which we have full view of the mouth of the Yazoo above and Vicksburg below. We are four miles from the latter place by the aid of the glass I have just made a very interesting observation. From this point it seems to be situated mainly on a hill gradually rising as it recedes from the river. I see its fortifications which from this point look very formidable. We are disembarking from the boat, having made it our home (or prison) for 38 days. My health is very poor indeed. I am weak and sick today but am on duty."(1)

General Grant arrived at Young's Point, Louisiana on January 30, 1863 and took command of all the armies in the area. Special Order number 210, from the War Department, split the western armies into five different corps. Major General John B. McClernand was given the command of the 13th

Corps. In middle Tennessee, Major General George H. Thomas was given command of the 14th Corps. Major General William T. Sherman was given the command of the 15th Corps, which included the 31st Missouri Infantry Regiment. Major General S. A. Hurlbut was given command of the 16th Corps which was then at or near Memphis, Tennessee. Finally, Major General James B. McPherson was given the command of the 17th Corps, also in the Memphis area.

Now began one of the most determined efforts of the war to get from one position to another. General Grant was bound and determined to get to Vicksburg and capture it. But how to perform this task was going to be easier to think about than to actually do. Vicksburg had massive defenses on the bluffs overlooking the river. The river from Young's Point turns in a north-easterly direction above Vicksburg and then makes a turn and runs south-westerly direction. This would prove to be a hazardous undertaking for the riverboats because they came under fire from the batteries below Vicksburg before they could come under fire from those above the river. The Confederates had quite a few cannons up on the defenses and could easily fire round after round at the riverboats and inflict heavy damage on them before, during, and after they could bypass the batteries on the river. The Confederates were in possession of all the land just north, south and east of the city and were familiar with the land. There was also natural barriers that surrounded them. There was a delta area just to their north that was formed by the meeting of the Yazoo and Mississippi Rivers. This delta was interlaced with little bodies of water, bayous and swamps. It was almost impossible to invade from the north. General Grant had tried in December to attack from the northeast of Tennessee and had to withdraw. General Sherman had been bloodily repulsed at Chickasaw Bayou. He could not attack directly from the west because of the cliffs and river that made direct assault from that direction virtually impossible. The land west of the Mississippi River, in all but a few places, was barely above the level of the river. The Mississippi River was in the hands of the Confederates almost all the way to New Orleans. All the land east of Vicksburg was in control of the Confederates.

The winter of 1862-1863 was one of continuous high water in the Mississippi River and of heavy rains down river. Because of the high water, there were almost no dry spots on

LIEUTENANT-GENERAL ULYSSES SIMPSON GRANT: National Archives, Washington D.C.

the west side of the river for which the Union army could camp. They camped on levees and the ground immediately in that area. It was so bad that because of the lack of room to camp his army General Grant sent General McPherson and his 17th Corps to establish his camp at Lake Providence, seventy miles above Vicksburg. Lieutenant William H. Lynch, Company I, 32nd Missouri Infantry Regiment, wrote in his diary, "The Company moved camp on the 6th February 1863, from near the Mississippi River, below Vicksburg and encamped above Vicksburg. There was much sickness in the Company, owing to a want of proper tents to shelter the men from the heavy rains and protect them against the cold."(2) Along this same train of thought Private Henry Kuck wrote a letter to his wife Metta about the conditions that he had to endure.

"My wound was quite unimportant and if I hadn't wished it, I would not have had to spend a single day in the hospital, but I wanted to rest up for a few days. We are stationed opposite Vicksburg, only the Mississippi River separates us from Vicksburg. It is very rainy and muddy weather here, it has already rained for seven days and continues to rain, and the mud is so deep that one isn't able to get through at all. Write me back soon, how the Winter Weather was and if you have enough to live on. I am now thoroughly well and active and hope that I'll stay that way. I have read in the newspaper here that the Health Conditions in our army have gotten much better, but to the contrary it is still very poor, as the sick are not treated as well as a dog. Then I wish to illustrate a clear incident: on our steamboat, a soldier was declared to be healthy and fit for duty, and the next day he died. Thousands of soldiers are lying sick on the wet ground in their tents, and when some straw is brought in, it isn't long before everything turns into muck; now they have to lie there without the necessary care being offered, instead of a better place being prepared for them, one lets them lie there without help until they die.

Mound upon mound of graves are being raised up where our strong young men are ending up; then it isn't only the thousands who are being sacrificed before enemy cannons through inept, ignorant officers, but many more will die through illness and through the inefficient and poor medical treatment of the doctors' assistants.

Also I have seen in the newspaper, that our General Blair has especially distinguished himself in Vicksburg: we haven't seen that he did such miraculous deeds there. Blair hasn't shown the least sign of heroic deeds, then I was a witness to his heroic deeds - what he did during the Attack near Vicksburg & Arkansas Post anybody who is dumber than Blair can do. The newspaper said further that not a single soldier doubted the Competence and Military Ability of Blair, but we believe that there are very few soldiers who (actually) believe in Blair. It has been said here that Blair has been commissioned a major-general. Therefore Warfare is so miserable that lawyers and politicians are leading our army, who don't care if thousands of soldiers are sacrificed, just so that their ambition and greed can be satisfied. We are not directly attacking Vicksburg here, or we would all be lost. We don't believe that Vicksburg will be taken this year, unless unexpected events take place.

P.S. Concerning the Health Conditions in the army I must reiterate: a man (soldier) in the 32nd Regiment Mo. Vols., posted next to us, said that in his Regiment 60 men have died in one week, then consider that the Regiments will not remain at full strength. In addition, the soldier that was declared able-bodied and the next day found dead, was (actually) very ill. The Doctor declared him fit for duty, he was sent on guard duty and the next morning found dead at his post; here one sees the incompetence of our doctors. And whoever doubts the bravery of Gen. Blair near Vicksburg: our company tambourine-man or drummer saw that he wasn't able to get his horse out of the bushes, then returned to Brigade Headquarters where he leisurely ate and drank. If you hear again that I was in the battle and you can't find out if I am alive or dead, then don't doubt as I could be a prisoner, then among our Company ten were left behind in the battle near Vicksburg. Also our major and Col. Fletcher were left behind there, but we don't yet know if they are dead or not, then we only buried 3 men there and the rest are all missing. Perhaps they are dead and have been buried by the Seceshers, or prisoners and can still come back after 1 or 2 years."(3)

From Haines Bluff, about eleven miles above Vicksburg, to Warrenton, including Vicksburg, was heavily entrenched with batteries and rifle pits connecting them. If he did not have enough to worry about, General Grant was concerned about the public opinion of how they perceived the war was progressing. There seemed to be a growing sentiment that the war was going on too long. The Republicans had lost some seats in congress in the 1862 elections. The voluntary enlistment of men had basically ceased throughout the north. People were becoming discouraged because they thought the war would be of short duration and had already been going on for about two years. General Grant decided instead of going north and then crossing the river to attack from Jackson, Mississippi, they would try different experiments in order to cross the Mississippi River and if successful they would attack from the place of the successful experiment. He states in his Memoirs, "I, myself, never felt great confidence that any of the experiments resorted to would prove sucessful. Nevertheless I was always prepared to take advantage of them in case they did."(4) He also thought that it was important that the men be kept busy to keep them in shape and that the folks back home might think that doing something was better than doing nothing.

One of General Grant's first plans was to widen a canal that was started by General Thomas Williams in 1862. He had started the canal straight from Young's Point to the river below. This canal was approximately one mile long. General McClernand, who had prior permission from President Lincoln to start this project, was given the task of widening and deepening the canal. He used about four thousand men to complete this task. All the corps, except McPherson's, would furnish up to a thousand men a day in order to help complete the canal. General Sherman's two divisions furnished five hundred men a day while they were stationed at Young's Plantation, at Young's Point, Louisiana. When they were almost complete it dawned on the Confederates what was going on and they set up a battery of artillery that was able to fire rounds at the two dredges, that were in use, they had to abandon their work. Then the river forced its way through the dam and flooded the canal. While it was being dug, General McPherson was ordered to cut the levee at Lake Providence in hopes of opening a channel that would make it navigable. This would enable the Union forces to reach the Mississippi River through the mouth of the Red River just above Port Hudson, which is approximately four hundred miles below Vicksburg traveling by river. Lake Providence at one time was part of the Mississippi River before the river changed course. This work was abandoned after the canal proved a failure on approximately March 27th. During the month of February, thirty to fifty men a day would die from malarial fevers, measles and small pox. This happened due to the low lying land and water. Once a disease like measles took hold, there were so many men who had no immunity to these illness that they easily became infected.

The weather for the month of February 1862 was terrible. Major A. J. Seay's diary has an almost daily entry about the weather they experienced. Listed below is his weather report for February in Louisiana.

"Sunday Feb. 1st, 1863. It is raining slowly today and very warm. Afternoon—The rain pours down while the sun is almost visible. The river is still rising.

Wednesday Feby. 4th, 1863. We have had dark dreary weather since Sunday. Today it is hailing, raining and sleeting a little.

Thursday 5th Feby, 1863. It rained heavily and incessantly last evening. The rain ceases, the wind blows, gloomy the howling of the wind from the north and darkness envelops us. This morning I rose early and went forth and beheld the beauty of the rising sun. The air was cold – ice ½ in. thick Wind is cold and bracing all day.

Friday 6th Feby. 1863. Ground frozen this morning slightly. A beautiful day but quite muddy. River on a stand still—high.

Saturday Feby. 7th. A nice day.

Thursday 12th Feby. 1863. This morning at daybreak it began to rain and in two hours the ground was covered. Water 3 inches deep in my tent.

Friday 13th Feby. 1863. A warm day – cloudy at night.

Saturday Feby 14th. Today the weather is hot and the sun shines out (strange Phenomona).

Sunday Feby 15th 1863. Last night we had a terrible thunder storm and heavy rain.

Monday Feby 16, 1863. Dark and rainy. Rained slowly all night, last night. Raining today—dark and gloomy.

Tuesday 17th Feby, 1863. Rained all night and day –
18th no better. I'm off today again everything flooded.

Feby 19th, 1863 Thursday. A fine sunny day everything
looks more cheerful than since I came.

Feby 20th, 1863. Friday. Another nice day – the air a
little "airish".

Feby 22th '63 – Sunday. The wind blows cold today –
fore noon cloudy.

25th Wednesday Feby. It begins to rain in the evening
very heavily.

Thursday 26th Feby. It rained all night and is raining
furiously this morning. Rains all day.

Friday 27th Feby. Dark and gloomy

Saturday 28th. Muddy and fair.

Sunday March 1st. 1863 Today is a fine day. The atmosphere clear and serene. The sun shines magnifi-
cently, but the air is cooler than ususal. All quiet
before Vicksburg. The river is still rising. The surface of the Mississippi about 3 ft. higher than the
ground on which we are encamped. We are only
protected from a deluge by the levee."(5)

Lieutenant-Colonel J. H. Wilson of General Grant's staff
was sent to Helena, Arkansas to find out if it was practical to
open a way through Moon Lake and Yazoo Pass. Mississippi
had built a levee, or dam, across this way prior to the war to
give them more land for planting. Prior to this it had been
navigable by steamships but it now had a narrow inlet. On
February 2nd, this levee was cut. Since the river was so high,
the force of the water washed out almost the entire levee and
started to fill up the bayous, and the surrounding land was
flooded. On February 24th General Ross and approximately
four thousand five hundred men from his brigade entered this
new waterway. The Confederates had felled trees into the water causing obstructions that had to be cleared away. After
much hard work General Ross and his men, accompanied by
Lieutenant-Commander Watson Smith and his two gunboats,
continued down this waterway until they came upon Fort
Pemberton. Fort Pemberton was on an island that was formed
where the Tallahatchie and Yallabusha Rivers unite and where
the Yazoo River begins. Since the island was unapproachable
by land, the infantry was useless. The most General Ross could
contribute was artillery fire. The gunboats attacked on March

11th and 13th and both attacks failed. One of the gunboats was disabled, six men were killed and twenty-five wounded. On March 22nd, on his way back from the attack, General Ross was met by General Quinby with reinforcements who took command and returned to Fort Pemberton to see for himself. Seeing that nothing further could be accomplished, the force returned.

Admiral Porter explored Steele's Bayou as far as Deer Creek and proclaimed that this way was navigable. On March 15th, five gunboats and four mortar-boats headed out. They went quite a distance, even with low hanging branches that did some damage to the super structure. General Sherman was ordered to take a division to reinforce the task force. General Sherman chose General Stuart's division of his corps and took transports to Eagle Bend on the Mississippi River. From here they debarked and marched across to Steele's Bayou where they boarded transports. Admiral Porter had proceeded farther and came upon some sharpshooters who were part of a four thousand Confederate force. The naval force was trapped and Admiral Porter had contemplated blowing up the boats when he saw Union infantry marching to his aid on a narrow strip of land. The navy then was able to back their vessels out of the trap and returned to the Mississippi River. This was the fourth effort and the fourth failure.

Another effort that was tried was to break another levee and flood the bayous. This led from Miliken's Bend and Young's Point that channels that could be navigable passing Richmond, Louisiana, entering the Mississippi River at Carthage approximately thirty miles above Grand Gulf, Mississippi. There were good roads in back of the levee that could support the infantry and artillery if the rain would stop and given a few days to dry out. These bayous, which would be dry if not for the rain that kept them wet, were grown up with trees that had to be cleared out before they could proceed. They had made good progress but then the river began to fall and like the other four attempts, it failed.

When the 31st Missouri Infantry Regiment wasn't part of the group helping with the digging of the canal or other jobs they were busy performing the important jobs while in camp in enemy territory. On March 14, 1863 they were ordered to furnish one lieutenant, three corporals and thirty men on the next day for the performance of pickett duty relieving the 30th Mis-

84

souri Infantry Regiment. It appears that the men were staying on the levee's or any type of suitable ground to camp on while their brigade commander was issuing orders from a steamship, where I assume he was camping. Then on March 18th they were to furnish a daily detail of twenty-five men, under the command of a non-commissioned officer, to meet the hospital steamer at the lower steamboat landing each morning to bury the dead. This had to be terrible duty. To have to bury men who had died aboard the ships and as described by Private Henry Kuck in his letter quoted earlier in this chapter, that mound after mound was covering a once brave soldier who was willing to die for his country by bullet but perished by sickness that was caused by exposure from the poor living conditions that the men had to endure at Young's Point. On March 20th they were ordered to furnish one non-commissioned officer and nine men for pickett duty on March 21st to perform their duty at the railroad on the left of the brigade near Ballard's Point, Louisiana relieving the 27th Missouri Infantry Regiment pickett.

Private Henry Kuck, Company G, 31st Missouri Infantry, wrote a letter to his wife on March 16th, 1863 that expresses not only what went through his mind but what might have went through the minds of countless men on both sides.

"I understand that you and the sweet little ones still aren't very healthy, and that little Elisa is so strong that she will be walking. How my heart would leap for joy if I could visit you soon again when the little one could walk, but it can still be awhile, for it could scarcely happen soon. As our Brigade goes there's hardly a regiment left; our Brigade has 4 (regiments) and together with Blair and his brigade and the whole artillery there are approximately 550 men who are fit to serve, thus it's expected, if they don't break our necks, that we will soon be sent away from here; and if it is true that we can leave, I believe that we will be granted leave and can visit you, but because our sweet children surely don't know me anymore they'll hide from me, at least little Elise won't know me at all, which will be really amusing. Oh, my sweet, good Metta, maybe I can stay for a few months, but perhaps not —

I hear that we'll soon be paid, but we still don't have it ..... Do let me know if the GREENBACKS were really devalued, we've heard they're only worth 50 cents. We're still stationed here by Vicksburg where the Canal I told you about will be or should be, built. Now two Mudd (Lt. Col. Mudd, Commander of Army Engineer Corps Unit) machines are working to give it a navigable depth. This canal has been dug about 40 feet wide, and if the machines can finish the rest of the work it could be good, but when? For one, the springtime is not helping because the dike has broken and the channel is too wide.

We don't know if Vicksburg should be attacked or whether we have to give up, but I believe the water will again overflow the channel and it will leave Vicksburg exactly as we found it. The war drags on, brings the United States farther into debt, for it's not so easy to defeat the Rebels, but according to the opinion of many of the sharp-eyed men is: we're coming closer to our goal, and if I would never have believed there would be so much grumbling as there is in the Army, I surely was and am a good Union Man and would for nothing in the world be an enemy, I have defeated the Rebels, but it seems to me now as if the fighting is not helping the enemy, thus I wish that the enemy would declare peace to protect the country from complete ruin. Thousands of people sacrificed, and perhaps for nothing if it's ended soon; of course the war demands sacrifice and this can't be changed if it's directed by conscientious leaders and not by traitors, and if we had millions of soldiers and our leaders are incompetent or traitors, then it won't help at all. We hear there's a Conscription Bill in effect, and that they have enlisted already, I'd like very much to know if this is true, and ask John Eggers if he would be so good as to write to me about this."(6)

General Grant was afraid that General Pemberton might recall his forces from the delta, that was described earlier, to strengthen further his forces around Vicksburg. So General Grant planned some different diversions in order to keep the Confederates guessing what his intentions were. One of these diversions was for General Sherman to send a division into this delta to keep the force of Confederates occupied. General Sherman chose General Frederick Steele's division for the task. They were sent one hundred miles up the river to Greenville where the men went ashore (described in more detail in the next chapter). The Federals were trying to give the impression that they were the advance element for the major force to follow for another drive upon Vicksburg from the north. After having thoroughly alarmed the population, and having done some damage, which was estimated at five hundred thousand bushels of corn burned, they reboarded the transports and returned to Young's Plantation in order to participate in another diversion. Because of this diversion, General Pemberton's second in command, Major General Carter L. Stevenson, ordered out a strong force in order to destroy this invasion. This move caused General Stevenson to be slow in recognizing that the Union could attack from the south from Miliken's Bend.

General Grant reported that there was an average of thirty to fifty men dying every day, although that was fewer than was expected. The 31st Missouri Infantry also had its share of men who died, deserted, became ill and were discharged. Company A's men who died of disease: Private John P. Hicenaugh of Hillsboro died on February 17,1863 and is buried at Jefferson Barracks, Missouri, Private Henry H. Jones Jr. of Desoto died on March 8,1863, Private William J. Reynolds of Victoria died on March 6, 1863 on a hospital steamer. The following men were discharged: Private Joseph Dickerman of Victoria on February 16, 1863 at Saint Louis, Missouri; Private Landon S. Williams of Victoria on April 22, 1863 at Saint Louis, Missouri. Private Nathaniel W. Rutherford of Victoria deserted on April 12, 1863 at Greenville, Mississippi. Company B losses were the following; by death, Private Samuel P. Coloway of Ironton on March 14, 1863 at Young's Point Louisiana, Private Thomas Linehan of Saint Louis on February 13, 1863 on a Hospital Boat, Private George Northcut of Washington County on March 27, 1863 at Young's Point, Louisiana, Private Yenno Polite of Washington County on March 6, 1863 near Vicksburg, Mississippi, Private George W. Staples of Washington County on April 26, 1863 at Saint Louis, Missouri and is buried at Jefferson Barracks, Missouri. Private Benjamin F. Staples of Washington County was discharged on April 22, 1863 at Saint Louis, Missouri by order of General Davidson. Company C's losses were the following: by death, Private Alfred Cain of Hopewell on February 8, 1863 at Jefferson Barracks, Missouri, Sergeant Rodney Caldwell of Hopewell on February 14, 1863 at Irondale, Missouri, Private Joseph Bone of Hopewell on April 5, 1863 at Memphis, Tennessee, Private Edward Anderson of

Hopewell on April 21, 1863 at Memphis, Tennessee, Sergeant George S. Cunningham of Hopewell on February 4, 1863 at Irondale, Missouri, Private William H. Dogget of Hopewell on March 27, 1863 at Memphis, Tennessee, Private John Elliott of Washington County on February 2, 1863 at Saint Louis, Missouri and is buried at Jefferson Barracks, Missouri, Private Thomas Fatchett of Washington County on February 23, 1863 at Saint Louis, Missouri, Private Joseph Jacko of Washington County on April 20, 1863 at Memphis, Tennessee, Private William F. Manker of Randolph County, Arkansas on February 24, 1863 at Saint Louis, Missouri and is buried at Jefferson Barracks, Missouri, Private Leander Martin of Butler County, Arkansas on April 3, 1863 at Saint Louis, Missouri and is buried at Jefferson Barracks, Missouri, Private Joe H. Marler of Washington County on March 16, 1863 at Young's Point, Louisiana, Sergeant Henry H. Stapp of Hopewell on February 16, 1863 on the hospital boat "City of Memphis," Private Richard T. Vaughn of Hopewell on February 10, 1863 at Young's Point, Louisiana, Private Sidney Wigger of Hopewell on March 30, 1863 at Memphis, Tennessee. Discharged, Private Matthew E. Mansker of Randolph County, Arkansas on March 16, 1863 at Jefferson Barracks, Missouri, Private Andrew J. Woods of Hopewell on April 22, 1863 for disability. Transferred, Sergent George Hughes of Belleview to Veteran Reserve Corps on Januray 16, 1863, Sergeant Francis Jolly of Washington County, to Invalid Corps (Company E, 5th Veteran Reserve Corps) on February 3, 1863. Company D losses were: death, Private John B. Sullivan of Greenville on April 12, 1863 at Memphis, Tennessee, Private Samuel K. Stockton of Greenville on March 21, 1863 at Young's Point, Louisiana, Private John W. Swiney of Greenville on February 13, 1863 at Saint Louis, Missouri, Corporal Pleasant V. Thomas of Greenville on February 5, 1863 at Young's Point, Louisiana. Discharged, Private James Brown of Patterson on April 16, 1863 at Memphis, Tennessee for disability. Private John M. Dale of Carter County on April 2, 1863 for disability, Private Jacob N. Williams of Greenville on April 3, 1863 for disability, Private William H. Wood of Greenville on April 6, 1863 for disability. Desertion, Private Nathan Stewart of Greenville on April 18, 1863 from a hospital in Saint Louis, Missouri. Company E lost the following men. Death, Private James H. Fisher of Franklin County on March 3, 1863 near Vicksburg, Private James Frazier of Franklin County on April 3, 1863 at Young's

Point, Louisiana, Private Moses M. Page of Moselle on March 16, 1863 on a hospital boat, Private I. E. Skeggs of Moselle on March 13, 1863 at Helena, Arkansas, Private James W. Studdard of Hillsboro on March 4, 1863 at Memphis, Tennessee, Private Jacob Wideman of Hillsboro on February 9, 1863 near Vicksburg, Mississippi, Private John B. Wilson of Moselle on March 4, 1863 near Vicksburg, Mississippi. Discharged, Private William H. Budwell of Leesburg on March 10, 1863 at Saint Louis, Missouri. Deserters, Private Michael Cowley of Moselle on March 1, 1863 at Young's Point, Louisiana. Company F's lost by death, Private Tipton B. Strain of Canaan on February 6, 1863 on a hospital steamer, Private Willas Pennington of Gasconade County on April 17, 1863 at Memphis, Tennessee, Private Francis M. Pryer of Canaan on February 6, 1863 at Young's Point, Louisiana, Private John H. Holt of Gasconade County on February 22, 1863 on the hospital boat "City of Memphis", Private Joseph A. Crower of Canaan on April 3, 1863 at Saint Louis, Missouri, Private William D. Gibbons of Gasconade County on February 28, 1863 at Young's Point, Louisiana, Private John H. Hall of Gasconade County on February 22, 1863 on the hospital boat City of Memphis. Discharged, Private Elijah H. Spear of Canaan on March 4, 1863 due to disability, Private George W. Strain of Canaan on April 20, 1863 due to disability, Private William R. Holt of Canaan on April 16, 1863 at Memphis, Tennessee, Private William J. McKean of Gasconade County on March 4, 1863, Private Thomas Meredith of Canaan on March 14, 1863, Private Shedreck Cuthlertion of Canaan on April 1, 1863 at Benton Barracks, Missouri because of disability. Company G lost the following men due to: death, Private Henry Bollt enlisted at Camp Fletcher on April 26, 1863 at Benton Barracks, Missouri, Private Frederick Dubbert of Greenville on February 26, 1863 at Helena, Arkansas, Private Peter Hamen of Washington on March 13, 1863 at a hospital in Saint Louis, Missouri, Private Michael Houndremont of Saint Louis on February 3, 1863 on the hospital boat "Pembina # 2", Private Herman Kasel of Warren County on March 12, 1863 at Memphis, Tennessee, Second Sergeant Justus Klinge of Saint Louis on March 3, 1863 at Memphis, Tennessee, Private John Stutzman of Dutzow on March 26, 1863 at Ballard's Plantation, Louisiana, Private Edward Schmidt of Saint Louis on April 11, 1863 on the hospital boat "January". Company H's losses were: death, Sergeant Columbus Baird of Wayne County on March

22, 1863 at Memphis, Tennessee, Private Daniel Clubb of Stoddard on March 3, 1863 at Grover Plantation, Louisiana, Sergeant Chesley Cozart of Wayne County on February 8, 1863 near Vicksburg, Mississippi, Private James Hause of Wayne County on February 25, 1863 at Groves Plantation, Louisiana, Private Alexander Helms of Wayne County on February 21, 1863 at Groves Plantation, Louisiana, Private Absalom Horton of Washington County on February 12, 1863 on the hospital boat "City of Memphis", Private Zanos Jordon of Wayne County on February 26, 1863 at Groves Plantation, Louisiana, Private Levi Luffy of Wayne County on February 21, 1863 on the hospital boat "City of Memphis" and is buried at Jefferson Barracks, Missouri, Private Nathan W. Midget of Wayne County on March 2,1863 at Jefferson Barracks, Missouri and is buried there, Private John J. Walker of Wayne County on April 23, 1863 at Saint Louis, Missouri and is buried at Jefferson Barracks, Missouri, Private Luke White of Wayne County on April 13, 1863 at New Orleans, Louisiana. Discharged, Private Wallace Kirkpatrick of Wayne County on March 6, 1863 at Saint Louis, Missouri, Private William C. Long of Wayne County on March 10, 1863 due to disability. Private James Richardson of Washington County deserted on March 6, 1863 from the hospital. Company I lost the following men: death: Private Charles Bone of Misneral Point on February 15, 1863 on a hospital steamer. Private William R. Clemens of Danville on April 30, 1863 at Saint Louis, Missouri and is buried at Jefferson Barracks, Missouri, Corporal David B. Cowan of Danville on February 14, 1863 at Young's Point, Louisiana, Private James Culton of Mineral Point on April 19, 1863 at Benton Barracks, Missouri, Private Carl Deirstein of Saint Louis on March 10, 1863 at Memphis, Tennessee, Private Meredith Helm of Calloway County on April 17, 1863, Private William Henderson of Moura, Illinois on April 8, 1863 at Young's Point, Louisiana, Corporal James Moffat of Jefferson County on April 30, 1863 at Miliken's Bend, Louisiana, Private Henry Schriver of Saint Louis on March 27, 1863 at Paducah, Kentucky and is buried at Mound City, Illinois National Cemetary, Private Thomas Sloan of Sulpher Springs on February 1, 1863 at Young's Point, Louisiana, Private Joseph Weller of Adams County, Arkansas on April 1, 1863 at Jefferson Barracks, Missouri. Discharged, Private James Monroe of Saint Louis on February 28, 1863, Private Wesley E. Norris of Sulpher Springs on March 7, 1863 due to disability,Private Harvey C. Wright of Carondelet on April 12, 1863. Company K's loss are as follows. Death, Private Thomas Campbell of Caledonia on February 23, 1863 on the hospital boat " Pembina", Private Lewis Boyer of Washington on March 25, 1863 in the hospital at New Orleans, Private Benjamin Coffman of Caledonia on February 17, 1863 at Young's Point, Louisiana, Private Jefferson C. Forrester of Caledonia on March 8, 1863 near Vicksburg, Mississippi, Private William W. Hopkins of Caledonia on March 20, 1863 at Memphis, Tennessee, Second Lieutenant William B. Ramsey of Ironton on April 11, 1863 at Memphis, Tennessee, Private Thomas Tinker of Potosi on February 8, 1863 at Young's Point, Louisiana. Discharged, Private William Thomas on February 7, 1863 at Benton Barracks, Missouri and Private William H. Woods of Ironton on April 6, 1863 due to disability.

CHAPTER FIVE:
ROAD TO JACKSON, MISSISSIPPI

On April 11, 1863, the "Daily Missouri Democrat" a newspaper in Saint Louis, printed the following article. The Daily Missouri Democrat had published this type of article, by other Missouri units in the field, in its paper in prior editions.

"THE VOICE OF THE ARMY,

RESOLUTIONS ADOPTED BY THE 31ST MISSOURI.

Whereas, We, the officers and soldiers of the 31st Regiment Missouri Infantry Volunteers, view with regret through the rebellion sympathizing newspapers of the North and Northwest, the efforts of the unreliable, unrighteous and unholy traitors to lead astray the loyal citizens at home and discourage and demoralize the good and faithful soldiers already in the field by their constant and vindictive complaints against the Government and Administration in the lawful prosecution of the war, for the suppression of the wicked rebellion.

Resolved, That we the officers and soldiers of the 31st Regiment Missouri Infantry Volunteers (Blair's Brigade) are for the preservation of the Union, the whole Union, and nothing but the Union, one and undivided, and do unanimously discountenance the treasonable acts of the rebellious sympathizers of whatsoever country, clime or party.

Resolved, That our whole object is to suppress the rebellion, punish treason, and hand down to our posterity the Constitution of the United States of America, so dearly bought and carefully preserved by the fathers of the revolution, as pure and unsullied as it was in the days of its ratification; and by this blood – bought soon we will stand as brothers, until peace and harmony shall be restored to our once happy, but now distracted country.

Resolved, That we will stand by and assist to our utmost, the present Administration in all its efforts to put down this unholy rebellion believing its policy to be that of wisdom and justice.

Resolved, That we fully indorse the late acts of Congress, and especially the conscription act, believing it to be one of the most fatal blows ever struck at this rebellion. That those traitors of the North and Northwest, as well as those of the South, will be compelled, despite all their hellish designs, to submit to the laws of our common country, for the faithful execution of which we shall ever hold ourselves ready to pledge our lives, our fortunes, and our most sacred honor.

Resolved, That we warn those unprincipled partisans who are too cowardly to join their allies of the South in an open campaign against us, but who seek by insidious threats to destroy the harmony and unity of purpose of our troops in the field, that there is a day of terrible retribution – when the men who have voluntarily left their homes, their fireside, their wives and little ones, and all that makes life sweet, and faced a hostile foe upon many a gory field, suffered the dreadful malaria of the hospitals – will return to pay them in their own coin for the kindness and encouragement they have received from those fiends in human shape.

Resolved, That we cordially give to the Administration a heavy support in the measures proposed for the vigorous prosecution of the war, believing that they are eminently wise and patriotic, and will greatly hasten a triumphant and glorious victory over all our foes, both North and South.

Resolved, That we pledge ourselves and our friends at home that we will never lay down our arms until this wicked and causeless rebellion is entirely crushed, and we call upon all good patriots and citizens everywhere – by all the memories of the past, by all the bright and glorious hopes of the future, by the memory of the brave men who have already fallen in this strife—to join with us in our efforts to vindicate the majesty and supremacy of the Constitution and the laws.

Resolved, That a copy of the proceedings and resolutions of this meeting be forwarded for publication to the DAILY MISSOURI DEMOCRAT, *Daily Union* and *Westliche Post*, of St. Louis, Mo."(1)

The rain had ceased falling in torrents and the sun began to come out and dry up the ground and the river was falling. The roads were becoming passable and General Grant had decided to proceed with a new offensive. He had described to Admiral Porter his ideas about running some of the gunboats, transports, yawls and barges past the defenses of Vicksburg. Admiral Porter agreed to the idea and set about to prepare his boats. Admiral Porter used bales of hay and cotton to protect the boilers from Confederate shot and shell. They used sacks of grain on the outside also to help protect the boats. They also planned to use the hay and grain once they were below Vicksburg because of the belief that such supplies would be scarce. General Grant stated "that I had been collecting, from St. Louis and Chicago, yawls and barges to be used as ferries when we got below."(2) On April 16, 1863, Admiral Porter took off around ten o'clock at night. Admiral Porter hoped to use the darkness to cover their approach as long as possible. Once the Confederates recognized what was happening they started firing their artillery at the naval force coming downstream. They set fire to bonfires, that they had prepared for this very thing, and houses on the Louisiana side of the river to help illuminate the boats as they moved past. Every boat was hit numerous times by this artillery barrage. There was only one transport that was so severely damaged that the crew abandoned ship. It caught fire and burned to the water line floating free and later grounded farther down the river along with one of its barges that it was towing. They were hauling coal for fuel in these barges to use down the river because it was believed that once they were below the river, they would not be able to return above Vicksburg for additional supplies.

General McClernand, with his corps, had started for New Carthage, by way of Richmond, Louisiana, on March 29th. The condition of the road and ground was muddy, due to all of the rain of that winter, he made slower progress than he hoped. On April 6th, General McClernand, with one division and some artillery, had reached New Carthage. Once deciding that it was not practical to attack Grand Gulf, Mississippi by this way it was decided to follow a different route. General McClernand's men ended up building four bridges across bayous, two of which were over six hundred feet long each. This increased the march from Miliken's Bend from twenty-seven to almost forty miles. General McPherson's corps were following behind General McClernand's.

While all of this was going, on General Sherman's forces were not sitting idle. Brigadier General Frederick Steele's division was sent out on an expedition in order to confuse the Confederates of the intent of General Grant's attack. The expedition started on April 2nd and their intent was to cause the Confederates to keep as many men as close to Vicksburg as possible. In his diary Major A. J. Seay wrote the following description of the expedition near Greenville, Mississippi.

"APRIL 2ND 1863.

Went on board the Chancellor with the 29th Mo. Started up the river late in the evening. Ran all night – stopped at Lake Providence a short time. My whole force 212.

APRIL 3rd. 1863.

Arrived at the Fanny Bullet Landing. We all disembark and Capt. Ballow scours the country for several miles around and finds no enemy. We had to cross a slough to get to the main levee. Many got a dunking — horses fell with them etc. Late in the evening we got orders to reembark which we did, (Companies) F. and K. being on picket.

APRIL 4th 1863

We started up the river at three a.m. this morning and arrived at Washington's landing at sun rise. Co's. F. and K. having been left behind Col. Manter sent for men and reprimanded me for leaving them. I defended myself telling him they were sent out by his order. I know not whither and that the order for their release should have come from his headquarters. He was quite mad but said very little. 10 A.M. – We are lying still and have sent the steamer Sun Flower down with Lt. Collins and ten men after them. They return we reembark – go down lake Washington til we strike the river –we then turn up the river and land at Greenville and tie up for the night.

SUNDAY APRIL 5th, 1863.

Moved at daybreak up the river 1 ½ or 2 miles. (a nice day) Started to the interior in search of Fergusion's and Adam's forces. Arrived at Black Bayou about 4 P.M. Drove the enemies pickets from the opposite bank and went to work to reconstruct the bridge which the rebels had destroyed. Finished the work about 11 o'clock P.M. This is Easter Sunday and according to a long established custom our friends are today eating printed eggs up North in perfect security.

MONDAY APRIL 6th, 1863.

A nice day. We start early in pursuit of the flying enemy and travel hard all day 18 or 20 miles. The men stumble slowly towards night they complain of sore feet. Captured abundance of corn, chickens, some beef and bacon. Burned two bridges out of which the rebels had taken a section in the center. Four of our men straggle and are probably lost.

TUESDAY 7th APRIL.

A nice day. We traveled 10 or 12 miles and come up to the enemies rear guard. They have some desultory artillery fighting. We advance in line of battle just in rear of Hoffman's battery which numbered and shot a few rounds into the ranks of the enemy. They fly cross the creek (Deer Creek) on double quick and go 4 miles into camp. We go into camp at Thompson's Plantation.

WEDNESDAY 8TH, 1863.

We counter march burning all the corn and fodder on the road and capturing all the molasses, honey, pigs, poultry, oxen wagon, jacks, asses et al.

THURSDAY APRIL 9TH 1863.

We march back and encamp where we did two days ago. Two rebel dutchman from Cincinnati deserted and came to their friends in the 30th Mo. Late in the evening we capture a straggling rebel Lt. The work of fire and confiscation still goes on and the blue army still moves towards the river. General Steele cannot control the men as he wishes and he uses his sword and revolver.

FRIDAY APRIL 10TH 1863.

Went into camp at Metcalf's Plantation last night. Poultry in abundance and the men pressed it freely and without compulsory process. We leave camp at 8 A.M. and move to Black Bayou bridge – one of our wagons broke thru which delayed the army two hours. In the meantime the enemy made a slight demonstration in our rear – were engaged by Gen. Steele's boat guard. They killed one of the latter – shot him thru the head. I saw him before he died – was frothing at the mouth. We formed line of battle in Capt. French's plantation, but the enemy came not. We then masked a battery behind

Black Bayou commanding the lane through which the troops would pass. Then we started the infantry across the bridge. No sooner had they disappeared than the enemy 20 in number – came into the lane. Capt. Hoffman gave them a couple of shot before they could get away, killing several among whom was the audacious fellow who rode on the white horse – the same who skidaddled at Thompson's plantation on Tuesday.

SATURDAY 11TH APRIL 1863.

The rebel pickets have been shooting at our men all day but have done no damage. About sunset a heavy rain storm comes up. The rain falls heavily for three hours. Mules and cattle break thru the corral and thunder is to pay generally.

WEDNESDAY 15TH APR. 1863

This morning cousin Jimmy died very suddenly – had not been sick at all. This is three cousins I have lost in the Federal army. Had him buried near Greenville as decently as possible.

APRIL 18TH 1863.

We go out foraging today with the 27th Mo. Col. Curley in command. We wade in water four feet deep – cross several pools. Go about 4 miles come to Black Bayou. The men pilliage a house taking everything they wanted. The bus. at this place too hard for the soldiers. We got horses, mules, cattle, onion, etc. and waded thru the water, got into camp about two hours after dark. Several of my men get drunk and I will have them punished.

TUESDAY APRIL 21ST 1863.

We marched to the boats taking all the contrabands property in our wake. Get wet and I being quite unwell was thrown into a fever which lasted me (confined me to my bed) till Friday 24th, at which time we got on board the Fanny Bullet and came to Young's Point arriving Saturday 25th at ten A.M. We went out to the old camp, but had not got to our places before we had an order to embark with every thing for Milliken's Bend – 15 miles up the river."(3)

The Federals marched approximately forty three miles down Deer Creek until they came near to a Dr. Thompsons' Plantation where the Confederates formed a line of battle with about six hundred to one thousand men with six pieces of artillery. The Confederate artillery opened up on the Federals while they formed a line of battle across an open field. The Federals then advanced upon the Confederates who then left the area without any farther action. The Federals spent the night of April 7, 1863 on Dr. Thompsons' Plantation, while the Confederates moved on. The next day General Steele sent a force to find out where the Confederates had gone when it was learned that they had gone to Rolling Fork where it was believed that they had received more re-enforcements. The Federals then headed back to Greenville, Mississippi driving much livestock and wagons loaded that caused General Steele to request six boats to carry all this new found material. Lieutenant William H. Lynch wrote in his diary his account of the campaign at Greenville, "The Company & Regiment left Young's Point, La, the 2d April 1863, on board the Steamer Chancellor and landed at Greenville, Miss. the 5th Apr. and marched to and encamped at Black Bayou. The 6th marched to and down Deer Creek. the enemy attacked our advance, but retreated as soon as fired upon by Huffman's Artillery. The 8th, 9th and 10th April we return to Greenville, Miss. The 19th embarked on transport and disembarked next day in Bolivar county, making a raid a short distance into the country, capturing a large quantity of stock, produce & etc. and returned to Greenville Miss. 22nd embarked on Transport, 24th & landed at Youngs Point, La. 25th 1863. Moved camp to Milliken's Bend April, 26th 1863."(4)

Private Henry Kuck wrote home, in a letter dated sometime after April 8,18 63 at Greenville, Mississippi;

"Last night I dreamed: that you and all the children were with me, that the little Nina & Emilie & Anna were all climbing on me and were pulling my legs and clothes, but as I awoke, I was lying alone in my (army) camp. We're no longer near Vicksburg, but our Division, commanded by Gen. Steele, has gone 151 miles further upriver, and we're now stationed in the small town of Greenville in the State of Mississippi. Our Division is supposed to receive its own physician. On Deer Creek the Rebels are supposed to have lots of supplies, that is whole warehoused full of foodstuffs are to be found there. On the 5th of April we went ashore by Deer Creek with our Reg. and the 29th Mo. stayed near the Steamboat in order to guard it. Our troops met there about 1200 men of Rebel Cavalry, who all withdrew with the arrival of our army. Because of the poor roads and underbrush, and the fact that our army marched on the only good road, they set themselves into a trap and returned a few days later. They brought to our camp more than 300 mules and many cattle, which will all remain here. All the neighboring houses and mills, excepting houses inhabited by families, were burned down. Many blacks are coming in to join up with us. The blacks are being exercised (trained) with their weapons, and a whole Brigade of these soldiers will be formed. It was announced, in ours and other regiments, that those who want to become officers should submit their applications, but most officer-candidates do not want to be officers in the Brigade of the Blacks. We're stationed here still and are living quite well. Often we eat chicken 3 times a day. When we run out, we simply go to the Seceshers and get more, and Uncle Sam pays for everything. How long we'll stay here, I don't know, but it has been said: we'll stay a few days longer to be paid, maybe we'll move out again to Vicksburg, and when I get money, I'll send it as quickly as possible."(5)

Probably one of the most famous of General Grant's diversions was what became known as "Grierson's Raid." Colonel Benjamin H. Grierson, was a reluctant cavalry officer, he was afraid of horses, who was placed in command of a cavalry force of one thousand seven hundred men and six 2-pounder guns. They started from LaGrange, Tennessee on April 17, 1863 hoping to get into the rear of Vicksburg and cause as much confusion as possible while causing the Confederates to use as many men as they could to chase after him. On April 21st, Colonel Grierson sent one hundred and fifty of his men back to LaGrange that were sick with lame horses. This was used as a diversion in hopes of confusing some of the Confederates that were chasing them. Plus he sent one cannon and a force of six hundred men to strike the Mobile & Ohio Railroad to the east and then once done there to head back to LaGrange. They did this so successfully that the Confederates were thrown off the main force and chased after this smaller force. On April 23rd Colonel Grierson and his remaining force of just under a thousand men, entered Newton's Station arriving two hundred miles deep into Mississippi and about one hundred miles east of Vicksburg. General Pemberton, when he heard of the cavalry force behind him, he asked for more cavalry from General Johnston. General Johnston replied that the cavalry he had could not be spared. General Pemberton sent almost his entire force of cavalry after Colonel Grierson's force. This left him without the valuable eyes of the cavalry to help keep him informed of exactly where General Grant's force was. By this date the Federal navy river force had made it below Vicksburg. Colonel Grierson made an effort to reach General Grant at Grand Gulf. Because of the amount of Confederates between them he gave this thought up and headed towards Baton Rouge, Louisiana where there was a force of Federal troops. Finally on May 2nd they were met by Federal troops who came out to investigate them. In just sixteen days Colonel Grierson and his men had covered six hundred miles loosing only twenty-six men while killing or wounding one hundred Confederates capturing around five hundred. They had destroyed fifty-five miles of railroad and telegraph lines and had exchanged their played out horses for horses of those in the state. The main reason for the raid was to confuse the Confederate high command in Mississippi and cause as many of their troops to pursue them as possible. In this alone they far exceeded the expectations of General Grant.

General Grant had planned another diversion issuing orders that General Sherman's men would demonstrate against Haines Bluff. General Sherman used ten small regiments from General Blair's division. They were in view of some of General Pemberton's forces on Haines Bluff. General Sherman's men would unload from one of the transports then march through the woods and then load up on a transport back up the river and start the process all over again. This hopefully gave the Confederates the idea that there was a major force building up to their front and that the major attack would again come from there. This was somewhat successful and did retain the forces that were already there until it became known exactly where the Union forces were crossing the river. This started on April 30, 1863 and continued into the next day. General Pemberton ordered three thousand men that were on their way to reinforce the troops at Grand Gulf to return to Vicksburg to meet this new threat. This was, in effect, caused by General Sherman's feint that caused Major General Carter Stevenson plea for reinforcements to counter this threat to his positions.

On April 29th, General Grant sent General McClernand and approximately ten thousand men to attack Grand Gulf, Mississippi. Grand Gulf was a strong artillery defensive position with infantry support under General J. S. Bowen. General Pemberton had ordered General Bowen there a few short weeks before the attack of Admiral David Porter's gunboats. After about five and one-half hours of firing from both the gunboats and Grand Gulf's defenses, Admiral Porter decided that because of the defenses he had encountered that the infantry would not be provided with the support that they would need and that it would be to costly for a direct assault. The Union force withdrew and the infantry was unloaded on the west side of the river where a levee was found to be suitable for marching. The Confederates had scored a decisive victory by preventing the Union forces from landing there. The Union forces lost eighteen men killed and fifty-six wounded, all lost by the navy. That night, Admiral Porter sailed down the river past the Grand Gulf defenses. At dawn the Confederates saw that the Union navy had managed to go by and were a few miles down river from them. General Grant was informed by a slave that he would not have to go all the way to Rodney to unload his men, there was another landing a few miles farther up river close to Bruinsburg. Finding this to be true, he then began to unload his men without any opposition. Once this landing was affected it made the position of Grand Gulf untenable and General Bowen moved his men toward Port Gibson in order to defend that town against the Union forces. General Pemberton was informed that the Union forces were crossing at Bruinsburg, Mississippi. General Bowen then asked for some reinforcements. General Pemberton had few men to send him because he had sent some of his, mostly his cavalry, throughout Mississippi chasing Colonel Benjamin Grierson in hopes of stopping him on his famous ride through Mississippi.

On April 30th General Grant's forces began their invasion of Mississippi. With approximately twenty-three thousand men from General McPherson's and General McClernand's corps, General Grant crossed the Mississippi River to Bruinsburg, Mississippi which is about eight miles below the artillery emplacements at Grand Gulf. After they were safely across the Mississippi, General Grant ordered General Sherman to march from Miliken's Bend and join him. General Sherman

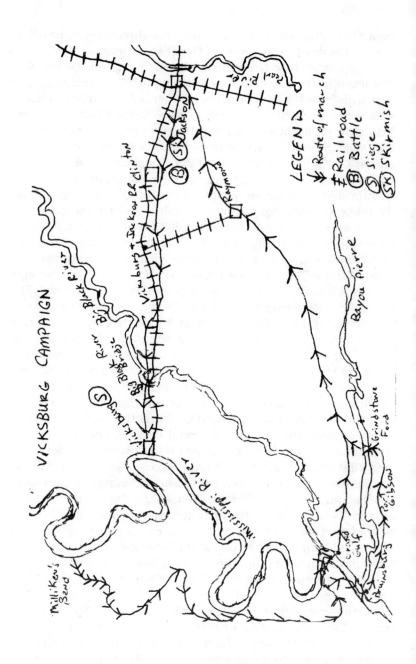

VICKSBURG CAMPAIGN

took with him from his 15th Corps, General Steele's and General Tuttles divisions. On May 1st, they left on their march, early the next morning while General Blair's division continued on with the diversion for a little longer so as not to alert the departure of the rest of the 15th Corps. General Blair's division was left at Miliken's Bend to guard the supply base. He was ordered to remain there until relieved by troops on their way from Memphis, Tennessee and then follow the rest of the 15th Corps. General Sherman in his "Memoirs" says, "Our route lay by Richmond and Roundabout Bayou; then, following Bayou Vidal we struck the Mississippi at Perkins Plantation. Thence the route followed Lake Saint Joseph to a plantation called Hard Times, about five miles above Grand Gulf. We reached Hard Times on the sixth of May."(6) The distance that they had marched was about sixty-three miles. General Sherman's troops crossed the Mississippi River from Perkin's Plantation to Grand Gulf, Mississippi and then marched to join the rest of the Federal Army. Lieutenant William H. Lynch records in his diary, "The Company and Regiment started from Milliken's Bend, La. the 2d May 1863, and marched to Grand Gulf, Miss. the 8th May."(7)

General McPherson's 17th Corps had been shifted approximately eight miles east to Rocky Springs, leaving Hankinson's Ferry to be occupied General Sherman's corps. General Sherman's Corps joined the rest of the army in Mississippi on the 7th of May. This raised General Grant's forces to about thirty-three thousand men. Most of the supplies that they were to receive, as far as ammunition and other military supplies, would follow the same route as described earlier. The Confederates had a strength of nearly sixty thousand spread throughout Mississippi at places such as Grand Gulf, Haine's Bluff, Jackson and Vicksburg.

The following is from the diary of Major Abraham J. Seay of the 32nd Missouri Infantry Regiment as they leave their camp at Milikens Bend, Louisiana to reaching Grand Gulf, Mississippi.

"SATURDAY 2D May 1863.

I reported for duty this morning but am not able. The weather is very hot. We start on the trip at 4 P.M. – march till 8 and go into camp.

SUNDAY MAY 3RD, 1863.

A warm day – we pass some very fine farms, the land

is wet. Cross a bayou in a bridge at Richmond. A small ville not large than a common plantation. We don't march till 5 P.M. and continue till 10.

MONDAY 4TH MAY, '63.

March till noon and stop in a shady grove on a fine plantation. Here I got some fine dew berries. There is here innumerable Buffalo gnats. They fly in your face and bite. They creep into a horse's ear and suck his blood at a terrible rate. We are now marching along the banks of the bayou Tenas which contains fish and is navigable for the largest boats in high water, but for the trees which grow in the stream promiscuously. We cross this and two other bayous by the light of the moon on pontoon bridges and march thru a bottom covered with young trees – 6 to 15 inches in diameter – straight and not a limb for 50 feet – a suffocating stench in the atmosphere. Road rough and men tired and hungry, yet they cheer lustily at intervals. While resting at noon – 438 prisoners passed us bound for Milikens Bend – they were taken in the Grand Gulf fight. I'm told we have 1700 more, our boys are working 'em up.

TUESDAY MAY 5TH 1863.

Went into camp at 11 P.M. last night and many had no supper. Started at 5 ½ A.M. without breakfast. We got two miles and go into camp once move on the banks of the Father Waters and draw rations for five days. This is Perkin's landing. The plantation of old Judge Perkins the brother-in-law of Jeff. Davis is at this landing. It is a fine plantation. The houses were burnt by himself in order that they should not be used by the Feds. This is 18 miles above Grand Gulf and 40 miles below Vicksburg by the river. The former is our probable place of our destination. We draw rations for 5 days and march at 5 p.m. Travel 6 miles thru a beautiful country and go into camp at Dr. Bowies' Plantation sit wait on the banks of Lake St. Joseph. This is a magnificent plantation. The florid garden here is remarkable for variety. Here I find the banana with its broad leaves. The house here is magnificent and of a different construction to any thing I have seen. The yard is filled with a variety of ornamental shade trees. Fine hedge here made principally of the Cherokee Rose. The osage orange black berry and other growths also used. Our men in fine spirits and march well.

MARCH 6TH, 1863.

We march thru a fine country. Not so boggy and wet as the land generally. I have seen today one field containing at least 500 acres of corn much of which is waist high. I have also seen a large field of Hungarian grass heading out. Also a field of rye and barley. The fields as level as a floor the dryest land I have seen. We marched all day on the bank of St. Joseph lake which has gradually widened till it is say ½ to ¾ ms. wide. Cross three small pontoons bridges over small bayous erupting into the lake. I have seen today three alligators which were shot in the lake by soldiers, the longest being about 5 ½ ft. All the land traveled over today belongs to one Ruth, who has seven large plantations and works 900 (or did) hands, exclusive of children and old folks. Go into camp 2 miles from Hard Times. It has been so cold today that I was chilly, with my great coat on.

MAY 7TH, 1863.

We embark on board the Forest Queen and down we go to Grand Gulf. I now stand on the apex of the hill at the foot of whose base were planted three heavy siege guns by the Rebels but are now in our hands. As I stand facing Northward to my right is the gulf into which empties Black River – before me is the Miss. and Hard Times in sight – to my left is a range of hills extending down the river rising abruptly and forming in some places a vertical precipice 11 feet high. At intervals are rebel works at the base stretching for three fourths of a mile is one capacious range of rifle pits, with here and there a double one. Diagonally, up the steep hill side is a deep ditch an army can evacuate the works and gain a position of safety in a deep ravine behind the hill. No stone of any kind is visible on the surface any where, but the yellow earth is cohesive, that although precipitiones a stone bluff it has not washed away. I now go across the hill to the residence of old Judge Maxwell whose yard is filled with a fine variety of shrubbery. There was considerable ville here which was burn't last summer. It is still cold today."(8)

General Grant's first objective was the taking of Grand

Gulf. The best route to attack Grand Gulf was by land. Bruinsburg is about two miles from the high ground that led to Grand Gulf. The best way to Grand Gulf was by way of Port Gibson, Mississippi. The Bayou Pierre was a stream that was very high because of all the rain during the winter and General Grant sent General McClernand's 13th Corps forward on the 30th of April with two days rations, which were supposed to last four days and ammunition. They reached the bluffs before sunset and pushed on in hopes of reaching the bridge across Bayou Pierre at Port Gibson. If they could secure this bridge they could have access to roads in Port Gibson that were starting points to Vicksburg and Jackson.

The 13th Corps were about five miles west of Port Gibson when they were met by the enemy. Because it was late, at night there was not much fighting but there was some skirmishing trying to discover the enemies position. The Confederate's were under the command of General Bowen and consisted of most of the Grand Gulf garrison of about eight thousand men. General Bowen had no hopes of defeating the Union forces but only hoped in delaying their forces long enough for reinforcements to arrive. The reinforcements never reached them. This part of Mississippi "stands on edge"(8). It is largely ridges with heavy forests and thick undergrowth which made it almost impossible to march across the country mainly having to march on the roads. The roads, for the most part ran, on top of the ridges except where there were roads that connected one ridge to another. These terrain features aided General Bowen in his defensive positions. The place chosen by General Bowen to defend was on a road that split and then went on two different ridges and did not join again until near Port Gibson. Even though the ridges were seldom more than two miles apart at its widest point, because of the obstacles before described it was impossible for the troops on one ridge to support the other. General McClernand had to divide his forces in order to engage the Confederate troops on both branches of the road. The Union force on the left, made up of General Peter Osterhaus' division, was meeting stiff resistance and receiving casualties. The Union force on the right was made up of Generals Hovey, Carr and A. J. Smith were pushing the enemy back. As soon as General McClernand's troops were clear of the main road, General McPherson's men were thrown into support of General Osterhaus' men. Two brigades of General Logan's division were sent with General John E. Smith's brigade on a flanking movement to drive the Confederates from their position. Once General Smith's brigade was seen to be in position, General Osterhaus was ordered to resume his attack. The attack was successful and the Confederates were driven back. The Union forces on the right and the left drove the Confederates for the rest of the day and by night were within two miles of Port Gibson, where they went into bivouac for the night.

The next morning the Union forces started for Port Gibson, finding that the Confederates had destroyed the bridge over the bayou. The soldiers then started to rebuild the bridge over the south fork of the Bayou Pierre. When it was finished, they crossed and one of General Logan's brigades were sent downstream to take care of a battery and infantry support. Two of his other brigades were sent up the bayou to rebuild the bridge that had been destroyed. When the enemy saw that they were rebuilding the bridge, they abandoned Port Gibson to the Yankees.

General Grant had the troops rest and wait for provisions. While they were waiting, he directed Generals McPherson and McClernand to send out reconnaissance patrols. This was to keep the Confederates guessing where he was going to strike next. The 15th Corps had spent May 6th and 7th crossing the Mississippi River into Grand Gulf, which was being used as a supply base. General Grant ordered General Sherman to bring up General Blair's division since General Hurlbut and part of the 16th Corps had arrived at Miliken's Bend on May 3rd. General Blair was to bring two hundred wagons loaded with hard tack, coffee, sugar, salt and one hundred thousand pounds of salt pork. General McPherson on May 7th, early in the morning, started his troops on the road to Jackson. That night, both Generals McPherson and McClernand were at Rocky Springs where they bivouacked. General McPherson's 17th Corps spent the next day there and General McClernand moved on to Big Sandy. General Sherman's 15th Corps marched from Grand Gulf to Hankinson's Ferry, which was about eighteen miles. Major A. J. Seay recorded in his diary, "Friday May 8th 1863. We march at 1 P.M. over short, abrupt, irregular and disproportionate hills, which are too steep in some places for a dog to climb. Yet it is cultivated. Can't tell which was the hollows go every thing looks abrupt and accidental. The road is graded all the same, cuts being 25 feet deep. The road is very broken, crooked and dusty. Water scarce-country poor. We march till late at night and travel 18 miles. The men tired and mad-stop in a corn field and lay down in the dirt. One of the ambulances got tipped over but no damage done."(9) On May 9th, the 13th and 15th Corps remained where they were with the 17th Corps moving to a position just west of Utica, Mississippi. Major A. J. Seay wrote in his diary, "Saturday 9th May. We move a mile and a half and go into camp in a black oak grove (fine timber) on a rolling hill, in line or battle."(10) On May 10th, the 17th Corps moved to Utica, the 15th Corps moved to Big Sandy, while the 13th Corps remained at Big Sandy. "Sunday May 10th, 1863. A beautiful morning. I see a fox squirrel sporting in the bough of a tree over my head and shot at him with my pistol, for which heinous offence I am first abused and then placed under arrest by the Tyrant Manter. We get orders to march at 2 o'clock suppose I will have to march in the rear. Move 9 miles by Rock Spring and to Big Sandy. There is a telegraph line on this road-the country not so hilly but still broken. Some pine timber and a little gravel."(11) May 11th found General McClernand and his 13th Corps marching almost straight north on the Telegraph Road towards Edward's Station, Mississippi stopping at Five Mile Creek General Sherman and his 15th Corps were at Auburn where they met General Grant, who stayed with them until they reached Jackson, Mississippi and then moved on to Dillon's Plantation and General McPherson's 17th Corps had advanced five miles from Utica. In his diary, Major A. J. Seay describes his day following his arrest. "Monday May 11th, 1863. We march 15 miles thru a broken country-considerable pine-not much water. Pass McClernands HdQrs. And meet Col. Warmouth was glad to see him. After we get into camp Col. Curley Brig officer of the day shot six times in the face of the enemy at a beef. At night I wrote a line to Gen. Steele asking to be released from arrest or charged and court martialed forthwith. Capt. House took it to the Brig headquarters. Campbell and Williams heard it read. Lawerence and Warmoth saw Curley shoot. There is a very strong feeling against the tyrant Manther thru the entire brig. Land –poor roads, dusty and water scarce. The men stand the march very well but are loud in their denunciations of Manter for placing me under arrest."(12) On the 12th, the 13th Corps was at Fourteen Mile Creek as was the 15th Corps and 17th Corps after the Battle of Raymond, Mississippi. The Battle of Raymond, Mississippi was an attack by General Gregg and his force against General McPherson's 17th Army Corps composed mainly of General Logan's division. The Confederates attacked with about five thousand men and two batteries about two miles from Raymond, Mississippi. The battle started about two o'clock p.m. and lasted almost four hours with the Federal's driving the Confederates from the field. General Logan's men then went in and took position of Raymond. The 17th Army Corps suffered sixty-six killed, three hundred and thirty-nine wounded and thirty-seven missing. The Confederates suffered one hundred killed, three hundred and five wounded and four hundred and fifteen men missing mostly men that were taken prisoner. Major A. J. Seay wrote the following in his diary. "Tuesday May 12th/63. A fine day-I am quite unwell with a cold. No meat but fresh pork. It is expected the ball will open today and I am still under arrest. Our advance has been skirmishing with the enemy-lost a few men- 5 or 6 killed- and wounded- are now at a halt and I am temporarily released in order to command the regiment, in the present campaign. We are on a halt woods covered with pine and other timber. Go into camp at 14 mile creek at 3 ½ P.M. the bridge being torn down Gen. Steele order me to his head-quarters forthwith. I go and take a drink with him after which he endeavors to convince that Col. Manter did his duty and winds up the confab by releasing me from arrest. The men cheer me when I take command. McPherson is doing some heavy fighting on the right at Raymond. We got as many mul-berries as we can use-pond water to drink."(13)

The Union line stretched from the Big Black River through to Raymond. General McClernand's 13th Corps were on the left, with his left on the Big Black River and he was also guarding all crossings to keep the Confederates from fording the river and attacking them from the rear. General Sherman's 15th Corps was on the Fourteen Mile Creek, a creek which ran almost parallel, but just a few miles south of the Vicksburg to Jackson Railroad. General McPherson's 17th Corps extended from the right of the 15th Corps to Raymond, Mississippi. This placed them in a position where they could attack Vicksburg or Jackson.

General Grant gave General Sherman his orders for the next day, May 13th, to leave his position across the Fourteen Mile Creek and proceed toward Jackson through Raymond. Lieutenant William H. Lynch recorded in his diary, "The next morning we resumed our march for Jackson Miss. The day was very warm & roads dry & dusty."(14) General McPherson's 17th Corps reached Clinton, Mississippi early in the day and started destroying the railroad. The 15th Corps reached Raymond before all of the troops of the 17th Corps had departed. Can you imagine the thoughts of those citizens who remained in Raymond concerning the number of Yankees in their town. General McClernand's 13th Corps withdrew from Edward's Station and the Confederates and reached their position that night. The orders for the next day were for the 17th Corps to head for Jackson from Clinton, about 15 miles away. The 15th Corps was to march for Jackson from their position in Raymond and time their arrival in Jackson close to the same time as the 17th Corps. General McClernand was to split his 13th Corps up sending a division to Clinton where they would be available to support the 17th Corps. Another division was to go within a few miles of Mississippi Springs, following the 15th Corps line of march. A third division was sent to Raymond where they were in a position to support either the 15th or 17th Corps if they should need help. General McClernand still had two other divisions available to him should he need it in case General Pemberton should try an attack from the rear. It poured down rain on the night of the thirteenth which made the roads almost impossible to march on. The 15th Army Corps had to march on these wet and muddy roads which slowed the speed of the march drastically. These roads were in a lowland area and the rain could not run off and had to be obsorbed into the already saturated ground.

On the 14th of May, the 15th Corps approached Lynch Creek, which was nearly overflowing, met a small Confederate detail covering a bridge over the creek. At approximately eleven a.m., it stopped raining and General Sherman ordered an immediate attack. The men quickly attacked the enemy and drove them back. This drove the Confederate detail to the safety of their main entrenchments were the Union attack came to an abrupt halt. At about the same time General McPherson's 17th Corps was coming into contact with the enemy in entrenchment's from a northwesterly direction. It was around nine a. m. when General Crocker's division met the enemy pickets and drove them back into their main entrenchments.

Major A. J. Seay of the 32nd Missouri Infantry Regiment wrote in his diary for May 13th and 14th , 1863.

"We right about and march towards Raymond 8 miles distant. Now we overlook the ground which McPherson fought and drove the enemy yesterday. The right began at 11 and lasted until sun down. Loss pretty heavy-victory complete Mc, then went into Raymond the enemy flying before him. Oh, how much anxiety is felt for me by mother, brothers and sisters. How I wish they knew I am yet unhurt. With what great anxiety they will search the papers. Uneven country-poor land- heavy pine groves. Pond water (a little cistern) and not much of that. Rebel accounts say Hooker beat them on Rapahannock, killing Stonewall and Longstreet, rumor said the rebels are re-enforcing from Charleston and Mobile. We shall see – men enthusiastic.

Rumor says we lost 150 killed and 400 wounded in the Raymond fight on yesterday. Rebels lost killed 200, wounded 500, prisoners 600, later 40 Feds and 61 rebels have been buried today by us. Small arms thick in the woods, 20th Ohio distinguished itself –7th Mo. ran. Logan's divisions were engaged yesterday. The fight was musketry and hand to hand. The troops were from Port Hudson- were Tenn. and Texas veterans. Fought well—charged on battery and came near taking it, were repulsed with heavy loss—hauled dead and wounded to Raymond during the fight, which are now in our hands. The battle field is undulated with heavy timber and underbrush—our forces had to advance thru an open field on the South and West. The 13th Ill. is lost—we halt for some purpose. Have seen a great quantity of cotton marked C.S.A. since we left Grand Gulf.

We pass thru Raymond of 800 inhabitants—court house (rather fine) filled with rebel wounded. Got a paper printed by Co. R. 32nd Ohio—a large frame house (hotel) filled with rebel prisoners. After passing thru town we take the right hand road and travel two or three miles over hills and go into camp distance marched 10 miles. The 13th Ill. comes in about bed time having marched 25 miles. A little rain shower. 11 o'clock the ball opens in front—it rained harder than I ever saw in my life—the men almost drowned in the rain, mud and water. Heavy cannonading in front—wagons and artillery sticking in the mud and men wading to their waits in mud and water. But they move forward with alacrity and yell occasionally. The fighting begun 2 miles from Jackson and we drove them into the town and then out of the town. My men marched to the top on the head and very tired, but they sent up cheers after cheer for an hour. I was wet to the skin from head to heel and covered with mud, all my bedding wet as water could make it. But I see the stars and stripes floating over the capital of Miss. The enemy has fled in hasty confusion to Canton a little town 25 miles North of Jackson. Joe Johnston arrived here yesterday morning but his stay was short.

We have beaten and driven them at every point from. Grand Gulf to this place as far as heard from. On our march we passed Miss. Spring a great place for invalids to resort to. It has a steam mill and a row of large buildings that have been lately used for a hospital. The rebels burned the depot containing all the commissary stores at this point estimated to be worth a million. Their retreat was so precipitate across Pearl River beyond town. I am told several got drowned."(15)

General Joseph E. Johnston, who had arrived at Jackson only a few days before, received reinforcements from Georgia and South Carolina on the night of the thirteenth. Once the pickets had returned to their entrenchments, the Union forces formed into battle lines trying to find a weak spot in the Confederate defenses. General Johnston, seeing that he was being attacked from two different directions, decided to withdraw and give the city to the enemy. Confederate Brigadier General John Gregg was the front line commander in the entrenchments on the outskirts of Jackson. He was preoccupied by the approach of the 17th Corps and wasn't aware of the approach of the 15th Corps. Colonel Thompson of the 3rd Kentucky Mounted Infantry of the Confederate forces, was ordered to take his unit and that of the 1st Georgia Sharpshooter Battalion and four guns of Martin's Georgia Battery. They were ordered to meet this new threat in the southwest and to hold the 15th Corps south of Lynch Creek if possible. Lieutenant William H. Lynch recorded in his diary, "On the 14th May 1863 (Thursday) we marched to & took Jackson the Capital of Miss. The advance had a short engagement with the enemy when we were about two miles from the Capitol. The engagement lasted but a short time, when they retreated leaving their Town & its contents all behind, we marched into town at one O'clock P.M.."(16)

General Tuttle's division of the 15th Corps went to the right trying to probe the Confederate line when he found a slave who informed him that the Confederates were all gone but just a few men. General Tuttle sent the 95th Ohio Infantry Regiment, which was commanded by Colonel William L. McMillen, into the entrenchments led by General Sherman's chief engineer, Captain Julius Pitzman, and some of his scouts. Prior to this, Captain Pitzman and his scouts had sneaked up and checked out the slave's story. The 95th Ohio was then led through the avenue found by Captain Pitzman's scouts and attacked the defenders manning the guns. They captured six guns and fifty-two prisoners who had been left behind to man the guns. It was about this time that General Steele's 1st Division of the 15th Corps arrived. General Sherman gave General Steele orders to take advantage of any success that General Tuttle's men might have. The way was now open for General Sherman's 15th Corps to storm the city. The 1st Division of the 15th Corps then followed the railroad into Jackson, which was the route that the 95th Ohio Regiment had opened. While heading toward the capitol General Sherman ordered General Steele and General Tuttle to camp for the night southwest of the city in some open fields. The 17th Corps, at approximately the same time, discovered that the enemy had left their front and began to enter the city. With General Crocker, a division commander in his corps, General McPherson entered Jackson capturing some artillery and their crews. They entered the capital building and hoisted the flag of the Union. General Grant is recorded to have slept in the same room that Confederate General Johnston had slept in the night before.

The Confederate losses are reported to be about eight hundred and forty-five with the Union forces suffering forty-one killed , two hundred and fifty-one wounded and seven missing. Considering the Union army was attacking a fortified position, it was an amazingly low cost victory over the Confederates guarding a state capitol. General Sherman's casualties totaled only thirty-two, included six killed, twenty-two wounded and four missing. The 31st Missouri Infantry had very few casualties in the skirmishes and the Battle of Jackson. Killed in action was First Lieutenant William Robinson of Danville who

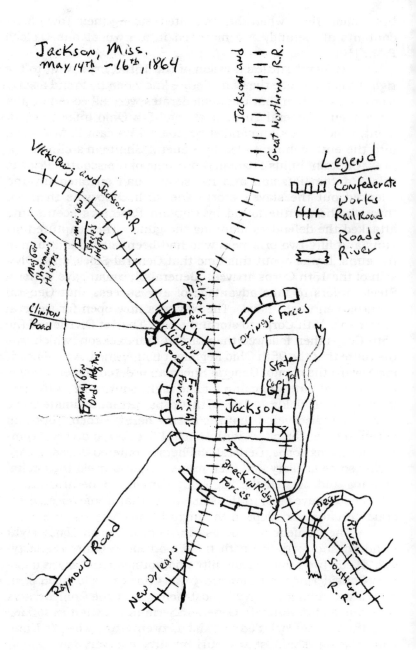

Jackson, Miss.
May 14th – 16th, 1864

Vicksburg and Jackson R.R.

Jackson and Great Northern R.R.

Legend
Confederate Works
Rail Road
Roads
River

Major Gen Shermans H.QTRS

Steeles Heights

Walkers Forces

Lorings Forces

Clinton Road

Clinton Road Forces

Frenchs Forces

State Capitol

Jackson

BreckinRidge Forces

Raymond Road

New Orleans

Pearl River

Southern R.R.

BATTLE OF JACKSON, MISSISSIPPI

was killed on May 10, 1863 while serving in Company I. Captain William Osterhorn of Carondelet was wounded in a skirmish while commanding Company G. Captured in the skirmishers on the way and around Jackson, Mississippi were Corporal Alexander McConnel of Company F from Washington County who died in Jackson Mississippi while a prisoner. Private Adolph Uckermann, from Dutzow, of Company G was a prisoner at Jackson, Mississippi and was retaken on May 17, 1863 in Jackson. He was listed as totally disabled and discharged if not dead. Private Ralney Ward of Company H from Wayne County died in Jackson, Mississippi while a prisoner. Corporal Orson Pierson of Hopewell died in Jackson, Mississippi in 1863. Private Adam Tarwate, of Company H, of Wayne County died on May 9, 1863 near Vicksburg.

The following men were lost to the service of the 31st Missouri Infantry due to death, desertion and discharged. The following men died from May 1st to the capture of Jackson, Mississippi. Company B's Private Dennis Ryan of Saint Louis deserted on May 2, 1863 at Miliken's Bend. Private John C. S. Stock of Saint Louis deserted on May 3, 1863 at Carondelet, Missouri. Private William Schofield of Ironton, Missouri was discharged on May 5, 1863 at Saint Louis, Missouri. Private Richard Veach of Washington County was discharged on May 13, 1863 at Saint Louis, Missouri. Private Peter Valley of Washington County died at Helena, Arkansas on May 3, 1863. Company C's Private John Eaton of Saint Francis County died on May 1, 1863 at Saint Louis, Missouri. Private Charles K. Mailer of Washington County died at Memphis, Tennessee on May 11, 1863. Private Samuel Vaughn of Hopewell died at Young's Point, Louisiana on May 14, 1863. Company D, Private Francis M. Rodgers of Greenville deserted on May 10, 1863 from Richmond, Louisiana. From Company E, Corporal William A. W. Whitmire from Moselle was discharged for disability on May 8, 1863. From Company F, Corporal William L. Shockley of Canaan died on May 13, 1863 at Mempis, Tennessee. Private Martin Brown of Canaan was discharged on May 8, 1863. Company H's, Corporal William M. Greene of Wayne County died on May 9, 1863 on the hospital steamer "City of Memphis." Company I's Private Benjamin M. Miller of Carondelet died on May 2, 1863. Company K's Corporal David S. Barger died on May 15, 1863 at Jefferson Barracks, Missouri and is buried there. Private Elijah Bayce of Ironton died on May 9, 1863 at Nashville, Tennessee.

The following is found in the Morning Report of Company G, 31st Missouri Infantry Regiment in the remarks column. It tells of where the 31st Missouri marched on their way to Vicksburg which is the subject of the next Chapter.

"May 1863   2nd- Left Milikens Bend, Louisiana
               5th- Arrived at Hard Times Landing
               7th- Crossed river on Gunboat
                      Carondelet
               8th- Left Grand Gulf
             10th- Camp near Rock Springs
             13th- Camp near Raymond
             14th- Arrived at Jackson
             16th- Left Jackson- Camp at Bolton
             17th- Crossed the Big Black River at
                      8 O'clock p.m.
             18th- Arrived in the rear of Vicksburg
             19th- Captain Osterhorn wounded in
                      the Rifle Pits
             27th- Left Camp near Vicksburg for
                      the Yazoo City Expedition
             29th- Arrived in Mechanicsburg
             31st- Returned to Haynes Bluff"(17)

CHAPTER SIX:
ON TO VICKSBURG

On May 14th, General Grant gave the following orders to his corps commanders. General Sherman's 15th Corps were ordered to stay in Jackson to destroy railroads, factories and any other building or property that could be used for the Confederate cause. General McPherson was ordered to leave in the morning march toward Bolton, Mississippi, about twenty miles west of Jackson. General McClernand was sent the following order, "It is evidently the design of the enemy to get north of us and cross the Big Black, and beat us into Vicksburg. We must not allow them to do this. Turn all your forces towards Bolton station, and make all dispatch in getting there. Move troops by the most direct road from wherever they may be on the receipt of this order."(1) He then ordered General Blair, whose division was at New Auburn with the two hundred wagons of supplies, to Bolton. He was to take his division, General Smith's division, supply trains and any other troops he could grab on the way.

On the night of May 15th, General McPherson and his 17th Corps were at Bolton, with General Carr and General Osterhaus were just south, facing west. General Blair along with the troops he had with him, were north of Raymond. General Sherman's men were up the next day ready to go about the business of destroying the Confederate material and buildings. General Steele's division of the 15th Corps were assigned the responsibility of destroying the railroad and public property to the south and east of Jackson, Mississippi. Major A. J. Seay recorded in his diary his impressions of the day.

"We got to work on the Southern R.R. today, 32nd, alone tore up ¾ mile of track. Did not go to the city during the day-busy-went up at night and met the Master at Jackson Lodge had a long, interesting friendly talk with him. He told me many things that I could not have known otherwise. Says good boots $75 per pair. Was a Union man as far as he dared to be. Is well pleased with the conduct of our troops. Says they have pilliaged no private houses, etc. They find all the drinkables in town and many indulge. I am disgusted with them a perfect rabble for 4 or 5 hours. Govt. buildings, arsenals, and stores are burned all day, but I am proud to say no private houses have been burned. The men got an immense quanity of tobacco, some rum, whiskey, wines, etc. – some clothing and some provisions. Also some stationary and shoes. 200 Secesh prisoners in the capital.

Some pretty fine public buildings and some nice private residences, but upon the whole it is a common town of perhaps 5,000 or 6,000 inhabitants. More shrubbery than vegetables. The people do not seem so much alarmed as I expected at our approach and while some are bitter others make strong professions of loyalty. They say 5 men have recently been hung in the town for disloyalty. The Rebs have here a cannon and ammunition foundary all of which we have destroyed. All the printing presses were also destroyed."(2)

They destroyed the bridges across the Pearl River. The railroad bridges were burned by being coated with tar. Some trestles and bridges across ravines were also destroyed. Jackson was a major rail center with tracks running east to Vicksburg and in other directions to such towns as Meridian, Mississippi and Memphis, Tennessee. The destruction of these vital rail lines slowed, if not halted transportation of vital material by railway for the duration of the war. The 15th Corps had went about their job of burning the buildings and railroad with great efficiency. They were starting to develop a reputation that followed them into Georgia and South Carolina. This is where they started making their famous "Sherman's neckties". A regiment would line up along a railroad track, the men would bend over and grab a tie and simultaneously lift up one side of the whole track, ties and rails. They would then set the railroad ties on fire and lay the rails across them. Once the rails were red hot in the middle, the men would then grab hold of each end and wrap them around a telegraph pole or tree and bend and twist them. They would throw them into water, if handy, or just leave them wrapped around the tree or pole. This would damage the rails to such an extent that they couldn't be used again, unless they were melted and remade into rails.

While they were busy doing this bit of business General's

McPherson's and McClernand's Corps were approaching what would later be known as the Battle of Champion Hill or Battle of Baker's Creek as it is referred to by the Confederates. May 16, 1863 found the Union Army approaching the Big Black River. General Grant knew what the plans of the Confederates were from information passed on to him by a spy. General Johnston had sent General Pemberton orders telling him to bring his force with him and they would then combine their forces, under the command of General Johnston. General Grant, with this knowledge, gave orders so that his troops could be in position to keep the joining of the Confederate forces. Contrary to the orders of General Johnston, for some reason General Pemberton decided to go ahead and attack the Union forces, this attack resulted in the Battle of Champion Hill. While this battle was going on, General Grant sent orders for General Sherman to send one of his divisions to support the attack. The other division was to finish up what they were doing and then to join with the rest of the army. General Sherman sent General Steele's 1st Division, along with the ammunition train, within an hour after he received the order. Not long afterward the division that finished the destruction of Jackson, Mississippi under the command of General Tuttle, was on its way accompanied by General Sherman. These two divisions of the 15th Corps were in Bolton, Mississippi late on the night of May 16th. It was to late for them to reach the battlefield in time to participate in the battle because they wouldn't have reached the battlefield till late the next day. It was late in the evening of the 16th when the Federals entered Edward's Station. Major A. J. Seay wrote in his diary the following,

"Saturday May 16th 1863. We tear R.R. until 10 A.M. and then march 18 miles to Bolton via Clinton, a small ville of 300 inhabitants, 10 miles west of Jackson–a fine church in it–five rebel Hosps. Arrived at Bolton Station late at night crossed the bridge and lay down in a corn field–men tired and hungry. hear Gen. McClernand had a hard fight today–loss in killed and wounded heavy on both sides–McClernand drives the enemy back across the bridge a distance of 4 miles and captures 1500 prisoners or 2000.

Country traveled over not so hilly and the soil a little better than that formerly traveled over. I announced McClernands victory to the 32d after arms are stacked and they give three lusty cheers. The report flies like wild fire thru the army that Richmond is ours many high officers believe it but I am doubtful. I wrap my overcoat around me spread my Poncho in the furrow of a corn row, put my saddle under my head, saddle blanket over me and lie down to sleep sweetly being quite unwell and very tired. The men do likewise, some of them have a bite to eat."(3)

From approximately thirty-thousand men, the Union forces lost four hundred and ten killed, one thousand eight hundred and forty-four wounded and one hundred and eighty-seven missing. The Confederates lost three hundred and eighty-one killed, one thousand and eighteen wounded and two thousand four hundred and forty-one missing, for a total of three thousand eight hundred and forty. These were men that the Confederates could not afford to lose, as they would need them later around Vicksburg. Most of those who were listed as missing were men of Major General William W. Loring's division who had become separated from the rest of General Pemberton's force. General Loring's division was later able to make it's way to Jackson, Mississippi and part of General Johnston force. The Confederates also lost twenty-seven artillery pieces. This was a small battle compared to others and many people have never heard of Champion Hill. But it was this battle that led to the siege of Vicksburg by keeping the Confederate forces of General Johnston and General Pemberton from uniting and if not outnumbering the forces of General Grant at least equalling his strength. After his defeat at Champion Hill, General Pemberton's force began retreating to Vicksburg and General Johnston's force withdrew to Jackson, once again taking control of the Mississippi state capitol along with some Federal soldiers who had been left there in a hospital.

On May 17, 1863 the 15th Army Corps reached Bolton around two o'clock in the morning. General Sherman at that time was informed of the victory of the Union Army. Around six o'clock that morning they again started marching toward the Big Black River on the road that would lead them to Bridgeport, Mississippi. General Blair was ordered to rejoin the 15th Corps along with a pontoon train as soon as he could. It was hoped that General Sherman could get across the Big Black River and come up behind, or flank the Confederates from their position and capture the army to keep them from going into

Vicksburg or joining General Johnston. General Pemberton had retreated to the Big Black holding some bridges open in hopes that General Loring's division would be able to link up with the army. It was here that General Lawler, a brigade commander in General Carr's division, made his charge for which he is best known for. He was a large man who it is reported weighed over two hundred and fifty pounds. His stomach was so large that his belt would not fit around it so his sword hung across his body from the shoulder. Being a large man he sweated very freely. At the Battle of Big Black River Bridge he led his men in his short sleeves. His brigade attacked the bridge with a mighty shout, the Confederates fired a few shots and then swiftly fled. They blew up the bridge which slowed the attackers because of the depth of the river and its swiftness due to the amount of rain that had been falling. The Confederates were in such a hurry to blow up the bridge that all of their troops had not yet made it across to safety. The Confederates lost eighteen guns and one thousand seven hundred and fifty-one men captured. Some Confederates drowned swimming the river trying to avoid being captured. The Union forces loss in this battle was thirty-nine killed, two hundred and thirty-seven wounded and three missing. By blowing up the bridge when they did, they slowed the Union forces enough that they could not keep on the heels of the Confederates and follow them into Vicksburg.

General Sherman's men reached Bridgeport about noon on May 17th. General Blair was already waiting for him with the pontoon train. The Confederates had some troops in defensive positions across the river to contest any crossing by the Federal troops. The Confederates had left a small force there who quickly surrendered once the 15th Corps attacked. Major A. J. Seay wrote in his diary the following, "Sunday May 17th, 1863. Started early this morning and marched hard to Big Black Ferry. Some cavalry came into Jackson just as we left and I saw them shot and bayonet several drunk straggling Yankees and negroes. Good for the stragglers. Arrived at the river at 3 P.M. – threw across a pontoon and move across at 9 P.M. Gen. Blair's div. taking the lead followed by Gen Steele – march 2 miles and go into a corn field and rest our weary limbs in its furrows."(4) The 15th Corps crossed two divisions that night with the third division crossing the next morning. Lieutenant William H. Lynch of Company I, 32nd Missouri Infantry Regiment, wrote in his diary, "Monday morning 18th May 1863. The command resumed the march to Vicksburg Miss. The day was beautiful, not a sound of a musket or cannon could be heard, all was profound silence till about 4 O'Clock P.M. when the thunder of Cannon & the sharp crack of the musket were heard in the rear of Vicksburg Miss. The enemy fell back at dark into their rifle pits & as the night grew dark, both sides ceased their firing. The federal army bivouacked & were in readiness next morning for a new conflict."(5) By ten o'clock that morning they reached Benton Road, which gave them control of the peninsula between the Big Black River and the Yazoo River. General Grant wanted General Sherman to establish contact with the navy on the Yazoo River in order to set up a supply base from which to supply his army. Continuing on to Vicksburg, General Steele's division was sent to the right marching on the graveyard road, which entered Vicksburg near a cemetery. It was General Steele's division who was sent to make contact with the navy in the Yazoo River. They ended up in positions on top of the Walnut Hills that were looking down on the Chickasaw Bayou Battlefield where they had first attacked the enemy in December 1862. "Our Division was posted on the right our Regt. (32nd MO) was on the extreme right near the river."(6)

On May 19, 1863 the battle for the city of Vicksburg officially began. Vicksburg, Mississippi was now surrounded by the Federal army. The army of General Grant was above, below and east of the city with the Union navy forces on the river within gun range of the city, the siege was now started. One of the major concerns of General Grant was that General Pemberton would be reinforced or he would try to break through to General Johnston. General Grant's forces at the time of the start of the siege were approximately fifty thousand men, with the Confederates having approximately twenty five thousand men in Vicksburg. There was almost constant skirmishing on the 19th of May while the Union army was trying to strengthen their position. It appeared that the Confederates had retreated into the defenses of Vicksburg in such a manner as to give the impression of a demoralized army. Because of this impression, which would be verified after the capture of Vicksburg, General Grant ordered an attack across the whole front. Around two o'clock p.m. there was an attack which resulted in a bloody repulse of the Federals. General Grant found out that the Confederate army was not as completely demoralized as he had thought. Major A. J. Seay wrote in his diary, "Tuesday 19ᵗʰ. We moved a mile skirmishing as we go. Now we take possession of the works we assaulted last winter and from which we were compelled to fall back. Here are the steepest hills and bluffs in confederate states and we scale them with bayonets fixed ready to meet the foe. A charge has been ordered and we stand in breathless suspense ready to obey, but the order is counter-manded. A fortunate occurrence for us. We go into the rifle pits."(7) This first attack cost the Federals one hundred and fifty-seven killed, seven hundred and seventy-seven wounded and eighty missing. The 31st Missouri Infantry Regiment losses in this attack was one officer wounded and one enlisted man wounded. The casualties of the Confederates were reported to have been about two hundred and fifty.

General Sherman sent the 1st Battalion, 13th U S Infantry and the rest of General Blair's division in the lead of the attack. General Blair was given the job of attacking the Stockade Redan Complex. They made a strong attack down the Graveyard Road but because of the terrain and some trees that the Confederates had cut down, their attack was impeded. Mississippi and Louisiana troops set up such a volume of fire that it stopped the attack. Some of the men were pinned down until after dark when they were successfully withdrawn. The 13th U. S. Infantry Regulars lost three color bearers when Captain Charles Ewing grabbed it and took it up to the ramparts. While doing this he lost a finger. The 13th U. S. Infantry Regulars commanding officer Captain Washington was mortally wounded and later died in the hands of the enemy. They lost a total of seventy-seven men with about two hundred men reported as casualties from the 83rd Indiana Infantry and 127th Illinois Infantry. Generals McPherson and McClernand's attacks were more successful, they drove in the enemy pickets and even drove some of the enemy out of their trenches, but then pulled back and returned to their original lines. General Grant said, "It resulted in securing more advanced positions for all our troops where they were fully covered from the fire of the enemy." (8)

Major A. J. Seay wrote the following in his diary for May 20, 1863.

"The most exciting thing that occurred yesterday was the advance of the flying Dutchman, Landgraber (of the

1st Mo. flying artillery) who charged over the hill with two pieces at a full gallop a distance of ½ mile while four rebel guns played fearfully on him. Got a horse killed and man wounded was thrown himself, lost his hat but soon remounted and brandished his sword in mid air cried "Forward" after he got his gun in position he did good fighting. The fight today is general from the extreme right to the center. Steele and Blair commanding. The rebels charge Blair but were repulsed. Sherman's corps has done all the fighting today as far as heard from. We are fighting at long range. Losing but few men. 32d has a position in a house which is riddled with shot and shell, Nobody hurt. We kept the rebs so completely driven from their guns they could not use them. 32d hard to beat as sharp shooters. I shot till my shoulder was sore from the kicking muskets. I'm worn out – not much to eat – nor to buy—but nobody grumbles—all cheerful. A mortar boat two miles from the city across the point is shelling the town. There seems to be no fighting on the extreme left."(9)

Both armies spent May 20th and 21st strengthening their positions and sharpshooting at the enemy. There were also men who were busy building roads to the river in the rear of the Federal lines. These roads were used to bring up the supplies that were brought in from the river. There was also liberal foraging by the Federals in the surrounding area. It was so liberal that it left those who were robbed without anything, if it could be found by the foragers. There was no want for food in the Federal lines but the one thing that was missing was bread. On the 21st, while passing around the left of the army, General Grant said, "A soldier, recognizing me, said in a rather low voice, but yet so that I heard him, 'Hard Tack'. In a moment the cry was taken up all along the line, 'Hard tack! Hard tack!' I told the men nearest to me that we had been engaged ever since the arrival of the troops in building a road over which to supply them with everything they needed. The cry was instantly changed to cheers. By the night of the 21st all the troops had full rations issued to them. The bread and coffee were highly appreciated."(10)

Lieutenant William H. Lynch wrote in his diary,

"Wednesday 20th May 1863. The 3rd days fight was not very severe, till about 2 O"lock when the fire was very heavy by our boys. The Gun Boats acted in front while the land forces operated in the rear of Vicksburg Miss. Thursday 21st, 4th day's engangement. The 32nd Inft. Regt. Mo. Vols. was engaged in the Rifle Pits from one to 6 P.M. when we were relieved by the 27th Mo. Inft. Vols. one of our Brigade. The Gun Boats acted upon the Town, Shelling the enemy, behind their breast works doing much injury to the Town. Our Regt. (32nd Mo.) Bivouacked in the Rifle pits, during the night of the 21st May '63 about 450 yards distant from the enemy's breast works."(11) Another member of the 32nd Missouri Infantry Regiment wrote in his diary, Major A. J. Seay. "Thursday May 21st. Position unchanged-we have mounted one and the enemy three more guns, but our sharp shooters annoy them so much they seldom get to fire. One of the men of Co. B. had the hair shaved from his head by a ball this evening. Our generals seem too slow, besides they do not use the spade enough. We should have dug rifle pits all night, but it was not done. Joe and I sit tonight and watch the shells from the mortar and signal lights. The shell can be seen gliding thru the air like a lightning bug. A bombardment is awfully sublime. The fortifications and earthworks against which we contended by the natural position were certainly never surpassed. But the rebels strong hold must fall."(12)

May 22, 1863 was the date of the second attack on the Confederate entrenchments around Vicksburg. The Federal army made ready to attack the enemy to their front. It was a Friday morning at ten o'clock when the 15th Corps, with the rest of the Federal army, again charged down the Graveyard Road to attack the Stockade Redan. This was the exact same route that General Frank Blair's division had taken on the 19th. In order to attack the stockade the road was about the only way into the area. It was like going into a funnel and then trying to reform to attack. The 15th Corps were led by about one hundred and fifty men who considered themselves a suicide mission they were so sure that their mission would be a failure that they named themselves the "Forlon Hope." They were volunteers who carried the ladders in which to throw upon the stockades walls in order to carry the walls. They also were to carry other material in which to help build a bridge over the ditch. They ended up being trapped in this ditch. Many of these men were wounded or killed in the initial charge. They were followed by the 30th Ohio Infantry which suffered about the same results as the Forlon Hope. The 37th Ohio Infantry came over the same road as the 30th Ohio Infantry. When they saw what happened, they refused to go on. The road was cut through a hill and when they emerged they were only about one hundred and fifty yards from the Confederate line. The 15th Corps attacked Stockade Redan three times this day and were repulsed every time. General Sherman called off the attack even though the 15th Corps which had around fifteen thousand men in it, had committed only around one thousand of its force. General Steele's division was not in line to attack because they had been given the task of making a strong demonstration about a mile to the right of the attack, towards the river.

General McPherson's corps attack was about as successful as that of General Sherman's. One of the reasons that the 15th Corps made three attacks was because General McClernand told General Grant that his men had made a successful attack and had taken some of the entrenchments to his front. He said that if supported by another attack from both General McClernand's and Sherman's corps, they would be able to keep the enemy from withdrawing men from their fronts in order to strengthen the enemy in his front. After consultation with Generals McPherson and Sherman, General Grant gave the order to attack again. All attacks failed. This last attack accomplished nothing except to increase the number of casualties that were suffered by all the corps. The Federal Army suffered three thousand two hundred and forty-one casualties while the Confederates suffered less than five hundred. The 15th Army Corps loss was about six hundred. On this attack the 31st Missouri Infantry Regiment suffered two more losses they lost one officer killed and one enlisted men wounded. Now began the Siege of Vicksburg. Major A. J. Seay of the 32nd Missouri Infantry Regiment records in his diary the following.

"Friday 22d May 1863.

We have been enjoying refreshing showers of rebel bullets and shells for quite a while and last night had one of rain. Hot and cloudy—we have advanced a little on the enemy. We command these batteries with our advanced position better than before. 11 A.M. We move hastily to the extreme left of our position to charge the enemy from their fortifications-a hazardous attempt.

Our brig was held in reserve. We were repulsed with heavy loss after approaching the enemies entrenchments. Our brig loss 4 killed and 10 wounded while under cover of a hill. The cries of the wounded is terrible and the sight of the mangled dead is horrible. Our loss in killed and wounded in the 2 brig must have been three hundred. We bivouack for the night 150 yards from the scene of action. At 10 P.M. we are aroused from the arms of Morpheous and ordered to the place from whence we started in the morning. 2 ½ miles distant-dark and raining. I have no horse blanket, overcoat or supper but get along almost exhausted. I have no doubt but that we will have a long bloody siege of Vicksburg (which must eventually surrender) and those of us who survive will be able to stand almost anything."(13)

The Confederates were trapped in Vicksburg with no possible way of escape. General Pemberton, who was in Vicksburg with his troops, was under the impression that the holding of the city of Vicksburg was his objective until relieved by General Johnston, who was his immediate commander. General Johnston, who was in command of this district, felt that saving the army who was trapped in Vicksburg was more important than saving the city. If the forces of General Johnston and General Pemberton would be able to unite, they would outnumber the forces of General Grant, and therefore endanger the Federal Army with the threat of capture or destruction. He was continually asking for more reinforcements to strengthen his forces and also to continue to tighten the ring around Vicksburg in order to keep the Confederates from escaping. The morale of the Confederate forces in Vicksburg was very high at the beginning of the siege, because they were sure that General Johnston would come to their aid. While the Confederates were retreating into the city from the Big Black River they brought with them livestock that they had picked up on the way into the city. They not only had a force of approximately thirty-two thousand men, they also had to worry about how to feed the remainder of the population of Vicksburg who had not fled the city.

The citizens that remained in the city had to endure a severe bombardment by not only the artillery but also from the Federal navy on the Mississippi River. Vicksburg was almost continuously under this bombardment for the whole time of the siege. The citizens endured hardships that would be hard for us to imagine today. Vicksburg became a city of caves. The citizens, along with some of the troops, dug into the hills and formed caves in which to live to escape the bombardment. Some of the caves were so big that they had rooms and doorways that lead into the rooms for privacy. They moved in furniture, rugs and other conviences that made life bearable. Some of these cave dwellings had porches that the residents used to do daily routines such as sewing and visiting with neighbors. They usually spent the night in the caves sleeping on beds or mats in order to protect themselves from the bombardment that usually went on at night. Some of the citizens still lived in their houses and refused to go to these shelters. Most businesses remained open as long as their stock lasted. There were still services in the churches held at the normal time. The local newspaper continued to print their paper until their last issue which was printed on the day of the surrender of Vicksburg. This last issue, was found on the back of wallpaper. During the long days of bombardment there were some people who were killed. There were children who were killed and wounded not only by bomblasts but also by cave-ins in the caves caused by bombs. Some children were severly hurt by picking up rounds for keepsakes or treasures that would explode while they were in the act of picking them up.

The major problem that became the final breaking point was the lack of food. As previously mentioned, because of the large amount of food that was consumed by all persons within the Confederate lines and in the city, food quickly became scarce. One of the benefits of the bombardment was that once in a while a mule or horse would be killed. Towards the end of the siege anyone who was in the area of the death of an animal would walk up and cut off a piece of meat and take it to their fire and cook it. At the beginning of the siege there were still restuarants who served their normal meals, but toward the end of the siege one such restuarant listed their menu for every meal as mule meat. The soldiers were quickly put on reduced rations because of the possible length of the siege. Once flour started to become harder to get, they began to mix pea flour and meal to make it stretch. This was not a very delicious combination and was hard to eat, but there was not much else to eat so the men had no choice but to eat it. The amount of food that was finally issued for each man was flour or meal and bacon, four ounces each, one and one-half ounces of rice, two ounces of peas that were not very appetizing, and three ounces of sugar. This reduction in food and the hectic schedule of daily fighting, strengthening the entrenchments, the disturbance of their sleep by the explosions and the sickness that began to become prevelant each day began to take it's toll on the soldiers. Another enemy in both trenches was the hot weather that was an almost constant companion for both sides.

There was constant shrinking of the lines throughout the siege. The Federal soldiers had constructed their trenches so that they could at least walk around in it without exposing themselves to the constant harassing fire of the Confederate sharpshooters. The trenches were built with a ledge that a man would stand upon to shoot while men could walk behind in an area that was low enough to walk past the person shooting and not be exposed. In times of attack there could be a regiment firing from the ledge with another regiment standing in the bottom of the trench ready to relieve them if they should run out of ammunition and to replace casualties. The trenches had a berm or a parapet in front with a head log on top of that. There was space enough under the log for a man to shoot through. It was called a head log because a man could shoot under the log, while his head would be protected by the log from any enemy fire except for sharpshooter fire. The log would normally be about twenty-four inches thick, or thicker, and would have logs that would support it. These support logs ran from the parapet across the trench to the back part of the trench. The reason for this was in case the head log was dislodged out of position by artillery fire, it would then land on the support logs or roll down them hopefully without falling into the trench and injuring any of the men. There were also trenches that were designed as those previously described but the head log was made of railroad ties layered so that they had firing slots in them just big enough to fire through. The only place where the soldier was exposed was in those slots. There were numerous casualties caused by Confederate sharpshooters firing through these slots and killing or wounding Federal soldiers who were standing in front of these slots.

As stated earlier, the Federal soldiers were slowly trying to get their lines closer to those of the Confederates so when it came time to attack they would have less ground to cover. Some of these trenches were so close that the two different sides could hold a conversation. One of the ways they were

SIEGE OF VICKSBURG, MISSISSIPPI: National Archives, Washington D.C.

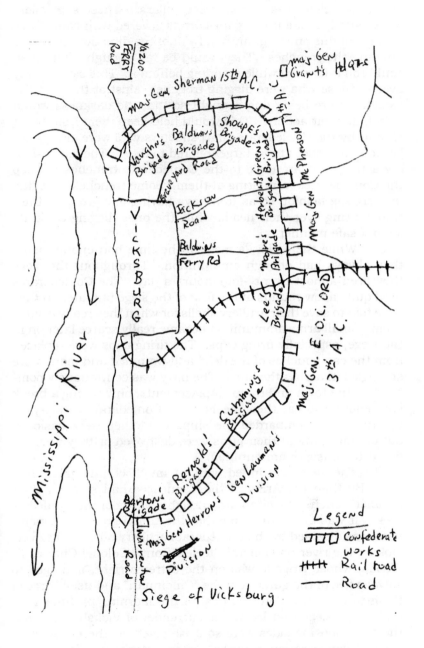

SIEGE OF VICKSBURG

131

able to get close was by using sap rollers. These sap rollers were usually made up of giant barrels covered with cane. They would roll this on the ground in front of the direction they were building the trenches. They would be tall enough where men could roll it forward while standing behind it. This saved many lives of those who were digging trenches. Most ot the time the trenches were being dug at night so that the darkness would help hide their actions. This would help keep them from being shot at by the Confederate sharpshooters who were always eager to take a shot at any target offered to them. The men would dig a trench at an angle to the Confederate trenches to keep the Confederates from firing at them. Some trenches were dug in a zig zag fashion so as to always having one group of their troops firing over their heads while the ones digging could do so in a safe manner.

While the Federals most of the time had enough food, they always had enough ammunition. Throughout the siege they fired almost twenty-four hours a day. The Confederates fired quite a few rounds at the first of the siege but later on they were told to save their artillery shells for when they really needed them. Small arms ammunition became really scarce later on in the siege, especially firing caps. The firing caps were replaced from the cap pouches of the dead and wounded and many were smuggled in across the lines. The navy was continuously bombarding the town and troop emplacements, only taking a break long enough to eat their meals. The Confederate artillery on the river side bombarded the ships until they were basically out of ammunition, their guns were destroyed or they were ordered to conserve ammunition.

The siege continued without much change until July 4th. By then the Army of the Tennessee had some of their parallel trenches to within about eighty yards of the Confederates. It was about this time that the Union gunboat "Cincinnati" was disabled by the Confederate artillery on the hills overlooking the river on General Steele's front. Colonel Charles R. Woods, whose Brigade was on the extreme right, managed to salvage five of the guns from the "Cincinnati" and used three of them to shell the Confederates on the morning of June 29th and in the siege that led to the surrender of Vicksburg. Since the two opposing sides were so close together, there was quite a lot of conversation between the two trenches. There were Missouri units not only in the Federal army but also in the

Confederate army. The Federal army had the following Missouri units the 3rd Infantry, 6th Infantry, 8th Infantry, 11th Infantry, 12th Infantry, 17th Infantry, 27th Infantry, 29th Infantry, 30th Infantry, 31st Infantry, 32nd Infantry, and the 6th Cavalry (seven companies), The Confederate army had the following units from Missouri the 1st and 4th Infantry (consolidated), 2nd Infantry, 3rd Infantry, 5th Infantry, 6th Infantry, 1st Cavalry (dismounted), 3rd Cavalry Battalion (dismounted), Lowe's Battery, Third Battery, Bledsoe's Battery, Clark Artillery, Wade's Battery, Landis' Battery and Cuibor's Battery. These Missouri Confederates had been at Grand Gulf with General John Bowen and remained with him throughout all the battles in the campaign until the surrender of Vicksburg. Missouri regiments fought Missouri regiments such as on the defensive position of the Stockade Redan on the Graveyard Road. They were defended by the 5th Missouri and the 1st and 4th Missouri combined with the 3rd Missouri in reserve. On May 22nd the 11th Missouri (Union) fought its way to the bottom of the ditch at the base of the stockade. The 1st Missouri Cavalry (Confederate) and the 3rd Cavalry Battalion held the line against the 8th Missouri (Union). After the battles of the 22nd of May these units were in the trenches opposite of each other.

At this time the 31st Missouri Infantry was in Major General Steele's division. While being in the 1st Brigade they were under the command of Colonel Francis H. Manter, who was the Colonel of the 32nd Missouri Infantry, from April 1 through June 12, 1863 and Colonel Bernard G. Farrar from June 13 through July 4, 1863. Colonel Farrar was the Colonel of the 30th Missouri Infantry. Each regiment usually had a detachment of sharpshooters that were there to kill or wound as many of the Confederates as possible. They were usually the best shots in the regiments. The 31st Missouri Regiments sharpshooters were on the line from June 5 through July 4,1863. They were facing some Tennessee troops and Louisiana troops.

The casualties that are listed for the 31st Missouri Infantry Regiment from May 16th thru May 31st. Company B's Private Lafayette Jackson from Washington County died on May 5, 1863 at a Van Buren, Louisiana hospital. Company C's Private Charles Dowine from Hopewell was discharged on May 28, 1863; Private James K. Marler from Washington County died on May 25, 1863 at Saint Louis, Missouri. Company D's Private Charles Jones from Butler County was discharged on May 19, 1863 at Saint Louis, Missouri. Company F's Private James C. Seaton of Canaan died of disease on May 25, 1863 at Memphis, Tennessee; 3rd Sergeant Theodore H. Snyder of Sullivan was discharged on May 23, 1863 due to disability because of the wound to his right hip while at Vicksburg. Sergeant Snyder was later drafted; Private Augustus Carman of Canaan deserted on May 18, 1863 at Young's Point, Louisiana. Company H's Private Richard Harkee of Wayne County died on May 21, 1863 at Van Buren, Louisiana hospital. Company I's Private Warren Moffat of Danville died on May 30, 1863 at Memphis, Tennessee. Company K's Private William D. Brown died of disease on May 20, 1863 at Benton Barracks, Missouri; Private Michael Gleason from Saint Louis was discharged on May 17, 1863 at Saint Louis, Missouri; Corporal Joseph G. Henderson of Caledonia died on May 23, 1863 at Saint Louis, Missouri.

The siege began in earnest after it was determined that any attack upon the Confederate line would continue to result in needless casualties. General Grant in his memoirs describes the opposing lines.

"My line was more than fifteen miles long, extending from Haines' Bluff to Vicksburg, thence to Warrenton. The line of the enemy was about seven. In addition to this, having an enemy at Canton and Jackson, in our rear, who was being constantly reinforced, we required a second line of defence facing the other way. I had not troops enough under my command to man these. General Halleck appreciated the situation and, without being asked, forwarded reinforcements with all possible dispatch.

The ground about Vicksburg is admirable for defence. On the north it is about two hundred feet above the Mississippi River at the highest point and very much cut up by the washing rains; the ravines were grown up with cane and underbrush, while the sides and tops were covered with a dense forest. Farther south the ground flattens out somewhat, and was in cultivation. But here, too, it was cut up by ravines and small streams. The enemy's line of defence followed the crest of a ridge from the river north of the city eastward, then southerly around to the Jackson road, full three miles back of the city; thence in a southwesterly direction to the river.

Deep ravines of the description given lay in front of these defences. As there is a succession of gullies cut out by rains along the side of the ridge, the line was necessarily very irregular. To follow each of these spurs with intrenchments, so as to command the slopes on either side, would have lengthened their line very much. Generally therefore, or in many places their line would run from near the head of one gully nearly straight to the head of another, and an outer work triangular in shape, generally open in the rear, was thrown up on the point; with a few men in this outer work they commanded the approaches to the main line completely."(14)

To show you what life was like for a regiment on the line during the siege the following diary entries of Lieutenant William H. Lynch. He was in Company I, 32nd Missouri Infantry Regiment that was in the same brigade as the 31st Missouri Infantry throughout almost the whole war.

"*May 23d,* 6th days engagement (Saturday). The land forces did but little fighting on the 23d May. But the gun boats kept up a continuous fire, shelling the Town, doing much damage to the enemy.

May 24th, Sunday 7th days engagement. The firing was not very heavy on the 24th May. Our Regt. (32d Mo.) was engaged in the rifle pits, Huffman's Battery was engaged the entire day. Huffman made several shots that damaged the Rebels very much. Our Regt. was during the time, erecting breast works.

May 25th, Monday 8th day's engagement. There was but little firing on the 25th. The pickets in the Rifle pits fired several shots during the day. About 5 o'clock P.M. a flag of Truce was hoisted by the Rebels & respected by General Grant, till 30 min. after 8 P.M. till that hour, all hostilities were abated, but after the time designated, had expired, the battle was renewed; but very little execution done, on the night of the 25th May.

May 26th, Tuesday 9th days attack. Our Regt. (32nd Mo.) & Brigade were ordered on an expedition Northward. We left at dark, marched about 2 miles & camped till next morning, at 5 O'Clock the command started for Mechanicsville, Miss.

May 27th, 10th days engagement. The command left Walnut Hill, early Wednesday morning, in the direction

135

of Yazoo City. We halted at 8 O'Clock A.M. for breakfast & recreation, as the weather was extremely hot. At 9 O'clock & 30 min. We resumed our march until noon, when we again halted, till evening, when we moved onward, again. The day was extremely hot & dry.

May 28th, Thursday, 11th day's engagement at Vicksburg Miss. There was not much fighting at Vicksburg from the 26th May till the month of June 1863. We resumed our march, the day was hot & threatened rain. We marched till 11 P.M., when we camped till next day about 7 O'Clock. There was no fighting up to Thursday evening when the pickets had a skirmish with the enemy.

May 29th, Friday, 12th day's engagement at Vicksburg Mississippi. We marched about 8 miles and camped. It rained in the afternoon, which made the roads muddy, that our march was very much hindered. We went into camp about 6 O'Clock P.M. camped in an old field, near a small Town, called Mechanicsville on the Road From Vicksburg to Yazoo City.

May 30th, 13 day's engagement. On the morning of the 30th the command returns to Vicksburg Miss., at 6 O'Clock A.M. (day cloudy & pleasant). We marched back on the Yazoo Road, about 4 miles, where we left the road & took the Telegraphic Road to Hanes Bluff, Miss. Camped in Yazoo Bottom at 12 P.M.

May 31st, 14th days attack. We marched to the Yazoo River at Hanes Bluff where the enemy had made strong defences to drive back our gun boats if they should offer to pass by. Digging rifle pits and forts we went into camp. The Regiment & Company remain here till Second day of June 1863."(15)

June was a hot month with temperatures reaching close to the one hundred degrees mark with high humidity. General McClernand was relieved from command of the 13th Corps in the latter part of June because of the publishing of a congratulatory order to his troops for their battles of May 22nd. In this order he congradulated his troops on their actions during these two charges. It was also implied that if they had received more support from the other commands, that they would now control Vickburg. It was standing orders from the War Department that such orders would not be sent to the papers for publication and the same orders were also issued by General Grant. General Grant already had permission from General Halleck to remove General McClernand from command, but General Grant did not exercise this option until this time. General McClernand was ordered to Springfield, Illinois to await further orders from the War Department. This publication offended both General McPherson and General Sherman with its inference to their respective corps lack of participation.

Meanwhile, the siege continued. The Federals continued to get closer to the Confederates. Reinforcements began to arrive as was promised to General Grant by General Halleck. Major A. J. Seay was worried about reinforcements as he states in his diary entry for June 1st.

"Monday June 1st, 1863.

The first day of summer and oh, how oppressive the heat. If we had to march today we would surely loose men from sunstroke. If we are to fight at Vicksburg in front or rear this kind of weather, the sufferings of the army have just begun. The expedition from which we have just returned went to Mechanicsville 42 miles from Vicksburg and from Big Black-found 1500 to 2000 rebs and drive them beyond the Big Black. Blair commands. We make a number of captures. The object was accomplished, we having got position of the country, the roads, etc, and frustrated the designs of Joe Johnson. The fact is authentic that Hill, Johnson, et al have 30 to 40,000 reenforcements from Bragg, Richmond, Charleston and Mobile-also that they are completing bridges at several points on Big Black to cross over and attack us in the rear. If Grant gets heavy reenforcements we are all right, if not we are gone up and must abandon the siege."(16)

On June 3rd, a brigade arrived from General Hurbut's command with General Kimball in command. Lieutenant William H. Lynch of Company I, 32nd Missouri Infantry Regiment, wrote, "Friday 5th June '63 19th days attack upon Vicksburg, Miss. Our Regiment and Brigade remained in Camp in a Hollow, near the enemy's Rifle Pits till sundown, when our Regt. (32nd Mo. Inft. Vols.) was detailed to stand picket in rifle pits.

There was but little firing by the pickets, but the gun boats shelled the Town during the entire night. During the early part of the night our Regt. (32nd Mo) assigned the Gun

Boat Boys by planting a large cannon. About 8 O'clock the gun was mounted, & fired once every hour, till day dawned. It was not fired any more till dark. It did great execution upon the Fort & Rifle pits. The gun boat boys lost their boat & were [forced to] land. Today their still on land."(17) On June 8th General Sooy Smith brought in a full division which also came from General Hurbut's command. On the 11th another division joined the forces around Vicksburg from the Department of Missouri. General Parke, with two divisions, joined the Federal forces from General Burnside's corps. This brought the total amount of men that General Grant had to around seventy-one thousand. General Grant, now for the first time, felt confident that he could keep the siege around Vicksburg going with enough forces to keep an eye on the army that General Johnston had with him in the Jackson area. On June 16, 1863 Private Samuel A. Garrison of Company D, 31st Missouri Infantry was killed in the trenches near Vicksburg.

Private Henry Kuck, Company G 31st Missouri Infantry Regiment, on June 20th wrote a letter to his wife informing her of what was going on in his life in the breast works at Vicksburg.

"I wrote in the last letter that we're still besieging Vicksburg. We're laying about opposite from the breastwork of the Rebels' fort, in a hollow, of deep valley, where at first the bombs and musketshot went off over our heads, without hurting us. The Rebels don't use cannon so much anymore, in the last few days they didn't shoot anything big to our side, our batteries came so close to them that they couldn't stay anymore at their cannons. Maybe they would have surrendered Vicksburg already, but they're probably waiting for reinforcements. Quite a few deserters came over to us; their reports vary, many say, or believe, they can't last much longer, for their supplies are almost gone, others think they have provision for a while yet, but they are short on ammunition. In the evenings scouts or front guards are sent out, and when they're sent out they often group together. Often it's not more than 50 steps away from each other. As soon as it's dark and the scouts are sent out, they don't shoot at each other, that is, these front guards don't do it, so their artillery has to be fired off if it seems necessary. We hope that Vicksburg surrenders soon, and I hope we'll come then to St. Louis in a short while. Our Col. Thomas Fletcher promised us, he's just now come back again from St. Louis himself, love to you sweet Metta and our children. Write right away."(18)

For sixteen days there was basically no change in what was happening on both sides. The routine in the trenches around Vicksburg became boring. Even at times of almost continuous danger you can become so used to what is happening, even someone shooting at you, a person becomes careless. Lieutenant William H. Lynch writes in his diary about the change in routine on June 20th.

"Our Regt. & Brigade remain in Camp, near the enemy's breast works, from the 4th June, till 20th day of June 1863, when we were ordered to be ready to move at a moments notice, (at 4 O'Clock A.M.) On the 20th June a general fire was opened on the entire Circuit of Rebel Breast works. The fireing was opened on the left & combined to the extreme right along the Miss. River we did not gain much ground but damaged the enemy very much. From every Hill, we had heavy cannon to act upon their works. The day was exciting, our Regt. and Brigade did not move, but were held in readiness to move where ever we might be called at a moments warning. We lost no men from our Regt. & Brigade & very few was killed at all, of our entire force."(19)

Colonel Thomas C. Fletcher when exchanged as a prisoner of war he reported to Vicksburg and then applied for a sick leave. He was in for a severe shock when he sees what is left of his regiment. While home in DeSoto, Missouri he wrote a letter dated June 22nd, 1863 in the letter he states, "On arriving at Vicksburg I found my once splendid Regiment with only 155 men for duty. I am confident that if I had it once in Mo. Again I could recruit it up and make it what it was before the battle of Chickasaw Bluff."(20) In this letter he seems confident that he can recruit the 31st Missouri Infantry if he could get it home. General Grant was not either approached or did not think it was important enough to worry about because it is not mentioned anywhere.

Federals started to dig a mine in order to blow up some of the formible defenses that the Confederates had erected. The men had dug a mine to a point where it was directly under the Confederate works. The Confederates had tried to find the mine by undermining but were unable to find it. They then dug another entrenchment farther back of the estimated place of the mine so that when it was exploded they still had a strong defensive position. Most of the Confederates in this position were in the secondary position but there were a few men manning the main works. General Grant in his "Memoirs" says,"There were a few men, however, left at the advance line, and others working in the countermine, which was still being pushed to finds ours. All that were there were thrown into the air, some of them coming down on our side, still alive. I remember one colored man, who had been under ground at work when the explosion took place, who was thrown to our side. He was not much hurt, but terribly frightened. Some one asked him how high he had gone up. 'Dun no, massa, but think 'bout tree mile', was his reply." (21) This man was used by General Logan for his orderly for the rest of the war. There were no exact count of casualties from the Confederates. The Federals had sent in two regiments to occupy the crater before the Confederates could regroup. They succeeded but the enemy kept rolling grenades and fused artillery shells. The crater had to be abandoned but another mine was dug and exploded on July 1st. It was decided not to occupy this crater. More mines were started and it was decided not to attack the craters until there were numerous craters along the whole front and they could attack them all at the same time.

On June 22nd, General Grant was informed that General Johnston was planning to attack the Federals from the rear in hopes of allowing part of the army trapped in Vicksburg to escape. General Johnston had already crossed the Big Black River on his way to relieve the Vicksburg troops. General Sherman was given command of all the forces from Haines' Bluff to the Big Black River. General Sherman was in charge of almost half of the Federal troops in the area. General Tuttle's division from the 15th Corps area covered from Haines' Bluff to Young's Plantation overlooking what was called Bear Creek valley. General McArthur's division, of the General McPherson's 17th Corps was assigned the area to General Osterhaus's division of McClernand's 13th Corps which held a strong position on the railroad-crossing of the Big Black River. These three divisions were now facing to the east to fight General Johnston. General Steele had taken command of the 15th Corps on the lines facing Vicksburg. This is when General J. M. Thayer was given command of the 1st Division of the 15th Corps. The 31st Missouri was part of the 1st Division.

Lieutenant William H. Lynch, Company I, 32nd Missouri Infantry Regiment wrote in his diary what happened from June 21st to July 4th.

"June 21st, On 21st June, there was very little fireing, except on the extreme right, where it was at times, very heavy & severe. The enemy very seldom replied to our boys, in the Rifle pits. Our Boys & Brigade remain in camp, near the Rifle Pits till Wednesday 24th June.

June 24th, At sundown we left our old camp and occupied a position, still on our left. There we were engaged in digging rifle pits and mounting heavy guns.

June 25th, We lay in Camp, except a heavy detail to dig rifle pits. Thus ends the 25th day of June 1863.

June 26th, Friday 26th day of June 1863, was a day of great excitement. It was on that day that our boys made the attack upon the Rebel Forts, called, the Key of Vicksburg. There the last & final assault was made upon the enemy. The Key was reduced & it was now one of the strongest positions the enemy had .

June 27th, Saturday, our Regt. & Brigade planted a new battery & it was opened upon the Rebel FortIfications, about 6 O'Clock P.M. It was aimed at the Stockades, & did much damage. I could see, at every shot, the effects of the Cannon Ball. I was standing by the Cannon where I could see, the result of every fire. It damaged the stockades & front & port of the Fort.

June 28th, Sunday, we remained in Camp in View of the enemy's breast works & Forts, except a heavy detail from the Reg't. (32nd Mo.) to dig rifle pits. Our boys were so near the Rebels, in their Rifle Pits & Forts, that they could converse freely with each other. They would ask our boys 'when they would take Vicksburg.' Our boys would tell them "we will take Vicksburg tomorrow.' Rebels answer, 'Albut the take Vicksburg.'(?) Some of our boys were standing picket, (it being contrary to fire at each other on picket), Would exchange some very sharp expressions, for

141

pass time. One of the rebel pickets asked one of our Boys on picket, 'why don't you shoot.' Fed. Answered, 'It is strictly against our principles to shoot prisoners.' Every evening, about dark could be heard, many pithy and sharp remarks. The 1st Brigade & Blair's Division, were constantly employed, in digging rifle pits, till the fourth day of July 1863.

July 4th, 1863, At about 9 O'Clock A.M. General Pemberton & his whole command 31,000 soldiers 217, pieces of artillery, 40,000 stand of arms & etc. Surrendered to General U.S. Grant, the hero of the present war. May we ever have such Generals, to lead us to victory, as Gen'l Grant. We repose all confidence & trust in him. He is a true patriot & a brave & tried soldier. He has met the enemy on many battle fields & met them only to conquer & defeat them. He is the man for the boys of the West. They will follow him, go where he may. He will be remembered by the Armies of Tennessee & Miss."(22)

While the Federals continued to try and reach the Confederate lines, the situation in the Rebel works kept getting worse and worse. The weather, lack of sleep and the strain of always being under fire was stressful, yet the most trying circumstance was the poor rations. General Pemberton had received the same order that General Grant had intercepted. In a letter General Johnston told General Pemberton to prepare to try and break out. General Pemberton then called a meeting of his four division commanders to get their opinion on the best course to take. Two of his generals stated that the men were in such poor condition that they could not undertake the long, trying march under fire that they would probably have to endure. There was a letter that had anomiously in effect stated that General Pemberton should go ahead and surrender instead of starving them to death. It was then decided that it was time to surrender. It was reported that General Pemberton had stated that they could get better terms on the Fourth of July than on any other day. He was from Pennsylvania and said that he knew his people. At ten o'clock A. M. on July 3rd white flags began to appear on a portion of the Confederate works. Fighting ceased and two men appeared bearing a white flag. They were General John S. Bowen, who was once an acquaintance of General Grant, and Colonel Montgomery, who was aide-de-camp to General Pemberton. The note sent by General Pemberton asked for an armistice to avoid further bloodshed so that they could discuss the terms for the surrender of the city. Major General U.(Unconditional) S.(Surrender) Grant in a note to General Pemberton stated, that if he was so worried about the further bloodshed that he should surrender unconditionaly right now. This was the terms that General Grant demanded. At three o'clock P.M. General Pemberton appeared at the place that General Grant had appointed to meet him at that time. Major General A. J. Smith and General Bowen discussed terms while General Pemberton and General Grant went off to the side under an apple tree to talk. This tree was completely destroyed after the surrender by those desiring souvenirs. Later that night General Grant sent a note to General Pemberton outlying his plans for the surrender of the Confederate troops in Vicksburg. He said that the men could march out after they had signed a parole with only their clothes. The general officers could keep their side-arms and field and staff officers and cavalry officers could keep one horse each. Later that night General Grant received a reply from General Pemberton asking that he be allowed to march his troops out under their colors and arms at ten o'clock A. M. on July 4th. General Grant sent back a reply that if General Pemberton meant for his men to march out in brigades, stack arms and then return to the entrenchments to await parole, then he would have no objections. By nine o'clock A. M. he would resume hostilities if General Pemberton did not send notice of acceptance of these terms. General Pemberton immediately accepted these terms. At the time specified the Confederates marched out, stacked arms and returned to their trenches. The Union army never uttered a cheer out of respect for those who suffered so much and fought so well. The Union men shared their rations with the Confederates. The Confederates were then marched to a camp where they awaited their paroles to be taken care of, some of the men went home.

To the men in the Federal army it was a day of happiness that they could walk around without the worry of being shot at. To the men who fought there, the surrender of Vicksburg would cause the future celebration of the Fourth of July to never have the same meaning as before. In a letter to his wife Private Henry Kuck of Company G, 31st Missouri Infantry Regiment wrote his feelings at the surrender of Vicksburg.

"Vicksburg surrendered on July 4: You imagine that we were excited, that this work was so wonderfully accomplished. On May 18 we arrived at Vicksburg and laid siege to it until July 4, that is, 6 weeks, when we heard nothing more than the barking of the cannon, banging of the muskets, when this stopped all at once, it was as if a clock had stopped ticking in the room, where we could hear the buzzing of the flies in summer, it was like that at Vicksburg, after the shooting stopped all of nature appeared suddenly to be so peaceful and it seemed as if we had suddenly traveled into a land of peace, even the birds seemed to share that feeling with us, and they wanted to announce that they were among us safe and sound."(23)

The total loss for the Federals were one thousand two hundred and forty-three killed, seven thousand and ninety-five wounded with five hundred and thirty-five missing, which comes to a total of eight thousand eight hundred and seventy-three total causalties. The following men, of the 31st Missouri Infantry Regiment, were killed at Vicksburg, Private Samuel A. Garrison of Company D was killed on June 16, 1863. 1st Lieutenant William Robinson of Company I was killed on May 10, 1863. Among the wounded were Private James Palmer of Company F who was wounded in May 1863, Private Arnold Crawer of Company F who died on June 23rd, 3rd Sergeant Theodore M. Snyder of Company F was wounded in the right hip. Private Klinge of Company G died of his wounds. There were approximately thirty-two thousand men surrendered at Vicksburg for the Confederates, this included the wounded. The Confederates also lost to capture about fourteen thousand additional men at Champion Hills, Big Black Bridge, Port Gibson and with General Loring. They also had ten thousand men killed and wounded in the above listed places. Along with all of this, the Confederates lost essential material such as arms, ammunition and artillery, but most importantly they lost control of the Mississippi River.

Not only was this Fourth of July the surrender date of Vicksburg, it was also the date when the Confederates were successfully withdrawing from Gettysburg after the terrible beating that the Confederates received. At Gettysburg the loss of manpower that the Confederates suffered was not easily replaced. Now the news of the fall of Vicksburg was another hard pill to swallow for the Confederacy. Many people think that these events were the beginning of the end of any chance of the

Confederate States to achieve independence. Many believe that General Pickett's charge, which is recalled as the high mark of the Confederacy, was in effect the beginning of the end. The battle of Gettysburg has long over shadowed the victory of Vicksburg. I believe that the victory at Vicksburg was much more significant. Gettysburg was just another battle between the Army of the Potomac and the Army of the Virginia. I am not taking anything away from, or calling the losses of both sides useless, but I feel that it really did not strategically change the war at that time. I will admit that it gave the Northern people a great morale boost and did reduce the effective strength of General Lee's army. The capture of Vicksburg not only successfully returned the Mississippi River to the Union, but it denied the use of essential war material to the Confederates. Most of the Confederate soldiers that were captured, later returned and served in the Army of Tennessee again. The successful conclusion of the siege of Vicksburg also established, in the mind of the northern people, the great generalship of General Grant. President Lincoln, who had for a while been a supporter, became a strong advocate of General Grant. In a telegram to General Grant, President Lincoln told him that when he headed south and crossed the river that the President thought that he had made a mistake, but was now glad that he was wrong.

After General Pemberton surrendered, General Grant then gave orders for General Sherman to go after General Johnston. General Sherman had been warned to be prepared to attack General Johnston after the surrender. General Steele, who had assumed command of the 15th Corps while General Sherman was in command of the troops facing General Johnston, and General Ord, who was in charge of the 13th Corps, were also directed to be prepared to join General Sherman. Once the order was received, preparations were made to leave.

The 15th Corps moved out on July 5th with General Thayer still in command of General Steele's division, they reached Messinger's Ford later in the afternoon. Private Henry Kuck in a letter to his wife wrote, "On the 5th July, 3 o'clock in the morning we left again, specifically, General Johston had arrived to attack us from the rear, that's why we had to leave right away; but as General Johston heard that Vicksburg fell, he retreated hurredly to Jackson."(24) Lieutenant William H. Lynch of Company I, 32nd Missouri Infantry Regiment wrote in his diary, "Our Regt. left Camp, in rear of Vicksburg Miss. July 5th '63 on a 'forced' march to Jackson Miss., in order to capture or drive Johnson & his forces, about 20,000 from the Miss. Valley."(25) While an unknown soldier in the 13th Illinois Infantry Regiment wrote, "Sunday, *July 5th, 1863.* – Our division took the road at 2 a.m. to reinforce General Sherman who is after Johnston. The day was excessively hot. Passed through the fortifications that had been erected as our rear line. We came fifteen miles and camped just at dark."(26)

On July 6th General Tuttle's division, who had been facing any possible attack from General Johnston's force, had completed a bridge over the Big Black River. Meeting some resistance, they attacked across the bridge and then went into camp a few miles down road after they had reached the Bridgeport road. The rest of the 15th Corps had crossed the bridge and camped in the rear of General Tuttle's division. An 13th Illinois Infantry Regiment soldier wrote, "*July 6th.*—Spent most of the day in a very pleasant camp. We found blackberries in great profusion and they were sought after and enjoyed. This kind of fruit was without doubly a great preserver of health during the siege. Much foraging was done during the day. Came two miles to Big Black river."(27) On July 7th General Frank Blair's division took the lead of the 15th Corps and they marched until they were in the Bolton, Mississippi area. It was extremely hot and there was not much water to be found on the way. The water they had found was poisoned by General Johnston's troops by killing animals and throwing them into the water. The men suffered terribly from these elements. The march was harder on them because while they were participating in the siege of Vicksburg they had not moved much for almost fifty days. Some unknown diarist from the 13th Illinois Infantry Regiment wrote, "*July 7th.* – Started early, crossed the river on pontoons, came twelve miles and camped near Bolton. The heat and dust was very severe on the army. Many men were sunstruck and some died from the heat. We passed General Tuttle's division. A kind providence gave us a shower of rain this evening."(28) Private Ephraim James, one of the men of the 31st Missouri Infantry, died of sunstroke on July 7th. Mr. Virgil Carroll, the Grandson of Private William Carroll, told me that he remembered his grandfather telling him of how men on the march would drink water out of cow hoof prints. The Federal men had been in the trenches as long as the Confederates and

146

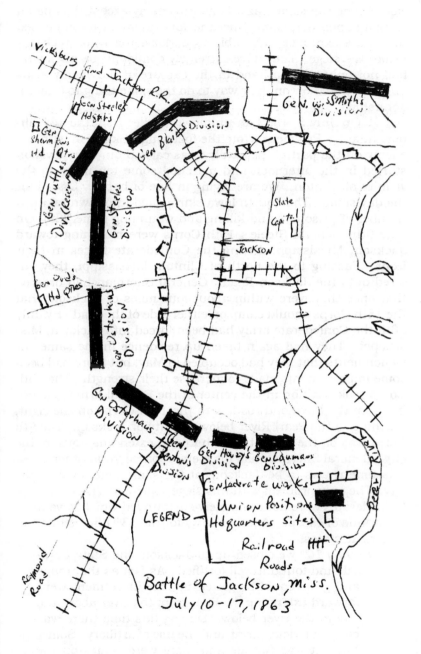

Vicksburg and Jackson R.R.

Gen Steeles Hdqtrs

Gen Sherman's Hd Qtrs

Gen Tuttle's Div (Reserve)

Gen Steeles Division

Gen Blair's Division

Gen W. Smith's Division

State Capitol

JACKSON

Gen Ord's Hd Qtrs

Gen Osterhaus Division

Gen Osterhaus Division

Gen Benton's Division

Gen Hovey's Division

Gen Lauman's Division

Pearl River

Raymond Road

LEGEND

Confederate works

Union Positions

Hdquarters sites

Railroad ┼┼┼

Roads ——

Battle of Jackson, Miss.
July 10-17, 1863

BATTLE OF JACKSON, MISSISSIPPI

were facing the same hazards as the enemy except they had a regular supply of rations. Once the surrender was accomplished they were expected to be able to perform the same tasks as before the siege. They were extremely confident because they had not only taken a hand in the capture of the enemy army but they were now on their way to do the same thing to General Johnston.

On July 8, 1863 an unknown soldier from the 13th Illinois Infantry Regiment wrote the following, "Skirmish with the enemy on the part of the cavalry was carried on. Our division started in the afternoon and marched some ten miles to the vicinity of Clinton. We are laying in line of battle. Losses for the day small. The Fourth Iowa skirmished into town taking a number of prisoners and killing and wounding some."(29) On July 9th, General Steele's 15th Corps were marching toward Jackson, Mississippi driving the Confederate forces in their front. Passing to the north of Clinton, Mississippi, they entered onto the Jackson Road. General Sherman had ordered that once they were within about four miles of Jackson, that the 15th Corps should camp on either side of the road. By July 10th the Confederate army had been forced into Jackson, Mississippi. They had again taken up residence in the same entrenchments that they had occupied in May, but there had been some improvements made to increase their strength. The 15th Corps took position in the center of the Federal army, extending from the Raymond road, with the 13th Corps on the right, reaching to the Pearl River below the city of Jackson. The 9th Corps was on the left of the 15th Corps, extending north of the city. General Sherman had his men prepared for another siege, this time it was to be Jackson, at the same time shelling the city. The only problem with this siege, unlike at Vicksburg, the Confederates were not completely surrounded which gave them an avenue of escape. Another entry for the 13th Illinois Infantry Regiment states,

> "On *July 10th* we closed up to Jackson, the State Capital, and found it well fortified. As fast as the troops and guns could be gotten up, the investment went forward extending the lines from the river above the city to the river below. During this time there was constant picket firing and the use of artillery. Sometimes it was furious and there were sallies on the part of the enemy, and charges on the part of our

troops with considerable loss. On the thirteenth General Lauman's division made a charge an was repulsed with severe loss. By this time General Sherman had brought up sufficient forces to make a demonstration on the opposite side of the river and the enemy's rear. General Johnson was too shrewd to have the same trick played on him that had cooped General Pemberton in Vicksburg."(30)

On July 16th, the remainder of the 15th Corps, except for Colonel Charles R. Woods brigade who had spent July 15th preparing to start destroying railroad tracks in Canton, Mississippi north of Jackson and Brookhaven south of Jackson, went into the trenches that the Confederates had built, and strengthened them turning them toward Jackson. The combat team was formed was made up of the 30th Iowa Infantry, 8th Missouri Infantry and the 31st Missouri Infantry, which was camped near what was then called the deaf and dumb asylum in Jackson. This combat team forded the Pearl River and marched eastward along the Brandon Road. They met no real resistance until they reached a point about five miles east of the Pearl River. They had encountered General Cosby's cavalry who was fighting a delaying action and falling steadily toward Brandon, Mississippi. General French's Confederate infantry came up to reinforce them. Not wishing to start a major skirmish or battle, this combat team returned to the Jackson area. General Johnston found himself out-numbered by the forces facing him and abandoned the city to the Federals.

An exert from a letter that Private Henry Kuck wrote home dated August 1st, 1863, "We pursued the Rebels right on their heels. General Johnston took a stand in Jackson; we occupied Jackson; because we had a large area to occupy, we couldn't control it completely; we arrived at Jackson on the 10th and by the 17th, As Gen. Johnston fought on, we needed reinforcements, which we got. We wanted to surround and capture them but they escaped, if he had stayed a few more days we would have captured him with his whole army."(31) The whole time that the Federal army was in front of the Confederates they were continuously digging rifle pits trying ever to get closer to the Confederate line. Water was a major concern to the soldiers on the line because of the extreme heat. A soldier in the 13th Illinois Infantry gives an example of what it was like.

"The drinking water was bad and scarce, the only good water being found in cisterns; these were soon used dry, some of the men going as far as three miles to get it, and some of the boys paying as high as fifty cents for a canteenful. There were some houses with cisterns at our advance lines, and between the two lines. These were sought after for the water. I myself took a load of canteens before daylight on the morning of the 17th and went to one of these houses to fill them; and some of our outposts were there."(32)

General Joseph E. Johnston performed a withdrawal from Jackson, Mississippi so successfully that the Federal army was not aware of it till the next day. He would perform the same movement many times in the future. Early in the morning on July 17th, the Federal forces discovered that the enemy had evacuated the city. They then went in and took possession of the city, destroying any parts of the city that had escaped their destruction in May. Jackson, Mississippi became what many cities would become in the future in the wake of General Sherman's troop, a town destroyed so thoroughly that it became known as chimneyville. General Sherman sent General Steele's division in pursuit of General Johnston. General Johnston had such a head start that it was really a fruitless pursuit. Maybe that is why he only sent one division. A description of this march is given by a diarist in the 13th Illinois Infantry Regiment wrote,

"*July 18th,* —Received orders to have three days' rations in haversacks and to march after the retreating army. Our regiment with others moved into town and laid in the street all night, delayed by a difficulty at the bridge. The next day we started to Brandon a town twelve miles out. Having gone about nine miles our forces were resisted and quite a fight ensued in which several were killed and wounded. Our regiment formed line and were ordered through a vast cornfield on the right of the main road, where the fighting was being carried on. In this field the heat was intolerable and it did seem that we would have died of suffocation, if a kind providence had not just then sent a brisk rain that wonderfully relieved matters. The advance was pushed and by dark we were in posesion of the town, the enemy having gone to

150

the east.

July 20th, — Many prisoners were picked up, and many of the parloled prisoners from Port Hudson, that had surrendered on the 9th.,came into town. Part of the town was burned and our troops began to tear up and burn the railroad. Our regiment was a part of the detail, and the work was thoroughly done. A whole regiment would form in line on one side of the track and just lift the thing bodily. Then it would be knocked to pieces, the ties piled up and the rails put across them. As the ties burned the rails would become sufficiently heated to bend and so become useless."(33)

After they had destroyed the railroad around Brandon, Mississippi, General Steele took his division and returned to Jackson, Mississippi arriving there on July 21, 1863, rejoining the rest of the army that had chased the Confederates from the city. While on this march to Brandon, Mississippi they lived mainly on green corn. In the 13th Illinois Infantry Regiments book they describe how they cooked it. "One feature of this campaign was, that the army lived largely on green corn, just then in season. When the army stopped for dinner it would just strip acres of it for a single meal. It would be cooked after this fashion. A fire would be kindled between two rails, and the corn with husks on would be laid upon the fire. By the time the husks were burned off the corn would be cooked by the steam and be in a delicious state to be eaten."(34) Private Henry Kuck of Company G, 31st Missouri Infantry Regiment describes Jackson, Mississippi in a letter to his wife.

"Everywhere our troops go everything is completely destroyed, for if the officers didn't agree to this, then it would be worse for the Rebels than it is now. The biggest and nicest part of Jackson has been burnt up, there everything was stolen and demolished and set in flames. The residents close to Vicksburg have nothing on which to live, most of them in the outlying area come to Jackson for food, otherwise they would have to travel over 40 miles from Jackson for it, we destroyed all the railroads and stations. If the army in Virginia would do as much as we've done, then the war would soon end, and every family man could go back to his wife and children, and every son to his mother; every single soldier hopes and wishes that this will soon happen."(35)

General Grant wrote in his memoirs the following, "The National loss in the second capture of Jackson was less than one thousand men, killed, wounded and missing. The Confederate loss was probably less, except in captured. More than this number fell into our hands as prisoners." (36) The 31st Missouri Infantry Regiment reported no casualties during what has been called the siege of Jackson, Mississippi.

In the August 11, 1863 Daily Missouri Democrat printed an article on "The Expedition against Joe Johnston's Army." It was sent in by an unknown person, it was listed as correspondence of the Missouri Democrat. The article is quoted below.

THE EXPEDITION AGAINST JOE JOHNSTON'S ARMY.

Interesting Resume of Gen. Sherman's Operations,
The March – Black River Works –
Champion's Hill – Bolton Station – Clinton – The
Country – Corn and Cotton Formation of Line
About the Enemy's Works – Lauman's Charge
and Advance of the Line – Rebel's Charge –
Osterhaus's Lines – Retreat of Rebels – Jackson
– Prisoners – Reason for Not Pursuing Them Return of Expedition

(Correspondence of Missouri Democrat)

The long, marvelous and bloody campaign against Vicksburg is ended. The last act, the discomfiture of Johnston's army and the recapture of Jackson by the Federals, was the last stone in the enduring temple, which Grant and his followers framed. On the heels of the news of surrender came the order to prepare ten days' rations, and be ready to move at a moment's notice. It was by no means wonderful that some surprise and disappointment should be manifested by those who had marched so far, and labored so long and well, when they were ordered away from the scenes of their victory before they could look on the prize.

Still the idea of 'doing something' soon swept away all other thought, and resuming their wonted merriment, they proceeded to make the necessary preparations. By eight, on the morning of the 5th, the whole column, consisting of about fifty or fifty-five thousand effective troops, composed of 13th, 15th and 9th army corps, all under the direction of General Sherman, was set in motion. The day was excessively hot, and many soldiers suffered from lack of water, and many fell by sun-strokes by the wayside. Each man got along as best he could, the men of the different divisions mingling and marching along together. The advance halted, and encamped on Baker's Creek near Champion Hill battle ground; the rear camping on Clear Creek about two miles from Black River bridge. The next day was spent in crossing the river, all passing over except General Hovey's division, and part of Lauman's. The works at Black River have been remodeled and greatly strengthened by General Osterhaus, who was stationed here during the greater part of the siege.

The works are constructed on the bluff, rising almost perpendicularly from the river bottom, and are about two and a half miles in length. They are constructed in a zigzag line, and afford complete protection for the riflemen occupying them. They are impregnable from the front. The Railroad beyond the bridge has been wholly destroyed by the rebels, for what object is wholly unknown to us. About noon on the seventh, the rear Division reached Champion's Hill. There was much here to interest the members of Hovey's Division. There nearly 1,400 of their comrades had fallen. Each one had friends and companions in arms, whose graves they sought out and paid their last tributes of respect. All was quiet. Each spoke and walked about, as if he moved on hallowed ground, and hallowed it was, if the noblest blood of the land can hallow any spot of creation, when ebbing from wounds received in defending liberty's banner and liberty's cause. It was an impressive sight to behold the bluff and hardened soldier, wipe from his bronzed cheek the silent tear. They visited the spot where their comrades fell. All around were evidences of the fierce conflict. Each tree, log and bush was scarred and torn by the balls. The graves are arranged along the summit of the hill. In many instances officers lie buried in the same grave with the common soldier. They died together, struggling for victory; it is meet that they should sleep in the same heroic graves. In future days, when the starry folds shall float over this united land, honored and respected by all, some memorial may be raised by their grateful countrymen to commemorate their deeds of valor in the greatest of the battles fought for the possession of Vicksburg.

The rear moved to Bolton station this evening, 9th, the 13th and 15th army corps being formed in line of battle. Osterhaus had skirmished here during a part of the day, and we confidently expected a battle on the following morning. It rained one of those Mississippi rains, which being interpreted, means a deluge. In the morning, one accustomed to such scenes, would very naturally have supposed we had all been on a bender, and with the carelessness of a drunken man, 'laid about loose' in the mud and water. Bolton has about four or five wooden buildings, a grocery and a blacksmith shop. The town was sacked long before, and nothing now remained but the ponderous evidences of its former magnificence. That night we passed through Clinton, close column with colors flying and bands playing. Clinton is a wooden town with low buildings and few inhabitants at present. From the number of grog signs one would suppose that the chivalry were in excellent spirits, and had spent much of their time in the enjoyment of them. The surface of the land, as we drew near to Jackson, became less rugged and hilly than about Vicksburg. The Plantations are well cultivated and well improved, but the soil, judging from the fields of growing corn, is generally very poor.

The Confederates have complied to the letter with the demands of their chief. I did not see an acre of cotton or anything but corn between the two cities. The corn was ripe enough for roasting, and it was surprising to see how quickly it disappeared, when the column would halt for meals. It is no exaggeration to state that forty acres of average corn would be stripped in half an hour. Peaches were ripening, and the orchards which are large, and contain well assorted varieties, were bending with fruit. Soldiers are fond of luxuries, and did not forget the orchards. Most of the plantations were destitute, with the exception of an old slave or two, who welcomed the Yankees to anything they had left them. The line was formed about the rebel works on the 11th and

12th, and the siege of Jackson commenced in earnest on the 13th. The 13th A. C. occupied the right of our line, Lauman's and Hovey's division forming the extreme right. The enemy made a slight show of opposition on the evening of the 12th as we approached his lines.

We lay in line of battle all night along the banks of a small creek, not daring to speak aloud, nor having time to get anything to eat, except what was in our haversacks. There was an open field in front, of perhaps forty rods in width, and those that had acted as skirmishers in front, now acted as pickets, and lay down where they were halted. About eight o'clock next morning fresh skirmishers were thrown out and line of battle formed. It seemed almost certain that the enemy was posted in the edge of the wood immediately opposite, awaiting an approach.

Now was the time to try men's souls. We almost fancied that we could see the muzzles of their guns, double-shotted and pointing toward us. A grim line of 'greybacks' seemed to stand in the rear, with bayonets fixed, ready to complete the destruction made by the cannon.

Whatever may be said of the discipline of the army generally, never did a line advance more steadily, regularly, and beautifully in battle, or on occasions of parades and military displays, than did this, advancing to meet its foe. There was not the excitement of a charge to animate and inspire their courage. It was cool, disciplined valor, nerved for the conflict – not anxious, but ready to meet its consequences. Each man moved forward at the same instant and in the same degree. It was a beautiful and impressive sight, one of which the soldiers were not conscious, but of which their commanders are proud. The orders issued to each of the commands, were to advance cautiously as near to the enemy's works as possible, without exposing themselves to the necessity of a charge or retreat. This was done by all the commands except Lauman's, a part of whose division for some reason, charged the enemy's works. It is stated that the rebels laughed when they saw his men approaching. His loss in killed, wounded, and prisoners, is estimated at eight or nine hundred. The repulse, it is needless to say, was complete. The other divisions remained in their places and prevented the rebels from following up their victory. Johnston made several attempts to break our lines, charging upon the division of General Osterhaus. He was each time handsomely repulsed, and full revenge taken for the misfortune of the 12th. I neglected to mention that during the time we were taking position one of General Osterhaus's orderlies was taken prisoner, and brutally shot by the rebels for having in his possession a commission to raise and command a company of negroes. The General, immediately upon receipt of the news, sent word to the rebel General that he would kill four of his men for that cowardly act. He took some prisoners; whether he executed the threat or not, I have not been informed; but if he did, he has only done what justice demanded. The soldiers now in the field appreciate the services of the negro as a warrior, and are prepared to carry out any mode or degree of retaliation for such offences, the Government shall adopt. Our lines were sufficiently close to the enemy's for him to shell us, and throw grape, canister and shrapnel into the ranks. Again we heard the cannon roaring at intervals, and the sharpshooters playing on each other in the advance, which sounded precisely like a great many wood choppers hewing away at the trees. All sieges are similar, and it is needless to describe this. Having no support, and no relief, it became necessary to fortify, to strengthen the line. Ere three days had elapsed, works were constructed behind which the boys felt secure. I say boys, for each regiment, without the aid of engineers, constructed its own fortifications. Had there been sufficient supply of provisions, each and all would have been satisified with the situation of affairs. Strangely enough, subsistence was shorter within thirty-five miles of Black river, whither the cars were running, than on the march from Grand Gulf to Vicksburg.

About day break, on the morning of the 17th, it was rumored that the rebs had evacuated the place. I immediately set out for the city. There was already a great number of soldiers there.

One, on entering the business part of the town,

would suppose that there was a lively trade in the articles of tobacco, sugar and molasses. Everywhere were to be seen groups of soldiers dividing the spoils. They labored hard and fast, for the guards were being stationed throughout the city, and the game would be up. One entire brick block, opposite the State House, had burned to the ground, either by our shells or the rebels themselves, the latter of which is probable from the appearance of the camp and garrison equipage mingled with the bricks and ashes. The soldiers afterwards set fire to the adjoining block, and burned it to the ground. Thus the central and business portion of the city - that immediately opposite the State House and adjoining grounds – is swept entirely away. The city, like Vicksburg, is extremely filthy. Everything bore the appearance of disuse and long neglect. The State House is a large building, but evidently in the decline, and sadly out of repair. Their railroads have been destroyed for twelve miles out of the city, and the cars remaining and the buildings burned. It will be impossible for the rebels to make Jackson, without much labor and time, a military post, should it become our policy to abandon it.

We captured nearly six hundred prisoners – stragglers who remained in the rear purposely; at least they were the most willing captives I saw two sitting off in the woods; I went up to them and told them to come with me; they had no guns and came along cheerfully. They were members of the 16th Louisiana. A division of our forces was marching out in pursuit. One of them inquired: Are your regiments no larger than that? No, sir. Is not any one of them large enough to whip any Southern regiment? No; the old 16th could whip any two of them. Why, then, do you not whip us? There are too *many* of them and it's no use fighting.

They have great confidence in the generalship of Johnston, but all are beginning to think there is something the matter, and attribute it to our numbers. Johnston's army probably consisted of 85,000 effective men. Why he was permitted to escape us, after besieging him five days is a little curious to some of us, but let those explain it who can. One thing is certain, we could not have charged upon his defenses with any hope of success. The works are in the form of a semi-circle, and nearly five miles in length. The trees in front of the works were fallen for twenty rods, forming an abattis over which it would have been utterly impossible to pass. Large guns were planted in a position to rake the roads, and protected by strong works. Still they did not deem this sufficient, and had several lines of defences in the rear of the main line. In some places they had made pits similar to those in Vicksburg to escape from our shells. There is no evidence of their having intended to with-stand a siege for any great length of time. But one day's rations was brought in per day, and that immediately issued to their troops. It was impossible to pursue them, the heat and dearth of water being very great. Johnston issued an order calling upon the people to kill their stock and throw the dead carcasses into the pools and wells to poison the water. Steele's division was left to occupy Jackson, and the column set out for V. on the morning of the 20th. The soldiers were on less than half rations. It was intensely hot and water scarce. Yet they marched 60 miles in two-and-a-half-days. This expedition will long be remembered for the strange manner in which it was conducted. The lack of sufficient and proper subsistence and the severity of the march on its return once passed all is forgotten, and we mingle our voices with the notes of those shouting – Victory. St. Louis."(37)

On July 23rd, the 15th Corps evacuated the capitol city of Mississippi at daybreak and by mid-day they had reached Clinton, Mississippi. Because of the heat General Steele had ordered that the 15th Corps go into camp early. On July 24th the 15th Corps marched to Champion Hill and camped for the night. July 25th found the 15th Corps crossing the Big Black River and into their assigned campground for a well deserved rest. July 27th found the 15th Corps camped along the Big Black River. The 1st Division, General Steele's, was camped near the railroad bridge, the 2nd Division, General Blair's, was next to the first, the 3rd Division, General Tuttle's, was on a ridge near the head of Bear Creek and the 4th Division, General Ewing's, was camped at Messinger's Ford.

Once their camp had been established each regiment was allowed to let five percent of those men in the regiment who were not sick to go home on a furlough. One of those who were given this furlough was Private Henry Kuck who went home. Also many of the sick who required hospitalization were sent north. Those who were to sick to be moved were left at Vicksburg. While in camp the troops who were left went through the tedious camp duties which were performed whenever in camp and the constant sound of drill could be heard.

This completed the action around Vicksburg. The 31st Missouri Infantry was in the trenches surrounding Vicksburg throughout the siege. Like all the other units, it had taken its share of casualties throughout the siege. In Company A, Private Josiah J. Brooks died aboard the steamer "Isabella" on June 24, 1863, Private James B. Ware died on July 16, 1863, Private George W. Hendrickson of Hillsboro received an honorable discharge on June 25, 1863. In Company B, Private Matthew Bouchard was discharged on June 13, 1863 at Saint Louis, Missouri, on June 30, 1863 Private James Flynn of Washington County died in the hospital. In Company C, Private David Barkley of Hopewell died on June 22, 1863 on the steamer "D. G. Taylor", Private Frederick Fear of Potosi died at Vicksburg on July 8, 1863, Private Andrew Orm of Hopewell died on July 2, 1863 at Memphis, Tennessee, Corporal William Wiley of Hopewell died on July 26, 1863 at Young's Point, Louisiana, Private David Yount of Hopewell also died at Young's Point, Louisiana a month earlier on June 21, 1863. Company D, Private Samuel A. Garrison of Randolph County died on June 16, 1863 at Vicksburg, Private Ephraim James of Butler County died at Bolton, Mississippi of sunstroke on July 7, 1863, Private Madison Cob of Patterson was transferred to Company B 5th Invalid Corps on July 29, 1863. In Company E, Private Henry H. Cain of Moselle died on June 25, 1863 on one of the hospital boats, Sergeant John H. Compton of Moselle died on June 18, 1863 from an unknown cause, Private Charles D. Ward of Moselle died at Vicksburg on July 16, 1863. In Company F, Private Thomas J. Branson died on July 29, 1863 at Benton Barracks in Saint Louis, Missouri, Wagoner Richard Parkins of Mineral Point died in July 1863 at Mineral Point, Private William W. Brandon of Canaan was discharged on July 6, 1863 at Jefferson Barracks due to disability, Private Eli Haines of Canaan was discharged on June 22, 1863 at Saint Louis, Missouri. In Company G, Private Henry Aherns was discharged on June 26, 1863 at Saint Louis, Missouri, Private Henry Wahl from Saint

Louis, Missouri deserted on July 26, 1863 while in camp on the Black River, Private Robert Oesker of Carondelet died on June 14, 1863 on a hospital steamer, Private Herman Winterberg of Washington died on July 30, 1863 at Memphis, Tennessee. In Company H, Second Lieutenant Burgen F. Tyler of Wayne County was discharged by order of the War Department for disability on July 8, 1863, Private Smith C. Wright of Wayne County died on the hospital steamer "City of Memphis" on June 1, 1863. In Company I, Private Sylvester B. Stoddard of Saint Louis, was discharged because of disability at a hospital in Saint Louis, Missouri on July 13, 1863, Sergeant Larkin Thompson of Danville was discharged on June 20, 1863 at Milikens Bend, Louisiana. In Company K, Private Madison Cobb of Ironton was transferred to the Invalid Corps on July 29, 1863. Whether this is the same person as Private Madison Cob, in Company D, I'm not sure but I went ahead and listed them separately.

The following is an article found in the "Daily Missouri Democrat", a Civil War period newspaper in Saint Louis, Missouri, that featured an article on the death of Lieutenant William Robinson. It is quoted as it appeared on Wednesday morning July 8, 1863.

"Lieut. William Robinson.

The history of 'The war for the Union' will not record the death of an officer more universally regretted by his companions in arms than that of First Lieutenant William Robinson, company I, 31st regiment Missouri Infantry, who fell while in command of his company in one of those brave assaults made by our forces on the works of the enemy at Vicksburg, soon after our army reached the rear of that city, had before Gen. Grant had decided on the slower process of capturing the city by parallel approaches.

Lieut. Robinson was a native of Missouri born in Danville, Montgomery county, a young man of rare acquirements and mental ability. Tall, graceful and of most prepossessing manner, he was the admiration of his brother officers, and by his many virtues endeared to the whole regiment. At the early age of his nineteenth year, he died a soldier's death. When his companions bore him from the field and laid him in the soldier's grave, eyes that with tears were seldom wet, rained genuine drops of sorrow. One of his brother officers, with a voice trembling with emotion, remarked, 'he was as full of joyous hopes, and was young man of such promise it was hard to see him fall, not weary or worn or oppressed, but while the earth was beautiful still to his eye, he sank into her bosom to rest.' In 1862 he was at the United States Naval Academy, but a desire to participate in the struggle of the loyal men of Missouri to restore the Federal authority in his native State, induced him to resign and return to the home of his father, James H. Robinson, Esq., of Danville, Missouri.

In July he was appointed a Second Lieutenant and in the following September, on the recommendation of his Colonel, he was promoted to First Lieutenant. He acted as Assistant Adjutant General while both Col. Chester Harding and Col. Fletcher were in command of the 1st brigade of Davidson's Division, in Southeast Missouri. He was detailed as aid to General John B. Gray, who commanded the same brigade, afterwards he acted as Assistant Adjutant General of Blair's Brigade up to the time General Blair took the field at Helena, and then acted as Adjutant of the regiment. Proficient in the drill, and distinguished for his soldierly bearing and moral deportment, his regiment was proud of him as a Missourian. At the battle of Chickasaw Bluff he was amongst the foremost of the gallant officers who led the memorable charge of Blair's Brigade, and received a severe wound, but paused not in the fight. A bright page in our country's history will be the record of the heroism of Missouri's sons, and with the names of the bravest and best, will be the name of Lieut. William Robinson, while his memory will ever be cherished by his companions in arms."(38)

CHAPTER SEVEN:
ON TO CHATTANOOGA

Not long after the fall of Vicksburg the Confederate forces defending the fort at Port Hudson surrendered to the Federal forces. The 31st Missouri Infantry Regiment now had a brief time in which to recover from the last few months of labor and fighting while camped along the Big Black River. While they were there, some Confederate cavalry under General Armstrong was watching them. Evidently Colonel Thomas C. Fletcher felt that the 31st Missouri Infantry Regiment was being watched more closely than other units because of a report he sent to General Sherman. This report, though not located, caused General Sherman some needless patrols in search of the Confederates in which he later remarks about Colonel Fletcher. On September 20, 1863 in a report to General Rawlins, General Grant's Assistant Adjutant-General, he states, "General Osterhaus this moment reports that the picket down by Hall's Ferry reports the appearance of camp-fires across the Black, rockets, &c. I will send all my cavalry down in that direction at once. Order McPherson to have his cavalry to look at Hankinson's Ferry, and look out on the south front. I was up at Oak Ridge yesterday, and saw and heard no signs in that quarter. (signed) W.T. Sherman, Major-General."(1) In three different reports, also dated September 20, 1863, to General Rawlins he states that "I will reprimand Colonel Fletcher for making such a report; Both my judgement and information unite in pronouncing the stories sent me by Colonel Fletcher and pickets as twaddle; There is no enemy to my front. Colonel Fletcher was humbugged purposely."(2)

General Grant at this time went to talk to General Banks in New Orleans. While there, he was inspecting the troops of General Banks and ended up taking a fall off his horse and injuring himself enough that he would be on crutches for some time. This is somewhat surprising because General Grant was known as a superior horseman. Some reported that General Grant, after the stress of his campaign against Vicksburg, was again on a drunken binge.

MAJOR GENERAL PETER JOSEPH OSTERHAUS
1st Division, 15th Army Corps Commander, September 1, 1863
through September 24, 1864. 15th Army Corps Commander,
September 23, 1864 through January 8, 1865

General Parke's 9th Corps was returned to Kentucky and later became part of General Burnside's forces. The 13th Corps, who was now commanded by General Ord, was sent to Natchez, where they captured about five thousand head of cattle and some other material. They became part of General Bank's force in New Orleans, and later were part of the force that was defeated in the Red River campaign. The 17th Corps, under General McPherson, remained in Vicksburg, while the 16th Corps, under General Hurlbut, returned to Memphis.

On October 7, 1863 the "Daily Missouri Democrat," copied a letter from Colonel James Peckham of the 29th Missouri Infantry Regiment to a friend in Saint Louis, Missouri.

"FROM MISSISSIPPI

A Voice from the Army – Return of Rebels to Missouri – The 29th and 31st Missouri Regiments – Rebels Well Supplied with Subsistence – A Saucy Little She Rebel.

{We publish the following interesting letter from Colonel Peckham, of the 29th Missouri Infantry, now in Mississippi, to a friend in this city: Ed.}

IN CAMP NEAR BLACK RIVER, SEPTEMBER 2O, 1863.

The mail has just arrived and a "big mail" it is too. And nearly all of us have letters from friends. These letters are angel visitors to us down here. They remind us what we are soldiering about. We are pushing our outposts farther off from home. But in doing so we somewhat fear we are giving chances for rebel visits at home. That is all the fear we have; not the foe in front, for he is beaten and demoralized. Brave man as he is he sees no chance for success and confesses it, but an inexorable despotism keeps him in the ranks and he says my duty calls upon me to die. It is his interpretation of duty. But the cowardly sneaks who fear to meet us in the field are smuggling themselves back into Missouri – nay encouraged to go there – and so we fear the fire of the incendiary and the blade of the assassin right at our own homes. You have no idea of the feelings that engross us as we read of affairs in Missouri. *Our indignation, our Venom is not so much toward the parties who commit as toward the policy which permits such return.* Those rebels are deserters from rebel ranks in our front through fear and not through repentence.

My own regiment, and the 31st, (Colonel Tom Fletcher) are encamped about eight miles from the railroad crossing of Black river near Baldwin's Ferry. We are on the summit of a very high hill, from which we can look over all creation. Away over yonder in the furthest distance are some ridges of blue mist, which seem to rub hard against the sky, and which people hereabouts say are hills in Hinds county, thirty miles off. How many million acres of bottom land there are between those misty ridges and this hill of ours I can't say, but I can say that those acres are here and there dotted with little patches of woodland, and are swarming with cattle. It is all a mistake about the South being at the point of starvation. I can't see it. Since our entry into Mississippi, we have not wanted, and we can now subsist our whole army upon what is running loose hereabouts. Every morning the farmers bring us in newly made butter, fresh butter-milk, and sweet milk in abundance. They will not take Confederate money at any rate, but lay by Lincoln greenbacks as they would treasures for Heaven. We pay fifty cents for butter, and five cents a pint for milk. Our boys have cleaned the country entirely of chickens left by the Confederates, so that we get no eggs.

Near by us is a family named Batchelor. There is the widow Batchelor and Miss. Vick. Batchelor and three other little Misses Batchelors, and baby Batchelor and widow Nugent and a Mr. Nugent, brother-in-law to the last and uncle and brother to the others. Miss Vick. has two dogtypes of men whom she calls her brothers; one of whom she says "has been in all the glorious battles in Virginia," and the other was taken a prisoner at Vicksburg. Vick. Is a stubborn traitor – draws rations and laughs at us for "giving them to such a spirited rebel," – declares she will fight against us when her brothers cease fighting, and thinks, (at least says she does,) that Yankeedom is gone up. Vick. is 18, and by no means pretty, but her people think her so, and are happy in her accomplishments. She can sing and play and do worsted work, and use her tongue very glibly; and she is peculiar in the employment of sarcasm and

165

thorough enunciation of hate. Fletcher, Captain Reed, and I went there last night. Vick. sat in the middle of the room, and carried on the conversation, and her people gazed at her with the utmost admiration, laughing heartily at her every denunciation of Yankees. She seemed to enjoy it herself, too, and was so extremely polite in abusing us, so courteous and willing to favor us with music and songs, (such as 'The Bonnie Blue Flag,' 'All Quiet on the Potomac To-Night,' 'The Red, White, and Red,') so anxious that we should stay, so anxious, also, that we should call again, that we could not get angry at her. And we didn't. We too, sang, or attempted to sing; and we sang 'John Brown,' 'The Union Forever,' 'Red, White, and Blue,' 'Yankee Doodle,' and 'Old Massa Run; Ha! Ha!' Vick. is a fair specimen of a she-rebel. She laughed sarcastically when we spoke of going to Mobile, and insinuated that when we got there, she would just like to see how we would look, just for the fun of it, although she abhorred suffering even in a foe. She didn't doubt but 'from the present light we enjoyed on the subject we really thought we would go into Mobile and where ignorance is bliss, 'twere folly to be wise.' I told her that the right by which we reading our history now as the light of victory, and we indeed happy in our ignorance of any other Vick. laughed, as much as to say, 'You'll be fooled at Mobile,' and Tom and I laughed, as much as to say we *wouldn't* be fooled at Mobile. So we counted ourselves *even* with Vick. And here we are giving regular rations to such people as these, who openly denounce and abuse us, who laugh at our charity at the same time they *demand* it, and whose male kindred are all in the armies in our front.

We are getting a good deal of cotton out of this country. Nearly all the farmers have saved much of their cotton by rolling it out in the cane and hiding it there. They come into camp now, sell it to us at eight cents per pound, and conduct our expeditions to the hiding places. This trade is being carried on exclusively by Government through its regular quartermasters.

We have just received the news from Rosecrans, Gilmore, Burnside, Steele, Blunt – glorious good news for us. It wakes the boys up who were drowsy on picket, for I shouted it to the nearest post, and he passed it on the next, and so it went around the entire line.

They must have heard it over at Batchelors', and did Miss Vick a heap of good. We are lessening the rebel area for conscription.

It is a beautiful night, though somewhat cold. I am chilly as I write. There are huge fires in camp which show for many miles, and up yonder the cloudless sky is glittering with stars, whose cheerful faces seem as though newly washed. There goes the old moon, just as calmly walking her nightly round as she did while Abraham was patriarch. What scenes like this has she looked upon since then, herself unchanged. But never did she look upon armed sentinels doing duty in as sublime a cause as this of ours. We are struggling to preserve the work of the good men of every age, for this Government is their work. The past is horrible with kingly rule and scaffold, stake and inquisition. They have been swept away. We are struggling to prevent their re-enthronement; We are fighting the devils who would call from their graves. Ours is the cause not of a family or of clique, but of all humanity – the cause of Divine Catholicism. I know what inspiration this though gives in front of battle.

Our purpose is founded upon this conviction, amounting to a religion. The rebels have only passion to back *their* purpose. *We* shall suceed.

Lieutenant Colonel Gage, of my regiment, is acting as Division inspector on the staff of General Osterhaus. Phil. Murphy, my Major, is close by me, in his new uniform. He makes a splendid Major. Willie Gray, of *News* renown, is now a lieutenant; so also Jo. Russell and Bill Henley, known each to many St. Louisians. Dan. O'Hanlan, of Kilkenny memory, is sutling for us, and making something for himself. Barney Dailey is sutling for the 27th. Colonel Curley has just got down from Missouri his tenth company – sixty – five men – and Curley feels mighty proud of his present *big* regiment. My own as also the 31st, are mightily re-duced. I went into the service this last time with seven hundred and fifty men. Lost nearly three hundred in battle, and two hundred and fifty in hospital from disease. Some have deserted

– some have stood true as milestones. What is to be done? Are we to be filled up? I hope so. If not, I want consolidation and my own muster-out. I do not desire a consolidated command, and I know of no one who does. Yet I am subject to orders, and know how to obey.

JAMES PECKHAM"(3)

Events in Chattanooga, Tennessee would soon be effecting the rest that the 31st Missouri Infantry was enjoying in camp on the Big Black River. General W. S. Rosecrans was driving Confederate General Braxton Bragg's Army of Tennessee, toward Chattanooga, Tennessee. The two armies met at the Battle of Stone's River where the Confederates and the Federals both claimed victory but the Federal's held the field. After the defeat of the Confederate army at the battle of Stone's River, Tennessee and their retreat toward Chattanooga gave General Rosecrans' enough confidence that he was not worried about being defeated. He continued to follow General Bragg's army towards Chattanooga. General Rosecrans made one of the tactical blunders of any military campaign against an enemy force of equal size, he split his forces in order to cut off the Confederate retreat. General Bragg, seeing that the enemy forces were seperated, decided to attack. In answer to a request for reinforcements, General Longstreet and his corps were on their way from General Lee's Army of Virginia, and this gave General Bragg some confidence. But all was not well with the Confederate general's in the Army of Tennessee.

General Bragg was not an easy man to like. He was not well liked or admired by either his general's or his men. Once General Bragg realized that he had the chance to fight the divided enemy army he gave the orders. For some reason, which has not really been explained completely, the Confederate army did not attack right away as General Bragg expected. This delay in the attack allowed General Rosecrans to perceive the danger that his army was in. Once informed that the Confederates were no longer running he ordered his army to hurry and regroup near Chattanooga. General Rosecrans immediately went on the defensive in order to see what General Bragg would do. Finally the Confederates began the attack.. On September 19-20, 1863 the Battle of Chickamauga was fought. It was probably the most famous victory that the Army of Tennessee achieved while under the command of General Bragg. This was a battle that was one that should have gone down as a great victory, which General Bragg informed Richmond it was, but because of the failure to follow the Federal army into Chattanooga and defeating it, it cannot be classified as a complete victory.

It was during this battle that Major General George H. Thomas received the nickname "Rock of Chickamauga." His men held the Confederates at bay while the rest of the Federal army made a mad stampede for Chattanooga. The Federal army made its retreat to Chattanooga and started to dig in. The Confederate army then began to surround the Federals by taking up positions on the high ground. To the south of Chattanooga there are three prominent terrain features. They are Missionary Ridge, Lookout Mountain and Raccoon Mountain. The Federals were penned in on the north by the Tennessee River. The Federals were almost completely invested by the natural terrain features that surrounded the city of Chattanooga. Their only supply line was what became known as the "Cracker Line." This was a sixty mile long trail that went through the ridges and mountains north of the river. Even in dry weather it was not the best way to bring in supplies but because of an extended period of rain this route was miserable. This caused the wagons to sink to the hubs and the horses and mules sank to their bellies in place. This wore the animals out so much that many just laid down and died from sheer exhaustion. Periodically the Confederates sent cavalry units to raid this supply line. They were successful in these raids destroying animals, supplies and the wagons. This slowed down even more the slim supplies that were managing to get through. Eventually, the men even ended up stealing the animals grain or following supply wagons in hopes that some food had fallen through the cracks of the beds of the wagons. The situation was somewhat the same as around Vicksburg except the roles were reversed. The only difference was the Confederates who held the high ground were suffering almost as much as the Federals. At this stage in the war the Confederates were finding it harder and harder to supply their men with food and clothing. General Bragg's men were cold, hungry and angry.

As stated earlier they had the opportunity to follow the disheartened, defeated and retreating Federal army into Chattanooga. For some reason General Bragg did not follow up his accomplishment, instead he kept his army where they were until the next day. The average soldier in his army, though not a military genius, knew enough after almost two and one-half years of fighting, that they should have followed the enemy into Chattanooga. His generals could not believe that he did not follow them either. They were so upset that they sent a petition to President Davis asking for the removal of General Bragg. General Bragg found this out and he eventually ended up removing General Leonidas Polk and General Daniel Harvey Hill from command. He blamed them for acting so slowly when he gave commands that they allowed the Federals to reunite prior to the battle of Chickamauga. General James Longstreet was also not on General Bragg's favorite subordinate list. These were the conditions that existed in and around Chattanooga in the Confederate high command.

Charles A. Dana, the same one who was sent to spy on General Grant, telegraphed the Secretary of War that in his opinion General Rosecrans was not fit to command. While General Grant was greatly admired by Charles Dana, General Rosecrans was not so lucky. After this report General Halleck ordered General Grant to send all available units to Memphis and then to Tuscumbia, Alabama where they would proceed to the relief of the Federal army in Chattanooga. Again, General Grant was ordered on September 15th to send as many units as he could to Chattanooga. At this time General Grant was bed ridden from his fall off the horse in New Orleans. He received the last telegram on the September 27th. By order of General Grant, General Sherman sent the 1st Division of the 15th Corps to Vicksburg to load on boats to head to Memphis, Tennessee. General Peter J. Osterhaus was now in command of the 1st Division since General Steele had been promoted to the command of the Department of Arkansas.

General Grant on October 3rd was ordered to report to Cairo as soon as possible and report by telegraph to the War Department. He left immediately, even though still crippled, and once he arrived at Cairo was "directed to report to the Galt House in Louisville, Kentucky where he would meet an officer of the War Department."(4) He met Secretary of War Edward McMasters Stanton. The Secretary gave General Grant his orders giving him command of the new, "Military Division of the Mississippi, (giving me the command) composed of the Departments of the Ohio, the Cumberland and the Tennessee, and all the territory from the Alleghanies to the Mississippi River north of Banks's command in the south-west."(5) It was in Louisville that he learned of the sad shape the Federal army was in at Chattanooga. He was given two orders with only one difference and that was the choice of relieving General Rosecrans or keeping him in command. General Grant chose the order that relieved General Rosecrans. General Thomas was placed in command of the army at Chattanooga. When General Grant arrived at Chattanooga he found conditions worse than he had imagined. This is coming from a man who had just observed the Confederate soldiers coming out of the city of Vicksburg in much the same condition as he found that the Federal soldiers.

The 31st Missouri was on the move again. They were at Camp Sherman from July 27th till September 22nd. They left Camp Sherman on the Big Black River and marched to Vicksburg on their way to Memphis, Tennessee. Lieutenant William H. Lynch of the 32nd Missouri Infantry Regiment records in his diary, "Next morning we marched to Vicksburg embarking on steamer 'South Western'. Passed Hellena (stayed all night Sept. 26) left Hellena Sept. 26th for Memphis, Tenn. Monday 28th disembarked at Memphis Tenn."(6) After they had arrived in Memphis, Tennessee they received orders to start "repairing the railroad on the way as far as Athens, Alabama."(7) This was being done so there would be a supply line to their rear since General Rosecrans wasn't even able to feed his own army. General Sherman's son Willie died on the way home, becoming sick on board a steamship and eventually dying on October 3rd in Memphis, Tennessee. This was a hard loss for General and Mrs. Sherman as it was also for Willie's adopted unit the 13th United States Infantry. Lieutenant Lynch continued in his diary the following, "Left Memphis Tenn. For Cornith 28th Sept. '63, arrived at Cornith about 3 O'Clock A.M. 29th Sept. '63. Go in camp near Cornith Miss. Sept. 29th 1863. Remained in camp till 9th October '63"(8) In the Official Records, Brigadier General Peter J. Osterhaus, commander of the 1st Division 15th Army Corps, wrote an itinerary for the 1st Division and in it he listed the division camping on Clear Creek one mile east of Cornith, Mississippi on September 30th. Because of the insufficient train cars to be able to move the whole brigade only about a half of the 1st Brigade of the 1st Division was sent to Cornith on September 29th while the rest came two days later.

Even though Lieutenant Lynch records in his diary that they arrive on the September 29th, an unknown diarist in the

13th Illinois Infantry Regiment does not arrive until October 1st. "On *October 1st*, 9 a. m., we took the cars and moved eastward and at 7 p.m. we found ourselves landed at Cornith, Mississippi, ninety-three mile east and a little south of our starting point. We noted that the railroad was strongly guarded and at many places fortified. This railroad was a bone of contention through most of the war after it fell into our hands, as raiding parties from Mississippi could so easily cross it and cut it."(9) The major problem that the Federal army had in the Cornith area was water. The area around Cornith was supporting Federal troops who were stationed in the area since the Confederate army left Cornith with the approach of the Federals in May 1862. The Confederates had attacked a Federal position called Battery Robinett. The Confederates made their final attack on October 4, 1862 and suffered severely during the battle finally leaving Cornith in the hands of the Federal army. "On *October 3d*, we marched three or four miles to the southeast of the town and went into camp. The ground was favorable for a camp, but water was not readily procured, nor was what we did secure, good water. We spent our time here until the 9th, in drill, parade, and duties incident to camp-life. The writer remembers the camp, as having had while there, the most lonesome sense that he knew in all the three years of service. The winds moaned through the pines and the leaves rustled in a way that the occasion was a most dismal time."(10) There is an interesting incident relating to General Sherman about the trip on the way to Cornith, Mississippi.

"It was at a station on this road that General Sherman barely escaped capture. Memphis was always full of spies. As his train was to leave, the news was borne to a body of rebel cavalry, and when his train drew up at one of the stations, a dash was made to capture him. The fight was made about the train and one of the General's horses was taken from the car and carried off. It was only with extreme gallantry on the part of his body-guard that the General was saved from capture. Had they succeeded, it would have been a sweet plum to that crowd."(11)

On October 9, 1863, General Sherman and his army left their camp in Cornith, Mississippi and marched to Iuka, Mississippi. Lieutenant William H. Lynch writes the following in his diary. "We left camp near Cornith Miss. Marched with the Division to near Burnsville, Miss. (a station on the Rail Road) leading from Cornith to Iuka, Miss. (day clear & pleasant) arrived and went into camp at Iuka Miss. about 3 O'Clock P.M. 10th October 1863. Remained in camp at Iuka Miss. Till Saturday 17th day of Oct. 1853. (Our Regt. was paid two months pay – paid up to Sept. 1st 1863 by Maj. Dean)."(12) An unknown diarist of the 13th Illinois Infantry Regiment writes the following.

> "*October 9th*, —Started on the road to Iuka Springs and came some twelve miles. The arrangement seems to be to extend the railroad to the east as parties are employed on repairing it. On the 10th continued our march some eleven miles and camped at Iuka. This is quite a fine little town. It has five mineral springs, and is fixed up as a pleasure resort. A sharp little battle was fought here just before the battle of Cornith in which General Price's army was the party who got worsted. We stayed at this place a full week. One of the things that characterized our stay here, and it was not an unknown thing in army life, was a series of preaching and prayer meetings that developed something of a revival. War is serious business and men who engage in it ought to be serious and thoughtful men. While the opposite spirit seemed to have a large place, it was not universal, perhaps not so generally as it seemed. As thoughfulness that is touched with pride, sometimes tries to hide itself by noisy demonstration, so as to put the world off the track of our thoughts."(13)

Private Henry Kuck of Company G, 31st Missouri Infantry Regiment, his furlough up, was on his way to rejoin his regiment arriving in Memphis, Tennessee on October 11, 1863. He wrote in a letter to his wife Metta, "We're just arrived in Memphis, and I found out that our regiment isn't at Memphis anymore, rather in Cornith in Tennessee about 90 miles outside of Memphis, early tomorrow I'll go there on the train. Since I have to stay here today I took up my pen to write one more quick letter to let you know that I'm not going back to Vicksburg."(14) By the time Private Kuck wrote this letter the 31st Missouri Infantry Regiment was already at Iuka, Mississippi. He finally rejoined his command on October 14, 1863.

In another letter he writes to his wife what he and his

regiment are doing.

"Dear Metta,

This is the 2nd letter I'm writing to you; one I wrote as soon as I arrived in Memphis. On the 14th of the month I joined my Regiment again, which is, as I already wrote you, no longer by Vicksburg but we're now about 155 miles from Memphis and are to guard the railroad which (we) rebuilt from Memphis to Chattanooga where General Rosencrans is headquartered.

For myself, I'm still healthy and better than I was as I left you. How speedily and hurriedly the time flies, just a short while ago I was on the way to visit you and I know I'm already back again at camp where we're awakened in the morning and put to bed in the evening with drums and whistles. I can and should admit that I felt much happier at home, although I can't complain about poor treatment.

Where else can one find a nice happy place than among one's own? 'I would say, for me there's nothing better'. No one can be pleased unless he has a happy family, and I wish and hope on and on that you, Dear Metta, stay healthy so you can care for our lovely little ones, for myself I have few cares, that is, I take care of myself, but I'm not afraid to lose my life on the battlefield if I can also die knowing that you are well, but we'll hope that I can see you safe and sound again, and can stay with you, where no gruesome war cry can tear me from your side and make the enemy happy.

Gerd Losmann is healthy again and Claus Gerdel, John Gerdel, is sick. Wilh. Schwarze is healthy too. Don't forget to write whether you received (my letter) and if you're already moved into the house."(15)

Lieutenant William H. Lynch writes the following in his diary, "On October 17th the 32nd Mo. Inft. Vols. & also the entire Division moved about four miles along the R. Road, towards Tuscumbia Alabama and went into camp, about 12 P.M. The enemy attacked our advance, killed none, but wounded one man of Comp. 'E' 32nd Mo. Inft. Vols. (shot through the shoulder – wound serious). Regt. & Div. Remain in camp doing picket & on camp duty till the evening of the 19th Oct. when we moved about two miles further on towards Tuscumbia Al. & camped nearby, the creek (called Bear Creek)."(16)

A soldier in the 13th Illinois Infantry Regiment writes in his diary, "*October 19th*. – Our regiment was detailed for picket duty and sent some four miles east. This took us into Alabama and across Bear Creek. This Bear Creek Valley at this time of year was one of the most beautiful I ever looked upon. The look down the stream gave the appearance of a series of terraces on the either hand; the foliage, dark green pines, the brilliant oak leaves turned red by the cold weather and the chestnut leaves a beautiful yellow, gave a variety that was most pleasing to the eye. We might say of this country, 'Every prospect pleases and only man is vile."(17) He continues in his diary for the next day. "*October 20th*. – Moved up about thirteen miles to Cherokee station. At this place we were opposed by a force of the rebel cavalry commanded by Stephen D. Lee, numbering some five thousand, strengthened with artillery. The days spent here were full of anxiety and excitement as the rebels hung around us and made dashes both day and night; for more than a week it was constant strain."(18)

There was quite a skirmish on October 20, 1863 that preceded a major skirmish or battle on the next day. Lieutenant William H. Lynch describes the skirmish of October 20th. "Tuesday 20th October '63, when we resume our march towards Tuscumbia Ala. Marched about 8 miles & went into camp about 3 O'Clock P.M. The enemy about 400 strong attacked our advance (5th Ohio Cavalry & 3rd Regulars, but they were driven back with loss. Our cavalry attacked and not but few being in the advance, were compelled to fall back a short distance. General Osterhause, being in front, sent a dispatch back ordering the 3rd Regulars up. They being brought up, formed a line & made a desperate charge upon about 400 rebels, stood & were cut to pieces & finally were compelled to retreat, losing about 30 taken prisoners (killed not yet known). The Infantry moved up near the place of the engagement & went into camp. Remain in camp from 3 O'Clock P.M. till 12 A.M."(19)

The 31st Missouri Infantry was involved in a skirmish on October 21, 1863 at Cherokee, Alabama. At the skirmish at Cherokee, Alabama the Federals of the 2nd Brigade, 1st Division, 15th Army Corps was ordered to advance to support two companies of cavalry left at Cane Creek, from a skirmish the day before, reported a strong Confederate cavalry force putting strong pressure on them. The 1st Brigade was positioned so they could go to the support of either flank. The Confederates

175

were driven back by the 2nd Brigade, the Confederate force then tried to go around the left of the Federals. The 29th Missouri, 31st Missouri and part of the 12th Missouri Infantry Regiments were ordered in this direction to repulse the Confederate attack on that flank if it should happen which it didn't. The 2nd Brigade then chased the Confederates till night when the chase was suspended. The Federals suffered thirty-five killed and wounded. It turned out that the Confederate force was a several thousand strong force of both cavalry and infantry.

Lieutenant William H. Lynch describes the above action in his diary. "Next day Wednesday 21st when the enemy, (reported to be about 3000) attacking our front, we were ordered in the line of Battle. Our Regt. (32nd Mo.) & Div. Were ordered up to the front. The 30th Iowa (2nd Brig.) was hotly engaged but several killed & about 30 enlisted men wounded. Their Col. killed & several Capt. wounded. The fight was commenced about 12 m. and kept up till almost dark, the Rebel force falling back. Our artillery continued to shell them till dark, driving them back at every point. Our Regt. & Brigade were on the right of the command engaged we were held back as a reserve & were not immediately engaged. Yet we moved about 1/2 mile from our camp towards the front, formed on the right stacked arms, remain in said position, till almost dark when we were ordered back to camp. We returned & remain in camp till next day Thursday 22nd Oct."(20) One diarist from the 13 Illinois Infantry Regiment records his impression of the skirmish. *"October 21st. – The Second Brigade of our Division had quite a fight and loss to-day. Our cavalry were on the picket line and Colonel Torrence of the Thirtieth Iowa told them not to fire, for those were our men in front. The rebels had put on blue clothes to deceive us. The Thirtieth Iowa was then flanked, and fired into. Colonel Torrence was killed and many wounded and missing. The Fourth Iowa, our near and good friends, had one orderly sergeant killed and six men wounded. Some of our pickets were taken last night. The rebels made dashes on our pickets and then fled. This was kept up at short intervals."(21)

It was at Iuka that General Grant was able to get a message through, by canoe, to General Sherman to stop repairing the railroad because they would never be able to complete it and get to Chattanooga in time to make a difference in the siege.

It was about this time that General Sherman was placed

in command of the Army of the Tennessee which included the 15th, 16th and 17th Army Corps. Major General Frank P. Blair was temporarily placed in command of the 15th Corps, he was at this time with General Osterhaus' division and General John E. Smith's division at the head of the 15th Corps. Lieutenant William H. Lynch wrote in his diary, "Our Regt. remain in camp till 23d Friday Oct. '63 when we marched about one mile towards the front stationed 16 men on picket & then returned to camp. The day was blustery & roads very muddy. On 24th Saturday 2 O'Clock A.M. about 60 Rebel cavalry made a charge upon our pickets. The Rebel picket were, after a short engagement repulsed & driven back several miles. We lost no men in this engagement. The 32nd had a part of its men in this engagement, yet we lost no one. At first our Infantry pickets was driven back. One of our Boys, Isaac Bounds of Company 'B' 32nd Mo. Inf. Vols. was on his post when the enemy about 20 made their appearance near him, he halted them & as he pronounced the word 'Halt' the enemy gave the word 'charge' & he fired his gun & retreated, they firing a volley at him but done no injury. He fell back to reinforcements."(22)

One of the 13th Illinois Infantry Regiment soldiers wrote in his diary, "*October 25th*. – At 1 o'clock a.m. Companies A and B of our regiment were sent out and stayed on the skirmish line till morning. General inspection was ordered to see that everything was in the best of shape; and an order left to move in the morning at 2 a.m., with three days' rations. Almost anything would be a relief from the present irritating surroundings."(23)

At three a.m. on October 26th the 1st Brigade led the 1st Division towards Tuscumbia, Alabama. The 1st Brigade was composed of the 12th Missouri Infantry, 13th Illinois Infantry, 27th Missouri Infantry, 76th Ohio Infantry, with the 32nd Missouri Infantry and 29th Missouri Infantry Regiments forming one battalion and the 17th Missouri Infantry and the 31st Missouri Infantry Regiments forming another battalion. The infantry was accompanied by the 1st Missouri Horse Artillery and the 4th Ohio battery. At the cemetery near Barton's Station on the Memphis and Charleston Railroad at four-thirty a.m., the enemy had taken up a strong position being chased there by the division cavalry. Two regiments were placed on the left of the railroad with the rest of the brigade being placed on the right. The two seperate battalions were placed in a tree line about three-quarters of a mile to the right. The brigade was then ordered forward with the 2nd Brigade having come up moving forward on the left. They drove the Confederates about one mile to Cane Creek where after a brief delay the Federals were able to drive the Confederates from that position. It was during this charge that the two battalions in the wood line were brought into the battle. The Confederate's then retreated to Little Bear Creek, three miles from Tuscumbia. The Confederates occupied a strong position on a hill from where they conducted a counter-attack which was successfully driven back by a volley from the 3rd Missouri and the 27th Missouri Infantry Regiments. It was during this volley that it was falsely believed that great Confederate cavalry leader Major-General Nathan Bedford Forrest was severely if not mortally wounded in both thighs. With night close approaching there was no more fighting. The next day the Federals advanced into Tucumbia and took possession around noon. The 2nd Division had come up during the night and was placed on the right of the 1st Brigade of the 1st Division. One of the soldiers in the 13th Illinois Infantry Regiment records his view of October 26th.

"*October 26.* – We were up at 12 o'clock. Tents, baggage and sick were sent back to Dickson Station. We were on the move at 3 a.m. A mile out we struck the rebel pickets; pushed them back with steady skirmishing for about six miles. At daylight we found their main body supported by artillery. A fire was kept up while a flank movement was made upon them. Two or our men were wounded. At 9 a.m. our flanking forces compelled them to abandon their position. At 11 a.m. they again made a stand at a small creek, but this was not intended as a real position.

At 3 p.m. we came upon them in a strong position, two miles west of Tuscumbia. They had been reinforced and had a couple of long range guns that reached us as soon as we came out of the woods across the valley opposite them. I suppose our commander thought they would soon abandon their position, as they had before, so that we were not thrown into line, but merely sheltered ourselves somewhat by moving out of the road among the scattered trees. Another regiment of the brigade came up beside us. The shells came unpleasantly near our heads. Finally one struck the regiment that had just come up and the men and rails flew in every direction as it burst. Several men were badly wounded. One man set up an unearthly yell that was very trying to our nerves. It was found out that the man who made the noise was not hurt at all, only covered with blood from the man next to him who had a leg torn off. Our regiment was then thrown into line of battle on the south side of the railroad and held this position till morning. In this position a shell struck the regiment just to the rear of us, killing one man and badly wounding two others. After it was over some one asked Norman Sterling, of Company A, if he got down when those shells were tearing through amongst us. 'Get down?' said he, 'why I'm spread all over like a pancake, and wished I could get thinner.

October 27th. – We laid in line of battle all last night. This morning one brigade of the second division moved to the right to flank the enemy's position. A full battery of twenty-pound Parrott guns were brought up and opened on the rebel battery. Their firing was so rapid and close, that without firing another shot they limbered up and fled at full gallop. We started to follow them by brigades in column. They offered no opposition, and before 1 o'clock we were in possession of Tuscumbia. This proved to be a fine village with a beautiful country surrounding it. At the time of writing this, it is a town of some fifteen hundred inhabitants.

We found some one hundred of the rebels wounded in the town and vicinity, among them Colonel Forrest mortally wounded. He was a brother of the famous General Forrest. They had some thirty killed. The enemy had spent all the night previous in destroying the railroad.

The plan of advance was evidently changed, for the next day found us on the back track, destroying what we had repaired on the railroad.

On the *29th*. – The rebels followed us closely, evidently determined to find out what our movement meant; the skirmish was kept up all day. We had one man killed and twelve wounded; the enemy had five killed and nineteen wounded and three taken prisoners.

On the night of the 31st three companies of our regiment were on guard. They were fired upon, and one man of Company C and one negro were wounded."(24)

In the Official Records Brigadier-General Charles R. Woods wrote in a report covering the dates from October 20 – 29 1863, which included the skirmishes involving his command at Cane Creek and at Barton's Station.

"HDQRS. FIRST BRIG., FIRST DIV. 15TH ARMY CORPS,

Cherokee Station, Ala., October 28,1863.

CAPTAIN: I have the honor to report that at 3 a.m. of the 26th instant, I left camp at this place with my brigade, having the advance of the division, and proceeded in the direction of Tuscumbia, Ala. The brigade is composed of the Twelfth Missouri Infantry, Col. Hugo Wangelin commanding; Thirteenth Illinois Infantry, Col. A. B. Gorgas commanding; Twenty-seventh Missouri Infantry, Col. Thomas Curly Commanding; Third Missouri Infantry, Lieut. Col. Theo. Meumann commanding; Seventy-sixth Ohio Infantry, Maj. W. Warner commanding; Thirty-second and Twenty-ninth Missouri Infantry, forming one battalion, Lieut. Col. H. C. Warmoth (Thirty-second Missouri) commanding; Seventeenth and Thirty-first Missouri Infantry, forming one battalion, Lieut. Col. S. P. Simpson (Thirty-first Missouri) commanding.

It was accompanied by the First Missouri Horse Artillery, Capt. C. Landgraeber commanding, and the Fourth Ohio Battery, Capt. George Froehlich commanding, and was followed by the Second Brigade of this division.

When I reached Barton's Station I found that the cavalry had driven the enemy to a strong position. I deployed two regiments the Thirteenth Illinois and Seventy-sixth Ohio – on the left of the railroad and the remainder of my brigade on the right, taking the two battalions, composed each of two regiments, to a position three-quarters of a mile to the right, and posting them in a piece of woods. Having completed these dispositions, and thrown skirmishers well to the front, I ordered the brigade to advance.

The Second Brigade, with skirmishers in front, advanced at the same time on my left. The skirmishers moved forward in gallant style, driving the enemy from their position and pushing them back to Cane Creek, a distance of 1 mile. Here they reformed, having five pieces of artillery posted on high ground, with open fields intervening, and skirmishers strongly posted along the creek bottom. After reconnoitering, I pushed my right forward to the edge of the woods. The skirmirshers soon reached the creek, and succeded in crossing. At this point the firing was very heavy, but of short duration. The enemy, abandoning their positions fell back to the Little Bear Creek, 3 miles from Tuscumbia. They made a stand upon a hill which commanded the valley between us I posted my brigade on the right of the road upon a hill. About the time the first two regiments were posted the enemy's cavalry made a charge across the open field on my right, with the evident intention of getting possession of the hill.

They were checked and driven back by a volley from the Third and Twenty-seventh Missouri, by which Colonel Forrest was severly, if not mortally, wounded by a Minie ball through both thighs. It being late, nothing further was done than to take a position and to hold it until dark. The troops, except three regiments, which were left on picket duty, were then withdrawn into a ravine. On the following morning, the 27th instant, I deployed the Seventeenth Missouri, Col. John F. Cramer commanding, as skirmishers, supported by the Third Missouri on the opposite side of the creek. At the same time the Second Brigade moved up on my left and the Second Division on my right. The movement was successful, and by 12 m. the troops were in Tuscumbia.

I append a list of killed and wounded.

I am, captain, very respectfully, your obedient servant,

> CHAS. R. WOODS,
> Brigadier-General, Commanding.

Capt. W. A. GORDON,

Asst. Adjt. Gen., First Div., 15th Army Corps."(25)

After their return to Tuscumbia, Alabama they crossed the Tennessee River and marched to Waterloo, Alabama where the 15th Corps split up at Florence, Alabama. Three divisions of the 15th Corps left Florence and proceeded to Pulaski, Tennessee toward Bridgeport, Alabama and then into Chattanooga, Tennessee. Two divisions which included the 31st Missouri

Infantry, marched towards Athens, Alabama to Huntsville, Woodville, through Taylors Gap and then into Chattanooga, Tennessee. These two divisions brought up the rear of the 15th Corps. The first of the 15th Corps reached Bridgeport, Alabama on November 15th. Leaving them there General Sherman proceeded into Chattanooga to meet with General Grant. When he saw that the Federal army in Chattanooga was surrounded he told General Grant, "Why, General Grant you are besieged;' and he said,' It is too true." (26)

The following are the dates that describe where the 31st Missouri Infantry Regiment's Company D were and other information found in this Company's Morning Report in the Remarks section.

"November 1863   3rd-Left Chickasaw Landing, Alabama march towards McPherson Alabama.

5th- Arrive at Harrison, Alabama Alabama. Distance marched 25 miles.

9th- Arrived at Pulaski, Tennessee Distance marched 42 miles.

11th- Arrived at Fayetteville, Tennessee. Marched 32 miles.

14th- arrived at Maysville, Alabama. Distance marched 50 miles.

17th- Arrived at Stephensville, Alabama. Distance marched 50 miles.

18th-Arrived at Bridgeport, Alabama. Distance marched 14 miles.

28th- Marshal B. Robbertson died of wounds Rec'd in Action at Ringgold, Georgia."(27)

Major A. J. Seay of the 32nd Missouri Volunteer Infantry Regiment, records in his diary for the march from November 1,1863 to November 17, 1863.

"Sunday, Nov. 1st,1863.. Warm and cloudy.

Nov. 2d.

Warmer-we get rations and supplies. Gens. Osterhaus and Wood dine with us. Osterhaus gets a telegram announcing that his wife is very sick. He will start home, on tomorrow. We move down the river and cross our teams and batteries during the whole night. Our division is the last to cross. The other three have gone on. My health poor.

Nov. 3rd.

Very hot, we start at noon and march 10 miles to Gravely Spring on Bluff Creek. Bottoms productive-hills steep and brushy-looks a little like the Boaring River. Guerrillas fired into our train burning 2 wagons, one was Gen. Blair's. He lost his hardware, 1 mule and 2 horses killed.

Nov. 4th.

Rained all day, muddy-hard marching. Camp at Cypress factory or cypress creek, a large stony Creek. Perpendicular bluff covered with evergreen. We stop in an old out house make a big fire which we enjoy being quite wet muddy and cold.

Friday, 5th November, 1863.

A fair day after the fog goes off. We march in front as cattle guard. We pass thru Florence Ala., a nice little town of say 2,000 inhabitants situated near Tenn. R. Traveled 16 miles. We leave the Huntsville and take the Pulaski road. No troops have traveled the road before. Country hilly red clay and covered with same kind of timber that grows on Mo. hills with addition of chestnut. Go into camp at _____ Spring a summer resort and water place. A good deal more Union sentiment thru here than I ever believed.

Friday, 6th November, 1863.

Camped at Taylor's Spring.

Saturday, 7th November, 1863,

Camped in the brush.

Sunday, 8th.

A beautiful day-pass over a heavy timber upland country-go into Camp at Squire Reynolds.

Monday, 9th.

Quite cold-ground frozen all day-pass thru Pulaski about 11 A.M. A nice little town in a basin of over 2,000 inhabitants. Memphis and Decatur R.R. pass thru here. Late in the evening we pass an old sacred spot-a camp meeting ground and shanties with 2 large wooden churches. Reminds me of my boy-hood days. A great deal of Union sentiment strong here. The steepest hills I have ever seen cultivated are here. Quite cold all day-we get into camp in the night.

Tuesday, 10th Nov.

Ground hard frozen this morning and has not thawed during the day. The finest water in the world. We are in the advance today. Go into camp at 5 P.M. Capt. Bland sick.

Wednesday, 11th.

Nice and frosty. We march at 11 A.M. Cross Cane creek a large creek. Soon pass thru Fayetteville a small ville of 1,200 inhabitants. It is on a high bottom on the South of a small hill. On the east is Elk River a pretty stream. Water as blue as the sky, runs south. We cross over on stone bridge made out of solid limestone masonary. A magnificent structure.

Thursday, 12th.

Go into camp at 8 P.M. last night, country traveled over a ridge of lime stone hills but land productive. Frost this morning. We march in front over 11 miles find but one house on the route. A post oak upland or ridge- every ravine so miry that the train could scarcely pass. Several mules and horses killed. A nice day. Camp near the fork of Winchester and Stephenson roads.

Friday, 13th.

Warm and cloudy. We are the rear today. Have taken the Stephenson road. Stayed at Branchville. Move south thru New Market at the foot of the Cumberland Mts. New Market is little ville of 150 inhabitants. At Branchville we were in Franklin Co. than Lincoln than Ala.

Saturday, 14th.

Cloudy, rain and mud. We direct our course south thru the towering spruces of the Cumberland Mts. To Maysville 11 miles easy of Huntsville-has been in possession of the Federals since August. Gen. Crook is camped here with 11 regiments cav and 5 mounted infantry. We got in from Maysville on the line of the Memphis and Charleston R.R. The people and country destitute of everything but corn. The mountainous region thru which we pass is romantic beautiful. The valley soil is red. Timber oak, beech and some chestnut and cedar.

Sunday, 15th, 1863.

Frost last night-clear and beautiful today. We pass Point Rock River and bridge. Here the R.R. bridge is being rebuilt and when the bridge is rebuilt across Fling river the Memphis and Charleston Road will be open from Stephenson to Huntsville. Point Rock R. is a narrow but deep stream. Go into camp at Larkinsville, Jackson Co.

Monday, 16.

Travel thru a less mountainous region than yesterday-hills covered with pine. We cross no streams today. Go into camp at Bellefonte a miserable dilipated country town.

Tuesday, Nov. 17th 1863.

March to Stephenson, crossing a muddy creek and a good deal of muddy roads on our route. Stephenson is situated at the foot of a stoney hill or mountain side on the east side of the creek. It is a small uncouth place important only for locality as a military depot and junction of the Memphis and Charleston and Nashville and Chattanooga R.R's. It is garrisoned by the 28th Ky. Mounted Inf. and the 20th Conn. Camp 2 miles east of town."(28)

On November 17, 1863 General Sherman's leading division left Bridgeport and marched about forty miles to Chattanooga to do join the rest of the Federal army, but because of the rain they were delayed. By November 20th the head of the Army of the Tennessee was only to Brown's Ferry and there was no way that they could be in position to begin an attack in time to participate with the rest of the army. So General Grant delayed the start till November 23rd. It rained again on the 21st of November which not only made the roads worse but also continued to add to the depth and speed of the current of the Tennessee River. An unknown diarist in the 13th Illinois Infantry Regiment records, "On the 21st we came some six miles and camped near a great cave called the Nickajack. This is said to be seventeen miles long. A lieutenant and four soldiers had gone in to explore it, and after four days had not returned. A relief party of soldiers and citizens had been sent to the rescue. *Sunday, Nov. 22d.* – We find the road through this ravine very bad, and we are now being stripped for the fight. Blankets over the shoulders, one hundred rounds of ammunition on our person, two days' bread in haversack and two in a single wagon to the regiment."(29)

Major A. J. Seay writes in his diary the following.

"Sunday, 22d. Nov.

Start toward Chattanooga with 4 days rations and one wagon passed at the foot of Raccoon Mt. And on the bank of the Tenn. The roughest road I ever saw. R.R. above the river beneath. The bluff an overhanging precipice of 250 or 300 feet-scene grand. Camp late after a hard days march of seven miles over the roughest road every traveled over in a civilized country. A vast mountain on either side-narrow ravine with a roaring creek the men had to wade it at least a dozen times in 2 miles. Pass Whiteside, a little place where the ravine is bridged.

Monday, 23rd. Nov.

Start on the march thru mud, water and splash at mid-night, wagons stalling and breaking down frequently. At dawn of day we come in sight of Lookout Mt. on whose side the traitors fires are distantly seen. Ours are also seen lighting a lesser range on hills ravines etc. known as lookout valley. It is the fire of Gen. Hooks (2 div 11th and all of 12th) The rebs are firing from their batteries on Lookout Mt. at short intervals directly upon Chattanooga. I have seen Gen. Hooker at his hdqrs. He has a fine personal appearance, straight as an Indian-gray side whiskers-plump well delimated face, a little red, looks like T. L. Price of Mo. We move down near the river and stack arms in an open field in full view of Lookout Mt and the Reb encampment. The Rebs sent down a log raft last night and broke down our pontoons so we cannot cross the R. as was intended. At 2 P.M. the fight begins briskly in front and on the left of Chattanooga continues till night with what result I do not know. Am told our forces drive them."(30)

General Sherman was to try and get his troops across the river, unobserved if possible, in order to attack Missionary Ridge from its northern flank. His troops were observed marching in that direction but the Confederates saw them from Lookout Mountain and were under the impression that they were the troops that were sent to reinforce General Thomas. On November 23rd, the 15th Corps crossed the rising Tennessee River, with everyone getting across except for General Osterhaus' 1st Division. The 1st Division was bringing up the rear of the 15th Army Corps and just as they were getting ready to cross, the pontoon bridge broke loose and began to float downstream. The 1st Division was then ordered to report to General Hooker if they had not crossed the river by eight o'clock in the morning on the 24th of November. In a letter, dated November 30, 1863 Private Henry Kuck wrote his wife, "...I came on October 14th with my regiment and marched the whole time until Nov. 25th, through thick and thin. As we arrived here at Chattanooga the 23rd of this mo. we thought we would get some rest, but the next morning we had to move on again, with 2 days rations and bread, and 2 days of rations packed on the wagon, and 100 bullets for everyone."(31)

The eastern army had started wearing corps badges early in the war. In most cases they were made of cloth and were sewn on the uniform somewhere, generally on the cap. This emblem was of different shapes which denoted the corps and then each division would have a different color. Their supply wagons would have this emblem painted on the canvass covering in the appropiate color so each corps could tell which was their supply wagons from a distance. As an example the 2nd Army Corps had a three leaf clover as their emblem. It's 1st Division flag had a white background with a red clover in the middle, red representing the first division. The 2nd Division flag had a blue background with a white clover in the center. The 3rd Division flag had a white background with a solid blue clover in the center. Most of the army corps flags, color wise, were the same as the 2nd Army Corps.

The western army was different in this respect. They did not have corps badges until almost the end of the war. The 15th Corps didn't have one approved until April 9, 1865. Here is the story on how the 15th Corps received their badge. The following is from General Sherman's memoirs:

"As the men were trudging along the deeply-cut, muddy road, on a cold, drizzly day, one of our western soldiers left his ranks and joined a party of the 12th Corps at their campfire. They got into conversation, the 12th Corps men asking what troops we were etc., etc. In turn, our fellow (who had never seen a corps badge, and noticed that everything was marked with a star) asked if they were all Brigadier General's of course they were not, but the star was their corps-badge, and every wagon, tent, hat, etc., had its star. Then when the 12th

187

Corps men inquired what corps he belonged to, and he answered, "the 15th Corps." "What is your badge?" "Why," said he (and he was an Irishman), suiting the action to the word, "forty rounds in the cartridge box, and twenty in the pocket." General Logan adopted the cartridge-box and forty rounds as the corps-badge, when he took command of the 15th Corps." (32)

The 15th Corps headquarters flag was unique in that it had all four division colors on the flag. It was cut into quarters with the top left color being the 1st Division's red, the top right corner was white which represented the 2nd Division, the bottom right was blue which represented the 3rd Division and the bottom left was yellow which represented the 4th Division. In the middle of this flag was an emblem of a cartridge box with the words "Forty Rounds" printed above it. Each division had its own flag with the color of the background of the flag the respective color of that division as listed above. Then the cartridge box and the words "forty rounds" in black. On General Sherman's mroument at his grave site in Calvary Cemetery in Saint Louis, Missouri, the cartridge box and "40 Rounds" are present.

Private Henry Kuck, Company G, 31st Missouri Infantry Regiment kept a record of the places he had been and called it an Inventory. The following is what he wrote for the months of October and November 1863.

"INVENTORY

The list of places we were during our field marches, with the dates we were there.

Date	Places
Octob.	
5	Home to St. Louis, there on a steamboat to Memphis
11	Reported at Fort Pickering in Memphis for Transportation
14	Reported to the Regiment, Iuka, Miss.
18	Was paid for 2 months; sent 26 doll. Home by express
26	From Cherokee Station to Tuscumbia, about 10 miles from Iuka, where we had Camped since Otober 21st.
27	Back to Cherokee Station
30	To Chattanooga

Nov.

3   Over the Tenn. Riv. at Chickasaw Landing to
        Waterloo, Alabama.

6   Colfax Mill

9   Polansky Tenn.

16   Bellfonte Ala.

17   Stevenson

19   Bridgeport, Ala.

20   Across Tenn. Riv. at Bridgeport by Lookout,
        Tenn."(33)

The 31st Missouri Infantry, as most of the other units in the Federal army suffered loss due to the usual reasons that they have experienced up to this time. In Company A, Corporal Joseph Adams of Victoria died on August 27, 1863 at Vicksburg, Mississippi. Private John Huckey of Hillsboro deserted on August 3, 1863. Private Benjamin R. Wallace of Victoria deserted from Miliken's Bend. Private Franklin W. Williams of Carondelet was discharged on August 20,1863 while in camp at Black River, Mississippi. In Company B, Private Paul Dumphrey of Washington County was discharged due to disability on November 20, 1863. Sergeant John Egan of Saint Louis deserted on November 2, 1863 at Saint Louis, Missouri. Private James W. Stevens of Washington County deserted on September 14, 1863 at Carondelet, Missouri. Corporal Marion Evans of Washington County on November 21, 1863 at Memphis, Tennessee. Private Lewis S. Gibson of Saint Louis died in the hospital at Camp Sherman, Mississippi on August 27, 1863. Sergeant Walter R. Stone of Saint Louis was discharged on August 15, 1863. Corporal Henry C. Trimbel of Saint Louis was discharged due to disability on September 2, 1863. Private William Wilson of Patterson died on August 29, 1863 at Vicksburg, Mississippi. In Company C, Private Charles East of Saint Francis County was discharged due to disability on September 5,1863. Private Joseph Stoney of Hopewell of Ironton, Missouri deserted on October 5, 1863. Private Willis McVey of Washington County died on a hospital boat on September 14, 1863. Private George W. Small of Hopewell died while at home in Hopewell, Missouri on October 13, 1863. Private Hiriam T. Smith of Hopewell died at Paducah, Kentucky on November 19, 1863. Corporal William W. Rogers of Hopewell was transferred to the Invalid Corps on September 3, 1863. In Company D, Private Elijah Vaughn died on October 3, 1863 at Jefferson Barracks, Missouri and is buried there. Private Wiliam J. Houghson of Ripley County was discharged at Jefferson Barracks on September 4, 1863. Corporal Ehraim C. Ruiticele of Greenville died at Detroit, Michigan on November 8, 1863. Private Elijah Vaughn of Greenville died of disease at Jefferson Barracks on October 3, 1863. Private Marcus Abernathy of Carondelet was transferred to the Invalid Corps on October 23, 1863. Private Claib D. Agee of Greenville was also transferred to the Invalid Corps on October 22, 1863. Private Jeremiah Eaton of Carter County was transferred to the Invalid Corps Company A 4th Regiment on August 2, 1863. Private Jeremiah Vaughn of Greenville was transferred Invalid Corps on September 1863. In Company E, Private Elijah Siles of Moselle deserted from Jefferson Barracks on September 25, 1863. Private A. W. Sterling of Moselle deserted from the hospital on September 28, 1863. Corporal Jonathon Hollingsworth of Gasconade County died on August 18, 1863 at Vicksburg, Mississippi. Private Alfred Patton of Moselle discharged on October 3, 1863 at Memphis, Tennessee. In Company F, Private Harland M. Smith of Canaan discharged at Jefferson Barracks because of disability. Private Daniel W. Turner of Canaan was discharged from Camp Sherman, Mississippi because of disability on September 5, 1863. Private Isaac E. Pounds of Canaan was discharged on November 6, 1863 from Jefferson Barracks. Private William R. Brown of Canaan deserted at Bridgeport, Alabama on November 18, 1863 but was honorably discharged on March 25, 1865. Private William Spaulding of Canaan also deserted from Bridgeport, Alabama on November 18, 1863 they evidently went together. Private Christopher L. Darbin of Canaan was transferred to the Invalid Corps on September 26, 1863. Private John Scandler of Canaan was also transferred to the Veteran Reserve Corps on September 1, 1863. Private James A. Vaughn of Canaan was also transferred to the Invalid Corps on September 1, 1863. Private John Thompson of Canaan was transferred to the Invalid Corps on August 19, 1863. In Company G, Second Lieutenant Adolph Frick of Washington was honorably discharged by order of General Grant on August 10, 1863. Company H had no losses during this time. In Company I, Private Ambrose Hughes of Monroe County was discharged from Camp Sherman, Mississippi on September 5, 1863. Private John F. Craft died on August 13, 1863 at Vicksburg, Mississippi. Private James M. Dulton of Carondelet died on August 30, 1863 at Danville, Missouri. Private Peter Dunn of Desoto died on September 17, 1863 at Victoria, Missouri. Private Peter Keern of Saint Louis died on August 4, 1863. Private John Kroft of Montgomery County died on August 12, 1863 at Vicksburg, Mississippi. Private Elisha Palmer of Potosi died on August 31, 1863 at Saint Louis, Missouri. Private James Skinner of Montgomery County died at Paduka, Kentucky on November 19, 1863. Private Benjamin Clemens of Montgomery was transferred to the Invalid Corps on November 1863. Corporal Abraham W. Rudd of Desoto was promoted to Sergeant on December 1862 and then transferred to the Invalid Corps on September 26, 1863. In Company K, Private Thomas J. Branson of Canaan died on October 3, 1863 at Benton Barracks. Private William H. Akers of Caledonia died on November 2, 1863 while at home in Caledonia. Private Herman H. Rahe of Saint Louis died on August 22, 1863 at Black River Bridge, Mississippi. Field and Staff lost their surgeon, Surgeon Churchill G. Strother some time in November 1863 at Saint Louis, Missouri.

CHAPTER EIGHT:
LOOKOUT MOUNTAIN THROUGH RINGGOLD GAP

On November 23, 1863, General Grant ordered Major-General Joseph H. Hooker to stay in Lookout Valley and be prepared to make a demonstration the following morning in order to keep the Confederate troops on Lookout Mountain pre-occupied so as to not be able to participate in the attack to be led by General Sherman on Missionary Ridge. This demonstration was also to keep the Confederate high command's attention diverted from the real attack and to confuse them about what the Federals were up to. It was on this same day that General Hooker was informed that General Osterhaus' 1st Division would probably be joining them the next day if the pontoon bridge at Brown's Ferry could not be repaired. Shortly after General Hooker received the telegram about the possibility of General Osterhaus joining him, he received another telegram informing him that if his demonstration against Lookout Mountain the next day looks like it could turn into a successful attack he was to attack the Confederates on Lookout Mountain. If he should be successful he was then to attack the southern end of Missionary Ridge.

The 31st Missouri Regiment's strength going into this battle was one hundred and twenty-three men, its sister regiment, the 32nd Missouri Regiment had one hundred and forty-nine in it, combined with the rest of the 1st Brigade the total strength was one thousand, eight hundred and sixty-three men. General Osterhaus' division reported to General Hooker at seven-thirty a.m. on November 24, 1863 and took up position on the left of the rest of the troops then formed up. The 31st Missouri Infantry Regiment was now part of Major General Joseph Hooker's thrown together army. It consisted of General Osterhaus' 1st Division, of the 15th Corps who had two brigades; the 1st Brigade was commanded by Brigadier-General Charles R. Woods of which the 31st Missouri was a part of, the 2nd Brigade was commanded by Colonel J. A. Williamson. The 1st Division had no 3rd Brigade at this time, it had been discontinued in September 1863 and would later be reinstated on

December 1,1863. Brigadier General John Geary's division of General Hooker's own 12th Corps. In General Geary's division there were three brigades, they were led by Colonel Charles Candy, Colonel George A. Cobham Jr. and Colonel David Ireland. Brigadier General Charles Cruft's division of the 4th Corps of the Army of the Cumberland was made up of Brigadier General Walter C. Whitaker's Brigade, whose size it is estimated totaled almost the same amount of men as General Geary's whole division, and Colonel William Grose's brigade, who would join General Hooker's force at about the same time as General Osterhaus' command joined. Later in the day Brigadier General William P. Carlin's brigade was also added to General Hooker's force. This placed approximately between nine and ten thousand men under General Hooker's command.

General Sherman and his three division's, plus Brigadier General Jefferson Davis, whose division was detached from General Palmer's Corps, had finally got into position in the hills where General Grant had wanted him to start his attack. They were about four miles northeast of Chattanooga. When General Sherman started his attack, he found out that he was in the wrong position. Instead of facing the north slope of Missionary Ridge he was actually ready to attack a hill in front of Missionary Ridge. This was probably an honest mistake. The terrain was very hilly and heavily forested. Being unfamiliar with the area and not performing a reconnaissance prior to the assault led to this mistake that would cost him the major role of the defeat of the Confederates on Missionary Ridge that General Grant had planned for him.

While General Sherman's force was preparing to attack what they thought was the northern slope of Missionary Ridge, Major General Joseph H. "Fighting Joe" Hooker was given the job of merely holding Lookout Valley and making a demonstration against Lookout Mountain. General Hooker, who at one time had been the commander of the Army of the Potomac, was not real happy with this secondary role in the attack. I would like to pass on some information of General Hooker that was recorded of him at the time. While in Washington D. C., General Hooker was a regular visitor to the ladies of ill-repute. His reputation of visiting the ladies of the oldest profession was so well known that they were being referred to as Hooker's ladies, which was eventually shortened to Hookers, a name that they are often still referred to as today.

Lookout Mountain is the highest point in the immediate area of Chattanooga. If you are standing in Chattanooga and looking up at the mountain you can not believe that men would charge up that mountain and make it to the top. There is a white house on Lookout Mountain called the "Craven's House." Parts of it is still there, with the rest being rebuilt, and if you ever go to Lookout Mountain you should visit the Craven's house. The mountain looks out over the city of Chattanooga and the bend in the Tennessee River, known as "Moccasin Bend" is clearly seen and you have an excellent view of Lookout Valley to the west. It was from this valley that General Hooker's force was to begin their assault. General Hooker described Lookout Mountain in this way. "Viewed from whatever point, Lookout Mountain, with its high palisaded crest, and its steep, rugged, rocky, and deeply-furrowed slopes, presented an imposing barrier to our advance, and when to these natural obstacles were added almost interminable, well-planned, and well-constructed defenses, held by Americans, the assault became an enterprise worthy of the ambition and renown of the troops to whom it was instrusted. On the northern slope, midway between the summit and the Tennessee, a plateau or belt of arable land encircles the crest. There are redans, and pits appeared lower down the slope, to repel an assault from the direction of the river. On each flank were rifle-pits, epaulments for batteries, walls of stone, and abatis to resist attacks from either the Chattanooga or Lookout Valleys. In the valleys themselves were earth-works of still greater extent." (1)

General Hooker described the position of the Confederates from his point of view and the ideal he had of maybe forcing them off the mountain. "At this time the enemy's pickets formed a continuous line along the right bank of Lookout Creek, with the reserves in the valley, while his main force was encamped in a hollow half way up the slope of the mountain. The summit itself was held by three brigades of Stevenson's division, and these were comparatively safe, as the only means of access from the west, for a distance of 20 miles up the valley, was by two or three trails, admitting of the passage of but 1 man at a time, and even those trails were held at the top by rebel pickets. For this reason no direct attempt was made for the dislodgment of this force. On the Chattanooga side, which is less precipitous, a road of easy grade has been made communicting with the summit by zig-zag lines running diagonally up the mountain side, and it was believed that before our troops should gain possession of this, the enemy on the top would evacuate his position, to avoid being cut off from his main body, to rejoin which would involve a march of 20 or 30 miles."(2)

At approximately eight o'clock a.m. on November 24th, the Battle of Lookout Mountain began, it is best known throughout history as the "Battle Above the Clouds." There was a heavy mist or clouds on top of the mountain which prevented the Confederates from observing the movements of Yankees. They did have a large amount of pickets stationed in a position so as to give early warning should the Federals try to attack the mountain. General Geary's division moved out first, some favoritism could be accused of here since they were part of General Hooker's Corps or they could have been the troops that General Hooker had the most faith in carrying out his orders. They crossed Lookout Creek at a ford they had found and started up the mountain, capturing Confederate pickets that they came in contact with. They were supported by General Whitaker's brigade. Colonel Grose's brigade was to seize a bridge over the creek. In the process of securing this bridge they had a brief skirmish with the Confederate pickets. This firing had attracted the attention of the Confederates on the mountain, the Confederates sent troops in the direction of Colonel Grose and the approach of General Geary's men were not noticed. General Woods' brigade, of General Osterhaus' division, went farther up the creek and built their own bridge which they completed around ten o'clock that morning. At eleven o'clock, General Geary's men finally made an advance which was the signal for General Osterhaus to advance with his troops. Both forces crossed their bridges and started forward. General Osterhaus' forces met the enemy and had a sharp skirmish. The Confederates were so outnumbered that they rapidly gave ground. General Geary's forces, at this time, were moving up the mountain. The enemy had occupied their rifle pits and were putting up some resistance. The Confederates noticed that General Geary's force was threatening their flank on the left with the possibility of getting in their rear.

General Osterhaus' line, still supported by Colonel Grose, and General Geary's line, still supported by General Whitaker, joined forces. General Osterhaus was on the left and General Geary was on his right. The Confederates had lost a lot of their pickets, General Moore lost two hundred and twenty-five and General Walthall lost at least that many or more. Most of these were captured. By noon General Geary's men had ran into the Confederate forces behind breast works in front of the Craven's House. They were on a small plateau, about half way up the mountain. The Federals had anchored their right with the right flank on some cliffs that were called the palisades. These cliffs were anywhere from seventy-five to one hundred feet high. General Osterhaus' and Colonel Grose's men, after almost two hours of fighting, climbed step by step up the steep mountain side over some of the worst type of terrain to make a charge. They had to march over and through gullies and ravines plus there were huge boulders that were almost everywhere on the mountain. The trees were also a problem. It was hard to keep alignment in the heavy woods and many of the trees had fallen in a way that they had to be climbed over. General Osterhaus' forces was still on General Greay's left. "General Wood's brigade was on the extreme left of the Federal line, on the slope of the mountain covering the area between the white house and the Chattanooga road at a point where it runs round a promontory about 250 feet above the level of the Tennessee river."(3)

The Federal artillery had been firing at the Confederate positions, they now began to increase their fire. The Army of the Cumberland were firing from Moccasin Point and there were also some artillery firing from the west of Lookout Creek where General Hooker had placed them. The Confederate artillery was having a few problems. The mountain was so steep that their guns could not be depressed enough to hit the Federal soldiers coming up the mountain. The Confederate infantrymen were able to fire their rifles into the Federal soldiers with better accuracy because they could fire almost straight down at the enemy.

The Confederate defenses were manned by Brigadier General Edward C. Walthall's brigade of approximately one thousand of his fifteen hundred men. The other five hundred had been on picket duty and had been in positions that should have been occupied by a larger force than what was there. As stated before most of these pickets had been captured. General Longstreet's corps had previously been in this position but had been pulled out of line and sent to Knoxville, Tennessee to try and defeat General Burnside's force there. The battle around the Craven's house was on a narrow shelf on the mountain. This was a strongly fought battle and around noon the Federal's gained possession of the Craven's house. The Confederates had used some of the stone fences as breast works. The howitzers of the Confederates were overrun and captured after their infantry support had retreated. Walthall's command fell back about four hundred yards to some more positions and remained there until relieved by three regiments of General Pettus' brigade. The rest of General Moore's brigade formed to the right of General Pettus'.

The weather was terrible. As mentioned earlier there was a mist that either was a cloud or fog that was wet enough to get the men damp. On the way up the mountain the 31st Missouri Infantry found that it had some men from the 104th Illinois Infantry on its skirmish line, the 104th Illinois having become separated with the 88th Indiana Infantry both being from the 14th Army Corps. They reached the white house later in the day where they spent the rest of the day and night. In a report Colonel Cyrus E. Briant of the 88th Indiana Infantry Regiment, writes "In advancing the regiment up and forming on the left of the Forty-second Indiana, we received a volley from the enemy before we could form our line, but the regiment came up to the work in an orderly manner, and we soon drove the enemy from their strong position, and then formed in line on the extreme left of the Forty-second Indiana, thus making a connection with the Thirty-seventh [Thirty-first] Missouri, of General Sherman's corps, forming a complete line of battle from the river to the ledge of rocks near the top of the mountain."(4) At two o'clock General Hooker called a cease fire because the men could not make out the enemy and any firing they did was at the enemy's flash from their rifles. The Federal's were also running out of ammunition and since they were about half way up the mountain, with no road behind them, the resupplying of the ammunition would take a while. At four o'clock p.m. General Hooker reported that he was in a position that the Confederates could probably not be able to penetrate. General Hooker's forces had not only carried the east side of Lookout Mountain they also were in a position that they had a commanding view of the Confederate defenses in Chattanooga Valley. Once the mountain was carried this made Chattanooga Valley untenable.

Major A. J. Seay records in his diary his view of the day

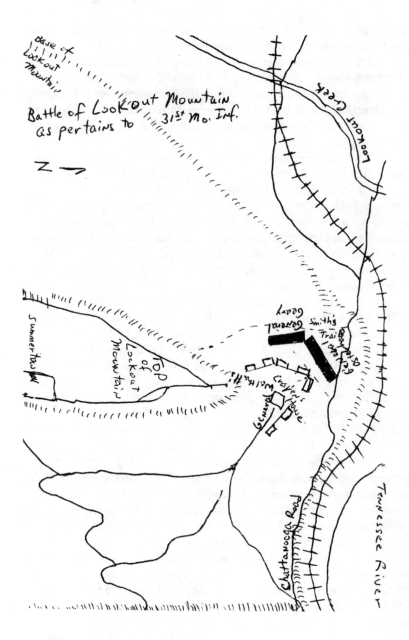

The following handwritten labels appear on the map:

- Base of Lookout Mountain
- Battle of Lookout Mountain as pertains to 31st Mo. Inf.
- N →
- Lookout Creek
- Summertown
- Top of Lookout Mountain
- General Geary
- Smiths Trail
- Craven's House
- General Walthall
- Chattanooga Road
- Tennessee River

BATTLE OF LOOKOUT MOUNTAIN, TENNESSEE

BATTLE OF LOOKOUT MOUNTAIN, TENNESSEE: National Archives, Washington D.C.

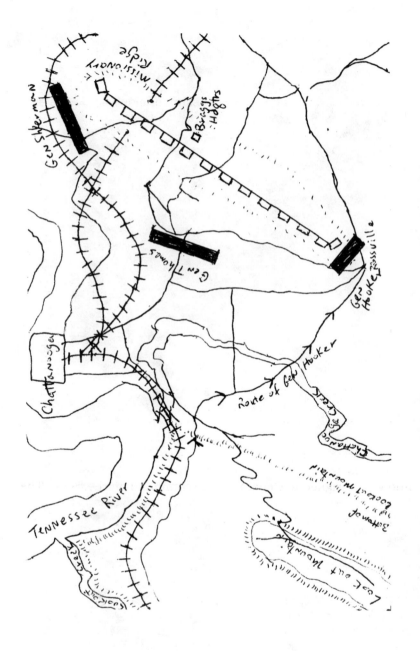

LOOKOUT MOUNTAIN TO MISSIONARY RIDGE

on Lookout Mountain.

"Tuesday, 24th, Nov. 1863.

10½ A.M. we were told that a general engagement would take place today but up to this hour all the fighting that has been done by our division on the point of Lookout Mt. which it being a cloudy misty day is obscured near the top by the passing of clouds. A grand spectacle. We have marched and counter-marched considerable and our skirmishers have driven the enemies' picket away from the creek at the foot of the Mt. and are now constructing a bridge over which we are to pass as soon as completed. All the part we play in the ensuing battle will probably be under Gen Hooker (having been cut off from our own corps by the breaking of the bridge. I do not clearly understand how things are. We will ship them. Advanced at 11 ½ A.M. across the creek and charged the enemy from point to point until we gained the front and side of the Mountain. Here the enemy kept up a brisk fire until 11 P.M. having made 2 charges without success. We have taken during the day about 2,000 prisoners with trophies or fruits of victory with us is the possession of Lookout Mt. with 3 cannon and the opening communication with Chattanooga on the side of the river. No fighting no where else in hearing. Been rainy and foggy all evening could not see a man at a 100 yards. Our loss one man slightly wounded. 4 ball holes in my blanket and one in my coat sleeve. Pass a cold hungry weary watchful night."(5)

At five-fifteen p.m. Brigadier-General Carlin and his brigade from the 14th Army Corps, reported to General Hooker and was assigned to General Geary command on the right. The Confederates had undermined the road and covered it with felled trees to keep the Federals from bringing up artillery. It was a miserable night for the men on both sides, they were wet, tired, cold from a wind that blew that night, and dreading another day of battle that was sure to start in the morning. That the night the Federal positions were easily spotted by their bivouac fires on the side of the mountain. All the federals were not idle during the night they were repairing the road earlier described. There was also firing throughout the rest of the day and well past midnight between the opposing forces. Once during the night the Confederates attacked the right trying to break through but were repulsed. The 1st Brigade, 1st Division 15th Army Corps under the command of General Woods was ordered by General Hooker to cover all the ground between Craven's House and the Chattanooga Road where it runs to a high elevation near the river. Private Henry Kuck, Company G, 31st Missouri Infantry Regiment, writes in a letter to his wife Metta,

"On the 24th of the month we had to fight the enemy first thing, on Lookout Mountain, and after a short while we drove them to the other side; the next morning the rebels had completely vacated the Lookout and our flag flew upon the peak of the Lookout. We took a goodly number of prisoners, they say 2 thousand on the first day, our regiment took almost 100 prisoners, for they ran there like a herd of sheep; we took their weapons away and ... they didn't know what they should do ... they seemed to step forward ...began to feed themselves ...they sputtered out nothing but good ... their faces lightened, they had not expected to be treated as they were."(6)

At two o'clock a.m. on the morning of November 25th the Confederates evacuated Lookout Mountain. These forces were pulled back to Missionary Ridge along with the forces in Chattanooga Valley. As they were retreating they destroyed the bridges over the Chattanooga Creek and did everything they could by placing obstructions in the roadway to slow the advance of the Federals. The Federals were bound to follow them once they realized the Confederates had made good their escape. The Confederates then took up positions on the southern end of Missionary Ridge.

The federals on Lookout Mountain were prepared to start the battle again the next morning when it was discovered that the Confederates had evacuated. The 8th Kentucky Infantry was the regiment that was given the honor of being the first unit to place their colors on top of Lookout Mountain. When the Federal troops around Chattanooga saw the Stars and Stripes flying on top of Lookout Mountain, they set up a loud cheer. This was a welcome sight after being held in seige in a defensive position in Chattanooga for so long. By clearing the Confederates from Lookout Mountain the Federals had secured the river for transportation of vital supplies into the city of Chattanooga. The Federals on Lookout Mountain had captured between two thousand and three thousand soldiers, five stands of colors, two pieces of artillery, and upward of five thousand muskets. General Hooker was ordered to leave two of his regiments on Lookout Mountain and take the rest of his force to Rossville Gap in order to assist in the attack on Missionary Ridge. He was also ordered to return Calin's Brigade to General Johnson's division in the Army of the Cumberland.

One of the 13th Illinois Infantry Regiment soldiers wrote in his diary, "Early the next morning, for some bungling reason, we marched down the mountain again and got our breadfast and then marched back over the mountain again into Chattanooga valley."(7) General Hooker was ordered to be ready to move at ten o'clock a.m. General Hooker troops, led by the 1st Division of the 15th Army Corps commanded by General Peter J. Osterhaus, started the march about one-half hour later they started for Rossville Gap as ordered. The reason the 1st Brigade, 1st Division of the 15th Army Corps marched out first was because they were the ones who had occupied the extreme left of General Hooker's force. They descended into the valley by the Chattanooga road, on which General Woods' left had spent the night. One of the men in the 13th Illinois Infantry Regiment wrote, "As we were marching down the mountain side, we could plainly see almost the whole of General Grant's army then in the valley, moving out toward the ridge, to battle; mostly infantry, but with it much artillery and some cavalry. It was a fine sight, such as few men ever see in a lifetime."(8) Upon arriving at Chattanooga Creek they saw the bridge had been destroyed by the Confederates it took them three hours to rebuild the destroyed bridge. General Hooker was severely criticized for this delay that held up the expected help for General Sherman's attack on the northern end of Missionary Ridge. Whenever the stringers for the bridge had been laid General Osterhaus ordered the 27th Missouri Infantry Regiment to cross over the stringers in order to provide security while the bridge was being finished. As soon as some of the other troops in the 1st Division, 15th Army Corps managed to get across, the 27th Missouri Infantry acting as skirmishers and soon came under fire from the Confederate artillery and infantry. This Confederate force was covering a train of wagons loading supplies at a Rossville house. While the 27th Missouri Infantry was keeping this Confederate force engaged, the rest of General Woods' brigade began attacking the ridge on the right with four regiments of Colonel Williamson's force attacked the ridge from the left. Once the Confederates realized that they were in danger of being flanked on both flanks the Confederates evacuated their position leaving much of the supplies that they were trying to guard. After a sharp skirmish the Confederates began to retreat towards Rossville Gap. General Osterhaus kept pushing the Confederates not allowing them much time to get into a strong position. After clearing the Rossville Gap, General Hooker reported that he had reached Rossville and was capturing some of the Confederates supply. From the diary of a soldier in the 13th Illinois Infantry Regiment, "Having got across the stream we, with the rest of our division, and General Hooker's forces, moved across the valley and down the ridge till opposite Rossville Gap, in and about which was stationed General Bragg's extreme left. They were soon driven out of this and we were in the gap and on the ridge."(9)

Once they reached Missionary Ridge, General Cruft moved up on top of the ridge. The ridge was very narrow so General Cruft reformed his men to accommodate this terrain feature. General Geary started on the west (left) side of Missionary Ridge with General Osterhaus on the east (right) side of the ridge. They began their attack together so rapidly that the Confederates continued to lose ground and were not having time to fortify.

At approximately four o'clock p.m. General Thomas' force began an attack on the center of Missionary Ridge. General Sherman's men were not having any success in driving the Confederates from their positions on the northern edge of Missionary Ridge. They had begun their attack against one of the most able Confederate generals in the western army. He was Major General Patrick Cleburne. He was in the dog house with General Bragg and with some of the other top brass of the Confederate hierarchy. He wrote a paper stating his belief that they should start using slaves as soldiers in the Confederate Army. His belief was that even if the Confederates did win the war the institution of slavery would no longer be acceptable by foreign countries. This paper was meant for only the eyes of those who were in the immediate area, but it made its way to the Confederate Secretary of War who became quite upset. Everything was finally smoothed over but this paper affected any promotion that he had earned because of his excellent fighting record. As previously stated he was probably one of the

204

best generals in the Army of Tennessee and his division deeply loved their general. He was a native of Ireland and had taken up residence in Arkansas, when the Civil War broke out he enlisted in the army of his adopted state. The sad thing is that later in the war the Confederate Government enlisted slaves as fighting men. They were promised if they would enlist that they would be given their freedom. This is almost exactly what General Cleburne suggested in his paper. Of course by the time the Confederate government had decided this General Cleburne was dead, he was killed at the Battle of Franklin, Tennessee in November 1864.

On the 24th of November, General Sherman's men began their attack and started to charge up what they thought was Missionary Ridge. Once they were on top of the hill they had attacked, they realized that they were on a hill that was in a range of hills before they were at Missionary Ridge. Not stopping they continued on, but the element of surprise was completely lost. The Federals dug in for the night to wait for the next day. General Grant had ordered General Sherman to attack as soon as possible. The next day, behind their entrenchment's, the Federals began their attack. The Federals greatly outnumbered the forces of General Cleburne because they attacked in piecemeal they were driven back. General Cleburne's men spent the whole afternoon repulsing the attacks of General Sherman's troops. General Bragg and General Hardee were sending reinforcements continuously from those who were in the positions in the center on Missionary Ridge. Because of the success on his part of Missionary Ridge, General Cleburne was shocked when he was ordered to abandon his position and to cover the retreat of the rest of the army. He thought that they had been winning all day.

According to the original orders, General Thomas' army, who was facing the center of Missionary Ridge, was to have a secondary role in the attack on the ridge. They were to demonstrate against the center to keep General Bragg from sending reinforcements to the troops fighting against General Sherman. There was some Confederate troops in rifle pits at the bottom of the ridge, in one position there were rifle pits about half way up and the rest of the army was on the crest of the hill. They were not on the military crest of the hill but on the real crest of the hill. The military crest is on the part of the hill which allowed the men to fire at the enemy without skylining themselves. This allowed the men to have a better field of fire and to be able to fire straight at the enemy. On the non-military crest of the hill, the men could not fire at the enemy without exposing themselves to the enemy. The cannons were also in poor position and could not fire at the enemy once they got to a point where the muzzles could not be depressed enough to hit the enemy. The men in the rifle pits were to fire one volley and then retreat up to the top. Most units fired and continued to fire until it was almost to late to withdraw. In these units there were a lot of casualties suffered primarily from being captured.

General Grant, General Thomas and General Granger were standing on Orchard Hill observing the troops charge the rifle pits at the base of the ridge. As the troops started toward the rifle pits they were fired on, they stopped and returned fire and then charged again. They over ran the rifle pits at the base of the ridge and halted as ordered. While trying to protect themselves from the Confederate fire they were receiving from those on top of Missionary Ridge. The Federals were taking casualties while trying to occupy the rifle pits at the base of Missionary Ridge. They couldn't retreat, they were being killed, so by common consent by their actions they started to attack the Confederate rifle pits midway up. They fought their way up the face of the ridge and the Confederates that had occupied the rifle pits mid way up the ridge began to withdraw to the main line. Once the Confederates started their planned withdrawal they were being closely pursued by the Federal troops.

The Confederates on the top of Missionary Ridge could not fire at the Federals for fear of hitting their own men. This was caused by the steepness of the terrain of the ridge. General Grant, while watching this charge, wanted to know who gave the order to continue the fight. Whoever gave the order was going beyond the scope of their orders. General Grant asked both General's Thomas and Granger if they had ordered such a charge, both replied in the negative. Once it was started, there was no way to stop the fighting. The men who were winded after their charge to the rifle pits stopped to rest behind some of the boulders that are on the ridge and also in some of the ravines that were present. There were some misunderstandings in the orders on where to stop, at the rifle pits or on top of the ridge, so some of the units kept on going after the Confederates. The Federals finally were able to break through the Confederates in the center of their line. Usually the center is one of the strongest parts of the line because that is where the attack is generally sent. Also reinforcements can be sent from the center to the right or left flank easier. General Bragg had weakened his center throughout the day by sending different units to aid in the defence against General Sherman. Also he had even sent some of his forces to strengthen his left against the new threat caused by the approach of General Hooker. Once the center was broken, it seemed that the whole Confederate line began to break causing a mad dash to the rear by most of the Confederates. Contrary to the original plan, it would be proven later, once all the reports were in, that the forces of General Thomas, the Army of the Cumberland, was the one who had caused the defeat of the Confederates on Missionary Ridge with both General Sherman and General Hooker and their forces providing a secondary role.

The 31st Missouri Infantry Regiment and the rest of General Hooker's army attacked from the south on Missionary Ridge driving the Confederate forces from their front. The Confederates facing General Hooker's men had been closely pursued and had not been able to build proper breast works to repel the attack. The Confederate forces were tired from their long night of marching and of fighting the day before. Once they got to the ridge General Hooker gave his orders on how to go up the ridge as earlier described. General Osterhaus' 1st Division was on the east side of the ridge with Colonel J. A. Williamson's Brigade connecting with the right of General Cruft's division which was on top of the ridge. General Woods' Brigade was to the left of Colonel Williamson's men extending down into the valley next to the ridge.

Attempting to stop General Hooker's force were five small regiments of Alabama infantry under the command of Colonel J. T. Holtzclaw. Major General John C. Breckinridge, who had been promoted to Corps Commander, had come from the center to help in defeating the Federals that were approaching from the south. Colonel Holtzclaw men consisted of the 18th, 32nd, 36th, 38th and 58th Alabama Infantry. These men faced three divisions of nearly eight thousand men. It was a hopeless situation for the Confederates, by the time they were ready to face the Federals, the center had already started to disintegrate. Some of the skirmishers of the 36th Alabama Infantry saw the 1st Division of the 15th Corps form up and move out. They fired a volley at the Federals and then withdrew to their unit.

The Federals began their attack. The Confederates were simply overwhelmed by the numbers, they put up a little bit of defense. With General Osterhaus trying to get behind them, General Cruft attacking them from the front and General Geary attacking them from the Federal left, there was only one thing to do. . . Run! And run they did but to no avail because by this time the Confederate center had started their hasty retreat and there was another Federal force coming up from behind. They were almost completely surrounded so their only alternative was to surrender. There were a little over seven hundred prisoners taken that day on the south end of Missionary Ridge. Private Henry Kuck of Company G, 31st Missouri writes home in a letter, "The morning of the 25th we heard heavy artillery on the left wing and at 10 o'clock that morning after our brigade moved forward, we were able to cross a creek and then 2 miles farther it started off on right side; here a whole brigade was taken prisoner with a general (General Breckinridge), the son of old Breckinridge."(10) A member of the 13th Illinois Infantry Regiment relates the same story.

"An incident that occurred just after we got possession of the gap, and while our regiment was resting on top of the ridge and facing the road that led down from the open country through this gap, is a striking illustration of nerve.

While resting, I, with others, saw a rebel officer ride down this road on a fine horse into our lines. As he found himself right upon our forces (not knowing we were in possession of the gap) he did not even draw a rein or give any sign but that what he intended to do was to come into our lines. He rode right on to General Osterhaus's headquarters in the gap, and asked for an ambulance to remove a wounded rebel officer up on the ridge. He then came back and rode up the hill on the North side of the gap. One of the men said, 'See, there goes that rebel again; I have a mind to put a ball into him before he gets away.' He put spurs to his horse and disappeared on the top of the ridge. He doubtless thought to get out of our lines and regain his own again, but just then he came upon the good old Fourth Iowa, some of whom were scattered along that part of the ridge as skirmishers. One of them quickly halted him and bade him dismount. It was the wise thing to do seeing he was looking down a loaded and cocked rifle in the hands of a determined soldier. So he did it. He found his way among other prisoners who were moving North. General Osterhaus rode his horse after that. Some of the boys will remember the little blooded roan. The man was Captain Breckenridge, the son of General Breckenridge."(11)

After all the Confederates were on the run, and it was beginning to get dark, the Federals went into camp on the ground that the Confederates had camped on the night before. Most of the Federals were given the orders to dig in and the men began to throw up breast works in case of a counter-attack by the Confederates. They were given an issue of food and ammunition, most of the men had depleted their supply during the day's battle. The hospital stewards, as well as concerned men, sought out friends or relatives, checking out the dead and wounded on Missionary Ridge. Major-General Philip H. Sheridan was the only leader in the Federal army who had his men to continue to pursue the enemy. This event was one of the primary reasons that General Grant took him with him when he went east. General Sheridan was an aggressive leader who had earned quite a reputation during this battle. On a tablet in Bragg Reservation on Missionary Ridge it describes the actions of Wood's Brigade, Osterhaus' Division – Blair's Corps. "At 10:30 A.M. Nov. 25 this brigade marched from Lookout Mountain for Rossvilled as the head of Hooker's Column. It was delayed about three hours at Chattanooga Creek by the burning of a bridge. About 4 P.M. assisted by Williamson's Brigade on its left with the 27th Missouri as skirmishers it forced its way through the gap which was defended by a part of Clayton's Brigade with four guns, and turned north along the eastern base of the ridge, finally charging obliquely to the summit capturing many prisoners and bivouacked here."(12) The following is taken from the first tablets placed in Chattanooga about the battles around Rossville and Missionary Ridge.

"No. 1.   HOOKER'S COLUMN.

U

MAJ.-GEN. JOSEPH HOOKER

(Nov. 25, 3 p.m.)

Osterhaus' Division, 15th Corps – Maj.-Gen. Peter J. Osterhaus.

Cruft's Division, 4th Corps – Brig.-Gen. Charles Cruft.

Geary's Division, 12th Corps – Brig.-Gen. John Geary.

This column, descending from Lookout Mountain at 10 a.m., Nov. 25, and marching in the order named, reached this point and about 3 p.m., after having been delayed about three hours by the destruction of a bridge over Chattanooga Creek. Osterhaus' Division pushed through the gap to the eastern base of Missionary Ridge driving back a small force of Stewart's Division, first turning northward in rear of the Confederate line which occupied the crest of the Ridge, and after proceeding over a mile assaulting and carrying the Ridge from the east.

Cruft's Division moved into the Gap and pushed northward with its center on the summit of the Ridge.

Geary's Division moved along the western base of the Ridge gradually nearing the crest and first Reaching it about a mile to the south of Johnson's Division of the 14th Corps.

All three Division were sharply engaged by Stewart's troops, but the latter being largely outnumbered and nearly surrounded, were obliged to withdraw with heavy loss of men and material.

[Tablet At Rossville.)

No. 4. – A

U

OSTERHAUS' DIVISION – 15TH CORPS
Brig. – Gen. Peter J. Osterhaus.
(Nov. 25, 1863, 3 p.m.)
1st Brigade – Brig. –Gen. Charles R. Woods.
2nd Brigade – Col. James A. Williamson.

This Division, being the head of Gen. Hooker's column, reached Rossville from Lookout Mountain at 3 p.m. Nov. 25th. It pushed through the Gap which was defended in front of this point by a small force of infantry and artillery and turned northward upon a road running parallel to and about 1000 yards east of Missionary Ridge. After marching nearly a mile the command was formed in echelons of brigades, the Second Brigade on the left and the First on the right. They moved northwesterly and obliquely up the slope of Missionary Ridge and carried the crest. The command bivouacked on the eastern slope of the Ridge in the vicinity of Bragg's headquarters. The enemy's line with which it had been engaged in co-operation with Cruft's and Geary's Divisions was held by the Division of Maj.-Gen. Stewart."(13)

After the joy of knowing that they wouldn't have to finish the charge up Lookout Mountain in the face of Confederate guns they then continued on to their next mission of attacking the south slope of Missionary Ridge. Major A. J. Seay wrote in his diary the following about his day.

"Wednesday, Nov. 25th.

All quiet with us this morning but the ball has opened with heavy music on our extreme left. I guess on Mission Ridge. 10 A.M. finds us moving towards Mission Ridge. We cross the creek on logs and move upon a battery that leads onto the ridge in the mouth of a hollow. They have burned the bridge and our artillery cannot cross so we move by the right flank thru valley being shelled with some loss all the way, then move by the left flank in battle line up a steep hill flanking their battery and forcing it to retreat. We then move forward on the road at right angles to a ridge and high point on which the Rebs. are in force. They are attacked furiously in front. We move across the hollow on their flank-our men running, yelling, shooting with furious impetuosity. The most restless charge I ever witnessed. Bland, Truce and Clouts in the right as skirmishers capture a gun, 7 prisoners-on we move as fast as our legs can carry us the Rebs falling in disorder before us. A Brig. Of 6 Ala regiments feeling that resistance was useless and escape hopeless laid down their arms. Then was yelling and cheering such as I never heard before. Gen. Hooker, Osterhaus, Ganger, ex-governor of Kansas, Woods and others were present with heads bare and hats waving aloft in air. We are exhausted and lay down to rest our weary limbs. I almost froze thru the night."(14)

As mentioned earlier what General Grant's assessment of the Battle of Lookout Mountain or more commonly referred to as the Battle Above the Clouds, was here is the impression of Captain W. W. Carnes of Bradenton, Florida as he wrote in an article to the Confederate Veteran.

"In refutation of the popular belief that a battle took place on Lookout Mountain 'above the clouds,' which was the inspiration of a movement in Chattanooga to stage a celebration on the top of the mountain and to christen the place as 'the Shrine of the Southland,' Capt. W. W. Carnes, of Bradenton, Fla., contributed the following, which, needless to say, put a quietus on the movement: 'No one can deny that there was battle on Lookout Mountain, but I can make affidavit that there was never a shot fired between Confederate and Federal soldiers on the top of that mountain, all of the fighting having been between Craven's farm and the river. That is shown by the location of the monuments to the troops which did the fighting and by an official iron tablet placed on top of the mountain. I will further say as Chief of Artillery of Stevenson's Division (to which position I was promoted after Chickamauga battle), I had control of every piece of artillery which fired a shot from the top of Lookout, as I will now explain.

When the pontoon bridge had been placed across the Tennessee River, one of the heaviest guns of our battalion of four batteries was driven to the point, by order of General Bragg, to ascertain whether that bridge was within our artillery range. A lieutenant with the gun detachment made the trial under my direction, and having found that none of our field pieces could throw shot to the bridge, the gun was at once returned to its battery in our lines of investment below the mountain. At a later date, Stevenson's Division was sent up on the mountain, but several miles from the point overlooking Chattanooga, to guard against any attempt of the enemy to cross over the low slope of the mountain to get to their rear of our investing force. One of the batteries under my command went with the division, and the other three were near Rossville on the lower end of Missionary Ridge, none being near the point.

When Hooker's forces were advancing, the firing on the morning of November 24 caused two guns of the battery to be sent, under one of the lieutenants, to see if they could be of any use on the side of Lookout on which the advance was moving, but it was found that the distance was far too great and the guns were brought near the point. Then, when the fighting was going on below, the lieutenant in charge fired a few shots in that direction, but the most extreme depression of the guns only threw shot or shell far over the combatants, and those artillery pieces remained there inoperative till the battery was brought down late in the afternoon under the General's orders.

I was then with the batteries on the ridge early opposite and had a good view of the whole mountain. There was no cloud near the top at any time, but there was a heavy mist from the river to the Craven farm above the road, and the ashes of fire from the guns of the fighters were plainly seen through the mist. That caused some newspaper correspondant to write of it as a battle in the clouds. The foregoing is from my personal experience.

Now, as to the force engaged, I write from the official recorded facts. The number of Hooker's troops engaged is given as 9,681 men. The first Confederate troops encountered were those of Walthall's Brigade which was surprised by an unexpected flanking force of superior numbers, and a large number of them captured. Moore's Brigade, of three Alabama regiments of infantry, and three regiments of Pettus' Brigade, were sent to re-enforce Walthall. The three brigades of Walthall, Moore, and Pettus were the Confederate troops that opposed the attack of General Hooker's army, advancing over the foot hills of Lookout Mountain toward the Craven house on the road from Lookout Valley to Chattanooga. The Confederates were forced back beyond the Craven house to junction of that road with the Summertown road, where they held their ground till all troops had come down the mountain by that road, and then all Confederate troops were withdrawn to prepare for what was evidently to be expected next day. After the mountain was abandoned by all Confederates, some of Hooker's men worked their way up to the top, without equipment they could not have carried, and raised their flag on the summit. That is the only way anyone could have reached the top of Lookout from that battle ground, and any man of common sense would know that schoolboys, armed only with stones, could have repelled any attack. Yet some persons are made to suppose that armed Confederate soldiers could be so driven from the top of Lookout, as guides there have stated to visitors. On a visit to Lookout Mountain many years ago, I saw the tablet headed by my name as in control of the guns shown there and heard the fabulous account of one of the guides. So I called on the chief member of the government commissioners with request to correct the false impression made. This he did by having another tablet placed by which visitors were informed that no fighting was done on the top of the mountain, but where the monuments were placed at and around the Craven house below.

If the tablet has not been removed, how could this movement succeed in making much of a historic shrine on top of the mountain? Or make it a great battle in which the three Confederate brigades engaged lost a total of 1,250 men killed, wounded and missing, of which number 845 of Walthall's brigade were captured in the first encounter, and some of Moore's brigade were captured in later fighting, so less than 300 were killed and wounded in this battle?

The report of General Hooker seems to have intended to give the impression that he had carried his assault to the top of the mountain, as had been suggested to him. When General John B. Gordon published his 'Reminiscences of the Civil War,' I was surprised to find that he had that impression, and I wrote to him about it. As he had served throughout in Virginia, he had no personal knowledge of events further west, and he informed me that he received from General Hooker, at Washington, his mistaken view of that battle, and he said that in any further publication he would correct the error.

Now, consider what General Grant said about that battle. He said: 'The battle of Lookout Mountain is one of the romances of the war. There was no action very worthy to be called a battle on Lookout Mountain. It is all poetry.' Those are what is said to be his words in Hon. John Russell Young's book, 'Around the World with Grant.' The official reports of the Confederates engaged and the casualties in their ranks, as hereinbefore given seem to have prompted General Grant's estimate. General Grant's estimate of Hooker's boastfulness can be learned from Grant's report of the battle of Missionary

Ridge, in which he made the following indorsement on Hooker's report: 'Attention is called to that part of the report giving the number of prisoners and small arms captured (by his commands), which is greater than the number of really captured by the whole army.'

This is the same Gen. Joseph Hooker who made a vile, slanderous charge against Tennessee soldiers in a communication to Hon. S.P. Chase, dated December 28,1863, and to be found on page 339, Series 1, Vol. XXI, part 2, 'Official Records of the Union and Confederate Armies.' In that communication he stated: 'Before the battle of Lookout, I had opened communication with Cheatham's Division, holding the summit of the mountain, and had good reason to believe that I would have succeeded in bring in all the enlisted men with some of the officers but for their untimely removal.' Cheatham's Division never occupied the summit of the mountain, and any reader of the operations of the two armies at that time will know that there was no opportunity for him to communicate with any command on the summit.

I have hereinbefore stated that my plain view of the mountain showed no cloud near the top, and in commenting on the fanciful account of a 'battle above the clouds,' a writer in the New York Tribune at that time said: 'There were no clouds to fight above; only a heavy mist which settled down and enveloped the base of the mountain.' It is incontestably true that Hooker's advance was across the foothills of the mountain to and beyond the Craven house, on the eastern bench of Lookout, in plain view from Chattanooga, and no one ever saw clouds that low down. So that 'battle above the clouds' is a war myth as false and fanciful as the Barbara Fritchie tale at Frederick, Md.

This writer, now in his 91st year, was an artillery officer in the Army of Tennessee on every occasion when the Confederates were in or around Chattanooga, and what is written herein is based on personal knowledge of facts and official reports."(15)

Another participant of the Battle of Lookout Mountain recalled his part of the battle. He was Colonel (later General) James A. Williamson, who was in command of the 2nd Brigade of General Osterhaus' 1ˢᵗ Division. In a speech to the Society of the Army of the Tennessee in 1895 he said,

"Heavy cannonading was begun at several points along our line; while clouds of white mist of smoke, or all combined, hung heavily along the side or point of the mountain. The ground in front of my line, as I remember it, was undulating and favorable for a forward movement. I soon received orders to move forward, and did so without difficulty till reaching the great masses of stone and underbrush at the base and on the side of the mountain. By this time the mist and clouds were clinging low down the side of the mountain, obscuring from view the position of the enemy, except as it was disclosed by the flashes of the musketry almost in our faces as we struggled up its rough side and dislodged the enemy from line to line, which he yielded stubbornly and only after making a gallant defense.

In this manner my command finally reached the top, or well nigh the top of that part of the mountain in its front. At that point what has been said in history and in song about fighting above the clouds became a literal and real fact. Finally the enemy gave way, and I formed my line again as well as it was possible on such ground and under such circumstances, and moved forward to a designated line without further opposition. Darkness settled down on the contending armies. It had been a day of fighting and climbing. My command and myself had had but scant food all that day and for several days before, having been marching rapidly through a country where supplies were not very abundant.

This will always stand out from the background as a memorable day and night for me and my command. All were exhausted almost beyond endurance. I was weak and sick, and hungry and cold, having neither overcoat nor blanket. Within a few months past a fellow-comrade has reminded me that he found me in this sore plight and forced me to drink from his canteen. He also remarked, with some regret in his voice, that I returned it to him empty. This may be true. I am grateful to him, and shall always be."(16)

General Cleburne and his force were given the task of covering the retreat of the Confederate army. His force was really the only unit that had not been routed during the day. There were units who had reassembled and prepared to meet the enemy but they had not abandoned their position in a military manner as had General Cleburne's force. The Confederates assembled around Chickasaw Station, where much to the anger of the men, there were plenty of supplies and food that they had been denied in their siege of the Federal forces around Chattanooga. These supplies were liberated by quite a few of these men. General Bragg ordered the army to retreat to Ringgold. The long retreat started and what supplies had not been carried off by the starving Confederates were supposed to be destroyed. Considering the large amount of supplies and the short amount of time that was allotted for this destruction, this project was not completed as thoroughly as it was hoped it would be.

On November 26th, while the Federal forces were pushing the Confederates, they fought a skirmish at Chickamauga Station and again near Graysville. General Hooker asked permission of General Thomas to follow the Confederates. The 32nd Missouri Infantry Regiment was left behind in camp to collect all arms and prisoners and to await there for further orders. General Thomas gave his permission and gave orders for General Palmer to follow General Hooker. By the time they had went into camp General Hooker was about five miles from Ringgold and General Palmer was in Graysville. General Bragg gave orders for General Cleburne to hold Ringgold Gap at all costs until the train had made it through. General Cleburne had enough of a head start to set up effective defenses. This extra time had been gained by destruction of bridges across most of the waterways that the Federals would have to cross. Every time the Federals stopped to repair or rebuild the bridges this gave the Confederates that much more time.

On November 27th, General Hooker's men started depart their camp at five thirty a. m. A soldier from the 13th Illinois Infantry Regiment wrote in his diary, "On the 27th the pursuit was continued with our division and brigade in the advance. We moved out of the camp at 6 a.m. We soon came upon the sights to be found in the wake of an army fleeing in haste. Broken-down gun-carrages, abandoned wagons, guns, ambulances, clothes, etc. For some reasons whether good or bad many rebels lingered in the woods. Some forty or fifty were picked up as prisoners.... The roads were bad and for some reason the artillery was not up – a mistake – had it been the enemy could have been driven out with much loss of life and limb."(17)   Shortly thereafter, Major General Peter Joseph Osterhaus 1st Division of the 15th Army Corps was in the lead of General Hooker's force, with General Geary's force behind him with General Cruft bringing up the rear. General Woods' 1st Brigade led the way with skirmishers thrown out with some mounted infantrymen commanded by Captain W. T. House. They brushed aside some of General Cleburne's rear guard, captured the bridge across the creek. They chased the Confederates, numbering around two hundred, into Ringgold. Captain House had with him only twelve men, once the Confederates realized how small the Federal force was, they counter-attacked driving the mounted Federals back to the bridge only to see the 17th Missouri Infantry and the 29th Missouri Infantry regiments, fighting as a tactical battalion, moving forward to the bridge forcing the Confederates back into town. The Federal forces entered Ringgold at approximately eight o'clock that morning. There is a gorge to the east of Ringgold and the Federals were approaching from the west. The Confederate rear guard put up some resistance in the town itself before they finally made a dash to Taylor's Ridge just on the outside of Ringgold Gap. "This is a break in Taylor's Ridge of sufficient width for the river to flow and on its north bank room for an ordinary road and a railroad, when the ridge rises with abruptness on both sides 400 or 500 feet, and from thence running nearly north and south, continues unbroken for many miles. Covering the entrance to it is a small patch of young trees and undergrowth."(18)   Once inside the town of Ringgold,Georgia the Federals reassembled and started toward Ringgold Gap. General Woods was orderd to deploy the following regiments from his brigade to the line that was just evacuated by the skirmishers who had led the way across the bridge, they were the 13th Illinois Infantry, 3rd Missouri, 12th Missouri and 31st Missouri Infantry Regiments. General Woods, of the 1st Brigade, 1st Division 15th Army Corps, sent out skirmishers that were made up of the 17th and 31st Missouri Infantry Regiments. They moved forward across the open fields to a stand of timber at the foot of a slope of Taylor's Ridge. Once these skirmishers were in range they come under a heavy fire from Colonel Granbury's men from Texas. A soldier in the 13th Illinois Infantry Regiment wrote in his diary the following.

218

"As our regiment came up, we passed to the right of the ford up the stream to the covered bridge over it, and through the town by flank. Just ahead of us were the Seventeenth, Twenty-ninth and Thirty-first Missouri Regiment that had been skirmishing up to the foot of Taylor's Ridge, where the enemy were strongly posted. The rebels pressed upon these and drove them back in some confusion. We then passed up near the depot and filed to the right into line squarely across the gap, in an open space. The boys were chipper as could be, and hardly expecting so much danger so near at hand. We had scarcely got faced to the front, when from a clump of young trees, a masked battery of two pieces belched forth grape and canister. This passed through the right wing of our regiment."(19)

The Federals immediately began to fall back. General Woods' immediately sent in the 29th Missouri Infantry to bolster the 17th and 31st Missouri Regiments. The 29th Missouri tried to flank the Texans but this threat was countered and all the Missourians began to retreat and running to the rear. During their retreat they ended up going through the rest of the brigade.

General Woods then sent the 3rd and 12th Missouri to renew the attack. They went right over the same ground that the three other regiments had just retreated over, climbing over the dead and wounded. The 13th Illinois was sent and formed to the right of the two Missouri regiments which led them to charge toward a wooded area. The 76th Ohio was sent to the left to attack up the side of White Oak Mountain in hopes of turning the right flank of the Confederates. General Cleburne saw these movements developing and was ready for them by reinforcing the areas that were being attacked. The 13th Illinois received a terrible fire from Lieutenant Richard W. Goldthwaite's artillery that opened terrible holes in the ranks of the men in the regiment. The Confederate artillery was supported by the 5th and 13th Arkansas (Consolidated) which opened fire at approximately the same time as the artillery. The men in the 13th Illinois almost immediately hit the dirt to escape this terrible fire directed at them. They tried later to charge the Confederates but the fire that they were facing was to fierce. They retreated to a farm house and used this house and outlying buildings to cover them as they tried to fire back.

They spent the rest of the battle firing from this position while their flag dangled from a tree about fifty yards from the Confederate lines. Their flag bearer had left it there, though he was near by, after advancing and realizing that he was alone had put it in the tree and fell to the ground. It spent the rest of the battle there. It was far enough away from the Confederate lines that to venture out and get it was to invite fire from the watching Federals.

Meanwhile, the 3rd and 12th Missouri Regiments had run into the same defensive line and rifle fire that had defeated the Missouri regiments before them, Colonel Granbury's Texans was the Confederate force that the Missourians had run into. The 3rd Missouri and the 12th Missouri Infantry Regiments managed to fall back to their brigade positions. The 76th Ohio, followed closely by the 4th Iowa, was making its way up the side of the mountain when they were spotted. General Cleburne sent orders for General Lucius Polk and General Mark Lowrey to bring their brigades up to meet this new threat to the right flank of the Confederates. They beat the Federals to the top of the mountain spur and drove them back down the mountainside which they had just climbed. The Confederates tried to follow up their success by charging after the Federals but soon ran into the 3rd Missouri, 12th Missouri and 31st Missouri Infantry Regiments who fired volleys direct into the charging Confederates forcing them to fall back to their own positions. Colonel Williamson sent the rest of his brigade up the mountainside to try and drive the Confederates off the mountain. The Confederates were bringing up reinforcements faster than the Federals could. The rest of Colonel Williamson fared no better than the 76th Ohio and 4th Ohio. Colonel Williamson related his view of this fight in a speech to the Society of the Army of the Tennessee.

"We caught up with the rear of Bragg's army at Ringgold in the forenoon of November 27th. Here I received orders to form a line of battle and move forward on the left side of the road where it passes through Taylor's ridge. I moved my command as directed, and soon came to the base of the ridge or hill, my right resting not far from the road. The enemy was strongly posted along the crest of the hill; its side being comparatively smooth, afforded but little shelter for an attacking force. I pushed my command forward as fast as it was possible to do in the face of the deadly fire to which we were subjected. My tried, brave veteran officers and soldiers fell about me like leaves in the autumn, and yet all this for some cause is lost to history. Many valuable lives were lost – and for what? Can any one reply? It would be untrue for me to state that we carried the crest of the ridge. It is true we passed over the crest, but not till after the enemy had inflicted heavy losses on us and withdrawn comparatively at his leisure. My command pursued the retreating enemy for a short distance, and drove off a force which was endeavoring to burn the bridge beyond the gap, after which I received orders to give up the pursuit and return. I was never in a harder or more fatal engagement than this, considering the numbers engaged, and yet I think it was reported as a slight skirmish, or something of the sort."[20]

General Hooker was not about to give up his attack. Once General Geary's lead brigade came up General Hooker told him to send it up the mountain and go to the left of Colonel Williamson's force. At about nine o'clock a.m., Colonel William Creighton's brigade went up the mountain and were met by the troops in General Polk's and General Lowrey's brigades. They didn't stay long, in fact they retreated so rapidly down the side of the mountain, that their descent almost caused panic in Colonel Williamson's men who had watched their ascent. General Hooker then ordered more men up the mountain to continue the assault. Around noon the Federal artillery arrived as did General Davis' division. General Cleburne saw all of these reinforcements coming with the knowledge that almost all of his men had been put into line without any replacements to relieve them. The Federals did not continue the assault and the battle became a sharpshooters battle. It was also around noon that General Hardee sent the welcome news to General Cleburne that the supply trains were now considered safe enough that he could retire from his position and continue to guard the rear of the rest of the army. General Cleburne then retreated to Taylor's Gap and took up defensive positions ready to repeat Ringgold Gap again if necessary. General Grant had arrived in Ringgold towards the end of the battle. He then ordered General Hooker to cease action and to remain at Ringgold during November 29th and 30th. General Hooker's force were to look for an opportunity to go to Dalton, Georgia if he could do so without fighting a battle, if not he was to return to Chattanooga. General Hooker had lost five hundred and nine men, two hundred and five from General Geary's 12th Army Corps and three hundred and four from General Osterhaus' 15th Army Corps. They both suffered sixty-five killed, four hundred and twenty-four wounded and twenty missing. General Cleburne had lost two hundred and twenty-one men, with only twenty men killed. This was probably one of the better delaying actions of the war. The battle of Ringgold Gap was the last action that occurred in the battles around Chattanooga.

From Chattanooga, Tennessee on November 30, 1863, Private Henry Kuck wrote in a letter to his wife what had been happening in his life, including the recent battle at Ringgold, Georgia. "On the morning of the 26th I went back on a ship ... had run, and I had a cold ... I'm on the wet ground, but you're thinking 'he's in the South', but I assure you that it's just as cold in the winter here as in Missouri; it froze last night and the night before and yesterday, so that after my watch I seemed to be nothing more that a frosted ice-clump. On the 27th our brigade had a hard battle, we pushed 20 miles ahead .... There our brigade lost many men, 1 man was shot dead, the next 2 were wounded; among the wounded is Wilh. Schwarze, but I have only a small wound on my right arm, yesterday our regt. was to return to camp, but we're not there yet. Concerning myself, I have a very bad cold, I think that it will be gone soon, for the time being I've heard in camp that we took a total of 90 cannons and 10 thousand prisoners from the Rebels. If we had not gone in close to Chattanooga, then we would have had to leave this place again; I do think we'll be able to defeat the Rebels again so much that we won't need these food supplies for them, for Bragg will then let his army go. ... We'll hope for the best. Your, Henry."(21)

The total loss for the Federals in the battles of Chattanooga, with a total of fifty-six thousand and three hundred and fifty-nine men engaged, were seven hundred and fifty-three killed, four thousand and seven hundred and twenty-two wounded, three hundred and forty-nine missing. This gave the Federals a total casualty amount of five thousand, five hundred and twenty-four. The 1st Brigade, 1st Division, 15th Corps suffered thirty-three killed, two hundred and three wounded, and forty-one missing which totaled two hundred and seventy-seven. One of the officers who was wounded that will later become the 31st Missouri Infantry Regiment's brigade commander is Colonel Hugo Wangelin of the 12th Missouri Infantry who was wounded in the right arm which was later amputated. The 31st Missouri Infantry Regiment suffered the following total of casualties in the battles of Lookout Mountain, Missionary Ridge, Ringgold Gap and Taylors Ridge, Georgia. They lost one enlisted man killed, two officers and nineteen enlisted men wounded and six enlisted men listed as missing in action for a total of twenty-eight casualties. Private Timothy Baird was wounded in the leg at Lookout Mountain on November 24, 1863. Some of the casualties listed were referred to as being wounded at Pigeon Mountain, but Pigeon Mountain has the same date as Ringgold Gap, they are Captain Francis Doherty of Company K who died of wounds received at Ringgold, Georgia dying on December 10, 1863. Captain William H. Judd of Company A, was wounded at Ringgold, Georgia on November 27, 1863. 1st Lieutenant Jonathon Burrows of Company I was wounded at Ringgold, Georgia on November 27, 1863. Corporal Cyprian Portelle of Company B was killed November 27, 1863 the battle at Ringgold, Georgia. Private Marshall V. Robertson of Company G died of wounds November 27, 1863 he received at Ringgold, Georgia. Private Henry Meyer was wounded at Ringgold and later discharged because of wounds on July 22, 1864. Private Samuel Washburne was wounded at Ringgold and he was also discharged because of wounds on November 19, 1864. Private Patrick Phillips of Company E from Moselle, was listed as missing in action on November 27, 1863 at Ringgold Gap. Corporal William Hamilton of Company E from Hillsboro, was also listed as missing in action on November 27, 1863 at Ringgold Gap. They both died at Andersonville Prison and or buried there. Private Phillips died on April 26, 1864 and Corporal Williams died September 17, 1864. Private Hiram L. Ramsey of Company K, according to records in Missouri State Archives in Jefferson City, Missouri was captured at Ringgold Gap and died while a prisoner at Andersonville Prison in April 1864. The following or also listed as missing in action after the battle at Ringgold, Georgia. Sergeant Robert G. Kinny of Company A, Private Boone Bryan of Company A (he was later listed as a paroled prisoner), Private John N. Williams of Company A (listed as dying while a prisoner, date unknown), Private John McKee of Company G, Private Ellis Schindler of Company I (listed as dying while a prisoner, date unknown). In an article on

Tuesday Morning, December 7, 1863 the Daily Missouri Democrat published a list of all the casualties of Missouri, Illinois, Iowa and Ohio Regiments in the 15th Army Corps, at late battles near Chattanooga.

"31st Missouri Volunteers

Killed.

Corp Cyprian Portal, B.

Total killed, 1.

Severely Wounded.

Corp. P. R. Haverstick, A	Sergt. Henry Finke, G
Henry Meyer, A	Pat Sullivan, K
Capt. Will. H. Judd, C	Sergt James Lanahan, K
Capt. Francis Doherty, K	Marshall Robinson, D, died
Henry Boedsker, A	

Total severly wounded, 9

Slightly Wounded.

Berry H. Landham, A	Wm. Schwarze, G
Sergt T. P. Baird, H	Fred Klingman, G
Sergt. Horace Hood, A	Wm. Hill, K
Sergt. Wm. F. Mitchel, C	Jos Kellerhand, I
John Druese, G.	Francis Schraub, I
Henry Meyers, G	Allice Schindler, I

Total slightly wounded, 12

Missing

Sergt. Robt. C. Kiney, A.	Corp. Wm. Hamilton, A
Boone Bryan, A	John N. Williams, A
H. F. Ramsey, K	Corp. Jno. E. McKee, I

Total missing, 6.

Recapitulation. – Killed , 1; severely wounded, 9; slightly wounded, 12; missing 6, total, 28"(22)

The Confederates had a total amount of forty-six thousand, and one hundred and sixty-five men engaged in these battles. They suffered three hundred and sixty-one killed, two thousand one hundred one hundred and sixty wounded, four thousand one hundred and forty-six missing. This does not include General Reynold's brigade or the cavalry for which there were no returns. After this series of battles General Braxton Bragg offered to President Davis his resignation. It was accepted and this left the Army of Tennessee without their commander, who the men no longer had faith in, including those in the ranks. General Bragg again blamed those immediately under him, even the privates for running from Missionary Ridge. Never is there an instance where General Bragg admitted that he was at fault. By losing Chattanooga they lost one of the most direct rail routes from the west to the east. Tennessee and Kentucky was effectively lost to the Confederacy and the road to Atlanta was now open for the Federals to take. The 1st Brigade, 1st Division of the 15th Army Corps captured one thousand, nine hundred and ninety-nine Confederates with the 31st Missouri Infantry being credited with capturing seventy-six of them.

The following is the official report of the 1st Brigade, 1st Division, 15th Army Corps under the command of Brigadier-General Charles R. Woods.

"November 24-27, 1863,
The Chattanooga & Ringgold Campaign.   No. 192
Report of Brig.-Gen. Charles R. Woods,
U.S. Army, commanding First Brigade.
HDQRS. FIRST BRIG., FIRST DIV. 15TH ARMY CORPS,
Ringgold, Ga., November 28,1863.

CAPTAIN: I have the honor to report that, on the morning of the 24th instant, this brigade, consisting of the Twelfth Missouri Volunteers, Col. Hugo Wangelin commanding; Thirteenth Illinois Volunteers, Lieut. Col. Theodore Meumann commanding, Seventy-sixth Ohio Volunteers, Maj. Williard Warner commanding, Twenty-seventh Missouri Volunteers, Col. Thomas Curly commanding, Thirty-second Missouri Volunteers, Lieut. Col. H. C. Warmouth commanding. Twenty-ninth Missouri Volunteers, Col. James Peckham commanding (until about 3 p.m., when being wounded, he was succeeded by Maj. P. H. Murphy), Seventeenth Missouri Volunteers, Lieut. Col. John F. Cramer commanding; Thirty-first Missouri Volunteers, Lieut.Col. Samuel P. Simpson commanding, was ordered to cross Lookout Creek, and, in connection with the other brigade of this division and troops of the Twelfth and Fourteenth Army Corps, to assault Lookout Mountain. It was necessary for this purpose to throw a bridge across the creek. This was done by the pioneers of the First Division, Fifteenth Army Corps, who were protected while at the work by the Third Missouri Volunteers. The bridge was soon finished, and the troops moved across the creek by the right flank up the hill, covered by the Third Missouri Volunteers as skirmishers. As soon as the brigade was across the creek it faced by the left flank and Moved along the slope of the mountain in line of battle, the left resting on the Chattanooga road. Owing to the broken and rough nature of the ground near the Chattanooga road, I took two regiments, the Twelfth Missouri and Seventy-sixth Ohio, and moved by the left flank up the road to a point near where the railroad debouches into the Chattanooga Valley, where I formed them in line of battle. I afterward placed other regiments on the same line, which I was directed by Major-General Hooker to hold.

On the right of my line the fighting was stubborn. The Twenty-seventh Missouri was ordered forward to relieve some regiment of General Whitakers brigade reported to be out of ammunition, and took possession of rifle-pits from which the enemy had been driven. The Third Missouri, the Twenty-ninth Missouri were placed on the same line. The latter two regiments were in the extreme front, and took possession of some rifle-pits from which they drove the enemy, taking a few prisoners. This disposition placed the brigade in two lines *en echelon,* the right thrown forward, and this was the situation during the night.

I cannot speak too highly of the conduct of the officers and men under my command during the engagement. They moved forward to the attack with an energy that overcame all opposition, and they held every inch of ground gained with a tenacity which foiled the enemy in every attempt to dislodge them.

On the morning of the 25th, this brigade led the advance of Major-General Hooker's column, taking the road to Rossville. When near that place we found the gap through Missionary Ridge strongly occupied by the enemy with infantry and artillery.

The Twenty-seventh Missouri formed the advance guard. The skirmishers attacked with vigor and occupied the attention of the enemy, while the remainder of the brigade moved off to the right, under fire of the enemy's artillery, and advanced up, and without further opposition gained the summit of the ridge, along which it moved to the gap, but upon arriving there found that the enemy had fallen back, and that it had been followed by the Twenty-seventh Missouri through the gap.

The brigade then moved forward, taking a road about 1,000 yards in rear of Missionary Ridge and running nearly parallel to it. Having gone about a mile to some fields, we discovered the enemy in force on Missionary Ridge moving toward the gap through which we had passed. They soon met the head of General Cruft's division, which engaged them sharply, and was driving them back. They endeavored to escape in the direction in which my brigade was stationed. I was ordered by General P. J. Osterhaus to move up the hill on their flank, which was done in the most gallant style, completely surprising the enemy, killing and wounding a number and capturing the remainder.

During this charge the Thirteenth Illinois captured the battle flag of the Eighteenth Alabama Regiment, and the battalion of my brigade, composed of the Thirty-second and Twenty-ninth Missouri Volunteer, captured one piece of artillery, with horses and cannoneers. The number of small arms captured will probably be over 1,000. During this day every officer and man did his duty.

On the 26th, my brigade had the rear of Major-General Hooker's column. One regiment, the Thirty-second Missouri, was left on Missionary Ridge to collect and turn over to the ordance officer the small-arms captured. The Twenty-seventh Missouri was left at the crossing of the Chickamauga to protect the bridge. Nothing of note occurred during this day's march. On the 27th, this brigade had the advance of Major-General Hooker's column and moved on Ringgold, Ga. We found the enemy strongly posted in a gap on the mountain and occupying the slopes and summits on either side in our front. As soon as the proper dispositions could be made, I sent forward the Seventeenth and Thirty-first Missouri as skirmishers. They moved forward across the open fields to the timber at the foot of the slope of the mountains, but were soon severely pressed by the enemy's skirmishers. I sent immediately forward the Twenty-ninth Missouri to support them, but the whole line of skirmishers and support was driven back upon the main line in confusion, and were not again entirely rallied until after the enemy retired. Shortly after forming the line, I pressed forward the Thirteenth Illinois on the extreme right to some houses within 100 yards of the enemy's artillery. Before this the Seventy-sixth Ohio was sent up the slope of the mountain well on the left. The Twelfth and Third Missouri occupied the center. The fighting on the extreme right was severe, the Thirteenth Illinois firing 100 rounds of cartridges per man, besides taking all the ammunition from their killed and wounded in order to hold their position. The Twelfth Missouri, although exposed to a severe fire, held its position with undaunted courage. The Seventy-sixth Ohio, after gaining the crest of the hill, held it against superior numbers, who poured a withering fire from the front and both flanks. The regiment held the crest until 8 color bearers were either killed or wounded, when it fell back, fighting and in good order, to a sheltered position under the crest of the hill, where it remained, holding the enemy in check, until the fighting was over.

I inclose the report of Col. J. A. Williamson, commanding the Second Brigade, of First Division, Fifteenth Army Corps, in reference to the action of the Seventy-sixth Ohio, he being near with a part of his command, also the report of Maj. Williard Warner, commanding the Seventy-sixth Ohio Volunteers, concerning the part taken in this action by that regiment.

I am glad to be able to speak most approvingly of the conduct of the officers generally of my command during the operations of the 24th, 25th, and 27th of November. They evinced the greatest alacrity in carrying out all orders, frequently in circumstances of great exposure and danger.

The mention of the names of some is proper, and I designate the following as conspicuous in bravery, viz: Col. Hugo Wangelin, wounded in arm at Ringgold (since amputated); Lieut. Col. J. Kaercher, Maj. Frederick T. Ledergerber, wounded at Ringgold – all of the Twelfth Missouri; Lieut. Col. F. W. Partridge, commanding Thirteenth Illinois Volunteers, wounded at Ringgold; Maj. Willard Warner, commanding Seventy-sixth Ohio Volunteers, Lieut. Col. Theodore Meumann, Third Missouri

Volunteers, Maj. James F. How, Twenty-seventh Missouri Volunteers, with 10 men, attacked and took prisoners 65 armed rebels.

I have to regret the loss of Maj. D.R. Bushnell, Thirteenth Illinois Volunteers; Capt. J.A. Ledergeber and Actg. Adjt. F. Kessler, both of Twelfth Missouri Volunteers, Capt. Ira P. French and First Lieut. John B. Miller, Seventy-sixth Ohio, who fell gallantly fighting at Ringgold for the country to which they gave their services and their lives; also First Lieut. S. B. Wall and Second Lieut. John A. Lemert, Seventy-sixth Ohio Volunteers, who were mortally wounded at Ringgold, and are since dead. Capt. H.A. Kircher, Twelfth Missouri, wounded at Ringgold and Actg. Adjt. John Wellmeyer, Twenty-seventh Missouri, wounded at Lookout Mountain, received their wounds while gallantly doing their duty.

To the members of my staff—Capt. C.H. Kibler, assistant adjutant-general, Lieut. Fred. H. Wilson, aide de camp, and Lieut. W. E. Ware, acting assistant inspector-general—my warmest thanks are due for the gallant and fearless manner in which all orders were executed.

The number of killed, wounded, and missing during the actions of the three days is 277, as will be seen by the inclosed list.

The number of prisoners reported captured by the different regiments of this brigade is 57 officers and 1,942 men, as appears by the inclosed lists.

I have the honor, captain, to be your obedient servant,

CHAS. R. WOODS,
Brigadier-General, Commanding.

Capt. W. A. GORDON,

A. G., First Division, Fifteenth Army Corps."(23)

Notice that General Woods did not mention the wounded officers of the 31st Missouri Infantry Regiment or the 17th Missouri Infantry Regiment in his report. It could have been he felt these two regiments which ran at Ringgold Gap did not deserve mention.

From the diary of a soldier in the 13th Illinois Infantry, "Following the battle of Ringgold, the days and the nights were very cold, so much so that many of the men suffered and could not sleep, as we had no shelter. The badly wounded were either put on flat-cars and the cars pushed by hand to Chattanooga, or carried on stretchers. Captain Blanchard was carried by his men some sixteen miles to a hospital near Chattanooga. We laid in camp near Ringgold for three days after the battle."(24) On November 30, 1863, General Hooker received orders from General Grant to move after dark as soon as the moon rises. General Hooker's force was to head back to Chattanooga and resume the positions that they held prior to the attack on Lookout Mountain. He was also instructed to leave General Osterhaus and his 1st Division somewhere between Rossville and Chattanooga. General Osterhaus was to report to General Grant for further orders.

A member of the 13th Illinois Infantry Regiment wrote in his diary, "On *November 30th* General Hooker ordered that his command move on the day following, in following order: General Cruft's Division was to move at 2 a.m. and return to its camp on the road to Bridgeport. General Geary's to move at 2:30 a.m. returning to his camp in Lookout Valley. General Osterhaus' Division to follow General Geary's and encamp in Chattanooga Valley, between Rossville and Chattanooga, and report to General Grant for instructions. The baggage and wagons to start as soon as the moon was up. General Geary was to destroy all the mills, railroad depots, tanneries and two bridges across the Chickamauga Creek before leaving."(25)

On December 1st, the 1st Division, under General Osterhaus, were on their way back to Chattanooga going into camp in Chattanooga Valley. A member of the 13th Illinois Infantry Regiment wrote, "*December 1st*, at 4 p.m., we were moving back over the road we had come, and in the evening after marching fourteen miles, camped between Missionary Ridge and Lookout Mountain."(26) While the 1st Division, 15th Army Corps were actively engaged with the Confederates the rest of the 15th Army Corps were not idle. General Sherman and the rest of the 15th Corps were on their way to relieve General Burnsides at Knoxville, Tennessee. General Sherman's men marched to the relief of General Burnsides forces, believing that they were almost out of food and that if not relieved soon they would be forced to surrender. Once they finally arrived in Knoxville, they found that General Longstreet had made his way towards Virginia to rejoin General Lee, and that there was no danger of General Burnside's men being starved into surrender. Most of the citizens in this section of Tennessee were loyal to the Union and once the Confederates had left they brought supplies to the Federal troops who were amply fed. In disgust General Sherman returned to Chattanooga and went into winter quarters in northern Alabama.

In the 1863 "Report of the Adjutant General of Missouri," he described the account of the 31st Missouri Infantry during the battles around Chattanooga.

"On the second day of November, it crossed the Tennessee river, and took up the line of that long and hurried march, via Pulaski, Tennessee, to Chattanooga, arriving at Lookout Mountain on the evening of the 23d of November. It bore a part in the splendid achievements of Osterhaus' Division, under Major General Hooker, in scaling the mountain side, and in capturing the mountain with the guns of the enemy upon it. On the 25th, it was in the charge on Missionary Ridge, and on the 27th, at Ringgold, was one of the advance Regiments which were forced to fall back for a time before a superior force of the enemy; in these engagements the loss of this Regiment was 30 killed, wounded and missing. Among the wounded was Captain Francis Doherty, commanding Company K, who subsequently died; he was a brave man, and universally esteemed by his brother officers. On the 25th and 27th, Lieutenant Colonel Simpson commanded the Regiment, Colonel Fletcher being, from exhaustion in the ascent of Lookout Mountain and physical weakness, unable to Longer lead the Regiment."(27)

The 31st Missouri Regiment again suffered a loss of man power that probably could not be blamed on direct battlefield causes. Company A experienced no casualties except for Private John M. Williams who was missing in action and it was later found out that he had died. Company B suffered the following losses during this campaign Private Paul Dumphrey of Washington County was discharged on November 20, 1863 because of disability; Corporal Marion Evans of Washington County died on November 21, 1863 at Memphis Tennessee; Private Cyprian Portell of Washington County died on November 27, 1863 at Ringgold Georgia. In Company C, Corporal William S. Cole of Hopewell died from disease at Patterson, Missouri on December 20, 1863; Private Aldophos Whaley of Hopewell died on December 14, 1863 in Louisville, Kentucky. Company D's Private Hiram Stags died on November 28, 1863.

In Company E they lost to their rolls; Private Patrick Phillip was listed as missing in action on Lookout Mountain and later listed as dead; Private Lewis J. Collins of Moselle was discharged on November 29, 1863 at Saint Louis, Missouri; Private Charles B. Musgraves of Stanton died in Cairo, Illinois in December 1863. Company F suffered no losses at this time. Company G's Private Philip Eckert of Saint Louis was transferred to Invalid Corps on December 12, 1863; Sergeant Jacob Roesner of Washinton was transferred to the Invalid Corps on November 28, 1863. Private Timothy Baird was listed as missing in action on Lookout Mountain and later listed as dead and he was the only loss for Company H. In Company I, Private Benjamin Clemens of Montgomery was transferred to Veteran Reserve Corps in November 1863. Company K's losses were Captain Francis Dougherty died on December 9, 1863 and is buried at the Chattanooga National Cemetery; Corporal William D. Forrester of Caledonia who died on December 31, 1863; Private Jacob F. Richardson of Potosi was discharged for disability on December 24, 1863; Private Thomas L. Williams of Ironton died on December 10, 1863 at Paducah, Kentucky; Private Lewis Ricter of Desoto was transferred to the Invalid Corps on December 12, 1863.

CHAPTER NINE:
WINTER CAMP

The Federal army went into winter camp in and around Chattanooga. The Army of the Ohio went into camp in eastern Tennessee around Knoxville and the Army of the Cumberland went into camp around Chattanooga. Most of the Army of the Tennessee returned to Mississippi where they went into camp. The 15th Army Corps spent the winter in northern Alabama. Because of the expiration of their enlistment, the Federal army, in the western theatre, was in danger of losing nearly one half of their veteran units. This was a serious problem that could effect the efficiency of the future of the army. The regiments that had enlisted in the early part of the war had spent almost three years in the war and their enlistment's were almost up or would expire before the campaign against Atlanta could be completed. Without these seasoned, battle wise veterans, there were many that believed that the war could not be successfully completed in the next year if at all. The government came up with an idea that was hoped to make the men in these units re-enlist. If any regiment had at least three-fourths of its members, who were eligible, to re-enlist they could keep their numerical designation and organizational status. This was an important incentive because a soldier's main identification was his regiment. His close friends were in his regiment, they had been family for three years, experienced many trials together and those who had fell in the defense of their country would always be remembered by those who lived in the regiment. The officers really pushed hard for their men to re-enlist as a unit, mainly because without their men they had nobody to command. If their unit did not meet this requirement they would lose their rank and position. There were meetings that almost equaled the intensity as a good old-fashioned brush arbor meeting. If the number was close to the required three-fourths there was a great amount of pressure put on the holdouts, there ws so much pressure put on them that many finally gave in and re-enlisted. Once a unit had re-enlisted they were given privileges that were special just for them. They were given the designation of a volunteer veteran and they were authorized to wear a veteran chevron on their sleeve. They could then be designated as a veteran regiment on their flag and correspondence. Another two reasons, which were probably the most decisive, were that the soldiers received a four hundred dollar bounty, plus whatever their home state or county might chip in, and a thirty-day pass. Since some of these men had not seen loved ones and home for three or more years this was probably one of the major reasons that a lot of the men re-enlisted.

The western army had more men to re-enlist than did the Army of the Potomac the army fighting the war in the east near Washington D.C. and in Virginia . The men in the west had experienced a long line of victories where ever they went, they had complete faith in General Grant, General Sherman and other generals. They were looking forward to a hasty end of the war while the men in the east had spent the last three years fighting in the same area and had suffered more defeats than victories. The Army of the Potomac had one general after another in command of them with the average soldier not having much faith in whoever was in charge at the time. Major General George Meade was in command of the Army of the Potomac at this time and had been in command just prior to the Battle of Gettysburg. The 31st Missouri Infantry Regiment and its sister units, who were mustered in as a regiment in September 1862, did not meet the requirements to be classified as a veteran unit.

The 1st Division of the 15th Army Corps, was still attached to General Hooker as of December 1, 1863. In the following order General Grant finally returned the 1st Division back to the command of General Sherman.

"SPECIAL FIELD ORDERS,   Number 22.
HDQRS. MIL. DIV. OF THE MISS.,
Chattanooga, Tennessee, December 2, 1863

  2.   Brigadier General P. J. Osterhaus, commanding First Division, Fifteenth Army Corps, Army of the Tennessee, will move with his command at an early hour on the morning of December 3, and proceed to Bridgeport, Ala., at which place he will await further orders.

By order of Major General U. S. Grant:
GEORGE K. LEET,

Assistant Adjutant-General."(1)

The 31st Missouri Infantry Regiment arrived at Bridgeport, Alabama on December 5, 1863. In a letter to his wife, Private Henry Kuck of Company G wrote the following.

"Bridgeport
Dec. 10, 1863

Dear Metta,

I got your letter from Nov. 1 and see from it that you are very worried about the battle you assumed we would have under Rosecrans: dear Metta, don't worry at all about it, this battle is already over, the Rebels were so beaten down that for the present they won't even think about attacking us. We arrived at Chattanooga on the 23rd, which I already mentioned in the last letter. Probably you've already read everything that happened here in the paper. I already wrote you in my last letter that Wilh. Schwarze was wounded; he's still in the hospital at Chattanooga and and will probably be here soon; that is, the whole hospital with all the wounded will be brought here. We're, that is the Army Corps Camp, about 25 miles from Chattanooga. I don't know how long we'll be here.

But we're all very happy, after having to withstand so much hard-ship, that we can finally rest. This area doesn't please me at all; the mountains are so high and the roads so bad that we can move forward only with very bad feet. The stock, that means the donkeys, drop and die from exhaustion, and as we came back I too was pulling my last bread and crackers from my bag. Here at Bridgeport it's somewhat better than at Chattanooga and here, 25 miles on the other side, we can receive our provisions by train, which we couldn't at Chattanooga; at Chattanooga they receive their provisions, or anything else they need, by steamboat from Nashville, because it's only 2 or 3 hours away, additionally the railroad brings it here and then it's loaded onto wagons, which move ahead only very slowly because of the bad roads. The railroad bridge over the Tennessee River and other big bridges over the Hollows (valleys), and then it will be easier to ship necessary items over there. Dear Metta, you write as if you felt completely hopeless; have our good neighbors deserted you? I don't think so; surely you are best off there, sweet child, but .... We will keep hoping my guardian angel will protect me and keep me healthy. I will come back to you, for my time is almost half over, and if God wills I will come back happily and hug you close to my heart; these good hopes should encourage you and make you strong, for if you lose your hope and faith, you lose your courage and you're like a ship without rudder or anchor and drift into desolateness. Take courage as long as we're alive and healthy, after the hard times, for after the rain comes the sunshine again. My little Elsie, I hope when this letter arrives that you'll already be getting better and that you will soon be well. That is my dearest wish. Sweet farewell, my dearest wife and children, and I wish you all a very merry Christmas and New Year's celebration, all the friends and neighbors too. Be happy, and then I can be happy too.

Your Henry

P. S. Dearest Metta, don't give little Elsie so much medicine. I worry that it will be bad for her. The main thing is: to take good care of her with (proper) food and drink and keep her quite warm and also give her only gruel and milk to eat, etc. She is so weak and still too young to tolerate medicine. You should understand that as you are looking after her."(2)

A diary entry of a 13th Illionis Infantry Regiment soldier, "The 4th we made our way to Whiteside station, and on the evening of the 5th, we camped near Bridgeport, having crossed the Tennessee again. We remained in camp at this place trying to keep warm and only doing those things essential to camp welfare, until December 21st, when we were on the move again."(3)

The roads were still in a terrible mess. A member of the 13th Illinois Infantry Regiment describes the conditions on the roads when they approached a small stream and how they were fixed. He describes this event after they started their first day of march which occurred on December 21, 1863.

"Camped the first night at Stevenson, and then had to await the work of the pioneer corps; they had to make roads for the teams and artillery to reach the high and more solid road near the foot of the mountain. These roads and the work that had to be done to make them passable would seem appalling to men not used to the fork. I remember in a special way the piece of road fitted up at this time. They first cut logs about two feet thick and laid them side by side. On these were laid logs about a foot thick, and on these poles of a smaller size and brush, in order to hold up the teams from sinking, and this had to be done not only for a narrow stream, but for many rods together before any advance could be made at all."(4)

Mostly this work was done by the pioneer corps that was assigned to the 1st Division. If the brigades had pioneer companies in them, which most did just for this kind of work, they were the ones that performed this task. Most of the time to speed the process up other men were assigned the task of helping out.

A continuation of the diary from the 13th Illinois Volunteer Infantry Regiment, that describes the way they celebrated Christmas. This was the second Christmas away from home for the 31st Missouri Infantry Regiment. They celebrated their first Christmas on Mississippi River on their way to the battle at Chickasaw Bayou.

"On *December 24th* we were on the road again, and a tramp of twelve miles brought us near Bellefonte. Christmas came, cold and cloudy and we celebrated the day by a tramp of sixteen miles over a rough road and put up for a night in the vicinity of the City of Larkinsville Alabama. The hotel accommodations not being such as we approved, we rolled up in our blankets and looked up at the twinkling stars until they put us to sleep.

After a rainy night and on a rainy morning we moved on our way to the West; our march, in this particular, that part of the day we took the railroad track leaving the more common road to the wagon trains and artillery. We moved on this way for about ten miles and at 3 p.m. went into camp at Woodville, a small railroad station.

We remained here the remaining day of the year, all of which were cold and wet and disagreeable. It was during this week that the order was read to us, which was a call for the older troops to re-enlist as veterans; with the re-enlistment was included a bounty and a thirty days' furlough."(5)

The 1st Division went into camp in and around Woodville, Alabama where it arrived on December 27, 1863. The 13th Illinois did not re-enlist as a unit, and when their three year were up they went home. They had suffered a total of sixty-seven officers and men killed or mortally wounded with another one hundred and twenty-five officers and men dying of disease for a total of one hundred and ninety-two. Because of their time almost being up, they were left behind as guards when the rest of the army marched to Atlanta. They were mustered out in June 1864 having fulfilled their obligation to the government and their families. They had done everything that was asked of them and more.

In his "Inventory", Private Henry Kuck of Company G, 31st Missouri Infantry Regiment wrote,

"Dec.

3	Back through Chattanooga, Tenn. cross the river.
4	Arrived at Bridgeport, remained until Debr. 21st.
7	was paid for 2 months, sent 30 dollars home by Adams Express.
21	March from Bridgeport, Ala. to Woodville, Ala.
28	Arrived in Woodville, very dirty from river crossing"(6)

On December 30, 1863 the 1st Division of the 15th Army Corps was between Larkinsville, Alabama and Huntsville Alabama. The 31st Missouri Infantry Regiment went into winter camp at Woodville, Alabama. In the month of January 1863 the 31st Missouri Infantry was on its way and fighting in its second battle at Arkansas Post, Arkansas, in Woodville it was a different story in January 1864. They actually got to experience what is called a winter camp. In a winter camp it is more relaxed. There were a few negatives that were involved. Instead of marching from one place to another seeking out the Confederates, the soldiers were busy with the mundane chores of camp life. There was fatique duties, guard duty, drill which consisted of regimental drill and brigade drill and the ever present inspections. No longer could the private just let his uniform go, he now had to keep it clean and shiny. To the men who had spent the last year chasing and fighting Confederates it was a bitter pill to swallow. Many did not care for the change and eventually they longed for the march even if it meant more battles.

Major A. J. Seay was left in command of the 32nd Missouri Volunteer Infantry Regiment while in Camp Proclamation in northern Alabama. In his diary he records the day to day weather and activities while in camp. The following information from his diary entries in January, will give you an idea of what was probably the daily activity of every officer if not soldier in a winter camp.

"JANUARY, FRIDAY, 1,1864.

In camp Proclamation near Woodville, Ala. Very cold snow last night, the wind tempestuous. Quite a contrast with one year ago then withdrawing, dis-spirited and sad from Chickasaw. Now gay and joyful, altho think of other days and lady friends.

SATURDAY, 2.

Cold. The men working busily on their camp ground getting building material in order to make themselves comfortable.

SUNDAY, 3.

Cold. Unprecedented in my experience of the climate in dixieland but beaver or bee like the men know no sabbath when they are exposed. They labor unceasingly and the chaplain has no sevices, unless in secret.

MONDAY, 4.

I go in search of supplies, find a little butter dried peaches and sweet potatoes, the latter hard frozen. Buy all. The woman treats me politely, but says "the boys took all my chickens and paid me nothing." This is wrong.

TUESDAY, 5.

Cold and cloudy. The axe and stone hammer ring merrily on the mountain side. Here comes two men with a stone as large as they can carry-there goes one with a load of wood and here comes one laden with boards.

WEDNESDAY, 6.

Heavy details from the 32d, something dead in the meal. Only 13 men for duty left in camp. Williams is out foraging. Brings in one pounds butter and 2 old hens, small favors thankfully received, Etc.

THURSDAY, 7.

Examine and compare muster pay rolls find some things of them in bad condition. False Muster on October rolls. I have much trouble in getting them straight badly blotched and interlined.

FRIDAY, 8.

Resume my labors. Today I finish the job and sign and forward rolls. Also monthly returns etc. Weather moderate, but cold yet.

SATURDAY, 9.

Busy in adjts. Office straightening up all day. A rumor rife comes into camp that we will soon move west. But the boys are still at work on their huts as though we would stay here all winter. This is commendable.

SUNDAY, 10.

Cold. This the longest cold spell and said by citizens here to be coldest weather that has been here for 30 years. The northern papers speak of men and animals freezing to death. We can hardly realize that it is so.

MONDAY, 11.

I am div. officer of the day. Ride all day. Find our front badly picketed, make some changes. Have been in all the camps. They are built up quite comfortably. Veteran volunteers all the talk-not very cold today.

TUESDAY, 12.

Moderating, ground thawing. Threatened with rain. Men done building their chimneys and Col. Simpson calls on me. A sharp fellow and a good soldier. A nice day warm-ground thawing. More mud than we have had for two weeks. All quiet in the regiment. Heavy details on us. Single gets tried tomorrow Warm clear tonight.

THURSDAY, 14.

Frosty and foggy in the morning-warm towards noon but damp and cloudy.

FRIDAY, 15.

Am detailed on a court martial. Meet and adjourn until next Monday. Dark and cloudy today, ground a little frozen.

SATURDAY, 16.

Are inspected by Capt. Parris. Our appearance, qtrs. Etc. very satisfactory. But we don't stand up like soldiers. Examine books, papers and records also hospital-quite well pleased takes dinner with us.

SUNDAY, 17.

A warm nice day. We have Co. inspection, Divine service. Articles of war read, and a nice dress parade. Got the Daily Democrat, last night and tonight. Get Cincinnati, Louisville and Nashville Dailies regularly.

MONDAY, 18.

Cloudy and in the P.M. cold. It snows about 2 in. deep last night, the biggest snow we had this winter-the 2nd. Tried three cases in court.

TUESDAY, 19.

A nice sun shiney day. All the snow has melted by noon. Jas. A. Duke, Co. A. dies poor fellow. It is no doubt better for him and all concerned. An interesting time in court. Dispose of three cases. Bohmann starts to Cin. After goods.

WEDNESDAY, 20.

A nice warm beautiful day. Tried three cases in court.

THURSDAY, 21.

A frosty morning and a beautiful day.

FRIDAY, 22.

Today looks like a spring of the year in Mo. Try 3 cases of the Mo. horse artillery. I got there too late. Every thing going well in camp.

SATURDAY, 23.

I am Pres. today. We try and dispose of three cases today. Horse Art., nice warm and smoky like Indian summer. I see Gen. Woods who does not wish me to leave the command. I'll not go.

SUNDAY, 24.

As nice a day as I ever saw. What a contrast between today and 2 months ago, we in deadly conflict we stormed Lookout. The skies bright today are bright and hope is buoyant. We started at 3 P.M. for a scout three days. March 10 miles by moonlight. Bivouac on Gunter's Mountain.

MONDAY, 25.

March at 5 P.M. arrive at landing on Tenn. R. at 8 thence back to Bucksnort and onto the mountain. Find poor degraded, ignorant, starving people, the roughest road in the South. Few rebels on the south bank of the Tenn. fired at us. I am in command of the expedition.

Weather as nice and pleasant as April.

TUESDAY, 26.

Camped on the mountain last night. Moved at day-light this morning arrived over rough roads etc. at 2 P.M. having marched 42 miles. The men were orderly. Did not jayhawk anything-disappointed about not getting a fight. Some of the country very poor. Pine on the Mt. top. Wind sighs thru its boughs.

WEDNESDAY, 27.

Slept well last night. Today took my seat in court martial as Pres. Tried Capt. Gibbons, 26th Iowa. Nice weather-no frost- all sunshine in day and moon shine at night.

THURSDAY, 28.

Fine weather. Tried two cases in court. I am Pres. Sick furloughs were granted for 3 of Co. B. and 1 Co. I. (Reeves) they will start on train on to-morrow. Stock of provisions running low.

FRIDAY, 29.

This P.M. had Brig drill in the old field. Truce and Campbell did poorly for officers who have been in so long.

SATURDAY, 30.

Cloudy, rainy and warm. Our brig except the 32d Mo. goes out on a seven day expedition. I am left in command of what is left. At night a heavy shower.

SUNDAY, 31.

Warm, fair and nice. 25th Iowa and 32d Mo. chaplain consolidated and held div. service in our half completed rail constructed sancturary. The former preached a very poor sermon-late papers."(7)

While they were in Woodville, Alabama the 1st Division was assigned a district to patrol and guard key areas within that district. The Federals, even though in winter camp, were still in the heart of the Confederacy. The 15th Army Corps was the western flank of the army around Chattanooga. There was not too much to worry about from the main Confederate army but there was always the regular Confederate cavalry and the local guerrillas in the area. For this reason there were different key terrain areas that were under guard by different regiments for short periods of time. One regiment would be assigned to one of these guard sites, where there was a camp, and then another regiment would relieve them. Once another regiment relieved them the first regiment would go back to the division camp at Woodville. The Tennessee River was the main concern of the 15th Army Corps. They were to patrol it and keep their area free from Confederate forces if possible. They were constantly patrolling the river between Paint Rock River and Flint River. They were at guard duty posts at places like Claysville and Vienna, Alabama. They went on patrols to places like Fearn's Landing, Deposit, Boyd's Switch, Farrens Ferry and Brownsborogh. Not only were they to be concerned about the Tennessee River they were also assigned to patrol the railroad in their district. The 1st Division was assigned with patrolling the railroad between Steven's Gap to Camden.

Major General Peter Joseph Osterhaus the 1st Division commander went on leave as did a lot of higher ranking officers. After the last year of fighting, marching and sickness most of the regiments had suffered the loss of many men. The 31st Missouri Infantry Regiment was down to one hundred and sixty nine men. In hopes of increasing the number of men in the regiment, some of the officers and some of the men were detached for recruiting services. One such soldier was Private William Carroll of Company F, 31st Missouri Infantry Regiment who arrived at Benton Barracks, Missouri on February 1,1864.(8) Some of the men who were recruited for the 31st Missouri Infantry Regiment during this time were, Private Charles Comball of Cuba was recruited on March 29, 1864 and assigned to Company E as also was Private Charles N. Comwall he enlisted on March 7, 1864; Private Hart Culton from Mineral Point who was enlisted on February 29,1864 and assigned to Company I; Private George W. Fisher of Middleton who enlisted in Company F on February 24, 1864; Private William J. Thornhill from Franklin County was assigned to Company A; Private William R. Cantrell from Laclede County was assigned to Company A; Private Andrew Goff of Pulaski County, Kentucky enlisted on February 10, 1864; Private William M. Goff of Washington County, Missouri enlisted on February 15, 1864; Private Walther Fredrick of Saint Charles, Missouri was assigned to Company I; Private Lorenzo D. Hawaly of Saint Louis, Missouri enlisted on February 24, 1864; Private George Priester of Saint Louis, Missouri enlisted on February 24, 1864; Private William A. McCrery of Franklin County, Missouri enlisted on March 7, 1864; Private George Jamison of Crawford County,

Missouri enlisted on March 10, 1864 and was assigned to Company E; Private Cultun Hart of Washington County, Missoouri enlisted on March 10, 1864; Private James Hamilton of Saint Louis, Missouri enlisted on March 17,1864; Private Hert Elicis of Saint Louis, Missouri enlisted on March 17, 1864 and assigned to Company G; Private Herman Holerness of Saint Louis, Missouri enlisted on March 22, 1864; Private Elijah Stephanes of Saint Louis, Missouri enlisted on April 5, 1864; Private Milton Stevens of Saint Louis, Missouri enlisted on April 11, 1864; Private Johnnie Calvin of Murphysboro, Tennessee enlisted on April 27, 1864 as an assistant Cook at Woodville, Alabama. He was the only ex-slave to enlist in the 31st Missouri Infantry Regiment. These are the only men that I have found a record on as enlisting during this time.

Private Henry Kuck of Company G, 31st Missouri Infantry Regiment writes in his inventory what has happened for the months of January through April 1864.

> "Jan. 3(64)   entered hospital with swollen legs, had felt sick for a long time.
> 26   out of hospital, back to company.
> 30   healthy.
> Feb. 12   cold, fever.
> 24   paid for 2 months, 26 dollars.
> March 4   practice in sharpshooting
> 12   new weapons
> April 3   sick, fever. Wrote a letter to Christ., Ill.
> 7   better again, reported for duty.
> 30   march orders.(9)

In a letter to his wife, Metta, Private Henry Kuck writes,
> "Camp Proclamation near Woodville
> Febr. 25th 1864

Dear Metta,

Your letter of the 16th I got on the 23rd of this month and I see that you received my letter from John Gerdel, and that you're all healthy and about, which pleases and comforts me. On the 17th of this month I wrote you a letter which probably is already in your hands. You write that John Gerdel said I'm not really well yet. For as he left us I was fairly pleased, that is, I felt very well, but since that time I've been sick again, but it didn't make so sick that I had to go to bed; now it's gone and I hope that Spring will kill off this illness completely, for now I'm as healthy as I've ever been and I believe I'm 20 pounds heavier as I was on leave. You write that Henry Muller wants to go into the military again: this is praiseworthy if he wants to serve his country, for we still need many men who will take weapons in hand for their Fatherland and will help establish Peace and Order again; but for whoever wants to be a soldier just to earn money it will seem as if he's gotten himself into a big muddy mess; a true soldier who knows this, and was already a soldier, can prove himself, for he already knows what it's like in the army.

Now I know what it's like in the army, and when I've served my time, if I were to enlist again and find out again that it's nothing for me, then that would be my own fault. But when I want to get out of the army with my life and health, then I won't go back in so easily, for we thought then that it would be impossible for the war to continue for 3 years, or however long it's been; when our time is up some of these ones will go who haven't yet served their land and are still young and single. One should hold no one back from military service, for the more hands, the sooner the work will be done and the earlier Peace and Order will be in the land.

There is not much new to write, and so my greetings to all friends and neighbors and to you, sweet Wife and children.

Your, Henry

We were paid for 2 months just as this letter was finished – 26 Dols. Since there's no Express Company close by, I'll have to wait for a better opportunity to send you the money, but I think an opportunity will soon present itself. I'll send it to (Mr.) Koln again."(10)

Major Abraham J. Seay filled in his diary for the month of February and the first five days of March. Some of the entries for February are much like those in January, so below are the dates that are a little different or have members of the 31st Missouri in them such as the reference of Private Pigg on February 1st. The 31st and 32nd Missouri went out on a reconnisance in force as described below that ended on March 5th.

MONDAY, FEBRUARY, 1.

Rained last night. This morning the sun shines out

upon us as genial as though it was spring time. Court gets thru business today. Tries Pigg, 31 Mo. (a big hog) House retiring from St. Louis. Looks fat.

FRIDAY, 5.

Nice weather. Drill at night, we had a debate-questions sutler, court martialed John Brown, Co. A for neglect of duty and absence without leave in Proclamation Hall

SATURDAY, 6.

Dark and rainy. Capt. Davis goes out in search of forage. The brig returns in the P.M. have been to Lebanon Ala., 31 miles from Larkins landing. It is said the 25th Iowa stampeded.

THURSDAY, 11.

Marched at sun up towards Bridgeport. Made 20 miles camped near Bellfort. A nice day. Marched fast-all anxious to know our particulars destination. None can tell. No foraging.

FRIDAY, 12.

Marched at day light-men sore-I have their knapsacks hauled only three wagons along. We make it to Stevenson. 18 miles and bivouach on the same ground. Get onions and potatoes, etc. Frosty nights.

SATURDAY, 13.

March at 9 A.M. and arrive at Bridgeport 3 P.M. camp near the fort distance 12 miles. Get two days rations and forage. Men stand the march very well. Military improvements going on-boats building-pressed.

SUNDAY, 14.

Get a valentine last night from Bland. Start to march at 7 A.M.-march 17 miles a slow rain All the way. Hard march, 32d in front-lead the whole brig.

MONDAY, 15.

Rained most all night and until we arrived in Chattanooga about 1 P.M. quite wet and muddy. A fine time to go ducking. Get a drink of whiskey for the men. A large number of troops in town, camp looks well.

TUESDAY, 16.

Having drawn rations last night we start today for Cleaveland Landing at 12 M. Pass thru town up across Mission Ridge, march 10 or 12 miles and go into camp. Has become quite cold. I suffer for the men, no tents.

WEDNESDAY, 17.

Cold as thunder. Wind sharp as lightening. Sun shines but does not thaw anything. Pass over White Oak Mt. which looks like Mission Ridge, larger, country very poor till we get near Cleaveland Tenn. Get better.

THURSDAY, 18.

Camped 1 ½ miles from Cleaveland, lost and move in today. Very cold. The snow or frost fell fast the first thing of the kind I ever witnessed in Dixie. Move thru town and ½ west-still cold. Go into camp.

MONDAY, 22.

The anniversary of Washington's birthday. Joe, Rob and Andy get drunk and go to town at 8:30 P.M. I get marching orders to report to Col. Dickerman commanding 1st Brig, 4th Div, 15 A.C. at 5 A.M., 23rd.

TUESDAY, 23.

March 12 miles to Red Clay by noon and report to Gen. Craft, commanding 1 div 4th A.C. move 12 miles further and bivouach near Ruigal at 11 P.M. A big march, we are rear guard. None but us from our div. We are the larckeys. I am tired and poor by providing fire.

WEDNESDAY, 24.

Move at 10 back on same road 2 miles to forks. Go into battle line and remain till night-then the whole regiment are detailed on picket. Very light skirmishing but heavy firing heard in the distance towards Dalton. I'm almost sick, nothing to eat but hard tack, etc.

THURSDAY, 25.

Move at 3 A.M. thence South at right angles to within four miles of Dolton, here skirmishing commences. Then heavy at 12 to 2 P.M. An artillery brisk duel-we under fire all day in line of battle, but not engaged. More or less fighting along the lines. Heavy guns on the extreme right silently withdraw at 9 P.M. and move backto the old camp-arriving at 2 A.M. Bright moon and good roads.

FRIDAY, 26.

Weather clear-draw three days rations and move out of the road yesterday traveled twice before. At 12 skirmishing commences-the enemy said to be in heavy forces. We lay in line till moon rises then move five miles west of near Ringgold and bivouach 2 A.M. Little to eat. Heard little firing today. We know not what is going on are befuddled and befogged. March and countermarch we know not whither.

SATURDAY, 27.

Leave camp at 12 M. Go near Ringgold Ga. Then turn north towards Cleaveland. Travel over pine hills (poor) 13 miles and bivouach. The enemy follow our rear a short distance. We are now returning after a strange combination of movements. We have accomplished our end.

SUNDAY, 28.

A beautiful day. We start at 7 and get to Cleaveland at 3, Col. Dickerman, 103 Ill. a good soldier commanding brig. March thru town by platoons. Give him three cheers. It seems that our movements brought three div from other points to Dalton. They being then much stronger than we we retire in safety.

MONDAY, 29.

It is muster day and cloudy and warm. Rains in the P.M. Officers have no time to get their muster and pay rolls in good shape. At night I go to brig Headquarters and have a game of sell. Dark and rainy.

MARCH, TUESDAY, 1,1864.

In line at 5 A.M. in anticipation of an attack. It rains-at 9 we get orders to march at ten towards Chattanooga, supplies baggage and the sick by the cars to Bridgeport-heavy rain.

WEDNESDAY, 2.

March at 8. Cold clear but windy, camp in the valley east of Chattanooga on the ground contested for, i.e. picket posted before the Nov. battle of Lookout Mountain and Mission Ridge.

THURSDAY, 3.

Tried to buy provisions in Chattanooga but the 15 A.C. could not buy. I gave one man a lecture on the importance of red tape, etc. Marched 20 miles, bivouacked near "Hell gate" (not guarded like Milton's gate was). Men tired. Wood hard to get.

FRIDAY,4.

The fifth anniversary of Abe's inauguration. A nice warm day. I think spring has opened. We get to Bridgeport at noon-send wagons on and take the cars. Run up and down the track puffing and blowing all night. It rained heavily on the men who were on top of the cars.

SATURDAY, 5.

Crowded and could not sleep last night-no breakfast-get to Stevenson at 7 A.M. Get a good sanitary dinner. A number of the men also get dinner. A good thing. The Chaplain gets religious papers for distribution-arrived at Woodville 10 ½ P.M. Men shout-go into the old camp."(11)

On March 12th, the 31st Missouri Infantry Regiment received new weapons. They had to turn in their old ones and were issued new Springfield Rifles. The following is an order issued on March 12th.

"Hd. Qrs. 31st Mo. Vols. Inft
Camp Proclimation Woodville,Ala. March 12/64
Special Order No. 139.

In obedience to order from Major General John A. Logan commanding 15th, A.C. dated Huntsville, Ala. Feb. 25th, 64 and to Special Orders No. 3 Hd. Qrts. 2d Brig. 1st Division 15th A.C. March 12th 1864.

The Commanding officer of Companies are hereby ordered to turn over to the commanding officer of the Regiment all ordinance & ordinance stores(cap pouches excluded) Now in their possession and to receive new armes & accoutrements for their

Frederick Jaensch
Major, 31st Mo. Vols. Inft. Regt.

Official

J.W. Evenden

A. Adjutant

Every company commander has to file a true copy of this order with their next returns."(12)

Not only did they receive new weapons they also had target practice. Major A. J. Seay in his diary for March refers to practicing with their new weapons. "Tuseday, 8. Men shot five shots each at 200 yards-do well. Wednesday,9. Target practice again at 200 yards."(13) Major A. J. Seay records later in the month the events of a battle of another kind. "Tuesday, 22. Snow falling and melting at the same time. Nearly knee deep, the deepest I ever saw. Ceases at 2 ½ feet and sun comes out at 3 P.M. Men have a great deal of fun. Snowball by regiments. Sutler sells beer and the men feel good. This is the equicnoctial storm. Will have more high water. Wednesday, 23. The sun has shown out most of the day and a great deal of the snow has melted off. We drink beer today and strange to say many of the officers take a nap this P.M. Boys snowballing again-no drill. We furnish 29 privates for guard."(14)

On Easter Sunday, March 27, 1864, General Osterhaus records that it was a warm, beautiful morning. General Sherman came from Huntsville, with Generals McPherson, Logan and Allen at eight o'clock that morning.(15) Normally you might think that it was a time when the soldier could relax and take it easy. It was not. It was a time when the thought of battle was something for the future or even the battles that were in the past. It was also the time when those who were in command decided that it was time to make the soldiers experience proper military camp life. In the case of Sergeant Fielding Jenkins Smith (my great-great Grandfather) it was a time for discipline. He was punished in the following order.

"Hd. Qrs. 31st Mo. Inf.
Camp Proclamation
Woodville Ala.

General Orders   Mar. 30th, 1864
No. 62
Sergt. Fielding J. <u>Smith</u> Co F, 31st Mo Vol Inf. is hereby reduced to the ranks for disobedience of orders and gross neglect of Duty.

By Order of
Fred Jaensch
Major Comdg.
J. W. Evenden
1st Lieut. & act adj."(16)

General Osterhaus records in his diary, "On April 1, Rain again, General Brody's Rebel cavalry reported in force on the South side of Tennessee River. Sent 31st Missouri Infantry to fork of Claysville."(17) The 32nd Missouri Infantry Regiment goes out on one of the frequent patrols as recorded by Major A. J. Seay. "Wednesday, 30. In the P.M. we were paid on December rolls. Got orders to march on expedition at 1 A.M. on tomorrow. I will take the bushwackers along with me. Some of the men drunk this evening. Thursday, 31. March at 1 A.M.

PRIVATE FIELDING JENKINS SMITH
COMPANY F, 31ST MISSOURI INFANTRY REGIMENT

PRIVATE JOHN W. TAYLOR
COMPANY I, 31ST MISSOURI INFANTRY REGIMENT
CARLISLE BARRACKS, CARLISE PENNYSLVANIA

Dark till moon rose. Marched 12 miles before daylight. At daybreak surrounded Sinclair's house and caught Lieut. — (Meads adjt.), 1st Surgeon Geo. Berry etal. On going Sinclair got away. We got three blankets, six prisoners, 3 horses and as much meat as the men wanted and came into camp having marched 30 miles."(18) Even though the Federals were in a strong winter camp the Confederates did not let them rest. On Saturday, March 26th, the long roll was sounded and they awoke and fell into formation to go and fight. The same thing happened again on Saturday April 2nd. Both of these were false alarms. Why the Confederates chose Saturday night to keep the Federals on their toes, is anyone's guess. Of course it could have been that the men on guard duty were drunk and seeing things that were not there. On Monday April 11th, General Osterhuas went on an inspection tour by train which took him to Cassville, Claysville and then return to Colton. He says in his diary "that seven miles from Claysville there seems to be a Rebel hiding place."(19)

"Thursday, April 21st, General Logan review at 12 noon a success! The troops appeared to all advantage. General Logan expresses himself very satisfied. The camp also inspected the men clean an looked healthy!" (20) It was during this winter, in camp, that the 15th Corps were being rearmed. Throughout early part of the war the army in the west was not as well supplied as that in the east. I guess it was because they were closer to the capitol than was the army in the west. General Osterhaus in his diary on the date of April 26,1864 states that "The rearming of my infantry and artillery pretty much completed."(21) "Friday April 29,1864-very warm and hot- -received third marching order. I believe we go at last- - Prisoners escape: the 32nd Missouri on guard; it is beyond a doubt the meanest regiment Missouri sent out."(22) I'm not sure what General Osterhaus meant by this but I found it very amusing. To be referred to in this manner in his diary it is evident that at some point in time they had developed quite a reputation.

The Confederates also went into camp at this time in northern Georgia. They were a demoralized army who had won a battle but lost the campaign. The commander of the Army of Tennessee, General Bragg, had resigned and was now an advisor to President Davis. The Confederate army needed help and needed it bad. Even though President Davis didn't like General Johnston, he ordered him to take command of the army in northern Georgia. When General Johnston arrived to take command of the Army of Tennessee he was sorely disappointed. He was not in command of an organized, well functioning army, but he found himself in command of an army whose supplies were almost non-existent. They were almost naked, hungry and short on tents. Most of the soldiers had never served under General Johnston before, but after serving under General Bragg, who not only had no respect for his men but was not adverse to executing his own men for desertion or other offenses, they were a little leery of the coming new commander.

Since winter had begun, some of the men had decided to spend the winter at home. They had done this on their own, without permission, and were classified as A. W. O. L. When General Johnston formally took command one of the first things that he did was send whole units home on furlough. This not only improved the morale of the men, it also gave them almost instant respect for their new commander. Once this was done General Johnston started work on improving the living conditions of the men. They started to get tents in which to live, clothing, that included shoes and socks, which was almost always a problem, and improved the quality and amount of the food. Not only was the men's morale improved, the major commanders in the army, who had come to despise and almost hate General Bragg, morale improved because they were glad to have General Johnston as their new commander.

With this new attitude the army still had a large number of men who were listed as A. W. O. L. or deserted. General Johnston then issued the orders to grant amnesty to these men if they would return by a set date with no questions asked. A large majority of these men, who fit into these categories, did return to duty, and were accepted back into the army. With these improvements started they got down to soldiering which included drill, inspections and more drill. It was while in this winter camp that a religious revival took place that spread throughout the army. Many soldiers turned toward God and accepted Christ as their Savior. Some believe that the amount of loss that they had experienced prior to this time caused many to turn toward God. Some theorize that it was the long separation from home and family or even boredom while in camp. Whatever the reason, many of those who had turned toward God would die within the next year in northern and central Georgia and in Tennessee.

CHAPTER 10:
THE BATTLE AT RESACA

The campaign for Atlanta began with most of the units leaving on May 1, 1864. While the army in the west began their campaign, Lieutenant General Grant was directing the campaign in the east. The eastern army was to engage the famed Army of Virginia under the command of the very capable General Robert E. Lee. There was also a campaign that was starting from New Orleans, Louisiana, with General Banks in command with the objective of taking Mobile, Alabama. General Banks had started a campaign, prior to General Grant taking command of all Union Forces, up the Red River. This proved to be an utter disaster with a defeat given to the Federal forces that prevented them from participating in a coordinated attack with the Army of the Potomac and the forces under General Sherman in his military division of the Mississippi.

In a report dated May 20th, Major-General Peter Joseph Osterhaus gives the strength of the 1st Division as listed below:

"Headquarters First Division, Fifteenth Army Corps Camp near Kingston, Georgia, May 20, 1864

Major: I have the honor to report on the part taken by my division in the engagement near Resaca, Georgia, which led to the surrender of that fortified place. My command consisted of the following:

Strength of First Division.

Effective Infantry Present.

First Brigade, Brigadier-General Woods:
76th Ohio Infantry.............................. 526
27th Missouri Infantry...................... 279
26th Iowa Infantry............................. 292
30th Iowa Infantry............................. 331
Total First Brigade........................... 1,428

Second Brigade, Colonel J. A. Williamson:
4th Iowa Infantry................................ 322

9th Iowa Infantry.................................. 431
25th Iowa Infantry.............................. 361
31st Iowa Infantry.............................. 315
Total Second Brigade........................ 1,429

Third Brigade, Colonel Hugo Wangelin:
3d Missouri Infantry............................ 218
12th Missouri Infantry......................... 289
17th Missouri Infantry......................... 157
29th Missouri Infantry......................... 179
31st Missouri Infantry......................... 163
32nd Missouri Infantry........................ 164
Total Third Brigade............................1,170
Total Infantry.....................................4,027

Artillery (Major Langraeber)
4th Ohio Battery:
20-Pounder Parrots ....2 pieces
12-Pounder light field pieces (Napoleons) .....4 pieces
          Total pieces: 6 pieces and 106 men

Battery F, 2d Missouri Artillery:
12-Pounder howitzers.................................... 2 pieces
3-inch ordnance... 2 pieces
          Total pieces: 4 pieces and 104 men
Total artillery ....10 pieces and 210 men

Detachment sharpshooters
     (Lieutenant H. E. Williams).......81
Detachment mounted infantry
     (Captain W. T. House)..............32
Detachment pioneers
     (Captain John Keis)..................70"(1)
     The men in the ranks, who started on this campaign,
were basically veterans of many battles. They were prepared
for the hard campaigning that was coming up and had the basic equipment to take along on this campaign. Each man carried on his person his rifle, bayonet, cartridge box, cap pouch,
canteen, haversack, knapsack, blanket, gum blanket that also
acted as a poncho and a shelter-half which usually did not last
long. Some even started out with their great coats but these
were so heavy that they were quickly disposed of because of

the weight and this was a summer campaign. Extra clothing was generally kept to the bare minimum of maybe a couple of pair of sock and some underwear. Personal items included diaries, letters that they had received from home and read many times already, paper, Bibles, cards and watches and these items were carried in the knapsack and pockets.

General Sherman started this campaign with approximately one hundred thousand men in all branches of the service besides those who were a part of his supply line. The Army of the Tennessee, under the command of Major General James McPherson, had twenty-two thousand four hundred and thirty-seven infantrymen; one thousand four hundred and four artillerymen who manned ninety-six guns, and six hundred and twenty-four cavalrymen this came to a total of twenty-four thousand four hundred and sixty-five men. The 15th Corps, which was part of the Army of the Tennessee, had only three of its four divisions with it on this march. They were the 1st Division, 2nd Division and the 4th Division. The 3rd Division was left behind to guard the railroad in northern Alabama and northern Georgia. The Army of the Ohio under Major General John M. Schofield had a total of thirteen thousand five hundred and fifty-nine men under his command. He had eleven thousand one hundred and eighty three infantrymen, six hundred and seventy-nine artillerymen and one thousand six hundred and seventy-nine cavalrymen. The largest amount of men was from Major General George Thomas' Army of the Cumberland. There were fifty-four thousand five hundred and sixty-eight infantrymen, two thousand three hundred and seventy-seven artillerymen who served one hundred and thirty guns and three thousand eight hundred and twenty-eight cavalrymen. (2)

On May 1st at six thirty a.m., the 31st Missouri Infantry Regiment was in the 2nd Brigade, 1st Division, 15th Army Corps and the 32nd Missouri Infantry Regiment was in the 3rd Brigade, 1st Division, 15th Army Corps. This was the first time that the 31st Missouri Infantry and the 32nd Missouri Infantry were not in the same brigade. They along with the rest of their division left their winter camp in Woodville, Alabama, and started out on what would prove to be a long campaign against Atlanta. They made seventeen miles on the first day and arrived at Rasberry Creek where they went into camp. "It rained last night and the morning broke cool which made for some fine marching weather."(3) This was especially beneficial for men who had not been marching very much for the last few months. While his fellow soldiers in the 31st Missouri Infantry were beginning their march of seventeen miles on May 1st, John T. Clarke, who was a member of Company I, who was at home in Mineral Point, Missouri, wrote in his diary, "Sunday, May 1,1864. Commenced chewing Tobacco. A remarkable event!!" A postscript dated February 1,1922, "after more than fifty-seven and one-half years of continuous use, abandoned tobacco."(4)

The following is entries into the diary of Major General Peter J. Osterhaus, the 1st Division commander, for the first few days in early May 1864.

"May 2nd, Marched at five-thirty in the morning. The first division, after only about two miles of marching caught up with the supply train of the second division. This stopped our march until about eleven a.m. when we marched to Bellefort where stopped for the day, totaling about eight miles. The first division train made it into camp today. It was on this night that the 17th Missouri Infantry lost its commander Colonel Cromer who committed suicide at eleven-thirty p.m.

May 3rd, Marched fourteen miles and went into camp at Stevenson, Alabama. We left the next day at six a.m. and arrived in Bridgeport, Alabama at ten a.m. After a two hour lay over we left Bridgeport and arrived in camp in Shillman that night at six-thirty after traveling about seventeen miles in total for the day.

On Thursday, May 5th, Left camp at seven-thirty a.m. Progress was slow because of the supply trains that were on the road. It was on this day that the 4th Iowa Veteran Infantry returned to the division from their veteran leave.

It's commander Colonel Williamson assumed command of the 2nd Brigade. The 1st Division had marched fifteen miles this day going into camp at the railroad junction in Wauhatchie."(5)

Friday, May 6th, was the day when the 15th Army Corps got rid of their excess baggage. Each regiment was allowed only three wagons per regiment, one for the officers, one for the companies and one for the medical department. Each brigade headquarters was allowed two wagons and each division head quarters were allowed three wagons. Also each division had fifty wagonloads of ammunition. The first division was issued

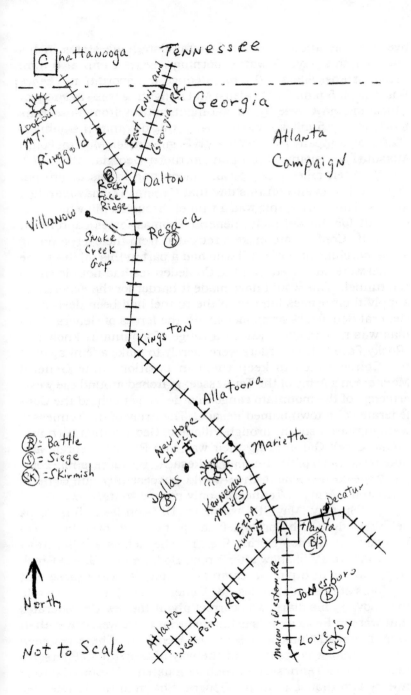

ATLANTA CAMPAIGN

five days of rations. Major General Osterhaus states in his diary for this day, "A warm morning. Leave camp at 6 a.m. Arrive at Rossville at 10 a.m. Reduce transportation- Leave Rossville at 5 p.m. for Gooden's Mill in fighting trim- in camp at Chickamauga Creek by 12 midnight not for from Rosecrans battlefield. 16 miles." (6) It was on this day that the John T. Clarke of Company I, 31st Missouri Regiment, left Mineral Point, Missouri to rejoin his unit in northern Georgia. "May 7th, marched ten miles. Leave camp noon and it was a very hot day."(7) It was also on this day that General Thomas marched against Tunnel Hill, this was a tunnel through a hill which was dug out for the railroad. General Thomas forces captured it when the Confederate pickets retreated from the overpowering force marching at them. All who had a part in this taking of the tunnel were surprised that the Confederates had not blown up the tunnel. This would have made it harder for the Federals to supply their armies later on if the tunnel had been destroyed. General Schofield's army along with the forces of General Thomas was now ready to attack a range of mountains known as "Rocky Face." Their orders were merely to make a feint against the Confederates to keep them in position while General McPherson's Army of the Tennessee; marched around the western edge of the mountain range in order to get behind the Confederates at a town named Resaca. The Army of the Tennessee were to march south through Villanow, Georgia then turn into Snake Creek Gap making their way into Resaca, Georgia and take possession of the railroad in Resaca. By successfully completing this movement they would successfully cut General Johnston's Army of Tennessee only escape route.

"Sunday, May 8th, warm 1st Division lead 15th Corps behind Dodge (16th Corps); left camp at 8 am go over the gap to Villanow; at Gordon Spring 9 a.m. The Rebels left Saturday Night. Arrive at Villanow after 1 p.m. Dodge enters Snake Creek Gap, I follow at 6 p.m. in camp at 8 p.m. sit clear course, but few Rebs at Resaca 12 miles."(8) General Osterhaus, who wrote the above in his diary, was correct about the few Confederates that were in Resaca. It is estimated that there were fewer than four thousand Confederates in the trenches. These few men were all that was standing in the way of General McPherson's Army of the Tennessee, which consisted of approximately twenty-two thousand men. General Sherman would later tell General McPherson that he had missed one of the great opportunities of the war to destroy an enemy army. The Confederates had failed to leave a guard in the Snake Creek Gap. The road that runs through the gap is bordered by substantial hills on both sides of the road. It is the perfect place for an ambush by determined defenders. Snake Creek Gap has high hills on both side of the gap that if properly defended would have made it almost impossible for a force to attack it directly without suffering severe casualties. Some historians can't believe that the Confederates without so much as a picket line did not defend this Gap. But as it had happened at Tunnel Hill, what good would a few pickets had been against a whole army of the enemy. It would have been at best an early warning but it also may have been just some more prisoners in the Federals hands. They camped that night in the Snake Creek Gap and it started to rain. It was a terrible downpour that drenched the men to the bone.

May 9th, at five in the morning the troops left camp and headed toward Resaca. When leaving the Snake Creek Gap they crossed Snake Creek, it was here that they made their first contact with a brigade of Confederate cavalry. One of the Confederate cavalrymen was sent to General Johnston to deliver the message that a large enemy force was spotted at Resaca and that his line of communication was now endangered. This was the first indication he had that a part of the Federal army had made its way to a position in his rear. The Confederate cavalry was being steadily pushed back by a division of the 16th Army Corps under the command of General Dodge. The Federal force then proceeded toward Resaca on the Lafayette Road, their progress was very slow. The 9th Illinois Infantry Regiment led the way and was being followed up by the 39th Iowa Infantry Regiment. When approximately a mile from Resaca they were fired at by the troops of General Leondias Polk consisting of about four thousand men. Not knowing who or how many of the enemy they were facing and with night coming on, the Federals retreated to the safety of the Snake Creek Gap. On a Georgia historical sign at the foot of Snake Creek Gap states,

"May 8, 1864. McPherson's 15th & 16th Corps seized Snake Creek Gap. On the 9th, attempting to destroy the R. R. at Resaca, (defended by Cantey's Div. of Polk's Corps). McPherson was forced to withdraw to the mouth of the gap where he intrenched.

This was the beginning of Sherman's move to outflank Johnston's forces at Dalton.

May 13-14. Sherman moved the 14th, 20th, & 23d Corps through the gap together with McPherson's troops, advanced toward Resaca ~ the 4th Corps marching due S. from Dalton. On the 14th began the two day battle of Resaca."(9)

Special Field Orders # 5, Headquarters Department and Army of the Tennessee in Sugar Valley, May 10,1864, says in section VII, "First. All the troops now in advance, consisting of the divisions of Brigadier General's Morgan L. Smith, Osterhaus, Sweeny, and Veatch, will be drawn back to-night and placed in position along the defensive line on which we have been working to-day, the first two taking positions on the left of the Resaca road, the right resting on the road, and the last two on the right of the Resaca road, the left resting on the road."(10) The orders that were given to General McPherson gave him the discretion to do this if in his opinion he could not defeat the Confederate force he might meet in Resaca. He waits here for the next three days for reinforcements to reach him so that he might then attack the force to his front. General Osterhaus in his diary says, "May 10th, Rain.. May 11th, A terrible thunder and rain storm in the night: during which we executed the order to change positions. It rains continuously- we are entrenching as we will remain here until something happens at Dalton. The 20th A. C. is with us."(11)

General Johnston, once he finds out that he is in danger of having one of the only major escape routes to his rear, starts what would become one of his major fighting techniques throughout the Atlanta campaign, the tactical withdrawal. This is probably one of the hardest movements to successfully complete of all military maneuvers. You are being engaged by an enemy with a superior force, you have to convince him that you are still there ready to defend your position, you have to be able to get all your men, artillery, horses and supplies to the rear, with the least loss to yourself. General Johnston successfully accomplished this maneuver and beat the rest of General Shermans force to Resaca. His success in this withdrawal completely surprised the Federals, but it also started his declining popularity among the citizens in Georgia and the Confederate capital. Later the Confederate government would relieve him to stand and fight. General Hood, who became his successor, was at this time writing letters to President Davis criticizing General Johnstons fighting ability. These letters were being written without the knowledge of anyone and this added with the dislike that President Jefferson Davis had for General Johnston, was fuel to the fire that led to the ultimate dismissal of General Johnston.

On May 12th, the army begins its preparations for the upcoming battle. This includes orders for the knapsacks to be left behind. "Special Field Orders No. 7 of the Headquarters Department and Army of the Tennessee, In the Field, Sugar Valley, Georgia, May 12, 1864, Section III. Corps commanders will at once cause their commands to be provided with three days' rations in haversacks from to-morrow morning, the 13th instant. The troops will behind them their knapsacks, and will be in light marching order, prepared for a fight. The only wagons accompanying them will be the ambulances and ammunition trains."(12) Also in section V. of the same order it states, "Major-General Logan's command will have the advance to-morrow, the leading division moving on the Resaca road at 6 a. m. precisely, the other divisions following as closely and compactly as possible. Brigadier-General Dodge's command will follow immediately in rear of Major-General Logan's. 2. The men will march in light fighting trim, carrying their haversacks with three days' cooked rations, canteens filled, and one blanket rolled in their poncho and slung across the shoulder. The knapsacks will be left behind with trains, under charge of a guard, consisting of convalescent soldiers."(13) The 15th Army Corps improves its entrenchment's just in case the Confederates decided to attack. General Schofield's 20th Army Corps arrives on this day.

The following is a description of the terrain around Resaca, Georgia as given in a response by General J. D. Cox in a toast named Resaca at the Reunion of the Society of the Army of the Tennessee at its twenty-second meeting at Cincinnati, Ohio on September 25 & 26, 1889.

"Now what made Resaca's consequence? Its geographical position. The Oostanuala river, which runs immediately south of Resaca, on the banks of which the little town is, runs eastward and then southward by the way of Rome. The railroad, which we were to follow and which was that on which we were to depend for our supplies, ran through Resaca, running also through

Dalton and Tunnel Hill, and it was along the line thus occupied by Johnston's army. The Oostanuala river is made up of two branches; one going directly into it from the north, and the other from the east; the north branch, known as the Conasauga river, and the eastern one called the Coosawattee, making the junction at Resaca, where the road crossed the bridge. Resaca thus became an important point for Johnston as a base of supplies, and was an important point for us, because if it were occupied in the rear of Johnston's army before he could get away, he must take his chances if finding fords across the Oostanuala river, or move off eastward away from his own source of supplies, and in a position of great difficulty to carry on the campaign.

Snake Creek Gap, as it was called, was a deep cleft in the rocks, a mere ravine through which we marched; where there was scarcely a pretense of a road; all there was of it was few wagon tracks that could be seen here and there, following the bed of the creek, with a tall forest rising on each side and precipitous hills beyond. We moved through this gap, where a mere company could have held an army at bay, finding it unoccupied, and marched to where McPherson's army through the opening into the valley of Camp creek, which lies just to the west of Resaca.

Just north of Resaca there was another rise of ground and long ridge, several miles in length, and bordering upon this Conasauga river that I have mentioned. Along the west side of it, in a rough and rocky bed, ran Camp creek, running into the Oostanuala river just at or near Resaca. This ridge seemed to be broken where the creek itself made a new opening near the town, with a shorter ridge upon our extreme right, as we faced the town, and then the more open country, leading up to the rough ridge north and to the left of the town as we faced it."(14)

May 13th was a cool day, with orders to prepare to fight, General Sherman had now made his way to Snake Creek Gap to take command of the Federal forces there. The 15th Army Corps deploys into a line of battle and started on their way towards Resaca. The 1st Division was in front of the corps with a strong skirmish line leading the way. The 2nd Brigade, commanded by General James Williamson, and the 1st Brigade, commanded by General Charles Woods, marched on either side of the Lafayette Road, with the 3rd Brigade and the 4th Ohio Battery forming the second line, the whole time meeting some resistance from Colonel Thomas M. Scott's force. Colonel Scott was part of the command of General Leonidas Polk's army. Once the Federals came in range of some Confederate artillery fired upon them from their positions on Bald Hill. Bald Hill is part of a range of hills that overlooked the Confederate entrenchment's near the town. Counter battery was then effected by two twelve pound howitzers from Battery F, 2nd Missouri Artillery. The infantry skirmishers were also involved in driving the Confederates back, after a battle of about one-half of an hour the Confederate skirmishers withdrew into the valley just in front of the main Confederate entrenchment's. The 1st Division of the 15th Army Corps then took up positions on these range of hills that put them in position in which to be able to fire upon the Confederates. They held this position for the remainder of the night and into the afternoon of the 14th. There was constant skirmishing between the two skirmish lines almost the whole time that the Federals were in this position.

About four p.m. on May 14th the fighting began along almost four miles of the front. General McPherson ordered General Logan to make a demonstration against General Polk's men. General Osterhaus' 1st Division was ordered to demonstrate along his whole front with support from his artillery that would be firing from the hills that they had taken the previous day. The 17th and 32nd Missouri Infantry Regiments, of Colonel Hugo Wangelin's 3rd Brigade of General Osterhaus' 1st Division, waded across Camp Creek while the 12th Missouri Regiment made it across the Lafayette Road bridge and entrenched to make a bridgehead on the Resaca side of Camp Creek. About five-fifty in the afternoon General Charles R. Woods' 1st Brigade pushed across the creek led by the 26th Iowa Regiment acting as skirmishers. They were supported on the right by the 1st Brigade of Morgan L. Smith's 2nd Division, led by General Giles A. Smith. The 57th Ohio Infantry Regiment were acting as skirmishers for the 2nd Division. The 30th Iowa Infantry and the 27th Missouri Infantry were the forward regiments in General Woods brigade with the 76th Ohio Infantry and the 3rd Missouri Infantry were the regiments in the second line. In a very short time the Federal units had forced the Confederates to abandon their first line of defenses with the 3rd Missouri attacking and securing the second line of defenses that consisted of another ridge line that they had been occupying. The rest of the brigade immediately followed and began to fortify to resist any Confederate counter-attack. They endured a severe artillery bombardment with little damage done. The Confederates then launched their attack around eight p. m., the Confederates after a determined attack were driven back with assistance from the 25th Wisconsin Infantry and the 35th New Jersey Infantry Regiments. They had been sent to relieve the 30th Iowa Infantry who had reported that they were running out of ammunition. Once the Confederate infantry had been driven back there was a severe artillery bombardment of the Federal line, that had once been theirs, which lasted about one-half of an hour. This bombardment inflicted few casualties but was very heavy and finally ceased about ten o'clock p. m. Around ten-thirty p. m. the 25th Iowa Infantry, Colonel George A. Stone commanding, and a battalion under the command of Lieutenant Colonel Joseph S. Gage, which consisted of the 29th Missouri and the 31st Missouri Infantry Regiments reported to General Woods, where they were put in reserve while the rest of his troops continued to strengthen their rifle pits. While attached to General Woods the battalion of the 29th Missouri and the 31st Missouri Infantry Regiments suffered one man killed and two wounded. The remainder of the night remained quiet. General Polk then reformed his line in a cemetery on the edge of Resaca. With the capture of this ridge the Federals could effectively fire their artillery at the railroad bridge and could observe the town of Resaca. This railroad bridge was one of the main arteries for the Confederates to escape across the Oostanula River.

When General Johnston decided to abandon Dalton, Georgia, the Federal army, under General Thomas', followed closely behind the fleeing Confederate army. With this movement the whole Federal army was now in place near Resaca. At about this same time the rest of General Schofield's army made it through the Snake Creek Gap and immediately went to take positions around Resaca. General Logan's 15th Corps was in front of Resaca with General Osterhaus' 1st Division in the center across the road to Resaca, General Morgan L. Smith's 2nd Division on the right and General William Harrow's 4th Division on the left. The 16th Corps was on the right of the 15th

BATTLE OF RESACA, GEORGIA: National Archives, Washington D.C.

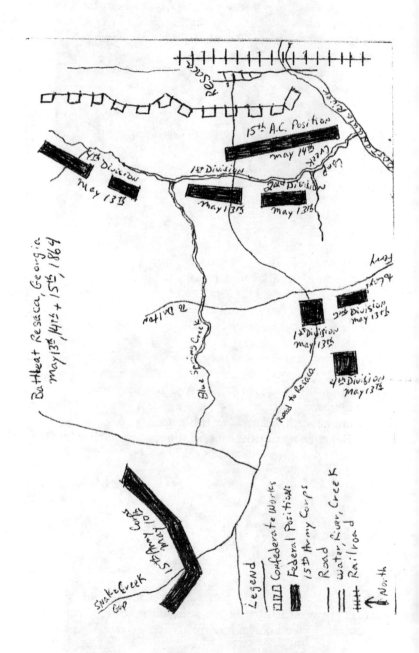

BATTLE AT RESACA, GEORGIA

Corps, with General James Veatch's 4th Division in front reaching to the banks of the Oostanaula River. General Thomas' army was on the left of General McPherson's army, which would be to the north.

General Johnston, realizing that the railroad bridge was now in range of the Federal artillery, ordered that a pontoon bridge be placed about a mile upstream hopefully out of range of the enemy artillery. The whole day of May 15th was spent in fighting and skirmishing. General McPherson ordered that there should be constant pressure put on the forces of General Polk. There was some serious fighting done during this day in which the Confederates lost approximately thirteen hundred men with about one hundred men captured. While the Federals had suffered six hundred dead and three thousand three hundred and seventy-five wounded.

During the night of the 15th the Confederates evacuated the town of Resaca. There were two reasons for this evacuation, the town of Resaca had Federal troops to the west and north of it and if the Confederates stayed in their trenches there would be a severe fight. Federal troops of the 16th Army Corps, under the command of General Sweeny had effected a crossing of the Oostanula River to the west of Resaca and if they were reinforced could then block any attempt by the Confederates to escape south across the bridges. Again General Johnston made a complete withdrawal of his forces across the Oostanula on the bridges setting them on fire, while the Federal forces set in their trenches and waited for the next day.

Below is a continuation of the speech earlier by General Cox. Even though he wasn't in the 15th Army Corps he gives a very good account of the battle around Resaca as he remembered it.

"The order which General Sherman had established for the attack was that upon the right and close to the Oostanuala river. Logan's corps of the Army of the Tennessee was to make an attack, supported by General Dodge, with the 16th Corps, who is here with us to-night. [Applause.] At the same time arrangements were being made to cross the Oostanuala river and intercept the rebel army still further on the south, one of the divisions of Dodge's corps having an active part in this also. On the left of Logan, and going partly toward Camp creek and toward the gap which that creek makes, as I have said, in the hill reaching north and south of us, were the various divisions of the Army of the Cumberland, except the 4th Corps, which was coming down from the north. Between the 4th Corps and the 20th of the Army of the Cumberland our little Army of the Ohio was to fall into its place, so that we would have the Army of the Cumberland, in the center, the Army of the Ohio on the left, with General Howard coming in with the 4th Corps, making a circuit and closing everything from the north, as far as possible, towards the Conasauga river.

I remember very well that our own duty was to find our place by a difficult and circuitous march across the country, away from roads. I know that some of the newspaper correspondents got it into the press that a portion of the army was lost in the woods; and we might have been, as far as our knowledge of the country was concerned. We, however, found our way out, and came into position at the time we were expected. My own division had come out into the country facing Camp creek, and ready to take the position assigned to it. I rode to the hills overlooking the creek, and that is the point of view from which my own memory always recalls what I know of the opening of the battle of Resaca most vividly. General Thomas, with that sturdy and rather ponderous equanimity, lymphatic character and quiet courage that so marked him, sat upon his horse, General Schofield opposite him, waiting for the troops to form in line. The Army of the Tennessee was already pushing forward, some of the advance guard sharply skirmishing with the enemy. We waited perhaps half an hour, waiting, as I supposed, until the 4th Corps could come within connecting distance from the north. When the time had arrived—and I see it to-night as plainly as though it were yesterday—General Thomas, sitting on the hill, having been entrusted, I believe, with the command of ours as well as of his own corps by Sherman, who was further to the right in person, said, in his business-like way, "General Schofield, the line may as well advance." General Schofield turned to me, and said, "General Cox, your division will advance." The same order was given to Judah's division on our right, and I galloped away from the hill. Before us, through a country more or less open, covered here and there with timber, was a slope reaching down to a thicket, below which was Camp creek. We marched forward through the thicket until we came to the creek. It was one of those little crooked creeks, with banks perhaps three or four feet high, and fifteen or twenty feet wide, not very deep; rising precipitously, we enter again a thicket, and exactly what was behind that we did not at the moment know. On our right and left was the line, probably three or four miles in extent from flank to flank, trying to keep shoulder to shoulder—trying to keep up that "tramp" which meant solidity of action and success in its result, which has been so well referred to in the poem which you have just listened to. We could see on the hill the enemy, and shot and shell would drop in or line; but that was not what our men were apprehensive of. Through the thicket we went, stopping to arrange the line and see that it was a line and in order, then with a cheer, forward and up they went, up against those rocky hills of Resaca which are mentioned in the couplet to which I am called upon to respond. Not far did they go before something different was heard—something the soldier had learned to dread more than the noisy explosion of shells—the rattling and hissing of Minie balls and the volleys of musketry! Cheer upon cheer, and away they went, and it was not long before part of the line over the rebel entrenchment and out-work, and the rebels in retreat.

We had risen on a height of ground probably a hundred feet high, from the shoulder of which we could look off and see a little of what was happening to our comrades. We saw the fire and smoke of the musketry along the right, reaching to the Oostanuala river. We saw the other division of our command in the valley, finding itself in a position unhappily worse than ours, and one in which they were suffering. I remember looking back and seeing the brigades of that division coming through the low ground on the right, and feeling a curious kind of interest in seeing the men falling, here and there, like ten-pins in an alley. There was no sound; they were too far away. We could see the cannon balls striking the ground and bounding through the ranks. We could see the men fall, but with that strange feeling that you have of things seen in a dream. We were not near enough to take any active share in that part of the battle; we had gone through the worst of our special conflict and risk, and this seemed like a pantomime, as it were, the roar of the batteries around us making those things at a distance seem to be enacted in silence. I wondered at the time that I did not feel a more humane and active interest in it; but it was strange thing to see men tumbling down in that way, the carnage of battle going on so far away that we could only see the dim outlines. But it was not long before I had the pleasure of meeting our friend, General Howard, riding from the left, informing me that the 4th Corps was in close support, and inquiring after our own position. The battle had continued long enough, for although I have only taken a few minutes to describe this part of it had taken an hour or two, probably, for the advance. By the road we had come it was utterly impossible that there should be any direct communication by wagon with the rear. Our artillery had not been able to follow us, or our ammunition wagons, and our line which had carried that portion of the rebel works was out of ammunition. General Howard ordered a portion of Wood's division, as I remember, to relieve those who were in the works, and our men took a position a little more in the rear. The brigade which was to relieve the right brigade of mine was commanded by that young hero,

Harker, who afterwards fell at Kenesaw. He rode up and asked some questions in regard to the situation. I was at the moment standing on the ground. General Manson, of Indiana, was near me, who commanded the brigade that was in the works, and Colonel Opdycke, who was second in rank in Harker's brigade, was with Harker. We stood, I remember very clearly, my own hand resting on Harker's saddle pommel, Manson standing near me, Opdycke just in front, when a shell from the right seemed to explode right in our midst. Harker was slightly wounded, Manson was knocked down senseless by the concussion of the explosion, from which he never entirely recovered; Opdycke was wounded at the same time, I think, however, by a rifle ball, and I was the only one of the group entirely unhurt.

Manson afterwards, (as showing another curious effect of the experiences of that time), was carried to the hospital, and there it was said, that as he partially recovered his senses, the first thing he said was "Well, General Cox is gone." "No," said somebody, "he is not gone." "Why," he said, "as I fell, I saw him go right up into the air." Such was his illusion; the shock and the fall making it look to him as though others had been blown upwards.

So much for such comparatively trifling personal incidents. I find it interesting to me simply because it helps to make a picture of the events on that day. Our real work was, of course, of another sort.

During the day, the Army of the Tennessee was, as I was saying, pressing in on the rebels on the right. They held this high and rocky prominence, and made, of course, a stout fight to maintain it. We gained advantages here and there, but the whole day was spent in that kind of bitter warfare that occurred in a broken and woody country in which no decisive results could be reached, because the country itself was what European military men called "impracticable;" a country in which armies cannot get together, and in which the maneuvers are confined to skirmishing on a great scale, skirmishes in which hundreds and thousands of men fall, and yet you see only a rattling irregular fight, with only the commander himself, able by means of reports coming to him, to tell what is being done, and how far his men really control that which to the onlooker seems to be so mixed and unformed, as such a battle is.

The next day Hooker's command was pressed around to the north, the Army of the Cumberland, more concentrated in that direction, and the Army of the Tennessee pushed forward more to the right. They captured the hills which look down upon Resaca. They had the position which commanded the railroad bridge to the town, and Sherman was hoping still further to surround Johnston and force him to retreat eastward, and so put him in circumstances which would make him lose the principal material of his army.

After another day spent in the same sort of continual

273

struggle, pressing onward, without having that range of battle which occurs upon a free and open field, the result was that the rebel army succeeded in getting across the river by pontoons and bridges and retreated.

Such, in short, was Resaca; not a battle in which two armies could maneuver on a field such as we imagine when we think of the European battle-fields, but where, over those rocky heights and through those rocky heights and through those thickly wooded valleys, we were fighting onward, scarcely able to see anything that was being done; it being an exceptional opportunity, such as I spoke of, when we were able to see a little of what was going on in some other part of the field. It resulted in the winning of a position. Johnston had lost control of all northern Georgia."(15)

Private Henry Kuck of Company G, 31st Missouri Infantry Regiment on May 20th in one of two letters to his wife wrote his estimate of the action leading to the Battle of Resaca.

"On the 9th we fought the Rebels who had occupied the Railroad about 12 to 14 miles from Dalton: this road goes from Dalton to Atlanta. On the 14th of the month as Claus Gerdel was with us we overwhelmed the Rebels and drove them out of their fortifications; whereby both we and the Rebels lost a lot of men; If we could have taken them faster and sooner we would have taken a lot of prisoners, but this way they all got away. Our army was divided so that Dalton was attacked while the rest of the troops were held back, we could have taken Resaca (Georgia) or the place stormed and thereby surrounding his whole army if all of us had attacked right away.

Concerning myself, I'm fine and so is Wm. Schwarze & John Gerdel & young Gerd Losmann was wounded on, or through, his neck on the 14th of the month, I don't know how bad it is; we were behind a battery by the rifle pits. I saw him get shot; the captain and another by him took him away and he was taking to the hospital; some say he's badly wounded, others say he's not badly wounded, I myself think it's not critical, but it will be a long time before he returns to duty."(16)

On May 16th, as pickets eased their way toward the Confederate trenches they found the trenches empty. General Osterhaus in his diary for Monday, May 16th, says, "Rain cloudy-

Resaca is ours.- At 9 a.m. received orders to advance- we go to Lay's Ferry. When in camp General Dodge sends for reinforcements-a scare- we bivouac on the south side of the Oostanula River-9 Miles."(17)   Sometime in the morning General Woods returned the 29th Missouri and the 31st Missouri Infantry Regiments to 2nd Brigade of the 1st Division of the 15th Army Corps. Also the 3rd Missouri and the 12th Missouri Infantry Regiments rejoined the 3rd Brigade at about the same time. The following is some excerpts from the Official Records relating to the movements for the following day, "Headquarters Department and Army of the Tennessee, Near Resaca, Georgia Special Field Orders Number 11, Section 1, The army will immediately be put in motion on the road to Rome, Georgia, crossing at Lay's Ferry, Brigadier-General Dodge having the advance, Major General John A. Logan, commanding 15th Corps, will follow promptly, and every precaution will be used to prevent delay." Section 2, "The command will be supplied with three days' rations in haversacks, cartridge-boxes and ammunition-chests will be refilled from the supply train." Section 4, "Major General John A. Logan, commanding 15th Corps, will cause to be detailed from his command a competent officer to act as commissary for the hospitals of this command at Resaca. He will report for instructions to Lieutenant-Colonel Morton, chief commissary of subsistence 15th Corps, who will see that a sufficient number of beef-cattle are turned over to the officer detailed as herein provided for the use of the hospitals." Section 6. "Major General John A. Logan, commanding 15th Army Corps, will have the advance to-morrow, and will move his command at seven o'clock on the Rome road. General Logan will (move) forward cautiously, feeling out well to the right and left, endeavoring to communicate on his left with the column of General Thomas." By order of Major General James B. McPherson."(18)

Private Henry Kuck of Company G, 31st Missouri Volunteer Infantry Regiment, wrote in his "Inventory" the dates for May 1st through May 16th, 1864.

"May 1   marching through Bellefonte
      3   by Stevenson
      6   by Lookout & Chattanooga
      9   fought the Rebels at Resaca, Ga., in
the evening back 4 miles.
     11   spoke with Edward Hickham from
Calhoun Co., Ill. He told me my brother John Henry

died of chronic diarrhea, both from 8. Reg. Mo. Vols., Co. E.

    14   Resaca, Ga., stormed Rebels' position and drove them off.

    15/16   Rebels left Resaca, Ga.

    16   . Marched over Consa. River, Dallas."(19)

The 31st Missouri Infantry Regiment suffered very few casualties in this battle. Private Nicholas Gerdel of Company G of Saint Louis, Missouri was severely wounded in the neck on May 15th at Resaca. Private John Bone of Company C of Hopewell, Missouri was wounded in the bowels on May 15,1864 and later died of his wounds. Private Frank Morse of Company H died from wounds at Resaca and is buried at Chattanooga National Cemetery. Corporal Robert Richardson of Company A, was slightly wounded in the hand on May 14, 1864. Private John Drenning of Company E, was severely wounded in the thigh on May 14, 1864.

The following members of the 31st Missouri Infantry were lost to the regiment due to reasons which will be listed with their names, beginning January 1,1864 until May 15, 1864, the last day of the battle of Resaca. In Company A, Sergeant James A. Blake of Victoria was transferred to the Veteran Reserve Corps on January 5th; Private Charles McNulty of Victoria was transferred to the Veteran Reserve Corps on April 2nd; Musician Barnard Reynor of Saint Louis was transferred to the Veteran Reserve Corps on March 16th; Private Austin Williams of Victoria was transferred to the Veteran Reserve Corps on May 15th; Private App. B. Hensley of Hillsboro deserted while at Woodville, Alabama on April 24th; Private S. R. Jemison died at Paducah on January 16th and is buried at Mound City National Cemetery in Illinois; Private John Morrison died on March 14th while at Paducah and is buried at Chattanooga National Cemetery. Company B lost the use for the following reasons: Private James Connelly of Saint Louis was transferred to the Veteran Reserve Corps on April 9th; Private Patrick Lavelle of Saint Louis was transferred to the Veteran Reserve Corps on May 1st; Corporal Samuel O. Staples of Washington County was discharged at Jefferson Barracks, Missouri on April 13th; Private M. Breckenridge died on January 16th at Paducah, Kentucky and was later buried at the National Cemetery in Mound City, Illinois. Company C lost due to the following reasons: Private John H. Forsha of Washington County died of disease at Ironton, Missouri on April 7th; Private Joseph F. Forshee of Washington County died at Young's Point, Louisiana in January; 2nd Lieutenant J. W. Disemling died on January 14th while at Paducah, Kentucky and is buried at the National Cemetery at Mound City, Illinois. Company D lost only one man during this time and he was Private James Wilson of Greenville who was transferred to the Veteran Reserve Corps on April 28th. Company E lost the following men: Private William Witt of Moselle was discharged because of disability on April 24th; Private Robert J. Jenkins of Cuba, Missouri died of disease in Memphis, Tennessee on February 6th; Private L. T. Goforth is buried at the National Cemetery in Mound City, Illinois, he died on February 7th; Private Jacob Rider died at Resaca and is buried at the National Cemetery at Chattanooga, Tennessee. Company F lost the following men: Private Fritz Hain(s) from Canaan was transferred to Company G, 14th Regiment Invalid Corps on April 22nd; Captain Egbert O. Hill resigned from the service on February 29th. Company G lost the following men due to the listed reasons: Private Frederick August Isermann of Warren County was transferred to the Veteran Reserve Corps on March 23rd; Private Jans Toft from Dutzow was transferred to the Veteran Reserve Corps on January 12th; 1st Lieutenant Frederick Ruderhausen from Saint Louis resigned on April 1, 1864. Company H losses were; Private Thomas J. Davidson of Wayne County was transferred to Company B, 2nd Veteran Reserve Corps on January 22nd; Private Francis M. Forrester of Wayne County was transferred to the Veteran Reserve Corps on January 16th, and later discharged on January 27, 1865; Private Robert M. Gregory of Van Buren, Arkansas deserted on March 3rd from the hospital at Benton Barracks, Missouri; Private Ezekial East of Wayne County died of disease at Memphis, Tennessee on March 11th; Private James H. Mallow of Wayne County died of disease on February 28th. Company I lost the following men: Private Martin Klingsliper of Montgomery County was transferred to the 15th Company, 2nd Battalion Invalid Corps sometime in 1864; Private William Lynch of Saint Louis was promoted to Hospital Steward on March 11th; Private Fred A. E. McNair of Carondelet was discharged for disability on March 16th; Private Charles J. Bone was transferred to the Invalid Corps on April 26th; Private John Clarke was promoted to Major and became part of the staff of the regiment sometime in 1864. Company K suffered the following losses: Private Barney

Rainer of Saint Louis was transferred to the Invalid Corps on March 16th; Private Michael Henry age 40 was transferred to the Invalid Corps on April 30th.

CHAPTER ELEVEN:
FROM DALLAS TO BIG SHANTY

"Tuesday May 17-Raining-the 15th Army Corps goes in advance of the 16th Army Corps today-[2-4-1 Division]- leave camp at 9 a.m. a little firing in front it is Cleburne's Division again, which covers the Reb's retreat (Ringgold). By 4 p.m. many firing near Adairsville in General Thomas front! In camp at the crossroad near McGuire on Rocky Creek a fine stream."(1) General Schofield's men were near Sallacoa and the 15th Army Corps was camped near McGuire, both of these areas were about a dozen miles from Adairsville in opposite directions. The 2nd and 4th Divisions of the 15th Corps, on their way to McGuire, were engaged in a battle with Cleburne's Division. General Cleburne and his army were continuing to be a thorn in the flesh of the Army of the Tennessee as they were at Missionary Ridge and Ringgold. This action, which is called the Battle of Rome Crossroads, achieved it's primary objective to delay the Federal army long enough for the Confederate army to retreat.

On Wednesday, May 18th they left camp at six a.m. and headed toward Adairsville where they arrived there around one p.m., resting until about four-thirty and then moved out with a destination of Kingston. General McPherson's army passed to the west of Adairsville arriving at Woodland, which is approximately six miles from Kingston, at about nine p.m., where they went into camp before they proceeded toward Kingston the next morning. General Sherman believed that the main part of the Confederate army had moved into Kingston and was forming there. General McPherson and General Thomas' armies were sent directly to Kingston while General Hooker's 20th Army Corps and General Schofield's Army of the Ohio were sent on the main road towards a town named Cassville. The Confederate army had a line running basically from north to south just east of Cassville to the railroad, about three miles south of town. General Polk's army was in the center with General Hood on his right, and General Hardee's army on his left. As always, when the two armies were within a close contact, there was skirmishing along the front. That night in a conference while at dinner General Johnston, Hardee, Hood and Polk were discussing the battle that would probably come in the morning. It was here that General Hood called attention to the fact that his troops were in danger of some artillery that had them under direct fire. He therefore thought that his position was untenable and that it was best for his force to pull back. General Johnston decided from this exchange to pull back so as to put the Etowah River and the Allatoona hills between them and the Federal troops. General Johnston felt it was better to retreat than to try and fight a battle with leaders who felt they were already beaten. So during the night the Confederate Army again made a successful retreat. It was here that Private John T. Clarke rejoined the 2nd Brigade from Missouri. The 31st Missouri was not involved in any fighting this day but they did march around fifteen miles.

On Thursday May 19th, General Osterhaus says in his diary, "foggy- we leave camp at seven a.m. in advance for Kingston. No enemy found- arrive at Kingston by ten and one-half a.m. go in camp two miles west of it on the Rome road and near the river. Firing in front of the left wing (General Schofield's)-seven miles."(2) Went into camp with General McPherson Corps about four miles west of Kingston at a place known as Woodlawn. While here they rested and were assigned to guard some bridges across the Etowah River to keep the Confederates from destroying them.

On Friday May 20th, Special Field Orders Number 9, were issued by General Sherman headquarters stating that the whole army was to be ready to march on May 23rd to head toward Dallas. Private John T. Clarke says in his diary, "Wolleys Plantation. We have a rest today. Have only marched one mile. We guard the bridge across Ethowak (sic) River in Cass County. I am a picket tonight. Post in a Gin House."(3) General Osterhaus puts in his diary, "fine morning-we remain in camp-My return of casualties near Resaca shows infantry's at two hundred and thirty-four killed and wounded."(4) In General Sherman's special field orders of this date says in section 5, "The ration will be for troops, one pound of bread flour, or meal, beef on the hoof, two days' allowance of bacon per week, and sugar, coffee, and salt; four pounds of grain will be allowed each animal and no more. All else must be gathered in the country. Brigade quarter-masters and commissaries will be instructed to forage and graze, but indiscriminate plunder must not be allowed."(5) On May 20, 1864 General Peter J. Osterhaus at Kingston, Georgia realigned the 1st Division again putting the 31st Missouri Infantry Regiment in the 3rd Brigade. Private Henry Kuck wrote a summary of what had been happening to him the last few days.

> "Kingston, Georgia
> May 20th 1864
>
> Dear Metta,
>   Yesterday I mailed a letter to you from the post office; in case this letter doesn't arrive I'm noting here what I write in the last letter. I'm perfectly fine now. On May 11th we marched from Woodville, Ala. To Dalton where the Rebels are well ensconsed. Here we have a huge army ready. The army was split up: one part went directly toward Dalton and the other part surrounded Dalton, where we wanted to take most of their army as prisoners. On the 14th we fought the Rebels at the Railroad by a small town which was strongly occupied in order to cut off their retreat from Dalton; we stormed it twice, once at 5 o'clock and on the next day, that is the 15th, we approached again and secured it for ourselves. Since then we've had skirmishes almost every day on the march. Yesterday we arrived here at Kingston and are guarding the bridge so the Rebels won't come back and burn it, not forgetting that the Rebels retreated quickly as we seized their entrenchments.
>   We chased the Rebels so fast that they didn't have time to burn the bridges. Don't forget where the fighting was: a small town called Resaca by a small river called Goose River. Nicolaus Gerdel was shot through the neck, but I don't think seriously, which Wm. Schwarze probably wrote in his letter. Young Gerd is still O.K. and says hello to his mother and to all of you. I spoke with Edward Kickam of Calhoun Co., Illinois, who said my brother John Henry is dead, he was in the 6th Reg. Mo. Vols. and was always quite close by, which I and the two of them didn't know; he died of diarrhea. Be of good hope, my dear wife, for He who leads and guides our ways will also protect me if he so chooses, and will give you your husband and our dear children their father back again, so we can live together again and can be happy and comfort each other in sorrow and

distress. You write how little Elsie still thinks about her father. This always reminds me of our last goodbye, when little Nina cried about me and Emilie was so worried when I had to leave. Take care of yourself by the coming birth and don't get up too soon. Greet all our friends and neighbors. Let us stay here in Eggers' house! Things can change with him. Love to you all.

Your Henry"(6)

"Saturday May 21,1864. Wooleys Plantation. We are still encamped here. It is a lovely place, nicely ornamented with flower gardens and everything indicative of wealth. Found a letter from Mrs. Stephan [name indecipherable] in the R [Rebel] Army. She wants the skull of a Yankee for a soup bowl and the jaw bone for a spear for her lover."(7) Nothing much happened on May 22nd except the preparation for departure on the next day for Dallas. Hot weather had set in on May 21st and continued making the march miserable for the men on May 23rd. John T. Clarke was ordered to report to the 15th Army Corps headquarters for office duty in the Assistant Adjutant General office.

May 23rd started out hazy but proceeded to get hotter and hotter as the day went along. This made marching miserable, the men suffered because of the heat and the dust that their feet kicked up on the march. The 1st Division brought up the rear of the 15th Corps which made for a lot of dust they had to eat. Major A.J. Seay of the 32nd Missouri Infantry Regiment recorded in his diary the following, "Monday, 23. We start across the Etowah on a bridge. Our div wagon guard and we travel most all night-march 16 miles thru wilderness-but as fine pine timber as I ever saw. We bivouack just before day in a cornfield."(8) The Army of the Tennessee marched to the right, spending that night at Euharlee Creek having marched approximately eighteen miles that day. The terrain was hilly and there was sand on some of these hills which made for hard marching. There was no water for about twelve miles in one stretch which made it miserable. General Osterhaus in his diary says, "A long tedious march: in camp on Euhrahee Creek: the rear of the division gets in only after 3 a.m. in the night. 18 miles."(9) This was the day that Private John T. Clarke reported to the Assistant Adjutant General Office for duty. This would enable them to approach Dallas from the west.

General Osterhaus says in his diary, "Tuesday, May 24th

hot and cloudy-(4,1,2) at Van Wert by 10 a.m.- camp on a little branch about four miles beyond Van Wirt; water is very scarce and it is sour. There is no water for 5 miles!- It is a good thing for the 1and 3 brigades, that todays march is so short; the poor mens did not get in camp last night before 3 a.m.-made 8 miles." (10) In the entry from his diary General Osterhaus states in parenthesis that the 4th Division was the lead division in the march of the 15th Army Corps, with the 1st Division following and the 2nd Division bringing up the rear. Some of the men who had got in around three a.m. in the morning they were again on the road after only a few hours of sleep. This, along with the lack of decent drinking water, made for men who were extremely tired and worn out.

May 25th, found all the columns converging toward Dallas, Georgia. It rained during the night bringing some relief to the soldiers in the Army of the Tennessee. The 1st Division of the 15th Army Corps led off in the march of the corps. As you will notice that one division would lead one day and the division that was second would lead the next day. There were many reasons for this procedure. One of these reasons was that the closer to the front you are the less likely it will be that you will eat the dust of the whole army. Another reason would be that in the event of constant skirmishing, if the same division was always in front they would be taking all of the early casualties from the fighting. Also the men in the rear always have to worry about closing up on the men to the front. The men in the front could be marching at a moderate speed and those in the rear at times would almost be running just to keep up. And as the case in most armies the division in the rear for the day were responsible for the security of the division supply train which usually followed the division. By rotating like this it would allow each division to bear all the burdens equally. It was on this night that General Logan, the commander of the 15th Army Corps, issued the following order.

"In the Field, on Pumpkin Vine Creek, May 25,1864- 10:15 p.m.
Brigadier General P.J. Osterhaus,
Commanding First Division:
The indications are that we will have a heavy battle to-morrow, the enemy having massed his entire available force, consisting of Hood's, Hardee's and Polk's corps at Dallas. Hardee is in our front. You will have

your command in readiness to move at a moment's notice, in light fighting trim. No wagons, except fifteen ammunition-wagons to each division and the ambulances, will be taken along. The rest will be parked on the west side of Pumpkin Vine Creek. Rations will be issued to the troops to-night, and care will be taken to see that each man has forty rounds of ammunition in his cartridge-box.

By order of Major-General Logan

R. R. TOWNES,

Assistant Adjutant-General"(11)

During the night General Hooker had tried to carry the woods near an intersection named New Hope because of the proximity of a Methodist Church by that name. The fight lasted well into the evening before the fighting ended for the night. Major A.J. Seay of the 32nd Missouri Infantry recorded in his diary, "Wednesday, 25. March 8 or 10 miles. Go into camp about 3 P.M. Heavy firing on our left-4 to 6 miles. Cannonaning very rapid poor country today. Go into camp three times, the last at dark and rainy. No eatables obtainable. Meat, crackers and coffee is all we have-plenty of that."(12)

May 26th, found the 15th Corps on the edge of Dallas with General Logan on the right of the Army of the Tennessee. General Osterhaus says in his diary, "Cool clear morning-Hardee's and Polk's Corps said to be near Dallas. Advance one-fourth to 11 a.m. get in position in front of Dallas by 1 p.m. on the right of General Smith. Skirmishers (unreadable) Cavalry-2nd Missouri Artillery in position exchange a few shots- Dallas is ours. Advance beyond M. L. Smith against a (unreadable) line, I go in position on his left. 5 miles".(13) Once through Dallas the Army of the Tennessee set up in formation with General Harrow and his division on the extreme right facing almost due south, General M. L. Smith was on his left with General P. J. Osterhaus to his left almost in the center of the Army of the Tennessee. General Sweeney division was in reserve with General Veatch to the left of General Osterhaus with General Davis' Division on the extreme left with some of his division facing almost due north. General Hooker again renewed the attack against entrenched enemy and was repulsed all day. General Thomas was between General McPherson and General Hooker with General Schofield eventually coming up on the left of General Thomas. While there was a general overall battle going on against the whole Confederate lines it was without much success. Major A. J. Seay recorded in his diary, "Thursday, 26. Leave camp at 11 A.M. March 2 ½ miles and go into battle line-skirmishing light, some artillery, etc. Late in the evening the fight waxes warm, but we don't go in. A fight between the lines all night, sometimes very heavy. We sleep but little."(14)

General McPherson had been ordered to turn the flank of the Confederates but on the 27th of May he found the enemy strongly entrenched to his front and determined to stay there and let the Federals attack. He had found that the lines of the Confederates appeared to extend past the Villa Rica road which was south of his position. The Army of the Tennessee could not afford to stretch any farther because there was already a gap between them and General Thomas to his north. If General McPherson extended farther to the right he would be in danger of having both of his flanks open where they could easily be attacked by the Confederates. General Osterhaus diary says, "fine- the pioneers cut a road on left of the 2d Bde which is in position on the left of the 2d Division, a gap between 16th C.- Reb's charge inside it at 6 a.m. just when I bought the 3rd Brig. on the left of the 2d (which had given way) the 12th Mo. check the enemy-forms 2 lines-drives the Rebs gradually back-relieve 2d by 1st Brig-Bring 2 Napoleons in battery-entrencments-2 more Napoleon's."(15) This is how the battle had gone along the whole front of the Federal line. When the Confederates thought that they had found a weak spot they would try and take advantage of it by trying to turn the Federals flanks. This is what exactly happened when it was reported to General Osterhaus that there was large masses of Confederates moving toward his left flank. At five a.m. Colonel Wangelin deployed his brigade in two lines to the left of Colonel Williamson. Just after they arrived the Confederates attacked causing the 2nd Brigade of the 1st Division to fall back slowly fighting the Confederates hard all the way. The 3rd Brigade's regiments started to arrive to help them out. The 12th Missouri Regiment led the way, with the 29th Missouri and 31st Missouri Infantry Regiments pulling up alongside the 12th Missouri Regiment, these three regiments made up a battalion that was commanded by Lieutenant-Colonel Joseph S. Gage, drove the Confederates back regaining all the ground that had been lost that day plus a little more. The 1st Brigade came up to relieve the 2nd Brigade while the rest of the 3rd Brigade came

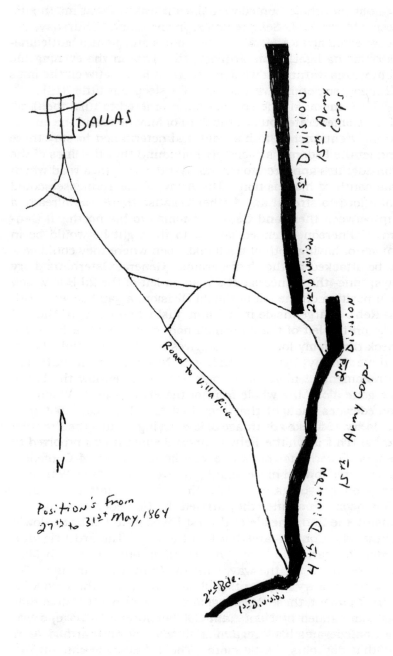

DALLAS

1st Division
15th Army Corps

2nd Division

2nd Division

2nd Army Corps

15th Army Corps

Road to Villa Rica

N

Position's from
27th to 31st May, 1864

4th Division

2nd Bde.

1st Division

BATTLE AT DALLAS, GEORGIA

up and eventually linked with the 16th Army Corps closing the gap between the two army corps. This was a day of almost constant struggles between the two opposing forces. Major A.J. Seay writes in his diary, "Friday, 27. We start in at 6 and fight till 5, one div at a time. Our loss four wounded-Capt. Zimmerman, Sergt. Clouts, Pots, Davis Co. A. and Rice, Co. B. and J.J. Lane Co G. killed. 17 Mo. lost four with the regiment. Reb lines stiff-16th corps amounts to but little."(16)

Saturday May 28th started out as a fine day as far as temperature goes, but it proved to be another hard day of skirmishing between the two opposing forces. It started at about four-thirty in the morning and continued all day until about four-thirty in the afternoon when the Confederates made an assault along the whole line. General Osterhaus in his diary says, "a most impetuous assault on this whole line commencing on our right, (4th Div), which became a little panic stricken, threw 2d Bde(reserve) on the right- Steady the line, 3 hot guns taken back. In my front proper the most terrible slaughter of rebels near(indiscernible) wounded and prisoners is on hand. Infantry and Artillery splendid."(17) This attack included a strong Confederate attack on the 1st and 3rd Brigades which led to a number of dead and wounded that were left for the Federals to bury and care for. Private John T. Clarke, who is now in the Assistant Adjutant General office, says in his diary, "Saturday 28. A sharp fight took place last night. Skirmishing and Artillery fire is going on this morn. We played Yankee on the Rebs. Moved our trains to the rear, our troops were hurried to the front. The Rebs thought we retreated and charged us but were repulsed with awful slaughter. Our men were in the ground."(18) The Confederate troops of General Bates were the ones that attacked General McPhersons men.

General Sherman had hoped to draw General McPherson from in front of the enemy where he was entrenched and have him move to General Hooker's right, but before he could obey these orders he was assaulted by the Confederates. At about three forty-five p.m., the Confederates made a determined attack against the Federals carrying the first line and capturing a three gun battery. General Armstrong's dismounted cavalrymen from Mississippi and Alabama, were the Confederates who had captured the battery and trenches. General Logan, after seeing this, ordered Colonel James A. Williamson's 2nd Brigade to the extreme right. General Osterhaus took personal command of this brigade. He and General Logan, though wounded slightly in the forearm, helped to beat back this attack. General Bates and his men were under furious counterattack by the Federals for about two hours when Major General Logan, on his horse, leaped over the entrenchment's and recaptured the three guns of the 1st Iowa Artillery that was lost and the entrenchment's.

Farther down the line, General Lewis' Orphan Brigade fought against Colonel Wangelin's 3rd Brigade, over-running the Federal line capturing some thirty prisoners and several artillery pieces while receiving terrible fire from the Federals just a few yards away. General Bullock's Florida Brigade attacked General Morgan L. Smith's 2nd Division. There were heavy losses in this Florida Brigade and they were ordered to withdraw once General Bates realized that the Federals were to strongly entrenched. General Lewis' Orphan Brigade did not receive the order to withdraw as soon as the Florida Brigade, and the 5th Kentucky Infantry Regiment was within a few yards of the Federal works and refused to withdraw until their commander, Lieutenant Colonel Hiram Hawkins, grabbed their colors and ordered his men to the rear. The Orphan Brigade lost approximately fifty-one percent of the almost eleven hundred men that went into this battle.

General Logan reported a loss of three hundred and seventy-nine casualties while estimating that the Confederates had lost about two thousand to three thousand casualties. General Bates reported a loss of four hundred and fifty men to his division which makes it appear that General Logan estimate was a little high. Since there was a tendency on both sides to exaggerate the enemy losses and sometimes the Confederates records lacked total casualties listed, it is estimated that there could have been as high as one-thousand Confederate casualties.

May 29th was a Sunday and as most Sundays during the war the Lord's Day was not observed in the traditional way. There was consistent firing along the whole front. General Sherman was trying to reach east in order to reach the railroad and his supply line and also trying to get around the flank of the Confederates. Again General McPherson was ordered to try and withdraw from the position that they were in to continue to new positions to the east. General Johnston who, had guessed at this, was ordering his men to keep constant pressure on the Federals so they could not evacuate their positions. Major A. J. Seay wrote in his diary, "Sunday, 29. Quite warm. I've been unwell three days. John Greenstreet wounded in Co. E. Under marching orders at 10 P.M. the Rebs pitch into us and we fight all night. The most terrific firing I ever witnessed. They did not move us. Our loss four men."(19) There was almost constant skirmishing between the two opposing forces. The 30th and 31st of May were spent in trying to get away from the position. At about midnight of the 30th the Confederates attacked the 15th Army Corps again. In his diary Major A. J. Seay wrote the following of May 30th and 31st. "Monday, 30. Weather hot and dry, sharp skirmishing all day, wounded last night-Cloutz and Reeves, Co. F., Leek Co. H. and A. Man of Co. I. Our line acted foolishly. Hard living loss of sleep and contant watchfulness. Jim and Mc get in from St. Louis. Tuesday, 31. Hot dry, heavy skirmishing, no fighting in the distance. Wangelin scould me on Joes account-calls him coward, etc. Nothing to feed on except a little green wheat. I am up most all night. Rough times."(20) In a letter to his wife Private Henry Kuck of Company G, 31st Missouri Infantry Regiment writes, "On May 21st in the evening we arrived here, where we have been fighting night and day since then and where some soldiers already ..... The worst part of it was when the Rebels attacked. The Front lines had no time run back because they were surprised by the Rebels, and then we had to open fire before they were all in; some of them were shot by their own people .. until the Rebels retreated again and came back into it. From our Regiment ... still about 28 to 30 miles away. Atlanta, which is close to the middle of Georgia, has ..."(21) General McPherson had come up with an idea on how to get away with the least possible of loss. He had decided that the best way was to have trenches prepared to the rear of the main trenches to get into in case the Confederates followed. General McPherson had decided to withdraw his army division by division. Some people credit General Sherman with this idea and others have given credit to General Logan. During the night the supply trains moved toward the north and then to the east. Surgeon Alexander W. Reese, age thirty-five, was mustered in the 31st Missouri Infantry Regiment on May 30, 1864 at New Hope Church, Georgia as their surgeon due to the death of Surgeon Churchill Strother.

At the twenty-second meeting of the Society of the Army

of the Tennessee in Cincinnati, Ohio on September 25 & 26, 1889, Major A.M. Van Dyke responded to a toast named "Dallas." Recorded below are parts of his speech to the society that relate to the battle.

"On the 26th, the 15th Corps, having the right of the army, moved forward from Pumpkin Vine creek toward Dallas, the march being enlivened by spirited skirmishing, and during the day passed through the town, taking position two miles beyond on the Powder Springs road. The necessity for stopping here manifested itself in a considerable body of rebels very strongly posted. This corps, which was the part of the army principally engaged, was placed in position in line of battle, with Harrow's division on the right and crossing the Villa Rica road; M. L. Smith, in the center, crossing the Marietta road, and Osterhaus, upon the left, connecting with General Dodge, of the 16th Corps. (Excuse these details, I thought they might be interesting to some of you.)

Although the battle of Dallas may be said to have begun on the 26th, continuing during the 27th with heavy skirmishing and artillery firing all day, yet it was not until the 28th that the matter in dispute between the two armies was hotly contested and definitely settle.

From early morning of that day until 3:30 P.M., there was heavy skirmishing so as sometimes to be very like a battle. At that hour the rebels in column of regiments made a determined assault upon Harrow's division, which for unavoidable reasons was the weakest part of our line. They came on with the usual rush and that same famous "rebel yell." The men of the Army of Tennessee had heard that yell so many times that they had come to regard it quite as much the despairing shriek of a forlorn hope as the exultant shout of anticipated victory. In their frantic rush, they came up to within eighty yard of our line, many of them nearer; the fighting was close and deadly, Logan says, and especially so in front of Walcutt's brigade. Line after line of the enemy came forward and was sent back a broken and disordered fragment. Walcutt stood amid the storm of bullets on the top of the breast works, animating and inspiring his men.

I am glad that he did not then present so broad a target as he would to-day, or we might have been denied

290

the gratification of his presence with us to-night. The 1ˢᵗ Iowa battery, in position some what forward of the main line, was at one time within the rebel line, but never in their possession.

The affair was short, sharp, brilliant, and the principal assault lasted but a half hour. It was followed by a feebler attempt against M. L. Smith's line, and a still feebler one against Osterhaus. It came upon us as suddenly as a furious summer thunder-storm from the west, and we heard the deep mutterings of its thunder as it passed away exhausted to the east.

Thus began, continued and ended the battle of Dallas, where Hardee's entire corps, twenty-five thousand men, under the belief that the right of the army had been weakened to strengthen the left, was dashed in mass like an avalanche against a single line of our troops, and like an avalanche was dashed into pieces against an immovable obstacle.

But who can describe a battle, the sublimest spectacle ever presented to human sight. The colors which the painter puts upon his canvas are but dead things, and the living words of the most impassioned eloquence seem but tame things with which to picture the frantic rush of an assault, the heroic steadfastness of the defense, the frightful fury of shot and shell, the rattle of musketry and the whiz of its leaden hail, the tense muscle, firmly set jaw, the distended nostril, the unflinching eyes that look death in the face and defy him, the havoc the ruin, the blood of gaping wounds, the stony stare of death, the dejected silence of the defeated, he ringing cheer of the victors.

The battle of Dallas was not a great battle, such as Antietam, or Gettysburg, or Shiloh, or Chickamauga. There was no grand strategy, no brilliant tactics, but a good square stand up and set to, and the best men won.

Johnston says it was trifling affair. Was Johnston so great a man that a disastrous failure of an attempt, with the loss of more than two thousand men, was to him a trifling affair? But it seems that in the written history of the war from a rebel point of view, their defeats were generally trifling affairs and their victories indescribably grand; and I have seen that, on paper at least, they often snatched victory from defeat.

But it was not a trivial affair to him and his cause. It was a link in that great chain of events, that coiling about it with ever tightening grasp, choked the life out of the hideous serpent that would have stung our liberty.

Nor was it a trivial affair to us and our cause. It is true that our loss was but thirty killed and three hundred wounded. But the loss of one patriot's life is an irreparable loss; and yet we know that such sacrifices found favor in the sight of God, for it was through such that he brought it about in his own good time, that this country of ours should be the land within whose shores there could rightly stand a "Statue of Liberty Enlightening the World." And let us hope too that he will continue henceforth to direct us in the paths of peace; but if war shall come, that he will again lead us to victory, and so guide us in all things that the states of this Union shall ever form one country having one glorious flag and one common destiny."(22)

On June 1st, in the morning the 15th Corps and the 16th Corps retreated back to the prepared positions division by division until they had all made it to the road where they could march to the north and then east. The 2nd Brigade of the 1st Division went into the works near Dallas at three-thirty a.m. to cover the withdrawal of the 15th Corps, they were able to leave Dallas by nine a.m.. General Osterhaus states in his diary, "The movement of the Division began at 4 a.m. 2nd Brigade leave Dallas by 9 a.m. Rebs follow very continuously. An awful march, hot and dusty. The men struggle a good deal. Met General Hooker. Malcontent!! 4th and 2nd Divisions in position the 1st Division in Reserve. Marched 7 miles."(23) The Army of the Tennessee then marched around the rest of the army to the north and then east, moving into the trenches of General Hooker's 20th Army Corps near the New Hope Church and remaining there through the 4th of June. While they were in these positions they were almost continuously skirmishing with the Confederates to their front. The 4th Army Corps was in position on the left of the Army of the Tennessee. The 1st Brigade was put on the front during the night of June 1st and 2nd because of a scare of an attack by the Confederates. It was on this day that the commander of the 31st Missouri Regiment, Colonel Thomas C. Fletcher, left sick. He would be discharged by Special Order Number 209 from the War Department on June 16,1864. During the night of June 2nd and 3rd there was a heavy rain and thunderstorm. Rain is sometimes called the best friend that an infantrymen can have, mainly because it helps to hide movements. The soldiers who were in the trenches, rifle pits or on picket duty would have had a tendency to disagree with that statement. There is nothing worse than trying to sleep when it is raining because when you get wet, unless you are extremely tired, you will wake up. Rifle pits are shallow pits scooped out of the dirt or are just low spots in the ground in which logs or stones were placed in front to act as a breastworks. These rifle pits, though they supplied adequate protection, also had the tendency to hold water. This was uncomfortable for the men who had picket duty. Another hazard of rain was the possibility of the paper cartridges getting wet, which ensured the powder got wet, causing the cartridges to misfire.

General Stoneman's cavalry captured the town of Allatoona. This assured the Federal army that the railroad could now be used to supply General Sherman's army. General Hooker's 20th Army Corps, once they were relieved from the front near New Hope Church by the 15th Army Corps and the rest of the Army of the Tennessee, was trying to march around to get into position on the flank of the Confederate army. General Hooker had lost a lot of his prestige among not only his superiors, but also those who served under him. Private John T. Clarke writes in his journal, "Friday 3. No intermission, but fire, fire all the time. Hooker with a large force is trying to flank Joe & Co.. Rumor has him very successful. We shall see."(24) The 1st Brigade was relieved by troops of the 16th Army Corps, again it was a rainy day. The 2nd Brigade were sent to the left and placed in the trenches of the 4th Army Corps. They occupied rifle pits that were only about one-hundred yards from the rifle pits of the Confederates to their front.

Saturday night June 4th and 5th was another night of rain. General Hooker had completed the task assigned to him by flanking the Confederate army. General Johnston, knowing that his position was now in danger, chose this dark, rainy night to withdraw from their positions. General Osterhaus in his diary states, "Sunday June 5th, Rain all night-Rebs skedaddles during the dark night from our front- a few prisoners:- Order to march for Acworth Creek- leave by 11 A.M.- in camp 2 miles N E of Burnt Church or Hogans Place (4 miles S. W. of Acworth Station) 6 miles- A very hot night."(25) General Sherman on June 4th issued Special Field Orders, Number 17, which addressed some items that had bothered commanders for years. He addressed the problem of soldiers who would abandon the battle to bring their wounded comrades to the aid station or hospital. Another problem that effected both sides was shirking, skulking and straggling. These were men, who when a battle was about to be fought would disappear by hiding, feigning sickness or on the march would start slowing down and fall behind their unit then head for the woods or get lost in a convenient building. General Sherman, for his part, thought the proper response was to shoot them. These type of men were many times captured by the enemy.

"Special Field Orders, Number 30.

Headquarters Department and Army of the Tennessee.

Near New Hope Church, June 5,1864.

I. Major-General Logan, commanding Fifteenth Army Corps, will move to the vicinity of Burnt Church, and one division, if possible, without wagons or artillery, will be pushed forward to the bridge across Allatoona Creek, near Acworth, where Major-General Thomas has a brigade. Two divisions of the Fifteenth Army Corps will march by the main road which runs, substantially parallel to the enemy's line; the other division will march by a road which runs in rear, guided by Capt. C. B. Reese.

III. The command will move to Acworth to-morrow, Major-General Logan, commanding Fifteenth Army Corps, having the advance, marching at 6 a.m.

By order of Maj. Gen. James B. McPherson

WM. T. Clark,

Assistant Adjutant-General"(26)

General Logan issued his Special Field Order, Number 22, assigned the duties for the 15th Army Corps for the following day starting at six a.m.. The 1st Division, commanded by General Osterhaus, was to be the first division to leave down the main road followed by the 4th Division, commanded by Brigadier General William Harrow. The 2nd Division, commanded by Brigadier General M. L. Smith, was given the task of relieving General Thomas' brigade that was guarding the bridge across Allatoona Creek.

General Osterhaus states in his diary, "Monday June

6th, fine- leave camp at 6 a.m. arrive at Acworth by 9 a.m. 7 miles water on both sides of town, it is quite a little place. Go into (unreadable)- position N E of town fronting S E-large mail."(27) General Sherman reaches Acworth and decides to go to General McPhersons camp along Proctor's Creek. The connection of the army with the railroad was one of the goals that General Sherman had while his troops were around New Hope Church. He was relieved because now he could resupply his army. He had not yet whole-heartedly adopted the concept of marching through Georgia, living off the land and the people who lived in the path of march. General Sherman's army spent the next few days in camp around the town of Acworth. The men who had just survived the battle of Dallas were ready for some time off. The men were refitted, casualties were removed to the north into hospitals, food was issued and the men were allowed to rest. An army at rest is really a busy army. Major A.J. Seay writes in his diary what occupied his and other officers in his unit. "Tuesday, 7. Lay in camp all day. Hot and cloudy. Our wounded in a good place and well cared for. We are busy trying to get our paper reports, returns, etc. right. Are required to do many things in the line of reporting. Thursday, 9. Make out tri-monthly return, write letters to Mother, Ed and Virginia and Capt. Clark. One letter from the Capt since I left. We have been gathering supplies for another forward. Got some fresh butter and milk."(28) The men were assigned to picket duty, to keep in contact with the Confederates, guard duty and other duties which kept them busy.

It was at times like this that the mail would finally catch up with the men and letters which they opened were read and reread over and over, there was nothing more welcome than news from home. Many soldiers also received newspapers from the town where they grew up and they were not only read by these men but also by their fellow soldiers. Confederate papers were read by the Federal soldiers as were the Federal papers read by Confederate soldiers. Some letters that were sent to the folks at home were very descriptive of what was happening, but lots of times it was just pleasantries and questions. This was done so as not to worry those at home, but also it was hard to adequately describe what was seen. Writing a letter and avoiding the subject of war was a form of escaping from the situations faced by the soldiers. If any information was put in a letter describing the war it was pretty basic and general. Most field grade officers, majors or above, were more explicit in their description of the overall battle events because most of them were more familiar with the information that came in from the line companies. Company officers through the ranks to private wrote more about the events that happened directly in their company or regiment area.

Private Henry Kuck of Company G, 31st Missouri Infantry Regiment, wrote in what he called his Inventory the important days in his life.

"May 18/19   camped near a plantation, a rebel Col.
                Was shot there in battle with our cavalry.
       20   by Kingston, Ga. On the Etowah
                River, we had to guard the bridge over the
                river
       23   over the bridge to Dallas.
       25   to Dallas.
       26   arrived at Dalton, lost many men
       27   our Rg. on the skirmish line. Rebels
                stormed our flank, were driven off, lost
                many men.
    29/30   last night, many skirmishes, they
                retreated
       30   Today we left our positions and
                marched to the left wing.
June 5   The Rebels left their positions and
                retreated.
       6   through Acworth Ga., camped there
                until June 10, had fever
       10   marched to Big Sandy Station near
                Acworth
       11   took our positions in front of Army
                divisions 15 to 19, guarded train.
       24   to the division hospital with swollen
                legs.
       26   back to regiment, in the night
                marched to Kennesaw Mountain."(29)

The losses to the 31st Missouri Regiment during May 16th through June 9th are listed as followed. The following men were wounded or killed at the Battle of Dallas, Georgia. Private James Cosgriff of Company B was slightly wounded in the head on May 27, 1864; Sergeant James C. Thomas of Company C was killed on May 28, 1864; Private Henry Now of Company G was killed on May 27, 1864. Private James H. Cozort of Company H was killed on May 29, 1864;   Private Thomas B. Self of Company C was slightly wounded in thigh on May 28, 1864; Private Thomas Duvalt of Company C, was killed on May 27, 1864. Other losses in the regiment were; Company C lost Private Lewis E. Lowe of Washington County was transferred to the Invalid Corps on June 6, 1864. In Company H Private Franklin Beaty of Wayne County was killed on May 24th at Dallas, Georgia; Private James H. Cozart of Wayne County was wounded in action at Dallas, Georgia and would later die of these wounds on May 29th, 1864. Company K lost Private Michael Henry of Saint Louis was transferred to the Invalid Corps on June 16, 1864.

CHAPTER 12:
KENNESAW MOUNTAIN

General Blair arrived in camp with the 2nd Division of the 17th Army Corps on June 8th. This division had gone home after they had re-enlisted as a veteran unit. The 15th Army Corps, as was the rest of the Federal army, were on their way towards Marietta starting on June 10th. General Osterhaus in his diary states, "Friday June 10, fine (weather), at 12 1/2 marching order for Marrietta (4.2.1) ready at 6 a.m.- massed at 'Big Shanty' by 10 3/4 a.m.- Rebs in front. Saw General Blair- 5 miles- Manuever for position- rotten town- Rebs like us not-very careful- bring in prisoners. I have nothing to (next two words unreadable) Show us all day."(1) Along the same lines as General Osterhaus, Major A. J. Seay wrote the following in his diary. "Friday, 10. We start about 8 in the rain—rain and sun shine all day. Move South to Big Shanty Station and bivouack for the night in sight of a reb signal station on the top os Lost Mt. at the base of which Joe is entrenched. Some skirmishing."(2) The Army of the Tennessee was on the left at Big Shanty, which was a station on the railroad that consisted of a few shantys and a hotel that were stretched across the railroad. General Thomas' army held the center with General Schofield's army on the right. The position which they were in was about four miles from Marietta. To their front was three mountains which were known as Kennesaw, Pine and Lost Mountain. The Army of the Tennessee was following the railroad which curved to the north of Kennesaw Mountain. They ended up about one mile south of Big Shanty heading toward Marietta looking at another mountain called Brush Mountain. From here the men that were sent ahead were able to see the Confederate troops making their defenses stronger. By marching in this direction General McPherson marched towards the defensive lines of General Hood's army. General Thomas' army was lining up south on Pine Mountain and General Schofield's army was on the far right facing Lost Mountain. The skirmishers were beginning to fire at each other from their positions, feeling each other out and locating one another.

Rain fell again on June 11th. The Federal army woke up to find the Confederate army still in position and themselves in a better defensive shape than they had been when the night had closed in on both armies. General Osterhaus states in his diary, "Order to make a reconnisance in force with 1st Division (1Division 17th A.C. & 1 Brigade 16 A.C. cooperating) Advance about 1 mile found the Rebs behind breastworks- Deployed in two lines- Some skirmishing- Have to wait for movements on the right."(3) The bad news for the Federal soldiers was that every move they made was under observation of the Confederates stationed on the mountains. On October 10th, 1864 when chasing General Hood and the Confederate army north towards Tennessee, Assistant Surgeon A. W. Reese the surgeon for the 31st Missouri Infantry, climbs Kenesaw Mountain and describes the view that the Confederates had.

"The view extended many miles on either hand — Atlanta — with its domes and spires glittering and sparkling in the gorgeous, Autumnal sunlight, slept in the blue and hazy distance. Stone Mountain, lifting its bold and barren front, far away to the left — Chattahoochee — classic stream! winding, like a thread of silver, through the tall, dark, forest pines — Lost Mountain — thrusting its lofty summit skyward on our right — Pine Mountain — with its plumy crest of eternal green, on whose summit fell the rebel General Polk — these were some of the most prominent features of this incomparable and matchless landscape, spread out, in living beauty, at our feet.

Forests dark and sombre with the gloomy Pine, stretched, for many miles away, on either hand. Far along the verge of the horizon's bar, wound the dim outline of the Alatoona range.

The Kenesaw mountains consist of two-lofty hills, connected by a long and narrow spur—one of these is called Big, and the other the little Kenesaw. At the base of the little Kenesaw is a long, spur like elevation.

It was through the woods — at the base of this spur — that our troops made the furious charge on the rebel works, June 27th, 1864.

Our line of works at that time, extended all along the base of the mountains from one end to the other.

Just opposite the peak of little Kenesaw, in the valley

beneath, during most of the month of June, the 31st Mo Infantry held its position in line."(4)

Major A. J. Seay records, "Saturday, 11. We move donw 1 ½ miles and take a position and have some skirmishing across a field. Artillery firing on our right, some distance. At night we go into the field and dig entrenchments for infantry and artillery. Rained all day. I am quite unwell. Sunday, 12. Rained all night last night. ½ the regiment in rifle pits all day covered the road. Some artillery today on our left, skirmishing brisk. Dark and cold in the rainy South. I am in bad health, very billious. No vegetables, water all around and above us."(5) It rained during most of the day, saturating the ground and pouring into the trenches where the men had to stand. Every day the men kept building trenches closer and closer. They would move from as far as an eighth of a mile to as close as a few yards from the Confederate line. The whole time it was like a siege, they were trying to force the Confederates off the mountains without making a frontal attack. There was artillery duels where the main objective was to demoralize and destroy as many of the enemy as possible.

The 2nd brigade relieved the 3rd Brigade on June 13th, with the 3rd Brigade going in reserve. It still was raining but there was hopes that the four days of almost constant rain would soon be ceasing. General Osterhaus states that "it was the most horrible time for campaigning I ever saw."(6) Lieutenant General Leonadis Polk was killed on June 14th while observing the movements of the Federals from on top of Pine Mountain. He was observing the Federals along with General Hardee and General Johnston, they were unhurt. General Polk was struck by an artillery round fired by a twenty pound Parrott of the 4th Ohio Artillery. This was a terrible blow to the Confederate army, not because of his expert military genius, but because he was loved by many of the men under his command. He was an Episcopal Bishop of Louisiana who had graduated from West Point who resigned to become a preacher. When the war started he again laid down the clothes of a preacher and put on the clothes of a soldier. Even as a soldier he was still concerned about his calling of the ministry and had baptized both General Johnston and General Hood not to long before the death of General Johnston at the battle of Shiloh.

General Sherman wanted to move his lines forward to put more pressure on the Confederates in hopes of finding a weak spot in the defenses in the Confederate line. Unknown to the Federals, the Confederates had withdrawn from Pine Mountain the previous night. This caused the Confederate lines to be drawn in closer and better able to support each other in case the Federals tried to cut off the mountains individually, isolating the troops. General Sherman ordered General McPherson to make a feint at noon in order to draw attention from General Thomas and Schofield to allow them to mount a sucessful attack. There were some prisoners taken by the 1st Division of the 15th Army Corps in their attack, and some ground taken from the Confederates that they were eager to get back because they attacked the Federals three times in order to retake the ground and failed. There was about five hundred Confederate soldiers taken prisoner by the Army of the Tennessee. General Thomas and Schofield had both moved about two miles closer to the Confederate lines while the Army of the Tennessee line extended around the north end of Kennesaw Mountain.

June 16th was a dry day as far as no rain fell giving the soldiers of both sides a chance to dry out. The men in the 1st Division had spent the night entrenching the positions that they had taken the previous day. Major A. J. Seay recorded in his diary, "Thursday, 16. A nice day, I feel better but puny-brisk skirmishing. Wounded come in frequently. Now and then an arm or leg is amputated. The booming cannon still does its work of death. One of our shell killed Gen. Polk yesterday."(7) General Hooker had come up to reinforce General Schofield and was moving forward at about the same pace as the rest of the Federal army. General Thomas men had been involved in a battle on the right and center during the day. The Confederate army had compacted itself to such an extent that they were able to observe most of the Federal army from Kennesaw Mountain. In abandoning Pine Mountain the Confederates were able to keep their men stationed on this mountain from being isolated. Not much happened on the 17th of June. There was a lot of artillery firing going on, mostly from the Federal side, with not much affect showing. The men on both sides spent the rest of the day making their positions more secure.

The 18th was another day of rain, John T. Clarke says in his journal, "Rain is falling in perfect torrents."(8) General McPherson's army had been facing General Hood's men on Brush Mountain and around the railroad. General Sherman, who was never really happy unless something was going on, ordered General McPherson to shift his forces to the right. Now instead of facing General Hood they were facing General Loring's Confederate Corps across from Kennesaw Mountain. General McPherson's men, as well as most of the Federal forces, kept up constant skirmishing with their pickets in hopes of finding a place that was lightly defended by the Confederates. General Osterhaus says in his diary on this date, "felt forward; found but few pickets."(9) Major A. J. Seay recorded in his diary, "Saturday, 18. Heavy musketry last night-rainy this morning and continues nearly all day. I witness two amputations. War is a bloody business. Men shot in every conceivable place. Our present fight will be known as the battle of Kenesaw Mts. It has rained every day but three in this month. I'm better today."(10)

Rumors were abounding about the Confederates abandoning Lost and Kennesaw Mountains, moving towards Atlanta. The Federals were hoping that this was true. But General Johnston, who was feeling some pressure from the people in Atlanta and the Confederate capitol in Richmond, Virginia about forcing General Sherman back toward Chattanooga, felt that he was in the best position since the campaign started. He only hoped that General Sherman would oblige him by making a frontal attack. And it was not long before his hopes were realized. Most of the Confederate army, especially the men in the ranks, had complete faith in General Johnston. So far whenever there was a chance of a retrograde movement instead of a hard battle, General Johnston had managed to expertly withdraw his men. The government in Richmond might not have appreciated his efforts but those who would have died certainly did. General Johnston had not needlessly wasted his men in worthless charges on the enemy. General Hood, who would replace General Johnston in a little over a month, could not be accused of such a statement.

Again there was concern in the Federal camp about their extensive supply line which ran all the way from Kennesaw to Chattanooga and then to Nashville. The Army of the Tennessee spent the next few days trying to force the Confederates off the railroad and Kennesaw Mountain. There were no real major battles but a lot of skirmishes which were short, fierce and deadly, but did not accomplish the desired result. General Osterhaus states in his diary,

"June 19th Cloudy and rainy of course- the rebs are gone. same for prisoners; we are getting ready for the pursuit. General Smith 2d Division has the advance. Cannonading on the right and same on the left;
The Rebs sure to be pushed back on the whole line. General Woods 1st Brigade supports General Smith; afterwards 2d and 3d Brigade follows.

Monday, June 20th Cloudy and rain still threatening- the 1st Division in line behind the Rebel breastworks Rebel rear guard near the R.R. xing at the foot of Pine (Kennesaw) Hill- Deploy 2d Brigade on the right of 2d Division. At 2 P.M. a very heavy cannoade on Thomas' front followed toward 5 P.M. by very heavy artillery continous musketry; lasting untill late after night; there was a general attempt of the center and right (Schofield) to carry a part of the Rebel line. We charge that all together!

Tuesday June 21- Rain! firing kept up all night and in the morning (9 a.m.) the Cannonade on the right re- sumes-General Woods 1st Brigade takes a position in front of 2d Brigade. The rebs burn a R. R. bridge in our rear." (11)

On June 20th the effective strength of the 1st Division of the 15th Army Corps was two hundred and thirty-nine Offic- ers, three thousand five hundred and sixty-five men with a to- tal of three thousand eight hundred and four. The men of the 15th Army Corps in the field around Big Shanty, Georgia came to a total of thirteen thousand two hundred and ninety-eight. General Sherman had ordered General McPherson to probe the right flank of General Johnston's defenses while General Tho- mas' artillery were bombarding Kennesaw Mountain. The ob- ject of General McPherson's probe was to see if he might be able to break through the Confederate line and reach the rail- road. This would enable the Federals to force the Confederates off the mountain or stand the chance of being cut off and sur- rounded. It was also in hopes of reaching the railroad in order to extend their supply line closer to the men. It was another day of rain and the Confederates were at the railroad crossing near the foot of Pine Mountain. For most of the day the infan- try were continuously firing at one another. The 1st Division had occupied some of the trenches that once had been in pos- session of the Confederates. June 22nd remainded the same as the previous days except for the rain, which had quit, and all the men hoped that it would hold off for awhile so everything could dry out.

On June 24th the 15th Army Corps received orders to make a secondary attack just to the south of Kennesaw Mountain with artillery and skirmish lines. The attack began as ordered with a heavy bombardment on the Confederate positions followed by the strong skirmish lines. General Logan's men attacked straight up the mountain into the teeth of the Confederate defenses. The men made it about halfway up the mountain before they began to withdraw. The losses were heavy including the loss of seven regimental commanders being killed or wounded. Sometimes these secondary attacks, though not as well reported as the main attack, were bloody and desperate affairs. If the attacks succeeded they could change the outcome of the battle if, causing the battle to become a victory or bringing on successful results that went beyond the expectations of the planners of the attack. Such as the case of the troops under General Thomas and their secondary part in the attack on Missionary Ridge.

General Sherman gave orders for an overall assault on the Confederate positions at Kennesaw Mountain and the surrounding mountains defended by the Confederates. General McPherson's Army of the Tennessee was to strike south of Kennesaw Mountain. General McPherson began moving his army to a position that would make the best jump-off spot. The 15th Army Corps at this time was north of Big Kennesaw Mountain, General McPherson moved them so they would be just west of Pigeon Hill. They replaced two divisions of the 14th Army Corps that was commanded by General Davis and General Baird. General Logan, the commander of the 15th Corps, was informed that his forces were to charge up the south and west slopes of Pigeon Hill. If they were successful this would allow them to reach the town of Marietta on the Burnt Hickory road, at the same time effectively cutting off any chance of retreat for the Confederate forces.

Major A. J. Seay of the 32nd Missouri Infantry Regiment, wrote in his diary the following for June 25th and 26th. "Saturday, 25. We are detailed on wagon guard and go two or three miles to the rear to the div. train. P.M. the Rebs open a furious cannonade from 25 guns upon our lines, but with poor effect. Train moves one mile to the front. Hot and dry. Sunday, 26.

Enter with vigor upon our new duties. Hot day. Much fatige to do—skirmishing not heavy—our Co. takes the right and 16th A. C. and center of Army of the Tenn. Clouts and I take a ride to the front."(12)

General Sherman had so successfully flanked General Johnston out of one position after another, it seemed ridiculous that he would now order a frontal attack on a strongly entrenched army. General Sherman was growing tired of waiting to see if he could force the Confederates out by forcing their hand, he had decided to attempt to drive them out. The men who had grown accustomed to the flanking movement, were upset when they found out that they were to make a frontal attack. Most of these men were veterans of up to three years, many had survived frontal attacks or had repelled Confederate attacks and knew that during these frontal attacks there were many casualties. General Sherman was concerned that these very men had become so accustomed to the flanking movement that they no longer had the nerve to participate in a frontal attack against a dug in enemy force. If the men would have found this out they would have really been mad. Many of those who would awaken on June 27th, the day the attack was to be made, would become a casualty during the battle that day.

Three o'clock in the morning, on June 27th, the men were awakened and prepared to leave the entrenchments to get in position to attack. At eight o'clock the artillery began their bombardment of the Confederate positions. At nine a.m. the Federal infantry began their attack along the whole line of the Confederates, this covered a front of about ten miles. General McPherson's forces were to attack the gap between Little Kennesaw Mountain and Pigeon Hill. General Logan's 15th Army Corps was to attack Pigeon Hill. Three brigades were picked to lead the assault against the Confederate positions. Pigeon Hill is a steep hill with a lot of trees up on the slopes and large boulders on the top of the hill that helped to protect the defenders. The units that General Logan picked were General Walcutt's brigade of General Harrow's division and two brigades from General Morgan L. Smith's division, commanded by Brigadier Generals Giles A. Smith and J. A. J. Lightburn. The Confederates on Pigeon Hill were commanded by General French and General Walker. Unlike most of the Federal brigades which attacked with brigades in column, General Logan had his men attack with each brigade attacking in a line formation with the brigade forming two lines. Instead of three or four brigades being under fire at the same time, only one would be under attack.

As General Logan's men attacked they lost their alignment because of the huge boulders, thick trees and some marsh land that was in their path. They approached the pickets on the run and captured the 63rd Georgia Infantry almost intact. They jumped in the trenches with the Georgians clubbing and bayoneting them, shooting some and capturing just a little under one hundred of the survivors. Once this was done they charged up the hill. They were charging towards the main Confederate lines when they were met by a withering fire from about twelve cannons that were firing shell and canister at the Federals. They also were met by stiff musketry that dropped many a brave man in his tracks. From this point on it was basically a fight for survival, firing when the opportunity afforded itself. Approxitmately two and one-half hours after the infantry attack began the battle was over. The Federals retreated off the hill to the entrenchments that they had drove the enemy out of that morning under the friendly cover of darkness. General Logan's troops suffered a total of five hundred and eighty-six killed and wounded. Because General Logan had his men attack in the line formation the casualties were lower in each regiment. General Thomas' army there was heavy losses in each regiment because of the brigades in column. General Thomas losses for the day was nearly two thousand men. General Walker and General French's divisions lost approximately three hundred on Pigeon Hill.

Colonel Hugo Wangelin's 3rd Brigade, of the 1st Division, were in reserve waiting for the opportunity to exploit any breakthrough that the Federals could gain and then continuing on to Marietta and the railroad. General Logan says in his official report, dated June 28th, 1864 that "Commanding officers state most positively that the position could not be gained in two hours without any opposing force. After vainly attempting to carry the works for some time, and finding that so many gallant men were being uselessly slain, they were ordered to retire to the last line of works captured, and hold them, which was done."(13) The attacks by the Federal army was a wanton waste of manpower and ammunition. Though I admire General Sherman's fighting ability that he exercised throughout the war, I am disgusted with this attack because it was such a

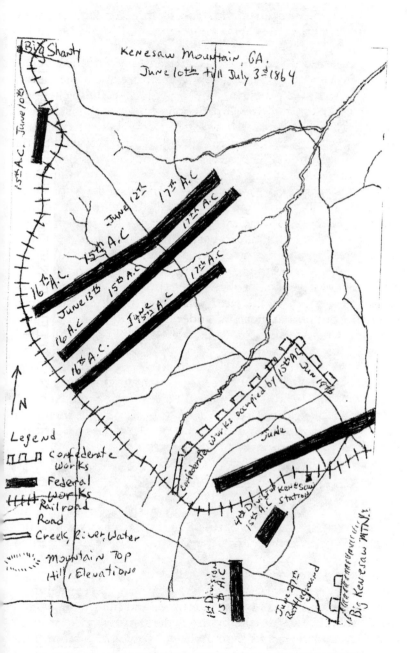

BATTLE AT KENNESAW MOUNTAIN, GEORGIA

KENNESAW MOUNTAIN, GEORGIA BATTLEFIELD: National Archives, Washington D.C.

waste of men with little if anything gained. Major A.J. Seay recorded in his diary, "Monday, 27. Gen. Sherman assailed the enemies works at 8 A.M. Repulsed with loss of 2,000 or 3,000 but gained some inconsideralble advantages. The rebel works and position are too strong to be carried by assault. We must flank 'em."(14)

In a speech to the Society of the Army of the Tennessee, Colonel G. D. Munson responded to a toast to Kenesaw. In his speech he describes his impression of Kenesaw Mountain.

"If the Kenesaw mountain had been specially created to bar an enemy's approach from the North to the "Gate City" of the South, it could not have been better planned or placed. Its wooded sides furrowed by deep ravines, its rugged slopes, its inaccessible cliffs, make it a natural barrier boldly blocking the way. Occupied and fortified by the Confederate General, Joe. Johnston, his lines contracted, forces concentrated, the mountain became a bristling fortress and seemed impregnable. With his sixty thousand infantry and one hundred pieces of artillery skillfully posted behind breastworks and in forts carefully constructed by trained engineers for the purpose of cross firing; with the flashings and entanglements of felled forest trees, the abatis in front, and with the clear view from the summit of every movement of approach, Johnston felt secure from successful assault. His men, steady and determined, believing themselves at last masters of the situation, serried ranks secure in intrenchments, cannon ready, gunners at post, stern and undaunted awaited Sherman's coming. Johnston invited attack, confident, in his lair, of victory.

Sherman, already crowding him closely, at 9 in the morning assaulted. The earth shook, as cannon sent shot and shell shrieking and hissing and roaring against the Kenesaw stronghold.

At that signal heavy lines of skirmishers leaped from their rifle pits and ran forward, while the devoted storming party of fifteen thousand men—six thousand from the Tennessee army, nine thousand from the Cumberland—moved from their position in the line to carry, if mortal men could carry, the fortifications in their front, and thus break the enemy's center.

Severe and continuous the cannonading; its like had

not before been heard in that army; it drowned the sound of musketry all along the line, and onward pressed the charging columns.

"Firm of step, though pale of face,
With lips compressed and eyes that glow with purpose strong,
And hands that grip their weapons tight.
Who meet those men must either kill or die,
They go to fight, naught else is their minds."

We think and talk of death, but ever since that bloody day 'tis vain to claim that mankind fear to die, and cower and tremble at the thought. I say not so; and point to Kenesaw—those thousands bravely storming the very gates of certain death; rushing through its yawning portals in solid phalanx, willing, obeying orders; willing, submitting to discipline cheerfully borne for love of country.

So died our men at Kenesaw. The two hours' struggle ended and the attack failed. Three thousand Union soldiers lay dead and dying on that ghastly mountain side. We drink our toast to them, the bravest of the brave."(15)

General Sherman now realized his men were not afraid to charge straight towards a dug in enemy. He started to make plans on how to flank the Confederates off the mountains. Private Clarke in his diary says on Tuesday June 28th," All is quiet today except skirmishing which is going on continually."(16) The 1st Division were occupying the position that was gained the day before. This position had been strengthened that night by the men and by some pioneers that had been bought up that day specifically for that purpose. During the night of June 29th, around two a.m., there was severe firing to the right of the 15th Army Corps about in the 4th Army Corps area. It was believed that both sides in the trenches thought the other one was attacking them. It was a vicious sounding battle but because there was no one who were in the direct firing area there was little if any damage. First Lieutenant William B. Pratt of the 31st Missouri Volunteer Infantry was assigned to duty as acting aide-de-camp in the field in general orders number 34 dated June 30, 1864. He then became part of the staff of General Logan and the 15th Army Corps command group.

General Schofield was busy as General McPherson and

General Thomas were attacking Kennesaw Mountains and Pigeon Hill. His troops crossed Olley's Creek gaining a position that was putting General Johnston's troops in danger of not being able to retreat. General Schofield's troops was now near the head of Nickajack Creek. General Sherman now began planning his next flanking move with the successful movement executed by General Schofield. He issued orders for General McPherson to leave his entrenchments and move to the right marching behind General Thomas' army to his new position on the extreme right. By doing this General Sherman was cutting his connection with the railroad and his supplies. Some of his officers were not sure this was such a good idea, especially those commanders who had served in the east and those who had starved in the siege at Chattanooga. But those officers who had participated in the campaign against Vicksburg, where they severed all ties to their supply line when they crossed the Mississippi River, knew that they could forage off the country and eat better than they could off of the government ration. General Sherman ordered General McPherson to start this movement on the night of July 2nd.

It was fine weather for July 2nd and the 15th Army Corps began to make preparations for the move that night. The Confederates were still on the mountains throughout the day occupying the positions that they had held since the attack of the Federals on the 27th of June. It looked like they were prepared to remain there. General Schofield crossed Olley's Creek and established such a strong position that they endangered the rear of the Confederate army. The movement of General McPherson's army was noticed by General Johnston, he realized that they were being flanked, again he followed the course that he had followed throughout this campaign. At the same time that the Army of the Tennessee was moving out of their entrenchments to extend the right of the Federal line, the Confederates abandoned their strong defensive positions on Kennesaw Mountain. The Army of the Tennessee was in position after a march during the night. In the morning it was noticed by the rest of the army that the Confederates seemed to have abandoned the trenches on the mountains. Skirmishers were sent to investigate the situation and discovered that the Confederates had abandoned their positions. Major A. J. Seay wrote in his diary, "Sunday, 3. Daylight reveals the fact that Wiley Joe took time by the forelock and retreated last night.

CAPTAIN WILLIAM BLANCHARD PRATT
AID-DE-CAMP, 31ST MISSOURI INFANTRY REGIMENT
CARLISLE BARRACKS CARLISLE, PENNSYLVANIA

Kenesaw Mt. Marietta and many prisoners are ours-glorious. We camp in Marietta, once a pretty town, now used up by her own men literally gutted. People destitute."(17)

The Confederates during the night had withdrawn to a fortified position north of the Chattahooche River. This position had been previously prepared and was such a good position that no matter how the Federals approached the position they would be under fire from more than one of the little forts at the same time. These positions were connected by trenches which could be used as a firing position. Fortifying the northern bank of the river eliminates the advantage of using the river as an obstacle to the Federals. It also means in order to retreat from the enemy, in the event that the position is flanked, the defenders must cross the river while being in danger of being under fire from the enemy. Some people believe that the same defensive position could have been built south of the river and used the river to make the fortified position even stronger. General Johnston occupied the position that he did in hopes of protecting railroad and the pontoon bridges that spanned the river.

While the Confederate began defending this position, the Federal armies, on orders from General Sherman, were to pursue the Confederates with all vigor. By the night of the 3rd, General Thomas' troops had come into contact with the rear guard and were involved in a battle near Smyrna camp ground which was about six miles below Marietta, Georgia. July 4th broke with a celebration of the Declaration of Independence with a minor battle, that of gun fire with the intent of keeping the Confederates in their fortified position. Major A.J. Seay wrote in his diary, "Monday, 4. The 1st anniversary of our Vicksburg campaign. Today we press Johnston's rear heavily-march 10 miles quite hot-at night we have music from band and the hills are made vocal with the joyous deafeninf cheers of the troops."(18) General Thomas' force were facing the Confederate position, with General Schofield on his right and General McPherson's men on the far right reaching the Chattahoochee River below Turner's Ferry. General Garrard and his cavalry had secured a position at the river near Roswell and were demonstrating against the Confederate cavalry in that area. The Army of the Tennessee was making a demonstration below Turner's Ferry trying to confuse General Johnston about the intent of their movement.

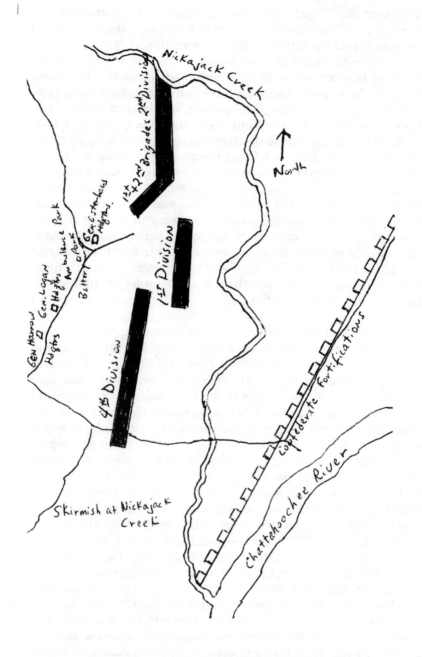

Nickajack Creek

1st + 2nd Brigades 2nd Division

North

Gen Litaulaus Hights

Gen. Logan Hights

Ambulance Park

Battery

Park

Gen Harrow Hights

1st Division

4th Division

Confederate Fortifications

Chattahoochee River

Skirmish at Nickajack Creek

SKIRMISH AT NICKAJACK CREEK, GEORGIA

In a report to General Sherman, General McPherson stated that, "Dodge moved across the Nickajack Creek at Ruff's Mill ran against General Stevenson's division, and as he developed his lines captured a few prisoners from each division of Hood's corps. The cavalry and infantry demonstration on the Turner's Ferry road reached a point, as they think, half a mile from Nickajack, and found it tolerably well fortified, with four guns in position. This brought the infantry to a halt, and they have not advanced since. They will, however, hold all the ground they have gained, and be ready to try the strength of the enemy's works, if it is deemed desirable. I have about fifteen thousand men across the creek with Dodge, and Logan's two divisions (Osterhaus' and Harrow's) in reserve at the forks of the road. They got in late and completely worn out. I do not think more than half of the divisions arrived."(19) General Osterhaus agreed with General McPherson's assessment about the condition of his troops. "Monday July 4th- breezy but warm- order to march at 5 1/2 a.m- go within 2 miles of Ruff's Mill. March 14 miles get into camp by (unreadable) p. m. the men were tired."(20)

In an article dated July 4, 1864, an anonymous author, writes about his experience of the celebration of the 4th of July at Kennesaw Mountain. I am not sure, but I think that Medicus, is Surgeon A. W. Reese. The reason I believe this is because of an article sent in to the Daily Missouri Democrat dated November 16, 1864 which refers to an instance on the way to Missouri after being mustered out November 9, 1864, that he later recounts in his book. This was a train wreck that happened in Tennessee.

"FROM SHERMAN'S ARMY.
The Stars and Stripes on top the Kinesaw-Marietta and the Madness of the South.
(Correspondence of the Missouri Democrat)

In Camp, 15th Army Corps,
Marietta, GA., July 4, 1864.

The 'glorious Fourth' is ushered in to day by the pealing of the 'national anthem' though the streets of another 'conquered city' of the South. Yesterday morning, June 30, we were aroused from our slumbers by the cheering of our boys. It began at the left of our line, and, one after another, each regiment caught up the cry, until one wild shout went up from one end of the corps to the other. We rushed out to see 'what was up.'

Casting our eye upward towards the bold crest of Kinesaw Mountains, 'we saw it,' for there floated in the morning sunlight 'the gorgeous ensign of the republic'- a long line of 'blue coats' stood on the enemy's works, and waved their hats and cheered our men below. The work was done. Kinesaw Mountain – the Georgia 'Gibraltar' –was ours.

The assault on the enemy's works (June 27th) has fully demonstrated the fact that these formidable defenses could not be carried by storm; put into execution one of his invertiable 'flank' movements, by which the rebels were compelled to 'evacuate' their position. It seemed to me impossible for us to dislodge them by main force, from these precipitous and rock-bound hights. I have seen no position since "Buzzard's Roost' at all comparable to it. The rebels fell back on Saturday night (July 2d) and on the morning of the 3d, the bugle sounded through our lines to advance in pursuit. Tents were struck and we were soon on the march. We wound around the base of Kinesaw till we struck the railroad. The 'rebs' had torn up the track for a mile and carried off the rails. This, however, will not amount to much, as far as obstructing our advance is concerned.

We entered Marietta at ten o'clock, A. M., Sunday morning, July 3d, 1864, in triumphal style—the 'stars and stripes' floating to the breezes, the drums beating, and bands playing 'Yankee Doodle.' It was a sublime spectacle! As the dense columns of troops moved through the streets with their shining bayonets and burnished arms to the sound of our national hymn, I could not help, but feel that 'Uncle Sam' was still a 'power in the land.' Marietta is the most beautiful place I have seen in Georgia. There are many elegant mansions with cool and spacious verandahs and porches, embowered among roses and wines and magical sway among cool and shady trees, interspersed with white gravel walks, winding here and there among these leafy bowers. This town, before the war, contained, I suppose, somewhere about three thousand inhabitants, and was a very flourishing place. As we entered it, however, we found it almost deserted—the major part of the citizens had fled in fear that the approach of the 'northern vandals' and

'Lincoln hirelings,' taking their property along with them to Atlanta. It is amusing to see the preciptancy with which the 'Secesh' skedaddle when we advance on their towns; and more amusing still to hear the absurd stories circulated among these poor ignorant creatures in advance of our appearance. They are all to be hung, shot, butchered, quartered, ravished, burnt up, and otherwise disrespectfully treated by our soldiers, according to the rebel authorities; and such is the ignorance of credulity of these people that such thing are believed and acted on accordingly. The schoolmaster is and has been abroad ever since the South was 'got up.' The people generally are illiterate and superstitious, though to this there are probably some exceptions. Alas! how these people are paying the cost for their folly.

'When the gods wish to destroy they first make mad.'

The South was mad—cotton mad and slave mad—and under complication of disorders it is more than probable that the patient will perish.

More anon.

Yours truly,   MEDICUS.

31st Missouri Vols. U. S. A."(21)

Private John T. Clarke states in his diary on Tuesday July 5,1864, "Our advance rests on the banks of the Chattahooche. The spires of the doomed Atlanta are visible! We are camped tonight 3 miles from the river! a few days more & a great battle must be fought or Johnston must make another disgraceful retreat."(22) The 1st Division advanced on the Southtown Road to the crossing at Widow Mitchell's place staying there untill around five p.m. They then advanced on the Tinner Ferry Road where they saw the Confederates safely crossing the Chattahoochee River from a piece of land between the River and Nickajack Creek. They marched about four miles that day.

General Schofield believed that he had a crossing just above where Soap's Creek ran into the Chattahoochee River. He informed General Sherman that this lookrd like a crossing and could be easily defended once across. General Sherman approved of General Schofield's idea and gave his permission to implement his plan, which was successfully executed on July 9th. This information with the news of General Garrard's cavalry crossing the river at Roswell driving the Confederate cavalry from the city, caused General Johnston to decide to withdraw his forces across the river to keep from being cut off from Atlanta by the Federal forces. They successfully withdrew on the night of July 9th. The Confederates left that night but not all the Confederates made it across, some of them fell into the hands of the Federals and were taken prisoners. Many of the officers in the Federal army went in to check out the fortifications and were very impressed with the way they were made. Because of his declining health General Osterhaus requested a leave of absence on July 10th.

The following is the entries of Major A. J. Seay for the days of July 5th through July 11th of 1864. These dates were almost all spent near the Chattahoochee River and the substantial works that the Confederates occupied.

"Tuesday, 5.

We march 2 ½ miles South. A very hot day-some fighting. The entire army is moving, as I suppose for position. Johnson has the Chattahooche in his rear and perhaps is cross with part of his forces.

Wednesday, 6.

We move 3 ½ miles North East within a mile of the reb works, which are very strong-3 forts in sight of our position. Late in the P.M. brisk skirmishing. I go and look at the works. Hilly hot and dry, country poor and barren.

Thursday, 7.

Hot and dry. We keep everything quiet during the day but all night shooting is brisk sometimes a volley comes and arouses us all. Movements going on. Important. I write to mother. A long letter giving her the news.

Friday, 8.

Hot and dry. King and Carringer have a fight, king whips. I arrest both. At night Col. Simpson arrests Padcock and says he will prefer charges against him. We move ½ miles to front and make pits.

Saturday, 9.

Still work on our pits make them strong. Construct fort Seay for Off. A very hot day. Very little fighting. Only a few balls whistled by us doing no damage. The men make arbors along the whole line of pits.

Sunday, 10.

One year ago today we beseiged Jackson. This morning we find Joe evacuated his ponderous works and has taken refuge behind the Chattoochee the fortifications abandoned by him were pits with stockades or pickets and forts or shell protectors a clumsy form of defense work.

Monday, 11.

Strange to day we have not moved yet. Hot. Some skirmishing with the enemy across the R. Artillery heard away off on the flank. I roll around in camp restless, etc. Others get letters. I get none. Some thunder and a light shower. Blues."(23)

In a letter to his wife, Metta, Private Henry Kuck writes about the good news that he received about her and his new son. His son was conceived when he went home on leave. As it has happened in all wars there was the worry of the new father that he would never get to see his newborn child.

> "Camp near Chattahoochee River
> July 11th, 64

Dear Metta,

I received yesterday evening your letter dated 28th June after I'd been asleep for half and hour. You can imagine how happy I was, sweet Metta, to receive again finally a letter from you. How long have I waited for this new, and at last it came. You can imagine how great my joy was to find out that you're healthy and happy and that you safely gave birth to a little boy, and that you're both doing well.

We'll hope that you and that dear child remain healthy until I knew if the Lord ordains for me the good fortune that I can hurry happily into your arms, and to the 5 children.

How happy I'll be then, this my small troop, born in my absence, to be peaceful and healthy with you, and then I can begin to relax; Papa; O, if only the time were not so long. Concerning myself I'm just fine. Wm. Schwarze fell off the wagon on June 27th and since then is in the hospital, but I don't know where he is. He lost 3 or 4 lower front teeth and has other injuries on his cheek, but it's not dangerous and I think he'll soon be better. Gerd Losmann is well and sent a letter off to his mother on June 18, addressed to you. We are close to the Chattahoochee River and from the hills can see Atlanta in the distance, still about 7 ½ miles from the river.

Word has it that we're to go back; that is, our brigade, back to the Railroad. I don't know if this is well-founded, the Rebels are staying back, and Atlanta will be ours in a very short time if Gen. Sherman wants it that way.

But it appears that Gen. Sherman is not at all in a hurry to take Atlanta. There's fighting here, too: Gen. Johnson sent Gen. Lee reinforcements; we also heard: Gen. Grant wanted to send reinforcements to Virginia, if that's true, then we'll probably all gather at a summer camp, where the army will regroup itself and begin again next fall. I have to hurry and finish, we could get marching orders any minute. Much love to all of you. Human speech is too poor to express my feelings for you, but your own feelings can show you how mine could be. Take care of the tiny little child and of yourself so that you'll be healthy. Thank the bricklayer's wife for the help she gave to you during your delivery and all the others who lent your support, I can't tell them myself, but I can do it in writing.

Don't worry about the baptism, there's time enough for that as long as the child is healthy and if it were up to me he would not be baptized until I come back; if I should die and not come back any more, then let him be baptized with my name, and tell him; while you're still with him, where his father was as he was born, and where he is. Don't be sad if I write such things, we have to be prepared for the worst, but I can bear up with it best in this way, if I think about my feelings along with the pleasant things.

Write soon again, for I'm very curious now about you and our sweet children, especially about our little screamer. Say hello to our friends and neighbors. Goodbye and kiss my dear, lovely children for me and especially the little baby.

Your husband

Henry

who loves you"(24)

July 12th the 1st Division, as well as the rest of the 15th Corps, was ordered to march at five p.m. toward Haswell factory in Roswell on the Chattahoochee River, via Marietta, Georgia. They marched four miles going into camp around eleven p.m.. The temperature was very hot this day. Many days there is no mention of fighting in diaries or reports, but Major A. J. Seay mentions the loss of two men in his regiment on July 12th. "Tuesday, 12. I lose two men, Co. G. and Co. K. Geister badly wounded. Can't swallow. I fear he will die. Dr. Watson extracts the ball from his throat. We march five miles and go into camp at midnight. Move short distance and stand. 1863 reenacted. I feel very tired. We ask to have, 29, 31 and 32 consolidated."(25)   General Osterhaus states in his diary, "Wednesday July 13-foggy- start from camp at 5 1/4 a. m., cross R.R. at 9 1/2 a.m. in Marietta- Sell my 2 horses to Jno. Schenk for $205.00- The Division marches to little Soap Creek under General Wood. Distance of today's march 13 miles."(26) General Charles R. Woods the commander of the 1st Brigade of the 1st Division, as senior brigade officer took command of the 1st Division because of General Osterhaus being too ill to continue in his position of command. General Sherman ordered General McPherson to send one of his other brigades to strengthen the 15th Corps at Roswell. During the night of July 14th there was a terrible thunder storm in which there were twenty men killed and wounded by lightning at Roswell, Georgia. The 15th Army Corps marched about 12 miles that day.

Another article wrote to the Daily Missouri Democrat dated July 13, 1864 that sounds more like a campaign instrument than any information that could be useful to the reader.

"Sherman beyond the Chattahoochee—The Soldiers' Interest in the Missouri Election—How we celebrated the Fourth—The Despondency of the Southern People.
HEADQUARTERS, 15TH ARMY CORPS,
Near Chattahoochee River, GA.
July 13, 1864.
The loyal people of the North are beyond doubt well posted in regard to the campaign in Georgia, and are anxiously awaiting the final blow which is to re-establish the supremacy of our Government and end the rebellion in this portion so the disaffected Union. It is enough, however, for them to know that all is well, and everything up to this time has been accomplished which the most sanguine expected. The enemy has been defeated, demoralized and driven with terrible loss over one hundred and thirty miles. Alatoona Pass, Kinesaw Mountain, and Marietta, no longer confront us, but are now garrisoned by Federal Soldiers while the brave and

victorious army of Sherman lies safely entrenched on the banks of the Chattahoochee, only six mile distant from Atlanta, the great centre of railroad communication, and is the wealthiest and most productive portion of the so called Confederacy. It is true we have occupied much time since the campaign began, but it is equally true that great results have been achieved, and the operations of this grand army are well deserving a bright page in the history of our country, and will go far towards the restoration of the Union and the day of peace, when the old flag shall triumphantly wave over every stronghold in the rebel States.

But while we are periling our lives in the open field, and are hourly battling for the preservation of our country's honor, we do not forget home and the great responsibility devolving upon the loyal citizens of Missouri, for we feel a lively interest and honest pride in the result of the election soon to take place, and we earnestly trust that the true Radical Union-loving men of our State will gain, at the ballot-box, a victor so demoralizing to the enemy and his abominable allies that he will never again dare to call in question the loyalty of Missouri.

The soldiers are united in their determination to blot out forever from their beloved State the blighting curse of human bondage, and what they have not already done with the sword they will do by their votes in November next. With this same determination substatly impressed upon the minds of all good citizens at home, success is inevitable, and the Radicals of Missouri will elect their nominee, than whom none are more worthy, and her sons in the field will hail with thanks and heartfelt rejoicings the selection of their fellow-soldier, Col. T. C. Fletcher, for the highest position in the gift of the people. But let us not be idle, and forget that the same foe, unable to accomplish his objet in the field is now lurking in the rear, seeking to destroy with his vote that which he failed to accomplish in battle. On the contrary, let us work incessantly, until an overwhelming victory repays us for our toil, and we can look abroad upon our beloved Missouri, and proudly exclaim slavery is no more; then, and not until then, let us cease working.

We celebrated the Fourth by a long and wearisome march through the dust and burning sun, while the vanguard hurled the Declaration of Independence from 3 lb. Parrots and Springfield muskets, into the rear of Joe Johnston's retreating army, driving him with fearful loss to and across the Chattahoochee river.

The people of Georgia are all disgusted and greatly tired of the despotism under which they have been compelled to live, and many welcome our advent as the dawn of a better time, from which they are to date their deliverance from the tyrannical oppression of Jeff. Davis. Not only is this the case with citizens, but hundreds of their soldiers embrace the opportunity to free themselves and escape into our lines seeming to be perfectly delighted to have escaped the vigilance of their commander and safety secured in our army.

Soldiers and citizens alike have lost all hope of success, and begin to realize that the end of their Confederacy is nigh, and the day of their strength gone. With this feeling among rebels who know and have experienced the severe teaching of their treason, let it simulate our friends in Missouri to renewed efforts in the great work of liberty and national unity; and when they go to the ballot box let them remember that the brave sons of Missouri are counting their votes for the gallant soldier and lifelong advocate of human freedom, Colonel Thomas C. Fletcher.

MINERAL POINT."(27)

General Osterhaus says in his diary, "Thursday July 14- leave Marietta at 4 a.m. the troops had left at 3 1/2 a.m. this camp. go in camp 2 miles west of Roswell the troops made 8 miles it is a very hot day! Leave camp again at 5 p.m. to cross the river- take a position on the left bank in a most miserable place 1 mile off the river. Marched in all 12 miles. A terrible lightning storm, many men killed."(28) The 15th Army Corps was to construct some bridges across the river to replace the ones that were burned by the Confederates. The Army of the Tennessee spent the 16th of July in camp preparing for the final push against Atlanta. General Osterhaus left his division because of his illness and left from Marietta on Monday July 18th for Nashville, Tennessee at seven a.m..

During the Battle for Kennesaw Mountain and the surrounding area the 31st Missouri Regiment lost the following men, Private Henry Drinckcorn, of Company A who was very slightly wounded in the back on June 14, 1864; Private John Moore of Company H, was died of his wounds to the shoulder, he died on June 30 1864; Private John M. Dale of Company D was severly wounded in the right arm on June 14, 1864; Private Solomon Reed of Company F was slightly wounded in the hand on June 27, 1864. This gave them a total casualties of four wounded near Kennesaw Mountain, Georgia. The losses that were received by the 31st Missouri Infantry Regiment from June 10th through July 16th are as follows. Company A lost Private John T. Huskey of Hillsboro was admitted to the hospital at Jefferson Barracks, where he occupied bed 2042 in Ward I, where he was later discharged on June 24th from Headquarters in the District of Saint Louis. Company D lost Private David F. Edwards of Wayne County was transferred to the Invalid Corps on July 16, 1864. Company F's, Private Jeremiah V. Hollingsworth of Cannan, was admitted to the hospital at Jefferson Barracks in bed 3426 Ward D, was transferred to the Invalid Corps. Private William Schwarze of Company G from Dutzow, Mo. was severly wounded on July 4th and was in the hospital; Sergeant Henry Finke of Washington was admitted to the hospital at Jefferson Barracks on June 27th having lost his left arm at Ringgold, Georgia on November 27th, 1863 he was later transferred to Alexander Barracks and the Invalid Corps on October 1,1864. Sergeant Gustavus K. Fulcher of Potosi was transferred to the Invalid Corps on June 10th. In Company I, Private John C. Powers of Saint Louis was admitted to the hospital at Jefferson Barracks on May 26th occupying bed 2085 Ward I, and later discharged on June 10th. In Company K Private Patrick Sullivan age 27 of Saint Louis was admitted on May 26th to the hospital at Jefferson Barracks with a gunshot to the middle third of the left leg, while in the hospital he deserted on June 23rd, probably to go home and see the family.

CHAPTER 13:
ON TO ATLANTA

Once the Federal army had successfully run the Confederates from their positions across the Chattahoochee, and the slight rest was over, General Sherman issued orders for the movements into Atlanta. Special Field Order # 70, issued by Major-General James B. McPherson, near Nancy's Creek, Georgia on July 17th ordered, "The Fifteenth Army Corps, Major-General Logan commanding, will march at 5 a.m., on the Decatur road to Widow Rainey's, thence on the Stone Mountain road, by Blake's Mill, to Browning's Court House, at the intersection of the Stone Mountain and Lawrenceville and Decatur roads, where he will hold his command in readiness to assist Brigadier-General Garrard, if he requires it, in his effort to make a break in the railroad."(1) General Garrard, and his cavalry, had the most important job that was assigned the Army of the Tennessee, and that was the job of damaging as much railroad as he could including bridges and culverts. This led to the special order number fifty-five, that was issued by the headquarters of Major-General John A. Logan. "Near Cross Keys, Georgia., on July 17,1864. II. Brigadier-General Woods' division will have the advance and be followed by the divisions of Brigadier-Generals M. L. Smith and William Harrow respectively."(2)

The railroad that General Garrard's cavalry was to destroy was the Georgia railroad that ran to important points in the Confederacy, such as the Carolina's, Virginia and some of the major cities in Georgia, that could send reinforcements to General Johnston once Atlanta was being attacked. Major A. J. Seay wrote in his diary, "Sunday, 17. Started on the march towards Decatur. Move out six miles and go into camp. Berries abundant-not many farms-wilderness-no water for six miles-cool and nice. Pine grove, we camp in. Monday, 18. Start at 5 A.M. Move south then east then south then west then north. Marching 15 miles. Go into camp"(3) Once the Army of the Tennessee, under General McPherson, started destroying the railroad east to Stone Mountain and effectively destroyed the railroad between there and Decatur. Decatur, Georgia is approximately six miles east of Atlanta. Major A. J. Seay wrote in his diary his impressions of Decatur. "Tuesday, 19. A pretty hot day. We move South West on Decatur R. to Town. About 800 inhabitants many of them left. Good court house. We camp in an old field North of town. I take cold and have headache. Considerable firing yesterday and today."(4) The railroad had been destroyed to within five miles of Atlanta. It was while here that the Army of the Tennessee found out some news that would change the whole method of fighting that they had become used to. The Federals, all the way from Chattanooga, had been forced to attack or try and flank the Confederates out of their positions. General Johnston had been replaced by a man who, if not a better soldier, was a man who was a fighter. He was General John Bell Hood. General Hood spent the next few days attacking the Federals trying to drive them back to their own country.

General John Bell Hood of Kentucky was thirty-three years old at the time that he replaced General Johnston. He had been in many of the major battles of General Lee's Army of Northern Virginia. He had suffered the loss of the use of his arm at Gettysburg and when he had been transferred to General Bragg in the west, he was wounded in the leg at the battle of Chicamauga. His leg was amputated almost at the hip which caused someone to have to actually tie him into the saddle in order to ride a horse. These two wounds would have forced any other man to retire from active service, but not General Hood. General Hood did not waste any time after taking command. On July 20th, General Hood and his army attacked General Thomas' army at a place called Peachtree Creek. The Confederates main assault landed on General Hooker's 20th Army Corps. The battle lasted approximately two hours and the Confederates suffered severely in casualties. General Hood was upset at his commanders because he felt that they did not attack as his orders had stated which caused them to attack almost separately instead as a combined force. This is the same complaint that his two predecessors had expressed. General Hood may have had a legitimate complaint but the terrain that they attacked across was rough and tortuous. General Hood did not take into account the amount of time that the terrain difficulties posed because he could not have checked this out due to his disabilities. After the failure of this attack the Confederates retreated to their entrenchments that had been prepared on the outskirts of Atlanta.

On the morning of July 20th the 15th Army Corps, at the time of the battle at Peachtree Creek, halted on the Charleston and Atlanta Railroad and proceeded to destroy it. Their entry into Decatur had not gone unopposed. They had to drive the Confederates from the town in a skirmish. After destroying the railroad to Stone Mountain they camped there that night. Major A. J. Seay recorded in his diary, "Wednesday, 20. We move thru Decatur and 2 ½ miles beyond and find the enemy in force. Brisk skirmishing and cannonading. A great many refugees gone from Decatur. We get plenty of black berries. Have onions for dinner."(5) The orders received from Major-General James B. McPherson during the day of the 20th were for the 15th Army Corps to start at five o'clock the next morning leading the Army of the Tennessee. The 17th Army Corps were to march in such a way that they would come up on the left of the 15th Army Corps at the point about three miles from Atlanta. The men were to march toward Atlanta ready for the battle.

July 20th found the Army of the Tennessee turning towards the west and resuming their march towards Atlanta, marching through Decatur and camping on the railroad approximately three miles from Atlanta that night. Private John T. Clarke in his diary for the 20th states, "Wednesday. Marched through Decatur and on the direct Atlanta road, camping on the R.R. within 3 miles of the city. Heavy skirmish and some sharp fighting. Batteries planted within easy range of the Town. Hot work tomorrow."(6) The Army of the Tennessee did not march very fast on their way towards Atlanta. General McPherson was most of the time an excellent commander, but at other times he could act rather slowly, such was the case at Snake Creek Gap. He was pretty sure that his army was going to end up as the main target. General Wheeler's cavalry was blocking the way of General McPherson's army. General Wheeler sent for help because of the amount of the Federals facing him. General Hood had no idea that the Army of the Tennessee was heading towards Atlanta from that direction. General Wheeler's note reached General Hardee just as he was getting ready to send his reserves into the battle of Peachtree Creek. General Hardee rushed his reserves to the point of danger to help hold the troops of the Army of the Tennessee where they were.

July 21st was a day of maneuvering for the Confederates and the Federals. Two divisions of General Blair's 17th Army Corps attacked General Cleburne's division on what was formally known as Bald Hill. After the battle took place, it would later become known as Leggett Hill. It was named after Brigadier-General Mortimer D. Leggett, whose division attacked, took the hill and defended it against strong opposition by the Confederates. They were at one time pushed off this hill but later it was regained. Major A. J. Seay wrote in his diary, "Thursday, 21. Very hot today. We got up and moved 1 mile to the Mt. last night. A lively time this morning. Skirmishers of 15th and 17th Corps advance and charge the enemy. Artillery and musketry played a tune fearful and terrible to tell but old soldiers."(7) The Federal line ended up with by the time of the battle on July 22nd the 16th Army Corps was on the extreme left with the 17th, 15th, 23rd, 4th, 20th Corps, in that order, to their right with the 14th Army Corps on the extreme right. The Confederates were busy on the night of the of the 21st. After participating in the savage fighting at Peachtree Creek, General Hood had plans for his men; he refused to allow them time to rest.

On July 21st, General Dodge's 16th Army Corps was given the task of destroying the railroad from Decatur to the position that they held. It was while the 16th Corps was performing the task assigned to them that it was reported to General Hood that the left flank of the Army of the Tennessee was completely open just asking to be attacked. General Hood ordered Lieutenant-General William J. Hardee and his Corps to go on a night march of about fifteen miles. As previously stated the men were hungry, tired and had suffered a defeat with a loss of many men in the battle of Peachtree Creek. Now General Hood ordered them to make a flanking movement that would take them almost all night to complete. This had to be very hard on the men's morale because of all of the conditions listed above. This flanking movement was to be executed so as to put General Hardee's corps on the flank of General McPherson. The intention of General Hood was for General Hardee to attack on the flank at the same time as Major-General Benjamin F. Cheatham, who was now in command of General Hood's old corps. Major-General Cheatham was to come out of the entrenchments around Atlanta and attack General McPherson in his front. Major-General Joseph Wheeler's cavalry was to go around the right flank of General McPherson and attack the

Army of the Tennessee's supply wagons that were at and near Decatur.

General Hardee's men endured the march and made it to their assigned positions, not at daybreak as General Hood had planned, but after twelve noon. Major-General Patrick R. Cleburne and Brigadier-General George E. Maney marched until they reached their position on the flank of General McPherson's army. Major-General William B. Bate and Major-General William H. T. Walker marched east until they reached Sugar Creek where they turned left and followed it to reach their position. General Walker was warned by his guide that to proceed along this route would lead them to a large mill pond that would be in their way and slow down their progress. General Walker didn't listen to his guide and continued on, and just as he had been warned the mill pond blocked their path. They finally made it around this obstacle and drew up into a line of battle and approached the crest of a ridge when a bullet from a Federal sharpshooter took the life of General Walker. Brigadier-General Hugh W. Mercer took command of General Walker's division and after a brief delay started the attack.

Approximately one-half hour after the attack of General Walker's command, the command of General Cleburne's and General Maney's divisions attacked the 4th Division of the 17th Corps under Major-General Giles A. Smith. The Federal's 4th Division was driven back to Bald Hill fighting an orderly withdrawal. This all took place on July 22, 1864. General McPherson, who heard the firing, sent his Chief of Staff, Colonel William E. Strong, to investigate the situation. General McPherson noticed a gap between General Blair's 17th Army Corps and General Logan's 15th Army Corps and sent orders that General Logan was to send the 1st Division, 3rd Brigade under the command of Colonel Hugo Wangelin, to fill this gap. This was the last command that General McPherson was to issue that would affect the 31st Missouri Regiment.

After issuing the above order General McPherson and two members of his staff proceeded toward General Smith's position when they were came into contact with a regiment of Confederate infantry. They were ordered to stop, but when General McPherson tried to make good his escape he was shot dead. General McPherson was killed at approximately two o'clock p.m., he had no idea that the Confederates were already in the gap. Once informed of his death Major-General John

Logan took command of the Army of the Tennessee and Major-General Morgan L. Smith took command of the 15th Army Corps.

The 15th Corps formed the right of the Army of the Tennessee, with the 3rd Brigade of the 1st Division filling in the gap that had opened between the 17th and 16th Corps. The 15th Corps fought a bloody battle against Cheatham's Corps with part of his corps fighting the 17th Corps under General Blair. The 15th Corps had occupied the entrenchments that the Confederates had built and used them against the Confederates when they attacked. General Hardee's men attacked them in these positions and were able to drive them out of some of the trenches capturing some pieces of artillery and then turned these same guns on the Federals. While in this position the Confederates having gained the position and able to hold it were driven from them by a personally led charge by General John A. Logan. The Federals were able to drive the Confederates from the position that they had just captured, and the guns were retaken. The Confederate left their dead and the wounded that they could not carry when they left the trenches. General Hood was not on the field of battle because of his disability but commanded from a house close to the battle. He could not see all the terrain features or what was going on as well as a general who was on the ground and this is the reason that he misjudged the situation on top of the hill that General Cheatham's men had recaptured. This possibly snatched victory from him and forced his men into the trenches about Atlanta. The trenches that the Confederates had just abandoned were reoccupied by the Federals of the 15th Army Corps.

General Hardee's Corps fought against the 16th Corps, under General Dodge, the rest of the 17th Corps, and Colonel Hugo Wangelin's 3rd Brigade, which included the 31st Missouri Infantry Regiment. General Maney's Division attacked around three-thirty p.m., almost three hours after the attack of General Cleburne. They attacked the Federals from one direction and then from another direction but at separate times. The Federals, on what became known as "Leggett Hill", repulsed at least four separate desperate attacks on their entrenchments. At one time they had to jump across the top of the entrenchments and use the back of them for protection. Again the Confederates failed to have a unified attack which meant instead of attacking all at the same time they went in piece meal which enabled the Federals to successfully withstand the Confederate onslaught.

The day ended with the Federals having defended the positions that they had taken that day and forced the Confederates to retreat to the prepared defensive positions closer to Atlanta. The new positions now occupied by the Federals were close enough to Atlanta that almost all of the Federal artillery pieces could reach the city. The Confederates, as reported by the Federals, lost seven thousand killed and wounded, some of the wounded were estimated since the Confederates were able to carry off about one thousand of their wounded. The Federals lost four hundred and thirty killed, one thousand five-hundred and fifty-nine wounded and one thousand seven hundred and thirty-three missing. This was a total of three thousand seven hundred and twenty-two. The Confederates could not continue to absorb these kind of losses without inflicting more casualties on the Federals than they had received on July 22nd. General Sherman in his memoirs states, "I purposely allowed the Army of the Tennessee to fight this battle almost unaided, save by demonstrations on the part of General Schofield and Thomas against the fortified lines to their immediate fronts, and by detaching, as described, one of Schofield's brigades to Decatur, because I knew that the attacking force could only be a part of Hood's army, and that, if any assistance were rendered by either of the other armies, the Army of the Tennessee would be jealous. Nobly did they do their work that day, and terrible was the slaughter done to our enemy, though at a sad cost to ourselves."(8) General Sherman took the loss of General McPherson personally because of their friendship. Private John T. Clarke says in his diary, "Friday 22. On the left and in front of the 15th., 16th., and 17th. Corps one of the most bloody and hard fought battles of the war occured. Our troops were assaulted by the whole force of the enemy, but stood firm. The field covered with dead & wounded. Many prisoners taken, some artillery lost." (9)

Private Henry Kuck wrote in a letter to his wife Metta, his impressions of the battle on July 22, 1864. He was a member of Company G, 31st Missouri Infantry Regiment, 3rd Brigade, 15th Army Corps.

"I wrote in the previous letter that the Rebels attacked on our left flank the 22nd July and afterwards our entire front line; they thought they could get around our left and break through our Center at the same time, forcing us to retreat. They took several hundred of our men prisoner as they surprised us, but their losses were 5 times as bad as our. The rebel newspapers say that on July 22 they lost more than 15 thousand men. They took some cannon away from us, which were meant to protect infantry units, but we took most of these back. Near one battery, which our 1st and 2nd Brigades recovered, there supposedly lay 1,000 dead rebels. We had built a breastworks near Atlanta, to defend ourselves against the rebels. They called 'charge' and many of them came across a large, open field, where we could take close aim on them. The whole field through which they came was full of dead and wounded lying close to each other. We also are supposed to have lost 4 thousand men. Our Brigade had to move to the left flank and due to our advance, the enemy retreated."(10)

Private Kuck may have given more credit to the 3rd Brigade overall impact in the battle than was really warranted. But to fill a gap in the lines was one of the important jobs of the reserve. If you will remember that it was such a gap at the battle of Chickamauga where General Longstreet marched through that gap caused by the withdrawal of General Thomas Woods brigade from the line. This allowed the Confederates to get in the rear of the Federals and start the route of most of the Federal army back to Chattanooga.

Colonel Hugo Wangelin issued the following report about his brigade on July 25th, it is quoted in its entirety.

"Hugo Wangelin
Colonel Twelfth Missouri Volunteers, Commanding Brigade.

Capt. W. A. Gordon,
Asst. Adjt. Gen., First Div., 15th Army Corps
Camp Scorpion, near Atlanta, Georgia., July 25, 1864
Colonel: Having been connected for the last four days with the Seventeenth Army Corps, I consider it my duty to report, for the Brigade during that time.
On July 22, 1864, at about 1 p.m., I received orders from General C. R. Woods, Commanding First Division, Fifteenth Army Corps, of which this brigade forms a part of, to march my troops to headquarters Fifteenth Army Corps, where a staff officer of General Logan would be

in readiness to assign the brigade its position. Arriving at the spot assigned, I found Captain Hoover, aide-de-camp to Major-General Logan, in waiting, who conducted the brigade about a mile or more to the left, and assigned as its position the edge of a woods across a hill, in the center of a gap left between the Sixteenth and Seventeenth Army Corps. I immediately caused the troops to construct breast-works along their front, which was speedily done, as rails were very abundant at that spot and thru a strong skirmish force forward to protect our front, give timely warning of an approach of an enemy in force, and take such prisoners as would come within their reach. In the mean time our litter-bearers were directed to search the woods for wounded men who had been left there from the engagement of one hour previous. Surgeon Joseph Spiegelhalter, Twelth Missouri Volunteer Infantry, went out to give the matter his personal attention, and succeeded in rescuing and delivering to their friends three wounded men of the Sixteenth Army Corps. At that time the distance of the left of this brigade and the next troops of the Sixteenth Army Corps was at least a quarter of a mile, and the gap on our right to Fourth Division, Seventeenth Army Corps, some 200 yards. The Sixteenth Army Corps soon after placed more troops on their right, thus lessening the distance, which troops were, however, soon withdrawn, re-establishing the original gap. Our skirmishers had by this time succeeded in capturing 20 prisoners, of whom 2 were commissioned officers, 1 of whom was wounded before he surrendered. This position the brigade held when Major-General Blair arrived at 4 or 5 p. m. when, after some delay, I was directed by him to close up on Fourth Division, Seventeeth Army Corps, and report to Brig. Gen. Giles A. Smith for orders. The skirmishers thrown forward were not withdrawn, to keep up appearance of force, although no support was in their rear. After our right had come up in the direction of the left of Fourth Division, Seventeenth Army Corps, General Smith directed a forward movement of the whole brigade, until our right came fully up with the left of his troops, when the right halted and the whole line performed a half or three-quarter wheel on its right and came to a stand. The whole movement was performed in thick woods and underbrush. The men keeping well closed up, however, a strong line was speedily established. By this movement our left was farther from connection and support than before at least half a mile of dense forest lay between it and the Sixteenth Army Corps, and night setting in I changed the position of my left by a half left wheel to the rear of my left regiment, and placed the Twenty-ninth Missouri some 150 yards from the left flank of the main line fronting toward the left. Skirmishers were thrown forward to cover our new position and connect with those left the preceding afternoon in their places, who in their turn, as was reported to me, connected with the picket-line of the Sixteenth Corps. About 12:30 a. m. July 23 I was put in possession of twenty-four spades, some picks and axes, and, under instructions from General Smith, commenced fortifying, selecting such a line as my limited number of men could well defend, and being entirely unsupported on the left, refused the works to such an extent that I was sure of our ability to hold the position against all attack. At daylight the works were pretty well complete, and the cutting of the small trees in our front formed such an effective abatis that no fear of a capture of our position could reasonable be entertained. The day passed quietly, our litter-bearers being engaged during a short truce in exchanging the rebel dead for those of our own fallen comrades, in which exchange, with accustomed liberality, they at least gave five for one, reversing the southern idea that one Southern man was worth as much as five Northern. The next day the officer in charge of skirmish line reported that three caissons of the Second U. S. Artillery, filled with ammunition, were in front of our lines. I therefore directed a temporary advance of our skirmish line, and with a strong fatigue party succeeded in bringing them safe within our line. One army wagon loaded with forage was still farther out, and in our endeavors to save it also the enemy opened fire; one round shot struck and broke one wheel; it was therefore abandoned as not of sufficient value to risk the lives of the men for it. The balance of the day passed quietly, with the exception of

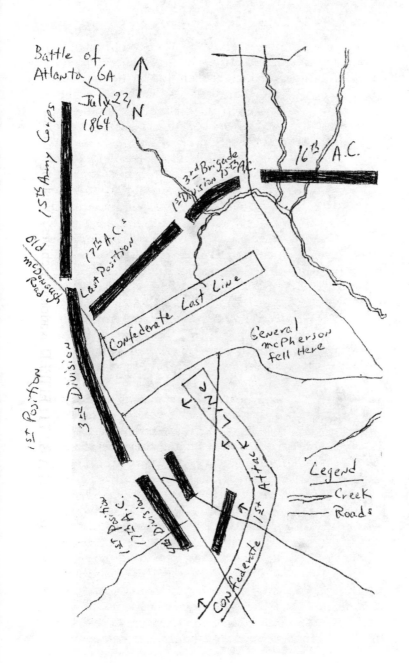

Battle of
Atlanta, GA
July 22
1864

N

15th Army Corps

16th A.C.

3rd Brigade
1st Division 15th A.C.

Old McDonough Road

17th A.C.s
Last Position

Confederate Last Line

General McPherson
fell Here

1st Position

3rd Division

2nd LINE

1st Attack

Legend
Creek
Roads

1st Position 17th A.C.
4th Division

Confederate 1st Attack

BATTLE OF ATLANTA, GEORGIA

ATLANTA GEORGIA BATTLEFIELD: National Archives, Washington D.C.

some little shelling, as did also this day.

The brigade consisted of the following regiments with the effective force (muskets) on the 22nd as herein set forth: Third Missouri Volunteer Infantry, Colonel Meumenn, 135; Twelfth Missouri Volunteer Infantry, Lieutenant-Colonel Kaercher 170; Seventeenth Missouri Volunteer Infantry, Lieutenant-Colonel Romer, 141; Twenty-ninth Missouri Volunteer Infantry, Major Murphy, 151; Thirty-first Missouri Volunteer Infantry, Lieutenant-Colonel Simpson, 122; Thirty-second Missouri Volunteer Infantry, Major Seay, 149; total, 868.

We captured 25 prisoners, including 2 commissioned officers, 20 during the day and 5 during the night, and lost 4 wounded, 3 of the Twelfth and 1 of the Third Missouri. Captain Burkhardt, Twenty-ninth Missouri, while out with the skirmishers, was taken prisoner. The only disappointment the officers and men of this brigade experienced was their inability to show by actual combat with the enemy that they were worthy to stand side by side in the defense of their country with the veterans of the Seventeenth Army Corps, whose fighting qualities they witnessed and admired on the memorable July 22, 1864, without being able, from their position, to participate therein.

Respectfully submitted.

Hugo Wangelin,

Colonel, Commanding Brigade.

Lieutenant-Colonel Alexander,

Asst. Adjt. Gen., Seventeeth Army Corps.(10)

Probably one of the most thorough speeches on the Battle of Atlanta is the one given by Major General Mortimer Dormer Leggett, of Leggett's Hill fame in the Battle of Atlanta on July 22, 1864, to the Society of the Army of the Tennessee on October 18, 1883 at their annual reunion in Cleveland, Ohio. It is quoted in its entirety in the next nineteen pages.

"The President (General W. T. Sherman) announced that General Leggett had prepared a paper, as requested by the Society at its last meeting, upon the "Battle of Atlanta," and would read it now if such was the pleasure of the Society. The desire that he should do so was universal, and General Leggett stepped to the stage and in a clear voice and forcible manner read his paper: At our St. Louis meeting last year, I was appointed to prepare for this meeting a paper on the battle of the 22nd of July, 1864, near Atlanta. I have presumed that I was not expected to give a complete description of that engagement, but to confine myself substantially to the battle as seen from the standpoint of my command, the 3d Division of the 17th Army Corps.

To do this understandingly, I must include the movements of the evening of the 20th, and during the day of the 21st of July. During the afternoon of the 20th, the 4th Division of the 17th Corps, under General W.Q. Gresham, was deployed and marched in front, while the 3d Division marched to the left and rear in echelon of brigades. Toward night General Gresham's division became quite sharply engaged; and just as the enemy were driven into the outer line of their works, General was severely wounded and carried from the field. Colonel Wm. Hall of the 11th Iowa, assumed command of the division, but turned it over to General Giles A. Smith the next morning.

The 4th Division pressed up as closely to the enemy's lines as they could, and availed themselves of the make of the ground for protection. To have placed my Division, the 3d, to the left of the 4th, and in prolongation of its line, would have thrown it into an open field in plain view and easy range of a battery, just in front of the 4th Division, and at the same time would have left a dense strip of woods between my line and the enemy in front.

While General F. P. Blair, who commanded the 17th Corps, and myself were discussing the disposition to be made of Division, General McPherson rode up, and suggested that we should occupy that strip of woods with a strong skirmish line. From the position where we were standing we could see that the enemy occupied a commanding position on Bald Hill in an open field to our left and front, and a short distance west of the strip of dense woodland before mentioned. General McPherson at once suggested that we should possess ourselves of that hill, and Colonel G. D. Munson, of my staff, was sent to press the skirmish line far enough, if possible, to discover the extreme right of the enemy. He soon fter reported that the Confederate line extended only a short distance south of the hill referred to. General McPherson decided that it was too late to assault the hill that night, but directed that we should do so in the morning, unless we got orders to the contrary.

I then moved my Division to the left, and forward into the woods, and bivouacked in two lines, with the 1st Brigade, General M. F. Force, on the right, the 2nd Brigade, General R. K. Scott, in the center, and the 3rd Brigade, Colonel Maloy of the 17th Wisconsin, on the left, refused so as to face south, while the other two brigades faced west, or nearly so. The skirmish line was pushed closely to the western edge of the woods. As the 3rd Division was bivouacked, General Force was directly in front of the Bald Hill occupied by the enemy's right. I then notified him of the orders I had received, and that we must make the assault early in the morning.

General Force expressed regret that he had not known of the order sooner, and before putting his Brigade in position—saying that he had the 12th Wisconsin in the front line, which would not have been the case if he had known he was to assault the enemy in works.

The 12th Wisconsin was a large regiment of veterans, who had campaigned in Missouri and Kansas for three years, but had never been under fire at the time it joined the 3rd Division, a few days before. It was a splendidly officered. When it reported for duty, its Colonel, George E. Bryant, said he had a good regiment of good men— that they had been long in the service, and had done much hard marching, but had never been under fire, and closed with, "Now General, if you have any fighting to do, give us a chance." I assured him that he would soon enough, probably, get all the chance he wanted, and assigned him to General Force's Brigade. General Force knew that this regiment had never been tried, while each of the others had a hundred times; yet he feared the effect upon the regiment, if he then should change its position.

Colonel Bryant and the other officers expressed the greatest confidence in their men, so they were left in the front line, and in that portion of it where most was to be done, and where the exposure was greatest. General Force and myself felt anxious about this regiment, but its officers were confident.

Our intention was to make the assault about daybreak on the morning of the 21st, but upon conference with General Blair, in the latter part of the night, I learned that the 4th Division had received no orders, and the support of that Division, in making the assault, was deemed important, if not necessary—hence, it was about eight o'clock when the order to advance was given.

It was found in the morning that the enemy had considerably strengthened their works on the hill during the night. General Force's Brigade consisted of the 20th, 30th, 31st, and 45th Illinois, and the 12th and 16th Wisconsin Regiments. General Scott's Brigade consisted on that day, of the 20th, 68th and 78th Ohio Regiments. The 3rd Brigade under Colonel Maloy was held in reserve. When the order to advance was given, the skirmish line, under the immediate command of Colonel Munson, was pushed forward to draw the first fire from the enemy. The front line followed closely after the skirmishers, and the second line only a few paces in the rear. The resistance to the first Brigade was determined and sanguinary. General Force's character for coolness, self-possession and utter indifference to danger was proverbial long before this, but here he even excelled himself. To lessen their exposure, he had directed all the field officers of his Brigade to leave their horses behind, only himself and a portion of his personal staff being mounted. He had directed his command to hold their fire until in the enemy's works, and his personal presence, conspicuously mounted, enabled him to enforce this order, and prevent a single moment's halt. His men fell thick and fast around him, but it was the work of only a short time, when his Brigade was in possession of the Bald Hill, and a considerable number of prisoners. The Confederate troops occupying this hill were a portion of General Cleburne's Division. Some of the prisoners said to General Force, with both pride and chagrin, that it was the first time that Pat. Cleburne's Division was ever routed.

General Force was now in possession of the Bald Hill. He made the charge through an open field, up the side of the hill, against a confident enemy, strongly entrenched upon its summit. The 4th Division on our immediate right, advanced at the same time, but finding the enemy too strongly entrenched, and too well supplied with artillery, were compelled to fall back into the temporary works they had erected the night before. This left General Force greatly exposed, for he was occupying the right of the enemy's line, while the enemy was still in possession of the same line to our right. We immediately began with a fatigue party to turn the works we had captured, but the enemy rallied in the woods at our right front in large force, and made several persistent and desperate efforts to dislodge General Force, but without avail. He was there to stay; and had the enemy known him as we did, they would have spared their ammunition, and saved their men. I have not been able to find General Cleburne's report of this affair of the 21st; but General Hardee, in his report of the military operations around Atlanta, says that General Cleburne described this fight for the hill on the 21st of July as "the bitterest of his life."

As soon as we could turn the enemy's works on the hill, we placed in position DeGolier's Michigan battery of Rodman guns, and shelled the enemy out of the woods in our immediate vicinity, and threw shot into Atlanta. As before stated, our line was a prolongation of the enemy's line. This brought the right of my Division facing toward Atlanta, in uncomfortably close proximity to the enemy's right, facing from Atlanta; and a continued galling fire was kept up until late in the afternoon. This hill was in an open field with nothing to protect against the direct rays of the sun. The day was extremely warm, and many of the officers and men suffered from sunstroke in the after part of the day. Among these were some of General Force's staff, whose constant activity and exposure had greatly exhausted them; and General Force himself suffered greatly from the same cause. This hill has since been known as "Leggett's Hill," but it ought to have been christened "Force's Hill," because General Force captured it and held it on the 21st by a display of most excellent generalship and unexcelled fighting qualities, and because in defending it the next

MAJOR-GENERAL JOHN ALEXANDER LOGAN
15th Army Corps Commander December 11, 1863 - July 22,
1863, and July 27, 1863 - May 23, 1865 Army of the Tennessee
Commander May 19 - August 1, 1865. Wendell W. Lang Jr.
Collection at US Army Military History Institute.

day, he there fell so terribly wounded. Although the hill was captured in less time that it takes to write it, yet it cost us dearly. Our loss was 38 killed, and 294 wounded. Of these numbers, 29 were killed and 108 wounded from the 12th Wisconsin. The steadiness and gallantry of this regiment could not have been excelled. Colonel Bryant said to me that evening, "Your prophecy was too true, and fulfilled much sooner than any of us expected."

Among the wounded was our gallant and witty Colonel Tom. Reynolds, of the 16th Wisconsin. He fell with his thigh terribly crushed. The surgeons pronounced his wound fatal. While they were examining it to determine whether or not his limb should be amputated, the Colonel replied and said, "Please spare that leg, gentleman. I think a great deal of it, for it is an imported article." It will be remembered the Colonel brought this leg over from Ireland with him. The surgeons determined that he would in all probability die anyhow, and concluded to let him keep his leg; and thank God, and the Colonel's indomitable pluck, he still has both his life and his leg. After the March to the Sea, and up through the Carolinas, much to our surprise, Colonel Reynolds met us at Raleigh, North Carolina. After congratulating him upon his resurrection, I said to him that his wound had considerably shortened his leg. He answered, "Well, I don't know, General; lying so long in bed my leg got crooked at the knee joint, and the doctors put me under the influence of chloroform to straighten it, and I believe the d——d fools stretched the wrong leg."

I will be pardoned for digressing so far as to correct a few errors of history. General Sherman, in his memoirs, has both General Gresham and Colonel Reynolds wounded in the assault upon this hill, and General Wm. T. Clark, McPherson's chief of staff, makes the same mistake in several published papers. General Gresham was wounded the day before, while capturing another hill, a half mile or more to the right and rear of the one captured by General Force. General Blair, in his official report, says, that in taking this hill on the 21st, General Force was severely wounded, while the fact is, General Force was not wounded at all when capturing the hill

MAJOR-GENERAL OLIVER OTIS HOWARD
Army of the Tennessee Commander July 1864 - May 1865
National Archives, Washington D.C.

on the 21st, but was wounded while holding it on the 22nd.

Late in the afternoon of the 21st, General Force called my attention to a column of Confederate troops moving out of Atlanta toward our left, and we both felt a little apprehensive as to their destination. This movement was witnessed also by all the officers and men in position on the hill, and on the skirmish line to the left, and the front of the hill. Notice of this movement was frequently sent back to General Blair, our corps commander, by Captain G. W. Porter, Captain A. W. Stewart, and others of my staff, with an urgent request that my left should be strengthened by additional troops.

What the destination of these troops was, is a mystery in the light of Hood's, Hardee's, and other Confederate reports, as they all agree in saying that the movement to our left commenced after dark, and a little after eight o'clock. Whatever they were, they caused our left to be strengthened by the 4th Division of the 17th Corps under General Giles A. Smith, and General John W. Fuller's Division of the 16th Corps. General Smith's Division occupied a refused line on the left of my Division, while Fuller's Brigade bivouacked directly in my rear. As soon as the Confederate movement referred to in the afternoon of the 21st was discovered, I gave orders to strengthen our works as much as possible, and throw out traverses to the rear facing South, on the left of each company. There was just enough apprehension of danger among the men, to cause them to work with a will. Just after dark, orders came, also from General McPherson, to strengthen our lines against an assault at daybreak next morning. The work of entrenching was carried on briskly all night. The works on the hill were considerably enlarged, and much strengthened. The DeGolier Battery of Rodman Guns were removed, and the McAllister Battery of 24 lb. Howitzers placed in position on the hill. At nightfall of the 21st, my Division was in bad shape. The first and second brigades occupied a prolongation of the enemy's line on what was then known as the McDonough road.

As before stated, in the assault of the morning of the 21st, General Giles A. Smith's Division, then on our right, found it impossible to dislodge the enemy in its front, and fell back into its works, some five or six hundred yards in the rear, leaving about five hundred yards between the right of Forces's Brigade, and the left of Smith's Division. When General Smith's Division moved to my left, 15th Corps extended to the left, occupying the position vacated by Smith's Division. Smith's Division relieved my third Brigade which I used to form a refused line on my right, extending from the right of Force's Brigade, to the left of Walcutt's Brigade of the 15th Corps. General Fuller furnished me two regiments from the 16th Corps to complete this line. There were three batteries attached to my Division—the 3rd Ohio, 20 lb. Parrots; DeGolier's, Michigan, Rodman Guns; and the McAllistar, Illinois, 24 lb. Howitzers. The McAllister was placed with General Force on the hill, while the DeGolier was adjusted to support the refused line on our right. My artillery was under charge of Captain W. S. Williams, acting as my Chief of Artillery.

The night was one of very little rest. Just after midnight, I called on Colonel George E. Wells, of the 68th Ohio, for two shrewd, reliable men, and sent them to the front with orders to go as far as they could safely. After an absence of an hour or more, they returned with a report that a column of troops was moving to our left from Atlanta.

I sent this report to General Blair, as my memoranda says, at half past one o'clock the morning of the 22nd.

At the break of day, the troops were on the alert, but no attack was made, and there was an ominous silence all along the line. It was soon discovered that the enemy had drawn out of the line at the right of General Force. I at once swung my third Brigade, Colonel Maloy, forward into the vacated works to the right of General Force, and the 15th corps did the same to the right of my Division, and all commenced changing the works to face toward Atlanta. The 3rd and 4th Divisions had an admirable line of works, with numerous traverses facing to the left, and as well arranged as they could have been on that line to resist the sanguinary assault so near at hand.

Soon after sunrise, Generals McPherson and Blair visited our lines. Both seemed impressed with the belief that the enemy had evacuated Atlanta, and both Smith's and my skirmish lines were advanced until we drew the fire of the enemy, and found Atlanta still guarded, but as was then thought, with a small force; and we could, and when properly constructed to move forward into them, General Smith and myself, with the brigade commanders, went to the front, and located a new line, and fatigue parties were sent forward with their entrenching tools.

For two days and nights the officers and men had obtained no rest. The weather was extremely warm, and General Force's command, both officers and men, had been constantly exposed both to the direct rays of the sun, and the galling fire of Cleburne's troops. General Force himself was so exhausted as to fall asleep on his horse, while locating the new line for works in the front. General Smith's Division had also been hard at work all night, and had been on the alert for two days before, with little or no rest.

About ten o'clock in the morning of the 22nd, I received word that our corps hospital, about two miles at the rear, was being menaced by Confederate cavalry, and I directed General Scott to send Colonel Wells with the 68th Ohio to protect it. About the same time Captain Peter Hitchcock, Quarter Master of my Second Brigade, sent word that the enemy had just captured a man standing picket only a short distance in rear of General Smith's left. I started to confer with General Smith on these matters but before reaching him, skirmish firing was heard in the rear, and I returned to the hill from which I could see the 68th Ohio deployed, and firing at the enemy, not visible at my standpoint. General Fuller quickly took in the position, faced his Division to the rear, and double-quicked back on to the ridge behind where he had been lying. The 68th Ohio was moving slowly towards us but kept up a constant fire toward their left.

The other Division of the 16th Corps was moving by the right flank toward Fuller's Division, but had not closed up to it. Colonel Alexander, of General Blair's Staff, at this point, joined Colonel Wells, and urged that he press the enemy hard to hold them back until the 16th Corps was closed up. Just as two Divisions of the 16th Corps had come together, the enemy in double line came out of the dense forest in their front. General Fuller by good luck had parked his artillery in exactly the right place, and it was very efficient. Both Divisions of the 16th Corps immediately became hotly engaged. The enemy were evidently greatly surprised at finding such a force in that position, and were easily repulsed, and fell back into the woods in a southeasterly direction.

Just at this time, I espied General McPherson upon the high ground in the immediate rear of General Fuller's command, and sent Captain John B. Raymond, of my staff, to enquire of General McPherson the expediency of having General Giles A. Smith and myself change our line so as to face south, and at the same time I sent Captain George W. Porter to ascertain whether or not the left of General Smith, and the right of General Fuller were sufficiently near together to antagonize any force seeking entrance there.

The enemy in front of the 16th Corps rallied in the woods, and then knowing what they had to meet, renewed their attack with increased vigor and bitterness; but the 16th Corps had also had time to dress its lines, and prepare for this second assault, and met it splendidly. The conflict continued for some time, with no appearance on either side of any disposition to yield the ground, when the enemy gave way, and fell back in confusion, followed by the 16th Corps. The attack was not again renewed from that direction. This flanking force of the enemy was Hardee's Corps, consisting of four Divisions, commanded by Generals Bate, Walker, Cleburne, and Maney respectively. Bate and Walker were on the right of Hardee's infantry, and Cleburne and Maney on his left, while Wheeler's cavalry was on his extreme right. The first attack upon the 16th was by Bate's, and part of Walker's Divisions, while the second was by the whole of these two divisions.

These conflicts between Fuller's and Sweeny's Divisions of General Dodge's 16th Corps, and Bate's and Walker's Divisions of Hardee's Corps, were among the few engagements of the War of the Rebellion, where the opposing forces met in the open field, with no works to protect or shield either side.

In Hardee's movements upon our left, it was his design to have his right reach to the right of our 15th Corps and assault it, while his left should reach to the left of our 17th Corps, hence, he swung his right more rapidly forward than he did his left, and Bate and Walker struck the 16th Corps before his left reached the left of the 17th. The second assault, however, was simultaneous with the attack upon Giles A. Smith's Division, which was the left of the 17th Corps.

To understand the disadvantageous position of Smith's line at this time, it must be remembered that my line was on the McDonough road running nearly north and south, and facing almost due west; while Smith's line was refused so as to guard against an assault upon our left flank, and consequently his line ran in a southeasterly direction. Hardee was seeking to strike us directly in the rear, and not in the flank, hence, as before stated, was more rapidly advancing his right, so he was marching in a northwesterly direction, the general direction of his line being northeast and southwest. Smith's line therefore was almost exactly perpendicular to Hardee's line of battle, so that the enemy struck it squarely on the flank, enveloped Smith's left regiment, and captured it before Smith could so change the front of the balance of his division as to resist and check Hardee's advance. In charge of front, General Smith was obliged to uncover two pieces of artillery belonging to an Illinois battery, and these were also captured. He succeeded, however, in repulsing the enemy's attack after a most desperate encounter of considerable duration.

In repulsing the Divisions of Bate and Walker, the 16th Corps had so advanced in following up the enemy as to materially widen the gap between Fuller's right and Smith's left, so that much of General Cleburne's command passed unmolested between the Divisions, and quickly appeared directly in the rear of the third Division. My Division, the third, was occupying the works it took from General Cleburne the morning of the day before, and Cleburne was now assaulting us from the same direction, and over the same ground we assaulted him. From the assertion made by the prisoners we captured from him, that it was "first time Pat. Cleburne's Division was ever routed;" and Cleburne's report to Hardee that his fight with us on the 21st was "the bitterest of his life," we may easily imagine the spirit that inspired him and his men, when they came upon us with their demoniac yells, so characteristic of Pat. Cleburne's Texans. Our men immediately leaped their works, putting their backs towards Atlanta, and for vindictive desperation, this encounter was probably never exceeded. When this assault was commenced, I was at the left of my line with General Smith, but immediately rode to the hill occupied by General Force.

The attack was finally repulsed, leaving many prisoners in our hands. Cleburne's troops were but just driven back to the strip of woods at the foot of the hill, when General Cheatham's Corps advanced upon us from toward Atlanta. This assault covered both my front and General Smith's, and other Confederate troops at the same time struck the 15th Corps to our right.

As soon as the first attack was made on the 16th Corps, we anticipated a co-operating attack from Atlanta, and I sent Colonel Munson, of my staff, to take charge of the skirmish line, and retard as much as possible any assault from that direction. Colonel Munson, probably, had no superior in ability to handle a skirmish line. A skirmish line under his control was equal to a line of battle in the hands of some others. He had a quick eye, excellent judgement, and that kind of fearless courage that gave him staying qualities, and a personal magnetism that inspired his men to stay with him. On this occasion he made his skirmishers fight so desperately as to retard Cheatham's advance, and thereby prevent his effective co-operation with Cleburne. Cheatham finally struck savagely, and found our men again upon the right side of their works facing Atlanta, where a sanguinary struggle ensued. The enemy began to waver when our men leaped the works, and forced them rapidly back at the point of the bayonet. Near the right of my Division, my Chief of Artillery, Captain Williams, had placed two pieces of the McAllister battery of 24 lb. Howitzers. The battery did magnificent service during the whole day.

Cheatham's Corps was but fairly repulsed, when Cleburne, who had fallen back into the woods in the immediate rear of my Division to readjust his line, again renewed his assault upon our rear with more anger, if possible, than before, but they were more easily repulsed, for General C. C. Walcutt, then Colonel Commanding the left Brigade of the 15th Corps, was on my immediate right, and so changed front as to obtain an enfilading fire on Cleburne's attacking troops, which quickly caused them to seek shelter in the strip of woods, followed a short distance by our men. There were indications that Cheatham's forces were again preparing for another assault from toward Atlanta, and our men were again called back to their works. At this time General Cleburne was unable to re-adjust his lines, and repeat his assault upon the same ground, for General Walcutt continued to pour in a galling fire upon his right flank, and General Fuller, becoming satisfied that the attack was not to be renewed, upon his front, had faced to the rear, and come to our assistance, by attacking Cleburne in the rear, compelling him to withdraw by the left flank. Immediately Cheatham was upon us again from toward Atlanta, supported by the Confederate troops upon his left. This assault was pressed with great vigor, causing the whole of the 15th Corps, except General Walcutt's Brigade, to give way, and fall back to the ridge in the rear, from which they had advanced early in the morning. Discovering this, I immediately went to the right of my Division and found General Walcutt still holding his position; but while with him, an order came from his Division Commander, directing him to fall back in line with the balance of the 15th Corps.

I said to him that the order was certainly a mistake; that my orders from General Blair, General Logan and directly from General Sherman were to hold the hill at any hazard and at whatever cost; but to do so would be impossible if the enemy were to have, undisputed, our front, and both our flanks. General Walcutt responded promptly that he could stay there as long as I could, and that he would take the responsibility of disobeying orders in doing so.

The position he held at the time was one of extreme exposure. The enemy, flushed with a temporary victory on his right, was pushing him with renewed vigor and determination. To determine to stay there and hold his position, even in violation of the orders of his superior officer, was a test of personal courage and good judgment to which very few officers were subjected. Yet to this action of this gallant officer, we were undoubtedly very largely indebted for our final victory on the 22nd July. The right of his Brigade was partially protected by a small swamp covered with a dense undergrowth of brush, while his left occupied a high point of land overlooking my 3rd Brigade, the highest point then held by our army north of the Hill captured by General Force the morning of the day before. If the enemy had got possession of this elevation, held by General Walcutt, the position of my 3rd Brigade would have been utterly untenable. If I had been compelled to withdraw my 3rd Brigade, I should also have been compelled to have abandoned the hill; and to have abandoned the Hill at that time would probably have resulted in a catastrophe not now pleasant to contemplate.

Up to this point in the battle, we had been extremely fortunate in being able to prevent the assaults in our front and rear, from being simultaneous. We had been able to repel the enemy from one side and then leaping the works repel it from the other.

Just about this time the 15th Corps was driven back from its position, Hardee having massed his divisions, or more strictly speaking, having shortened his line by closing more compactly, and having moved his whole line more to his left with his artillery at short range, so posted as to enfilade the whole line of our works, made an irresistible charge directly upon Smith's left flank, and doubled back his Division upon mine. For a time the two Divisions were thoroughly intermingled, and fought as if they belonged to the same regiments and brigades. The traverses thrown out the night before were a great protection to our troops, and enabled them to greatly retard the enemy's progress.

It at once became apparent that we must make a change of our front. At this moment Colonel George E.

Wells with the 68th Ohio, whose instincts always seemed to guide him exactly to the place where most needed, having made a detour to the right, made his appearance upon the hill at this critical moment. Colonel Munson immediately aided Colonel Wells in placing the 68th Ohio in a new line nearly at right angles with the former line, and its right resting against the works on the hill and facing south.

While my staff were busily engaged moving my second Brigade back to this new line, to aid them and to further retard the enemy, I swung my Third Brigade forward, wheeling to the left on the Atlanta side of our works, so as to face southerly, and by aid of our 24 lb. Howitzer guns, the enemy's advance was so held in check as to enable our troops to form on the new line, with Smith's Division to the left of mine. The 16th Corps also changed front and closed on General Smith's left. As soon as the new line was partially established the Third Brigade of my Division was again swung back into the works. Probably no occasion during the war, displayed so strikingly the discipline and soldierly qualities of the Army of the Tennessee, as did this change of front under the circumstances. Hardee's Corps, compactly formed, was charging and rapidly doubling our left flank, while his artillery was enfilading our whole line, and a galling cross-fire was being poured upon us from Shoupe's battery in Atlanta. The new line was but partially formed, however, when it was struck with great vigor, by Hardee's advancing columns, and a hand to hand conflict ensued not exceeded in fierceness by any assault during the day, but our men held their position, and repulsed the enemy.

No time was lost by our troops, and defensive works sprang up as if by magic all along the line. The day was now nearly spent. My first Brigade still held the hill. The 15th Corps had recovered its line and was again in the same position as when the battle opened. My Third Brigade held its position throughout the struggle, and so did so much of the first Brigade as was on the north of the Hill, but immediately south of the Hill, our line broke abruptly to the rear, facing south.

Our line therefore was so formed as to present a right

angle at the Hill—the apex of the Hill being within the angle. We felt that this was an awkward position, but one forced upon us against our will. This angle was a tempting exposure to the enemy, consequently they reformed, and just at twilight they made a bitter and persistent assault directly upon this angle, and came up against our works, leaving only the embankment between the two maddened lines. This last and bloodiest assault lasted until long after dark, when the enemy receded a few yards to works abandoned by us in our change of front, where they remained until toward the next morning and then withdrew. This ended the battle of the 22nd of July, 1864, or the battle of Atlanta, as it has generally been called.

The struggle to recover from us the Hill was fierce and desperate beyond description. The carnage at this point was terrible and sickening. The ground from close to our works to one hundred yards or more away, was literally covered with the dead.

During the whole of the battle, General Hood, the commander in chief, of the Confederate forces in and about Atlanta, occupied a position where the Hill and most of the 17th Corps' line were plainly within his view, and he witnessed all the movements and personally directed the assaults from toward Atlanta. Shoupe's Battery was close by his position, and he kept it playing upon us all the afternoon and much of the night.

The fortunate position of Colonel Wells, with the 68th Ohio Infantry, at the first appearance of the enemy in force, giving us full warning of their design before reaching our lines; the more than magnificent fighting of the 16th Corps, utterly defeating the enemy in the plan of striking the whole Army of the Tennessee in the rear; and the patriotic personal courage of General C. C. Walcutt, in assuming the responsibility of disobeying the orders of his immediate superior and protecting the right of flank of the 17th Corps in its most exposed and trying moment, were winning features of this bloody battle; yet the heaviest struggle and hardest fighting undoubtedly fell upon the 17th Corps. From the opening to the close of the engagement, from 11:30 A.M. to 8 P.M., the 3rd and 4th Divisions of this Corps were continually and most of the time fiercely engaged.

Often the conflict was a hand to hand encounter, with instances of brilliant personal valor all along the line, too numerous to mention in this paper. Almost at the very opening of the battle the gallant McPherson, who as our former 17th Corps Commander, and now as the Commander of our Army of the Tennessee, had led us so successfully through so many tiresome marches and hard fought engagements, was shot by the enemy and fell dead from his horse.

As a commander he was most thoroughly respected, and as a man loved by every officer and man in the old 17th Corps, and probably in the whole Army of the Tennessee. Captain Raymond, as before stated, was sent to him for orders. He rode up to him, obtained orders, and started to return to me by a road entering the woods by my headquarters. He had but just entered the woods, when General McPherson rapidly followed him. Captain Raymond had ridden but a short distance into the woods, before he found himself closely in front of Cleburne's line of battle, parallel with the road, moving from south toward it. They cried out "halt" to him and commenced firing; but his horse was shot, and he fell into the enemy's hands. He says he had scarcely extricated himself from his horse, when he heard the word, "halt," followed by some rapid firing, and General McPherson fell.

McPherson knew that Captain Raymond had cone to him on this road, and was returning on it, and consequently had no reason to apprehend danger from following him.

The death of General McPherson was quickly known to all our troops, and also the fact that General Logan had succeeded to the command. In General Logan, all had confidence. He was personally known to every man in the Army of the Tennessee, and his presence in battle was always a power. He always seemed to have a kind of magnetic influence, exciting to deeds of valor, every officer and man.

General R. K. Scott, commanding my 2d Brigade, rode out to the 68th Ohio as soon as he discovered it was engaged, but hearing firing on the front, he started to return and followed General McPherson into the woods. He had gone but a few yards when his horse was shot, himself slightly wounded, and he captured.

The same force that had killed General McPherson captured General Scott, a few moments later presented itself at the foot of the hill held by General Force, and commenced the assault, in which General Force, and his Adjutant-General, Captain Walker, both fell severely wounded, Captain Walker in his thigh, from which he subsequently died and General Force by a minnie ball through his head, entering just below the outer corner of the left eye, and coming out close by the right ear. That General Force recovered, and was able four months later, to go with us on the march to the sea seemed almost miraculous.

Thus the Army was deprived of its loved commander, and my Division of its 1st and 2d Brigade Commanders, by General Cleburne's advanced line in his first assault. General R. K. Scott was a discreet, but a brave, daring, officer, and his services in such an engagement would have been invaluable. General Force was the idol, not only of his Brigade, but of the whole Division. His loss was severely felt, and at first threatened to be disastrous. The next officer in rank, in his command, was Colonel Bryant, of the 12th Wisconsin Infantry, who as a commanding officer had never been under fire until the day previous.

When directed to assume command of the Brigade, and to hold the hill, Colonel Bryant modestly preferred to be left with his regiment, but reluctantly obeyed the order to take command. He very soon won the confidence of the officers and men, by his cool, self-possessed manner, and his careful handling of his troops. Lieutenant-Colonel G. F. Wiles of the 78th Ohio, assumed command of the 2d Brigade, and had the confidence of the men from the beginning.

General Smith had been in command of the 4th Division only 24 hours when the battle opened, and could hardly have had his command well in hand, when called upon to resist a most vigorous assault directly upon his left flank. The assaults upon the flank of the 4th Division so mixed its companies and men of different companies together, as would have made troops of less patriotism and nerve, utterly worthless, and an easy prey for the enemy. The same was true later in the day, of the 3rd Division, and in fact the men of the two divisions became thoroughly inter mixed about the time of our change of front, yet all this did not seem to materially affect the fighting or staying qualities of these commands. Wherever the men were, their faces were to the enemy, and every man doing soldierly work. The use of the clubbed musket, and hand to hand conflicts were frequent all along the line. General W. W. Belknap personally seized the Colonel of the 45th Alabama by the coat collar, and dragged him over the works, and made him prisoner. Some privates in the 17th Wisconsin, of the 3rd Division, seized the horse of a Lieutenant of a Confederate battery by the bridle, and pulled him over our works with its rider; and many prisoners all along our lines were captured in the same way. Captain Orr, of the 78th Ohio, discovered a Confederate soldier just in the act of bayoneting the color-bearer of his regiment, and springing upon him with the sword, cut his head almost clean from his body, for which act he was awarded a gold medal. Very many instances of individual prowess might be sighted, for probably very few battles of our late war were equally characterized by so much man to man fighting.

The number of men engaged in this battle must have been over sixty thousand.

On the 20th of July there was present for duty in the 15th, 16th and 17th Corps, of our army , including artillery 27,593.

While on the 10th of July, there was present for duty in Hardee's and Cheatham's Corps and Wheeler's Cavalry, including artillery, 37,455.

On the 20th, at Peach-tree Creek, the enemy's loss had been more that ours, and on the 21st about the same.

The assistance afforded from men and artillery in Atlanta on the 22nd, not belonging to Cheatham's Corps, probably fully compensated for their losses referred to, so they must have brought into battle of the 22nd fully 37,000 men, against 27,000 in our Army of the Tennessee, making in all about 64,000 men engaged.

Respectfully submitted,

M. D. Leggett."(12)'

The 23rd of July was used for the burying of the dead. There was a truce arranged between the two opposing armies so that this task could be accomplished. Major-General Charles Woods was given orders to take his 1st Division towards Decatur destroying the railroad on the way and what had not been destroyed in Decatur before would now be destroyed. Major A. J. Seay wrote in his diary, "Saturday, 23. We lay in line in hearing of the rebs in thick woods in line of battle till 1 A.M. we begin to entrench. Our suspense was great all night, our line partially shattered and disconnected. We were secure only in the weakness of the enemy and another assault expected at daylight this morning. No fight today, we fortify, bury the dead and steal a little sleep which is sweet."(13) They were also instructed that if they should learn that General Dodge's men came under attack they should attack the flank of the enemy. There was some firing on the right flank of the army but the left flank was quiet, which included the 15th Corps.

Private John T. Clarke states, in his diary, "Sunday 24. The day was occupied by our Corps in burning and destroying the R.R. Some cannonading and skirmishing on the Right. All quiet in our front. Some Rebs captured."(14) Major A. J. Seay of the 32nd Missouri Infantry Regiment records in his diary, "Sunday, 24. Very cold last night. I sleep cold under 2 blankets and overcoat. Some shelling this morning-a good deal on our right. Logan commands Dept. Tenn. Morgan and L. Smith, 15 A.C. Our div scattered I can't tell where. Wish Osterhaus was here. We are getting the rebs in a desperate condition. Repulsed 6 determined assaults 22nd inflicting a loss of 6,000 our loss, 2,500."(15) General Logan, who had assumed command of the Army of the Tennessee because of the death of Major-General James McPherson, led the Army of the Tennessee with great ability on July 22nd. He was loved by his men and had led them ably throughout the war. Surgeon Alexander W. Reese of the 31st Missouri Infantry Regiment records his impressions of General Logan in a book that he wrote in 1870.

"In a letter to my wife dated 'Coker's Ferry, Ala. Oct 26th,1864', speaking of Gen Logan, I said. 'I wish you could see him, riding along the lines on the eve of a battle—just as he did at Dallas, on the 28th May, and in front of Atlanta, on the 28th July—with his hat in hand—

his large dark eye flashing like the glance of an eagle—his swarthy complexion relieved by his huge mustache—and his long, glossy, black hair falling, in tangled masses, about his neck—he is a picture for an artist's pencil. Brave as a lion—heedless of personal danger—full of a patriot's enthusiasm and fire—no wonder that his soldiers love and venerate the man!!' I have seen him on many a bloody field, and I can truly say that a braver man than John A. Logan, never buckled on warrior's sword, or wore the good, old Lincoln blue."(16)

The major problem with General Logan was that he was a political general. He had not graduated from West Point, which had generated much jealously from those who had. General Sherman who had graduated from West Point, was not overly fond of political generals, one such general was General McClernand, even though General Sherman had high praise for General Logan and General Blair. On July 24th Major-General Oliver Otis Howard, sometimes referred to as the Christian general because of his strong religious beliefs and practices, even in war time, was named as commander of the Army of the Tennessee. This angered many of the men in the Army of the Tennessee as well as some senior commanders in the army that were not West Point graduates and could not believe the appointment. General Logan, the one who should have been the most offended, refused to let this instance alter his vision of the final goal of the war, which was the restoration of the Union.

General Logan served nobly and ably throughout the rest of the war. General Logan resumed command of the 15th Army Corps. I find this amazing that a general officer who had no formal training in war could turn over the command of an army, return to an army corps, and then serve under the command of the one who had replaced him. I think that this speaks volumes of the General Logans character. After the war General Logan returned to Congress. In a speech, on September 14, 1887 in the year following General Logan's death, to the members of the "Society of the Army of the Tennessee", General Sherman states, "Logan soon manifested his hostility to these last, and in a speech of March 10th, 1870, displayed his antagonism to West Point, attributing the fact that he, as a 'volunteer,' had been outraged by the selection of a West Pointer to succeed McPherson."(17) General Sherman and General

Logan did finally come to terms of reconcilliation at a later date. In 1903, Mrs. John A. Logan in a speech told of the circumstances that brought these two men back together.

"It may not be inappropriate for me on this occasion to say that whatever of misunderstanding and estrangement may have existed between the two great commanders of the Army of the Tennessee at one time, was wholly obliterated by General Logan's tribute to General Sherman at a notable banquet given by Colonel Corkhill to General Sherman on his retirement as General of the army, in which he said in replying to the toast, 'The Volunteer Soldier:' 'There was no questions of numbers or time, and for General Sherman I will say there was not a soldier who bore the American flag, or followed it; not a soldier who carried a musket or drew a saber who did not respect him as his commander. There was not one, sir, but would have drawn his sword at any time to have preserved his life. There is not one today, no matter what may have been said that would dim, in the slightest degree, the luster of that bright name, achieved by ability, by integrity and true bravery of an officer. And, in conclusion, let me say this: while that army, when it was disbanded, was absorbed in the community like rain drops in the sand; all citizens in the twinkling of an eye and back to their professions and their business; there is not one of these men, scattered, as they are, from ocean to ocean, who does not honor the name of the man who led them in triumph through the enemy's land. Wherever he may go, wherever he may be, whatever may be his condition in life, there is not one who would not stretch out a helping hand to that brave commander who led them to glory. Speaking for that army, if I may be permitted to speak for it, I have to say: May the choicest blessings that God showers upon the head of man go with him along down through his life is the prayer of every soldier who served under Sherman.'

When General Logan finished General Sherman arose, went around to General Logan, put his arm about his neck and shook his hand cordially while the tears ran down his cheeks. His emotions were too great for words."(18)

General Hooker is an example of how having hurt feelings affects how a person may react in about the same situation but only different conclusions. General Hooker had at one time ascended to the command of the Army of the Potomac and had more time in rank and in experience as an army commander than anybody else that was on the scene at Atlanta. When it was announced to the command under General Sherman that, with presidential approval, Major-General Howard would become commander of the Army of the Tennessee, General Hooker asked to be relieved as commander of the 20th Army Corps. General Hooker was a very vain man and as most men had a lot of pride. He felt that he should have been chosen instead of General Howard because of the above mentioned reasons. But because of his unpopularity with his peers around Atlanta and his immediate commander, Major-General Thomas, General Hooker's request to be relieved was accepted by General Thomas who then passed it on to General Sherman, heartily recommended. General Halleck was notified that General Hooker had resigned and that his resignation had been accepted, plus General Sherman requested that Major-General H. W. Slocum, who was then at Vicksburg, be ordered to Atlanta to take command of the 20th Army Corps. The above was approved and the proper orders were issued. General Slocum joined his new command in the latter part of August.

There was new plans being made by General Sherman to continue the offensive and eventual capture of Atlanta. Atlanta was a major railroad center in the deep south, as well as being a manufacturing center for the Confederacy. They manufactured war materials such as guns, ammunition, wagons and clothing as well as being a source of food for the Confederate troops. Much of what they made was sent to General Robert E. Lee's, Army of Northern Virginia, via their railroad system that went through Atlanta. The Georgia Railroad, which the 1st Division were busily destroying, traveled east towards Augusta, Georgia ending at Richmond, Virginia via South Carolina and North Carolina. Then the Western and Atlantic rail line ran northward towards Chattanooga. The Macon and Western railroad ran to Savannah with the city of Mobile, Alabama being connected to Atlanta by the Atlanta and West Point Railroad. These railroad lines could have kept the Confederate armies in Atlanta supplied for quite a while.

General Peter J. Osterhaus who was still on sick leave,

on July 24th, General Sherman was notified that General Osterhaus had been appointed as a Major-General. General Sherman planned to try and cut the railroad lines therefore cutting off the supplies and forcing General Hood to retreat or to suffer through a siege. Major A.J. Seay wrote in his diary, "Monday, 25. More cold. I have slept under 2 blankets and overcoat for three nights. A good deal of firing on the right. Rumor says Hooker had a fight last night. Skirmishing goes on lazily. We have one during the day. At night 6 rockets go up as signals. Gage got back."(19)

The Army of the Tennessee which was on the left flank of the whole army was on July 26th ordered to march to the extreme right flank of the army. This movement was executed at night to keep it hidden from the enemy so they would not have an idea of what was happening. Private John T. Clarke reports in his diary, "Tuesday, July 26,1864. Late this evening the whole Army of the Tennessee received orders to march to the extreme right of our lines and take up positions. We silently withdrew, marching all night over bad roads, traveling about seven miles. Cannonading."(20) Major A. J. Seay of the 32nd Missouri Infantry records in his diary, "Tuesday, 26. The usual routine of skirmishing. I get four letters one from Ed., one from mother, etc, one from Capt. Joe and one from Collins. Last night six rockets were sent up from our lines. I have a bad cold. We fall back and move towards the right at midnight."(21)

"Wednesday, 27. At daylight the enemy shell our empty pits, funny. we move on towards the right. Raining some, slept little last night headache. hard living, hard fighting, glorious results. We move on till midnight and lay ourselves down to rest a few short hours before the deadly conflict begins."(22) Thus records Major A. J. Seay in his diary. The Army of the Tennessee continued their march crossing the Chattanooga and Atlanta Railroad camping about three miles northwest of the city assuming their new position on the right of the 14th Army Corps, becoming the new right flank of the army. On this date Major-General Howard assumed command of the Army of the Tennessee. Their orders for this date was to march southward to East Point which was a key point in the railroad. General Blair's 17th Army Corps was in the lead of the Army of the Tennessee, but because of the severe battle of the 22nd they were down to barely four thousand men. The 15th Army Corps, under the command of General Logan, was marching behind the 17th Corps.

General Howard, who had never been known as an overly aggressive commander, asked General Sherman for permission to march his men in a division at a time while keeping in constant touch with the division next to them in order to keep them from being cut off by the enemy and maybe being destroyed. Even though General Sherman was confident that General Howard's men would not meet with any sizable enemy force he gave in to General Howard's request to be prepared for a rapid deployment. One of the reasons that General Howard was concerned was because of the reports coming back to him of the increasing resistance by the Confederate cavalry. Cavalry will generally not put up much resistance in the face of a strong infantry force, unless they are expecting infantry support to come to their aid a short time.

While the Federal infantry was making their move the cavalry was sent out to destroy as much of the Macon and Western Railroad that they could around Jonesboro, which was approximately twenty-six miles south of Atlanta. Major-General George Stoneman was overall commander of this cavalry command and he asked permission to proceed to Macon, Georgia to rescue Federal prisoners held there and then to march on to Andersonville Prison to free the prisoners in that rat hole. General Sherman gave his permission to fulfill his request as long as General Stoneman destroyed the railroad around Jonesboro' and that General Garrard's division was sent back to the left flank of the army. General Stoneman failed in his mission, primarily because he did not go to Jonesboro. He instead went straight into Macon to accomplish his own task. General McCook troops were to have met General Stoneman near Lovejoy's Station and start working on destroying of the railroad. General McCook began to destroy a couple of miles of track when he was informed that he was being pressed by the enemy. He found that he was surrounded and had to fight his way out. He lost about six hundred of his men as casualties, most of them were captured. The whereabouts of General Stoneman was still a mystery to General Sherman, after the report of General McCook there was a rumor that General Stoneman's unit had been wiped out. What was thought to be a rumor was later confirmed when two small brigades made it back to Federal lines from General Stoneman's force. They reported how General Stoneman had formed a unit of around seven hundred cavalrymen to hold off the Confederates until he was sure that these two groups were on their way and then surrendered the whole force that was left. This event was what convinced General Sherman that the cavalry could not or would not willingly destroy the railroad. He decided that he would have to use the infantry to do this task. The rumor of General Stoneman and his cavalry surrender, was confirmed on the 4th of August. General Sherman, who had not been a strong proponent of the cavalry, never put much faith in that branch after this incident.

Meanwhile, General Howard had marched close to a Methodist Church called Ezra Church which was approximately three miles west of Atlanta. General Hood had issued orders for Lieutenant General Stephen D. Lee to keep the Federals from gaining Lick Skillet Road but not to attack the Federals, only to defend themselves. The Confederate force that was facing him were the troops under the command of General Lee, no relation to General Robert E. Lee. Later engaged in the battle was Major-General A. P. Stewart's Corps and some of General French's Corps were also brought up for support. In General Lee's Corps, General Hoods old corps, there were two divisions under the command of Brigadier-General John C. Brown and Major-General Henry D. Clayton. General Clayton's Division was the one who led the initial attack against the Federal's 1st Division of the 15th Army Corps commanded by Major-General Charles R. Woods. The 3rd Brigade, commanded by Colonel Hugo Wangelin of the 1st Division, established hurried defensive positions a little ways in front of Ezra Church when they were ordered to prepare for battle. The troops that built these hasty defensive positions in front of the church were the 12th Missouri, 31st Missouri and 32nd Missouri who formed the first line. After they finished these hasty defensive positions they sat down to eat a hurried breakfast. The Confederates could be seen coming but there was no time to dig entrenchments so the soldiers of the 3rd Brigade grabbed whatever was available, which included the pews out of the church along with knapsacks, logs or whatever happened to be at hand. Even though the pews were outside the church building there was probably some praying going on.

The attack was to begin at twelve-thirty p.m. on July 28, 1864 using the forces of: Brigadier-General Randall Gibson's Louisiana Brigade, Brigadier-General Alpheus Baker's Alabama

Brigade and Clayton's Alabama Brigade now commanded by Brigadier James T. Holtzclaw. General Clayton was moving General Baker and General Holtzclaw into position when General Gibson started his attack right on time. Because the two other brigades were being moved around at this time, they were unable to support General Gibson's brigade. General Gibson, who attacked, was attacking a whole Federal division with his one brigade and he was greatly outnumbered. But attack he did and his brigade struck Colonel Wangelin's 3rd Brigade. Once the Federals realized that this Confederate brigade was on its own with no support, Colonel Wangelin's men, with some help from Colonel Walcutt's and Colonel Oliver's men, counterattacked General Gibson's outnumbered men. The battle was short and deadly with the Confederates being driven back. Once the Confederates had been chased off the Federals returned to their rough barricades. The other Confederate brigades also charged the Federals in other sections of the defensive position but with no better luck than General Gibson. There was a total of six charges throughout the day and around four p.m. the battle was finally over with the Federals still holding the field.

From the diary of Major A. J. Seay, "Thursday, 28. Move before day-skirmish and advance until 10, halt in line at 12. The enemy charge us impetuously 5 times withdraw at dark butchered at every point. The work was hot and heavy, but the 15 A.C. did it all well and effectually. Our loss (15 A.C.) 500. Enemies loss 6,000. My loss 2 wounded."(23)   In a letter to his wife Private Henry Kuck, Company G, 31st Missouri Infantry Regiment, wrote,

"On the 27th of July, we marched over to the right flank, in order to move our front line to the right. On the morning of the 28th, we took our position as far forward as our generals thought best and built a small breast works out of window frames and old logs. At about 12 o'clock the Rebels came and thought they could drive us back, but the same thing happened as did on the 22nd. According to the reackoning of our Officers, they must have lost once more between 7 and 8 thousand men. We didn't lose anyone in our regiment, but if we had not had our breast works, many of us would have had to bite the dust. Our Army lost some men, but compared to the Rebels, our losses weren't a quarter as much. You think that perhaps I could come home

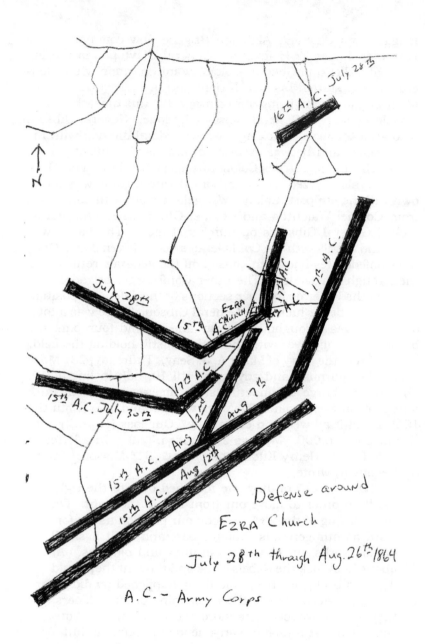

BATTLE AT EZRA CHURCH HOUSE NEAR ATLANTA

next Fall, but you don't have to get up your hopes on this. Then I don't think I'll get the chance, as it seems that this campaign will have no end to it."(24)

The casualties for the Battle at Ezra Church for the 31st Missouri Infantry Regiment was five wounded in this battle. One of the casualties was Sergeant Timothy Baird of Company H from Wayne County he was slightly wounded in the neck he was also wounded at the Battle of Lookout Mountain and was later discharged on November 14, 1864, Sergeant William Foctdman of Company G was slightly wounded in the jaw, Corporal Jasper W. Chatman of Company H was slightly wounded in the face, Corporal John C. Breckinridge of Company B was slightly wounded in the hand and Private Charles Withrow of Company C was slightly wounded in the brow. Colonel Hugo Wangelin the 3rd Brigade commander of the 15th Army Corps commander, gives his report on the battle.

"Forming a line of battle, whereof the First Brigade held the left, the Second the center, and the Third the right. Immediately after arriving, the Twelfth, Thirty-first, and Thirty- Second Missouri, which formed my first line, threw up log breast-works and then sat down to a hasty breakfast. A strong line of skirmishers had been thrown forward as soon as our position had been assigned to us, who soon commenced exchanging with the enemy, whose skirmish line they encountered. About one hour after, a forward movement of all the troops being ordered, with instructions to keep well closed up on Second Brigade, as the forward movement was somewhat in the nature of a left wheel of the Army of the Tennessee, we advanced steadily.

The country in our immediate front was covered by a thick growth of small trees, which our skirmish line was ordered to penetrate as far as possible, keeping in connection with the line of Fourth Division on our right and Second Brigade, First Division on our right and Second Brigade, First Division, on our left. About 1 p. m. our skirmish line was driven in by the enemy. The men reported that the enemy were advancing in three heavy lines ready to charge our works. The men were not allowed to fire until the enemy appeared in sight, which brought them to the distance of some eighty yards, when such a terrific fire was opened upon them that no mortal could stand, and the enemy fell back. Rallying his troops, however, the enemy advanced again, and to strengthen my defensive powers, I caused my last reserve regiment, the Third Missouri, to fill up all weekly manned points on the right of my line, which was principally attacked, thereby securing such a strong line that all apprehensions were put at rest. The enemy attacked again and again, and although the brunt of the attack was directed against the Fourth Division, their lines overlapped this division and attacked the right of this brigade, but all and every assault was repulsed as speedily as their first main charge. Thus, with more or less firing, the day passed, and tools having been procured, part of the men were digging and fortifying, while others kept firing; and when night set in we had not only repulsed the enemy, but put up field-works and a fifty-yard wide abatis of such strength that a single line of determined soldiers would have been able to hold them against all attack.

The loss this brigade sustained was light in comparison with the enemy's loss, of whom 72 were buried in our immediate front. This brigade lost 1 man killed and 34 wounded, of whom 5 were officers. All men behaved gallantly and felt sorry that no further attacks were made on them, as they felt invincible in their position, and would have proved it."(25)

The 15th Army Corps total losses for this battle was fifty killed, four hundred and forty-nine wounded, and seventy-three missing for a total of five-hundred and seventy-two. The rest of the Army of the Tennessee suffered only about sixty casualties which gave General Howard in his first battle as the commander of the 15th Army Corps, a total casualty amount of six hundred and thirty-two. He was happy and the men under him were happy about the victory. It was estimated, by the Federals, that the Confederates suffered about six or seven thousand total casualties. In front of the 15th Army Corps there were one hundred and seventy-nine prisoners captured, of which seventy-three wounded prisoners were sent to the hospital. There was between seven hundred to eight hundred dead Confederates that were buried by the Federals. The Confederates estimated that they suffered four thousand one hundred killed and wounded with two hundred missing for a total of four thousand three hundred casualties.

In a speech by General O. O. Howard to the Society of the Army of the Tennessee describes the action as he saw it at the Battle of Ezra Church.

"Now, in order to make this battle as plain as possible, we can do at this time what we could not do on the 27th or 28th of July, 1864. We can step over to the other side and see what our opponents were doing. I cannot do better, perhaps, than to give you what our good General Cox has ferreted out from Confederate reports: 'He (Hood) determined upon another effort to crush Sherman's flank; and since the thing was to be again tried, it must be admitted that he was wise in determining to strike Howard's right while in motion, and before he could intrench. He withdrew Loring's and Walthall's divisions of Stewart's corps to support General S. D. Lee, who, with his corps (lately commanded by Cheatham), was ordered to move out on the Lickskillet road, attack Howard, and drive him from that road and the one by Ezra Church. Stewart's orders directed him to remain in support of Lee near the fortifications till needed, and next morning (29th) re-enforced by his other division (French's) to move beyond Lee and turn completely the flank of Howard, attacking him in the rear. Hardee's corps and Smith's Georgians were ordered to occupy the works in front of Thomas and Schofield.' Perhaps General Hood himself makes it even plainer. His official statement is as follows: 'Sherman began to mass his forces in that quarter. On the 28th, it became manifest that the enemy (Howard) desired to place his right on Utoy creek. I determined to hold the Lickskillet road, and accordingly ordered Lieutenant-General Lee, who, on the 26th, relieved Major-General Cheatham from command of the corps formerly commanded by myself, to move his forces so as to prevent the enemy from gaining that road. He was ordered to hold the enemy in check on a line nearly parallel with the Lickskillet road, running through Ezra Church. General Lee, finding that the enemy had already gained that position, engaged him with the intention to recover that line. This brought on the engagement of the 28th,' to-wit: the Battle of Ezra Church. It is yet difficult to estimate the numbers which

General Hood brought to bear mainly upon the 15th Corps, which constituted my right flank. My old classmate, General S. D. Lee, whom our men reported as riding, in the thickest of the fight, a white horse all that exciting day, says of his movement. 'The (Confederate) army was then in position and intrenched around Atlanta, daily shifting its position to meet the flank movements of the enemy. On the 27th, Hindman's and Clayton's divisions were withdrawn from the trenches, and massed on the Lickskillet road. On the 28th, about 11 A.M., I received orders to move out on the Lickskillet road, and check the enemy (Howard) who was then moving to our left, as it was desirable to hold that road to be used for a contemplated movement; I soon found that the enemy (Howard's skirmishers) had gained that road, and was gradually driving back our cavalry.'

I met, since I have been here, Major Charles Hipp who lost his arm there. He was away out, I think it was the 37th Ohio. He had gotten quite to that road. There were two other regiments just to his left, that came in a measure around the flank, and the battle began with them necessarily, because we were working in front of our line, just as at the battle of Waterloo the troops were thrust out in front of the right flank.

'Brown's division was at once formed on the left of and obliquely to the road, and Clayton's division on the right, connecting by a line of skirmishers with the main works around the city. As soon as Brown was formed, he moved forward, handsomely driving the enemy (Lightburn's men) across the road and to a distance half a mile beyond, where he encountered temporary breastworks, from which he was driven back with considerable loss. Clayton's division moved forward as soon as formed, and about ten minutes after Brown's advance and met with similar results. I found it difficult to rally Brown's division, and moved it against the enemy a second time. The consequence was that one or two brigades of this division, as also of Clayton's division, sustained heavy losses because of the failure in the attack of portions of their lines. Walthall's division, of Stewart's corps, had moved out on the Lickskillet road, while Brown's and Clayton's divisions were engaged with the enemy. At

my suggestion, this division was thrown agai
enemy where Brown had attacked. The enemy
line) was still within easy range of the Lickskili
and I believed that he would yield before a determ
attack. The effort was however a failure.'

As Dodge and Blair were occupied with the Confederate forces inside of the Atlanta works, it is evident that
the moving Confederate column greatly outnumbered
our men, who were engaged at the points of attack.

Some writers think that Hood, after his sad experience at the two battles of the 22nd of July and Peach
Tree creek, should have managed to stand on the defensive, and have waited for our coming. If he had done
so, we would have had his railroad communications cut
off by two hours after sunrise of the 28th. Once there,
he could not have dislodged us, and the siege of Atlanta
would soon have ended in prompt abandonment or surrender. Certainly our movement would have forced even
Johnston to have attacked us as Hood did.

All the morning of the 28th, Logan kept moving steadily
forward, well covered by his skirmish line. With my staff
and small escort, I kept him in sight, following up the
movement. Between seven or eight, Sherman joined
me as we were passing through a heavily wooded country. As we were conversing, the skirmishing became
more brisk, and what I took to be grape-shot, cut through
the trees over our heads, breaking off the limbs. We
both felt that the enemy was becoming more obstinate.

I said: 'General Hood will attack me here.'

'I guess not; he will hardly try it again,' Sherman replied.

I then remarked that I was three years at West Point
with Hood, and pronounced him 'indomitable in heart.'
Now, as the sounds of battle kept on increasing.
Sherman turned back to Thomas, probably having a
double motive; first to be where he could best re-enforce, and second to let me exercise my new command
without embarrassment. On many occasions, I noticed
that Sherman took this course with subordinates in
whom he had confidence.

From the direction of the enemy's firing, I had no great
fear for my right flank, and knew from the shape of my

position that I could easily and largely re-enforce the right, if necessity should require. I watched Logan as he gained the higher ground, and saw, with satisfaction, thousands of men running forward with rails and such logs as they could seize upon, with which they were making a continuous pile. The shelter at best was but little, but was a fair one to men when kneeling, and better when lying down; of course, it was too late for intrenching.

It did not take long to verify my prediction. That shrill, terrifying yell, who can ever forget it! Hood's men charged and fired as they came. All along the lines, our men remained in place. I saw that a few straggled back from one cause or another, but not many. These few Logan and officers, who were with him, rushed to meet; and back they went to duty, impelled by the shrill fierceness of his indignant voice. Though it seems hardly possible that so much time had passed since Sherman had left, yet all the diaries place the hour of the first assault after 11 A.M.

From Harrow's and Smith's front, the first charge was met with rapid and well-directed firing. Nothing could stand against it, and the most of the Confederates either fell to the earth, or turned and fled protecting themselves as best they could by the trees and the incidents of the ground. Our right was slightly overlapped, and a number of the enemy appeared beyond us. Permit me to repeat an account I gave some years ago of this part of the battle when it was fresher in my memory than now.

To withstand them, four regiments came from Dodge including the 64th and 66th Illinois, armed with repeating rifles; General Strong led thither also two regiments from Blair, and my chief of artillery placed several batteries, so as to sweep that exposed flank. There were twenty-six guns in a row, all of them brought to bear upon that right flank. It was impossible for men to get around there alive.

These were brought in at the exact moment, and after a few rapid discharges, the repeating rifles being remarkable in their execution, all the groups of flankers were either cut down, or had sought safety in flight. This battle was prolonged for hours. We expected help all that day from Morgan's division of Palmer's corps, coming back from Turner's ferry; but the Confederate cavalry kept that division in check. Our troops exhibited nerve and persistency; Logan was cheerful and hearty and full of enthusiasm. He stopped stragglers, as we have seen, and sent them back, and gave every needed order. Blair was watchful and helpful, so was Dodge. After the last charge had been repelled, I went along my lines, and felt proud and happy to be entrusted with such brave and efficient soldiers. Hood, having again lost three times as many as we, withdrew within his fortified lines. Our skirmishers cleared the field, and the battle of Ezra Chapel was won; and with this result, I contented myself. One officer, who was a little panic-stricken, ran with the first stragglers to Sherman, and cried substantially, as I remember: 'You've made a mistake in McPherson's successor. Everything is going to pieces!'

Sherman said: 'Is General Howard there?'

'Yes, I suppose he is.'

'Well, I'll wait before taking action till I hear from him.'

So Sherman sustained and trusted me, and I was content."(26)

The three last days of July as recorded by Major A. J. Seay of the 32nd Missouri Infantry Regiment. He writes in his diary, "Friday, 29. I went upon the field this A.M. The most fearful slaughter I ever witnessed. The enmey lay dead in solid lines, many in a shooting posture. Oh, how sanguinary is the strife. But they will soon change their tactics or be annihilate. Get a letter from Dear sister. Saturday, 30. We move out of our strong pits and 17th A.C. move in. We encamp in a field ½ mile from the line as reserve. Our men go to work and put up good brush arbors to shade them. Shells occasionally burst with uncomfortable near proximity. A 64 lb gun is bearing directly on us. Sunday, 31. This morning one of the 64 pound visitors called upon us but did not burst. I write a long letter to my sister. It rains very heavily from 12 to 3 or 4. We (31 and 32) go off to picket the flank, three miles-rains all night, dark, rough. We relieve the 9th Iowa. Can't find anything good to eat. This is soldiering."(27) The 15th Army Corps' flank reached to the Sandtown Road with the division of General Jefferson C. Davis being on their right. Private John T. Clarke writes in his diary, "Saturday 30. Comparative quiet prevails. Our lines advanced last night and found 120 dead Rebels left-by their comrades unburied. Some skirmishing. Sunday 31. The 23rd. Corps is moving and our lines are being extended toward the Right. It is very warm, and I am quite busy making out lists of killed & wounded and captured."(28)

The Daily Missouri Democrat copied an article from the Cincinnati Commercial which gave a description of the Battle at Ezra Church near Atlanta. The article was written on July 29, 1864 which is the day after the battle. It is included in its entirety because it has some interesting views of the battle, plus a thorough description of some of the Confederate dead left on the battlefield.

"SHERMAN'S ARMY.

The Third Battle Before Atlanta

FULL PARTICULARS.

(Correspondence Cincinnati Commercial)

Two Miles West of Atlanta, July 29, 1864.

The New Position.

When I wrote you last I dated my letter two-miles east of Atlanta, and, to-day, the center of interest and activity is as far to the west. Immediately after the great battle fought by the Army of the Tennessee on the 22nd, in which they ran so near upon the perilous edge of disaster, but saved themselves at the last, and gave the rebels a severe punishment, preparations were begun to transfer this part of the army from the left to the right wing. The 17th corps was busily employed a good part of a day in tearing up the rails and ties of the Atlanta and Augusta railroad, to render it useless to the rebels when we should abandon it; and the hospitals were transferred from the rear of the three corps which had been engaged, around behind the 4th corps, to a place of safety. It was a hard necessity which compelled the removal of all those hundreds of wounded men, just as their wounds were beginning to heal, but it must be done. When they were all safely removed and provided for the left wing took up its march quietly, in order to evade the attention of the rebel pickets, and passing nearly two-thirds of the way around Atlanta, took up a new position on the right. It was expected the rebels would discover the movement at an early hour, and endeavor to harass the columns on the march, and preparations were made accordingly. The left of the 22nd corps, which was now to be the extreme left, was swung around back, so as to face to the rear, and occupied the old rebel works, which were the first we had encountered on approaching the city, while General Stanley's division, of the 4th corps, which lay next the wed, completed this rear line, extending it far around to the rear of the 4th corps. Thus the hospitals, with their thronging crowds of helpless men, were completely surrounded, and, as it were, folded in by a friendly wall of strong men, who would look well to it that no harm came to their suffering comrades.

On the morning of the 27th Major General Howard acceded to the command of the Army of the Tennessee, in place of General Logan, who had temporarily held the command since the death of General McPherson. This was by the appointment of the President.

On the morning of the 28th the three corps came into position on the right, in the following order from left to right: 16th, 17th, 15th—the 16th lying next to the 14th on its left. The two first corps were extended in a continuous line, almost due north and south, and about a mile an a half from Atlanta, while the 15th occupying the flank, was bent back almost at right angles with the other two, and faced to the south. The Georgia and West Point Railroad track was about two miles in rear of the 17th corps, and, turning west, approached the line of the 15th considerably nearer. The average distance of the line of the three corps from Proctor's Creek, which was north of them was about one mile.

Such was the situation, briefly set forth, with which the army met the fourth rebel assault, or sortie, about Atlanta, on the 28th.

POSITION OF THE 15TH CORPS.

Since it was this corps alone which bore the brunt of the rebel assault, it is necessary to give, a little more in detail, the order of its divisions and the nature of the ground on which the fight was made.

Colonel Wanglen's brigade of the 1st division, held the left the 4th division the center, the 2d the right. The remainder of the 1st division was held in reserve, until the severity of the attack rendered it necessary for its various regiments to reinforce weak and wavering portions of line, which they did, with promptness and efficiency that save them from probable defeat. Their line was drawn up in dense woods, part of the distance just in the edge of it, fronting a cleared field, across which the rebels charged, but mostly in the depths of the forest, rendering the employment of the artillery extremely difficult. Not a cannon was fired till into the afternoon, nor did the rebels hold positions on which they could plant artillery with advantage, so that the fight was almost entirely one of musketry. The batteries were not at all lacking in endeavors to secure points attack, but were, for some time, unable to plant their pieces where they would not inflict as much loss on our lines as on those of the enemy.

THE ASSAULT.

About half-past ten in the forenoon, Lieutenant Worley, a signal officer of the 15th corps, reported to General Logan that a heavy column of infantry could be seen issuing out of Atlanta, going southward, with the evident intention of attempting to turn our right flank. Hitherto the skirmishers had encountered nothing but cavalry, but upon this announcement they halted at once, and began to throw up works. They had time only to complete rude defenses of rails and poles, without throwing a shovel full of earth, when the rebels drove in the skirmishers, and rus!ied, upon them with their usual impetuosity. This was about noon. They evidently thought that they had made a circuit sufficiently wide to bring them upon our flank; but they were mistaken, and came up front to front with the works. The woods were so thick that I am persuaded they could not see the extent of our works, and besides that, prisoners stated that their leaders had represented to them that we were retreating, and needed only to be attacked with spirit to be put to utter rout. The heaviest shock of the assault fell upon the 2d and 4th divisions, and for a time it was not absolutely certain that they would be able to maintain themselves. A timely reinforcement of a single regiment, judiciously distributed, quickly determined the question, and the rebels were driven back with heavy loss. But they were not to be thus easily and expeditiously discomited.

From twelve o'clock till nearly night the firing was incessant, swelling out, as the rebels charged, into a fierce and steady roar, and again dying away as they receded, to a fitful rattling, and during the afternoon, the rebels made seven distinct charges, and after nightfall two more, in the vain attempt to recover the hundreds of dead and dying who had fallen near our lines. Nine fearfully obstinate charges in the afternoon of a summer's day, when the fierce rays of a Southern sun were intercepted by no passing cloud! Could human pertinacity do more? It is useless to urge that such men had been made drunk, or that they are demoralized and ready to abandon their desperate cause; and it is a source of sad pride that such valor was displayed by men who though deluded and traitors, are yet American citizens, and not foreigners.

All this however, was worse than useless though they kept gradually moving to our right, so that each assault threatened more and more to swing around and flank us. Still our reserve regiments were enough, and only enough, to prevent any disaster from this source. There was not a man to spare, and a few regiments were detached from the 17the corps, finally, and dispatched to the right, which saved this wing.

It was a vain attempt—a ruinous, utter failure—as all their other assaults have been here before Atlanta, and the field was left in our possession. They were able to carry off a part of their wounded, but left their dead in our front, and their pickets withdrew half a mile, and in the morning of the next day they were quiet. I walked over a small portion of the open field and witnessed the bloody effects of that half day's work. The dead were yet scattered as they had fallen, and lay exposed to the rays of the sun, in all the attitudes of fierce despair, of agony, or placid repose, and some even, with a pleasant smile upon their upturned faces, such as have been depicted so often but must be seen to be felt in all their grim fearfulness. All along a little rivulet of muddy water the poor wretched had crawled down into it, in their dying agony to quench their thirst, and made its banks bloody from their wounds. One had snatched in his feeble hand a bunch of dry leaves with which he had vainly attempted to staunch the blood with which his life was flowing slowly but certainly away. Two members of the 1st Missouri battery, stated that they counted on a tract of ground which they estimate at six acres, eight hundred dead rebels, and I am little disposed to question the statement, as I counted in the rear of a fence, where they had attempted to screen themselves, ten bodies in the space of a rod. Among the dead I noticed a colonel and a captain, lying not more than one hundred yards in front of our works.

OUR LOSSES.

The happy precaution which our men have learned, after so much bloody experience, and which had been newly and ineffaceably impressed upon them by recent events at Atlanta, secured to them on this occasion a protecting line of works which, though rude and irregular, turned aside many a bullet from its mission of death. The losses on this occasion were greatly unequal, and the disparity was greatly owing to the fact that our forces were protected, while the rebels were exposed to the full sweep of our missles. From the reports of the various division commanders to the losses of their several commands, I am enabled to give the loss with a near approach to accuracy. In the 15th corps the losses in killed, wounded and missing, foot up to 537; in the 17th corps, which was but very slightly engaged, and in the manner I have stated above, the number lost was not above twenty. Few prisoners were taken by the rebels, as they were unable to become closely engaged with our men, and were little entangled with them in the conflict. Before the skirmish line could get behind the breastworks, a few of them, and only a few, were overtaken or surrounded and carried off.

REBEL LOSS.

I have given some partial statements of the rebel losses above, and from the estimates of various officers combined, I am inclined to put their loss in killed alone at about one thousand. The proportion wounded was smaller than usual, from the fact that they fought so much of the time at very close range. The number of their prisoners brought in during the day did not exceed one hundred. It appears to have been Hood's old corps alone that made the attack, as I saw prisoners from no other, and when it is remembered that this is the third singularly bloody assault that this corps has made upon us since our arrival before Atlanta, it may well be imagined that there is a great thinning out of its numbers. One of the prisoners from it remarked with a doleful smile, that 'there were not enough men left in it for another killing.' The 30th Louisiana, composed largely of very wealthy inhabitants of New Orleans, was almost annihilated. The Colonel commanding was one Shields, formerly from Franklin county, Ohio, who bravely led the regiment to the assault, and fell at the head of it, only a few rods from our works, and was recognized next morning by men who had seen him in Ohio. His native state had no cause to be ashamed of any quality which makes a brave soldier, but only of his treason. The battle-flag of the regiment was captured, and a magnificent one it is. The border is of buff moiré antique, the ground work of beautifully fine, re worsted, and diagonal bars of blue silk, edged with white, and dotted their entire length with stars. For several minutes our men hesitated to fire upon it, thinking it was the national colors.

Next morning a lieutenant of the 10th South Carolina came in as a deserter, and stated that the rebels had four generals wounded—Brown, Stevenson, Loring, and Gibson—two of them mortally. Of course this must be accepted with caution. His regiment had thirty-five left fit for duty.

INCIDENTS OF THE ASSAULT.

The rebels rushed right upon our works—so many of them as lived to get there—and were sometimes killed in the very act of vaulting over. A rebel color-bearer ran up with his colors, and with the spear head annexed to the top of the flag-staff transfixed a member of the 26th Illinois, who was on the other side of the works, and killed him. Instantly another member of the same regiment shot the daring rebel through the head, and, leaping over the works, captured his colors in safety.

The colors of the 30th Louisiana were captured by private Harry Davis, of the 46th Ohio.

The 4th division of the corps brought off from the contest five rebel stand of colors. The whole corps captured at least 1,000 stand of small arms.

THE CENTER AND LEFT.

Confined their operations during the day entirely to making a demonstration to attract attention from the attempt on the right wing. The rebels doubtless, understood the matter, confident as they were that we would not have the audacity to assault their tremendous breastworks and forts directly in front, and replied to with shells and round-shot only. The troops did not come into close quarters on this part of the line; consequently the losses were nothing more than the trivial wear and tear of the skirmish line, such as every day brings with it.

I append a list of names of commissioned officers killed and wounded, which embraces all I was able to collect. Q. P. F.

OFFICERS KILLED AND WOUNDED BEFORE
ATLANTA.
JULY 28.

Maj. Ennis. 6th Iowa, killed

Maj. Hall, 40th Ill, arm, severe.

Capt. V. W. Harolson, 40th Ill. severe

Capt Nance, 40th Ill. leg amputated.

Capt. Lingenfelter, 40th Ill. severe.

Maj. Brop, 30th Ohio, arm amputated.

Maj. Flynn, 40th Ill. severe.

Capt. Lindley, 48th Ill. killed.

Lieut. Smith, 40th Ill. severe.

Capt. Summers, 79th Ohio, killed.

Lieut. Kroff, 70th Ohio, Killed.

Captain Nelson, 70th Ohio, wounded.

Lieutenant Maxwell, 48th Illinois, killed.

Captain Farrell, 48th Illinois, killed.

Captain Weems, 48th Illinois, wounded.

Lieutenant Stoval, 48th Illinois, wounded.

Lieutenant Ingersoll, 48th Illinois, wounded.

Captain Solean, 15th Michigan, wounded.

Lieutenant Crasedy, 15th Michigan, wounded.

Captain Ulrich, 6th Iowa, killed.

Colonel Karcher, 12th Missouri, abdomen dangerous.
Captain A. Afleck, 12th Missouri, severe.
Lieutenant Sellentin, 12th Missouri, severe.
Major Murphy, 20th Missouri, lung, dangerous.
Colonel Carskadden, 9th Iowa, head, severe.
Lieutenant Byng, A.A.A.G. 1st Brigade, 1st Division 15th Corps, shoulder, flesh."(29)

General Hood had suffered his third defeat in the month of July and was ordered by President Davis not to fight any more battles for fear of running out of men. General Hood then withdrew into the prepared defenses around Atlanta. General Sherman ordered that the shelling of Atlanta was to become serious. Before this time most of the emphasis of the Federal army had been directed at the Confederate army with periodically shelling of military targets inside of Atlanta. Once General Hood went into the trenches the artillery began a bombardment of Atlanta in earnest. General Hood sent a letter to General Sherman stressing that the Confederate army was in trenches that were about one mile from the outskirts of Atlanta and that the Federals were killing innocent civilians. General Sherman replied to this statement that Atlanta was a military target because of the military material in the city and the facilities that could manufacture war material. Needless to say, General Sherman continued to bombard the city.

The siege of Atlanta began approximately on August 1st even though some people believe it actually started after the battle on July 22nd. August started out hot and the men in the trenches were in the same situation as the siege of Vicksburg. The major difference was that the Confederates still had a railroad line that was available to the south for the delivery of supplies. Plus there were not enough men on the Federal side to completely surround the city. On August 2nd the 1st Division was put in reserve taking up a position in a field behind the 4th Division with no part of the 1st Division being placed on the front. Colonel Hugo Wangelin, who commanded the 3rd Brigade comments on the events of August 3rd later in a report dated September 5th states, "I received orders to occupy part of the advanced line. The Third, Thirty-first, and Thirty-second Missouri were ordered out, the two latter regiments, however relieved before night. The Third remained until evening of August 4, when it was also relieved by a regiment of the Second Brigade. Our loss was light, and resulted mainly from stray shots of shell and ball, which aimed at the pits in our front fell amongst our men. Here in this camp we remained, being but seldom called upon to assist in demonstrations made against the enemy."(30) Major A. J. Seay, who was regimental commander of 32nd Missouri Infantry, in a report dated August 5th to Brigadier-General John B. Gray the Adjutant-General of Missouri states, "The Army of the Tennessee has had heavy skirmishing at this point (southwest of Atlanta) for four days, in which we took an active part on Yesterday and the day before; are in reserve."(31)

On August 4th the movement to try and reach the railroad south of Atlanta was commenced with General Schofield's 23rd Army Corps marching around the 15th Army Corps along the Sandstone Road heading towards the railroad near East Point. General Palmer refused to take orders from General Schofield until he received confirmation from General Sherman because he believed that he ranked General Schofield. General Sherman finally convinced General Palmer that General Schofield out ranked him and that they needed to take action. But because of it was so late in the day, General Sherman ordered them to start the next day. This is an instance of pettiness that could have affected the outcome of a battle. The 15th Army Corps was one of the few corps where such petty arguing was openly reported. While this arguing was going on by the generals in the 23rd Corps the 3rd Brigade of the 15th Army Corps was being shelled by the Confederates. Major A. J. Seay writes his account in his diary. "Thursday, 4. We are cruelly shelled, every man has to hunt his own hole. Shells explode in our midst. W go out to make a charge get a good wetting in a rain storm and are ordered back at dark. I write to Col. Fletcher."(32)

On August 6th the Battle of Utoy Creek took place with General Schofield's 23rd Corps and General Palmer's 14th Corps fighting this battle. The battle was not much of a battle with the attack of one Federal division against a division of Confederates. In some of the accounts of the battle it is stated that there were three charges against the Confederates with each charge being repulsed. It finally ended with the Confederates being ordered to withdraw back to Atlanta and to abandon their strong trenches, which the Federals immediately took into their possession. Major A. J. Seay recorded, "Saturday, 6. During the evening the 14 A.C. on our right had a very lively time advancing their line and taking two rows of pits after a sharp fight.

During the night the Johneys undertook the job of recapturing them. After a terrific fire of musketry for ¾ of an hour. Then all was quiet. We hold the pits."(33)

In Special Field Orders Number Eighty-Eight, General Howard ordered,

"1. At 2:30 p.m., to-day the line of skirmishers will be doubled, and the enemy pressed hard along the whole line.

2. All the men in the trenches will stand under arms during the demonstration without their knapsacks.

3. Major-General Logan's division will be held where it now is, in readiness to move to any point at a moment's warning."(34)

The rest of the month of August was spent in trench warfare around Atlanta which included regular skirmishing between pickets. Private John T. Clarke's time of service with the 31st Missouri Infantry Regiment was just about up and he was ready to head home. There was not much going on according to his diary. Such as his daily entry on Sunday August 21st, "Another monotonous day is gone. The random shot of the skirmisher or the occasional discharge of a cannon is all to remind one of the presence of the enemy. Gen'l Kilpatrick cut the R.R. & burnt train of cars."(35) John T. Clarke left Atlanta on furlough starting from August 27th to end on September 26th, 1865 and on August 23rd arriving in Mineral Point, Missouri on the morning of August 30th. On September 22, 1864, from Saint Louis, Missouri Special Orders No. 263 from Head Quarters, Department of Missouri, Office of the Provost Marshal General, states, "Private John T. Clark, Company "I" 31st Mo Infy is hereby detailed on special Service as clerk at these Head Quarters & will report at once for duty to Lt. Col. Joseph Dan 1st Assst. Pro. Marshal General. By command of Major General Rosecrans." (36)

In the afternoon of August 13, 1864, the 1st Division of the 15th Army Corps, under General Charles R. Woods, advanced and took the Confederate rifle pits to their front capturing four officers and sixty-one men. The brand new appointed Major-General Peter J. Osterhaus reported back to duty from sick leave on Friday, August 15th and resumed command of the 1st Division. Brigadier-General Charles R. Woods was relieved from command of his old brigade and took command of the 3rd Division of the 17th Army Corps a well deserved promotion. On this date orders were issued by General Howard for the 15th Army Corps to withdraw from their trenches at eight o'clock p.m. and march on the Green's Ferry road, crossing Utoy Creek at Judge Wilson's. Then they were to march by the most direct route toward Fairburn, marching as far as Camp Creek. The 17th Army Corps was to pass through their old lines at Ezra Church and then follow the 15th Army Corps. The 16th Army Corps was to draw back and then occupy the old positions of the 15th Army Corps at the battle of Ezra Church and once the 16th Army Corps had finished passing their positions they were to follow them. Since this was not supposed to happen for the next two days, all the corps were to continue to press the enemy, taking Confederate skirmishers and pickets whenever possible in order to convince the Confederates that the main goal of the Federal army was to capture the Confederate army in their trenches. For some reason the movement that had been anticipated for the 19th was then postponed to the night of August 26th.

Major-General Dodge, the commander of the 16th Army Corps, was wounded in the forehead. This sent him to the rear and he was replaced by General T. E. G. Ransom as commander of the 16th Army Corps. Captain Henry I. Smith, 7th Iowa Infantry Regiment, writes a letter to his mother describing the wounding of General Dodge.

"Dear Mother:-I have only a few minutes to write before the mail goes out, so will just drop a few lines which will be better than no letter at all. I am well. We have not got Atlanta yet, although we can look over and see the town. We have got to take it by siege, as it would be almost impossible to take it by assault, the works are so heavy and every obstruction that man can think of is placed in the way. Two rows of palisades around the works besides a heaby abattis of fallen trees which would make it almost impossible to get in without anybody behind the works. I have just got out of the ditch. The rebels have been shelling us. They cannot hurt us much if we keep in our works. I am getting almost humpbacked with walking along the works with my head down to keep from being shot by the rebel sharpshooters.

Unless a man is careless and sticks his head above the works they cannot hit him. It is very tiresome. I am afraid if you should see me you would hardly own me as your son, I am so dirty. I stood beside Major General Dodge when he was shot. I was on the skirmish line. I had a hole through the top of the rifle pit to look through. He asked me some questions about their works and I told him to look through the hole and a rebel sharp-shooter shot him in the head, but fortunately the ball just cut across the top of his head and did not enter his skull. He fell right back on me, as I was squatted down behind him. He is doing well and expects to go home before long. I send you a lock of his hair that I picked up after they had carried him away that the ball cut off. The scalp is yet on it. They are packing up the mail, so I must close.

Your affectionate son,
Henry I. Smith."(37)

On August 18th in compliance to orders issued by Major-General John A. Logan, General Osterhaus, commanding the 1st Division of the 15th Army Corps, gave the following report.

"COLONEL: In pursuance of instructions from headquarters Fifteenth Army Corps, I made a demonstration with a view to develop the enemy's force at 4 p.m., while the artillery opened a lively fire on the rebel lines. At the appointed hour I pushed strong re-enforcement's forward to the lines held by the reserve of our pickets. The pickets themselves advanced in converging lines toward and in neck of timber in my front held by the enemy's sharpshooters. My pickets advanced from 200 to 300 yards and dislodged the rebels from their first line of rifle-pits. The ground gained is now occupied by my troops, and will be intrenched in compliance with your orders received since."(38)

Lieutenant-Colonel Samuel P. Simpson, 31st Missouri Infantry Regiment commanding officer, sent a list of all the casualties that the 31st Missouri Infantry had suffered during the campaign so far in 1864. He sent this article to the "Daily Missouri Democrat" in Saint Louis, Missouri. The following is an exact quote of this article in its entirety.

"List of Casualties in the 31st Missouri Volunteers during the Campaign of 1864.

Corp'l Robert Richardson, A, May 14, wounded in hand,

slight.

Nicholas Gerdel, G, May 14, wounded in neck, severe.

John Drenning, E, May 14, wounded in thigh, severe.

John Bone, C, May 15, wounded in bowels, since died.

James Cosgriff, B, May 27, wounded in head, slight.

Serg't James C. Thomas, C, May 28, killed.

Henry Now, G, May 27, killed.

James H. Cozort, H, May 29, killed.

Harry Russell, I, May 28, killed.

Thomas B. Self, C, May 28, wounded in thigh, slight.

Thomas Duvalt, May 27, killed.

Henry Drinckcorn, A, June 14, wounded in back, very slight.

John Moore, H, June 14, wounded in shoulder, since died.

John M. Dale, D, June 14, wounded in right arm, severe.

Solomon Reed, F, June 27, wounded in hand, slight.

Corp'l John C. Breckinridge, B, July 28, wounded in hand, slight.

Chas. Withrow, C, July 28, wounded in brow, slight.

Serg't Timothy P. Baird, July 28, wounded in neck, slight.

Corp'l Jasper W. Chatman, H, July 28, wounded in face slight.

Serg't Wm. Foctdman, G, July 28, wounded in jaw, slight.

Mark Wideman, A, August 8, killed.

John Jolly, C, August 8, wounded in arm and side severe.

Wm. Kuntz, G, August 8, wounded in bowels, slightly.

Recapitulation.

Killed.................6

Wounded.........17

Samuel P. Simpson,
Lieutenant-Colonel 31st Mo. Volunteerd,
Commanding Regiment.

Headquarters 31st Missouri Volunteer Infantry, before Atlanta, GA., August 28, 1864."(39)

On August 24th, General Howard issued orders that would have went into effect on the 19th of August were now to take effect on August 26th. Major-General Osterhaus in his diary states, "Thursday August 25- fine. Preparations for a move to X by and Utoy Creek. Write M. tell her that I am disgusted with the service."(40) The 20th Army Corps and the 4th Army Corps withdrew from their positions on the night of the 25th of August closing upon the 14th Army Corps near Utoy Creek. Once their positions were abandoned General Garrard's cavalry, minus their horses, moved in to fill these positions in hopes of fooling the Confederates into believing that the Federal infantry were still there.

The next night the Army of the Tennessee was given the task of trying to successfully break contact with the Confederates without them knowing. The order in which the army were supposed to withdraw was the same as the order issued on August 17th to the 15th, 17th and 16th Army Corps. In the 15th Army Corps the 1st Division, under the command of General Osterhaus, was to withdraw first. They were to be followed by the 2nd Division under the command of Brigadier-General Hazen, with Brigadier-Harrow's 4th Division following behind them. This movement was to start at eight o'clock p.m. and was hopefully to be done in such secrecy that the Confederates would not know what was happening until after the fact. A strong skirmish line was to be left in their positions until the movement had been accomplished then they were to return to their respective commands at the earliest opportunities. In his diary General Osterhaus states, "Friday August 26, fine but hot morning- order to march at 8 p.m. the left of our army withdrawn already- Rebs shelling a little. Colonel Connard command passes: he is in the same fix as the other Dutch. We break camp precisely at 8 p.m."(41) The 1st Division had marched during the night to Parker's Place, about four miles west of Fairburn which was on the Atlanta and Montgomery Railroad where they arrived on the morning of the 27th of August. Major A. J. Seay of the 32nd Missouri Infantry Regiment, writes in his diary, "Friday, 26. Quite hot-I take a bath, under marching orders-move out at 8 P.M. Rebels discover our movements and shell our camps vigorously, but we move on silently all night and till 10 in the morning. So dark and road so dim that we have to mark out our course by fires along the route."(42) The movement was done successfully with no reported casualties caused by enemy fire. General Osterhaus states in his diary on Saturday, August 27th, "A very tedious night march; it was very dark and a great many of men drown, general scatteration; hold from 2-6 a.m. to close up. Then march on - into camp on Perkins Plantation. It was a hot day."(43)

The Confederates on the 27th sent forward elements of their army to investigate whether the Federals were still there. Much to their great joy they discovered the enemy gone. Some how the impression or rumor got started that the Federals had finally gave up on the plan of successfully taking Atlanta and had withdrawn back up north. General Sherman in his memoirs states, "It was afterward related that there was great rejoicing in Atlanta that the Yankees were gone; the fact was telegraphed all over the South, and several trains of cars (with ladies) came up from Macon to assist in the celebration of their grand victory."(44) The rumor would prove to be sadly wrong. Can you imagine the great joy this news must have brought the South only to have the cold, hard facts, take the wind right out of their sails.

While the South was celebrating, according to General Sherman, the Federal army was preparing to continue on their way. General Howard issued orders for the General Logan and Major-General Frank P. Blair to build two bridges each over Wolf Creek and Camp Creek. These bridges were to be built at suitable sights in their fronts. They were to leave camp the next day at eight a.m. in two columns until they came to Shadna Church, which was between Fairburn and Red Oak. The 15th Army Corps followed by the general train and one brigade of the 16th Army Corps were to operate as the rear guard this column would comprise the left column, with the 17th Army Corps and the 16th Army Corps as the right column. General Logan was to provide for the construction of a road through a heavy forest in case one suitable for the moving of the army could not be found. They eventually ended up cutting three miles of road.

General Logan issued his orders on how the 15th Army Corps was to move. The following is the order in its entirety.
"SPECIAL FIELD ORDERS, HDQRS. 15TH ARMY CORPS,
In the Field, on Wolf Creek, Ga.,
No. 88   August 27,1864
1. Brig. Gen. William Harrow, commanding Fourth Division, will extend his picket-line on the left in a northeasterly direction to Camp Creek, and join on the right with the picket -line of Brig. Gen. W. B. Hazen, commanding Second Division.
2. Maj. Gen. P. Joseph Osterhaus will connect his

picket line on the left with that of the Seventeenth Army Corps.

3. The picket-line must be thrown well forward, and the pickets instructed to be unusually vigilant. Division picket officers must make frequent visits to the picket-lines of their respective commands and see that the duty is performed properly.

7. In accordance with instructions from headquarters Department of Army of the Tennessee, the command forming the left column will move at 7 a.m. to the vicinity of New Hope Church, situated between Fairburn and Red Oak.

First. Maj. Gen. P. Joseph Osterhaus' command will have the advance and will be followed by the commands of Brigadier-Generals Hazen and Harrow respectively.

Second. Ten wagons of ammunition, the ambulance and medicine wagons, will follow each division. All other wagons will follow the corps in the order of march superintended by the chief quartermaster of the corps.

Third. Brig. Gen. William Harrow will detail two regiments as train guard, to be disposed at proper intervals through the train. The ranking officer of the two regiments selected will have charge of the entire guard and train and will see that it is kept well closed up.

Fourth. Division commanders must cause their troops to march in good order and keep well closed up, and to this end will designate a staff officer to ride along the line of march frequently and give notice to brigade commanders of any break that may occur in their lines, with orders to at once close it up by marching in quick, and if necessary in double quick, time.

Fifth. Straggling must under no circumstances be allowed. Division commanders must give the most stringent instructions regarding it, for they will themselves be held responsible here. Each regiment should detach a small rear guard, under an officer who can be relied on to prevent it in his command.

Sixth. The route to be taken will be indicated before

the hour of march.

By order of Maj. Gen. John A. Logan

R. R. Townes,"(45)

It is surprising that this deep in enemy territory, there are still men who were classified as stragglers. Stragglers are men who would not keep up with their units while on the march. There were various reasons that this was done by these men. One of them was that they didn't want to get shot at, another reason that would continue throughout the rest of the war, was the appropriation of food, clothing, books or whatever met their fancy. But most of the time the closer to the time of battle the more straggling would occur.

On August 28th General Osterhaus writes in his diary, "Cool night. After considerable deliberation and reconnoitering we leave camp at 8 a. m. on a Fairburn Road to a point where it runs into the Sandtown Road. Which the 17 Corps marched on. Cut 3 mile road through timber and astride the R. R. by noon- Some Rebels in front. It was a hot day."(46) Major A. J. Seay recorded in his diary, "Sunday, 28. Move at 7-have a big scare at 10. At 2 arrive on and take possession Western and Montgomery R.R. and begin the work of destruction. Apples, potatoes (sweet), pigs, green corn, etc. We all live well except salt meat. Quite cold."(47) The 29th of August found the 4th Division of the 15th Army Corps destroying the railroad on the night of the 28th and 29th of August. The West Point Railroad was completely destroyed in such a manner that it was of no further use to the Confederates. Major A. J. Seay wrote in his diary, "Monday, 29. Very cold. We tear up R.R. all day-most effectually filling the cuts and planting shells etc. for torpedos. We got apples, corn, fresh meat, etc. I go to the wagons and get a good supper with Williams and a canteen full of bust head from Keiser."(48) Orders were issued that the 15th Army Corps was to march toward Jonesborough, crossing Pond Creek and Shoal Creek with the intention of reaching Renfroe Place. The 15th Army Corps was led by Brigadier-General W. B. Hazen's division with the division of Brigadier-General William Harrow with Major-General Peter J. Osterhaus bringing up the rear of the corps. The 1st Division, since they were in the rear of the corps were responsible for supplying the guard for the wagons that were in marching in the rear of the 15th Army Corps.

The march for Jonesborough began Tuesday the 30th of August. They started at seven o'clock a.m. as ordered. On the way to Jonesborough the Confederate cavalry kept up a harrassing fire which kept the guards busy fighting as well as the skirmishers in front of the army. General Howard had been ordered to halt at Renfro Place for the night, which they reached around three-thirty in the afternoon. It had been a very hot day and the march was a difficult one with almost constant contact with the Confederate cavalry which tired out the men. There was very little water to be had at Renfro Place and it was in great demand. There was a creek a little distance behind them and the Flint River about six miles ahead. General Howard had been instructed that if by chance he reached Renfro Place and decided that he could go farther, he should if the opportunity presented itself. General Howard decided that since the water situation was critical, he should try and reach the Flint River.

General Wheeler's cavalry thinking that the Federals were going into camp for the night were probably getting ready to go into camp themselves. All of a sudden some of General Kilpatrick's cavalry, followed by General Hazen's infantrymen, emerged from some woods that completely took the Confederate cavalry by surprise. The retreat that the Confederates executed was fast but the Federals were right behind them. The heat and their thirst was forgotten by the Federal troops because of the excitement of the chase. The Confederates made it across Flint River bridge setting it on fire but the Federals were able to extinguish it and take up positions on the east side of Flint River within sight of Jonesborough. General Howard got most of his 15th Army Corps across the bridge onto a wooded ridge about one-half of a mile from the bridge. By this time it was starting to get close to dusk and they spent the rest of the day building defensive positions to repel the counter attack that they were sure was going to happen. That night skirmishers were sent forward to protect the Federals from a surprise night attack by the Confederates. But the Confederates were not going to attack because they only had approximately twenty-five hundred men around Jonesborough. That night the Federals in the trenches on the Confederate side of the Flint River spent the night listening to trains arriving in town all night. There was no doubt in the minds of the Federals that the Confederates were bringing in reinforcements for the next day. General Osterhaus wrote in his diary, "Tuesday August 30- March to Jonesboro in rear of Army Corps. Rear of

Column constantly opposed by Rebel Cavalry- very hard march arrive within range of Jonesboro by 10 p. m."(49) The 1st Division crossed the bridge over the Flint River after eleven p.m. with the 1st Division going into the reserve position behind the other divisions of the 15th Army Corps. The 25th Iowa Infantry Regiment of the 2nd Brigade of the 1st Division, was placed on the right to guard the right flank. This position became more important with the coming of the morning of August 31st when it was strengthened with the sending of the 2nd and 3rd Brigades of the 1st Division to extend this line and make it stronger.

Even though informed that the Federal army was on the move, General Hood sent General Hardee to take overall command of the two army corps that were under the command of General Lee and General Cleburne. General Hood was not convinced that the whole Federal army was on the move but that it was only a small force to feel out the Confederate position. General Hardee's job was to keep the Federals out of Jonesboro and back across the Flint River and to protect the railroad in that town. During the night General Patrick Cleburne's Corps arrived with General Stephen D. Lee's Corps arriving later on in the day bringing the Confederate strength to around twenty-four thousand men. General Hood was wrong, General Hardee's forces were facing all of the Army of the Tennessee with almost all the rest of the Federal army on the move in the same direction.

General Howard wasted no time, he moved most of his army across the river sending elements of the 16th and the 17th Army Corps to support the 15th Corps. August 31st, morning broke with the troops of the 15th Army Corps continuously trying to strengthen their position against the expected Confederate attack. General Howard was hoping that the Confederates would attack because this would be to his advantage since; it is easier to defend than to attack. The attacking force can expect to suffer at least twice the casualties of the defending force and General Howard was hoping that his men would suffer the least amount of casualties. General Sherman, who was not known for being a patient commander, wanted General Howard to take position of the railroad in that vicinity as a high priority even to the extent of bringing on a major battle. The Confederates who had been moving into Jonesboro throughout the night did not seem to be in any hurry to attack the Federals. Around noon General Howard decided that someone had to attack so he issued orders for General Logan to be prepared to advance and attack the Confederates at three o'clock p.m. The veteran Federal troops in their entrenchments made preparations to attack.

General Hardee's plans for the attack was for a preparatory artillery barrage with the infantry two attack the whole line at the same time. The Confederates forces that were on the attack had more men than the Federals had in the trenches. The Federals numbered around twelve thousand men in the defensive positions with approximately seven thousand five-hundred men in reserve on the other side of the Flint River with a force of about one thousand men of the 1st Missouri Engineers who had arrived from the Army of the Cumberland. The Federal troops, in some places had abatis in front of their positions as obstacles to slow the Confederates down. There was also a fair amount of artillery in the positions to help against the expected charge. General Hardee ordered that General Cleburne's men, his old corps, were to initiate the attack with an attack from the south east heading north on the flank of Federal army against the troops of the 16th Corps. General Lee, once he heard the fire of General Cleburne's, was to make a frontal attack against the 15th Army Corps after the attack of General Cleburne's was proceeding for a while.

Approximately two forty-five p.m. the Confederate troops line of attack came into view with General Cleburne's troops on the left and General Lee's troops on the right. Colonel Hugo Wangelin, commanding the 3rd Brigade of the 1st Division, which included the 31st Missouri Infantry Regiment, saw this movement and had his men fire at the Confederates making this movement, along with two pieces of Napoleon twelve pounders. The Confederates did not stop and managed to get around to the position that they desired. The two pieces of artillery and their infantry support returned to the main line closely followed by the Confederates. The Federals unleashed a terrible fire on the charging Confederates which staggered them and they fell back to a tree line to reform and charged again but not with as much heart. Again they fell back not to return. The rest of the day and night was used to strengthen their entrenchments with the skirmishers keeping up a steady fire for the whole time.

According to the plans, General Cleburne sent out his

skirmishers as described above, which immediately came under fire of the Federals. General Lee hearing this fire gave the orders for the attack to begin. The generalship of General Lee was again showed wanting. He had jumped the gun and his attack went in basically unsupported. The Confederates overran the rifle pits of the Federals but were bloodily repulsed by the men in the entrenchments. After the repulse of the first line of General Lee's attack, his second line attacked, marching through the retreating first line and over those who had taken refuge from the furious fire that the Federals were sending their way. The second line met the same fate as that of the first line with the same reaction as the first line. General Hardee, once informed of the fate of General Lee's attack, called off the rest of the attack. The Confederates withdrew to the entrenchments they had occupied prior to the attack to try and regroup and prepare for the expected attack. Major A. J. Seay wrote in his diary, "Wednesday, 31. Today our corps has a hot fight-the Rebs charge our whole line-a feeble effort, which utterly failed-our loss very light. Enemies very heavy-32nd, 5-2 died. Hood is a sad failure. Our batteries throw into Jonesboro."(50)

While this attack at Jonesboro was going on, part of General Schofield's 17th Army Corps and General Stanley's 4th Army Corps reached the railroad at Rough and Ready and took position of the railroad north of Jonesboro. The Federals had driven off a force of Confederate cavalry from this position to make it secure. General Hood learning of this issued an order telling General Hardee to send General Lee's Corps back to Atlanta. Again this shows that General Hood who, was commanding from a spot not at the battlefield, did not realize the condition of General Lee's troops. That night General Lee and what was left of his corps marched back to Atlanta. This withdrawal of General Lee's corps was not unnoticed. The Signal Detachment of the 15th Army Corps had their men in a tree observing the movement of the enemy throughout the day, and were making reports to General Logan. In his report, 1st Lieutenant Samuel Edge chief acting Signal Officer, states, "Found a very heavy column of the enemy, both infantry and artillery, moving to their right. This column was nearly an hour and a half passing a given point. The infantry and two of these batteries passed on through town toward Atlanta; the other three batteries were parked in town. I remained at my station until 7 p.m."(51)

The Federals seemed content to sit in their entrenchments to await the coming decision of what to do next. They were left in their entrenchments for the night. The Confederate's casualties for this battle were one thousand, seven hundred and twenty-five killed and wounded with most of the casualties coming from General Lee's corps. The Federals suffered one hundred and seventy-nine killed and wounded with most of these casualties happening in General Logan's 15th Army Corps.

With the withdrawal of General Lee's men back toward Atlanta, General Hardee was left with under fourteen thousand men facing a force with a little over twenty thousand men. General Hardee's force being cut in half was trying to defend a position that was made for two corps but was now being defended by one. The attack scheduled by the Federals for September 1st, which did not begin until four p.m., had the 15th Army Corps attacking the Confederates in a frontal attack from the west with General Jefferson C. Davis' 14th Army Corps attacking from the north. General Osterhaus states in his diary that, "Thursday, September 1st, The 4th Division, 14th Corps have progress of the RR near Rough and Ready, march down, we demonstrate during the whole day to keep the Rebs from reinforcing their right."(52) Colonel Wangelin ordered his skirmishers forward followed closely by the 29th Missouri Infantry, with Colonel Joseph S. Gage having the honor of being the first man over the rifle pits, followed by the 31st and 32nd Missouri Infantry Regiments with these two regiments totaling barely over two hundred men. These three regiments charged the Confederate rifle pits driving them back to their main lines then occupying the Confederate rifle pits forming a new line for the Federals far in advance of their old one. Major A. J. Seay wrote in his diary, "Thursday, September, 1. Today we have fighting all day-in the P.M. we make a charge-I get so near the Rebs that I have to hug mother earth in an open field till sundown-my men in the meantime mourning my loss-I escape altho balls and shells whiz fearfully about me and me with dirt."(53) There were skirmishes throughout the rest of the day with the Federals trying to keep reinforcements from being sent to other parts of the line. Dark finally came to the beleaguered Confederates with the Federal attack not really materializing, General Hardee withdrew his forces to Lovejoy's Station which was about six miles south of Jonesboro. General Hardee informed General Hood of the events that had taken place with the Federals who were now in possession of the last railroad that was supplying the Confederates in Atlanta.

The demonstrating of the 1st Division of the 15th Army Corps was costly for the 31st Missouri Infantry. Their casualties for September 1st are; killed, Captain Roderick O'Doherty of Company D from Ironton, Missouri, Corporal Andrew Lawerence of Company H from Wayne County, Missouri, Private Louis Luping of Company G from Saint Louis, Missouri; wounded, Private John Drus of Company G from Saint Louis, Missouri was discharged on December 1, 1864 because of these wounds, Private Samuel Washburn of Company A from Victoria, Missouri. I have found no other record of casualties for this day in any reports.

General Hood was forced to do something that he didn't want to do, abandon Atlanta. He ordered General Stewart's and General Lee's Corps to leave the city heading to Lovejoy's Station in an attempt to join General Hardee's Corps and consolidate his army. General Hood ordered his cavalry to destroy seven locomotives and eighty-one cars of ammunition on the Georgia Railroad tracks near Rolling Mill. The explosion that occurred literally destroyed the railroad area and sent projectiles flying in all directions. General Sherman states in his memoirs, "That night I was so restless and impatient that I could not sleep, and about midnight there arose toward Atlanta sounds of shells exploding, and other sound like that of musketry. I walked to the house of a farmer close by bivouac, called him out to listen to the reverberations which came from the direction of Atlanta (twenty miles to the north of us), and inquired of him if he had resided there long. He said he had, and that these sounds were just like those of a battle. An interval of quiet then ensued, when again, about 4 A.M., arose other similar explosions, but I still remained in doubt whether the enemy was engaged in blowing up his own magazines, or whether General Slocum had not felt forward, and become engaged in a real battle."(54)

September 2, 1864 was the day President Abraham Lincoln's re-election was secured. Major-General Henry W. Slocum and his 20th Army Corps marched into the heart of Atlanta and took possession of the city. He sent a note to General Sherman informing him of this fact. General Sherman sent a report to General Halleck informing him that Atlanta had been taken and fairly won. The re-election of President Lincoln was

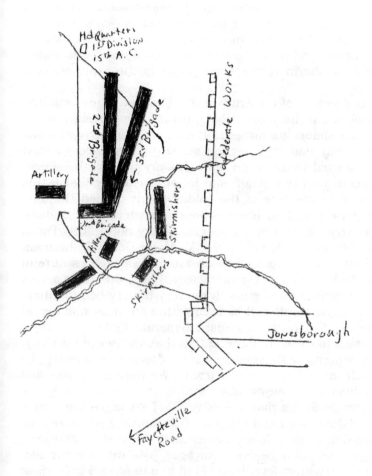

1ˢᵗ Division, 15ᵗʰ Army Corps Position Near Jonesborough, GA.

N

Headquarters
1ˢᵗ Division
15ᵗʰ A. C.

2ⁿᵈ Brigade

3ʳᵈ Brigade

Confederate Works

Artillery

2ⁿᵈ Brigade

Skirmishers

Artillery

Skirmishers

Jonesborough

Fayetteville Road

BATTLE OF JONESBOROUGH, GEORGIA

not guaranteed because of the way the war was going on. The people in the north were getting sick and tired of the war. Almost every family in some way had been affected by this ongoing war with no end in sight. Many families had lost a son through death, missing, terrible wounds or disability due to disease which had rendered them almost useless to their families. The Democratic Party was backing a man who was campaigning on a peace platform. He was Major-General George B. McClellan, who many in the military, especially in the west had felt that he had disgraced himself by accepting the nomination of the Democrats. The election was to take place in November, President Lincoln was hoping for some miracle because he was pretty sure that he was losing. General Grant was in a siege at Petersburg and prior to the capture of Atlanta it was feared that General Sherman was about to be in the same predicament.

The victory of the Army of the West sent the north into such celebration that their willing, continuing participation in the war was almost guaranteed. The democratic party who was sure that they had this election sewed up, watched as their chances started to drop and fast. History reports that President Lincoln won re-election and lot of people say that it was mostly due to the vote of the soldiers that carried the day. General Grant was so happy about the success of General Sherman that he sent him a congratulatory note. "City Point, Virginia, September 4, 1864— 9 P.M. Major-General Sherman: I have just received your dispatch announcing the capture of Atlanta. In honor of your great victory, I have ordered a salute to be fired with shotted guns from every battery bearing upon the enemy. The salute will be fired within an hour, amid great rejoicing. U. S. Grant, Lieutenant-General." (55)

Back to the war. General Osterhaus writes in his diary, "Friday, September 2- Rebs are gone. Jonesboro is ours! The enemy left immediately in our front. We pursue 7 miles find Rebs in lines near Lovejoy take a strong position."(56) Major A. J. Seay wrote in his diary, "Friday, 2. Last night the enemy evacuated Jonesboro and Atlanta. This morning we move thru Joesboro-doing the R.R.'s come up with the enemy and skirmishing immediately begins. Our army jubilant over our success. Country more level here. Find him in force 5 miles S. of Jonesbor."(57) General Howard had the 15th Army Corps on the attack by about three-thirty p.m. He sent them against the

Confederate line with Brigadier-General Charles C. Walcutt 2nd Brigade of the 4th Division led the attack against the Confederates and had carried the rifle pits capturing the troops in them and had taken possession of a good defensive position on a high hill about four hundred yards from the main defensive postion of the Confederates, with General Osterhaus' 1st Division on the right, General Hazen in the center and General Harrow's 4th Division on the right, when at four p.m General Howard received the following communication from General Sherman,

"Headquarters Military Division of the Mississippi,
In the Field,   September 2, 1864 p.m.
General Howard,

You know that General Garrard reports General Slocum in possession of Atlanta. I have sent couriers to learn the exact truth. If it be so, we don't care about pushing the enemy any farther at this time. Had we prevented his making intrenchments it would have been well, but, as he has a strong line, I do not wish to waste lives by an assault. You may therefore order the skirmishers close up, but hold your lines so as not to suffer much. If the enemy be gone in the morning occupy his lines to your front and await orders.

Yours,
W. T. Sherman
Major-General."(58)

General O. O. Howard, in his autobiography records the events that were called the skirmish of Lovejoy's Station as briefly described briefly.

"We came upon Hardee's skirmishers, where he was waiting for us, near Lovejoy's; the approaches to his position were exceedingly difficult; yet, as rapidly as possible, my command was extended into line, the Fifteenth Corps on the left, the Seventeenth on the right, while the Sixteenth was held in reserve.

By strengthening our skirmish line and pressing it along from right to left Hardee's gave back, until by our sudden dash a favorable height of great importance to us was seized and firmly held. And then by the usual processes our main lines were moved nearer and nearer to the Confederate works, strange to say, were as well constructed and as strong as if the Confederates had

had a week to prepare them.

It was between three and four in the afternoon when I was ready to move forward to the assault. At that hour I received orders from Sherman not to take the offensive, but wait where I was for the present.

General Thomas had also moved one corps forward from Jonesboro (Stanley's). He marched along the east side of the railroad. He had left Davis's corps at Jonesboro to gather up the captured property, and to care for the wounded and bury the dead. Stanley struck the enemy's lines about midday, and he had the same difficulty in developing the lines, in making his approaches to the enemy's works, that I had had; so that it was near dark when he was ready to make an attack. Thomas, probably not aware of my orders, pushed his troops well forward and had a lively combat.

About half an hour later one of Stanley's divisions made an endeavor to carry the enemy's works but did not succeed.

After this partial attack, a little later in the day, Schofield's army came up to support the left of Thomas. The effort resulted in about 100 prisoners, several of whom were commissioned officers.

Now we notice that from this time on, the two armies were facing each other, and each commander had full purpose to do nothing which would bring on a general action, though, as we were very near together, we had each day upon the skirmish line many men wounded and some killed. We thus watched each other and skirmished for four days."(59)

The losses that were suffered in the short battle of Lovejoy's Station were the Confederates lost fifty-seven dead with ninety-two men captured, the 16th Army Corps losses were one officer and one enlisted man killed and sixteen wounded. The 17th Army Corps reports two hundred and fifty Confederate dead and wounded with twelve prisoners taken and their losses as eleven men wounded. There were no reports of casualties listed for the 15th Army Corps.

September 3rd, orders were issued for the wishes of General Sherman to be carried out. General Logan was to hold his position gained in the capture of the rifle pits and the hill that they had gained and to let the rest of his corps go into camp within easy supporting distance from the front positions and relax a little. There were to be as few men as practical on the front line. Even though there were few men who were in the front line there were still skirmishing and men were being killed and wounded. Major A. J. Seay wrote about this in his diary. The following is his entries for September 4th through 5th. "Sunday, 4. It rains-stormy-McClellan nominated for the Pres. by the Anti-war-copperhead-rebel party. Skirmishing heavy several men killed and wounded today. We have no mail since leaving Atlanta, but we have been amply repaid for all our pains in another great victory. Monday, 5. Today skirmishing not so heavy. We will withdraw tonight to Jonesboro. I am officer of the day and have instructions to draw out my pickets at 12. Today many an anxious week-kneed copperhead is watching with terror at the wheels that grind out soldiers."(60)

Once the command was given to begin the expected withdrawal to Atlanta for relaxation and refitting the 15th Army Corps was to be the rear guard. The end of the month report of casualties for August in the 15th Army Corps were killed twenty-four men, there were five officers and one hundred and twenty-one men wounded and four men were listed as missing. This gave a total of one hundred and fifty-four casualties. The 1st Division of the 15th Army Corps listed one officer and two men killed, two officers and thirty men wounded which gave the 1st Division a total of thirty five casualties. The Battle of Jonesboro on September 1st cost the 1st Division more casualties than for the whole month of August. The total of casualties for the 15th Army Corps for this one day were three officers and twelve men killed, five officers and sixty-seven men wounded and two men listed as missing for a total of eighty-nine casualties.

General Sherman decided that it was time to bring his army closer to Atlanta and told his army corps commanders to withdraw to assigned positions within three or so days. The Army of the Tennessee was assigned to East Point, the Army of Cumberland were to camp in and about Atlanta and the Army of the Ohio were to go into camp at Decatur. On September 5th orders were issued for the 1st Division and the 4th Division to withdraw from their positions in front of Lovejoy's Station at eight p.m. marching to their old positions that they had occupied in Jonesboro. Brigadier-General W. B. Hazen's 2nd Division acted as the rear guard for the 15th Army Corps and thus acted as the rear guard for the whole Army of the Tennessee.

Major A. J. Seay writes in his diary, "Tuesday, 6. Last night was one of the dark, muddy dreary nights that soldiers often march in. I rode all night splash, splash and thunder, rain and darkness. Am pretty well used up today. We lay all day in our old positions at Joesboro. Our labors for the present are nearly ended."(61) September 6th orders were issued for the 15th Army Corps to proceed on September 7th at seven a.m. with the 1st Division leading the way and the other two divisions were to follow with the 4th Division bringing up the rear. General Osterhaus was to provide one of his regiments as train guard. The 15th Army Corps proceeded on September 7th across the Flint River to Morrow's Mill, Georgia in the order as described above. Major A. J. Seay rocorded in his diary, "Wednesday, 7. We march at 8 ½ back towards East Point and go into camp at a church 8 miles distant-dark cold and cloudy. After we get into camp an order from Lincoln, Grant and Sherman is read to the troops who make the woods ring with prolonged and deafening cheers."(62) Orders were issued for the Army of the Tennessee to move on to East Point on the 8th of September. The 15th Army Corps was to leave at eight a.m. with the 16th Army Corps was to leave at seven a.m. with the 17th Army Corps scheduled to leave at eight-thirty a.m. The 15th Army Corps was to march and the 2nd Division was to lead the way with the 4th Division following and the 1st Division bringing up the rear. General Osterhaus was told to make sure that there were no stragglers from any division and to bring them forward.

The Army of the Tennessee arrived at East Point, Georgia on September 8th without a hint of what was in their future. They knew that they were to use this time to replenish the equipment that they had lost and to rest, catch up on lost sleep and relax. In a report to Brigadier-General John B. Gray the Adjutant General of Missouri, Major A. J. Seay who commanded the 32nd Missouri Infantry Regiment states.

"Headquarters Thirty-Second Missouri Volunteer Infantry,
East Point, Georgia,   September 8, 1864.

General: I will give you a synopsis of our recent movements:

From the 5th to the 26th of August the regiment was engaged in the pits and on the skirmish line. On the night of the 26th we withdrew silently (with First Division, Fifteenth Army Corps) at 8 p.m., and marched all night southwest toward Sandtown, and rested at noon 27th. On the 28th we moved due south and took possession of the Montgomery railroad, after slight resistance by the enemy, and destroyed several miles, continuing our labors during the 29th. On the 30th we moved southeast with the design of striking for Macon railroad at Jonesborough. The enemy contested every foot of ground, but despite their desperate resistance 11 p.m. found us in position. During the night and early on the morning of the 31st we threw up earth-works. We had not finished them when J. B. Hood, after the style of 28th of July, charged our whole on our left, had taken possession of, and destroyed a portion of, the railroad. My regiment lost 2 killed and 3 wounded to-day (31st of August).

September 1, the Thirty-second, together with the other regiments of the Third Brigade, charged the enemy's works in front of Jonesborough, in which my loss was 7 wounded. It is needless to say (for the country knows) Atlanta was evacuated that night, the enemy destroying immense quantities of ammunition, &c. He also evacuated Jonesborough the same night, moving toward the Gulf of Mexico. Thus you see our work for the present is done, and General Sherman pronounces it "well done." On to-morrow we will go into camp for rest and reorganization. Our present station and post-office address is East Point, Georgia.

Hoping soon to receive from the draft depot men enough to fill my thinned ranks, at least to the minimum, I am, with high respect, your obedient servant.

A. J. Seay,

Major, Commanding."(63)

September 9th found the troops doing what they do best, writing letters, reading papers, repairing equipment and trying to rest and eat. The officers were taking the opportunity to catch up on their reports to their home states, as the report above, to the department commander. Each brigade commander sent a report to General Logan who then used the reports of his brigade commanders to write his reports to General Howard and General Howard used the reports to write his report to General Sherman who used these reports from his army commanders to send his reports to the commander of all the armies, General Grant. The 3rd Brigade of the 1st Division of the 15th Army Corps under the command of Colonel Hugo Wangelin.

"Third Brigade, Colonel Hugo Wangelin,

3d Missouri—5 men killed, 43 men wounded, 3 men missing, total 51.

19th Missouri—1 Officer & 5 men killed, 7 Officers & 51 men wounded, 3 men missing, total 67.

17th Missouri—2 Officers & 10 men killed, 24 men wounded, total 36.

29th Missouri— 3 men killed, 5 Officers & 31 men wounded, 1 Officer & 4 men missing, total 44.

31st Missouri— 1 Officer & 9 men killed, 18 men wounded, total 28.

32nd Missouri— 3 men killed, 2 Officers & 31 men wounded, 2 men missing, total 38.

Total 3rd Brigade—4 Officers & 35 men killed, 14 Officers & 198 men wounded, 1 Officer & 12

men missing, total 264." (64)

The following is an article that was printed in the "Daily Missouri Democrat" that describes the actions of the what he refers to as Colonel Vaughn's Missouri Brigade. He writes it while encamped at East Point, Georgia.

"FROM GEORGIA.

Col. Vaghn's Missouri Brigade.

It's Prt in the Capture of Atlanta.

An Interesting Narrative.

(Correspondence Missouri Democrat.)

Camp 32d Missouri Volunteer Infantry,

East Point, GA. Sept. 11, 1864.

Editors Missouri Democrat:

This brigade consists of the 29th, 17th, 31st and 32d regiments Missouri Infantry Volunteers, under Colonel Wanglin, of the 12th Missouri. It has been greatly reduced in numbers since leaving winter quarters at Woodville, Ala., not a little by battle and disease, but mostly by the return home of the greater part of the 3d and 12th Missouri, their term of enlistment having expired; but the few that are left have testified, in the severe battles at Jonesboro, that they are of the 'true grit.'

Colonel Wanglin is extremely popular with the men of his brigade, who, on account of the kind and fatherly care which he exercises towards them, affectionately call him 'Pap.'

We withdrew from our pits around Atlanta when the greater part of Sherman's army did so, on the night of August 26th and took part in the expedition which resulted so successfully in compelling Hood to evacuate his stronghold. The troops moved on parallel roads within supporting distance of each other, in a southeasterly direction, and reached Montgomery road at a point some ten miles below East Point, August 28th. The next day this road was most effectually demolished for a distance of several miles. Proceeding onward, we reached Jonesboro at midnight, August 30th, tired and sleepy from the long and tedious day's march; yet before daylight next morning, our boys were engaged in fortifying in order to be ready, for any emergency. As I afterward learned form a prisoner the main rebel forced did not reach the place until nine o'clock that morning. This force, consisting of Hardee's corps and Hood's old corps, attacked us with great fury at four o'clock in the afternoon; General Hood, well aware of the exact number of roads in the vicinity, supposed that as yet but a comparatively small Federal force had been able to reach Jonesboro. But in this he 'reckoned without his host,' not surmising that Sherman had made another road as he advanced on which more than double the numbers that he had counted upon had been brought forward and placed in position. When the rebels charged, therefore, all were impatiently expecting them for since morning the enemy had been seen rapidly moving to the right, so that the terrific slaughter they were hurled back, and another great Hood victory had been won. On the morning of Thursday, September 1st, a slight demonstration was made by our skirmishers in favor of Schofield, who had reached the Macon railroad near Rough and Ready, and was then advancing on it towards Jonesboro. Later in the afternoon General Osterhaus, who was standing behind a tree, passed in the rear of the works occupied by our brigade, suddenly ordered the men to jump over and charge. This order, though totally unlooked for, was obeyed with alacrity, for it is yet to be recorded that the 3d Brigade ever refused to advance upon the foe.

Forward they went with wild cheers, meeting at first with but a feeble fire from the enemy" works, which was certainly fortunate, for so weak was the line that it seemed a mere skirmish line which a couple well directed discharges of grape would annihilate. It was the double quick that took the boys forward with the hope that they would be able to capture the skirmish line, which, as was thought, was all the breastworks then shielded from the scantiness of the fire. As we advanced the 'Johnnies' in the skirmish pits took up the same time with ourselves, with their yellow looking blankets thrown over their shoulders and their guns at 'trail arms,' a little however, in advance of us. But when within twenty five yards of the main works the skirmish line, aided by the two batteries vomited forth such a fire as would have done credit to any heavy 'line of battle,' and had it been well directed none of us would have returned unscathed. Just as the fire rang along the pits not a Yankee stood as a target. So sudden did every one fall, that undoubtedly the rebels thought the venturesome Yankees had been swept away; therefore only a comparatively few shots were fired after the first volleys, though, one after the other the dead 'Yankees' arose from their reclining postures and rapidly withdrew over 'the brow of the hill.' Knowing that had the rebel aim been a little lower, the result of our charge would have been as they had at first anticipated, and too, that this aim would improve with a little practice. Major Seay, whose regiment was the most advanced, resolved to await further orders under cover of the hill, ere he should sacrifice his greatly reduced regiment. The Major though careful of his men where it is proper that he should be, is as brave an officer as any in the army, always leading where dangers thicken when duty calls. Here he was with Sergeant Wool, of same regiment, the very last to leave his position nearest the rebel breastworks, so that much search was made in order to bring off, if possible, the dead, or wounded body of our much esteemed commander. As it is not pleasant to record a 'fall back,' I will only say that we did so, having most fortunately escaped with a loss of twelve men killed and wounded in the 31st and 32nd (temporarily consolidated,)—among the former the gallant Captain Dougherty, of the 31st. During the night Jonesboro was evacuated, and the next day we pushed on after the enemy to Lovejoy, six miles down the railroad, where Hood had again made a stand. Here we heard of the capture of Atlanta, but supposed that the rumor would turn out as its predecessors of like import had. Its truth, however, was soon established by a characteristic order from General Sherman, which was read to the troops, stating that on the 1st day of September, 1864, Major General Slocum, commanding 20th army corps, U.S.A., relieved General Hood, C.S.A., of the command of Atlanta.

Marshall."(65)

The 31st Missouri Infantry Regiment had a total of twenty-eight casualties for the battle of Atlanta. The list of casualties as follows and non battle losses October 1, 1864. The losses suffered by Company A are, Sergeant Alexander Adeu from Victoria was transferred to the Invalid Corps on August 7, 1864, Private Henry Duckhom of Victoria deserted on July 25, 1864 at Atlanta, Georgia, Private Henry Meyer of Morse Mill was discharged on September 22, 1864, Private John Klipshine of Hillsboro died of disease on August 6, 1864 at Memphis, Tennessee, Private Mark Wideman of Victoria was killed by enemy fire near Atlanta, Georgia on August 6, 1864 and is buried at the National Cemetery in that city; Company D lost Private William H. Williams of Greenville died on July 26, 1864 and is buried at the Marietta-Atlanta National Cemetery, Private John Jolly of Butler County was killed in action near Atlanta, Georgia on August 16, 1864; Company E lost Private John Druing from Moselle, Missouri because of wounds suffered at Atlanta and was later discharged on October 22, 1864; Company G suffered the following losses, Private Joseph Kuip of Saint Louis was transferred to the Invalid Corps and was mustered out on September 6, 1864 at Detroit, Michigan, Private William Schwarze of Dutzow, Missouri was severely wounded on July 4, 1864 and was in the hospital, Private William Kuntz was slightly wounded in the bowels on August 6, 1864; Company H losses were Private William N. Humphrey of Wayne County died of disease on July 20, 1864 at Marietta, Georgia.

Private John Jolly of Butler County, Missouri, a member of Company D, as listed above was killed at Atlanta, Georgia. He had been transferred to the Invalid Corps. The Invalid Corps, sometimes referred as the Veteran Reserve Corps, was authorized to be formed in General Orders # 105 dated April 28, 1863. The Invalid Corps was composed of men who had served time in the service already. That is why it is sometimes referred to as the Veteran Reserve Corps. There were certain conditions that the men had to fufill before they could enlist in the corps. They are that "1. They are unfit for active field service on account of wounds or disease contracted in the line of duty; this fact being certified by a medical officer in the service, after personal examination. 2. That they are fit for garrison duty; this fact being likewise certified by the medical officer, as above, after personal examination. 3. That are, in the opinion of their commanding officers, meritorious and deserving."(66) They also had to be in such a physical condition that rendered them unfit for duty in the field. Another requirement was that if he was no longer in the active service that he could prove that he was honorably discharged from the service. The men came from different areas. Some of the men who were in the hospital suffering from wounds or disease that kept them from performing duties in the field. Some of the things that would prevent a person from qualifying was epilepsy, total loss of sight or other serious diseases of the eye, affecting its integrity and use, loss of nose, deafness, dumbness, total loss of tongue or partial loss in such a way that it affects their ability to communicate clearly, wounds or fractures tumors or chronic diseases of the joints or bone that would prevent marching or any considerable muscular exertion. I have listed just a few of the twenty-six physical infirmities that would keep the prospective enlistees of the Invalid Corps. In the list of reasons why an ex-soldier could enlist into the Invalid Corps was to include a loss of the left arm or hand but not the right so if a soldier lost his right arm he could not enlist.

The term of enlistment was for three years or until the end of the war. If the wounds or disease that had caused an individual to be forced out of the service previously allowed him to receive a pensions or bounty he would not be allowed to receive the money until his time in the Invalid Corps was up. Once his enlistment was up he then would be eligible to again draw such money. The Invalid Corps would be under the jurisdiction of the Provost-Marshal-General James B. Fry in Washington D.C., with the assistant provost-marshal-general in each state with opening a recruiting station in his area as soon as possible. Invalid Corps commander stationed with the Provost-Marshal-General in Washington D.C. was Colonel Richard H. Rush of the 6th Pennsylvania Cavalry. The assistant provost-marshal-general was to select officers and enlisted men to serve as recruiting officers and recruiting N.C.O.'s in the State's. He was also to establish a camp for the new enlistees, in their State, to go to await further orders. Once someone enlisted he would be sent to one of these camps where he would go through an examination by a doctor and if he passed this examination he would be immediately mustered into the Invalid Corps. If he failed this examination he would be supplied with transportation back to the headquarters of the district where he first enlisted. Each state in the north was to have sights for the amount of companies expected from their state. Missouri was to have eight companies and Illinois was to have camps set up for ten companies.

Men who transferred into the Invalid Corps from the active Regular Army, from hospitals and those home sick on leave because of disease will be transferred in the same rank as they currently held. Also there was a general order authorizing Army Corps commanders to have examined and those who were found to be unable to continue further active service could be transferred to the Invalid Corps. As soon as the original enlistment of these men were up they could re-enlist into the Invalid Corps or go home. The men who were sent from the Army Corps of Major-General's Grant and Schofield were sent to Camp Alexander. An officer who was appointed to the Invalid Corps was to resign his commission dated the day before his appointment into the Invalid Corps. Only men who had been in the infantry were to be allowed into the Invalid Corps. Detachment of recruits they were to be given at least two days cooked rations before going from one depot to another. One of the depots that was listed was in Saint Louis, Missouri known as Camp Alexander under the command of Colonel E. B. Alexander. Once they were on their way, for some reason or another, if they were delayed they were to march to the soldiers rest to get more rations and to continue this until they reached their destination. It was desirous that the Invalid Corps be known as a corps of honor, without any chance of the veterans feeling that they were not an intregal part of the military. Once they became part of the military they were to take the places of able bodied men in the hospitals as nurses and stewards, as guards in prisoner-of-war camps and military prisons, and clerks in any area of operations that they could be used to relieve able bodied men.

At the start of the Invalid Corps there were to be two battalions. The 1st Battalion was to be made up of men who were able-bodied enough that they could handle a musket, perform guard duty and able to perform light marches. Mostly these were men who had became sick with disease that further exposure to the elements, common to the men in the field, would cause their death or permanent disability. The 2nd Battalion and later the 3rd Battalion were to be made up of men who could not perform the above duties but capable of performing other duties such as duty in the hospitals, offices, store houses and depots of supplies. Those in the 2nd and 3rd Battalions were to be issued swords and pistols. As soon as a company was filled they were to be transferred to an area where they are needed to relieve a company of men for active duty. Regiments were formed consisting of the ten companies with six companies of the 1st Battalion and four companies of the 2nd Battalion. By October 31, 1863 there were seventeen thousand seven hundred and sixty-four enlisted men, with approximately sixteen thousand four hundred and forty-eight men transferred to the Invalid Corps from the army corps in the field, with four hundred and ninety-one officers for a total eighteen thousand two hundred and fifty-five. Below is a copy of a published handbill for men to enlist in the Invalid Corps.

"MEN WANTED FOR THE INVALID CORPS.

Only those faithful soldiers who, from wounds or the hardships of war, are no longer fit for active field duty will be received in this corps of honor. Enlistment's will be for three years unless sooner discharged. Pay and allowances same as for officers and men of the U. S. infantry; except that no premium or bounty for enticements will be allowed. This will not invalidate any pensions or bounties which may be due for previous services. The following uniform has been adopted for officers and men of the Invalid Corps: For officers. Frock coat: Of sky-blue cloth, with dark-blue velvet collar and cuffs; in all other respects, according to the present pattern for officers of infantry. Shoulder straps: According to present regulations, but worked on dark-blue velvet.

Pantaloons: Of sky-blue cloth, with double stripe of dark-blue cloth down the outer seam, each stripe one-half inch wide, with space between of three-eighths of an inch. Forage cap: Present regulation. For enlisted men.— Jacket: of sky-blue kersey, with dark-blue trimmings, cut like the cavalry jacket, to come well down on the abdomen. Trowsers: Present regulation, sky-blue. Forage cap: Present regulation. Men who are still in the service and unable to perform effective field duty may be transferred to this corps. Medical inspectors, surgeons in charge of hospitals, military commanders, and all others having authority to discharge, under existing laws and regulations, are forbidden to grant discharges to any men under their control who may be fit for service in the Invalid Corps. For the convenience of service the men will be selected for three grades of duty. Those who are most efficient and able-bodied and capable of performing guard duty, &c., will be armed with muskets and assigned to companies of the First Battalion those of the next degree of efficiency, including those who have lost a hand or an arm and the least effective, including those who have lost a foot or leg, to the companies of the Second or Third Battalion. They will be armed with swords. The duties will be chiefly to act as provost guards and garrisons for cities, guards for hospital and other public buildings, and as clerks, orderlies, &c. If found necessary they may be assigned to forts, &c. Acting assistant provost-marshals-general are authorized to appoint officers of the regular service, or of the Invalid Corps, to administer the oath of enlistment to those men who have completely fulfilled the prescribed conditions of admission to the Invalid Corps, viz:

1. That the applicant is unfit for service in the field.

2. That he is fit for the duties, or some of them, indicated above.

3. That, if not now in the service, he was honorably discharged.

4. That he is meritorious and deserving.

For enlistment or further information apply to the Board of Enrollment for the district in which the app-

411

licant is a resident."(67)

The above information on the Invalid Corps is really brief, but about the only information that I could find on this corps was found in the Official Records. It is interesting that so many men in the Federal army were transferred to this corps throughout the war and that they played an important part in the war by relieving able bodied men so that they could become an active participant in the war. By the time the war had come to this point the enlistment's in the army were almost non-existent. The draft was supplying a good number of men but some of the commanders in the army were complaining about the quality of the material the men they were receiving. The great draft riots in some of the towns in the north such as New York had proven that the popularity of the war was waning. The need for manpower was increasing for terrible battles had greatly reduced the Federal armed forces.

CHAPTER 14:
CHASING GENERAL HOOD AND THE CONFEDERATE ARMY

What was General Sherman's next move? That was the question that was being asked by the men, his subordinate commanders and his commanding officer, General Grant. For the mean time rest and relaxation for the men and re-equipping for the upcoming campaign. Now began one of the most bizarre events between two opposing commanders that happened during the war. General Sherman wrote to Major-General Halleck, who was the Chief-of-Staff, informing him what he had done. He wrote a letter to General John B. Hood, the commanding officer of the Confederate Army, that he was going to evacuate the civilian population from Atlanta. This was a shocking letter to General Hood. He could not believe it. In his letter, in response to the one from General Sherman, he admitted that he had no other course but to accept the terms that he had stated he also wrote, "And now, sir, permit me to say that the unprecedented measure you propose transcends, in studied and ingenious cruelty, all acts ever before brought to my attention in the dark history of war. In the name of God and humanity, I protest, believing that you will find that you are expelling from their homes and firesides the wives and children of a brave people."(1)

The people in Atlanta were given the option of moving north to Tennessee or Kentucky, with their transportation being provided by General Sherman, or south to those who wished to go in that direction with transportation being provided to Rough and Ready a railroad station south of Atlanta. General Sherman proclaimed September 15th as the close of the battle for Atlanta. The Confederate Army stayed in and about Lovejoy's Station without making any move that would indicate their plans. General Wheeler and his cavalry were now threatening General Shermans supply line in Tennessee. There was a strong rumor going around that General Nathan Bedford Forrest was on his way to do the same thing. Major A. J. Seay wrote in his diary the day to day events that transpired for the idle time around Atlanta.

413

"Thursday, 15. Gen. Osterhaus sends for me and Col. Simpson and desires that we go to Mo. to get recruits for the regiments. Has already sent Gage for that purpose.

Friday, 16. Now we have a good deal of rain, hot weather and cold nights. The officers are forwarding resignations and leaves of absence. The enlisted men are trying to go home. We are feasted with congratulatory orders from our generals recount in brief the successes which have crowned our arms and hinting to us that our rest will be a short one so for all are preparing by clothing our men, recuperating our animals, repairing our wagons, condemning our worthless camp and garrison equipage. Rubbing a little rust off our soldiers in the way of drill, discharging or furloughing the sick and disabled-writing to my friends and urging them to support Lincoln as the only way to uphold the soldiers and save the country. McClellan men in the army few and far between. If McClellan is elected he will recognize the South and discharge us all, and plunge us into irreparable ruin as a National Republic. God save us from such an awful calamity. It would paralize and neutralize the Republic and its defenders. The blows which we have struck and the great apertures we have made in the Rebel Oak have been labor in vain. The weather is windy, stormy and rainy. This seems to be the equinoctial storm."(2)

Some of the regiments in the Federal army enlistment's had expired and they were starting to go home. General Osterhaus assumed command of the 15th Army Corps on September 22nd while General Logan had taken a leave of absence to conduct some political campaigning in his home district in Illinois. General Blair was doing campaigning in his home state of Missouri. After staying at Lovejoy for awhile General Hood finally made a move in a direction that convinced General Sherman that, like General Hood's two cavalry commander, he was going to try to get in the Federal rear, between Atlanta and Chattanooga, to cut off their supply route. General Hood knew he couldn't keep the Federal army out of Atlanta, but he might be able to cause them to follow him north thus drawing them out of Atlanta.

General Osterhaus in his diary dated Sunday September 25th, "Visit battlefield of 22 July."(3) After so long a period of almost constant fighting and marching it probably seemed strange to have some time off. Things were changing in the Federal army at this time. General Thomas and some of the troops were sent back to Chattanooga in hopes of helping to convince General Wheeler and General Forrest to give up on the destruction and harassment of the Federal supply line. The 16th Army Corps was disbanded with one of its divisions going to the 15th Army Corps and the other division going to the 17th Army Corps, with two corps making up the Army of the Tennessee under the command of Major-General O. O. Howard. The Federal Army effective fighting strength had been reduced to approximately sixty-thousand men.

The 31st Missouri Infantry was still in camp near East Point. The following is some exerpts from Major A. J. Seay's diary. The 32nd Missouri Infantry was camped in the same area as the 31st Missouri.

"Sunday, 25. The chaplain gives us a sermon. Well attended. It is a hot day but the nights are cold. Col. Simpson and I are great friends and stay together a great deal. He is intelligent, sharp and interesting.

Monday, 26. We get an order quite suddenly to move 2 miles West in the camp of the 9th ILL. mounted infantry. Find plenty of lumber. The men go to making shanties to protect themselves from the storms, etc.

Tuesday, 27. Warm Col Simpson and I get orders to proceed to St. Louis to fill up our ranks with drafted men. The col is quite sick today but I guess we will start on tomorrow. I have got my business about straight

Wednesday, 28. Col. Simpson and I go to Atlanta in an ambulance. Start for Chattanooga at 12. We get into a cattle car and ride to Chattanooga without change arriving at noon 29th. Put up at Crutchfield house, a hard time at night."(4)

He arrived home in Missouri at 1 A.M. on Wednesday morning October 5th. He did not rejoin his regiment again until October 31st near Rome, Georgia.

While at East Point the organization of the 15th Army Corps changed somewhat due to the disbanding of the 16th Army Corps. The 31st Missouri Infantry Regiment that had been in the 3rd Brigade, 1st Division during most of the campaign against Atlanta, now became part of the 1st Brigade, 1st Division. When

Colonel Simpson and Major Seay went home to try and enlist men into their respective regiments. Captain Andrew A. Harrison took over the command of the 31st Missouri Infantry Regiment, and the 32nd Missouri Infantry Regiment was commanded by Captain Charles C. Bland. The 1st Brigade, 1st Division, 15th Army Corps was made up of the following regiments. 27th, 29th, 31st and 32nd Missouri Regiments; 76th Ohio Infantry Regiment; 26th Iowa Infantry Regiment; 12th Indiana Infantry Regiment.

General Hood had crossed the Chattahoochee River and was heading north. He had with him about forty thousand infantry and artillery forces on the march, not counting both of the cavalry units that were available to him further north which totaled about eleven thousand men. On October 2nd General Sherman issued marching orders, which General Osterhaus received that evening. General Sherman in a telegraphed message mentioned what his hope and plans were for the immediate future. He states in his memoirs, "Hood is evidently across the Chattahoochee, below Sweetwater. If he tries to get on our road, this side of the Etowah, I shall attack him; but if he goes to the Selma & Talladega road, why will it not do to leave Tennessee to the forces which Thomas has, and the reserves soon to come to Nashville, and for me to destroy Atlanta and march across Georgia to Savannah or Charleston, breaking roads and doing irreparable damage? We cannot remain on the defensive."(5)

The day of October 3rd was spent in preparing for the march north in hopes of defeating the Confederate force. The task of holding the city of Atlanta was left to the 20th Army Corps under the command of Major-General Slocum while the rest of the army was put into motion for Marietta, Georgia. General Osterhaus wrote the following in his diary for Tuesday October 4th, "Rainy- March at 5 a.m. arrive at 3 p.m. at the Chattahoochee (River); by 6 p.m. arrive camp near Ruff's Station a terrible night without tents. 22 miles (marched)."(6) The Federal army had been informed through a newspaper and scouts that the Confederate president, Jefferson Davis had made a speech in Macon, Georgia that he intended to cut the supply line of General Sherman and force him out of the state of Georgia into Tennessee. This was some speech considering General Hood was still out numbered. If the politicians can stay out of the business of war and leave it to those who are trained to fight the war, the results may have been different. Maybe President Davis was just making a speech to encourage the men. General Hood then proceeded to do exactly what President Davis stated and it did work for awhile. General Hood main goal was to cause General Sherman and the Federal army to follow him and abandon Atlanta. This to a small degree he achieved. While on his way north General Hood would attack some of the supply depots that were generally guarded by a small force of Federals in a fort. In his attacks upon these supply depots, General Hood not only hoped to destroy the supplies that were being stored or shipped to General Sherman, he also hoped to replenish some of the much needed supplies for his army.

Surgeon A. W. Reese of the 31st Missouri Infantry Regiment wrote a two volume book after the war in 1870 describing his life. He was appointed as an assistant-surgeon in May of 1864. The following quote is from the second volume of his unpublished book, volume one has not been found. "On the evening of the 4th of Oct, (1864) we received orders to strike tent, and be ready at a moments warning, to move out on the road. Great, therefore, was the bustle and activity in camp, the monotony of which had been undisturbed for so many long, listless, idle days—save by the shriek of fife, and roll of tenor drum, at 'reveille', 'tattoo', and other 'calls'. When 'the shades of eve were falling fast', we moved out (Tuesday, Oct 4th 1864) taking the Marietta road. The army was full — as usual — of rumors — One said, we were going to Mobile — another, that we were on the march to reinforce Grant — while a third, solemnly declared, that we were ordered to Missouri to help 'clean out' 'old Pap'."(7)

The Federal army reached Kennesaw Mountain, the site of terrible fighting in the month of June 1864, on October 5th. General Osterhaus in his diary states, "Wednesday, October 5- Rainy- leave camp at 8 a.m. Cross Nickajack Creek at Ruff's Mill. Take at Wade's thru Marietta Road go within 3 miles of the place, when camps- Rebel works fronting west and south. There was a fight at Allatoona- Raining all night."(8) Ruff's Mill had played a part in the 1st Division of the 15th Army Corps where they had marched within two miles of the place on July 4th.

At a place called Allatoona, the Federal forces had a small garrison to guard the railroad and was used as a supply storage area. The Confederates attacked this garrison, which had been reinforced by General Corse and one thousand and forty-four men. The Federals managed to beat back the Confederates and forced them to withdraw. One of the main reasons they withdrew was that the rest of the Federal army, under General Sherman, was starting to close in on them. The Confederates left their dead and wounded on the field for the Federals to take care of them. Surgeon A. W. Reese of the 31st Missouri Infantry Regiment, wrote in his book,

"Our own destination was no longer doubtful. We were hurrying to the support of Gen. Corse. The roads were, already, in an awful condition, and it rained, incessantly, the whole blessed night through.

The mud was fearful in the extreme. Our artillery horses were thin, poor and jaded up — so that they could scarcely drag the huge 20 and 30 lb. Parrott guns over the miry and, almost, impassable roads.

Frequently the mules and horse dropped down exhausted in the road — to rise, 'ah! nevermore'. Woe to the army mule, or horse, that drops exhausted on the march. The vultures shall chant his funeral hymn!

We marched on apace, amid the thick darkness of the Autumnal night, and erewhile, the hills and the glimmer of the Chattahoochee — with its grim outline of rifle-pits along the swells of its uplands — appeared to view. The vast columns of infantry — the grim batteries of Parrott, Rodman, and Napoleon guns — the long trains of white-covered ordnance wagons — the Ambulance and supply trains, crossed the river on two pontoon bridges.

Our line of march extended up the Marietta road, which soon became completely crowded and jammed with wagons, ambulances, artillery, ordnance, Supply and Head-Quarter trains.

We marched nearly all night. I said we marched, but I should have said, we crawled along the road, at the slowest of all possible 'snail paces', for it seemed impossible to get along any faster.

To render matters still more uncomfortable (if that were within the range of possibilities) a part of the 1st Division took the wrong road — got lost — and had to march 5 or 6 miles further than any of the rest of the troops in order to regain their proper position in the Corps.

Our Brigade (the 1st) was among this lot of 'stray sheep' and, as our venerated 'Uncle Samuel', in all human probability, would not care to pay us any 'extra mileage' for this part of the trip, we really need not have gone to the trouble of making it.

When it was discovered that the Brigade was on the wrong road we had marched till near the mid-hour of this starless night.

The troops were cold, weary, and hungry, and in no mood to enjoy the joke. At least we came to a dead halt, of about one hour's duration, during which time it seemed that nobody in particular was in command. Everybody speculated on the situation, and nobody could make head or tail of it. During this lull in our affairs, I slid off the back of 'honest Abe', and, spreading my poncho on the ground, prepared to take a nap.

I was roused from pleasant dreams by a nudge from the faithful Herman Bruns — who was holding the rein of my horse, hard by.

I rubbed open my eyes. The troops were moving in the direction whence we had come.

How those men grumbled it would be useless in me to write — and I am afraid there was a considerable amount of profanity indulged in, by 'the boys in blue', on that memorable occcasion.

Down the miry road we plunged.

The troops indulged in various pleasantries in order to pass away the time. Some fellow — away at the head of the column — began to hallo out, at the top of his voice, 'Whoa, whoa, whoa!' — as if he were engaged in the familiar occupation of driving cattle.

This started the rest, and 'whoa! whoa! whoa!' resounded from one end of the line to the other, till 'the night was hideous' with the clamor and din. Presently some accomplished individual, away down in the line, burst out with such a genuine 'Cock-adoodle-doo', as to set the whole brigade in a roar of laughter, and pleasantly suggested the idea of hot coffee for breakfast.

But soft! methinks I scent the morning air. Scarcely had the echoes of the horn of this pseudo-Chanticleer died upon the breeze, when the refrain was caught up, by other enterprising artistes in that line, and the midnight air was soon vocal with the music of the barnyard.

One big, strapping fellow — of Herculean frame and stentorian lungs — marching just at the end of my horse's nose, opened out with such a coarse, loud, brazen 'Cock-a-doodle-do', that I could not refrain from the conviction that we had a veritable live 'Shanghai rooster' in the crowd.

Sundry 'cat-calls' were also indulged — besides other pleasant imitations of the voices of the inferior animals, familiar to the youth of America — such as the bleating of goats — the grunting of swine — the braying of donkeys and mules, and the squealing of pigs.

These interesting exercised were varied and diversified by numerous sapient, witty, or sarcastic, and non-complimentary remarks on 'the military situation' — that would have provoked the gravity of a saint, and 'Drawn iron tears (of laughter) down Pluto's cheek.' The continual halting of the column (as something would get out of gear at the front) was a perpetual source of vexation and kept my nerves strung up to the highest pitch. I felt like the good, old Job, when, in his bodily discomfort, he exclaimed, 'Would that the morning were come!!' Sometimes we would not march a dozen paces before the column would be brought to a dead halt. Fifteen — twenty — perhaps thirty minutes would elapse, when we would again move up, a few paces, and again come to a halt. At the conclusion of one of these brief advances of the 'command', my big Shanghai friend bawled out 'Nine inches more' — which pleasant sarcasm on 'the march', elicited a roar of laughter from the 'rank and file.'

It was pleasant to contemplate that portion of the 'Grand Army of the Republic' — long since filled with 'hard-tack', 'sow-belly', and good, hot coffee, — now sound asleep around their blazing camp fires, while we, poor devils, were ploughing along, knee deep in the mud, and chilled to the bone by the keen, biting tooth of the night air!

When, at last, the glimmer of the camp-fires of the 15th Corps greeted our longing and eager eyes, such a cheer went up, along the lines of that wearied Brigade, as would have done your soul good to hear."(9)

After they got into camp they lay down for the rest of the night. If you think that they would get to sleep late because they got lost, that didn't happen. Surgeon A. W. Reese continued his story with the events of the next day. When you read the following story remember at Vicksburg when General Grant was riding by the men in trenches and they started to say "Hard-Tack", because they were wanting bread. General Grant didn't get mad but explained to the men that the supply of hard tack was coming but the roads had to be repaired first. General Osterhaus in a similar circumstance did not react in the same way.

"Wed. morning. Oct 5th, we were again upon the line of march. All long day long we marched over the miry roads. The rations had begun to fail, and the boys were beginning to feel the pangs of hunger. This did not add to their stock of patience, as you may well suppose.

Towards night-fall we went into camp, near some old, and deserted rebel earth-works and rifle-pits. Our Brigade went into camp immediately along the main road. The rebel-works consisted of a circular fort, pierced for 8 guns, and a long line of excellent breast-works.

The night came on with a cold, raw, piercing wind. It was about the most uncomfortable 'scrape' I had ever been in. We had but little to eat, and there was, absolutely, nothing in the country to forage.

The 29th Mo infantry, Col Gage, being in our Brigade, was encamped near us along the road. Just after the Brigade had stacked arms, Gen. P. Joseph Osterhouse, commanding the 1st Division, with his staff, passed up the road by us. The 29th Mo boys sung out, as the old General rode along by us, 'Sow-belly! Sow-belly,' (meaning thereby that they were out of rations) The General took it as a personal insult, and, as soon as he reached his tent, sent an order to Col Wangelin (commanding the Brigade) to put the 29th Mo immediately on picket duty.

The whole regiment was, accordingly, put out on Picket, & were not allowed to come in till the following evening — when, just as the sun flashed his dying glories through the somber gloom of the pine-forest, the

29th Mo, with muskets at 'right-shoulder-shift', came marching into camp.

Then you should have heard the peals of laughter that greeted their arrival in camp, and the shouts of 'Sow belly! Sow-belly!' that the rent the air."(10)

The Army of the Tennessee lay in camp at Smyrna Camp Ground, where they endured another day of hard rain. Finally the rain stopped and Colonel Woods led two of his regiments on a reconnaissance toward Powder Spring but did not encounter any of the Confederates. General Sherman nor any of his commanders could figure out what General Hood was up to or where he was going. General Osterhaus writes in his diary, "Saturday October 8- Cold and Clear- At 3 p.m. orders to march north of Kennesaw. At 4 p.m. march and got into camp after a 8 mile march after night pretty much in the old Big Shanty position fronting N. W. Enemy all gone."(11) Surgeon A. W. Reese writes in his book his perspective on October 8th. "Saturday Evening, Oct 8th, (1864) at sunset orders came in 'Prepare to move, at a moment's warning'. Pretty soon the word came round — 'Attention! Fall in!', and, once more, the command rang out, 'Forward — march!' But O such roads! 'The mud was here — the mud was there — the mud was everywhere' — Night came upon us before we entered the town of Marietta. We passed through this without making a stop. As we filed silenty through the streets in the lonely hours' of the night, I could not but contrast the scenes around me with those of our triumphal entrée, into that subjugated town, just three months before. We marched till mid-night when, on emerging from a wood, we came upon our advance guard, (we having been in the rear) encamped on our old ground, at the foot of Kenesaw, not far from Big Shanty Station on the rail-road."(12)

On October 9th General Sherman sent a telegram to General Grant, who was at City Point where he was conducting the siege of Petersburg, that was one of General Sherman most quoted lines in reference to the campaign in Georgia. The telegram is listed below;

"It will be a physical impossibility to protect the roads, now that Hood, Forrest, Wheeler, and the whole batch of devils, are turned loose without home or habitation. I think Hood's movements indicate a diversion to the end of the Selma & Talladega road, at Blue Mountain, about sixty miles southwest of Rome, from which he will threaten Kingston, Bridgeport, and Decatur, Alabama. I propose that we break up the railroad from Chattanooga forward, and that we strike out with our wagons for Milledgeville, Millen, and Savannah. Until we can repopulate Georgia, it is useless for us to occupy it; but the utter destruction of its roads, houses, and people, will cripple their military resources. By attempting to hold the roads, we will lose a thousand men each month, and will gain no result. I can make this march, and make Georgia howl! We have on hand over eight thousand head of cattle and three million rations of bread, but no corn. We can find plenty of forage in the interior of the State."(13)

This is probably has one of my favorite quotes from General Sherman. "I can make this march, and make Georgia howl!" To think that a commander would be so confident in himself and his men that he could make a statement like this and believe that he could actually do it, and did. General Sherman, as stated before, was a very impatient man and he was not going to chase General Hood all over the south.

"Monday October 10- In the afternoon at 4 orders to march to Kingston: start at once and reach by midnight Allatoona Creek, where we camp, 12 miles."(14) General Osterhaus tells how he and the men under him spent the day in his diary. The Confederates had made it to Rome, Georgia on the south side of the Etawah River preparing to cross to the north side. From this crossing nothing was heard from General Hood until it was reported that he was near Resaca, Georgia and the Federal commander was sent some re-enforcement's and he believed that with these re-enforcement's he could hold Resaca. Surgeon A. W. Reese wrote the following in his book of some of the events that he saw on October 10th.

"Our line of march extended up the rail-road from Alatoona Pass, and I soon learned that we had the agreeable prospect before us of again marching all night. We found that the 'rebs' had completely destroyed the road. They had torn up the track — fired the ties — twisted the rails — and burned the 'cattle guards' and bridges along their route. Such were the scenes of destruction which 'grim-visaged war' now offered to our view.

The toilsome night march 'dragged its slow length along'. It was a cold, clear, chilly, night — 'an eager and a nipping air' — but, praised be Mahomet, we did not have the mud to contend with on the rail-road track. The full-orbed, lustrous moon illumined the dark recesses of the forest's gloom with flashes of nocturnal glory, and the stars — silently burning, like isles of fire, in the far, blue sea of heaven — filled the Autumn night with indescribable grandeur — such as I had never looked upon before.

The troops moved rapidly up the road, and we soon reached the town of Ackworth. At this little town we found the debris of a train of freight cars' — the property of Uncle Sam — which the rebs had captured and burned.

Passing through Ackworth we moved on towards Alatoona Pass. After we passed beyond the former we found that the enemy had not totally destroyed the road any further towards the Pass than two miles.

About midway between the two towns we came upon a locomotive and freight train pitched from the track. It was a frightful wreck; battered, splintered, and crushed up — like a passenger's trunk on a western rail-road.

Soon after this we came to a 'middlin-sized' creek, the bridge over which had been burned.

A little further on and we came to another locomotive, and freight train, pitched from the track, and dashed in pieces.

March! march! march! through the long and weary night, till the 'small hours' came in apace, and then, far away like the twinkling of ten thousand stars, through the dense foliage of the massive Pines, the camp fires of the Army of the Tennessee flashed upon the eye. Cheer after cheer went up along our lines as this welcome sight met our view."(15)

Meanwhile, on the 11th of October, leaving camp at five-thirty in the morning, the 15th Army Corps reached about two miles east of Kingston after a march of sixteen miles arriving at four p.m. Surgeon A. W. Reese writes in his book for October 11th,

"Tuesday morning. Oct 11th, the sound of the reveille called us from slumber. The morning sun gleamed through the forest, and his red light flashed from the tall crest of the Alatoona Peaks. We moved out and soon reached the famous Alatoona Pass.   About noon we passed through Cartersville, and crossed the Etowah, (or High-Tower) river, at which point we were joined by the 63d Ill Infantry, Colonel James Isaminger, commanding the force. This regiment had been on duty, at Cartersville for some time, guarding the bridge over the Etowah.

Our boys had grown very tired and hungry, and many of them straggled along, and fell behind the main column of march, for the distance of two or three miles. One of the ambulance drivers I observed sitting on a bank by the road-side while one of his horses had dropped down completely exhausted on the march.

A citizen, whom I met near Cartersville, told me that the country around was swarming with 'bushwhacker's' belonging to 'Gatewood's band', and that it was very dangerous for our men to straggle.

I was about a mile behind the main column myself, so, as you may presume, this was not a very tranquilizing piece of news — and I immediately spurred up the 'honest Abe' till I caught up with 'the boys in blue.'

After getting into camp, that night, I learned that several of our stragglers had been killed, during the day, by these prowling bands. I learned, further, that the ambulance driver, whom I had seen sitting by the roadside, in the morning, was among the number – so that I had, myself, made a narrow escape. Six of the murdered men belonged to the 26th Iowa Infantry — which force formed part of my own Brigade.

Night found us encamped four miles from Kingston, on the abandoned plantation of one Doctor Solomon — who had 'refugeed' further South in 'search of his rights'."(16)

It was about this time that General Sherman began to run out of patience and sent telegrams to General Grant at City Point and General Thomas who was at Nashville, that he thought that it would be better for him to go back to Atlanta and head for the Atlantic Ocean. General Sherman was pretty sure that General Thomas could defend Tennessee from General Hood. He informed General Grant that he believed that it would be more beneficial for him and his men to leave General Hood to General Thomas and head for Savannah or Charleston and if

General Hood wanted to follow him then so be it, or if he wanted to head into Tennessee, then General Sherman was willing to let General Thomas deal with him.

General Sherman, with thoughts and plans running through his head about heading towards the Atlantic Ocean, was still on the trail of the Confederate Army. General Osterhaus states in his diary, " Tuesday October 11- fine morning- marched 16 miles leave at 5 1/2 a.m.- In camp at 4 p.m. 2 miles east of Kingston."(17)

Surgeon A. W. Reese of the 31st Missouri Infantry wrote the following in his book for October 12th.

"Morn came, at last, with sound of everlasting fife and drum — Tweedle-tweedle, tweedle dee-tweedle-tweedle tweedle dee — rub-a-dub-dub — rub-adub-dub—rub-a-dub—rub-a-dub—rub-adub-dub 'confound your noise! hush up, out there, you ragged rascals, in your dirty shirts!!' Soon a familiar sound 'Fall in! Forward-march', and we were again on the road. Four miles further on, and we passed Kingston—an old, dingy town—lonely, dilapidated, and 'tentless of its heroic dwellers.' A halt here! where would we go now? A half hour's pause—and then, a 'blast upon the bugle-horn,' and the vast column of troops, like the 'great anaconda', began to uncoil itself along the road. Down the railroad diverging to the right! 'Hurrah! to Rome, boys', is the cry.

Two miles down the road—then a halt! 'Stack arms!' 'Rest!' We tumble out, under the trees then for a nap. By the roadside—in the woods—in the ruts of deserted cornfields—trampled by the hoof of war—anywhere, anywhere—the toil-worn, weary soldiers drop down to rest their aching limbs.

But alas! what sound is that now rising on the air? 'The d—d old bugle'— escapes from many a disappointed lip, and a moment more, 'Fall in!!' and away we go.

'Tramp, tramp, tramp, the boys are marching', and when the evening sun went down behind the tall-old, forest trees, we went into camp in an old, fallow-fields, where the 'hog-weeds' were as high as your head, four miles from Rome, 'the eternal city'——— of Georgia."(18)

On October 12th General Hood had demanded that the garrison in Resaca surrender with the promise that if the white officers and men were to surrender that they would soon be paroled, if not there would be no prisoners taken if the Confederate force had to storm the garrison. Colonel Clark R. Weaver, commander of the garrison, replied to the demand of General Hood.

> "HEADQUARTERS SECOND BRIGADE,
> THIRD DIVISION, FIFTEENTH CORPS,
> RESACA, GEORGIA, October 12,1864
> To General J. B. Hood:
> Your communication of this date just received. In reply, I have to state that I am somewhat surprised at the concluding paragraph, to the effect that, if the place is carried by assault, no prisoners will be taken. In my opinion I can hold this post. If you want it, come and take it.
>
> I am, general, very respectfully, your most obedient servant,
>
> CLARK R. WEAVER,
> Commanding Officer."(19)

If General Hood was hoping that they would just surrender without a fight he was sadly disappointed with this response. Colonel Weaver's command, with the exception of the cavalry that had managed to join him, were of the 3rd Division of the 15th Army Corps that had been left in this area while the rest of the 15th Army Corps marched on to the defeat of Atlanta. This allowed them the chance to take an active part in the fighting if it came to that, but being veterans of many battles they probably were just as happy to be able to just hear and read about it. General Hood, after the losses his men suffered at Allatoona Pass, did not carry out the threats of his letter and by-passed them destroying many miles of track on his way to Dalton, Georgia.

On Thursday October 13, General Osterhaus recorded in his diary, "At 4 p.m. marching order for Resaca which is threatened by Rebs. Arrive after midnight at McGuires where camp-10 miles."(20) The 15th Army Corps left camp the next morning at seven arriving at Calhoun, Georgia at three in the afternoon where General Sherman ordered the 15th Army Corps to guard Rice crossing. This allowed the men a time to rest while the rest of the army kept marching in hopes of catching General Hood by surprise or to rescue the garrison at Resaca. The 15th Army Corps had marched 14 miles after only a few hours of sleep that night, if that much.

"Saturday October 15- fine- leave Calhoun at 4 a.m. arrive at Resaca by 7. advance towards Snake Creek Gap following 17th Corps. Enemy's rear guard was dislodged. Advanced very slowly owing to the Gap being likely held by the Rebs- in camp at the west end of Gap."(21) General Osterhaus described October 15th as he saw it as the 15th Army Corps commander. Here is how Surgeon A. W. Reese remembered October 15th in his book.

"We learned, in Resaca, that the rebels were in our front, in force, at a place called 'Snake Creek Gap'—a wild, rocky gorge, or 'Pass', through the mountains, seven miles long. This famous 'Gap' was just five miles from the town of Resaca.

The 17th Army Corps, Gen Francis P. Blair, took the advance, while the 15th Corps stacked arms in the town, and had rations distributed to the men.

About 4 P.M. the sharp crack of musketry, up the valley, in the direction of Snake Creek Gap, was the signal that the 17th Corps had come upon the rear-guard of the foe, and that the 'skirmish line' had opened up the fight. It did not last very long, however, for the rebs retreated 'in hot haste', into the gap.

When the sound of small arms first smote upon our ears the 15th Corps was ordered up to the support of Blair. Two hours march brought us to the scene of strife. The massive pines were torn and scarred by Minie balls on every hand. By the roadside, as I passed, laid six dead soldiers clad in Federal blue. A detail from the 'Pioneer Corps' were digging their graves—under the supervision of the Chaplain of the 35th New Jersey Vols. (Zouaves)

The rebel army fell back, as our columns advanced, retreating through the 'Gap'. They fell immense trees across the narrow road, thus seeking to retard the pursuit on our part.

All night long as we toiled through this narrow pass. Our progress was, naturally, and necessarily, slow—for we had to remove the obstructions the rebels had placed in our way. The 'Pioneer Corps' was hard at work, and, all night long, the sound of 2,000 axes rang through the gorge, and the glimmer of a thousand watch-fires flashed up the slopes of the somber hills.

Major Hudson, Surgeon of the 26th Iowa—and myself sat by somebody's watch-fire, for hours and hours, waiting for the seemingly interminable train of white-covered wagons to pass by. There was cold, drizzling rain, and, as we sat there, couched about the smouldering embers of the camp-fire, under the overshadowing branches of a majestic oak, I thought it the longest night of my life. The soldiers, tired and sleepy, tumbled down and slept anywhere that they could stretch out their wearied and aching limbs. In my opinion the most trying feature of the service is these dreadful night marches. I am sure that the night, spent on the march through Snake Creek Gap, which I have just described, was the longest, most cheerless, and, altogether, most uncomfortable night I ever experienced in all my life. Its vivid discomforts are a living memory to day."(22)

It had been a long time since the 15th Army Corps had been in Snake Creek Gap. The Army of the Tennessee had entered Snake Creek Gap on May 9, 1864 on its way to try and get in the rear of the Confederate Army, then commanded by General Johnston, but because of the resistance that they had met near Resaca they fell back to the end of the gap closest to Resaca to await reinforcements. Before the Army of the Tennessee had entered Snake Creek Gap they had marched through Villanow, Georgia on their way south towards Atlanta but now were on their way north chasing General Hood. If General Hood had as his main objective the forcing of the Federal army out of the southern part of Georgia he had succeeded. Except for the 20th Army Corps and the garrisons left in different towns along the railroad almost all of the Federal Army was now on its way back to Chattanooga. If he could keep on running north and forcing General Sherman to chase him and not bring on a major engagement causing the destruction of his army he could keep this up for an unlimited amount of time.

"Sunday October 16- 15 A.C. in advance- leave camp by 7 a.m. find Rebel Pickets at Villanow- drive them to the summit of Ship Creek Gap- after a good resistance- freed the pass (1 Brigade 1 Div) takes about 40 prisoners, quite a nice affair- in camp in the gap."(23) This attack of the 1st Division was recorded in the 31st Missouri Infantry Regiment's battle record as a skirmish at Taylor's Gap, Georgia. The Confederate picket was manned by members of the 24th South Carolina Regiment that had been left there to slow the Federal force down long enough to allow the Confederates to pull farther away. The following is a rather long description of the battle and an operation described by Surgeon A. W. Reese in his book. It is included in its entirety.

"Sunday, Oct 16th (1864) 'Morn bringeth cheer!!' The weary night is past—its discomforts no longer stare us in the face—its miseries are at an end! A beautiful, bright, Autumnal day!

The bugle sounds 'the advance' and the troops shoulder arms, and fall in line. The 15th Corps is at the head of the column to day, and the 1st Brigade at the head of the Corps—the post of honor on the march. A brisk march through the forenoon. At 12M we ascended a mountain spur, called 'Taylor's Ridge'—the road passing on thence through a narrow defile known as 'Ship's gap'. We were pushing the enemy close and hard, and constantly picking up stragglers from his ranks.

As the 1st Brigade approached 'Ship's gap' the crash of musketry saluted our ears'. We were up with the rearguard of Gen. Hood, and in immediate proximity to the main column of his force. The sound of small arms in our front grew sharper and sharper, until it swelled up almost into the grand diapason of the battle-field. A halt for the 15th Corps, which formed rapidly in line of battle—standing to their arms—while the chorus, in front, swelled and undulated, with its waves of sound, just as the rebs advanced, gave back, or opened, in some new quarter, on our troops.

At length the Surgeon in Chief of the Division, Major B. W. Bond, of the 27th Mo, sent orders for the 'Operating Corps' to go forward to the front. As we galloped—two abreast—eight surgeons in all—up the narrow, winding mountain-road towards the front, the roar of musketry grew louder and plainer every moment of time. The troops in reserve, standing in the middle of the road, ready to 'go in',—parted ranks and allowed us to pass towards the field. As we rode through, a solemn silence pervaded the ranks, and more than one muttered, 'Surgeons to the front! Heavy work, boys!!' In our rear, thundering up the rocky road, came the ambulance train—

to remove the wounded to the rear.

In a few moments we were at 'the front' and, just below the crest of 'Taylor's Ridge', we made a halt. Here we spread out our 'Field cases'—sponges, bandages &c, and went to work. Very soon we had our hands full of business, for the stretcher bearers began to pour in on us, with the wounded men. We were in a pretty safe place—being protected, by the crest of the hill, over which the Minie balls whizzed and sang, among the tree tops over our heads, at a most lively and suggestive rate.

In about an hour our men drove the rebs out of the Gap, and then the fierce roar of battle died out, and was succeeded by the cheers of the 1st Brigade as they 'about faced', and marched, with triumphal colors, back to camp; and then silence and darkness settled over the mountain peaks, and deepened the gloom of the valleys beneath. Thus ended the fight at 'Shipp's Gap', near Resaca, Ga, Sunday, Oct 16th, 1864.

Some incidents occurred during this engagement worthy of note. The 29th Mo Infantry was in the advance of the Brigade, and their skirmishers brought on the engagement with the rebs. A good many of the 29th were killed and wounded that afternoon. A great deal of coolness and gallantry were exhibited on the part of these men. During the progress of the fight a German private belonging to the 29th Mo, came limping down the hill towards the spot, where, floated from a pole, our red hospital flag. He was carrying his left hand in his right, and the bright-red, arterial blood was dripping from it to the ground, as he slowly limped along.

He came up to my table, and I examined the wound. It proved to be a compound, comminuted fracture of the lower portions of the radius and ulna, and, also, involving the carpal bones (the wrist joint). The injury was so serious that I was obliged to amputate the hand. He refused chloroform, but bore the operation with more than Spartan heroism and fortitude—not even wincing under the knife.

After operating on this man I went up to the crest of the hill, in company with Major Thos J. Watson, Surgeon 32nd Mo—then in charge of the 1st Division Field Hospital—to see what I could of the fight. While we were standing by the road side, on the crest of the hill, 46 Confederate prisoners were marched by, under guard, to the rear. A good many rebel dead and wounded were lying about, under the trees, on the far-side of the slope of the hill. I thought they were all dead—they laid so still—but I afterwards learned, from the wounded rebs brought back to us, that they were afraid to move, lest 'the Yankees might shoot them on the ground'. (These were wounded men)

On my return to the hospital depot I found my German friend, sitting on a log hard by, smokin his pipe with as much nonchalance as it was possible to imagine. 'How ish te fight, Surgeon?' he asked, as I approached. 'O! all right', said I, 'our boys have whipped the rebs!! They've driven the 'Johnies' out of the gap! I just now counted 46 prisoners going back to the rear!!' 'Brishioners is notting!' ejaculated my practical Teuton, from which remark I inferred that he would have preferred to see the aforesaid rebs laid out to dry rather than taken prisoners of war.

At length, taking his pipe from his mouth, this humane soldier remarked, 'Doctor, I believes I hash anoder wound.' On examination this proved correct, and, to my surprise, I found a musket ball had passed entirely through the fleshy part of the thigh—but had, fortunately, missed the bone. Here was a specimen of coolness refreshing to behold. I applied a roller bandage, and sent my honest Dutch friend, in an ambulance, down to camp.

A first Lieut of the 29th Mo was brought back to me, from the field, with a gun shot wound of the left shoulder joint. He was much exhausted from loss of blood. A careful examination revealed the fact that there was compound fracture of the head of the humerus. There was not very extensive laceration of the soft parts, and I therefore, concluded it to be a good case for resection of the head of the bone. Fortunately for the future prospects of the usefulness of the arm, the long head of the biceps flexor muscle was not injured. Cutting down, then upon the head of the bone, and disengaging it from its ligamentous connections with the socket, I turned the head of the humerus out at the opening, and sawed off the bone, having in the mean-time, been careful not to divide the biceps tendon. The wound was then approximated by means of the interrupted suture and adhesive strips, and the Lieut, with his arm in a sling, was allowed to walk about.

As the sun was slowly sinking in the west the roar of battle ceased, and the troops fell back to their encampment, in the forest, at the base of Taylor's Ridge. The work of dressing the wounded was about at an end, and the Surgeons, composing the Operating Corps, were making preparations to leave the field. In fact several of them had already gone back to camp.

At this juncture one of the stretcher bearers—a man named Harper, who belonged to my own regiment—approached me, and remarked, 'Surgeon! We've got all the men off the field, except a couple of wounded rebs, lying out yonder under the trees. We didn't know whether it was worth while to bother with them, or not. One of em—a youngish sort of fellow, is makin' a heap o' noise'. 'O" that wont do, boys,' said I, 'go up and bring them down, and I will see what can be done for them before dark sets in. Harper lingered awhile, and said, 'That's more than they would do for us! Look how they serve our boys at Andersonville!' 'Harper!' said I, 'do you want our cause to succeed?' 'Certainly I do!' 'Well then let us do right—-no difference what the rebels do. I firmly believe that God Allmighty will blast any cause whose agents perpetrate such horrible cruelties on defenseless prisoners of war. I could not believe in the existence of just God, and think otherwise. His blessing can not rest upon the cause that sanctions such deeds. Go, fetch those men down at once!' He turned away—called another stretcher bearer to his assistance—and away they went. In a short time they brought down the two wounded rebs. One was private soldier (who later died), and the other, I saw—from the chevrons on his arm—was an Orderly Sergeant. Both belonged to the 24th South Carolina Veteran Infantry."(24)

It was while at Ship's Gap that the official word for General Sherman's plan to march to Savannah had arrived with approval for such a move. He was to meet the navy at Ossabaw Sound which was below Savannah, Georgia. This was good news for General Sherman because he now had official sanction to go to Savannah which would allow him to stop playing cat and mouse with General Hood. He still had hopes of catching the Confederates and bringing him to battle with the hopes of destroying his army as a strong fighting force in his rear.

General Hood was getting ready to head into Alabama because he was drawing to near Chattanooga where General Thomas had ordered General Schofield with two divisions to help in trying to catch General Hood in a trap. The Confederates had headed south through the Chattooga Valley and was heading towards Gadsden, Alabama. "Monday October 17- Fine- Reduce transportation. At 3 p.m. order to march to Layfayette. At 4 p.m. meeting General Sherman of Corps Commanders he describes his general idea of the campaign- arrive in camp by 9 p.m. 7 miles."(25) Lafayette, Georgia was about five miles west of Villanow, Georgia. Surgeon A. W. Reese wrote in his book for the 17th of October the following. "At sundown we again received orders to march—so we shouldered our 'traps,' and move out from the classic precincts of Rome. A weary night march brought us to the ancient town of Lafayette, Walker Co, Georgia— a fitting name to be sure. Near this place, an hour, or two before day, we went into camp."(26)

The next day the Federal army proceeded south toward Summersville, Georgia which is about eighteen miles south of Lafayette.   Surgeon A. W. Reese writes, "Tuesday, October 18th, (1864) we marched from Lafayette to Summerville, Chattooga Co, (Georgia) Here we camped for the night in the edge of town."(27) After the Federal army had reached Lafayette they established a supply line from Chattanooga to Ringgold by rail and then to use supply wagons to reach the camps around Gaylesville. The Army of the Tennessee went into camp about four miles north of Summersville. At Summersville the 31st and 32nd Missouri Infantry Regiments were detailed to guard a baggage train back to Chattanooga.

October 19th found the 1st Division of the 15th Army Corps near the town of Alpine, Georgia twelve miles from their starting point north of Summersville. Surgeon A. W. Reese writes, "Wed. Oct 19th, we passed through 'Seneca Gap', and moved on towards the Alabama state line, which we crossed, near a small town, called 'Alpine', situated on the Georgia side. We camped near this place during the night. Thursday, Oct. 20th. We passed through 'Davis' Gap', in the night, and camped, towards morning, near the town of Galesville, Alabama."(28)

General Sherman telegraphed General Halleck to explain to him his plans for the near future. He informed General Halleck that he would not pursue General Hood any farther than Gaylesville. The 4th Army Corps was sent to General Thomas to bring him to a strength that General Sherman felt that General Thomas could then face General Hood with a confidence that he could beat General Hood. General Hood was in the Gadsden, Alabama area deciding that he was going to continue to proceed south to draw the Federal forces after him. "Thursday October 20- fine day- leave camp at 6 1/2 a.m. for Gaylesville, Ala. March via Shinbone Road and Davis X Road- The Rebs have apparently given up this idea of invading Tennessee- by making for Talladega, Alabama. I camp by 5 p.m. 22 miles."(29) This was the belief of a lot of the men of the army that they were just chasing General Hood and that he was going to continue to draw them farther and farther south into Alabama. When President Davis had talked to the troops around Atlanta, Georgia he had promised the men and the South that General Hood was going to invade Tennessee. Some of the men that were following General Hood believed that he had abandoned the plan of marching into Tennessee and now he was heading south in his attempt to flee the Federal army. General Sherman though still believed that General Hood had every intention of crossing into Tennessee as planned. Surgeon A. W. Reese of the 31st Missouri records, "On the 20th of Oct (1864) we went into camp on 'Little River', in the State of Alabama, at a place called 'Coker's Ferry', where we remained about a week."(30)

General Sherman arrived in Gaylesville, Alabama on the 21st of October and stayed in this area until the 28th of October. It was here at Gaylesville that General Sherman says, "The pursuit of Hood by the army under my immediate command may be said to have ceased."(31) He had ordered that the there was to be nothing left in northern Georgia that belonged to the Federal Army. He did not want to start his campaign to Savannah and have to worry about leaving a force large enough to secure Atlanta and all the little garrisons that guarded supply depots along the railroad. He also wanted to leave nothing in Atlanta that would require a guard or that the Confederates could use for themselves. He was planning to abandon Atlanta and wanted only a thirty day supply of food on hand with some forage. The rest was to be sent north to Chattanooga. General Schofield and the two divisions that were with him arrived on October 21st at the camp of Federal army. General Schofield was then given command of his old corps the 23rd Army Corps which had about twelve thousand men in it which was later sent to General Thomas at Nashville, Tennessee. "Friday October 21- very foggy afterwards fine- leave camp at 8 a.m. in order to take a position on Little River near mouth of Chattaooga River (opposite Blue Pond) 7 miles. 2 Bridges across Little River; throw 1 Brigade across & entrench camp."(32) Blue Pond was a town about eight miles west of Gaylesville just on the other side of the Little River.

In a letter dated October 23, 1864, Private Henry Kuck writes his wife from Chattanooga, Tennessee while on guard duty with the supply train.

"Dear Metta,

We're now at Chattanooga in Tenn. Left East Point, Ga. on Oct. 4th. The Rebels had cut off our path between Atlanta and Chattanooga, that is, they tore up the railroad ties in several places and threatened to cut us off completely. The Rebels attacked Allatoona Hill on October 8th or 9th with 4 thousand men, there were 14 hundred of our troops stationed on the hill in order to hold it. The Rebels lost over 2,000 men and we lost 700. On Octob. 11th we got to the hill and saw many rebel prisoners, almost all of who came from Missouri. Dalton was taken from the Rebels without a shot being fired. The commander in this town surrendered on his own accord without fighting. In addition we've heard that Dalton was occupied by 1800 black soldiers who would have liked to fight. After the blacks were taken prisoner they were used to rip out the railroad. All of these places are in our hands again and the railroad is almost finished. General Hood, the rebel general, thought he could cut us off and so force us to leave Atlanta; thus our army had to follow them and drive them off; he's running like the wind, our army can't go fast enough after him.

100 wagons were sent to Chattanooga, and our Regiment and Regiment 30(32nd) from Missouri had to go with them as guard. We arrived here yesterday and are waiting for further orders. And now we've heard that we

436

will be paid here; if this should happen, I'll send it to you right away. I'm fine right now. Claus Gerdel & John Gerdel and young Gerd Losmann are all fine and Gerd says hellos to his mother. You write that Ziegler rented John Eggers' land again.

Ziegler can perhaps arrange for you to stay there next summer, until I come and pay him a fair price. Dear Metta, don't lose hope! Sunshine always comes after rain, and the good times also come again after bad times. Write me again how Wm. Schwarze is doing, whether he's coming again or not, and what's wrong with him, anyway. Say hello to Ziegler and his family, Ehlers' family and Fick and all our friends and neighbors.

Write right away.

Your husband who loves you

Henry Kuck

P.S. Write and tell me something about the Draft, whether men have been drafted there where you are and if General Price is still in Missouri and how close he was to you."(33)

"Monday October 24- fine- At noon orders to march with cavalry towards Gadson- leave at 2 p.m. arrive at Leesburg by 5 p.m. a little pickets firing- Rebs skeddadle- no cavalry."(34) Leesburg, Alabama is about ten miles southwest of Blue Pond, Alabama. The excerpt from General Osterhaus' diary quoted above was the beginning of the Turkeytown Valley, Alabama battle that lasted from the 24th through the 26th of October 1864. "Tuesday October 25- fine- Break camp at 5 1/2 a.m. find Rebel cavalry at Kingshill, drive them back to the Rebel fortifications at Blounts where the cavalry left them on the 23rd- Dislodge them- they fall back to beyond Turkeytown on a forti- fied hill commanding the whole valley. Attack them in front & Right flank and drive them out- no cavalry to pursue. Return to camp 5 miles back near Blounts. 18 miles."(35) The troops on the front consisted of the 1st Division of the 15th Army Corps with the troops on the right flank those of the 2nd Division of the same corps. The Confederates had successfully withdrawn from the Federal army that was attacking them and since there was no cavalry to chase the Confederates and force them to stand and fight so the Federal infantry would be able to close with them again they were able to succeed in their escape. "Wednesday October 26- Rain threatening- leave camp at 8 a.m.

and march back to Little River. No sign of enemy. The rear of column arrives at 2 p.m. 17 miles."(36)

General Hood was then in the area between Tuscumbia and Decatur, which was in the north-western corner of the state, trying to resupply his army and found out that the supplies he so desperately needed were hard. He then spent about a month just across the river from Florence, Tennessee getting ready for his campaign into Tennessee. "Saturday October 29- fine but cool. Leave at 7 1/2 a.m. had to stop at Cedarbluff for the 17th A.C. to pass the pontoon till 3 p.m.: got the command over in 3 hours - destroy the bridge in 1 hour- go into camp 1 Division 6 miles, 2d division 3 miles south of bridge. Terrible roads 11 miles."(37) In a letter home to his wife dated October 29th, 1864, Surgeon A. W. Reese writes,

"We are lying on the banks of the Coosa river, at this little town, called 'Cedar Bluffs', while the 17th Army Corps (Major Gen: F.P. Blair) is crossing the stream on a pontoon bridge. In my last letter I told you that a rumor had reached us that the 31st and 32nd Mo, which had been detained as train guard, and sent back to Chattanooga, had been attacked by a force of the enemy, and captured.

I am happy to tell you that these reports are unfounded, and that these regiments rejoined the command this morning, safe and well, having performed the journey—a distance of 100 miles—in 4 days. They met no enemy, with the exception of a few, straggling guerrillas, belonging to 'Gatewood's Band', and had no difficulty in getting through to Chattanooga and back again.

We never hear the term 'Federal' or 'Feds' as we are so accustomed to hear the loyal soldiers called in Mo. Our boys like the term 'Yankee', and use it altogether themselves. The men, in our army, call the rebels 'Johnies', 'Johny-rebs', or simply 'rebs'. The origin, or significance, of the term 'Johny' I have never been able to learn."(38)

On October 30, the 15th Army Corps left the state of Alabama and crossed into Georgia going into camp four miles west of the town of Cave Springs marching fifteen miles. The army is returning in the direction of Atlanta and they are taking a different route back moving in a south-easterly direction. Surgeon A. W. Reese writes in his book the following,

"Sunday Morning, Oct 30th we finished crossing the

Coosa River. We took up line of march, as soon as the command was given, across the river, and did not get into camp till twelve o'clock at night. The road was a new one—cut through the pine forest by the Pioneer Corps—was dreadfully cut up by teams, and awfully muddy to behold. After one fourth of the army has passed over this road, it became almost a bog—in fact, well nigh impassable to man or mule. Unfortunately our Corps was in the rear, and, when we got to this part of the line, such a scene ensued, as I had never before witnessed.

The wagons floundered and plunged, like so many boats in a storm—the teamsters whipped and swore, at a fearful rate—teams frequently became entangled in the darkness, giving, thereby, fresh license while the whole woods was vocal with the neighings of mules, the halloaing of drivers—the splashing of horses feet, and the usual uproar of the march—in all 'making night hideous' with the din.

When, at last, we reached camp there was a rough, cold gale blowing through the forest, so that we were chilled to the bone. The boys managed, however, to get a huge pile of fence rails and pine-knots heaped up, and set on fire, by whose blazing light, and genial heat, we soon got thawed out, and ready for our coffee. How much good a hot cup of good, strong coffee does a man under such circumstances! It is far better for him than all the alcoholic stimulants in the world.

It had often struck me that there will be one branch of trade that much surely thrive well, 'when this cruel war is over', and that will be the manufacture of fence-rails. The way an army, like this, makes fence-rails fly is 'a sin to Crockett'. I remember a night march we made, about two weeks previous, which illustrates, most forcibly, this point.

It was an excessively, cold chilly, and disagreeable night. We marched the whole night long. The soldiers would set fire to the corners of the fences as they marched along the road. Squads of men would halt around these—warm awhile—then go ahead again, and halt at another fire, a few hundred yards further on—then on again. These were succeeded, in their turn, by other squads, who repeated the process, and thus, through the long, and, seemingly, interminable hours of the night. They kept up one, long, continuous line of 'bon-fires' along the whole route. It was a grand sight (to any of us) to look back, and see the thousands of fires flickering, flashing, and blazing through the thick darkness of the night, for miles and miles along the road behind us. I presume, however, that the secesh gazed upon the conflagration with emotions of a far different kind."(39)

"Monday October 31- Cloudy- no rain leave camp at 6 a.m. march to Cave Spring. Day of Muster- Prepare for striking South- 4 miles."(40) Major Abraham J. Seay rejoined his regiment near Rome Georgia. Muster is a time when the men are assembled and roll call is called. It is here that the men are counted absent or present which will determine what they will be paid. It is determined at this time what they might owe for transportation or clothing is then deducted. At the muster on the 31st of October the following numbers were present for muster. The Staff and Field, which is the regimental commander, surgeons and other non company men were assigned, had a total of seven men present with four men not present. Company A had two non-commissioned officers and eleven men present for duty, two men on extra or daily duty, three on detached service, two absent with leave and sixteen absent because of being sick which gave the company with a total strength of forty. Company A had present on September 2, 1862 seventy nine enlisted men and now they were down to thirteen. Company B had three sergeants, two corporals, one musician and fifteen privates present for duty, they had three men on extra or daily duty, five men on detached service, one absent with leave, two men absent without leave and eleven men absent sick which gives them a total of forty-five men. Company C had one 1st Lieutenant, one sergeant and thirteen privates, one on extra duty or daily duty, five men on detached service, one being absent with leave and five being absent because of being sick. This gives the company a total of twenty-seven. Company D had one captain, one 1st Lieutenant, two sergeants, two corporals, eight privates with a total of fourteen men present, one of these included John Calvin who had enlisted as a cook on April 27, 1864 the only enlisted black man in the regiment, one man on detached service, nine absent without leave, one in arrest or confinement with a total of twenty-five men in the company. Company E had one Captain, one 1st Lieutenant, one sergeant, two corporals, one musician and six privates were present for a total of twelve in the company present for duty, with one man on extra duty, three men on detached duty, one man absent without leave, seven men absent sick and one in arrest or assignment for a total of twenty-five men in the company. Company F had one 1st Lieutenant and twelve privates present, two were absent with leave including the Captain, with nine being absent sick, this gives the company a total of twenty-four men. Company G had one Captain, two sergeants, five corporals, one musician, and nineteen privates with three men on extra or daily duty, three men are on detached service, one absent with leave, with seven being absent on due to being sick, for a total of forty two men in the company. Company H had one Captain, four sergeants, two corporals and six privates present for duty, with one on detached service and four absent because of sickness which gives the company a total of eighteen. Company I had one 1st Lieutenant, one sergeant, two corporals and six privates, three were on detached service, and seventeen absent because of sickness for a total of thirty-four men in the company. Company K had one 2nd Lieutenant, one corporal, and eight privates, two men were in arrest, four men on detached service, one man absent with leave and five men absent sick, with a total strength of twenty-two. This gave the 31st Missouri Infantry Regiment a total of one hundred and forty-nine men present for duty. Some of the men who were present were assigned as ambulance drivers, teamsters with seven men who were awaiting court martial or awaiting sentence of court martial. Many of those who were listed as absent were listed as sick, or wounded in the hospital, on detached service to different organization, deserted, discharged, absent without leave or A. W. O. L., transferred to V.R.C. or Invalid Corps, died of disease, prisoner of war with two being listed as killed in action.

Captain A. A. Harrison wrote on the Muster Roll for Company D where they had marched since October 4, 1864. "The Co. with the Regt. marched from East Pt., Ga. Oct. 4' 64 via Marietta, Allatoona, Resaca, Kingston, Lafayette to Summerville Ga. Thence to Chattanooga from Chattanooga to Galesville thence by way Cedar Bluff to Cave Spring. Distance marched since last Muster 350 miles." Captain Samuel R. Maclay wrote on the Muster Roll for Company B, "Was last mustered at Jonesboro and marched to East Point, Ga. and remained in camp from Sept. 9th '64 to Oct. 4 '64 when we marched after the Rebel General Hood via Kennesaw Mountain, Alatoona, Kingston, Rome, Resaca, Snake Gap, Lafayette, Summersville where we were ordered to guard a train of wagons to Chattanooga. Rejoined our Div. via Lafayette, Summersville, Alpine, Gailsville, Cedar River marched with the Div. to this place." 1st Lieutenant Franklin D. Heaton wrote on the Muster Roll the following information for Company C. "This Company marched with the Regt. East Point, Ga. Oct 4th/64 via Marietta, Altoonia, Kingston Rome, Resaca, Fayette (Lafayette), to Summersville, Ga. Thence by way of Fayette & Chickamauga Battle Field. To Chattanooga Tenn. from Chattanooga via Fayette, Summerville Ga, Alpine, Galesville to Cedar Valley, Ala. thence by way of Cedar Town. & Carlton to Cave Spring, Ga.. Distance marched since last muster Three Hundred and fifty (350) miles and was engaged in the Battle at Jonesborough Ga. Sept. 1st, 1864." Captain William Burch of Company H wrote on the Muster Roll his report of what the company had been through since the last muster. "Hay Co. with the Regt. marched from East Point Ga. Oct. 4, 64 via Marrietta Ga. Altoona, Kingston, Resaca to Summerville, Ga. thence to Chattanooga from Chattanooga via Lafayette, Summerville Ga. to Galesville, Ala. from Galesville via Cedar Bluffs to Cave Springs. Distance marched 350 miles and was engaged with the enemy at Jonesboro Ga. Sept. 1st and all the engagements with the division during the present campaign." Captain John Reed the company commander of Company I wrote on the Muster Roll for October 31, 1864. "This Company with the Regt. was last mustered at Jonesboro, Ga. has moved since that with the Regt. and marching to East Point, Ga. from there to Vinings Station, Ga. by way of Marrietta, Kingston, Ressaca, Fayette, Summerville, Rome was sent Oct. 19' 64 Guard Baggage trains to Chattanooga and again joined the army at Cedar Bluffs Oct. 29 '64."(41)

"Tuesday November 1- fine- leave Cave Spring at 7 a.m. for Adamstown. A very good camp. everybody and thing in at 3 p.m."(42) Surgeon A. W. Reese wrote the following in his book.

"On the 1st day of November we took up line of march, our route lay through a fertile valley, dotted thickly with splendid farms, (or, plantations, as they call them in the South) and elegant mansions. This was called 'Cedar Valley' and was, by far, the best region of the country I had seen in the state—not even excepting that fine region along the valley of the Alatoona Mountains, through which we had passed, on the march from Rome to Resaca, a short time before.

The soldiers 'lived high' on this march. Gen Sherman had issued orders for the troops to subsist themselves on this trip. Foraging parties were, therefore, regularly detailed, to scour the adjacent country, and bring in supplies. The soldiers, with the main column, had liberty to take anything to eat that they could lay their hands on, but they were forbidden to enter any dwelling, or to take anything there-from. A guard was stationed at each door, as we passed along, to keep the soldiers out. The guard consisted of but a single man. But the way the chickens, ducks, pigs, guinea-hens, calves, sheep, cows, hogs, and potatoe patches suffered, along the route, was a fearful sight, for the secesh woman and 'folks' to look upon.

Those soldiers could 'grab' sweet potatoes on principles truly scientific, as I often had abundant opportunities to see. It was striking feature of the march. In an incredibly short space of time, a 'secesh' citizen would find his sweet potatoes all dug, and nicely stowed away in—haversacks. We encamped, at night, near a small place, called 'Cedar-town'—the county seat of Polk Co, Ga. This was nine miles from Spring Cave."(43)

General Forrest on October 31st had captured two gunboats with five transports and was on the Tennessee River looking like he was ready to head for Nashville. When this was reported to General Grant he became nervous at City Point. He also became nervous when he started receiving the reports of what General Hood was doing in Alabama. He asked General Sherman if he thought it was possible could he go take care of General Hood and then, as a secondary movement, his trip through Georgia. In Rome, Georgia, General Sherman, on November 2nd, sent a telegram to General Grant assuring him that there was no way that he could catch the Confederate Army unless they wanted to be caught and that if he did finally cross the Tennessee River, General Sherman assured General Grant that he would cut off his line of retreat. But if General Hood did cross into Tennessee he would be fulfilling President Davis' promise about driving General Sherman and his army north. General Sherman believed that the best thing he could do was to go through Georgia. In a telegram on November 2nd, later that day, General Sherman received permission from General Grant to make his now famous "March to the Sea." Meanwhile, the men in the 31st Missouri Regiment kept doing what they did so much of, march. "Wednesday November 2- Rain all night and all day; a very disagreeable march, the 1st Div crosses the mountains and camps at the x roads at Tallapoosa. 2nd Div remains at the foot of mountain 2 miles S.E. at Yellowstone."(44) Tallapoosa was about fifty miles, in a straight line distance, west of Atlanta. Surgeon A. W. Reese of the 31st Missouri Infantry Regiment wrote the following in his book.

"The next morning, Nov 2nd, we again set out on the march. We found the weather once more unfavorable and bad. A cold drizzling, uncomfortable rain distilled from the dull and leaden sky. It was one of those damp, sullen, dreary days, when a man feels ill and cross, and when everything looks gloomy, dismal, and dark. To add to our discomfort the roads proved miserable indeed! It rained almost incessantly, for two days and two nights, and the troops (many without stockings or shoes) splashed along, through the mire and mud, as though it were the prettiest work in the world. I pitied the poor fellows, as I saw them trudging along, so uncomplainingly, many of them with red, cold feet—day after day, in the cold November rain and mud. And yet the men were cheerful, and the morale of the army fine. One, big, strapping fellow splashed by me one day, as I was sitting under a tree on my horse, wrapped in my poncho, while the rain came down in torrents, and shouted out. 'Here's where you git your ice cream!' Truly!, thought I, the American soldier must have his joke. We camped, that night, within three miles of a small town, called Van Wirt.

Thursday, Nov 3d we marched, all day long, in a cold, raw, and dreary rain, and camped, at night, not a great ways from Dallas, as a little place called, 'Villa Ricca.' Nothing of note transpired during this march, except its extreme discomfort, to make us remember the day.

Friday's march (Nov 4th) brought us to the little town of Powder Springs, Cobb Co, Ga, 12 miles from Marietta and 21 from Atlanta. This town derives its name from a Sulpher Spring, of some notoriety, near the place."(45)

The next day the men were on the road by six-thirty a.m. continually making their way toward Atlanta to meet with the rest of the Federal Army. "Thursday November 3- Rainy- Leave camp simultaneously at 6 1/2 a.m. Roads good rain not withstanding. March via New Babylon (Little Mills) to x roads on the Powder Spring Road 7 miles north of Villa Rica and 8 miles south of Dallas. 16 miles."(46) When General Grant issued the order for General Sherman to march to the sea, the army had a definite goal in sight. The Federal troops in Atlanta were making sure that all men who were sick and were estimated that they could not successfully make the march to Savannah were to be sent to Chattanooga, as also were all surplus equipment that was not needed by those on the march. The railroad had been repaired enough all along the line that these things could be successfully completed. The wagons that were to go on the march were being packed and made ready to go so as not to slow down the departure in packing them.

Major-General Francis P. Blair Jr. returned to his 17th Army Corps with other men who had been on furlough and new recruits which were shipped to their companies helping to build the strength of the Federal army. Here are the diary entrees for General Osterhaus for the following days, "Friday November 4- Cool- cloudy- a little drizzlying- leave camp at 7 a.m. for Powder Spring. The road is generally indifferent for about 3 miles terrible. 14 miles. Saturday November 5- Cool but clear- a fine day- leave camp at 7 a.m. The road is very good march to within 3 miles of Chattahoochee R.R. bridge. A.C. in camp 6 1/2 p.m. 14 miles. Sunday November 6- Cloudy & Rain- The Paymasters are coming the men will be paid off till August 31."(47) Surgeon A. W. Reese writes in his book. "On Saturday, Nov 5th, we reached 'Vining's Station' on the rail-road, 5 miles from Marietta, Ga. This was the last encampment we made before Gen Sherman cut loose from his base at the city of Atlanta, and started southward on his famous 'march to the sea'. We remained here about two weeks, resting up the men and horses, getting new supplies of ammunition, drawing fresh clothing, shoeing up the animals, and preparing, generally, for the winter campaign which was so soon to set in. The Hospital Head Quarters were about half a mile from the regiment where still remained with the 'Operating Corps' of the division."(48) A new diary by William H. Lynch who was a member of the 32nd Missouri Infantry Regiment will start to be used as of this date. He will later become a member of the 31st and 32nd Consolidated Battalion Missouri Infantry. "November 6, Regiment remained in camp near Vinings Station, Ga. Mustered in as 1st Lt. Co. H 32nd Mo. Vols."(49) The following is an entry into the diary of Major A. J. Seay on November 7th. "Monday, 7. Frosty nights. We get up a petition for consolidation signed by all the officers of the 31st and 32nd Mo."(50)

November 8, 1864, the day that most of the nation had been waiting for. I will let General Osterhaus tell you what day it is. "Tuesday November 8- Rain- Presidential Election- Old Abe will have a glorious vote."(51) This was no walk away election for President Lincoln. It was so close that many people then, as well as today believe that it was the vote of the men in the army that won the election for President Lincoln. The men in the military referred to him as "Old Abe" both the men in the ranks and general officers like General Osterhaus. It was not a derogatory term it was a expression of endearment. The men in the military didn't vote by absentee ballot as it is used today. States sent election commissioners to the different armies to take the vote of men from their own state. This allowed the men to participate in the Presidential election the same as if they were at home. Surgeon A. W. Reese wrote the following in his book.

"I believe that our noble, old Mo will cast her vote for 'Father Abraham'. I do not speak thus, however, without 'fear and trembling'. The contest will be close—but I have no doubt Price's raid will prove a great advantage to the Union cause, as he, doubtless, carried off a good many McClellan voters, in the shape of Volunteers, when he left the state. Those warriors, 'good and true'. 'Who left their country for their country's good'. Tuesday Evening, November 8, 1864. The election, in the grand army of Gen Sherman, and throughout the loyal North, is over. This day has been big with the fate of millions yet unborn! The destiny of this Nation has been pronounced at the ballot-box to day!

In the 31st Mo not a McClellan vote was polled to day. Two of our men—I learn—did not cast their votes. One of these assigned no reason for his course. The other offered a quaint one indeed. He had declared, at the time when Vallandingham returned 'without leave', from his banishment from home, by the military order of the Gov't, that if 'Old Abe' didn't hang this eminent 'Copperhead', for 'contempt of court'—he'd be d-d if he would ever vote for Lincoln again. And he kept his word! So, you see that, if 'Val' had been hanged, Father Abraham would have gained one more vote in the 31st Mo Volunteers. In the 76th Ohio (of our Brigade) I learn that quite a number of votes were polled for Gen McClellan."(52)

Another group of men were on hand, and these men might be considered the most important people in the whole army, they are the paymasters. When the men received their pay there was usually a renewed interest in games of chance, buying items that they had not been able to purchase since they had run out of money such as food from the sutler, purchasing items for writing letters home and sending money home. Surgeon A. W. Reese wrote in his book the following.

"For several days there had been some talk, among the officers of the 31st and 32nd Mo, about an impending 'consolidation' of those two regiments, (both of which had been reduced, much below the minimum strength, by the casualties of war) and a consequent 'muster out' of the supernumerary officers, some of whom were anxious to go home, while others were indifferent about the matter, or preferred to remain with the command.

A 'caucus' was held, one night, at the tent of Major Jaensch, (of the 31st) and a 'slate' agreed upon, as to the parties who should be mustered out. The Major sent an Orderly to my tent, requesting my presence, and asking, in the event that I could not be there, whether I wished to remain in the service, or to go home. As I was indifferent about the matter, I sent word that I did not care which was done in my case; indeed I had no idea that any change would be made in the organization, before the conclusion of the winter campaign.

Later Geo Culton—our regimental wagon-master, poked his head in at the tent door, and said, 'Well, Dock, I guess you're a citizen!' 'How's that, George?' I asked. 'Major Jaensch wants to see you, immediately, at his tent. Go over there, and you will find out all about it. Sorry to lose you, Dock!!'

I gave Herman Bruns orders to saddle my horse, and

(late as it was) being near midnight, I repaired to the Major's tent. Several commissioned officers were there, assembled, all of whom seemed in high glee at the prospect of going home. My feelings were somewhat strange, I must confess—a sort of mixture of pleasure and regret. I felt reconciled to the 'situation'."(53)

The following is taken from Surgeon A. W. Reese's book. It is order handed to him from Major Fred Jaensch that gave the specifications of the new 31st and 32nd Consolidated Battalion.

"Headquarters Army & Dept of the Tennessee.
Smyrna Camp Ground, Ga. Nov 11th, 1864.
Special Field Orders
No 164
XIV.   In order to form a battallion, to be designated and reported as the Consolidated

Battallion of the 31st and 32nd Mo Infantry Vols, each of these regiments will be immediately reorganized as follows to wit,

First. The 31st Mo into three (3) companies, viz: A, B and C, with the following named commissioned officers.

Co A.   Capt W. N. Judd.
        1st Lieut David H. Middendorf.
Co. B. Capt Wm Burch.
        1st Lieut John W. Wilson.
Co. C. Capt Mathias Neuner
        1st Lieut John Burrows.

Second. The 32nd Mo into three (3) companies, D, E, & F, with the following named officers:

Co. D. Capt John A. McArthur.
        1st Lieut Wm H. Lynch.
Co. E. Capt Robert M. Askin.
        1st Lieut Beverly A. Davis
Co. F. Capt Andy B. Freece
        1st Lieut Charles G. Warner

Third. The two regiments, as reorganized, will be consolidated together, and the following name officers are assigned to the Field and Staff of the Battallion thus formed, viz:

Lieut Col Sam'l P. Simpson,   31st Mo.
Major Abraham Seay,   32nd Mo.
Surgeon Thomas J. Watson,   32nd Mo.

Ass't: Surgeon Addison Elston, 31st Mo.

1st Lieut & regt Q. M. Wm H. Barlow,   31st Mo.

The officers of each regt, other than those herein named and assigned, will be immediateily mustered out of the service, and all non-commissioned officers, who cannot be assigned to fill vacancies, and who become supernumeraries by this consolidation, will, also be mustered out.

The necessary transfer of public property and records will be made, and a full report of the changes, effected in the present organization of each reg't by virtue of the Order, will be reported to these headquarters, and to the Adjutant General of the Army and State.

By order of Major Gen O. O. Howard,

Samuel L. Taggart, Asst: Ad. Gen."(54)

General Osterhaus wrote in his diary, "Wednesday November 9- Rain- Order to be ready to march- 1st Brigade will leave tomorrow with the Pontoons to Turners Ferry. Everything not combatants goes to the rear."(55) As was being done in Atlanta, those who were not expected to be able to endure the long march that was about to begin and all men and equipment or material that would not be considered an important part of the combat team would also be sent north. As far as General Sherman was concerned November 10th was start of the next campaign, the march toward the sea. He ordered that all the troops that were designated to make the march to get to Atlanta. General Osterhaus recorded in his diary, "Thursday November 10- After a tremendous rain in the night- a cool breezy morning. The 31 & 32 Mo. are consolidated by Dept. H. Q. under Major Seay into 6 companies- 2 important orders from Sherman. We will go South- 200 recruits for 4th Iowa."(56) The 31st and the 32nd Missouri Infantry Regiments, both were first formed in 1862 they each had ten companies with approximately one hundred men in each company. They both started the war at the same time and had spent the war together in the same brigade except for a brief three month period. By this time in the war they were both below two hundred men each in their regiments. They became known as the 31st and 32nd Consolidated Battalion Missouri Infantry. The 31st Missouri Regiment men were divided into the first three companies in the consolidated battalion with the 32nd Missouri Infantry Regiment made up the second three companies. Lieutenant Lynch

449

recorded in his diary, "Thursday November 10th- Regt. get orders to be consolidated into 3 companies."(57)

The following quote is from the 1864 diary of 1st Lieutenant William H. Lynch. "Friday November 11th- Regt. in camp surplus officers ordered to be mustered out & 31st & 32nd to be consolidated into 6 companies. Day clear & cold."(58) In his book Surgeon A. W. Reese wrote the following story about how sometimes even when they thought they were safe a soldiers life was always in danger.

"Our first adventure occurred about 2 P M on the 11th. The train had stopped, at a wood-station, just beyond a curve in the road through a 'dirt –cut' about 12 or 15 feet deep. We stopped here about half an hour. The Conductor neglected to send a flag back which was, really, the cause of the disaster to our train.

It was bright, sunny afternoon, and the soldiers belonging to the train—worn out by the previous nights travel—it being impossible to sleep—had, most of them, disembarked and were strolling about, in the adjacent fields, enjoying the genial sunshine.

I was sitting, on the top of a box car, engaged in conversation with Captain Harrison & Lieut Webber, of the 31st Mo—all of us enjoying ourselves hugely, and having a 'gay time' generally, when suddenly my ear caught the near rumble of an approaching train in our rear. Glancing quickly in the direction of the sound, I saw the top of a locomotive chimney rushing towards us, at fearful speed, through the cut behind us. The curved shape of the cut prevented the engineer of the approaching train from seeing us.

With incredible speed the iron monster came rushing through the deep curve, and in a moment or two more, would be into our train. I instantly gave the alarm, and in less time than I can relate the story, was on the ground, and fifty feet from the rail-road track. As I passed the open door of the 'caboose', I saw three ladies inside, who seemed totally unconscious of the impending danger. 'Jump out!' I shouted, 'or you'll be killed in a minute!' They needed no second warning, but leaped out instanter, and were borne to a place of safety in the stout arms of the soldiers.

The engineer, all at once, discovering the impending

450

peril, shut off steam, and reversed his engine—whistled 'down brakes' frantically, and then, finding the collision inevitable, leaped, with a face, pallid, as a sheet, from the train. The locomotive rushed onward, like a mad bull, and dashed into the rear end of our cars' like the plunge of a cannon ball. The crash was tremendous— was appalling, and yet sublime! Our caboose, and several 'box cars' were splintered into 'oven-wood', and, as 'Daddy Corder' would say, 'mashed all to flinders.'

The caboose—being 'in the extreme rear', was 'knocked higher than a kite', and, had there been any person inside this unfortunate structure, at the time, it is more than probable that his nearest relative would have been unable to recognize, in the event of their discovery, the pieces of his 'frail mortality'. Providence so ordered it, however, that 'nobody was hurt', on either train. The locomotive, of the assaulting column', was knocked from the track, and badly battered up, and the platform cars, of which this train was composed, were 'considerably jammed'—but no soldiers were reported 'killed or wounded'—though a good many of them, like the Dutchman's pig, 'came up missing', for the time being. The platform cars of this train were covered with soldiers going home on furlough, and I observed, as the train came rushing furiously onward, the 'boys in blue' 'light out' in a manner truly refreshing and lively to behold. This accident detained us some hours on the road. Our brave soldiers set to work to clear the track of the debris made by the 'wreck of matter'. Our locomotive, being 'at the front' escaped being wrecked, and although some bolts were sprung, and a portion of the machinery somewhat deranged, for the tremendous shock, still, by a little work, she was soon set to rights, and, in a brief period, she was again speeding away on her fiery course. We arrived in the renowned city of Chattanooga on the 11th Nov about 4 P M. I observed, as we passed the battle-grounds of 'Missionary Ridge', a party engaged in disenterring some of the bodies of the gallant men who perished in that sanguinary conflict."(59)

General Peter J. Osterhaus recorded in his diary, "Saturday November 12- fine- beautiful- at 11 a.m. order to destroy the R. R. today. In the afternoon marching order for White Hall near Atlanta."(60) Major A. J. Seay recorded in his diary the following, "Saturday, 12. The whole army is tearing up R.R. today from Resaca to Atlanta. I effectually destroy ½ mile with my batt of 220 muskets. It makes six nice companies, 2 officers each. Coll. day."(61) All lines of communication with the rear was destroyed including railroad and telegraph lines. It had to be a lonely feeling knowing that now you were on your own in enemy country trying to feed yourself and protect yourself from any enemy force that you might encounter. The following are successive days in General Osterhaus' diary. He is still the commander of the 15th Army Corps until the return of Major-General John A. Logan. "Sunday November 13- beautiful- leave with 2nd Division at 7 a.m. by Turners Ferry- 1 Div goes by R. R. bridge. Arrive at White hall at 1 1/2 p.m. the 1st Div via Atlanta at 2 1/2 p. m. good march 15 miles. Monday November 14- 3d Div arrives and the 4 Div will be at the river. Everything is hustle, to get ready. We march tomorrow surely."(62)

In preparation for the next phase of General Sherman's conquest of the Confederacy, the Army around Atlanta, Georgia was divided into two wings, the right wing was commanded by Major-General O. O. Howard and the left wing was commanded by Major-General H. W. Slocum. The right wing was made up of the 15th Army Corps commanded by Major-General Peter J. Osterhaus and the 17th Army Corps commanded by Major-General Frank P. Blair. The 15th Army Corps had four divisions commanded by Brigadier-Generals Charles R. Woods, William. B. Hazen, John E. Smith and John M. Corse. The 17th Army Corps was made up of three divisions commanded by Major-General Joseph A. Mower, and Brigadier-Generals Mortimer D. Leggett and Giles A. Smith. The left wing was made up of the 14th Army Corps commanded by Major-General Jefferson C. Davis and the 20th Army Corps commanded by Brigadier-General Alpheus S. Williams. The 14th Army Corps had three divisions commanded by Brigadier-Generals William P. Carlin, James D. Morgan, and Absalom Baird. The 20th Army Corps had three divisions commanded by Brigadier-Generals Nathaniel J. Jackson, John W. Geary, and William T. Ward. The Cavalry division was under the command of Brigadier-General Judson Kilpatrick which was broken down into two brigades commanded by Colonel Eli H. Murray and Colonel Smith D. Atkins. General Kilpatrick had a nickname that followed him throughout the war. He was known as "Kill-Cavalry." He earned this name earlier in the war when he had ordered a charge into Richmond that caused quite a few of his men to be killed uselessly.

Casualties from October 1st to the start of the campaign to Savannah on November 16th are as follows. Company A lost Sergeant Elbert Ogle of Victoria due to discharge on November 11, 1864 and also Private Jarvis Konuts of Morse Mills who died of disease on October 25, 1864 and is buried at Marietta and Atlanta National Cemetary, Captain John Reed of Victoria, Missouri was mustered out on November 11, 1864; Company B lost by discharge Private Ezekial Willams of Saint Louis on October 29, 1864; Company D lost their Captain Andrew A. Harrison from Leesburg, Missouri on November 9, 1864 when he was Mustered out; Company E lost Private John W. Wright of Moselle, Missouri was discharged on November 14, 1864 and 1st Lieutenant W. I. Wilson of Cuba, Missouri who was mustered out on November 14, 1864; Company F lost their commander Captain Jonathon W. Evenden of Saint Louis, Missouri who was mustered out on November 9, 1864; Company G lost Corporal William Toetman of Carondelet was discharged by special order on November 11, 1864; Company K lost 2nd Lieutenant William P. Singer of Potosi, Missouri who was mustered out on November 9, 1864 The General Staff lost the services of Surgeon Alexander Reese who was mustered out On November 9, 1864.

The following men were in the hospital at Jefferson Barracks, Missouri on the following dates and were lost to the Regiment. Private Samuel Washburne of Company A was in the hospital in bed 5639 Ward G on October 14, 1864; Private William Still of Company K was in the hospital in bed 5591 Ward I on October 10, 1864 and later died on November 4, 1864. His brother came and picked up his effects sometime in 1865.

CHAPTER 15: ON TO SAVANNAH

General Sherman arrived in Atlanta on November 14th and found that everything that had been ordered to be done, in preparation for leaving, was done. There was enough ammunition for the men that each man would be able to fire two hundred rounds on this trip. Each man carried on his person at least forty rounds in his cartridge box and some of the soldiers carried an additional twenty rounds in their pockets. There was approximately a twenty day supply of rations for the men which amounted to one million two hundred thousand rations. There was not much forage for the horses of the cavalry and artillery, there was also all the horses that were required by the officers and staff men. There was only enough forage to last for five days for these animals. It was expected that there would be plenty of forage to be found on the way to Savannah along with the men who were expected to live off the land. This is no small expectation for the Federals to make. There were approximately sixty-two thousand men who would be going on this march. About fifty-five thousand of these men were in the infantry with five thousand in the cavalry and two thousand in the artillery manning approximately sixty-four artillery pieces. If they ran out of rations, it would take a lot of foraging to feed all these men. A fact that Georgia was going to experience.

The men of the infantry traveled much lighter than they had in previous campaigns. Each man carried his rifle and ammunition, canteen, tin cup, and eating utensils. The men were divided into a mess. The men usually divided into three men groups, that made up the mess, and divided the chores so that each man would do something different in the preparation of the meal, such as gathering firewood and water, another would cook the meal while the other would pack up the mess' gear. These men would sleep under the same tent. Most of the men would carry their own coffee and when ever the column would stop it wasn't unusual for men to fall out, start little fires and start making coffee, the soldiers go-go juice. Each regiment had pack mules or wagons in which to haul cooking and camping equipment so the men would not have to carry it. If the foragers did not find enough food to be distributed to all the men they would then draw on the rations that were being carried.

Major A. J. Seay, commanding the Consolidated Battalion of the 31st and 32nd Missouri Infantry Regiments, wrote in his diary of the preparation and start of the upcoming campaign.

"Sunday, 13. Cold. We march 16 miles and camp 1½ miles S. of Atlanta. The army very mobile and active. Pretty well supplied. We all make 15 miles per day with ease.

Monday, 14. We lay in camp all day, every officer at work on his record. We are trying to reduce our load to the smallest possible amount.

Tuesday, 15. Today we cut loose from our communication and start South from Atlanta relying only on our strength and the Providence of God. The army will number 50,000 muskets and it is buoyant and confident. March 17 miles and have some skirmishing, nice day."[1]

General Osterhaus describes the way most of the army felt to finally be on the way. "Tuesday November 15- Cloudy we are off for Savannah Ho! Leave promptly at 6 1/2. 1. 2. & 3 Div in 1 part, 4 Div starts from the river. We make good time- Some Rebels at Rough and Ready and near Stockbridge- They open artillery and skeddadle. 17 A. C. on wrong road. 1. 2. 3 Div close together 4 Div north of Rough and Ready. 18 miles."[2] If Major-General Peter J. Osterhaus, who was still in command of the 15th Army Corps, was worried about feeding his men in the upcoming march his diary did not give such an indication. Major-General Oliver O. Howard, who was in command of the right wing, had a military force with him which totaled about thirty-three thousand men, which consisted of the 15th and 17th Army Corps. General Sherman, who had kept the route that the army was to march a secret from his army, expected to be in Milledgeville in seven days. He kept the route secret from the men because he had hopes that the Confederates not knowing exactly which way he was going they would have to split their forces up to cover all practical routes to Savannah. This would allow his two wings to meet with forces that in all probability could not defeat either of the wings singularly.

General Sherman finally left Atlanta on November 16th at seven in the morning. He had stayed behind with the 14th

Army Corps to make sure that his forces all withdrew from Atlanta. On a hill outside of Atlanta General Sherman wrote in his memoirs the following lines. "We stood upon the very ground whereon was fought the bloody battle of July 22d, and could see the copse of wood where McPherson fell. Behind us lay Atlanta, smoldering and in ruins, the black smoke rising high in air, and hanging like a pall over the ruined city."(3) With most of the citizens of Atlanta no longer in the city the fires that were set burned down a large part of the city. It was supposed to have been just military establishments that were to have been burned, but some of the soldiers were just a little over zealous and set some of the private residences on fire. "Wednesday November 16- cloudy- threats to rain- Start at 6- 2 via Stockbridge, 3. 1 & 4. via Lee's Mill to McDonough. 2 & 3 Div camp South the others west of town. Fine roads & camps good forage for men & beasts- Rebs fired a little from town, but the fabulous charge of the 29th Mo, Signal Corps and orderlies made them get- 16 miles."(4) General Osterhaus who wrote the above information in his diary recorded this small skirmish that was to become a common occurance throughout the march. Major A. J. Seay wrote in his diary the following, "Wednesday, 16. Nice day. We march 16 miles and go into camp at McDonough the county seat of _____ county. It is a small dilipated town. We get plenty forage for the men and animals and have a nice camp in grassy field. Some skirmishing."(5) As the right wing marched to McDonough and went into camp, the left wing had marched down the Decatur road and then went into camp near Lithonia near Stone Mountain. Once in camp the men began the destruction of the railroad by burning ties and heating rails then wrapping the rails around trees making them unusable.

In a letter dated December 2nd, 1864, Elizabeth Perkerson wrote her brother, Angus M. Perkerson, a Confederate artilleryman who was in General Longstreet's Corps in Virginia, of her experiences during the occupation of Atlanta by the Federal forces. The letter was never delivered to her brother because it was part of the mail that was being burned at a railroad depot that had been captured in Charleston, South Carolina. It was rescued and sent home by Samuel A. Wildman, of the 25th Ohio Infantry Volunteer Regiment. The letter was wrote on the back of an army hospital muster roll that had been picked up at a Federal camp on the outskirts of Atlanta. Following is some exerpts from her five thousand word letter.

"On Sunday morning an officer rode up to the gate and told Ma it she had any chickens she had better put them out of sight, for there was a large body of soldiers coming. And they did come. The ambulance train were passing continually for three days. On Sunday they took pretty well all the chickens, all the bee gums and pretty near all our cooking vessels. We were cooking dinner in the kitchen and they took dinner, pots and all. All we saved was what we snatched from them and brought into the house. They didn't come in. I suppose several of the officers being on the porch all the while restrained them some.

The house never was plundered by them except the ones that come first. They were for a whole week picking up board to build their camps, and when they got done you never saw a place as nicely cleaned up as our was. You couldn't have found a board or a piece of plank as large as your hand on the place. And Till's (a sister) place they didn't leave a symptom of a house or anything else.

They stayed here five weeks. And the maddest set when they found that Hood was in their rear and they had to leave you ever saw, I reckon. They thought that Hood had moved to Macon until he was clean across the river. They moved off then, all except the garrison at Atlanta, and we saw but few afterward. They didn't bother us any more. The picket line was at the Loften place. We knew nothing more what they were doing until they left for good. We kept hoping they would leave, and when we failed to hear their drum for a day or two we would think they were gone, but to our sorrow we would hear it again. After they had been in town about six weeks someone called Pa up one night, and when he went out he found it was some Southern soldiers and they told him that the Yankees were leaving and they were going into Atlanta.

Next morning early a woman that is living in Jim McCool's house sent for some of us to come over, that her child was dying. I went, and when I got there she wanted me to go up after Mrs. Sylvie, so I put out and directly heard cannonading in the direction of town, and when I got in sight of the Holland crossing I could see the guns. Our soldiers were firing from the hill at Sally Whit's place. So I began to feel sort of squeamish, but I ran up to the house, and while I was there they began to bring out our wounded to Sylvie's to dress their wounds. The fight continued for two hours. But finding the Yankees in strong force, our men withdrew. But not until they had driven them in the works round the city.

Well it went on the same way until we began to see large fires in town, and then we were sure they were going to leave. That was on Saturday night. The fires continued until Monday night, and we discovered several large fires in the country. Till and I were on the porch looking at the fires when we heard the clanking of the swords and spurs coming up the road. Well, Ang. if I had seen them building the fire to this house, I would never have felt more certain that we were gone up. But they come up to the poplar tree and turned out in this road and stood a few minutes and went back. In about two hours we heard them coming again. This time they rode up in front of the house and hollered. Till went to the door. They asked her what 'them dogs' were making such a fuss about. She told them she didn't know but supposed they were barking at soldiers that were riding around here, so they turned and went off and we soon discovered they were on picket on top of the hill, and next morning by sun-up the whole road was full of them and we found they were leaving sure enough, but going down the country instead of up.

Well they were passing all day and until 11 o'clock the next day, and since then I felt free as a bird turned out of a cage. They didn't bother us much in passing. They sent in a guard without being asked for it. They told us they were going to play smash with the Confederacy, just going to sweep it out at one lick. But I find they didn't do as much as they calculated. They didn't injure the R.R.'s at all the cars will run up to Jonesborough in a few days. They are building up that road and the West Point Road as fast as they can. I don't know what they are doing on the Georgia Road. We are cut off form the world as yet, but I hope we will be all right soon.

Atlanta is a perfect mass of ruins. I haven't been

there as yet, but from what they tell me it is awful. All the public buildings are gone except City Hall. Whitehall street swept completely. Cousin Dan was up last week. He says he hasn't the shape of a house in the place, although he is coming back just as quick as he can get a place to go into. All the citizens are pushing back. Ang. it would make you sick to see this country now. Pa's place has not got 200 rails on it, and not a building of any kind except the house and smoke house. We have got one hog, four chickens, two old Yankee mules and ten dogs. That is the sum total of the live stock. We have 10 cows down in Clarke County, and Dempse has Gray with him. All or Negroes are at home, and they are the only ones in the neighborhood. You can't imagine how it would take the Yankees down to see a whole gang of old Negroes and children go straggling along. We would tell them to look, yonder are some more of Sherman's reinforcements."(6)

"Thursday November 17, Regt. moved out at Nine o'clock a.m. Day clear and pleasant. Camped near Indian Creek Day clear and mild, roads good country rich."(7) This will give you a perspective of how a regimental officer, 1st Lieutenant William H. Lynch, feels about the march that he was starting on as he wrote the above in his diary. Maybe a lot of the men were apprehensive but they all believed that it was a job to be done and that it would end the war at an earlier date than if they had not made the march. General Osterhaus writes in his diary, "Thursday November 17- fine 3d Div breaks out at 5 1/2, 4-1-2 following- 3d to Indian Spring, 4th near Jackson, 1& 2 near (5 miles west) Indian Spring; good roads, fine weather splendid horses, superb mules and an abundance of grub. The soldiers feel glorious- Some prisoners- 20 miles."(8) It was at Locust Grove, Georgia that the 15th Army Corps split up into two columns to help speed the rate of march. Both columns were marching toward Planters' Factory, on the Ocmulgee River. The 29th Missouri Infantry (mounted) had marched to the river and secured both river banks awaiting the pontoon bridges to march the army across. As soon as the bridges were put up General Smith marched his division across and set up a defensive position on the opposite bank. The left wing on this day marched through the town of Covington and then turned toward the State capitol at Milledgeville. They made the march through Shady

Dale, Madison and Eatonton.

General Osterhaus in his diary, "Friday November 18-Warm- 3d Div crosses the River at Mechanicsville 4th Div goes in afternoon to Iron Spring in order to cross tomorrow- 1 & 2 Div enter Indian Spring in splendid style. 6 miles Rain by night."(9) Major A. J. Seay wrote in his diary the following, "Friday, 18. March 6 miles and go into camp at Indian Springs. Plenty of everything in the country. This place a country village, small and dirty. Some cotton. Warm day."(10) If there was any doubt as to the direction in which the right wing was going to march, it was soon extinguished when General Howard ordered the right wing to turn southeast from Jonesboro in the direction of Milledgeville. The men were allowed to forage liberally. Forage means that assigned men would go out into the country in advance or on the flanks of the column, and take from the people living in the area the supplies that could be used by his comrades in the army. They were informed of the direction and the estimated destination for the day so they could meet the column with the food that they had appropriated. Each brigade commander had the authority to detail a company of fifty men as foragers under the command of one or two officers. Most of the time the men who were given the responsibility of gathering this vital substance for their fellow soldiers required appropriate transportation. The foragers would take a family horse and carriage or wagon to carry the food that was taken. They would take all sorts of meats, cornmeal and poultry. The men would also take some materials that were not food, such as pieces of furniture, clothing men and women's, silverware, money, horses and cattle. The animals were handed over to the brigade to be used in the areas where they would be the most beneficial. The next day they would again start out on foot as the day before and again return usually with another form of transportation.

The foragers, or bummers as they were commonly referred to, were not liked by the Confederates. There was terrible stories of rape, murder, robbery and destruction of private property. The civilian population did not meekly submit to the bummers or foragers. There are stories of having buried valuables in a grave yard in an empty grave. The foragers eventually caught on to this ruse, being informed a lot of the time by slaves, and would dig the valuables up. There were sometimes when they would dig up the fresh graves and actually find a body. The civilians would hide jewels, gold and silverware in gardens, flowerbeds, under floor boards, in beds with sick women in hopes that the foragers would not be brazen enough to search the bed, women would sew them into their dresses, throw the valuables down wells and other places that they thought the Federal soldiers would not search. They would also hide their animals in various places such as in swamps, in clearings deep in the woods that could not be seen from the edge of woods, sometimes in house or under, they would ride them in another direction in hopes of evading the oncoming enemy. Sometimes the foragers were reported to have used torture to get the information out of the people of where these animals might be.

The Confederate army was not overly happy about these bands of robbers running around throughout the country committing these crimes. They made it their business to try and find the foragers and kill them if they could. There are reports of foragers being found killed with notes on their bodies describing that the same fate awaited other such criminals. That is why the foragers were ordered to travel in groups for protection. There are some of these men who were listed as missing in action were killed by roving patrols of Confederate cavalry. A lot of the crimes that were reported by the civilian population was in fact committed by Federal soldiers who were not legal foragers. They were men who saw an opportunity to take advantage to get rich quick, or just a chance to destroy what they saw was the reason that they were fighting in a war, kind of an anger release.

General Osterhaus wrote in his diary, "Saturday November 19- Raining all night- 3d Div to Hillsboro, 2d Div commences crossing at 7 1/2 a.m., 1st Div follows at 9 1/2 a.m., all going to Hillsboro 4th Div falls in rear and marches to Mankinville(not sure of spelling) through to Hillsboro. 17 miles."(11) So far the men had marched a total of seventy-seven miles in five days for an average fifteen and four tenths of a mile a day. This is right on schedule with what General Sherman was hoping to achieve at the start of the march of averaging fifteen miles a day. Major A. J. Seay wrote in his diary, "Saturday, 19. Get up at 5, march at 8. Cloudy and warm. Cross Ocmutgee R. at noon. Get into camp at dark- made 15- I court martial Jim. Druning and dock his pay $16.00."(12) On this date the 17th Army Corps gave the right of way to the 15th Army Corps and they crossed in the order described in General Osterhaus' diary. General Corse's division was ordered to stay behind and destroy the cotton factory and other installations that might be used by the Confederates. The traffic on the road that the Federal army was using became rutted and muddy due to the rain. By the time General Corse was ready to march, it was a muddy quagmire that slowed his march so much that he could only make it to Monticello, Georgia on the next day, while the other three divisions had reached Clinton, Georgia. General Kilpatrick and his cavalry had entered into the town of Clinton on November 19th and were setting up camp for the night. The cavalry, which was a highly mobile force that was used for reconnaissance and to drive the enemy cavalry back from the main column.

General Osterhaus records in his diary, "Sunday November 20- Rains in torrents- 1 & 2 Div camps within 7 miles Hillsboro leave at 6 a.m. 3d Div 1 mile beyond Clinton, 1st Div at Clinton, 2d Div 2 miles north of it and 4th Div at Monticello. 14 miles."(13) Major A. J. Seay. commander of the Consolidated Battalion 31st and 32nd Missouri Infantry Regiments, wrote in his diary the following, "Sunday, 20. Dark and drizzly. Road heavy-we make a hard march. Pass thru Hillsboro and bivouack 11½ miles. In the mud men wet and muddy from head to foot. Jordan are a hard road to travel."(14) The right wing was making its way deep into Confederate territory on its way to Milledgeville. General Joseph Wheeler's cavalry ran into a small group of the Federal cavalry on its way to Clinton. Getting by the Federal cavalry the Confederate cavalry ran right into the 1st Division of the 15th Army Corps on the road just below Clinton. The Confederate cavalry continued to harass the Federal army around the town of Clinton throughout the day without much if any effect. Meanwhile General Kilpatrick had marched in the direction of Macon. The left wing, on this date, were near Eatonton Factory which was about four miles west of the town of Eatonton.

Major A. J. Seay wrote in his diary the following, "Monday, 21. Weather and roads worse than yesterday. It is quite cold, windy and rains all day. We pass thru Clinton Ga. at noon. Draw three days rations and start for Macon, 13 miles distant, have skirmished and crossed the R.R."(15) General Osterhaus wrote in his diary, "Monday November 21- Still raining- Roads almost impassable- 3d Div with all trains to Gordon, 1. to the R R Xing on the Irwinton Road 2d Div on the Macon and Milledgeville X Road 4 Div not heard from. Cut unto the 29th Mo the R.R. by 10 a.m. 10 miles."(16) The movement of the right wing, once they left Jonesboro, was made in such a way as to cause the Confederate forces to think that he was heading to Macon, Georgia. The 29th Missouri Infantry (Mounted) was sent by General Osterhaus to tear up the railroad near Macon, Georgia. The right wing then turned in the direction of Gordon, Georgia on their way toward Milledgeville. General Howard used General Kilpatrick's cavalry with the 1st Division 15th Army Corps as a rear guard to fight off the Confederate army. This force set up defensive positions near Griswoldville, Georgia about nine miles from Macon, Georgia on the Central Georgia Railroad, which was the basic route of the right wing. General Woods and the 1st Division of the 15th Army Corps and the 2nd Division commanded by General Hazen were marching toward Irwinton, Georgia. The 1st Division was the outside column on the march and was under almost constant attack by Confederate army forces. That evening they went into camp near the railroad destroying it during their time there while suffering more attacks. The army destroyed miles of railroad tracks on its march towards Gordon.

1st Lieutenant William H. Lynch, of the Consolidated 31st and 32nd Regiments of Missouri Infantry, says in his diary, "Sunday November 22-Regiment lay in R. Pits (thrown up during the night) and moved at 7 a.m. one mile and again fortified. Remained till 22 in Rifle pits. Heavy firing by our side. Day clear & windy."(17) The 15th Army Corps, accompanied by General Howard, arrived in Gordon. It would take two days for the rest of the column to arrive in and around Gordon. This would give the right wing a little time to recuperate and rest from the days of march. General Osterhaus wrote in his diary, 'Tuesday November 22- Very cold but better than rain Walcutts Brig demonstrates towards Macon- drives the Cavalry splendidly- He however entrenches a line 2 miles in front of the 2 other Brigades of 1st Div. A whole division of Rebs came out and assaulted in the afternoon, then they drive them back after a very hard fight. We took 35 prisoners and had some 30 wounded. 6 miles."(18) Major A. J. Seay wrote in his diary the following, "Tuesday, 22. We build rifle pits move and build again, etc. The 2nd. Brig, Gen Walcott fought nearly all day, repulsing the enemy 4 times with the loss of 1,000 our loss 76.

Very cold, windy, and freezing all day. I move out but not engaged."(19) In a letter dated January 5th, 1865, Private Henry Kuck wrote to his wife from Bridgeport, Alabama telling her that he and four other men from the 31st Missouri Infantry Regiment were being kept at Bridgeport for some reason. There is no record that he ever returned to the regiment.

While General Walcutt and his brigade were getting ready to fight the Battle of Griswoldville the rest of the 15th Army Corps was marching toward Gordon. The rest of the 1st Division was to stay within a reasonable supporting distance of General Walcutt's brigade if the need for assistance should be needed. This is primarily the reason that Lieutenant Lynch wrote of marching only one mile and throwing up rifle pits. On this same day the 76th Ohio Veteran Volunteer Infantry, under the command the command of Colonel William B. Woods, General Charles R. Woods' brother, was ordered to report to General Woods to destroy the railroad near there. They destroyed approximately three miles of the railroad, getting within three miles of Gordon, Georgia, including one large bridge and trestlework over a steam near Gordon Junction. The rest of the brigade moved about three miles farther putting portions of the brigade on both sides of the road from Gordon to Griswoldville, Georgia digging entrenchments.

The Battle of Griswoldville or Griswold Station was one of the tragedies of the war. General Walcutt's brigade was in trenches facing toward Macon, Georgia, General Kilpatrick's cavalry had attacked the Confederate cavalry and drove them into Macon attacking the trenches, even possessing some of them but because of the threat of being overpowered, they retreated to the infantry support in the trenches. The Federal troops had chosen some high ground at the edge of a woods with an open field to their front in which to build breastworks made out of primarily rails. The Federals had a brigade of infantry, cavalry and artillery in this position waiting for what they thought might be a light probing attack from General Wheeler. Confederate General G. W. Smith marched toward the Federal forces with an infantry division and some artillery. They attacked General Walcutt's brigade head on, this brigade was placed across the railroad, the Confederates made several brave charges getting to within fifty yards of the Federal defenses before being driven back. It wasn't what you would call a fair fight. The men under General Walcutt were some of the hardened veterans that had marched all the way from Missouri and other central States and had participated in many battles. This fight was just another fight to the Federals but to the Confederate forces it was a totally new experience. Most of the troops who attacked this Federal brigade were men who were to old for the draft and boys who were to young for the draft. Part of General Walcutt's brigade had been armed with Spencer repeating rifles, which one Confederate soldier had stated, "that the Yankee's could load these guns on Sunday and shoot them all week." General Smith who was an inexperienced officer made these brave but futile charges against a protected enemy. The Confederate artillery was efficient that they put the Federal line in great danger with fairly accurate fire. General Walcutt was wounded in the leg by a piece of shell and had to be carried off the field. He was replaced by Colonel Catterson who was the senior Colonel in the brigade. The casualties in this battle were not very severe for the Federals, they suffered thirteen killed, seventy-nine wounded and two missing. Another reason that the casualties were so low for the Federal was because they were firing from protected positions, and they were being attacked by a force that did not have experience and were poorly led. The attack had lasted throughout the afternoon and in the evening the Confederates departed leaving over three hundred dead men on the field, with estimates of as high as one thousand wounded.

At the start of the battle the 1st Brigade was ordered to go to the support of the 2nd Brigade, but after only marching a little less than a mile, they were ordered to return to their works and extend them on both flanks to cover more than their front. The 12th Indiana Infantry Regiment, under the command of Major E. D. Baldwin, was sent to support the 2nd Brigade, where they went into line on the right of the line and advanced skirmishers meeting the Confederate skirmishers preventing the 2nd Brigade from being flanked. The 12th Indiana Infantry received one man wounded in the advance upon the enemy.

Lieutenant William Lynch wrote in his diary, "Wednesday November 23- Regiment still in R. Pits. Enemy in strong works moved at about noon. 2nd Brigade fought the enemy. Kill and wounded about 1100 feel our loss small."(20) General Osterhaus writes in his diary for the day, "Wednesday November 23- Cold but clear- the Rebs were sorely punished in yesterdays fight; they left about 300 dead and 125 arms on the ground. Walcutt is but slightly wounded. 1 Div moves to 2 m. south of Gordon. 2 Div to 7 miles west of Irwinton. 4 Div within range of Gordon at East."(21) Major A. J. Seay wrote in his diary, "Wednesday, 23. Ice 1 inch thick. We march east 14 miles and put up works. Cold and clear all day. The country poor, hilly, sandy and piney. I have a very bad cold."(22) If you read Lieutenant Lynch's entry in his diary and the entry of Major Seay there seems to be a difference of opinion of what happened that day. There is the possibility that the battalion was in the rifle pits until noon or shortly thereafter. After the Confederate forces left they could have started their march that was referred to by Major Seay. General Smith's division was also destroying railroad track around Gordon making its way toward General Woods Division. General Hazen's division arrived within seven miles of Irwinton, Georgia along with General Woods' division had rejoined the rest of the 15th Army Corps and entrenched south of Gordon, Georgia while in this position they were able to guard almost all roads leading into Irwinton, Georgia. The left wing arrived in Milledgeville, Georgia on this date. General Sherman, who was marching with this wing, wrote in his Memoirs, "At Milledgeville we found newspapers from all the South, and learned the consternation which had filled the Southern mind at our temerity; many charging that we were actually fleeing for our lives and seeking safety at the hands of our fleet on the sea-coast. All demanded that we should be assailed, front, flank, and rear; that provisions should be destroyed in advance, so that we would starve; that bridges should be burned, roads obstructed, and no mercy shown us."(23)

As previously stated Milledgeville was the capital of Georgia. Governor Brown residence was in this city along with the state senate. They were all absent when the Federals marched into the city along with many, of what was considered, important State papers that they didn't want to fall into the Federal hands. The men in the left wing who entered the city took upon themselves to become the new representatives of the state and debated for awhile before bringing it to a vote, the new Georgia legislature voted to repeal the vote of secession. The residences of the town were not burned or molested most of the citizens of the city did no evacuate the city when the Federals had arrived. The next stage of the march, about one hundred miles, was to begin with the left wing to head toward Millen, Georgia from Milledgeville via Sandersville, Davisboro' and Louisville and the right wing was to continue eastward along the Savannah Railroad. There was an alternate reason to march to Millen because there were Federal prisoners in that town. The hope was to reach Millen in time to free the prisoners before the Confederates were able to move them.

"Thursday November 24- Cold, beautiful- 1&2 Div at Irwinton 3d at Gordon 4 Div at the X roads 2 miles south of Gordon."(24) General Osterhaus records in his diary the above. It was a day when the army took to rest itself and get ready for the next stage of the march. General Corse's division finally arrived in Irwinton to at last bring all the divisions of the right wing together again. The next day the right wing was to cross the Oconee River at Ball's Ferry. General Hardee was now assigned to this part of Georgia he did not take any troops with him because the Confederates were counting on the native son of Georgia to cause his fellow Georgians to rally around the flag and beat the invading enemy into the ground.

"Friday November 25- Regt. left Irwinton, Ga. at 7 a.m. marched to and camped near Oconee River. Some cannonading at the river Day clear & mild Country broken a continuous forest of pine."(25) Lieutenant Lynch with the rest of the Consolidated Battalion of 31st and 32nd Missouri Infantry Regiments were on the march arriving at Ball's Ferry where they went into camp and waited their turn to cross over the river. The Confederates had a force which was reported to be at a place called Big Sandy Creek. In order to keep this enemy force from harassing the Federal forces General Osterhaus sent the 29th Missouri Infantry (Mounted) to guard the stream and to burn the bridges that they come to while keeping the Confederate force at bay. They ran into a force at a bridge called Light Wood Knot bridge, driving the Confederates away then burning the bridge. Another mounted force, the 1st Alabama Calvary (Federal) made a reconnaissance and reported that their were Confederate forces across the river on the spot where the Federals planned to cross. General Osterhaus records in his diary, "Friday November 25- fine weather- March towards Balls Ferry- 2 & 1 Div reach the river (Oconee) 4 Div at Milton 3d at Irwinton. 12 Miles."(26) Major A. J. Seay wrote in his diary, "Friday, 25. One year ago today we fought the battle of mission ridge. Move towards the Oconee R. 14 miles and bivouach. A fight progressing at the river. Gen Blair engaged. I have a severe headache. Saturday, 26. We are traveling thru a sand, pine, poor hilly country where peanuts and sweet potatoes grow, but little. Move 4 miles thru swampy quicksand bottom and cross the Oconee R. an camp at Irvings Road ten miles from the R."(27)

Lieutenant William H. Lynch records in his diary, "Saturday November 26-Regt. crossed Oconee River on Pontoons at four o'clock p.m. marched 10 miles & camped at Irwin Crossroads, Ga. Country from Roads good."(28) General Osterhaus, who commanded the 15th Army Corps records in his diary, "Saturday November 26- fine weather- begin to lay pontoon at 9 a.m. and commence crossing by noon 4 Div first, 1 Div after both march to Irwin X roads. 2d cross the river and camp 2 mile east of bridge- 3 Div on other side yet 10 miles."(29). The left wing reached Sandersville, Georgia on November 26th and waited they were notified that the right wing had arrived in a position on the Savannah Railroad even with their position. General Sherman left the left wing on November 27th and joined the right wing to resume the march with them. "Sunday November 27- fine- The 2d Div came up in the morning- The 3rd in the afternoon, the 4th & 1st are partly engaged in destroying the remaining parts and trains march in the afternoon from Augusta Road to the Savannah Road."(30) The plans were for them to march to railroad station No. 11 arriving there the next day on the Savannah Road. All that is recorded in most of the diaries are that the Battalion 31st and 32nd Missouri Infantry Regiments marched fourteen miles that day while according to General Osterhaus he marched seventeen miles. Major A. J. Seay wrote in his diary, "Sunday, 27. Start at noon and march 12 miles thru a poor pine sandy desert and bivouach at Riddleville. The country East of Oconee R. is the poorest I have seen. It is flat and a little swampy in places."(31) The 15th Army Corps had marched to within seven miles of station No. 11 when they went into camp for the day. Whenever the opportunity afforded itself the Federal army would destroy as much of the railroad and any buildings associated with the railroad in order to disrupt communications in Georgia. General Kilpatrick meanwhile had ridden near Waynesboro on the railroad that lead to Augusta from Millen and found General Wheeler and his troops which they engaged in a sharp skirmish. General Kilpatrick had found out the information about the Federal prisoners in Millen and found out that they were no longer there, they had been removed on November 26th.

They returned to General Sherman and reported this information. General Sherman gave them a couple of days in which to give his horses and men a rest and return to find General Wheeler's force and to engage him in battle until General Wheeler decides he has had enough.

"Tuesday November 29- Regt. moved about 12 miles & camped near Summersville, Ga. Day clear & pleasant. Roads good Country poor."(32) Lieutenant William H. Lynch recorded the above in his diary, and had in previous days made mention of the condition of the roads and the shape of the country. The reason it was important to him as well as to any other foot soldier is that if the roads are in good shape it is easier to march and takes less time to reach their destination. But if the roads are bad due to an excessive amount of rain it takes longer to march and it may involve helping to pull wagons or artillery pieces out of the mud they become mired in. Since the soldiers were basically living off the land, if the country was poor that meant that there was not as much food to be taken from the civilian population and the men would be forced to eat the rations that was furnished for them which would not come close to the meals they had eaten since they had left Atlanta. Major A. J. Seay wrote in his diary, "Tuesday, 29. Foggy morning. Poor people live here and are losing all their provisions. We move S.E. 13 miles and bivouach in the edge of a swamp. Hot day, wagons get stuck in the swamp."(33)

"Tuesday November 30-fine weather leave at 7 a.m. march southeast on Southerland's Mill or old Savannah Road. 1 Div 6 miles ahead the roads a complete wilderness, only pine trees the most stupid place God created 17 miles."(34) General Osterhaus, the above is his diary entry, led his 15th Army Corps toward the town of Summerville, Georgia. The 2nd, 3rd and 4th Divisions were moving abreast of each other on this route with the 1st Division leading the way reaching a point where they were only three and one-half miles of railroad Station No. 9 1/2. The 15th Army Corps was getting ready to split again. They had been marching together for the last few miles but now came upon a road system where they could march separately yet within supporting distance of each other. The 29th Missouri Infantry Regiment (Mounted) was to have the job of riding in between these two columns keeping them informed of what was going on. They were to also ride through this area exploring the land in between the columns to find out if there were enemy troops in this area. The 1st Division, under Brigadier-General Charles R. Woods, and the 4th Division, under Brigadier-General John M. Corse were to make up the left column would be taking the inner route. The 2nd Division, under Brigadier-General W. B. Hazen, and the 3rd Division, under the command of Brigadier-General John E. Smith, were to make up the right column and they would be taking the outer route which would make them more susceptible to the attacks of the Confederate forces. "Wednesday November 31- Beautiful warm and nice- the 4th Div starts at 6 a.m. R. R. hope it will meet 1Div. 2 & 3 Div march to Summersville and camp there 18 miles."(35) The 1st Division and the 4th Division finally made contact with each other and went into camp about three and one-half miles from railroad Station No. 9 1/2 destroying all railroad equipment and tracks.

December 1st found the now divided columns leaving their respective camps at seven in the morning marching ten miles. General Osterhaus writes in his diary, "Thursday December 1- beautiful spring day the 2 columns (1 & 4 left) (2 & 3 right) left simultaneously at 7 a.m. and marched about 10 miles. Left camp near Greensbridge to R R 85(I think he means Station 8 1/2)."(36) It must have been a rather routine day marching because there is not much information out about this day. It is routine if you can call marching into enemy territory, without a line of communication with the troops in the rear, and the only other reinforcements that you could call on besides the rest of your wing, was another wing maybe as much as forty miles away a good days march anyway. Being confident that they could beat anything that they come against, it might not have been as scary a proposition as one who sits back and thinks about it. All except for some of the troops of the 1st Division which were ordered to cross the Ogeechee River at Green's Bridge, which had been partially destroyed by the Confederate forces which was repaired, and spent some of the day destroying the railroad around Station No. 8. Major A. J. Seay wrote in his diary the following, "Thursday, December, 1. Weather still quite warm. We have to corduroy much of our roads are moving E. parallel with Ogeeche R. Country very poor. Men get sugar cane which is buried in holes like potatoes. Plenty chickens."(37)

Major A. J. Seay wrote in his diary, "Friday, 2. March 13 miles and cross Scull Creek and bivouack. Plenty of potatoes and pork. Nice day, fine weather, everybody gay and jolly. We have passed no stone since Macon all sand."(38) General Osterhaus wrote in his diary, "Friday December 2- another fine day- the right Column on the Statebrook Rd to Sculls Creek- The left on the Savannah Road across Sculls Creek & camp 1 Brig. to destroy R. R. 15 miles."(39) A pontoon bridge was put across the river near Railroad Station No. 7, most of the divisions of General Woods and General Corse, was put across the pontoon bridge to destroy the railroad station and the track surrounding area. As they marched in this area of the country it changed. It became less populated and the food started to become more scarce. There started to appear a new crop, while the old staples became scarce, it was rice. It was used by both man and beast as a source of food. Many of the troops did not know how to prepare rice as a food. they finally solved this problem by beating the hulls off the rice with their rifle butts on blankets then tossing the rice in the air and the wind would blow the chaff away. It seems a crude way to do it, but whatever works.

General Osterhaus wrote the following in his diary, "Saturday December 3- Cloudy & Threatening- Right had trouble with swamps this is terrible country & worse people."(40) This was a day of rest for the right wing in order to give the left wing a chance to catch up. Its progress was somewhat slower than the right wing. Major A. J. Seay wrote in his diary, "Saturday, 3. The army lays in camp. Our brig goes across Ogeechee R. and tears up R.R. at Paeamours Hill. Comes back and camps on same ground. We have had no frost 24th inst."(41) General Sherman in his memoirs wrote, "On the 3d of December I entered Millen with the Seventeenth Corps (General Frank P. Blair), and there paused one day, to communicate with all parts of the army. General Howard was south of the Ogeechee River, with the Fifteeenth Corps, opposite Scarboro'. General Slocum was at Buckhead Church, four miles north of Millen, with the Twentieth Corps. The Fourteenth (General Davis) was at Lumpkin's Station, on the Augusta road, about ten miles north of Millen, and the cavalry division was within easy support of this wing."(42)

"Sunday December 4- Cloudy but fair- the right at Statesboro (skirmish Reb cav)- The left marches on the Savannah Road to a point 5.5 great road 18 miles."(43) The 15th Army Corps was marching through Bulloch County. They were marching in such a way that they were leaving a ten mile wide area of destruction. When the army went into camp that night they were warned that there was a force of Confederates estimated to be about ten thousand in the area under the command of General Bragg. General Osterhaus advised his division commanders that they should place their divisions flanks next to swamps and creeks in order to enhance their defensive position and deter the Confederates from attacking these flanks. Major A. J. Seay wrote in his diary, "Sunday, 4. Today, we march 18 miles S.E. crossing a wide creek. Country better than usual. We get another wagon, are now 52 miles from Savannah. The regiment was never in better health or spirits. We are destroying all the R.R. from Macon."(44) The 15th Army Corps went into camp near the town of Statesboro establishing a strong defensive position in preparation of the attack that they were expecting to receive that night. A strong picket was set up that night, this was something that had not been practiced for quite a while.

The attack so feared did not materialize that night and the next morning the march was resumed. As is common with soldiers throughout history there was probably quite a bit of complaining about all the wasted time and energy building the useless defensive positions in order to stop a phantom army. General Osterhaus wrote in his diary, "Monday December 5 - fine - Blair had to do a little skirmishing yesterday - Continue to march the left opposite Georgetown (No 8) the right to a point about 4 miles south of the left column. 15 miles."(45) The left column went into camp opposite Guyton which is also known as Station No. 3 on the Railroad, and the right column was about four miles off going into camp at the headwaters on Black Creek. General Wheeler forces were once again active attacking the Federal forces. After a hard, short fight at Statesborough General Wheeler retreated and was not active again for awhile. Major A. J. Seay wrote in his diary, "Monday, 5. Nice day. We move 17 miles S.E. crossing Belcher's Mill creek. Burn the mill-have good roads flat poor country. Men get sweet potatoes, pork etc. No fighting in hearing. Camp 38 miles from Savanah."(46)

1st Lieutenant William H. Lynch wrote the following in his diary, "Tuesday December 6- Rgt moved a few miles & camped. Day clear & pleasant. Some fighting. 1st Bde not engaged."(47) While Major A. J. Seay wrote, "Tuesday, 6. We do not march till P. M. go 8 miles and throw up temporary works near the R. crossing near No. 2 or Edw. Station. Brisk skirmishing at the river. Poor country and piney."(48) The objective for the day was Ogeechee River where they were to capture Jenks Bridge and Wright's Bridge. The 29th Missouri Infantry Regiment (Mounted) was sent to secure these bridges but when they arrived they found that the bridges had been burned. Once this was reported to General Osterhaus he ordered General Woods to send one of his brigades, Colonel Williamson's brigade, to Wright's Bridge to build a foot bridge across the bridge.

"The commanding officer of the brigade (Colonel Williamson) threw a regiment across the Ogeechee, and constructed on the east side breast-works, and then pushed a detachment of fifty men, under Captain McSweeney (Ninth Iowa), to the railroad with orders to break it, and thus prevent the columns on the east side of the river. Captain McSweeney moved directly for the railroad about two miles off and broke in plain view of a train coming down loaded with troops. He then fell back pursued by the rebels, but he kept them in check. When in the evening the enemy attempted to drive Colonel Williamson's men from the breast-works thrown up in the afternoon, he was repulsed with some loss. Our appearance on the flank of the rebels drew their attention to the lower crossing, and they sent a detachment of infantry to Jenk's Bridge, three miles below Wright's."(49)

General Osterhaus wrote in his diary, "Tuesday December 6- fine - remain in position- a reconnaissance by the 29th Mo. gave us control of the bridges near Eden; push 1 Brigade of Woods to Wright Bridge and 1 Brigade of Morgans to Jenks bridge- at Wrights's at little bit of skirmish some Rebs suffered."(50) General Hardee had General Laws division in front of the Federals with some home guard units making a force about ten thousand men. Even though this is a sizable force, it was not any where big enough to fight the Federal force that numbered close to sixty-six thousand. General Laws made a very wise military decision, seeing that he was in danger of having both his flanks turned he withdrew.

"Wednesday December 7 - Concentrated whole command at Jenk's Bridge (Eden) leaving Woods at Wrights."(51) Colonel Oliver's brigade was sent to the Cannouchee River with orders to get possession of a bridge near Bryan Court House. The bridge that Colonel Oliver was to have secured had been partly destroyed and they were unable to get over because there was a strong force of Confederates on the other side. When Colonel Oliver withdrew from his position he left Colonel Stuart and his 90th Illinois Infantry Regiment to keep an eye on the Confederates. Shortly after Colonel Oliver left the 90th Illinois was strongly attacked by the Confederate force. General John M. Corse and his 4th Division arrived giving Colonel Stuart some artillery support with which they were able to keep the Confederates from being successful in their attack. The pontoons were broke out and launched being manned by the 90th Illinois they were able to get a foothold on the east bank of the river. Once the Confederates saw that the Federals had successfully made it across the river they withdrew to a prepared position that was a dam which connected the swamp and the river with some high land. The Confederates in this position could not fire on the men putting the pontoons together, this enabled the pontoons to be laid without having to worry about the men being killed or wounded from Confederate rifle fire.

While the pontoons were being laid General Corse sent some of his men, in boats, across the river, where they made their way toward the Confederate position through the swamp and thick trees. Colonel Williamson's brigade, of the 1st Division, crossed Wright's Bridge and were ordered to march in the direction of the Confederates down the road from the direction of Wright's Bridge and intersected with the road from Jenk's Bridge, in order to be able to attack them in the flank. It was at this crossroads that the Confederates had established strong entrenchment's. Once it was estimated that Colonel Williamson was in supporting position, General Rice who commanded a brigade in General Corse's division, sent the 2nd Iowa Infantry Regiment to attack the Confederates. The 2nd Iowa Infantry rushed upon the Confederate works being able to over come the Confederates, killing and wounding some of them and capturing approximately thirty of them. Once the breast works were taken Colonel Willimson's brigade arrived on the scene. The Confederates were able to retreat to the railroad in their rear. Colonel Williamson's brigade then moved on toward the railroad station with General Rice's brigade moving in the same direction by a different route, the Confederates chose the better part of valor and escaped from the trap. Part of General

Corse's division stayed at the railroad while the rest of his division and the brigade of Colonel Williamson returned to the Confederate breast works at the crossroads before mentioned and established defensive positions.

"Thursday December 8 - March 2 & 1 towards Bryant C. H. 3d Remains at Jenk's Bridge to guard train- 4 Div marches down east side of Ogeechee."(52) The 1st Division minus Colonel Williamson's brigade, marched toward Bryant Court House and were halted about four miles above where the road forks and heads towards Fort Argyle. Major A. J. Seay wrote in his diary, "Thursday, 8. Marched at daylight South 15 miles and bivouach in Bryan Co. between Bld Crossing and Cannouchee R. 5 miles W. of Bryan's C. H. (eden) very few farms and little forage. Only 15 miles from Savannah hear fighting at Canoochee R. bridge. My foragers not yet in. Firing late in the night."(53) The 2nd Division continued on to the bridge that crosses the Cannouchee River near Bryant Court House. The Confederates had built a impregnable defensive position on the south side of the river.

"The enemy's position on the south side of the Cannouchee was naturally strong. Wide, impassable swamps line both sides of that stream, and there are but very few points where a crossing is practicable. There is none below Bryan Court-House, and parties sent twelve miles upstream could not learn of another above. From the Court-House a good road leads to the bridge, but an impenetrable live-oaks swamp is on the other side of it. A levee and three bridges, of an aggregate length of 800 feet, lead through the swamp to the highland; the levee and bridges were swept by a section of artillery and by infantry covered by breast-works."(54)

There seemed to be only one way to get across the river and that was straight across the bridges into the direct fire of the Confederates. Nothing can cause a soldier to lose sleep at night like trying to go to sleep thinking of having to be ordered to cross a bridge into the teeth of the Confederate defenses. General Osterhaus was informed that before the bridges had been built there had been a ferry across the river. A small force was sent to investigate the possibility of making a crossing there. This force ran into a Confederate picket force and a fire fight started that spread to the main Confederate camp which involved not only the infantry but also the artillery. The Confederates had been tipped off about what was going on but instead of strengthening this position at around two a.m. they left their camp. It was later learned that if the Federals had been able to successfully secure a foot hold at the old ferry crossing they would have easily flanked the Confederates.

The 15th Army Corps reached the Gulf Railroad and went into camp about nine miles from Savannah, Georgia. They were fired on by their own cavalry because the cavalry was sure that any troops this close to Savannah had to be Confederate. General Osterhaus writes in his diary the following, "Friday December 9- with 1& 2 Div. Throw up breastworks in preparation for forcing of the ferry- All swamp- Reb's skedaddle- Repair of bridge & lay pontoons destroy RR."(55) Swamps were to become something in which Federal Army was going to be spending a lot of time. Once they entered South Carolina they would then find themselves wading through a lot of swampy territory. Major A. J. Seay wrote in his diary, "Friday, 9. Some cooler. At 8 A.M. we hear heavy guns in direction of Savannah. Think it is guns boats. We hear that Schofield and Hood had a fight on the 2nd near Nashville. $5.00 offered for a paper. We are isolated but do not mean to be so long. We intend to bag the Rebs. We move three miles to Bryan C.H."(56) General Woods sent the 1st Brigade to Eden Court-House where they occupied positions and could cover movements that were being made beyond the Ogeechee River.

"Saturday December 10- all 4 Divisions demonstrate on Little Ogeechee. 1 & 3 on the Canal, 2 & 4 on Savannah Road."(57) Lieutenant William H. Lynch records in his diary the movements of the 31st and 32nd Consolidated Battalion's movement. "Saturday December 10- Rgt. crossed the Ogeechee River on Pontoons crossed the canal and marched about 7 miles towards Savannah and camped. Cloudy day- Heavy Cannonading."(58) Major A. J. Seay in his diary refers to the swamps. "Saturday, 10. Move at 5-cross Ogechee R. and move on Ogechee canal to within 4½ miles of Savannah-then turn right and take position late in the night. This country is the most dismal and swampy I have seen. We came up the tow path. Dark clouds and some rain. Warm."(59) The Confederate forces were not idly sitting back and letting the Federals approach Savannah without contesting their advance. As had been the case since the "March to the Sea" began they had to little of a force to stop the amount of men that was approaching them.

The 1st Division crossed the river at Dillon's Crossing, they started marching eastward following the towpath of the Ogechee Canal. The head of the column marched about nine miles when they struck the Augusta and Darien Road, and bearing to the right continued on about three miles, going into position and fortifying just in case the Confederates should attack them. General Corse's Division, accompanied by General Osterhaus, ran into a fortified position that had a strong artillery force, which after trading a few shots with them it was thought the best not to engage in an artillery duel that night.

Orders for movement had come down during the night for the 15th Army Corps to march on the right side of the Savannah Road. General Corse's Division shifted to the right as near to the Gulf Railroad as the terrain would allow with General Wood's Division to march to the left of General Corse with his left flank to march on the Savannah Road. "Sunday, December 11. Regiment moved to the right about 4 miles and camped Day clear and cool. Some fighting. Regiment not engaged."(60) Lieutenant Lynch recorded in his diary as always the weather which was of vast importance to all the troops even to General Osterhaus who records the weather to be of a different sort than where Lieutenant Lynch is. "Sunday December 11- Rain- Order the Corps to the right of Savannah Road- Roads abominable no sign of the fleet."(61) The roads were slowing the march up so much that General Osterhaus ordered the pioneers to construct a double corduroy track from the front to the rear. Major A. J. Seay wrote in his diary, "Sunday, 11. Fighting on the right yesterday. Very heavy artillery this morning. We start to move and get stuck in the swamp. Come back and run the blockade in the night. Warm and rainey this morning. Freezing cold to-night. Move three miles to the right."(62)

December 12th saw the preparations made for the attack on the Confederate Fort McAllister. The taking of this strong defensive position was important because of one main reason. General Sherman was expecting to make communication with the Federal fleet, who was supposed to be waiting in Ossabaw Sound with supplies and clothing for his army. The navy had no way to be sure that the Federal army was where it was supposed to be so Sherman was anxious to open communications with them. He went to such extremes as to send a couple of men in a canoe and cavalry along the shore. General Howard sent General Hazen's Division to King's Bridge, which was fourteen and a half miles southwest of Savannah, to rebuild it. General Hazen's engineers spent the night rebuilding the bridge. General Howard ordered General Osterhaus to send some of his artillery along with some of his infantry to support General Hazens force. General Osterhaus sent a section of 20-Pounder Parrots along with the 27th Missouri Infantry Regiment. They went to Cheves' rice mill and were later bombing the fort from about three miles away and the Confederates at the fort replied in kind. General Sherman spent the night at the King's house near the bridge. General Osterhaus records in his diary, "Monday December 12- Cool — Movement difficult because of road- it is late in the night when Woods comes up the 3 (Smith's) Div could not make it- some little firing." (63)

General Hazen started his attack on Fort McAllister at about three forty-five p.m. on December 13th, capturing the fort and all that was within it with the loss of only about ninety-two dead and wounded men. The Confederates in held the fort suffered the loss of around two hundred and fifty men the complete garrison which included about fifty men wounded and killed. Shortly after the fort was taken General Sherman had a signal man to signal the ship that the Fort had fallen. General Sherman took a rowboat and went in search of the navy and about six miles below the fort was able to establish communications with the ship and was greeted on board the U.S.S Dandelion.

Lieutenant Lynch wrote in his diary, "Tuesday December 13- Regiment did Picket and Guard Duty, Cannonading around the lines. Day clear and cool- Regiment at dark go on Picket."(64) General Osterhaus writes in his diary, "Tuesday December 13- General Smith goes to No. 1 Station in the R.R.. I sent some of Degress artillery and the 27th Mo. orders to the vicinity of Fort McAllister. No Fleet."(65) General Woods, as well as other division commanders, was at this time looking for the best place to cross the swamps in hopes of forcing General Hardee and the Confederate forces, in the trenches around Savannah, Georgia, into battle at least in hopes that they might retreat. The swamps formed a natural obstacle to hinder the progress of the troops. The swamps had to be waded and any of the dry ground that the troops came to was used for fortifications. Because of the swamps, the Confederates must have felt pretty safe with a smaller force facing a much larger force.

"Wednesday, December 14. Regiment still remained on

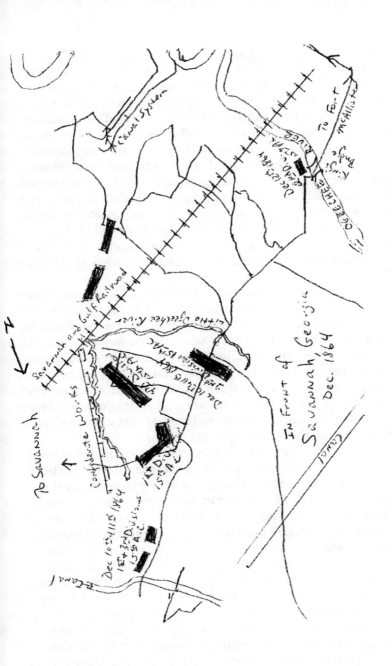

IN FRONT OF SAVANNAH, GEORGIA

Picket- Day cloudy and pleasant. Not much firing along the line. Battalion was relieved at dark."(66) Lieutenant Lynch recorded this in his diary. This has been the second day that they had been on picket. As far as I can tell the 31st Mo. Infantry is still in the approximate location that they were on December 11th. Here is one of General Osterhaus' last entries in his diary for 1864. "Wednesday December 14- fine weather. 2nd Division has gone to McAllister- Fort McAllister taken." (67) Why he waits one day to record in his diary what I would think is probably the most important event that happened at the battle for Savannah is beyond me, especially since the troops were in his Corps. Maybe communication is not what it should have been. It seems that the Federal forces, after a few days off, began to press the Confederates slowly driving them back to Savannah.

John Sherman, the brother of General Sherman, wrote in his "John Sherman's Recollections of Forty Years in the House, Senate and Cabinet. Volume I" the concern he had for his brother in his march to the sea. We are familiar with the results but those who were living at the time were concerned about the army. There was the fear that they would be wiped out or forced to surrender which would not help the war effort and morale at home. General Grant at this time was still being held at bay by the Confederate army at Petersburg. John Sherman wrote the following in his book.

"I was naturally deeply interested in the movements of General Sherman's march to the sea. Towards the close of November we had all sorts of rumors from the south, that General Sherman was surrounded by Confederate troops, that his supplies were cut off, that successful attacks had been made upon his scattered forces. I naturally became uneasy, and went to President Lincoln for consolation and such news as he could properly give me. He said: 'Oh no, we have no news from General Sherman. We know what hole he went in at, but we do not know what hole he will come out of,' but he expressed his opinion that General Sherman was all right. Soon after, authentic information came that General Sherman had arrived at Savannah, that Fort McAllister was taken, and the army was in communication with the naval forces."(68)

The Confederate army around Savannah was effectively

surrounded with nothing but water to their back. The Federal army had been in their current position for a few days. They were trying to find the weakest spot to attack the Confederate. General Sherman had the Confederates in the same position that they had been in around Vicksburg, Mississippi. General Hardee was no General Pemberton. He had served under the command of General Johnston and as will be shown he made a movement that would be similar to what you may expect from General Johnston. Major A. J. Seay writes in his diary for the days of December 14th through 20th, 1864.

"Wednesday, 14.

On duty at the grave yard battery. Very little fighting today, heavy cannonading in the distance. Gen Sherman went down to the fleet last night. All is going well. The troops rejoice, warm.

Thursday, 15.

We are cleaning up preparatory to inspection. I am writing to Ed. and Mother, write 12 pages and then do not tell all I want to. The weather is quite warm. The evergreens on all sides and especially the stately live oak gives the appearance of spring.

Friday, 16.

Capt. Strong inspects and pronounces us in good condition especially the arms. It is hot. Thermoneter stand 81 degrees. All are scarce of food. Men beat out rice with their vessels.

Saturday, 17.

We go on duty at the grave yard battery. Get nobody hurt. Are relieved by 12 Ind. Men are parching corn. Say they are horses and want to be curried.

Sunday, 18.

Nothing done by our artillery, skirmishing brisk as usual and does as little damage as it usually does. I write to Bland and Williams. Work some on my record return. We get some mail.

Monday, 19.

Warm and nice except the heavy fogs which saturate ones clothing blankets etc, every night rendering the air chilly and in my opinion will provide sickness when the winter is past.

Tuesday, 20.

Baldwin and I go to Fort McAlaster-down the Oheeche

see the wreck of the Nashville Lodge on Str. Delaware, on board scooner Ala. Thomas and other sail vessels. Visit the fort. Very strong. We loose our all and have to stay all night. Gay time."(69)

On December 17th General Hardee was extended the invitation to surrender. General Hardee, the old soldier that he was, declined the invitation and another siege was on the way. The Confederates were in a pretty tight spot. The Federal army had formed a line in the shape of a crescent, matching the shape of the lines that the Confederates had established. The 14th and 20th Army Corps of General Slocum's Left wing were facing the Confederates from the Savannah River to the Ogeechee Canal, with the 15th and 17th Army Corps occupying the front from the Ogeechee Canal to the Little Ogeechee River. General Hardee's only hope was to evacuate the town of Savannah, Georgia. The Federals had kept up constant pressure on the Confederate forces in the main trenches in hopes that by doing this they would not be able to freely move around. "Sunday December 18 - Regiment was on Picket. Some cannonading around the lines. Day clear and mild."(70) Lieutenant Lynch records in his diary about some of the pressure that was to keep the Confederates in the trenches.

On December 19th orders were issued for the Federal army to be prepared to attack the Confederates on December 21st. Preparations were being made and the Federals increased the pressure on the Confederates by the pickets and snipers increasing their rate of fire at them during the day and night in hopes of making them keep their heads down. General Woods had advanced his 1st Division of the 15th Army Corps to within one hundred and fifty to two hundred yards of the main line of the Confederates. "Tuesday December 20- Regiment in camp. Day cloudy. Heavy cannonading from our fronts all day. Get orders to be ready to move at short notice."(71) The Federals were afraid that the Confederates would sneak off and their fears proved correct. The Confederates leaving their main guns and ammunition in the forts they evacuated the city of Savannah by a pontoon bridge across the Savannah River. They used the same trick that they had used previously by covering the pontoons with green corn and sand to deaden the noise that marching feet, horses, wagons and artillery made on the wood on top of the pontoons.

During this time General Sherman was receiving letters from General Grant expressing his opinion on what should be the next step of the campaign. General Sherman had hopes of carrying the war into the Carolinas, especially South Carolina, since they had been the start of the rebellion by being the first state to secede from the Union. General Grant in his letters to General Sherman stated that since it was just a matter of time until Savannah was taken, he believed that the next logical objective was the destruction or capture of General Lee's force in Petersburg. This so greatly alarmed General Sherman that he replied to these letters pushing his own ideas. General Grant stated that he thought General Sherman should leave his cavalry and artillery at Savannah, plus enough infantry to help drive off any attacks by the Confederate forces. This also was an incentive for the Confederates to maintain their forces that already were stationed in that area. The rest of his forces were to be boarded on ships and brought up the Atlantic coast where they would land and be able to attack the rear of General Lee. General Sherman responded that he would follow orders but requested General Grant to reconsider. Like the good soldier that he was General Sherman began making plans to follow the requests in General Grants letters.

General Sherman went to Hilton Head to discuss strategy with General Foster while the army was preparing for the assault on December 21st. While General Sherman was returning to Savannah he received word that the Confederates had evacuated the city of Savannah on the night of December 20th and had blown up his ironclads and navy yard. Lieutenant Lynch wrote in his diary the following entry, "Wednesday-December 21- Enemy evacuated town. Regiment moved to Savannah, Georgia. Day clear and windy and cold."(72) It was an exciting day for the Federals because another important city had been taken in the south, but this one was taken without very much bloodshed which made the private soldiers glad since they do most of the bleeding. There was the usual argument of who was the first one in the city with General Geary's Division of General Slocum's wing getting the credit. The 6th Iowa Infantry entered the Confederate trenches before daylight on the right. This allowed them the honor of being given credit as the first unit in the 15th Army Corps into Savannah. Major A. J. Seay wrote in his diary, "Wednesday, 21. Get to Savannah at night ride 18 miles in 2½ hours. The city with all its forts, guns, wealth and great strength is our and its defenders fly for safety into S. Carolina. Another proud day for us and the nation. We go into camp ½ miles west of city."(73) Savannah was now captured and being occupied by the Federal forces, the Confederates had again successfully evaded sure capture by evacuating the town in another night march. It makes a person wonder how upset the Federal soldiers really were that they didn't have to attack an enemy in a fortified position. I think that they were probably grateful.

On December 22, 1864 General Sherman sent the following telegram to President Lincoln:

"Savannah, Georgia, December 22, 1864.

To His Excellency President Lincoln, Washington, D. C. :
I beg to present you as a Christmas-gift the city of Savannah, with one hundred and fifty heavy guns and plenty of ammunition, also about twenty-five thousand bales of cotton.

W. T. Sherman, Major-General"(74)

This message actually reached President Lincoln on Christmas Eve. The battle for Savannah was another great victory for General Sherman and his army, one that had shown that the South was nothing but an empty shell. The Federal army had marched through Georgia and had not hardly slowed down. They had successfully pushed the Confederate army from one position to another with numbers more numerous than the Confederates, but they were operating in a hostile country with no supply line once they had left Atlanta. This was a feat that was unequaled by a force of that size in history. They not only lived off the land but they were able to live very well and destroyed a large part of the country that they marched through. Other states now feared where General Sherman would go next. They knew that what he had done in Mississippi and Georgia, he would surely do in their states.

General Howard and his headquarters soon moved into the city with most of his troops in camps outside the city. General Sherman moved his headquarters into the city also taking residence in the house of a Mister Charles Green. General Osterhaus in a report written on December 26, 1864 gives the following overview of the campaign.

"In order to recapitulate, I state that since October 4 to December 21, the Fifteenth Army Corps had marched, in forty-six actual marching days, 684 miles; cut, corduroyued, and otherwise constructed thirty-two miles of road, and built 1,502 yards of bridge; while it destroyed most effectually over 60 miles of railroad. Being on an exposed flank, the corps had a large share of the fighting during the campaign, and the actions at Allatoona, Griswoldville, and McAllister will shine as bright stars in the record of the corps.

Our losses in battle were comparatively light, and I am happy to state that, thanks to the very efficient and skillful medical corps under the direction of Doctor Niccolls, surgeon of volunteers, not a single man of our wounded was left behind and given up to the mercies of a prejudiced enemy." (75)

The total casualties suffered by the 15th Army Corps on the campaign in pursuit of General Hood's army and the Savanah campaign was a total of one thousand four hundred and fifty-two with the 1st Division suffering a total of ninety-four of these casualties. The whole of the army, in their march to the sea, they fired one million two-hundred and fifty thousand rounds of ammunition for their rifles, three thousand five-hundred and seventy-six artillery rounds. The 1st Division of the 15th Army Corps lost fifteen enlisted men killed, eight commissioned officers and eighty enlisted men wounded and two enlisted men missing giving a total of one hundred and eight casualties. The 1st Brigade, 1st Division , 15th Army Corps, suffered the loss of one man captured and two slightly wounded.

Lieutenant Lynch records his diary, "Saturday- December 24- Battalion went on review through the city of Savannah. Day clear and pleasant. Enemy attack on our pickets north of town."(76) Major A. J. Seay wrote in his diary the following, "Saturday, 24. We have a grand review of 15 A.C. Gen Sherman, Howard, Slocum, Osterhaus, Woods, etal present. A big time, we march in column all over town. The streets are not paved-sand 3-4 inchs deep."(77) General Sherman let the civil authorities continue to run the city much as they had before the occupation by the Federal forces. The only difference was that if there was a clash between civil and military authority the military authority would have the final word. There was the problem of some greedy people from the north coming into the city of Savannah to help get rid of the twenty-five thousand bales of cotton. General Sherman soon got rid of these people, who later became better known as carpetbaggers, a most disgusting group of people who after the war caused much anger, pain and heartache for the people of the south. Overall during the time that the Federals occupied the city before their next march, they were a pretty well behaved bunch of men. This was due primarily to the fact that they were being watched by military police and the camps of the infantry soldiers outside the city. Even though they were in what could be called a safe setting, they were still in the deep south without many sympathizers. This is proven by the entry of Lieutenant Lynch which states there was shooting at his pickets. Colonel Milo Smith of the 26th Iowa Infantry, commanding the 1st Brigade on January 2, 1865, wrote in his report that his brigade was garrisoned at the following locations.

"The Twenty-seventh Missouri Infantry has been on detached service from 14th of December, guarding the rice mill of Doctor Cheves', on the Ogeechee, and in garrisoning Forts Rosedew and Beaulieu, on Wassaw Sound; the Seventy-sixth Ohio Veteran Volunteer Infantry are on duty as provost guard in the city; the Twenty-ninth Missouri Volunteer Infantry, being yet on duty at corps headquarters is encamped in the city; the Twelfth Indiana, consolidated battalion Thirty-first and Thirty-second Missouri, and Twenty-sixth Iowa, are encamped on the left of the Ogeechee road, and inside of the inner works."(78)

The last entries of Major A. J. Seay to finish the year 1864 is included below. It starts with Chritmas day and ends with New Years Eve.

"Sunday, 25.

Dr. and I go to church hear preaching and good music in a fine church. Then we go to the Com. (Rebel) get bacon, flour, spirits fermented, tents, Milton's Paradise Lost and Roscoe's Crime Evidence, biscuits and ham for supper. Improvement on my dinner.

Monday, 26.

Warm Rained hard last night. Wrote to sister. Weather windy and blustery. Rations quite scarce. Much business to do.

Tuesday, 27.

Don't remember what occurred today. A.J. Seay

Wednesday, 28.

I write a spread eagle letter to John and Sue Marsh.

SHERMAN'S MARCH THROUGH GEORGIA: THE REAR GUARD

Massachusetts Commandery Military Order of the Loyal Legion and US Army Military History Institute

Windy and cold. I am officer of the day.

Thursday, 29.

Rainey and blustery, the weather is quite unsettled one day is warm the next is cold, winds blow at a rapid gale.

Friday, 30.

Start foraging at daylight. Go 18 miles on Ohechee after rice for the animals, a nice day-we get Raccoons, oysters and have a nice supper. Boys get plenty of rice.

Saturday, 31.

We move to camp by noon and muster for pay P.M. Heavy wind and some rain."(79)

The losses of the 31st Missouri Infantry Regiment were as follows. Company A lost Private James H. Martin of Victoria who deserted on December 4th; Private Philip R. Haverstick of Victoria who was discharged on December 19th. The losses of the Consolidated Battalion 31st and 32nd Missouri Infantry Regiments, according to the December 1864 morning reports, were as follows. Lieutenant Colonel Samuel P. Simpson who was detached at Headquarters Missouri, per Special Field Order 216 Headquarters Military District of Missouri. Company D lost Captain Jonathon A. McArther who had been absent without leave since November 24th, whose resignation was accepted per Special Order Headquarters Department Army of Tennessee. This seems amazing that the Regiment lost no more men than this since they left Atlanta until they reached Savannah, Georgia. In a report dated December 31, 1864, Major Abraham J. Seay, who was the Battalion commanding officer, officially reported one man missing.

CHAPTER 16:
COLUMBIA, SOUTH CAROLINA IS BURNING

Probably one of the most debated questions of the war and shortly thereafter was the burning of the Capitol of South Carolina. Columbia was a fairly large city in the state of South Carolina and it seems that the attitude of the Federal privates, as well as many of the officers, was one of disgust and anger because South Carolina was the first state to succeed from the Union. They felt hostility towards Columbia and blamed them for the separation from those they loved and the death of many a man who they had served with and many times had grown up with as children. Many of those in later years attribute this common acknowledged fact to be the reason for the wanton burning of this city. General Sherman was mainly charged with the destruction of this city since he was the overall commander on the scene. He continued to defend himself throughout his life by stating that it was the Confederate cavalry, under General Hampton, blaming him for setting fire to the cotton bales to keep them from falling into the hands of the Federal government. The Confederates denied setting any fires, especially to the cotton. The fire destroyed over one third of the city, especially the business district.

General Sherman had a meeting with his generals in charge of the army corps and the two generals in charge of his wings on January 1st, 1865. It was at this meeting that his plans were officially made known to his commanders. General Howard was still to remain the commander of the Right Wing of the Federal army's march to Goldsborough, North Carolina. In his official report General Howard records the following;

"The part assigned to me contemplated the moving of a whole or a part of the Right Wing to Beaufort, S.C., to occupy Pocotaligo by the 15th of January, while the Left Wing crossed the Savannah at Sister's Ferry and moved to Robertsville. I expressed my fear that it would be impossible to transport my whole force in the time required, whereupon the general decided that one corps would be sufficient, and that the rest could cross the Savannah and form a junction with me at Pocotaligo after I had occupied that place."(1)

1st Lieutenant Lynch records in his journal, "From January 1 thru 9th Battalion remained in camp and worked on fortifications, reviewed by General Sherman on 7th."(2) Private Fielding Jenkins Smith records "Sunday, January 1st, 1865- Lay by all day near Swarmat (?), Georgia."(3) This is a short diary and of brief description by Private F.J. Smith who was a member of Company A , Consolidated Battalion 31st and 32nd Missouri Infantry. It has a preface which states, "Preface, This little journal was hastily written by F.J. Smith (Private) Co. A. Consolidated Battalion 31st & 32nd Mo. Infty. It relates primarily to his daily life but is done in stances report to the Regt. and Brigade to which he belongs, it is not written to be criticized by the public eye but for his own and his Parents satisfaction. — — Signed F.J.S. - - P.S. It dates from Jan. 1st to Mar. 31st. 1865."(4)

While around Savannah, Georgia the 15th Army Corps was kept busy. The 17th Army Corps had started to depart the city, preparing to cross the Savannah River into South Carolina, leaving the job of fortifying Savannah to the 15th Army Corps. The reason for the fortification was that the Federals were leaving a force in Savannah to keep it from falling back into Confederate hands. The 15th Army Corps had approximately three thousand infantrymen working on these fortifications besides the pioneers plus another one thousand men were assigned duties working with the chief quartermaster of the military division. While the men knew that they were going to be leaving shortly they also were required to build fortifications for another force. Here are some of the dates that Private Smith recorded in his diary.

"Monday 2nd Jan. A heavy detail to build washes.
Tuesday 3rd on review and inspection of the Brigade.
Wed 4th. on fatique building works.
Thur. 5th. Spent 35 cents. on fatique Again.
Fri. 6th. Drew clothing one pair of pants- - one blouse - one knapsack— one haversack- - one shelter tent. — one pair of socks.
Sat. 7th received of the 15th. A card and spent 25 cents.
Sun. 8th Jan. 1865. Detailed to work but was all sent to Quarters wrote a letter T.W.S. and we had orders

to march at 8 a.m. the next day.

Mon. 9th. did not march spent 65 cents and lay by all
day."(5)

In a letter to the Society of the Army of the Tennesee,
Colonel A. H. Markham writes of the timetable set by General
Sherman to deliver the mail to his army. If you think that this
campaign was not thought out, planned and had a strict time
table this letter may change your mind.

"At daylight on the second morning after the fall of Fort
McAllister, General Sherman called to me from the Fort to tell
me how anxious he was that the little steamboat Island City,
on which I had the mail, should get through the obstructions
of the Ogeeche river, below Fort McAllister, and reach King's
Bridge, where the Army was, so as to deliver the mail to the
soldiers before the dusk of that day. He said: 'I'll go over to the
rice mill, and signal all over the army that you are here with the
mail, and they will all be on the lookout for you.' He did signal.
The army did look out for the mailboat, and before the going
down of the sun of that day the connection between the army,
home, family and friends, had been made. What a bewildering
reception that was. All the boys brought out their canteens to
show them to me, as if they were a novelty. Those quiet fellows
like Poe, of the engineers; Beckwith, of the commissariat, and
Moore of the medical department, laughed and danced to think
that old times had come again. You boys of the Army of the
Tennessee left me again at Savannah, and took up your march
through the Carolinas. But General Sherman made for me,
before leaving, the closest military calculation of the campaign.
He told me about how long to remain in Savannah, then to go
to Charleston. He thought it would be evacuated by the time I
got there. I got there the morning after the evacuation, on the
tug Grant, and breakfasted with General Schimmelpfening, who
was in command."(6)

Major-General John A. Logan finally returned to duty
on January 8, 1865, to lead his 15th Army Corps into South
Carolina. While the 15th Army Corps were in camp performing
the above duties and others the 17th Army Corps, under the
command of Major-General Francis P. Blair began moving on
January 3rd. They had crossed the river and had all gone over
to Beaufort Island by January 11th, as had one division of the
15th Army Corps, waiting for a pontoon bridge to help cross
over into South Carolina.

Now that the idle time is over the expected campaign begins. "Tues. 10th. Marched a few miles camped near Savannah river at a place called Thunderbolt G. on guard."(7) They left the comfort of the works that they had been occupying and marched towards the place where they would embark for the shore of South Carolina. Lieutenant Lynch records in his diary. "Tuesday January 10- Batt. Marches to Thunderbolt and went into camp. Day cloudy- some rain in the evening."(8) When reading the diaries that I use for reference, I have noticed that it seemed that the private didn't seem to enter into his diary the weather as did the officers. It makes one wonder if the private knew that no matter what the weather was he would be in it. The officer was in the same weather as the private but he had to be more concerned with how the weather might affect the watchfulness of those who were on guard duty. He also realized that on the next day they would have to cross the Savannah River whether it was raining or not.

When the march began the Federal army had a strength of a little over sixty-thousand men. While the Confederate forces numbered no more than twenty-five thousand, this includes the depleted Army of Tennesse after the defeat at Franklin and Nashville, Tennessee. The Confederates were operating on guess work trying to decide the real target of the Federals. Since they were uncertain, they distributed their forces to cover all possible main targets; Charleston, Augusta or Columbia. Many of the Confederates, military and civilian, were so sure that the Federals were going to attack Charleston that they sent much of their prized possessions and military goods to Columbia. The reason that they thought that Charleston was going to be the target was because of firing the first shot of the war at Fort Sumpter. The Confederates had to few men to cover effectively all the possible main targets with any hope of stopping the Federals, only of delaying them long enough in hopes of rushing them reinforcements from the other suspected targets.

Private Fielding J. Smith wrote in his diary, "Wed. 11, Got aboard a vessel moved down to the mouth of the river and anchored till morning."(9) It had been awhile since the 31st Missouri Infantry Regiment had spent a night on board any type of boat. Lieutenant Lynch records in his diary, "Wed. January 11- Batt embarked on Steamer Matagorda at sunset."(10) The Confederate soldier's were not laying by, or retreating in disorder in front of this mass of Federal troops. Those who were not around the cities before described, were using the natural obstacles to slow the march of the Federals and hoping to force them to reveal their destination. The Confederates main use of terrain, in which the Federals were to become all to familiar, was to find a swamp and build entrenchments on some good land forcing the Federals to have to wade the swamp under fire. This could be used as a delaying action because generally there were not enough Confederates to turn back a major attack. These forces usually consisted of one or two regiments of infantry, maybe some artillery or manned by a small force of cavalry. Once it was evident that they could no longer safely defend this position without being captured, they would make a retrograde movement to the rear to another prepared position or past another unit already in that position.

Private Fielding Jenkins Smith wrote in his diary, "Thur. 12, Vessel moved out to sea at day light, passed Hilton Head and arrived at Beaufort, S. C. about 2 a.m. marched about 3 miles and camped for the night."(11) This is the first time that the 31st Missouri Infantry Regiment has ever entered the sea or any salt water to get to their destination. All of their previous experience on water had been primarily on riverboats. Lieutenant Lynch recorded in his diary, " Thurs. Jan. 12- Batt arrived at Beaufort S.C."(12)

Private Fielding Jenkins Smith wrote in his diary, "Fri. Jan. 13th 1865 Wrote a letter to father spent 10cts. and moved a short distance."(13) Not much information is found about January 12th and 13th, but soon things were to change. One can only speculate why there wasn't much movement. Primarily it was for the Left Wing to pull even along with the 17th Army Corps so that they could start out on the campaign together. 1st Lieutenant William Lynch wrote in his diary, "Fri. Jan 13- Batt camped near Beaufort. The wagons & mules still at Thunderbolt, GA."(14) During the night a small force of the 17th Army Corps secured a foothold on the other side of a body of water called Whale Branch and intrenched. A six hundred foot bridge was then spanned allowing more men to cross and support the bridgehead.

General Blair's 17th Army Corps crossed Whale Branch on the morning of January 14th at a place called Port Royal Ferry at daybreak. It took quite awhile for the Federals to cross the bridge because of the poor quality of the canvass of the pontoons. After the Federals gathered and formed a line of

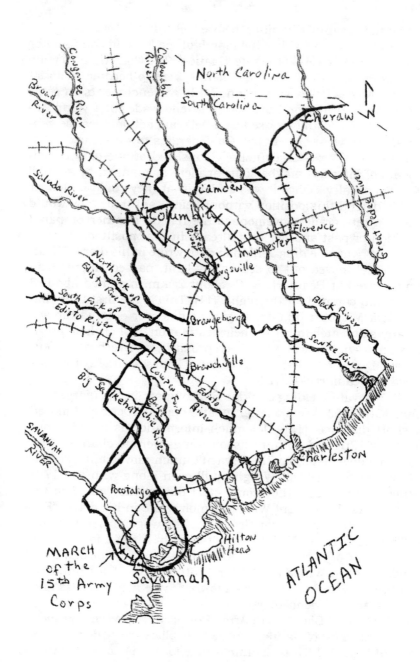

MARCH THROUGH SOUTH CAROLINA'S

battle, they attacked a strong force of Confederates about one mile north of Garden's Corner, South Carolina. General Leggett attacked and turned the left flank of the Confederate force, which consisted of about one regiment and a couple pieces of artillery, causing them to abandon the position. The Federals continued on until they met some more Confederates in a position in front of Stony Creek, which they quickly abandoned without a fight. The Federals then marched on to Poctaligo, South Carolina around sundown which was defended by the same kind of defensive positions as before described. The two skirmish lines then opened up on each other causing between eight to ten casualties. Artillery fire was kept up between the two forces until dark. Private Fielding Jenkins Smith wrote in his diary, "Sat. 14th. moved out crossed a pontoon bridge over x river and camped 10 miles from where we started."(15)

The next morning, much to the relief of the men, the works to their front were found to be abandoned. The Confederates had withdrawn their infantry across the Salkehatchie River putting up defensive positions near a railroad bridge. General Blair's bridgehead began to expand with part of his force making contact with General Foster's forces at Coosawhatchie River and another part was moving towards Robertsville, South Carolina hoping to make contact with the Left Wing. The brigade from the 15th Army Corps was stationed at Garden's Corners holding a cross-roads and watching the crossing of the Combahee River. Near Garden's Corners three pieces of artillery were found buried. Private Fielding Jenkins Smith records in his diary, "Sun. 15th. moved out at 4 a.m. and went 4 miles and had breakfast and came back to a place called Gardens Corner and went into camp."(16)

General Logan received information from General Sherman that the movement on Pocotaligo had been accomplished and that he was to cooperate with General Blair and his mounted infantry. Immediately the 29th Missouri Mounted Infantry and the 7th Illinois Mounted Infantry crossed the Savannah River and headed in the direction of General Blair. Their orders, on the way to link up with General Blair's forces, was to see if the route that they were marching on was solid enough to allow the supply wagons, artillery and infantry to proceed without much difficulty. Private Smith's entry into his diary was, "Mon. 16th. Lay by all day."(17)

"Tues. 17th. The Battalion inspected by the Brigade inspector."(18) While Private Smith and the Consolidated Battalion 31st and 32nd Missouri Infantry Regiments were being inspected, the rest of the 1st Division were doing the same things waiting for the rest of the 15th Army Corps to cross over into South Carolina. The 2nd Division was across the river, they were waiting for the rest of the 15th Army Corps to come across before proceeding on. General Logan was transporting all of his men and material by boat, because this method was taking so long he was ordered to march the rest of his troops by the Union Causeway. Orders were issued to the 3rd Division to be prepared to cross over the pontoon bridge to the South Carolina to begin on the morning of the 19th. As so many times happens, the plans made were to be changed by the weather. On January 18th a rainstorm came into the area and literally soaked and flooded everything. It rained for several days making the pontoon bridge unsafe to cross so General Logan again returned to transporting of his men by boat. Private Smith writes in his diary, "Wed. 18th. Wrote a letter to Mother and N.S."(19) Lieutenant Lynch wrote in his diary, "Wed. Jan. 18- Batt. encamped 17 miles from Beaufort City at Gardens Point-S.C."(20) Major-General John A. Logan wrote in his report dated March 31, 1865,

"A severe storm had set in on the 18th and continued through the morning of the 19th, but General (John E.) Smith succeeded in crossing the pontoon with his Second Brigade and a portion of his ordance train, and stretched out on the South Carolina side of the river, but the rains were so heavy, swelling the streams and bursting the dikes confining the headwaters of the great swamp river, that the roads soon became submerged and entirely impassable for man or team and only navigable in boats. His division was divided- General Smith with a portion of his command beyond the break and the balance still on the Savannah side of the river. Under these circumstances I ordered General Smith to push through to Pocotaligo with his Second Brigade and put the rest of the troops in camp to await a subsiding of the flood. The storm continued during that night and the next morning with unabated fury, and in consequence thereof I received instructions from the commander-in-chief to continue the shipping of my command to Beaufort, reserving the Fourth Division to move by land with the Left Wing of the army. As fast as boats arrived at Savannah they were loaded with troops, animals, and wagons to their fullest capacity, and on the morning of the 26th I transferred my headquarters to Beaufort."(21)

While all this was transpiring with one part of the 15th Army Corps, the rest of the army was quietly probing forward. Lieutenant Lynch recorded in his diary, "Thurs. Jan 19- Batt went out foraging- Had a short engagement with the enemy Drove him about 2 miles & returned to camp with a load of Sweet Potatoes. We receive orders to prepare for an immediate campaign. Each Regiment allowed 1 wagon & but one & will carry 4 boxes ammunition & 3 days forage for the animals. (He) was in mess with Major Seay & Captain Freece."(22) Private Smith records in his diary, "Thur. 19th. I am guard at the Wagons and a detail was sent foraging and being fired on, sent in for reinforcement and the Battalion went out as support and skirmished a little but no one hurt."(23)

Lieutenant Lynch wrote in his diary, "From Jan 19 - 29th remained in camp."(24) Again there was time for rest, to write letters and prepare for the march that was soon coming. The Federal troops were confident, they had taken Atlanta, marched to and captured Savannah and were now in South Carolina, all within six months. The Army of Potomac was still around Petersburg fighting the troops of the Army of North Virginia and General Robert E. Lee. Lieutenant Lynch added to his diary, "Mon. Jan 21- Batt. remained in camp doing picket & guard Duty. Day cloudy & rainy issued clothing to Batt."(25) Private Fielding Jenkins Smith wrote in his diary for these days.

"Fri. 20th. Lay by all day.

Sat. 21st. Wrote a letter to A. P. Jenkins.

Sun. 22nd. Co(mpany). Inspection in the A.M. and dress parade in the P.M.

Mon. 23rd. Co. Drill in the A.M. and dress parade in the P.M.

Tues. 24th. Co. Drill in the A.M. and dress parade in the P.M.

Wed. 25th. Inspection of Arms in A.M. and Dress parade in the P.M.

Thur. 26th. Washed my clothes and got a letter from father and a letter from A. P. Jenkins.

Fri. 27th. Jan. 1865 Wrote a letter to Father and one

to A. P. Jenkins.

Sat. 28th. On wagon guard.

Sun. 29th. On fatique in the A.M. "(26)

Lieutenant-Colonel A. J. Seay, commander of the Consolidated Battalion 31st and 32nd Missouri Infantry, wrote in a report dated March 25, 1865 to Missouri Adjutant-General Colonel Samuel P. Simpson, who was the commander of the battalion before Lieutenant-Colonel Seay, "The battalion broke camp at Savannah, Ga., on the 11th of January; embarked on transports at Thunderbolt for Beaufort, S.C.; marched out the Charleston Railroad to Garden's Corners, at which place our brigade did picket and outpost duty, and had frequent light skirmishes with the enemy."(27)

In his book, Major George W. Nichols Aide-De-Camp to General Sherman, wrote the following:

"Pocotaligo, January 27th.--- From Beaufort to this place there is the same character of country as in the rear of Savannah---impentrable swamps and wide-extended rice-fields, crossed by raised dykes or causeways. The heads of these were defended by finely-constructed forts, where it seems as if a few men could hold at bay an army. How it is that our soldiers are able to outflank and outmanoeuvre the Rebels it is hard to tell, unless we take into account an advantage which is illustrated in an incident which took place on the skirmish-line a short distance from here when the two line came within speaking distance.

Johnny Reb. commenced the conversation with the remark, 'Who the ___ are you? Strikes me you're pushing things!'

'You're right there, Johnny. We're Bill Sherman's raiders; you'd better git--we're coming for you straight!' The Rebels left the same morning.

From present appearances I judge we shall not move for several days. The balmy South, which I have heard of so long, is something we have yet to experience. We have either very heavy rains, or a harsh, biting wind, such as is now sweeping over the country to our great discomfort."(28)

Lieutenant-General W.J. Hardee, in command of Confederate forces in his home state South Carolina, reported, "Enemy have failed so far in all attempts to cross the Combahee.

Indications are that the Fifteenth and Seventeenth Corps, now in Carolina, will cross the Savannah and unite with the column moving toward Augusta."(29) This report was sent and received at ten o'clock p.m., by daylight the next morning the Federals were already moving out. Private Fielding Jenkins Smith recorded in his diary, "Mon. 30th. Started to march at daylight went 12 miles and camped at McPhersonville for the night."(29) 1st Lieutenant William Lynch recorded his views of the move, "Mon. Jan 30- Batt moved at 6: a.m. passed Pocataligo at 11: a.m. a small station on R.R. moved to & encamped at McPhersonville, S.C."(31) The 1st Brigade, 1st Division, 15th Army Corps was now commanded by Brevet Brigadier-General William B. Woods, whose brother was Brevet Major-General Charles R Woods the division commander. The 1st Brigade on this date had a total strength of one-thousand four-hundred and eight officers and men present for duty.

January 31, 1865 was used to send empty wagons to a place called Hatch's Landing to get supplies and other stores. Private Smith records, "Tues. 31st. Lay by all day and night."(32) The day was spent to rest up for the campaigning that was to begin tomorrow in earnest. The army had spent a little over a month doing short marches, improving works, and other camp duties. The anticipation of what was to come may have prevented some from getting sleep, but most of the Federals were seasoned veterans of long campaigns and as is common among veterans, when the opportunity presented itself they were able to rest quite easily.

The march resumed on February 1st, marching to Hickory Hill, on the left of Cooswhatchie River, arriving early in the afternoon. As a sign to come, before the rear of the 15th Army Corps had passed through McPhersonville it was in flames. General Logan wrote in his report about his regret of this circumstance but yet it doesn't mention of trying to find the guilty members of his command who were guilty of arson. Private Smith records in his diary, "Feb. 1st. 1865 Moved about 15 miles and about 2 p.m. formed in a line of Battle at or near a place called Hickory Hill and Co's B and F deployed as Skirmishers and waded a swamp 1/2 to three quarters of a mile in width and from knee deep to hip deep."(33) Lieutenant Lynch wrote in his diary, " Wed- Feb 1- Batt moved about 10 miles & went into camp. 1st Div. was engaged. Had short skirmish with the enemy. Batt. did not fire a gun but the rebels retreated."(34) What was it like to wade through a swamp in the face of the enemy? I don't know and I have a hard time even imagining wading through a swamp with the thoughts of snakes and other swamp creatures that may be in there. It is also winter and though they may be marching in the south it does get cold walking through the water. They were met by a regimental size force of Confederate cavalry under General Joseph Wheeler, who were in strong defensive positions on the bridge and road. General William Woods reports on this skirmish in the Official Records which follows;

"By direction of Brevet Major-General Woods, commanding First Division, I deployed three regiments, namely, the Twenty-seventh Missouri Infantry, Colonel Curly; Thirty-first and Thirty-second Missouri Infantry, consolidated, Major (now Lieutenant-Colonel) Seay and the Twenty-sixth Iowa, Major Lubbers, and throwing forward a strong line of skirmishers, advanced to the bank of the river, intending to cross in line of battle and drive off the enemy. It was found, however, that the passage of the stream was impracticable for so large a body of troops, as the river flowed through a dense cypress swamp nearly a mile wide, in which in many places the water was waist deep. I therefore pushed forward the skirmishers only, who with great difficulty advanced through the swamp, and under the fire of the enemy carried the bridge and causeway and drove him from the opposite bank of the river. In this affair I lost none in either killed or wounded."(35)

It seems that it was another case of the Confederates trying to do too much with to little. There was a whole Army Corps numbering almost fifteen thousand men, coming at a small regiment of cavalry. Not that the Confederates had much choice in the matter, but even if they had defended to the last man they may have delayed the Federals, at the most, maybe another hour. If their main goal was to inflict as many casualties as they could upon the Federals, before they abandoned the position, they failed to even inflict one casualty upon them. If the Confederates could have inflicted some casualties in this skirmish, it probably would have forced some of the wagons to transport the wounded back to Hatch's Landing in order to get them to Savannah to a hospital. Did this show of resistance have any effect on the Federals in the long run, I think not.

While the 15th Army Corps had arrived at Hickory Hill, South Carolina, General Blair and his 17th Army Corps was moving towards Whippy Swamp Creek arriving there shortly after noon. the Confederates had cut trees down so that they obstructed the road so much that they had to be removed before the march could be resumed. They had destroyed five bridges that also had to be replaced before General Mower's Division could move to the other side. There was a skirmish here with about six hundred Confederate cavalrymen. During this skirmish an assistant to General Howard's chief of artillery, Lieutenant William N. Taylor, was severely wounded. General Sherman was marching along with the Right Wing at this time.

"Thurs. 2nd. Marched 4 or 5 miles."(36) This is how Private Smith entry into his diary was made. Lieutenant Lynch recorded the day as, "Thurs. Feb 2- moved about 10 miles & went into camp."(37) I'm not sure how this difference of mileage can be explained by two different men in the same unit, but it is a matter of record. The next few days were basically the same, marching for a short time, going into camp and so forth. Private Smith records in his diary, "Fri. 3rd. Marched about 15 miles and camped near a mill."(38) While Lieutenant Lynch recorded, " Fri. Feb 3- B. moved at 7 a.m. marched about 12 miles & went into camp at _____ Mills on _____ creek. B. was in the advance of Brig. & Division."(39)

While these marches were going on the 17th Army Corps was meeting a determined force of Confederates. The Federals, under General Mower, worked all day in mud and water waist deep in order to be able to approach the Confederate from the right. At dark, two of General Mower's brigades had finally got into position and attacked the Confederate right flank. The Confederates, after a short fight, were able to withdraw having about thirty men captured. General Giles A. Smith had been sent about two miles below and secured a position that prevented the Confederates to send reinforcements from near Broxton's Bridge. The 17th Army Corps suffered around ten or twelve killed and seventy wounded for a total of eighty two. The Confederates suffered a loss of twenty killed, one-hundred and fifty wounded and the above thirty men captured for a total of around two-hundred casualties. This is the severest fight up to this time. If the Federals, who faced these men, had any thoughts that the Confederates would not fight to defend South

Carolina they no longer had to wonder. General Sherman held back the march of the 15th Army Corps so that the head of the corps only reached Angley's Post-Office on the evening of February 3rd, later than General Howard had ordered them to be there. The reason General Sherman slowed them down was so that the Left Wing could keep pace with them.

"Sat. Feb 4- marched about 6 miles & went into camp. All quiet troops in excellent health & full of sport. The Brass Bands play delightfully."(40) Lieutenant Lynch wrote in his diary another day of short marches and not much action. It sounds the same in Private Smith's diary. "Sat. 4th. Moved a short distance Co. A, B, D and F stopped to guard a lane until division train passed, went a distance of 5 miles camped for the night."(41) General Logan moved two of his divisions to Buford's Bridge while the rest of his corps finally entered Angley's Post-Office. One of the divisions sent to Buford's Bridge was the 1st Division. When they arrived there they found that the enemy had evacuated their position with the bridge destroyed and a total of twenty-six lagoon bridges broken down. There was not much fighting except some skirmishers from Confederate cavalry. One of the reasons that the troops did not march very far was in order to be able to move the supply wagons, ambulances and artillery, it required corduroying the roads. This was required because of the ground being swampy and the excessive amount of rain. They would corduroy the roads by cutting down small trees or saplings and lay them in the roadway for a base. This was a backbreaking and time consuming effort not only on the pioneers of the army but on regiments and at times whole divisions were often given this job. It was not a glamorous job but a muddy and dirty one that sometimes required standing in water to cut down the material needed.

Bummers or foragers, were men who were selected or volunteered to go out and try to secure food, forage, livestock and many other items needed by the army. They were to be organized and under the command of an officer, who would be held responsible for the action of the men under him. General Sherman was made famous in Georgia for what his bummers did. They were compared to common criminals stealing not only from the owners of the plantations but also from the quarters of the slaves. They became so proficient in finding the valuables that were hidden that hardly anything escaped their grasp. In South Carolina this activity was continued even though General Sherman had issued orders forbidding entering into a private residence to steal valuables. Many of these men who once had been in the infantry, as bummers could supply themselves with horses for their own transportation with the excess livestock being turned over to the quartermaster of their brigade. There is a down side to this job, they were subject to being killed by the Confederates, who compared them to nothing more than common thieves, rapist and murders. There are instances of the bummers being found tied and shot in execution style or even hanged. It was safer for them to travel in groups.

The 15th Army Corps spent the day of February 5th in crossing the Big Salkehatchie River and went into camp with the 1st Division entrenching and going into camp on the road that leads to Bamberg. The 2nd Division, also entrenching, camped on the road to Barnwell with the 3rd Division going into camp on the road leading to Rivers' Bridge. They didn't entrench so they could go to the support of the 17th Army Corps, who had spent the day crossing the Big Salkehatchie at Rivers' Bridge, in case of an attack by the Confederates. Private Smith wrote in his diary, "Sun. 5th. Marched 4 or 5 miles crossed a stream called the Salkehatchie River on the route and camped for the night."(42) Lieutenant Lynch records in his diary, "Sun. Feb 5- Batt moved at 6 1/2 a.m. crossed Salt-Catcher Swamp at 7 a.m. Marched 5 miles and went into camp."(43)

The 15th Army Corps marched to the Little Salkehatchie River where they were met by a force of Confederate near Duncansville. After a brief fight the Confederates left the area with the bridge destroyed. The bridge, which was around one-hundred feet long, was rebuilt. Once the bridge was done the 1st Division and their supply train moved across the bridge during the afternoon with the rest of the corps following going into camp near a place called the Springtown Meeting-House. During the night it rained hard and continued to rain well into the morning. The 17th Army Corps had reached the Little Salkehatchie River at a place called Cowpen Ford, where they also had to replace the bridge. "Mon. Feb 6- B.(attalion) marched about 8 miles camp at 4 p.m."(44) Lieutenant Lynch in his diary mentioned only what seems to be important to him. Not mentioning the fight or the rebuilding of the bridge. Private Smith writes almost the same thing in his diary, "Mon. 6th. Marched 5 or 6 miles and camped for the night."(45)

Lieutenant Lynch records the following in his diary, "Tues. Feb 7- moved 6 a.m. struck the R. Road at 9 a.m. Destroyed the R.R. & Depot at x near Bamburg & went into camp." (46) Private Smith who was going to be actively working on the destruction of the railroad records, "Tues. 7th. Marched a short distance Struck the Charleston and Augusta R. Road at Bamberg Station and Destroyed the road."(47) The roads were in bad shape from the rain of the previous day. It made the marching of the army slow and miserable and for the troops farther back in the column the marching was even worse. The 1st Division lead the way, followed by the 2nd Division, followed by the 3rd Division. The Confederate troops did not interfere with the march, except where there were a few trees that had been chopped down in Lemon Swamp. The rest of the day was spent in the destruction of the railroad. General Woods' 1st Division went into camp two miles north of the railroad covering the Cannon's Bridge road. General Hazen's 2nd Division went into camp on the left of the 15th Army Corps covering the approaches from Orangeburg and the 3rd Division, under General Smith, was covering the division supply train in a position south of the railroad tracks.

Lieutenant Lynch wrote in his diary, "Wed Feb 8- destroyed R.R. X stayed in camp."(48) Private Smith wrote in his diary for the same day, "Wed. 8th. Our regiment destroyed R.R. all day and lay in our previous camps all night."(49) The 1st Brigade, 1st Division, 15th Army Corps destroyed about four miles of railroad track. The rest of the Right Wing destroyed about twenty more miles of railroad. The infantry tore the tracks up, piling the railroad ties and setting them on fire. They then would take the rails, laying them across the ties getting them hot in the middle and using hooks and levers to bend the rails, twisting them in such a manner that they would no longer be of use to the Confederacy as a rail.

Private Smith records in his diary, "Thur. 9th. Started in the morning marched 10 or 12 miles and camped for the night."(50) Lieutenant Lynch wrote in his diary, "Thurs Feb 9 - marched 12m. camped at R. R. leading to Augusta, Ga."(51) The 1st and 3rd Divisions marched from their camps to Graham's Station going into camp just north of the railroad. From their camps they were able to cover the approaches that the Confederates could use to attack them from Binnaker's and Holman's Bridges. The 2nd Division moved to the crossroads on the Augusta road to near Holman's Bridge, going into camp and facing the river where the bridge had been destroyed. It was here that General Logan finally heard from a staff officer of General Corse and his 4th Division. The 17th Army Corps moved his command to Binnaker's Bridge where the Confederates opened up on them with artillery and infantry rifle fire from across the South Edisto River. General Mower, whose division was in the lead, constructed a raft and got some of his men across the river to form a bridgehead. He then had a pontoon bridge across by 6 p.m. where his men went across, wading through a swamp sometimes up to three feet deep. By 9 p.m. they got into the rear and left of the Confederates forcing them to flee from the entrenchment's.

The 2nd Division, with the division pontoon bridges, crossed the South Edisto River going into camp on the north side of the river. The Confederates had a small force that watched the 2nd Division come up the night before and when the Federals crossed that morning the Confederate forces were gone. The 1st and 3rd Divisions spent most of the day until 3 p.m. destroying the railroad when the 3rd Division moved out to Holman's Bridge to cross the South Edisto River the next morning. Lieutenant Lynch writes in his diary, "Fri. Feb 10 - in camp Division destroyed the R.R."(52) Private Smith records in his diary, "Fri. 10th. Lay by all day."(53) General Corse and the 4th Division were now within supporting distance of the rest of the 15th Army Corps going into camp within six miles of them.

1st Lieutenant William Lynch writes in his diary, "Sat. Feb 11 - moved at 6 a.m. crossed the Edisto River at 11 a.m. marched about 15 mile."(54) Private Smith wrote, "Sat 11th. Marched 15 or 16 miles crossed the South Edisto River and camped at a popular spring."(55) Even though these two diarists don't mention it, on this date their brigade commander mentions destroying another mile section of railroad track near Lee's turnout in his report in the Official Records. General Logan and his 15th Army Corps moved to Popular Springs, sending some of his mounted men to Shilling's Bridge which is about six miles above Orangeburg, South Carolina. The 2nd Division led the march for the 15th Army Corps on the Orangeburg Road with the 3rd Division and the 1st Division following with the 4th Division finally joining the rest of the corps for the first time since leaving Savannah, Georgia. Orangeburg was the next destination assigned the Right Wing by General Sherman.

The 17th Army Corps reached Orangeburg bridge about eleven a.m., this bridge goes over the North Edisto River.

Private Smith wrote in his diary, "Sun. 12th. Marched about two miles and camped for the night."(56) Lieutenant-Colonel Abraham J. Seay mentions in his report to the Adjutant-General of Missouri, that they were continuously pushing the Confederates with frequent skirmishes. One of these skirmishes was described by General Logan in his report.

"The corps moved from camp with General Hazen in the advance, and on reaching the bridge a strong skirmish line was deployed and pushed to the bank of the stream with the design of developing the position to the bank of the stream, while at the same time an effort was made to effect a crossing above and below the bridge. The Second Brigade of the Second Division, Col. W. S. Jones commanding, with a regiment at each of the crossings above and below the bridge skirmished heavily with the enemy in front, and so entirely engaged his attention that the flank demonstration was perfectly successful. A crossing below the bridge having been first effected General Hazen moved the First and Third Brigades of his division to that point and threw them across the river on a hastily constructed bridge of rafts fastened together, but found a dense and tangled swamp still in his front, through which he pushed his command, however, reaching the mainland without encountering resistance. In the meanwhile Colonel Jones had been equally successful in effecting a crossing above the bridge, and, with the Thirty-seventh Ohio Infantry, pushed down on the left bank of the river, taking the enemy's position at the bridge in flank and reverse. The moment the enemy discovered our forces on their side of the river they broke and ran from their works, throwing aside arms and accouterments in their flight. The enemy was driven from his works at 2:30 p.m. The Third Division of the corps was moved in support at the bridge, while the Fourth Division was held in reserve at a point equally distant from the two crossings.

The enemy lost killed 3, wounded unknown, with 80 prisoners and about 200 stands of arms left in our hands; my loss was very slight, being 1 man killed and 5 wounded."(57)

Some of the 15th Army Corps had crossed the river at a place called Shilling's Bridge. The 1st Division went into camp about three-fourths of a mile from Shilling's Bridge camping on the right side of the road facing the North Edisto River with one of the brigades on the Orangeburg Road. Lieutenant Lynch writes in his diary, "Sun. Feb 12- marched at 7 a.m. moved 3 miles & camped at 1 p.m."(58) The 17th Army Corps had reached the objective Orangeburg, South Carolina after flanking the Confederates out of their trenches by the river capturing about a dozen prisoners. They destroyed about six miles of railroad toward Branchville. While in Orangeburg a part of the town was destroyed by fire. There was a stiff wind blowing which helped to spread the fire. It was reported that the fire was started by a Jew who was angry that the Confederate cavalry had tried to burn his cotton. About two hundred bales of cotton that the Confederate cavalry had not destroyed was later destroyed by the Federal soldiers. Another incident of burning of the town that was to continue to follow the Federal Army wherever they marched. Whether it was an accident or on purpose is something that history has judged. My personal opinion is that it was on purpose. The story of the Jew in the community starting the fire seems like an excuse to take the blame from the Federal troops.

On the morning of February 13th the 15th Army Corps moved out on two separate roads on their way to the state capitol, Columbia, South Carolina. They were marching around a swamp called Caw Caw Swamp on two separate roads. The 2nd and 3rd Divisions were marching on a road on the east side of the swamp and the 1st and 4th Divisions were marching on a plantation road on the west side of the swamp. They went into camp that night almost straight across from each other. The 1st Division went into camp at Rucker's Plantation about one mile to the left of the main road facing norhtwest. Lieutenant Lynch wrote in his diary, "Mon Feb. 13 - Batt moved at 5 a.m. crossed the River. Ate breakfast and marched in the direction of Columbia, the capitol of S.C. marched about 18 miles & went into camp at dark."(59) Private Smith wrote in his diary, "Mon. 13th. Started before day crossed the North Edisto marched 15 miles and camped."(60) The two roads that the 15th Army Corps was marching on would bring them together at a place called Sandy Run Post Office.

"Tuesday Feb 14, Batt marched at 7 a.m. moved about

8 miles & camped. Some rain. Batt. was in the advance, skirmished with the enemy. Rebels fell back. Losses not known."(61) This was Lieutenant Lynch's entry into his diary. The 1st Division marched at the head of the column on the plantation road. The 1st Brigade was the lead brigade in the 1st Division with the Consolidated Battalion 31st and 32nd Missouri Infantry Regiments leading the brigade. Being in the lead had its good points and its bad points. The good points were that you didn't have to walk down a road that had been cut up by those ahead of you. The lead unit set the pace. If it was dusty you didn't have to swallow the dust of all those who had marched in front of you. The bad thing is that usually the lead unit was the one who suffered the casualties in a fight with the Confederates who were trying to slow the Federals down. They usually were the first to leave camp and they were responsible for pushing past the campground assigned for the night to make sure that there were no Confederates in their immediate front and if there were, how big they were and what were they doing. Private Smith records in his diary, "Tues. Feb. 14th, 1865, Marched 15 miles and camped for the night and 3 Co's was sent out to the river and Skirmished a little across the river. Shot several shots but we had no one hurt and one or two Co's was sent out as skirmishers but had no one hurt all returning at or before night."(62)

Brevet Major-General Charles R. Woods the 1st Division commander writes in Report No. 12, "That leaving my camp at Rucker's plantation the morning of February 14, I marched by a plantation road as far as Sandy Run. I here struck the State road, and, crossing the stream about 2 p.m., I continued for some four miles farther in the direction of Columbia, reaching with my head of column the camp-ground assigned me at Wolf's plantation at 4 o'clock in the afternoon."(63) Four companies of the 31st and 32nd Missouri Regiments were marching along the road as skirmishers and skirmished with some Confederate cavalry that was acting as an outpost. While the 31st and 32nd Missouri Regiments were exchanging shots, as described by Private Smith, the rest of the brigade and the 1st Division began throwing up earthworks on some hills overlooking the river in case the Confederates tried to attack them that night. A Confederate cavalry force made an attack on the pickets capturing three of them as well as 1st Lieutenant David Rorick, G Company 31st Iowa Infantry, who was picket officer that night of the 3rd Brigade, and was out checking on his picket line.

Described earlier in this book is General Sherman's story of how the 15th Army Corps received its design for its badge, but here is the order taken from the Official Records.

"GENERAL ORDERS, } HDQRS. FIFTEENTH ARMY CORPS, NUMBERS 10 } Baker's Plantation, S.C., February 14, 1865.

1. The following is announced as the badge of this corps: A miniature cartridge-box, black, one-eighth of an inch thick, fifteen-sixteenths of an inch wide, and thirteen-sixteenths of an inch deep, transversely on a field of cloth or metal one and five-eighths of an inch square; above the cartridge-box plate will be stamped or marked in a curve the motto, "Forty Rounds." The field on which the cartridge-box is set will be red for the First Division, white for the Second Division, blue for the Third Division, and yellow for the Fourth Division. For the headquarters of the corps the field will be particolored, of red, white, blue, and yellow.

2. The badge will be invariably worn upon the hat or cap.

3. It is expected that this badge will be worn constantly by everyone to take pride in its badge, surely that has which looks back through the long and glorious line of Wilson's Creek, Henry, Donelson, Shiloh, Russel House, Cornith, Iuka, Town Creek, Chickasaw Bayou, Vicksburg, Jackson, Cherokee Station, Lookout Mountain, Missionary Ridge, Ringgold, Knoxville, Resaca, Kingston, Dallas, New Hope Church, Big Shanty, Kenesaw Mountain, Nickajack, Decatur, the 22nd and 28th of July before Atlanta, Jonesborough, Lovejoy's, Allatoona Pass, Grahamville, Fort McAllister and scores of minor struggles; the corps which had its birth under Grant and Sherman in the darker days of our struggle; the corps which will keep on striking until the death of the rebellion.

4. For the present, good temporary badges can be made easily by any soldier in the corps. When communication is re-established with the North commanders can procure very handsome ones for their men at a nominal cost.

5. Division and brigade commanders are requested

to examine plans for division and brigade flags at these headquarters.

By order of Major General John A. Logan:

Max. Woodhull,

Assistant Adjutant-General"(64)

In his book, Major George W. Nichols wrote about the march that they made through a pine forest that was on fire. His entry was dated on February 14, 1865.

"The magnificent spectacle of a fire in the woods was the striking episode of our march yesterday. The army moved through a tract of hilly country which was thickly clothed with pine forests. Many of the trees were dead, and all had been scarped in order to obtain the resinous substance which formed their fruit and life. Accidentally or otherwise, the dry leaves and pine cones had caught fire, which ignited these trees, and for miles the woods were on fire. It was grand and sometimes awful to see the flames flying over the ground like a frightened steed. As we approached one of these forests, filled with flames and pitch-black smoke, it appeared as if we were about to realize the imaginings of childhood, and see dragons and terrible beasts guarding the entrance to some forbidden ground. Wagons, horsemen, and foot-soldiers, one by one disappeared in the gloom, to reappear here and there bathed in lurid light. Within, the fire singed our hair and clothes, while our maddened animals dashed hither and thither in an agony of fear. There was a terrible sublimity in this scene which I shall never forget; but it subsequently partook largely of the ridiculous when the column went into camp, each man so sooty and begrimed that it was almost impossible to distinguish African from Caucasian."(65)

While the 1st Division was digging in, the 2nd Division went into camp behind the 1st Division and the 3rd and 4th Divisions went into camp two miles behind the 1st and 2nd Divisions.

"Wed. 15th. The whole Battalion detailed as train guards marched 2 miles and lay by until morning."(66) This is the report of Private Smith in his diary for this date. While Lieutenant Lynch wrote, "Wed. Feb 15 - was rear guard for Div. Train. Moved to within 7 miles of Columbia."(67) The 3rd Division was given the task of making a feint at crossing the Great

Congaree River while the main crossing was to be in front of the earthworks of where the 1st Division spent the night. The attack was started at seven a.m. with the 1st Division in the lead. Almost immediately after leaving their works, they ran into the Confederate cavalry skirmishers who started firing at them while withdrawing fighting. The Confederates were easily pushed back, being greatly outnumbered, until they hit their main defensive positions. The rest of the 1st Brigade was in the rear of the 1st Division and took no part in the early part of the fight. Once the Confederates were forced across the stream and had taken up positions in their main line of works, the 1st Brigade then assumed a position on the extreme left flank. In the attack on these works the 1st Brigade had to attack a high ridge that was being held by a unit of Confederate cavalry. The 26th Iowa Infantry, commanded by Major Lubbers, was sent out as skirmishers. The 1st Brigade attacked the ridge driving off the Confederates.

The 1st Division started out early in the morning to drive the Confederates across the river but they put up such a strong resistance that it was sometime in the afternoon before they reached the Little Congaree Creek, which was only about five miles from their starting point. They finally crossed the creek with the 2nd Brigade, under the command of Colonel R. F. Catterson, with orders to try and force the Confederates from their works on their left. The 3rd Brigade, commanded by Colonel George A. Stone, was moved to the left with the same objective as the 2nd Brigade, except they were to drive the Confederates from their works on their right. The 3rd Brigade was successful in driving the Confederates, forcing them to prepared works nearer the main Congaree River. The 2nd and 4th Divisions were brought up in support, with the 2nd Division crossing the creek to the right of the 1st Division. General Woods' men then crossed the creek across a bridge that the Confederates had set on fire but was successfully put out by the Federals. The Confederates had fallen back to their prepared works about two miles closer to Columbia. The Confederates had set up camp on one side of the Congaree River with the Federals on the other.

Lieutenant Lynch records in his diary, "Thurs Feb. 16 - moved about 3 miles & camped. Still train guard."(68) The Consolidated Battalion 31st and 32nd Missouri Regiments again had the duty of train guard. Private Smith records in his diary,

"Thur. 16th. Moved 8 or 10 miles and lay by until 2 o'clock next morning and marched on."(69) The Confederates abandoned their works on the night of February 15th, burning the bridges behind them. Because of the width of the Congaree River at this point the Federals had decided that it would be best to cross the Saluda River and Broad River, which ran together and formed the Congaree River above Columbia, with the pontoon bridges. General Howard was ordered by General Sherman to cross the Saluda River at a factory about a mile from where it ran together with the Broad River. There was a demonstration ordered by the artillery to shell the Confederate artillery across the river that had caused so much trouble the night before. This artillery fire was used to try and keep the Confederates from moving military material from the city and to keep the Confederate soldiers from bunching up. It was during this fire that the Federal artillery fired upon the capitol building itself.

The 2nd Division, 15th Army Corps, under the command of Major-General W. B. Hazen, had the lead of the corps with the 1st Division, 3rd Division and 4th Division following respectively on the assigned march to the Saluda Factory on the Saluda River. General Hazen was ordered to try and force a crossing at this sight in order to get into Columbia. A small force crossed the Saluda River in pontoon boats and secured a small bridge-head on the other side. This afforded more safety for the engineers to build the pontoon bridge across the river. Once the pontoon bridge was completed, a mounted infantry unit was sent across first with some infantrymen following who rushed to the Broad River in hopes of saving it's bridge. They were to late, when the Confederate forces saw the Federals coming they set the bridge on fire. They had covered the bridge with resin and when it was set on fire it went up almost immediately. All the Confederate cavalry had not made it across, those still on the south side of the river made their escape to the north. Meanwhile, the 1st Division was given the task of crossing a brigade across the Broad River by daylight if at all possible. The river was so swift at this point that it was around three a.m. before a rope was finally crossed which allowed a ferry to be set up. Colonel Stone and his 3rd Brigade crossed the river boatload by boatload landing on the other shore and marched in the direction of Coumbia, South Carolina, meeting with little opposition from the Confederate forces in front of the city. The 1st Brigade of the 1st Division spent the night in camp on the banks across the river from Columbia while the 3rd Brigade tried to get across.

Private Smith records in his diary, "Fri. 17th. Crossed the Saluda River before daylight on a pontoon bridge went a few miles and lay up until next morning."(70) The Confederate forces had abandoned the city during the night except for a small cavalry force that was used for delaying the Federals as much as possible. The mayor of Coumbia came out under a flag of truce to surrender the city to the Federals assuring Colonel Stone that the Confederates had evacuated the city. Colonel Stone then marched in and took possession of the city. The 15th Army Corps marched to the east side of the city of Columbia. After marching through Columbia they went to the Columbia and South Carolina Railroad and began throwing up defensive works to their front. Colonel Stone and his brigade had remained in the city as a provost guard. These men who first entered the city received an ample supply of alcoholic beverages to the extent that they became exceedingly drunk. They were in such bad shape that the 1st Brigade was brought in to relieve them of the job of provost guard.

The burning of Columbia, as stated earlier, became one of the most debated discussions during and even well after the war. General Sherman had ordered that certain public buildings be destroyed but to spare all institutions of learning, asylums and private buildings. General Logan notes in his official report that there were men trying to put out fires in cotton bales as they entered the city. One saying, that was attributed to General Logan was quoted as, "Hail Columbia, Happy Land, If I don't burn you, I'll be damned." Whether he really said this or not is any ones guess but it will be seen that Columbia did burn. General Sherman later blamed the Confederate forces of setting these bales on fire to destroy them so they did not fall into the Federals hands. General Howard wrote in his official report that the fires that destroyed over one-half of the city were, if not started, spread by drunken soldiers made drunk by liberal offerings of the citizens of the city, and by criminals who had escaped from the prisons and those escaping an insane asylum. General Howard also notes that it was exceedingly dry and a very stiff wind was blowing. Much to the credit of the Federal soldier who had not become drunk, they were actively trying to put out the fire but without any success. Lieutenant Lynch records in his diary, "Feb 17. - Columbia was evacuated by the Rebs at 9 a.m. 3rd Brig. 1st Div. 15th A.C. were the first to enter the city. Columbia was the Eden of the South. But it was burned by our troops. It was a great military post. Containing a vast amount of supplies."(71) It was the opinion of Lieutenant Lynch that it was definitely burned by Federal troops.

This is the opinion of many of the common soldiers, that the city got what it deserved for being the start of the war that cost the Federal men so many of their friends and family members. Even though over one half the city was destroyed, there were not as many people killed as normally would be expected in a fire of that size.

Major George W. Nichols wrote in his book what he thought was the cause of the fire.

"Various causes are assigned to explain the orgin of the fire. I am quite sure that it originated in sparks flying form the hundreds of bales of cotton which the Rebels had placed along the middle of the main street, and fired as they left the city. Fire from a tightly-compressed bale of cotton is unlike that of a more open material, which burns itself out. The fire lies smouldering in a bale of cotton long after it appears to be extinguished; and in this instance, when our soldirs supposed they had extinguished the fire, it suddenly broke out again with the most disastrous effect.

There were fires, however, which must have been started independent of the above-named cause. The source of these is ascribed to the desire for revenge from some two hundred of our prisoners, who had escaped from the cars as they were being conveyed from this city to Charlotte, and, with the memories of long sufferings in the miserable pens I visited yesterday on the other side of the river, sought this means of retaliation. Again, it is said that the soldiers who first entered the town, intoxicated with the success and a liberal supply of bad liquor, which was freely distributed among them by designing citizens, in an insanity of exhilaration set fire to unoccupied houses.

Whatever may have been the cause of the disaster, the direful result is deprecated by General Sherman most emphatically; for however heinous the crimes of this people against our common country, we do not war against women and children and helpless persons."(72)

At nine o'clock p.m. the 1st Brigade was brought into the city to relieve the 3rd Brigade, but the fire was already burning fiercely. The efforts by the 1st Brigade, 1st Division to bring control of the city was not very effective. There was another brigade brought in to help establish control. They had arrested three hundred and seventy soldiers, two of these were killed and thirty wounded. Major-General Charles R. Woods in his report in the Official Records says that the fire broke out in the western part of the city spreading rapidly because of the high wind that his men didn't have a chance to stop it. The only thing that saved the city itself was the change in wind direction. He said that one-third of the city was destroyed, while his brother, Brigadier-General William B. Woods, 1st Brigade commander, stated that though his men did their best but that only two-fifths of the city was saved from destruction. General William Woods states that upon entering the city they were told by citizens that negro inhabitants were setting fires.

Some of the Confederate reports of the burning was that it was a planned, deliberate destruction of the city. There were reports that when the army came in, the general officers even appeared to look the other way. Some of the citizens of the city said that right when the fires started there was a firing of a rocket and then fires broke out in three separate sections of the city. Even though there was orders not to enter private buildings, there are numerous reports of soldiers who were drunk, came in and rifled through different rooms looking for valuables, told the occupants to leave and then set fires, burning down the residence. Even though they are not confirmed there were reports of some rapes. The soldiers committed wanton acts of destruction of businesses with the taking of anything they wanted. Many people were kicked out of their houses with nothing more than what they had on, which was insufficient for the cold night. The reason there was so much military material, alcohol and valuable possessions in the city of Columbia was that it was shipped there from Charleston and other places in South Carolina because it was believed that Columbia would be the last place the Federal army would go. Many people believed that Charleston was the likely target because of the attack on Fort Sumpter.

Lieutenant Lynch records in his diary, "Sat. Feb. 18th - B.(attalion) moved into the City. Crossed the Broad River at 10 a.m. on Pontoon Bridges."(73) Private Smith writes in his diary, "Sat. 18th. Crossed the Wateree marched through Columbia S.C. and I was on Provost guard in town. Spent 1.60 cents."(74) Major-General O. O. Howard was appointed post commander of all the part of Columbia lying south of Taylor street, Brevet Brigadier-General William B. Woods added to his force the 103rd Illinois, 40th Illinois and 97th Indiana while he appointed Colonel Reuben Williams commander of the 12th Indiana Infantry, as provost-marshal of the post. General Charles R. Woods on this date had a total of eight regiments on provost duty with orders that every enlisted man who was found on the streets after five o'clock p.m., without a pass from his division commander, was to be arrested and confined. The provost guard was to use any means possible to effect an arrest. During the night of the fire the provost guard arrested one hundred and thrity-six enlisted men from the 15th Army Corps and two hundred and sixty men from the 17th Army Corps. It was on this date that one of the unfortunate accidents of the war happened. The Federal were taking all the powder and ammunition from the city and taking it to a ditch outside of the city when somehow the powder exploded killing and wounding one officer and twenty-three men, all being from General John E. Smith's Division.

Sunday, as was common in the army during the Civil War, was again not a day set aside for rest. Lieutenant Lynch writes in his diary, "Sun. Feb 19th - B.(attalion) moved near the Capitol & camped. Brig.(Brigade) was Provost guard. Command destroyed R. Roads & Depots."(75) While Private Smith recorded in his diary the following, "Sun. 19th. Moved camp near the new State house and camped for the night."(76) The army remained in and around Columbia on the 18th and 19th of February, destroying as much material as they could that would prove useful to the Confederacy. They continued to destroy the railroad, military goods that they couldn't use, government buildings and supplies and some mounted men were sent to destroy bridges across the Wateree River. While the 15th Army Corps was destroying material, General Blair's 17th Army Corps was doing the same in a northerly direction. One of the buildings that was completely destroyed was the old United States arsenal that the Confederates took over during the war, using it to manufacture war material for themselves. It was with great joy that this building was torn down because the soldiers felt that the weaponry that was manufactured here had killed or wounded many of their friends.   The estimate of material destroyed would stagger the Confederacy, items that could not readily be replaced.   There was an estimated one thousand bales of cotton destroyed, nineteen locomotives that the South could not afford to loose, twenty-five powder mills, one million two-hundred thousand ball cartridges, one-hundred thousand percussion caps, thousands of rounds of ammunition for artillery, forty-four pieces of different sizes of artillery, thirteen ton's of powder and other items that are to numerous to mention. If the loss of Columbia as a strong hold in the South was acceptable, the loss of so much desperately needed war material was not. General Sherman, by destroying this material of war, was stating that no matter what you do you can not replace everything that has been destroyed. If the object of this march was to show the Confederacy what a hollow shell they had become, then the Federal army under General Sherman was achieving their objective. It was hard on the Confederate soldiers that were from North and South Carolina, who had been fighting at Petersburg for over eight months and had successfully kept General Grant and the Army of the Potomac out of Richmond, to stay in the trenches knowing that there was no way that the Confederate forces trying to stop the Federal army in those states, could even slow General Sherman down let alone protect their families from the outrages that these same troops were reported to have done in Georgia.   It is reported that once the soldiers from these states heard about what General Sherman and his army were doing, that many of them started to desert and went home to see about their families and properties. Who could really blame them. Many of the soldiers knew and would admit that the cause was lost even if some of the senior officers did not.

　　At last the Federal Army was going to leave what was left of Columbia to its citizens, though it was not much.   General Sherman left some food sources for the people in the city and surrounding community that was now destitute.   He left them a lot of rice and salt and even some five hundred head of his beef, though not good quality. Someone said that the only reason that General Sherman left the beef was because they would have died in the next day or two on the march.   He also, after some persuasion from the city leaders, left some arms and ammunition to help deal with the groups of ruffians who were in the countryside and who the city leaders were sure would come in and take what little the Federal forces had left behind. The weapons that were left behind were useless to the army so there was no great sacrifice on the part of General Sherman in this humanitarian gesture. There was a refugee train established for all those who wanted to go north with the army. This refugee train would follow the 15th Army Corps. Not only were the inhabitants of Columbia allowed to go but also those in the surrounding country side. The farther north they went the more the train expanded.

The 15th Army Corps left Columbia on the morning of February 20th. The 1st Brigade 1st Division, who were still pulling provost duty, was the last brigade to leave Columbia. They were the rear guard of the Right Wing and had the responsibility of driving all stragglers and camp followers in the city in front of them. Stragglers is a term that was given to those who always seemed to fall behind to avoid getting in the fight, marching hard or to so some mischief. Many of the buildings that had been burned, were burned by these stragglers. Some of the worst crimes that had been committed had been committed by these individuals. When soldiers were captured behind the march of the army, they were more often than not these stragglers who were looked down upon by men in there own unit because they very seldom nvolved in combat, so they were not sorely missed when captured. Private Smith and Lieutenant Lynch finally agree in their diaries about how far they marched on this date, Lieutenant Lynch's entry. "Mon. Feb 20 - B. moved with command at 2 p.m. marched 14 miles and camped at 2 a.m."(1) The destination was Muddy Springs but when they got there they found that there was not enough water to take care of the needs of the army so they proceeded several miles farther till they reached Rice Creek where they went into camp. The 3rd Division leading the march with the 2nd and 4th Divisions went into camp at Rice Creek while the 1st Division marching on Camden road going into camp near Muddy Springs with the 1st Brigade finally arriving at two o'clock in the morning.

The 1st Division started the next morning about nine a.m. behind the 2nd Division which they followed for about ten miles when they veered off heading towards the town of Longtown, South Carolina going into camp around eight p.m. that evening. The country that they marched through on this day was nothing but sand hills being characterized as miserable poor country. The 2nd Division went into camp at a place called Dutchman's Creek, with the 4th Division camping near by while the 3rd Division went into camp at Harrison's Cross-roads. Lieutenant Lynch recorded in his diary, "Tues. Feb 21 - .moved at 6 a.m. marched 16 miles- camped at dark"(2) Private Smith recorded in his diary, "Tues. 21st. Marched about 16 miles and I was on picket."(3) Private Smith as well as other men in the army had picket duty. Private Smith had been on provost duty in Columbia dealing with armed men who were drunk or committing some crime forcing him to participate in his arrest, then leaving Columbia in the rear of the army forcing those who do not want to go on the march, then marching fourteen miles arriving in camp at two a.m., having to get up and leave the next morning at six a.m. which usually required them to get up at four-thirty a.m., marching sixteen miles arriving in camp, receiving picket duty.

Picket duty requires that a soldier be assigned in front of his unit at a distance that would vary depending on the terrain and the distance of the enemy from their front lines. They were the eyes and ears of the army at night. Their job was to give early warning in case of an attack of the enemy. Many times these men were killed or captured. Sometimes they would spend the night shooting at the enemy pickets or in certain circumstances they would call a truce and meet between the lines and talk, trade newspapers, coffee or tobacco and at times try to figure out why they were fighting each other. Most officers did not agree with this fraternizing with the enemy and when he would get in the area his men on picket would yell at the picket on the other side to keep his head down because he would have to shoot at him.

The 17th Army Corps had been in the town of Winnsborough, South Carolina destroying the railroad joining the 20th Army Corps where they marched towards Poplar Spring Post-Office. The Confederates had destroyed the bridge across the Wateree River and the Federals began to rebuild the bridge. The 15th Army Corps approached the Wateree River at Peay's Ferry where it was directed to cross the river. General Woods' 1st Division was ordered to send a portion of his division on a road to Nichols' Ferry to fake a crossing there in order to draw Confederate troops to that point from Peay's Ferry. The Confederates had not positioned troops at either of these crossings. The pontoon bridges were then laid across the river and the 4th Division went across the river and set up a bridge-head on the other bank to secure a safe crossing spot for the next day. The rest of the 15th Army Corps went into camp at Peay's Ferry.

It was at the bridge crossing the Wateree River that foragers and all other people who were not authorized to be in possession of a horse were to surrender their horses or any other animal used for riding or hauling, before they could cross the bridge. It was an order that was not very popular with either those foragers or bummers who had become accustomed to riding a horse instead of walking or some of their commanding officers who were worried about how they were going to feed their men. All the animals that were deemed worthless were left on the side of the river that the Federals were leaving while those animals that could be used were issued to the cavalry, artillery or used as animals to haul ambulances or supply wagons. Private Smith recorded in his diary, "Wed. 22nd. Marched 9 or 10 miles and camped for the night."(4) Lieutenant Lynch recorded in his diary, "Wed. Feb 22 - moved at 8 a.m. marched to the Wateree River and camped."(5)

The foragers of the 1st Division, 15th Army Corps lost two men being captured, one each, on February 22nd and February 23rd, the one on the twenty-third was captured while out foraging. Even though these soldiers were within supporting distance of a large army they were still subject to be captured by small roaming bands of Confederate cavalry. The average soldier knew, after marching across Georgia and most of South Carolina, that for all intents and purposes the war was over and all that was left was to impress this fact upon the Confederate government and generals.

Lieutenant Lynch wrote in his diary, "Thurs. Feb 23 - moved at sunrise-crossed River at 8 a.m. passed Liberty Hill at about 10 a.m."(6) Private Smith wrote in his diary, "Thur 23rd. Crossed the Wateree River crossed Liberty Hill and marched 16 miles and camped."(7) The 1st and Brigade and the 2nd Brigade left their camp of the night before about seven a.m., while the 3rd Brigade was left at Red Hill, South Carolina awaited orders from the 15th Army Corps. Having marched all day until around five o'clock p.m. they went into camp near Flat Rock Church camping on the Camden Road facing southeast. The 3rd Division had proceeded the 1st Division on the march and also camped near Flat Rock Church, while the 2nd Division was camped near White Oak Creek. The 4th Division being the last division to leave their camp of the night before arrived at

White Oak Creek around ten o'clock p.m.

The 15th Army Corps was still divided into two columns, with the left column consisting of the 1st and 3rd Divisions with the right column was made up of the 2nd and 4th Divisions. Private Smith wrote in his diary, "Fri. Feb. 24th 1865 Marched about 12 miles and camped for the night."(8) While Lieutenant Lynch writes basically the same, "Fri. Feb 24 - moved at 6 1/2 a.m. marched 12 miles went into camp."(9) The march that Private Smith and Lieutenant Lynch talked about might not have been as easy at they make it sound. The 3rd Brigade of the 1st Division, 15th Army Corps was still waiting at Red Hill waiting for the pontoon bridges to be taken up while the other two brigades were marching along, corduroying the road. At one stream they built a bridge of about fifty feet over a small stream that they had to cross. The two brigades of the 1st Division left their camp at Flat Rock Church and marched to West's Cross-Roads where they went into camp for the day facing eastward. General Charles R. Woods stated that his forces had not met any enemy forces during the days march. The 2nd Division went into camp at Hughes' Mills, South Carolina going into camp around four p.m. The 3rd Division went into camp at West's Cross-Roads in the same general area as the 1st Division only they were facing north and northeast. Unlike the 1st and 3rd Divisions who met no resistance, the 12th Illinois Infantry Volunteer Regiment and four companies of the 66th Illinois Infantry Volunteer Regiment of the 4th Division were sent into Camden, South Carolina to destroy any material that may prove useful to the Confederate government. They met a small force of Confederate Cavalry and drove them from the town capturing around sixteen men. They destroyed almost one-thousand bales of cotton along with a lot of flour, meal, sugar, rice, corn, wheat and the buildings where the food was stored. They also cut the telegraph wires disrupting communications. Here they found seven men of the 2nd Division who had been captured while out foraging, but were released and returned to their forces. The 17th Army Corps was marching toward Flat Rock, South Carolina but while on the way ran into unpassable quicksand and had to march farther south and then turn north going into camp about five miles short of Flat Rock.

Lieutenant Lynch recorded in his diary, "Sat. Feb. 25 - remained in Camp. Batt. built breastworks."(10) Private Smith recorded much the same. "Sat. 25th. Lay by all day and strengthened our work."(11) While camped at this spot for the day the Confederate cavalry was moving on the flanks of the 15th Army Corps and were able to capture a few foragers and some of the ever present stragglers. General Logan sent the right column forwards till they arrived about twelve or thirteen miles from Tiller's Bridge, an easy day's march. General Logan had also sent his mounted infantry to secure the bridge which they were able to do surprising and capturing about one-hundred militia-men. Major-General Charles R. Woods sent out a regiment of the 2nd Brigade toward Camden on a reconnaissance and sent another eighty mounted men to the rear looking for the Confederates, but they found none. He reports that some of his foragers had been captured in the direction of Camden, in response General Logan sent him an extract of General Sherman's orders on this subject.

"He (General Kilpatrick) reports that two of his foraging parties were murdered after being captured by the enemy and labeled "Death to all foragers." Now, it is clearly our war right to subsist our army on the enemy. Napoleon always did it, but could avail himself of the civil powers he found in existence to collect forage and provisions by regular impressments. We cannot do that here, and I contend if the enemy fails to defend his country we may rightfully appropriate what we want. If our foragers act under mine, yours, or other proper authority, they must be protected. I have ordered Kilpatrick to select of his prisoners man for man, shoot them, and leave them by the roadside labeled, so that our enemy will see that for every man he executes he takes the life of one of his own. I want the foragers, however, to be kept within reasonable bounds for the sake of discipline. I will not protect them when they enter dwellings and commit wanton waste, such as woman's apparel, jewelry, and such things as are not needed by our army. They may destroy cotton and tobacco, because these things are assumed by the rebel Government to belong to it, and are used as valuable source of revenue. Nor will I consent to the enemy taking the lives of our men of their judgement. They have lost all title to property and can lose nothing not already forfeited, but we should punish for a departure from orders, and if the people resist our foragers I will not deem it wrong, but the Confederate army must not be supposed the champions of any people. I lay these general rules and wish you to be governed by them. If any of your foragers are murdered, take life for life, leaving of each case."(12)

Again General Sherman made a decision that was considered harsh and unjustified but it did effectively curtail the execution of foragers by the Confederates. Many of the Confederates considered it unjustified death by revenge on men who may not have participated in the execution of the Federal foragers.

The 2nd Division reached Sandy Grove Church and went into camp. General Hazen sent a force of his foragers who successfully took Tiller's Bridge. The 2nd Division was also requested to send a brigade to McCaskill's Bridge to take possession of it. General Hazen had not received this order, but did later receive another one with the note that two 15th Army Corps headquarter orderlies had been captured along with some foragers listed as missing. He sent his brigade as ordered. The 3rd Division, in camp at West's Plantation, South Carolina, reported to the 15th Army Corps headquarters that there was a large force of Confederate cavalry in the rear of the army. The 4th Division marched about eight miles and went into camp at a place called Pine Tree Meeting-House where three regiments went to McCaskill's Cross-roads and set up a defensive position.

"HDQRS. FOURTH DIVISION, FIFTEENTH ARMY CORPS,

In Field, Pine Tree Meeting-House, February 25, 1865.

Colonel F.J. Hurlbut,

Commanding Third Brigade:

COLONEL: You will pay particular attention to the posting of your pickets to-night, connecting on the right with those of General Rice, and instructing them to be on the alert and very watchful toward morning. Hampton's cavalry, said to be about 5,000 strong, are in our vicinity, and captured most of the foragers of the First Division to-day and some wagons.

By order of Bvt. Major General J.M. Corse:

L. H. Everts,

Assistant Adjutant-General."(13)

The 29th Missouri Infantry(Mounted), under the command of Major Charles Burkhardt, had captured Tiller's Bridge taking twenty prisoners while taking the bridge and later seventeen more prisoners of the State militia were captured by his vedettes. He had taken the bridge without listing any casualties.

The 1st Division and the 4th Division marched to Tiller's Bridge that crossed Lynch Creek. Private Smith recorded in his diary the days events, "Sun 26th. Marched about 8 miles and camped for the night."(14) Lieutenant Lynch recorded the following in his diary, "Sun. Feb. 26 - moved at 7 a.m. marched near Tiller's Bridge over Lynch's Creek and camped at 1 p.m."(15) Lynch Creek, which normally did not provide a serious obstacle, was to have an impact on the progress of the Federal army. There had been a lot of rain during the previous week causing the water in Lynch Creek to be high enough to endanger the crossing of the supply train to cross the creek. General John M. Corse, commanding 4th Division, was able to get two brigades of his division across the creek by having his men wade across the creek with water coming up to their arm pits while they held their rifles and cartridge boxes over their heads. Once the 4th Division got across, they had a small skirmish with the Confederate forces and then went into a defensive position to hold the bridge. It was decided that it was best that the rest of the forces stay on their side of the creek until the water went down. This was the first serious obstacle that the 15th Army Corps had encountered on the march through South Carolina. While the 1st and 4th Divisions was being detained by Lynch Creek, the 2nd and 3rd Divisions were having the same problems with high water and dangerous bridge crossing at Kelly's Bridge. The 15th Army Corps then went into camp for the next two or three days. While they were waiting the pioneer forces were building a foot bridge across Lynch Creek for the infantry to cross.

The 1st Division camped for the night about one mile from Tiller's Bridge where the Camden and Cheraw road crossed with the Young's Bridge and Bishopville Road. The three brigades faced in three different directions with one brigade front facing Bishopville, which meant they were facing south, another brigade faced west toward Camden and the last brigade was facing north towards Young's Bridge. A Confederate prisoner captured by the 1st Division, told the Federals that Lieutenant-General Hardee's army was probably near Cheraw with the intention of uniting at Charlotte. With the various reports of General Hardee's being in the immediate area there were many warnings about the possible presence of Confederate troops in any area. The orders issued by the 15th Army Corps headquarters was to keep the supply trains safe by having a large and alert guard. Such an order was sent to Colonel George A. Stone whose 3rd Brigade was still guarding the pontoon bridge on its way to get back to the main army. The 2nd Division and the 3rd Division were both camped at Kelly's Bridge, South Carolina on the evening of February 26, 1865. The 2nd Division was able to move two brigades and their battery of artillery across Lynch Creek before the river rose high enough to prevent the crossing of the creek. They were able to put up defensive positions in case the Confederates decided to attack.

The 17th Army Corps, under the command of General Blair, was able to get over the creek and marched a few miles and then went into camp by February 28th. The 17th Army Corps then had to wait for the crossing of the 15th Army Corps. The water had risen so much that it covered the road for almost a mile, rising to a depth as much as three to four feet over the road. The 1st Division of the 15th Army Corps spent the next few days in camp not crossing the bridge across Lynch Creek until March 1st, with most of the division crossing the next day. Lieutenant Lynch records in his diary the following, "Feb 26 & 28 - Remained in camp. - March 1 also. unwell."(16) Private Smith writes the following in his diary about the last days of February. "Mon. 27th. Lay by all day and night. Tues. 28th Mustered for pay but did not move."(17)

It was hoped that once the 1st Division was able to get across Lynch Creek, that they would resume the march to New Market, South Carolina. While there it was hoped that they would be able to fill their supply wagons. On March 1, 1865 the rest of the 4th Division and their supply train moved across the bridge followed by one brigade of the 1st Division along with the headquarters. Once across, the 4th Division moved to Black Creek arriving at eight-thirty p.m. where they went into camp to await further orders and the 1st Division. The 1st Brigade did not cross the bridge but spent another night on the same side of the creek they had been on February 27th and 28th. Private Smith records in his diary. "Wed. Mar. 1st. Moved a short distance late in the evening and I was on Fatique carrying forage."(18) The 2nd Division's, 2nd and 3rd Brigades, marched about six and one-half miles to Kellytown, South Carolina losing two men on the way. These two men were listed as deserters. There was also sixteen prisoners that were captured by this force. The 3rd Division was in the same position that they had occupied since February 26th.

Private Smith records in his diary, "Thur. 2nd. Crossed Lynches Creek marched 8 miles and camped for the night."(19) Lieutenant Lynch reports in his diary, "Thurs. Mar. 2 - Batt. moved with the command crossed Lynch's Creek on Tiller's Bridge. We marched to & went into camp at Black Creek 6 miles."(20) After the delay to get over Lynch Creek the 15th Army Corps was heading toward Black Creek which on this date had deep water for about one hundred and fifty feet but not so deep that it caused a delay for the army as had Lynch Creek. It was believed that the road leading up to the bridge was solid enough to support the wagons and artillery without them sinking and becoming stuck. The main concern would be that the drivers would run off the road causing a delay in the march. This concern proved to be valid. The drivers were unfamiliar with the road and it being under water they could only guess where it lead. The Confederate forces were not present and it was believed that the majority of the Confederates were still across Lynch Creek. The 1st Division finally was able to leave the east side and got across Lynch Creek and marched toward New Market, South Carolina, crossing Big Black Creek which was about as bad as Lynch Creek. They were able to use the pontoon bridges to get across the creek. General Smith and the 3rd Division reached Kellytown where they went into camp for the night.

Lieutenant Lynch recorded in his diary, "Fri. Mar 3 - Crossed Black Creek marched to and went into camp at Cheraw about 22 miles - The town was destroyed by our troops."(21) While Private Smith wrote in his diary, "Fri. Mar 3rd 1865. Crossed a creek before daylight marched 27 miles camped for the night."(22) The 15th Army Corps, and the rest of the Right Wing marched towards Cheraw, South Carolina. The 4th Division was marching down the Camden and Cheraw Road to Thompson's Creek where they went into camp for the night. The 1st and 2nd Divisions marched down plantation roads across from New Market and Society Hill Road to the Cheraw road coming up in position behind 4th Division going into camp at Thompson's Creek near the bridge that the men of the 17th

Army Corps forces had stomped out the fire. The 1st Division went into camp on a high ridge about one mile from the creek facing towards the east. The 2nd Division did not march as far as the 1st Division, marching about eighteen miles going into camp after crossing Juniper Creek, South Carolina. The 3rd Division brought up the rear of the 15th Army Corps and went into camp on the opposite side of Juniper Creek as the 2nd Division, facing southwest, provided rear security for the 15th Army Corps in case of an attack from that direction. The 17th Army Corps had entered the town of Cheraw, South Carolina and there was now no hurry to get the 15th Army Corps into Cheraw. General Sherman had issued orders that it was important that some part of the army get into city of Cheraw as fast as possible. Since this was accomplished it allowed the rest of the army to proceed at a normal rate of march.

The 17th Army Corps entered Cheraw across a bridge on Thompson's Creek following the Confederates, skirmishing with them all the way. The Confederates made it across a bridge over the Pee Dee River setting it on fire successfully destroying it before the Federal soldiers could save the bridge. General Hardee had set up a strong defensive position at Thompson's Creek but the Left Wing had taken possession of the town of Chesterfield the night before and endangered his flank forcing him to abandon Cheraw. The 17th Army Corps captured twenty-eight pieces of artillery and somewhere in the area of two-thousand to three-thousand stands of small arms and a large amount of ammunition.

General Sherman was with the Left Wing and ordered them to cross the Pee Dee River as soon as possible. The Left Wing soon was able to cross the river. He then sent orders for General Howard to cross the Pee Dee River as soon as possible and set up defensive positions. General Sherman was worried about General Johnston bringing his army to the opposite banks and making the crossing of the Pee Dee River difficult and inflicting a large amount of casualties on the Federal force while trying to cross.

General Sherman joined the Right Wing on March 4, 1865. Lieutenant Lynch wrote in his diary, "Sat. Mar. 4 - did not cross Pedee River but moved through at 8 a.m. & went into camp 2 miles above town."(23) Private Smith recorded in his diary, "Sat. 4th Marched 5 or 6 miles passed through Cheraw and camped 1 mile from town."(24) The 1st Division moved into position about one mile above the town facing northeast, with their left flank coming into contact with the right flank of the 4th Division and the right flank of the 1st Division moving into position so that they come into contact with the left flank of the 2nd Division. The 2nd Division while moving into position had one man wounded. The 3rd Division went into position behind the 4th Division.

March 5th was a day of remembrance for many of the men in the Federal Army. It was the day that President Abraham Lincoln was inaugurated for his second term as President. Private Smith wrote in his diary, "Sun 5th. Lay by all day and night."(25) Lieutenant Lynch writes in his diary, "Sun. March 5 - remained in camp - Troops were busily engaged destroying Govt. Stores that our army had captured here."(26) The 1st Division stayed in camp for the day destroying Confederate government material that could be used by the government. Orders were issued for the 1st Division to be prepared to move the next day and proceed to Phill's Creek and go into camp.

The 3rd Division left camp at six-thirty a.m. crossed the Pee Dee River and driving the Confederates in front of them going about four miles before going into camp. They had taken over three grist mills and started grinding grain for their own use. The 2nd Division was to wait until the 17th Army Corps had crossed over, then they were to follow. The 2nd Division finally was able to cross over the river at three p.m. marching on the Fayetteville Road to a place called Harrington's Plantation which was a distance about five miles. While on the way they captured eight Confederate prisoners. The 4th Division remained in camp on the south side of the Pee Dee River with the 1st Division and would remain in that position until all of the known Federal forces in the area had made it across the pontoon bridge. Once everyone else had made it across they were to cross over on the pontoon bridge after which it would be brought across the river.

Private Smith writes in his diary, "Mon. 6th. Crossed Big Pedee River continued 5 or 6 miles & camped for the night."(27) Lieutenant Lynch recorded in his diary basically the same thing, "Mon. Mar 6 - crossed the Pedee in the morning marched about 6 miles and went into camp."(28) There was another tragic accident happened at Cheraw, South Carolina just like the one that happened at Columbia, South Carolina. The troops were destroying ammunition and gun powder by putting them in a ditch when a terrible explosion happened. General Woods' infantry was resting nearby along with some of the supply train when it exploded killing one officer and three men and wounding nine other men along with several teamsters who suffered injuries caused by their teams stampeding. Brevet Brigadier-General William B. Woods as requested handed in this report of the accident:

"HDQRS. FIRST BRIG., FIRST DIV.,
FIFTEENTH ARMY CORPS
Phill's Creek, S.C., March 6, 1865.

Capt. Fred. H. Wilson,

Actg. Asst. Adjt. Gen., First Div., Fifteenth Army Corps:

Captain: In reply to your communication of this date asking detail of the circumstances attending the explosion which occurred near this command to-day, I have the honor to state that the explosion was caused by the accidental ignition of a large quanity of rebel ammunition which had been found in the town of Cheraw and hauled out and thrown in a deep ravine lying between the town and the pontoon bridge. The ammunition consisted of loaded shells and loose powder. The bottom of the ravine to the depth of four or five feet was filled with it, and powder was scattered up the banks of the ravine, and for several rods from the edge of the ravine. While the brigade was halting, having stacked arms to await the passage of the train, of which it was the rear guard, some of the men at a distance of several rods from the edge of the ravine are reported to have applied fire to some small cakes of powder found upon the ground. The fire immediately ran to the edge of the ravine down the bank, and exploded the immense piles of ammunition in the bottom of the ravine. One man of this brigade was killed and 1 officer and 4 men wounded. After dilligent inquiry I am unable to ascertain the names of the men who set fire to the powder, but have no doubt they were ignorant, as I was myself, that any explosive material was in the ravine. The following named officers and men were near the ravine when or shortly before the explosion occurred: Capt. Edward H. Webster and Lieutenant George H. Williams (both of the 12th Indiana Infantry), and Private John Werden, Company G, Seventy-sixth Ohio Infantry. Sergeants Clark and

King, Company A, Twelfth Indiana Infantry have been implicated by rumor in setting fire to the powder. Corporal Sergeant and Private Freeman of the same company and Thomas McPeak, of H Company, all of the Twelfth Indiana Infantry , are reported to know who ignited the powder.

I have the honor to be, captain, very respectfully, your obedient servant,

W.B.WOODS,
Brevet Brigadier-General Commanding."(29)

The 1st Division started leaving camp at six o'clock a.m., crossed the Pee Dee River and marched five miles to Phill's Creek where they went into camp facing eastward. The 2nd Division did not march that day staying in camp at Harrington's Plantation to rest and use the mills to resupply their food source while their pickets and foragers captured eleven prisoners. The 3rd Division also stayed at their camp site of the previous day at Phill's Creek. The 4th Division lost their 3rd Brigade as guard for the pontoon train as far as Springfield. They were the last brigade over the Pee Dee River and stayed with the pontoon train while the rest of the 4th Division marched about eight miles going into camp near Irby's Plantation forming a defensive position on the Sand Hill Road. Meanwhile the Left Wing had crossed the state line and was now entering the State of North Carolina.

Lieutenant Lynch wrote in his diary, "Tues. Mar. 7 - moved at 7 a.m. marched 8 miles & went into camp. Troops foraged freely upon the country."(30) The men in the army did what they did best, they took from those in the community in the path of march. No matter where they went it was just like in Georgia. What one group of men didn't take there was another group right behind them who would take what the proceeding group had failed to take. There was complaints, very valid complaints, about trunks being broken open jewelry and other valuables being taken. General Sherman had to issue orders, again, that this kind of stealing would have to stop or there would no longer be an opportunity to legally forage off the land. Private Smith recorded in his diary, "Tues. 7th. Marched 6 or 7 miles and camped for the night."(31)

The 1st Division had marched along a plantation road crossing over a creek named Naked Creek then they went into camp near a place called Goodwin's Mill, South Carolina on the

Fayetteville stage line. The camp was situated in such a way that they were facing north and east. This was the estimated direction which the Confederates were. They were given orders to start the march at seven o'clock a.m. the next morning along the same road that they were camped on. The 2nd Division went into camp at Crooked Creek at six p.m. after marching about eleven miles that day capturing two prisoners enroute. The 3rd Division followed the 2nd Division and went into camp in the same area with the men being on the north side of the road facing east. The 4th Division went into camp near the 1st Division near Goodwin's Mill marching on the old Stage Road leading directly to Springfield, North Carolina.

Now, South Carolina could finally feel safe and no longer fear the invading armies of the North that included the 15th Army Corps. In certain parts of South Carolina, such as Columbia, it was a feeling that they would not be able to feel for a very long time. South Carolina had indeed felt the cruel hand of the private soldier of the North on the State that many felt was the birth place of so much of the loss that they had been experiencing for so long. Private Smith records in his diary the following, "Wed. 8th. On this date we crossed the state line between S.C. & N.C. and camped after going 8 miles."(32) Lieutenant Lynch wrote in his diary, "Wed. Mar. 8 - moved at 8 a.m. marched 8 miles went into camp at 1 p.m." (33) The Consolidated Battalion of 31st Missouri Infantry and 32nd Missouri Infantry Regiments, had again suffered loss. The losses of the 31st Missouri Infantry Regiment up to March 8th are as follows. Private Thomas L. Porter Company I of Victoria was discharged from Company D 17th Veteran Reserve Corps on January 17, 1865. Lieutenant - Colonel Samuel P. Simpson resigned from his position on January 7, 1865 to become Adjutant-General of Missouri.

CHAPTER 18: BATTLE OF BENTONVILLE, NORTH CAROLINA

The Federal army was becoming more confident every mile they marched. There was a feeling among the common soldier that nothing could stop them. The Confederate forces that they had faced were simply just pushed aside and were not a threat to them at all. It looked like the end was very near with this march and the next object was to help General Grant at Petersburg. The Confederate General Joseph Johnston who was in command had other ideas. He knew that there was no way that they could get enough men to stop the Federal army, but if they could find a portion of the Federal army split off from the other then they could attack them and hopefully destroy them. This was their only hope. The strategy of General Johnston was calling all the forces that he could to meet at a central location where they would be able to carry out his plans. If you remember this was exactly what General Johnston was trying to do at Cassville, Georgia when his plans were not carried out and the ambush of General Schofield's corps was abandoned.

Major George W. Nicols wrote in his book the following:
"Laurel Hill, N.C., March 8th.---The central columns have advanced fourteen miles to-day, and, as was anticipated, without any opposition whatever. The conduct of the soldiers is perceptibly changed. I have seen no evidence of plundering; the men keep their ranks closely; and, more remarkable yet, not a single column of the fire or smoke which a few days ago marked the positions of heads of column, can be seen upon the horizon. Our men seem to understand that they are entering a state which has suffered for its Union sentiment, and whose inhabitants would gladly embrace the old flag again if they can have the opportunity, which we mean to give them, or I am mistaken as to our future campaigns.

Rain has fallen all day with a most disagreeable pertinacity. A more striking and unromantic contrast to the beautiful scenes of yesterday one does not care to imagine, much less experience. Pitching camp in the mud, with a torrent of water drenching every thing about you, and especially yourself, is not the most cheerful business that any person, civilian or soldier, can engage in. There is no help for it, and I am painfully concious that the impertinent floods of water will deluge me before morning, and even waterproof blankets will not save me. Ill to bed, and try to bear it with patience. The camp is still as a grave-yard, except that I have never heard that dead men snore, and our quarter-master (a quiet, good-hearted man when his eyes are open) is snorting under the adjoining fly like a locomotive getting up steam. Now for the blankets and a good sleep!"(1)

Lieutenant Lynch recorded in his diary, "Thurs. Mar. 8 - moved at 7 a.m. marched to Laurel Hill, N.C. 10 miles & went into camp. The Batt. entered the State from S.C. at 20 mins. after 8 a.m."(2) Lieutenant Lynch and Private Smith did not agree on which day they entered North Carolina, but they did agree that they entered North Carolina. Private Smith wrote in his diary, "Thur. 9 Mar. 1865 Started about noon and was all night crossing swamp about 4 or 5 miles wide."(3) It rained during the afternoon causing the troops that were marching to have to corduroy the road, slowing them down considerably. The troops did not reach their destinations for the day due to rain. The 1st Division went into camp at a plantation near Shoe Heel Creek, North Carolina. The reason they went into camp there was that they came upon the 3rd Division's train about four miles from Gilchrist's Bridge and the roads were in such bad condition that they would be almost impassable after the passing of the train. General Woods decided that this was where he would go into camp for the night.

The 2nd Division left camp at six-thirty a.m. marching on the Fayetteville Road reaching Lumber River at Gilchrist's Bridge at eleven-thirty a.m., being followed by the 4th Division. The Confederate forces had destroyed the wagon bridge across the river which forced the Federals to put up a pontoon bridge in order to cross the river. They then marched to Bethel Church near Raft Swamp, where after marching fourteen miles they went into camp. The 3rd Division moved out at nine a.m. and marched along the Fayetteville Road going into camp along the road with the rear of the command arriving in camp at three-thirty a.m. It is sometimes a long day for those who are in the rear. They may be the last to leave a camp but they are also the last to arrive into the new camp, and if the roads are in bad condition, it could take a long time before you finally are able to go to sleep.

The whole 15th Army Corps spent the day of the ninth corduroying the roads so all the men, when they finally were able to sleep, were wet, muddy and tired. Because they did not reach the objectives that were established for the ninth they were ordered to move as soon as possible the next morning and to go as far as possible. On March 10th, something happened to Major-General Kilpatrick that he never lived down. After spending the previous few days fighting Lieutenant-General Wade Hampton's cavalry they went into camp near Monroe's Crossroads. General Kilpatrick had escaped on March 9th from Major-General Matthew Calbaraith Butler when he had captured sixteen Federals of the 5th Kentucky Cavalry, along with their regimental colors, who were part of General Kilpatrick's escort. While General Kilpatrick slept the night away in Mr. Charles Monroe's house, who was not present, General Wade's forces were approaching the Federal force camped at Monroe's Crossing.

The Confederate cavalry attacked the sleeping Federal cavalry just at dawn. It was basically every man for himself with General Kilpatrick escaping in his night shirt. Seeing that his men for the most part were on the run General Kilpatrick didn't even take time to put on his uniform. He beat a retreat for a nearby swamp where Federal cavalrymen were beginning to form, starting to fire at the Confederates from their position causing the Confederates some confusion. Also near a house there were some Federals who were starting to put up a defense. The Federals, after the initial shock, began to reform and started to put up a strong defense and then counterattacked regaining some of the ground that they had just lost. During the battle some of the Confederate cavalrymen had stopped to loot the Federal supply wagons. After the battle had gone on for awhile, the Confederates decided that they had better head on toward Fayetteville leaving their dead behind. Again the Spencer carbines that the Federal cavalrymen carried allowed them to have superior fire power over the Confederate cavalrymen and their single shot carbines. The Federal cavalrymen were beginning to go through their camp when an infantry brigade from the 14th Army Corps was seen marching down the road to come to their assistance. Both sides claimed a victory, General Hampton claimed that he had recovered some of the Confederate cavalrymen who had been Federal prisoners, had opened the roads to enable them to reach Fayetteville, North Carolina, and had inflicted more casualties on the Federals than they had received. General Kilpatrick claimed victory by stating that he had regained the position that they had lost and were in possession of the battlefield and had inflicted more casualties than they had received. No matter how you look at it, General Kilpatrick had escaped by the tails of his night shirt and because of insufficient pickets or guards had been caught asleep in camp at a time when he knew he was in close proximity of the Confederate cavalry force that outnumbered him.

Lieutenant Lynch records in his diary, "Fri. Mar. 10 - moved at 11 o'clock A.M. in the direction of Fayetteville, N. C. marched about 6 miles & went into camp. Roads had to be corduroyed & before we could advance. William R. Hunter - Co. "D" Consolidated died in the evening - he had been sick several days with Fever & Chronic Diarrhea, died in Ambulance."(4) Private Smith wrote, "Fri. 10th. Got breakfast after marching all night and then traveled all day crossing Lumber River on the way."(5) The 1st Division began moving out at five a.m. down roads that required corduroying almost the whole way. They finally reached a stage road where they saw the 4th Division already marching on it. It took the 1st Division two hours to cross the Lumber River going into camp two miles beyond Randalsville going into camp around eight p.m. after having marched twelve miles that day. When they went into camp the troops set up defensive positions facing towards the south and southwest.

The 2nd Division managed to march about six miles on March 10th having to corduroy the whole way. The 3rd Division went into camp on the west side of Big Raft Swamp after crossing this swamp and another swamp which was called Lowry Swamp marching only four miles that day having to corduroy three of those miles. They went into camp on ground that they had finally found that was solid enough to hold up under the weight of their wagon train. The 4th Division went into camp near Juniper Creek after marching twelve miles having to corduroy four of them. The men were tired and worn out after these two days of some of the hardest work that many of these men had done for a long time.

Private Smith records in his diary, "Sat. 11th. Was all day marching 8 miles and working on the road. Co. Foraging it."(6) Lieutenant Lynch recorded in his diary, "Sat. Mar 11 - moved at 6 a.m.- Roads very muddy crossed Lowery Swamp in the evening & marched during the day only 10 miles. W. R. Hunter was buried in a field on the right hand side of the road leading from Laurel Hill a few miles from that place. We camped in Robinson Co., N.C. (passed Spring Hill Church in the forenoon. Church situated on Spring Creek) Passed Montpelier in the evening."(7) For most of the day, the 1st Division marched continuously across swamps. The soldiers of the division spent another long day of corduroying the road. They marched eight miles with General Woods headquarters camping at the crossroads near Nelson's Post-Office finally going into camp around eight p.m.

The 2nd Division went into camp at Little Rockfish Creek, North Carolina after marching nearly twenty miles. In a brief skirmish they experienced the loss of three men. One killed and two men missing. The 3rd Division went into camp in the same vicinity as the 1st Division. The 3rd Division was being followed by the small-pox train which had closed to within five-hundred yards of the division when they were attacked by a small force of Confederate cavalry dressed in Federal uniforms. They were able to capture a few horses and make their escape through the swamp making pursuit impossible. The 3rd Division was to follow the 1st Division on the march for the next day. The 4th Division went into camp near the same area as the 3rd Division.

The Left Wing had entered the outskirts of Fayetteville, North Carolina driving the Confederates from the part of the town they occupied. General Hardee, whose forces were guarding the town had ordered that the supply wagons and artillery be moved across the Cape Fear River with preparations being made for the destruction of the bridge. It was a case of the Federal cavalry being to anxious to take possession and getting credit for being the first troops in the city. Once the Left Wing came into the city they greatly outnumbered the Confederate forces in Fayetteville causing the Confederates to flee from the city. The Confederates were able to destroy the bridge causing the Federal army to build a pontoon bridge across the river once across they established a bridge head on the other side.

Lieutenant Lynch wrote in his diary, "Sun. Mar 12 - moved 5 a.m. marched about 8 miles & went into camp. The Batt. repaired the road all day & went into camp at sunset."(8) Private Smith wrote in his diary, "Sun. 12th. Marched about 12 miles passing through Rock Fish Village and camped for the night near Fayetteville."(9) The 1st Division marched till they came in contact with the 4th Division which was trying to cross over Little Rock Creek. The 1st Division then halted waiting for the 4th Division to finish crossing which they completed around noon. The 1st Division then proceeded to cross marching to within about three miles of Fayetteville where they went into camp with the division camping on the left side of the road facing to the rear. General Woods was ordered, at three a.m. the next morning, to send an efficient officer along with two regiments to the pontoon bridge where they were to prevent any of the 15th Army Corps men from crossing until the corps was ready to cross.

The 2nd Division left their camp at seven a.m. marched six miles arriving one mile southeast of Fayetteville, North Carolina and going into camp in this position. They had casualties on this date which consisted of six men and one officer captured and one man killed. The 3rd Division marched thirteen miles following the 1st Division going into camp two miles from Fayetteville, North Carolina on the west side of the road facing to the southwest. The 4th Division broke camp around eight a.m., crossed the Big Rockfish Creek over a bridge that his pioneers had built, finally going into camp at two p.m.

Private Smith wrote in his diary, "Mon. 13. Lay by all day and I wrote a letter to Father and went on pickett in the evening."(10) Lieutenant Lynch wrote, "Mon. March 13 - remained in camp near Fayettesville, N. C."(11) While the men of the 31st and 32nd Missouri Regiments were laying by in camp during the day other regiments of the division were busy escorting a forage detail, sixty wagons, and going to Rockfish Bridge for the purpose of protecting the bridge. It was believed that there was a Confederate cavalry force that was trying to destroy the bridge in order to entrap a force of Federal soldiers between two creeks with the intention of destroying or capturing the Federal force. It seems that the foragers who had been going out were getting wild again. There was an order issued by General Woods removing all foragers from their jobs and giving up of the animals that they had managed to obtain. There was now to be a new policy where each brigade was to have twenty men and one officer as foragers. All forage that these foragers managed to get would be equally distributed to the regiments in their brigade. The other three divisions in the 15th Army Corps, like the 1st Division, remained in the position they had the day before.

March 13th and 14th the 15th Army Corps was given some supplies that they needed from steamboats that had left Wilmington after being informed by some dispatches from General Sherman that Fayetteville was now in the hands of the Federal army and could they bring some needed supplies. They bought with them some sugar and coffee, a few shoes and some oats. This wasn't much in the way of supplies but it was a great morale booster to know that again they had contact with the outside world.

"Tues. March 14th - marched into Fayetteville, N.C."(12) This is the brief entry of Lieutenant Lynch's diary. Private Smith records in his diary, "Tues. Mar. 14, 1865. Fine day passed through Fayetteville and camped on the bank of Cape Fear River."(13) At two p.m. the 1st Division started moving through Fayetteville, North Carolina going to the pontoon bridge following the 3rd Division. It took so long for the 3rd Division to get across that it was ten p.m. before the first men of the 1st Division were able to cross the bridge. They started to cross with the lead element of the division going into camp about one mile beyond the Cape Fear River. Major-General Charles R. Woods, 1st Division commander, wasn't able to get across until around two a.m. Since he realized that it would be well into the morning before his whole division could get across, General Woods ordered that those already not across were to go into camp where they had stopped and to come across the next day. Each division, as they crossed the bridge, was to turn any of the refugees that had been following them and extra animals that the bummers had accumulated. It was hoped that the refugees could get a ride down the river on the returning steamboats to Wilmington, but if not they would all have to walk. By doing this the army hoped to reduce the amount of mouths they would have to feed but also to make sure that the refugees were not hurt in case they were attacked by the Confederates.

No longer was each division going to have their supply

trains following behind the division. They were to combine all brigade trains, except for wagons carrying ammunition and ambulances which would follow their respective divisions, into a 15th Army Corps train with each division supplying a brigade at different times, to guard the train from enemy attacks. The 1st Brigade of the 1st Division was going to be the first brigade that would be attached to the train until they reached Faison's Depot. Brigadier-General William B. Woods, commanding 1st Brigade, would also have attached to him one-half of the divisions pioneer corps, with their tools, to help them with moving the wagons along. There were five hundred and fifty wagons in the supply train which covered a distance of four and one-half miles when they were on the march. The 90th Illinois Infantry Regiment and the 39th Iowa Infantry Regiment along with the 29th Missouri Mounted Infantry Regiment were also attached to the 1st Brigade. They were expecting, as had been in the past few days, more corduroying of the roads to get the wagons to their designated camp grounds for each day.

The 2nd Division broke camp at three-thirty p.m. and started crossing the lower pontoon bridge at five p.m. going into camp about one and one-half miles east of the bridge. The 3rd Division left at eleven a.m. marching to the pontoon bridge and started crossing the bridge at five-thirty p.m. finally getting across at eight forty-five p.m. A division could take as much as four hours to get across an obstacle such as this river. One of the problems that the 3rd Division experienced was the rapid falling of the Cape Fear River. They had to keep adjusting the pontoon bridge and dig out more of the bank to be able to get to the pontoon bridge without such a sharp angle of descent. The 4th Division moved out at daylight reaching the pontoon bridge at around nine a.m. but had to wait till around twelve-thirty p.m for the 17th Army Corps to finish getting across. It was a long day for many of the men in the 15th Army Corps. Each division seemed to experience the army standard policy of hurry up and wait so you can stand in line.

Private Smith records in his diary, "Wed. 15th. Moved 1 mile and camped for the night."(14) Lieutenant Lynch wrote in his diary, "Wed. Mar. 15 - B.(attalion) remained in camp. B. drew 3 days rations to last 6 days."(15) The 1st Division, under the command of General Charles R. Woods, that had not crossed the day before were finally able to get across by four-thirty p.m. on this date. The main reason that it took so long for the 1st

Division to get over was that General Kilpatrick's cavalry was given the right of way to get over the bridge. The bank on the other side of the river was so steep that it was difficult for the infantrymen to climb. It rained all afternoon and into the evening during the day making it that much harder to climb up the bank. General Howard sent orders that on the next day the 15th Army Corps were to cross the South River and march on the Fayetteville and Bentonville Road while their wagons and those guarding the wagons were to march on the direct road to Beaman's Cross-Roads. The 17th Army Corps were to march toward Clinton, North Carolina on the road from Owensville.

The 2nd Division left their camp at eleven a.m. marching about ten miles on March 15, 1865 going into camp at Bethany Church near the South River. The 3rd Division left their camp at two o'clock p.m. marching about twelve miles going into camp behind the 2nd Division. The 3rd Division lost a total of twenty-three officers and two hundred and eighty-four enlisted, men due to their terms of enlistment being up. They were assigned the duty of marching with the refugee train to Wilmington, North Carolina. Looking back it seems that they should have stuck it out until the end of the war, but if you were in their shoes you would probably be sick and tired of marching in swamps chasing an enemy force. The 4th Division, under the command of Major-General John M. Corse, marched to the South River where a force of Confederate cavalry were occupying a strong position on the north bank. There was a strong skirmish across the river which drove the Confederates from their position with part of the 4th Division establishing a bridgehead while the bridge across the South River was repaired.

Private Smith writes in his diary, "Thur. 16th. On this day we was left back with the Corps train moved 6 miles and lay up until morning."(16) Lieutenant Lynch records in his diary, "Thur. Mar. 16 - B. moved at 6 a.m. marched 6 m. camped at Black River."(17) Lieutenant Lynch records that they camped at the Black River but I believe that it was the South River because all other correspondence refers to the South River. As Private Smith stated this was the first day for the start of using a brigade to guard the corps supply train. This was not a duty to take lightly. A person might think that it was good duty because you were in the rear of the corps, but it was usually the supply train that was attacked by the Confederate cavalry. The 1st Division was the last division in the line of march for the 15th Army Corps so they could supply support in the form of reinforcements in case the Confederates did attack the 1st Brigade. The privates really suffered because they were used not only for guard duty if during the day the roads were bad they would supplement the pioneers by laying corduroy roads, helping to pull out stuck wagons and other tasks that they would not have to normally perform.

The rest of the 1st Division was having problems of their own. They marched about three miles after crossing the river then they went into camp. The rain had caused a problem to the 1st Division by causing the river to rise making it hard for the ordnance and ambulance trains to cross the South River. It was so bad that General Woods was thinking of leaving his trains behind in order to catch up with the rest of the 15th Army Corps. He sent word of the conditions of the road to General William B. Woods so he could prepare the material that he would need to cross. The ordnance and ambulance train for the 1st Division were able to get across but it was finally decided that the corps supply train would not be able to cross unless they got a bridge. The 1st Division left camp and moved out again reaching the South River at three o'clock p.m. They finished crossing the river and went into camp three miles on the north side of the river. They finally got their last wagon over the river at ten-thirty that night.

The 2nd Division left camp at nine a.m. crossing the Black River at Maxwell's Bridge continuing the march about eight more miles before going into camp. The 3rd Division left camp at nine a.m. and followed the 2nd Division arriving in camp at the fork of the main Goldsborough and Graham Roads between seven p.m. and one a.m. having marched about nine miles. The 4th Division had again moved forward about nine miles which brought them to within six miles from the Little Cohera Creek where they learned from some civilians that a small force of Confederate cavalry force had established a defensive position. General Corse sent one of his regiments and a section of artillery to attack this force which they did successfully. The Confederates then retreated from this position. It was on this date, late in the evening, when the Right Wing commander General Howard learned of the battle between forces under General Slocum fought against forces under the Confederate General Hardee at the Battle of Averasborough where the Confederates were beaten and many prisoners were taken.

Lieutenant Lynch recorded in his diary, "Fri. Mar. 17th - B. moved short distance crossed Black River & went into camp."(18) Again Lieutenant Lynch states they crossed the Black River but I think it is the South River. Private Smith writes in his diary, "Fri. 17th. Marched 5 miles crossing a creek by wading & camped for the night."(19) The 1st Brigade was still on 15th Army Corps train guard. The 1st Brigade was finally able to get across the South River by filling in the holes in the river by using bricks and logs pinning them down to keep them from being washed away. They took almost twenty-four hours to finally get all the train across the South River. The rest of the 1st Division was following the 3rd Division, who was following the 2nd Division who was following the 4th Division. By the time the 1st Division was on the road it was almost a bottomless pit which required almost continuous corduroying by the men in the division. The 1st Division finally went into camp that night near dark.

The 2nd Division left camp at nine a.m. and marched until about two p.m. going into camp at a place called Peter's Cross-Roads. The 3rd Division left camp at eight a.m. marching about eight miles going into camp at three p.m. at a place called Jackson's Cross-Roads. The 4th Division broke camp at seven a.m and marched about six miles entrenching at a place called Jackson's Cross-Roads.

Lieutenant Smith recorded in his diary, "Sat. Mar. 18 - B. Train guard marched 8 miles & went into camp."(20) Brevet Brigadier-General William B. Woods reported to the 15th Army Corps Assistant Adjutant-General Major Max. Woodhull the following,

"HDQRS. TRAIN GUARD, FIFTEENTH ARMY CORPS,
    Near South River, March 18, 1865 - 3 a.m.
    Major Max. Woodhull,
    Assistant Adjutant-General, Fifteenth Army Corps:
    Major: I have the honor to report that I am camped about one mile and a half east of South River, having crossed the last wagons at 5:30 o'clock yesterday afternoon. If General Blair's pontoons are sent to the Little Cohera so as not to detain me, I can cross that stream to-day. The roads for several miles ahead are said to be very bad. I cannot promise to make Beaman's Cross-

Roads before day after to-morrow some time in the day-
that is to say, on the 20th.

I am, very respectfully, your obedient servant,
W.B. Woods,
Brevet Brigadier-General, Commanding.

HDQRS. TRAIN GUARD, FIFTEENTH ARMY CORPS,
On the Road, March 18, 1865 - 8 a.m.
Major Max. Woodhull,
Assistant Adjutant-General, Fifteenth Army Corps:
MAJOR: I think I made a mistake in my note of this
morning as to the time I expect to reach Beaman's Cross-
Roads. I think I named day after to-morrow, the 20th. I
meant to say to-morrow, the 19th. I have just heard
from the river and learn that the pontoons will be ready
for use by the time we reach there. We are making very
good progress this morning, but the roads are awful.

Very respectfully, your obedient servant,
W. B. WOODS,
Brevet Brigadier-General,
Commanding Train Guard."(21)

The rest of the 1st Division left their camp at nine a.m. marching to Ingram's Plantation, North Carolina going into camp
around five-thirty p.m. There were four men believed to have
been captured by Confederate cavalry that were sent out during the day as foragers from the 1st Division headquarters.

The 3rd Division left camp at seven a.m. marching eleven
miles on the Bentonville road to Monk's plantation going into
camp around three p.m. at the Benton's Cross-Roads. They
had followed behind the 2nd Division with their right flank connecting with the 2nd Division. The 4th Division left camp at
nine-thirty a.m following the 1st Division on the Goldsborough
road marching ten miles crossing both the Little and Big Cohera
Rivers going into camp at Newton's Grove.

This was a date of decision for General Joseph E.
Johnston. Even though he was pretty sure that the South had
lost the war, he was determined to try and deal General Sherman
a severe blow by defeating one of his wings or a corps. The
opportunity was presenting itself by the route of march the
Federal army was taking. General Johnston sent a letter to his
generals asking if anyone knew exactly where the Federal forces
were so he could plan his attack. General Wade Hampton had

sent a note to General Johnston informing him that the best place to attack was Johnston's current position. General Hampton and his cavalry was camped near the junction of the Goldsborough and Smithfield Roads a couple miles from the town of Bentonville, North Carolina. He made his headquarters in the Cole house located near the crossroads.

General Johnston, after receiving General Hampton's note, ordered General's Stewart and Bragg to bring their commands to Bentonville and he also ordered General Hardee to bring his command there, which was twelve miles away. General Johnston figured that the two wings of the Federal army were approximately twelve miles apart by the information that he had received from General Hampton. This would place the divided wings a days march from each other enabling him to attack the closest wing hopefully destroying it before troops of the other wing could arrive. The Left Wing under General Slocum was the closest to Bentonville so they were the target. This was the same situation that General Johnston tried to get in his retreat in Georgia. Maybe this time he would be successful.

Events soon transpired that started to turn against General Johnston's plans. The route that General Johnston had ordered General Hardee to take turned out to be a lot longer than the originally estimated twelve miles. Early on March 18th some of General Hampton's cavalry was sent out to delay the march of the Left Wing in order to allow the Confederate infantry time to get in position. You might think that this would tip the Federal army commanders hands that they were getting closer to Goldsborough. It was believed by some and hoped by General Sherman that the Confederates would defend Goldsborough so the extra force was just another delaying action that could be easily brushed aside. After delaying the Federal army by forcing them to go into line of battle, the Confederate force withdrew back to the position that General Hampton occupied having left the Cole house.

The Left Wing on March 18th was facing the whole of General Johnston's Confederate army even though at this time they didn't know it. The Federals were able to drive the Confederate cavalry past the Cole Plantation, which had once been their headquarters. The Confederate cavalry then dismounted and went into position in some woods. Here they hastily put up some breastworks and General Hampton placed his artillery in the middle of the cavalry and was pretty determined to hold his position until the infantry could come.

Once the Confederate cavalry was in postion it wasn't long before some of the Federal foragers came into sight numbering around one-hundred. The foragers were confident that they could drive what they thought was another small force of Confederate cavalry that they had been battling with for so long, they charged the Confederates coming under immediate fire from artillery and the cavalrymen. The Federal cavalrymen were driven back and both sides exchanged fire for awhile when the Federal cavalry finally decided to retreat. Excluding the Confederate cavalry delaying action earlier in the day, this was the first stand by the Confederate army at the battle of Bentonville.

Major-General Robert F. Hoke and his division finally came into Bentonville on the evening of March 18th. His division was part of the Army of Northern Virginia which was made up of seven different North Carolina infantry regiments, five South Carolina infantry regiments, five Georgia regiments, some of North Carolina artillery battalions, and four regiments of North Carolina Junior Reserves. Later in the evening the remnants of the proud Army of Tennessee marched in ready to fight once again the same men they had faced in their tactical withdrawal through Georgia. General Hardee's Corps was still about six miles from Bentonville after marching about fourteen miles during the day. General Johnston was also in Bentonville and after receiving the message from General Hardee informing him that he would start around four a.m. hoping to reach Bentonville before the attack began.

Lieutenant Lynch records in his diary, "Sun Mar. 19 - B.(attalion) Train guard moved at 6 a.m. marched 12 miles went into camp. B.(attalion) crossed the Moharah Cr. in the morning passed Gocean Church at dusk it is the Methodist Church & camped at Sampson Co., N.C."(22) Private Smith wrote in his diary, "Sun. 19th. Marched 10 miles and camped for the night."(23) The 1st Brigade and the 15th Army Corps supply train crossed the Little Cohera River on March 18th with the last of the supply train pulling into camp at Beaman's Cross-Roads at four a.m. on March 19th. According to Brevet Brigadier-General William B. Woods, the 1st Brigade commander, they had marched thirteen miles on March 18th. The 1st Division left camp in the morning following the 3rd Division going into position approximately three and one-half miles from Cox's

Bridge across the Neuse River. Instead of just going into camp as normal they went into a position assigned to them facing west putting the artillery on a defensive line placing them between the two brigades of infantry. The infantry were quickly building strong breastworks and they were building a barbetter defensive position for the guns in the artillery. The 1st Divisions left flank was connected to the right flank of the 3rd Division.

The 3rd Division left their camp at six a.m. and marched down the Goldsborough Road arriving at Falling Creek Post-Office around eleven-thirty a.m. They halted there long enough for the division to close up, having become spread out by some of the wagons traveling with the division becoming stuck in the mud. The 3rd Division sent out a regiment as an advance guard and also sent out flankers to the sides of the division to make sure that they would not be surprised by an attack on their flanks. The 10th Iowa Volunteer Infantry, 2nd Brigade, was sent forward to drive a force of Confederate cavalry across Cox's Bridge. They came into contact with about two-hundred of the Confederates driving them back to within a mile of Cox's Bridge where they quickly put up such a strong defense that they were in danger of being driven back themselves. The rest of the 2nd Brigade was ordered forward to come to the aid of the 10th Iowa Veteran Infantry driving the Confederate cavalry away. Later it was this same 2nd Brigade that the 1st Division moved into postition next to. The 1st Brigade, 3rd Division was then moved forward to link with the 2nd Brigade. Later in the evening two companies were sent to the Falling Creek Bridge. The 3rd Division had marched approximately fifteen miles that day. The 4th Division was following the 1st Division going into camp two miles from Neuse River on the Goldsborough Road. They were having trouble getting their wagons across Falling Creek so they started setting up defensive positions being pretty sure that they could hold their position in case attacked.

General Sherman was pretty sure that the Confederates had given up the idea of holding out at Bentonville and had retreated towards Raleigh, North Carolina. He was so sure that he issued the orders for the objective for the next day. General Howard sent orders for the 15th Army Corps to head for Cox's Bridge on the 20th and to try and get possession before it could be destroyed by the Confederates. General Blair's 17th Army Corps was to move as fast as possible to Falling

Creek Church and capture the road taking a position to the left of the 15th Army Corps. Then all of a sudden the situation changed. The 1st Division of the 14th Army Corps of the Left Wing, numbering about two-thousand men, was ordered to move on the Goldsborough Road on their way to Bentonville. The foragers for the 14th Army Corps proceeded forward of the corps as was their custom and immediately came under fire. The 1st Division of the 14th Army Corps immediately went forward not sure of what they were going up against. General Slocum rode up and asked why they didn't drive the Confederate cavalry force of less than a thousand men. Brigadier-General Harrison C. Hobart, who commanded the 1st Brigade of the 1st Division, ordered his men forward and the skirmish line that led the way soon came into contact with the Confederate cavalrymen who were in the woods. Even though the cavalrymen were firing at the Federals with everything they had they were simply out-numbered and were forced to evacuate their positions. They retreated through a swamp and were followed by the Federals with the swamp at times being knee deep in mud and water. This was the official start of the battle. General Slocum had sent a message to General Sherman stating that his men were driving a force of Confederate cavalry from their positions and believed that he would soon be able to start on his march again. But the 1st Division of the 14th Army Corps were heading straight for Major-General Robert Hoke's Division which numbered almost six-thousand men. While this was going on Lieutenant-General Alexander Peter Stewart was moving his contingent of the Army of Tennessee into position. This proud army had been reduced to an extent that General Stewart was able to bring about four-thousand five-hundred men into battle with him. General Slocum was still unaware of what he was facing.

Then everything began to fall apart for General Slocum. The cavalry force to his front was suddenly infantrymen in trenches facing the coming Federals. The battle took on a serious turn now with infantry facing infantry the Federals which had driven the Confederate cavalry back was halted by this unexpected turn of events. The Federals attacked the Confederates with confidence that they could drive them but they ran straight into the prepared works of the Confederates who out-numbered them almost three to one. In attacking an entrenched position it was believed in order to have a successful attack the attacker should have a three to one advantage. Part of the line that they attacked was held by the Army of Tennessee which defeated the attacking Federals causing them to retreat to their starting point.

General Slocum was now convinced that they were in trouble and sent a report to General Sherman stating that he had all the Confederate army to his front with General Johnston in command. General Sherman, once convinced that this was true, began to issue orders to help the Left Wing. He ordered that the 3rd Division should move up with it's artillery and the position they occupied should be taken by the 1st Division. He then ordered that the 2nd Division should backtrack and then link up with the Left Wing and go into a position directed by General Slocum. This was relayed to General Hazen in the following order.

"HEADQUARTERS FIFTEENTH ARMY CORPS,
  Falling Creek Post-Office, March 19,1865.
  Major General W. B. Hazen,
  Commanding Second Division, Fifteenth Army Corps:
  GENERAL: Major-General Slocum needs aid quick. You will please move your command back via Blackman Lee's Store, and from there, under direction of General Slocum's senior aide-de-camp, across to the Left Wing, reporting to Major-General Slocum.
  I am, general, very respectfully, your obedient servant,
  MAX. WOODHULL,
  Assistant Adjutant-General"(24)

Believing that the Federals were still well strung out and facing just a few of the Left Wing, General Johnston ordered an attack. It was something that he was not well known for, he was viewed as an expert at retreat and was replaced by General Hood at Atlanta because of this reputation. General Hardee who was now in command of Brigadier-General William B. Taliaferro's Division and the Army of Tennesse contingent. General Braxton Bragg was in command of General McLaws' and General Hoke's divisions. At two-forty-five the attack began. The troops under General Hardee moved forward driving the Federals from the positions that they held. They put up a spirited defense but the numbers were just to overwhelming and it was either stand and surrender or run and live to fight another day. For some reason that was never satisfactorily explained, General Bragg failed to attack as ordered. Finally General Bragg did attack. It was General Hoke's division, of General Bragg's command, that attacked General Morgan's men. The men in General Morgan's division were able to successfully hold their position causing the Confederates to fall back where they reformed and attacked again. Their second attack was no more successful than their first. General Hardee's men kept charging the Federal works until it was almost to dark to see. General Johnston decided at dark that it was time to call it a day.

Lieutenant Lynch records in his diary, "Mon. Mar.20 - B.(attalion) moved at 6 a.m. in the direction of Goldsboro, N.C. The 1st Div. was engaged with the enemy, but the 1st Brig. being train guards were not in the 1st days skirmish. The division drove back the enemy. We received orders to move up to the Div. then 15 miles from our camp. Trains were left back & the Brig. proceeded on their way. Moved all night. Roads bad."(25) Private Smith wrote in his diary, "Mon. Mar. 20th. Marced about 8 miles wading another swamp from ankle to hip deep and arrived at camp at 3 o'clock A.M. and then I had to go on pickett duty."(26) The 1st Division of the 15th Army Corps began their march to the battle near five a.m. The 1st Division was the head of the 15th Army Corps on the march, marching on the Goldsborough Road marching west toward Bentonville when they ran into Confederate cavalry. Colonel Robert F. Catterson's 2nd Brigade was in advance of the 1st Division. A sharp skirmish started that at times sounded almost like a battle. There were about forty casualties for the 1st Division during this engagement with the Confederates. The 1st Division took a position facing the Confederates where they started to build entrenchments. The Confederates were well dug in and waiting for the Federal force to attack them. The right flank of the 1st Division was in contact with the left flank of the 4th Division. The following is a portion of Major-General Charles R. Woods report of March 20, 1865:

"The next morning, the 20th instant, in compliance with the orders given me by Major-General Logan, with Colonel Catterson in the advance, I moved out on the road toward the bridge until reaching the point of intersection above referred to, when I took the road leading to the left toward Bentonville. I marched about four miles before I struck the outposts of the enemy, but from that time forward my advance had to be made under cover of a good line of skirmishers, and about 11 a.m., or when I had advanced some eight miles on this road, the Forty-sixth Ohio Infantry, then deployed as skirmishers, became so actively engaged with the enemy that I immediately deployed the two brigades of my division on either side of the road, selecting the most advantageous ground and throwing up light rail-works in front of my line. The Forty-sixth Ohio Infantry having dislodged the rebels, and by a most gallant charge driven them from a strong and extensive line of rail pits that they had established covering the road at the fork leading toward Smithfield, in obedience to the directions received from Major-General Logan I immediately moved my lines up to this point and at once took position, extending my lines so as to include both roads beyond the forks. The Forty-sixth Ohio Infantry, still deployed as skirmishers, was moved down the road leading toward Smithfield, supported by the One hundredth Indiana Infantry. The Twenty-fifth Iowa Infantry was promptly deployed forward, covering the road upon which I had been marching. The Forty-sixth Ohio Infantry soon struck the main line of the enemy, discovering him admirably posted behind well-constructed works. The right of the Twenty-fifth Iowa also had not gone far before meeting the rebels behind their works. The left of this regiment, that had by this time connected itself with the Second Division skirmish line, moved forward with it and gradually swung around to the right leaving the road entirely in the rear, so that the enemy's line was now developed as running almost parallel to the road on which my column had been marching and extending across the Smithfield fork about one-fourth of a mile from where the main road branched."(27)

The 2nd Division of the 15th Army Corps, was the division that was sent to General Slocum. They arrived at the Left Wing at sunrise after marching about fourteen miles going into a reserve role. Around eleven a.m. the 2nd Division was ordered by General Slocum to send skirmishers to the right of his lines and see if they can find the enemy lines. It sounds so simple but they were marching through swamps for about three hours when they finally ran into the Confederate pickett line.

The Confederates were bent back in a refuse line. The 2nd Division picketts were quickly re-inforced by a brigade when they attacked the Confederate picketts driving them back to the main Confederate line. The 2nd Division in this movement lost five men killed and nine wounded. The 2nd Division went into position to the left of the 14th Army Corps and their right was finally linked up with elements of the 1st Division.

The 3rd Division of the 15th Army Corps sent out the 2nd Brigade, Colonel Clark Russell Wever commanding, with one section of Battery B, 1st Michigan Artillery, to try and get to Cox's Bridge across the Neuse River and to destroy it if possible to keep the Confederates from sending re-inforcements to General Johnston. At about seven forty-five a.m. the Federals found a side road around the swamp that was not protected by a strong artillery presence as was the main road to Cox's Bridge. The Confederates consisted of a force of cavalry and four pieces of artillery that once they realized they were flanked, went across the river destroying the bridge. This was exactly what both sides wanted. The rest of the division followed the 1st Division going into position to the right of the 4th Division with the 2nd Brigade being ordered to stay in position until the corps train came up where they would then revert to the train guard. The 2nd Brigade suffered three men wounded during the skirmish at the bridge with two being severely wounded. The 4th Division of the 15th Army Corps left their camp at seven a.m. following the 1st Division going into position after a march of eight miles. They strongly fortified themselves preparing for an attack from the Confederates that did not materialize.

On March 20th the Confederate forces that had the day before fought one wing of the Federal army, were now preparing to face the other wing. With the knowledge of the 1st Division moving down the road toward them they moved their lines to form a horse shoe shaped defense position. General Hardee's men were on the west side of the horse shoe, General Stewart's Army of Tennesse formed the curve of the horse shoe facing south and General Bragg's army formed the east side. General Hoke's men were in a wooded area with a steep ravine in front of them. They had moved to this position after learning that the Right Wing was heading their way. It was a natural defensive position because the Federals would have to cross the ravine in order to attack them. The Confederates had spent part of the day burying their dead and caring for their wounded. It was another busy day for the surgeons who were going about their gruesome task of cutting off limbs of those who had been shot with the bones shattered. General Johnston decided to stay and fight the next day. It was a decision that many have wondered about. He received about five-hundred reinforcements from Smithfield, North Carolina, which consisted of two brigades of the Army of Tennessee. Instead of sending them to General Stewart he gave one of them to General Hardee and the other he sent to General Bragg. He also placed General Wheeler's cavalry on his extreme left. The two ends of the horse shoe defensive line came to almost meet at the end of the day. This gave General Johnston a total force of almost twenty thousand men compared to General Shermans approximately fifty-five thousand.

The Left Wing spent a part of the day burying their dead from the day before but also bringing in some of their wounded who had spent the night where they fell. General Slocum had ordered that his corps commanders send out skirmishers but not to bring on a general battle. Around two p.m. the 14th Army Corps commander, Major-General Jefferson C. Davis, sent orders for the 3rd Division, under the command of Major-General Absalom Baird to send two of his brigades on a reconnaissance to see if the Confederates were still to his front. They were there all right, the Army of Tennessee under Lieutenant-General Stewart, and part of General Hoke's forces which were made up primarily of the North Carolina Junior Reserves, behind strong entrenchments which made the Federal veterans knew that if they were ordered to attack many of them wouldn't be going home. The Federal's began digging in themselves preparing for a Confederate attack if it should come to that point. The 20th Army Corps, under the command of Brevet Major-General Alpheus S. Williams, was facing the men under General Hardee. They were experiencing the same thing as the 14th Army Corps. There was not much interest of either of these corps to bring on a strong battle.

Lieutenant Lynch records in his diary, "Tues. Mar. 21 - Batt. moved at 7 a.m. joined the Div. at about noon. The B.(attalion) was on the skirmish line from noon till the next day. The enemy charged our lines several times, endeavoring to drive us from our pits that we had taken from them the same day but were repulsed with heavy loss. B.(attalion) lost Wm. Burch CPT Co "B" mortally wounded in left shoulder. Elberton

Clounts - Priv. Co "F" lost one of his legs, James O. R. Reaves Pvt Co "D" wounded in wrist & several others slightly. Day cloudy & rainy."(28) Private Smith wrote in his diary, "Tues. 21st. On this day we rejoined our Division the whole Brigade having left the train and started to the front the evening before when we arrived at the front, the order came that we might stay 3 or 4 days and to put up camp in the regular order and just as we got our tents up and all fixed the order came get ready to move immediately in all out 15 minutes we was all ready to move and went out, the whole Brigade on the front line and a heavy detail was made to go out as Skirmishers but I being on guard the night before did not have to go but the Regt. went all but their Skirmisher lay in reserve and built works and the balls flew over us thick and fast but as the Rebels line of battle could not drive our skirmishers. I never fired a shot in this engagement we lost one Captain and 3 privates wounded, at night the enemy evacuated leaving dead and wounded and prisoners in our hands."(29) General Logan ordered all of his division commanders to strengthen their lines and to send skirmishers out in the morning to find out if the Confederates were still in their trenches. In response to General Logan's order the 1st Division did exactly that and the skirmishers found out that the Confederates were not only still there they had spent the night improving the strength of their positions. The 1st Division was facing the Confederate troops in General Hoke's division. General Charles Woods, he now had his whole division together for the first time since March 15th, three brigades were facing two of General Hoke's brigades. Colonel George A. Stone's 3rd Brigade was facing Colonel Charles T. Zachry who was commanding Colquitt's Brigade as was the 1st Brigade under the command of Brevet Brigadier-General William B. Woods. Colonel Robert F. Catterson's 2nd Brigade was facing Colonel William S. Devane who was commanding Clingman's Brigade. This was the first time that the 1st Division ever fought troops of the Army of Northern Virginia. The division front looked like this, the 3rd Brigade on the left, the 1st Brigade in the middle and the 2nd Brigade on the right.

The 1st Brigade commander Brevet Brigadier-General William B. Woods submitted his view of the attack they made on March 21st.

"I marched until 3 a.m., halted until 6:30 a. m., when I resumed the march and rejoined the division about 11 a.m., about three miles from Bentonville. The enemy was here in force and intrenched.

Pursuant to orders I placed the brigade in the front line between, the Second and Third Brigades, of the First Division, leaving the Twelfth Indiana Infantry in reserve. Under a sharp skirmish fire and within 350 yards of the enemy's main line a strong line of earthworks was built. Pursuant to orders I made preparations to advance a line of skirmishers and drive the enemy from their skirmish pits. I detailed 100 men as skirmishers, with Capt. William Burch, of the Thirty-first and Thirty-second Missouri Consolidated Battalion, as officer in charge, and directed Capt. Edward S. Lenfesty, picket officer on my staff, to take the general supervision of the movement. The skirmishers moving at the same time with those of the Second Third Brigades advanced briskly, and after a hot skirmish, almost amounting to a battle, drove the enemy's skirmishers from their intrenched position and immediately commenced to reverse the pits. Before this was completed the enemy came out in strong force from their main line and retook a part of the pits.

They were again driven out and again retook them. I then sent out a re-enforcement of forty men, and with their assistance the pits were again taken and held, and the enemy driven to his main line. The line thus taken and held was within eighty-eight paces of the enemy's main line. The loss of the brigade in this affair was 1 killed and 21 wounded."(30)

Colonel Robert F. Catterson, commanding the 2nd Brigade, wrote the following in his report of the part his brigade played in the battle of March 21st.

"On the morning of the 21st my skirmishers - - One hundred and third Illinois – drove the enemy from a line of strong rifle - pits, which at some portions of the line were within forty paces of his main works. This move was made in a very satisfactory manner, and fully developed the enemy's position. During this advance Adjt. Frank Lermond, One hundred and third Illinois, was severely wounded while gallantly urging his men forward. My brigade was again advanced and its position fortified. The Twenty-sixth Illinois was sent forward to relieve the One hundred and third Illinois, and taking position suffered some from a flank fire caused by the falling back of a portion of the line on my left. On the morning of the 22nd my skirmishers again moved forward at daylight and found the enemy's works evacuated. Two companies of the Twenty-sixth Illinois, supported by the remainder of the regiment, were moved forward as skirmishers on the road leading to Bentonville, and reached the bridge across Mill Creek, near that place, in time to extinguish the flames (the enemy having fired it), and in a very few moments after the enemy's rear guard had crossed. I immediately crossed with my brigade, and skirmishing again commenced, we driving our opponents in wild confusion beyond Hannah's Creek. The bridge over this stream was also on fire, and was saved only by the fearless daring of my men, who rushed forward and extinguished the flames. At this point I received orders to recross Mill Creek and take a position covering the bridge. This I immediately did and bivouacked for the night. At Bentonville the enemy was so closely pressed that he left 40 of our wounded and 12 rebel wounded in our possession. The brigade also captured 91 prisoners and 82 stands of arms and accroutements.

During the three days' skirmishing mentioned all, both officers and men, deserve great credit for their gallant conduct. The casualities during the campaign were as follows: Killed, 5; wounded, 30; prisoners, 8; total, 43. Total number of prisoners captured from enemy 166."(31)

The 3rd Brigade commander Colonel George A. Stone in his report of March 26, 1865 gave the following account of what his brigade did on March 21st.

"On the 21st instant I had orders to erect a line of works on the skirmish line, and at 1 p.m. I moved three regiments to the front line, the Fourth Iowa on the right, connecting with the left of the First Brigade, Brevet Brigadier-General Woods commanding, the Thirtieth Iowa in the center and the Ninth Iowa on the left. The Twenty-fifth Iowa and the Thirty-first Iowa were in the rear, held in reserve. We put up a temporary line of works under fire of the enemy, and at 2 o'clock I received orders to charge the enemy's skirmish pits. We captured the pits with but slight loss, but the enemy evinced so much determination to regain them that the fighting became very sharp. The enemy's main line of battle, behind good works, was by actual measurement but 100 yards from these skirmish pits, and he fired from the works by volley. At three different times they followed up the fire by volley by an assault on my skirmishers. Their men swarmed over the charged gallantly, but I had re-enforced the line till I had nearly a line of battle, and our incessant firing prevented them from charging as a perfect organization and every charge was repulsed. The orders came to me so positive to hold the ground I had already gained, even from Generals Howard and Logan, that I should have done so or ruined the brigade."(32)

These reports were given just a few days after the battle. The total of the casualties for what some people might call just a fight between skirmishers were pretty heavy. The Consolidated Battalion of the 31st and 32nd Missouri Infantry Regiments, who sent forward approximately one hundred and forty men suffered six casualties. They were Captain William Burch of Company B who was severely wounded in the left shoulder but did recover and was discharged for disability on May 15, 1865. Other casualties included Private Patrick Kain of Company B was wounded in the arm slightly; Private J. O. R. Reaves of Company D was wounded severely in the wrist; Private Burt Clounts of Company F, was wounded in his left leg causing it to be amputated at the knee; Private Daniel Payne of Company F was wounded in the arm slightly; Private Arthur Rawlins also of Company F was wounded in the arm slightly.

The 2nd Division went into line with the rest of the 15th Army Corps taking a position about two hundred and fifty yards from the Confederates. Their new position was to the left of the 1st Division with their right flank connecting with the left flank of the 1st Division. They tried to make a connection with the 14th Army Corps but were unable to because the 14th Army Corps right flank was about five hundred yards farther back from the Confederate entrenchments than they were. This caused a gap between the two army corps that General Hazen filled with his reserve brigade. Their skirmish line, much like the skirmish line of the 1st Division were constantly battling through the day. The 2nd Division reported a casualty list of three killed and twenty wounded. The 3rd Division was held in

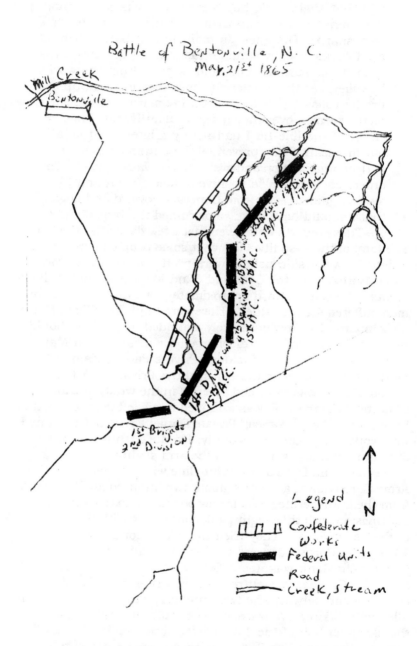

Battle of Bentonville, N. C.
May. 21st 1865

Mill Creek
Bentonville

1st Division
17th A.C.

3rd Division
17th A.C.

4th Division
17th A.C.

15th N.C.
17th A.C.

1st Division
15th A.C.

1st Brigade
2nd Division

Legend

Confederate Works

Federal Units

Road

Creek, Stream

N

BATTLE OF BENTONVILLE, NORTH CAROLINA

N

MARCH THROUGH NORTH CAROLINA

reserve for the day prepared to move at a moments notice. The 4th Division, who was on the extreme right of the 15th Army Corps, skirmishers attacked the Confederate line and occupied their rifle pits for awhile but soon had to retreat because their left flank was being attacked because the brigade to their left of the 1st Division was farther back than they were. General Corse reported that he didn't think that he had more than forty casualties for the action of the day.

The Left Wing was given orders to try and avoid a battle with the Confederates in their front and be prepared to march in the rear of the Right Wing the next day on their way to Goldsborough, North Carolina with the 20th Army Corps moving out first with the 14th Army Corps following on March 23rd. The Confederates, on their right flank, were withdrawing trying to get across the Mill Creek Bridge while leaving enough men in position to throw back any Federal skirmishers that might try and attack them. There were several attempts by the Federals on this day that were easily thrown back.

Probably one of the hardest fights of the day was the charge of Major-General Joseph A. Mowers 1st Division of the 17th Army Corps. Colonel John Tillson's 3rd Brigade, of General Mowers division, moved forward in a line of battle but before they could make an attack on the Confederate cavalry under General Wheeler they halted and waited for Brigadier-General John W. Fuller whose 1st Brigade was having difficulty getting across a swamp that was in their path of march. Once they made it through the swamp they lost valuable time reforming their lines. The two brigades advanced charging the Confederates. The Confederate cavalry, already outnumbered, were further reduced when one of their brigades fled across the Mill Creek bridge. The other two brigades were able to hold their positions. Upon being informed that his left was in the air General Mower ordered his division to move to the left in order to come in contact with the right flank of the rest of the 17th Army Corps. The 64th Illinois Infantry Regiment, who were the skirmishers for General Fuller's 1st Brigade, continued to press the Confederates to their front. When the Confederate brigade left their positions the 64th Illinois Infantry charged through the very headquarters of General Johnston, who, with his staff officers, left on foot. The 64th Illinois had entered the town of Bentonville and were within a few hundred feet of taking possession of Mill Creek Bridge when they stopped to wait for reinforcements. General Mower had sent word to General Blair that he was in sight of the bridge and was confident that he could take it if he could get some re-inforcements. If General Mower had succeeded in capturing the bridge the Confederates would have been cut-off from their only escape route. The 64th Illinois Infantry were suddenly thrown back by an attack by General Cummings Brigade of four Georgia infantry regiments, under the command of Colonel Robert J. Henderson. Then they were attacked by the 4th Tennessee Cavalry Regiment and the 8th Texas Cavalry Regiment. This attack was led by General Hardee himself on a borrowed horse. General Mower's division was under constant attack now by Confederate infantry and cavalry that had come up as re-inforcements and were giving the Federals a hard fight.

General Sherman, when informed of what was happening, ordered General Mower to pull back and let General Johnston break off the battle. General Sherman did not want an all out battle because he felt that he would gain nothing by such a fight except more casualties. Fearing that if he let General Mower retreat he would then come under fire from all of the Confederates in the area, which came close to happening, he ordered General Howard to order the rest of his wing to send out their skirmishers to engage the Confederates in their front to keep any more Confederate regiments from being thrown at General Mower's division. General Hardee was well satisfied with how the battle went until he saw his only son, sixteen year-old Private Willie Hardee of the 8th Texas Cavalry Regiment, was mortally wounded in the chest dying a few days later. General Johnston had depleted his right flank in order to re-inforce the left flank that there was great danger of being over-run should the Federals attack.

Lieutenant Lynch records in his diary, "Wed. March 22 - B.(attalion) in rifle pits some firing. During the night of the 21st the enemy withdrew their forces. A heavy fire was kept all night. B.(attalion) followed up the retreating host of Gen. Joseph Johnston's to beyond Bentonville, Wayne Co., N. C. The enemy having retreated across the River - & our campaign ended & we went into camp at Goldsboro, N. C."(33) Private Smith wrote in his diary, "Wed. 22nd. Followed the enemy to Bentonville and returned to our works and camped for the night."(34) It was a long night for both sides not only was it raining, they were forbidden to light fires in order not to give away their positions. As recorded by Lieutenant Lynch in his diary there was almost constant fire between both armies all night with finally the firing stopping around three a.m. on March 22nd. General Sherman ordered Colonel Catterson's brigade to find out if the Confederates were still to their front. Much to the joy of the men when they reached the Confederate lines they were gone. Once they found that the Confederates were gone the 2nd Brigade was ordered to see if the Confederates were on there way to Smithfield, North Carolina or whether they had crossed the river and were on their way to attack General Schofields army.

Colonel Catterson's 2nd Brigade, after passing Mill Creek at Bentonville, came into contact with the Confederate rear guard. They then skirmished with them until they reached Hannah's Creek where they destroyed the bridge. They then returned to Bentonville where they took up positions guarding the bridge and a pontoon bridge that had also been put across Hannah's Creek. The rest of the 1st Division was bought up to be in supporting position in case the Confederates try to return and cross the creek. Around six p.m. the 1st Division then returned to the works that they had built and stayed in the night before. Colonel Catterson was then given the task of destroying the bridges across the creek.

The 2nd Division had stopped at Grantham's House, North Carolina which was eight miles from where they started. The 3rd Division was still in camp where they were the night before at Mill Creek. The 4th Division left their campsite at three a.m. marching forward to the bridge across Hannah's Creek capturing some prisoners, where they occupied the old Confederate works.

This effectively ended the battle for Bentonville. It was the last major battle that the troops under General Sherman would have to go through. With the surrender of General Robert E. Lee and General Joseph Johnston so close it is a shame that men, on both sides, would have to die and be horribly wounded losing limbs that would effect them for the rest of their lives. The losses suffered by the Federals were one hundred and ninety-four killed, one thousand, one hundred and twelve wounded and two hundred and twenty-one missing for a total number of casualties of one thousand, five hundred and twenty-seven. The exact number of Confederate losses are not known but the official records state that there were two hundred and thirty-nine killed, one thousand six hundred and ninety-four wounded and six hundred and seventy-three missing. Brigadier-General Roswell S. Ripley who was in command of Brown's Division of Cheatham's Corps gave no list of casualties even though his division arriving on the battlefield on March 21st participating in the battle by helping to drive General Tillson and his brigade back.

Major-General Oliver Otis Howard, in a speech to the Society of the Army of the Tennessee gives the following account of the Battle of Bentonville, North Carolina.

"Ladies and Gentlemen, Comrades of the Army of the Tennessee:

In this annual address, we will attempt to place before you a few sketches to remind you of the operations of the Army of the Tennessee, in and near the last two battles which our great leader fought in North Carolina,— they were indeed the last of the war for Sherman's column.

We have reached Fayetteville, N. C., and the Cape Fear river. Slocum, with his two army corps, the 14th and 20th, was behind his crossing at the city. Our army, the 15th and 17th Corps, had a good bridge across the Cape Fear a mile below, and were encamped west of the river at convenient distances behind the bridge. Of course, we had some troops beyond the river, as advance guards, with cavalry and pickets handsomely covering our front. In this position we remained for nearly three days—from the 13th to the 16th of March, 1865.

Sherman had, some days before, expressed his desire to communicate with Wilmington, as he was confident that Schofield, with his 23rd Corps, after the battle of Nashville, had come around by rail, and had by this time secured Wilmington. Thereupon, the daring Captain Duncan had selected two enlisted men, the same that had with him floated down the Ogechee, through the enemy's lines two months before to bring our army and navy into conjunction. These men, Sergeant Amick, 15th Illinois Cavalry, and George W. Quimby, 32d Wisconsin, loaded with as much mail matter as they could carry without suspicion, had set off boldly across the Carolinas for Wilmington. Later Sherman had caused another scout to float down the Cape Fear river. The first party succeeded in getting through in forty-eight hours, where-upon a small river steamer started up the river for Fayetteville. Immediately after the first brisk excitement of our skirmish with Hardee had subsided, and his forces were well over the Cape Fear, we heard the shrill whistle of a steam tug coming from below. It proved to be the message-bearing vessel from Wilmington. Not long before the vessel came in sight, fortunately for its safety, Blair's men, reconnoitering along the river banks, had come upon a Confederate steamer and captured it. The day before our departure one of our gun-boats, carefully working up stream, reached our position, and soon other steamers arrived. With them came the coveted mails; also sugar, coffee, shoes and forage,-most welcome supplies. The returning steamers bore from us our sick to better accommodations, and carried mail matter for the entire command. The remaining spaces were occupied by the most of our white refugees, that had been gathering and increasing from Columbia to Fayetteville. Here it was that we organized that motley column of freed people that we set in motion towards the promised lands of Sea Island cotton. Using our soldiers, whose time had expired, we put a guard and wagons, with enough supplies, ahead, and a sufficient guard in the rear. That main body in the middle of the road beggars my description.

It took at least forty minutes for this singular column to pass a given point. There was in the air the music of a multitude, the cries of children, the shouting of drivers, the snatches of jubilee songs and prayerful ejaculations; and above all the murmur could be heard the shrill whistling and singing of saucy youngsters of negro refrains. It was the out bubbling of young hearts which no circumstances can ever repress. Comrades will recall that phenomenal refugee army, some 4,500 strong, which passed near Fayetteville on the road, leaving behind the much lauded contentment of slavery, and hopefully marching to the fields of freedom. Those human hearts, at whatever cost, greatly preferred the freedom.

Looking ahead toward Goldsboro and Raleigh, we were sure that Joe. Johnston, called back, was somewhere in our path. So that, now, the entire command under

Sherman's instructions, stripped for battle; the trains, except wagons absolutely essential, were thrown back, kept well together and placed under special escort and covered, of course, by a good rear guard.

Before setting out from the Cape Fear, let us delay a moment to reproduce such a picture of the country before us which was photographed upon our minds at the time. If we connect Fayetteville with Averasboro northward by a right line, then Averasboro with Smithfield to the northeast, and Smithfield southward with Goldsboro, and then join Goldsboro with Fayetteville, we have an oblong, four-sided figure. The distance from Fayetteville to Goldsboro is fifty miles. The other distances are about twenty miles each. This oblong figure is the terrain which covers the maneuvers and the two battles of Averasboro and Bentonville. Bentonville is a point as near the middle of this terrain as you can place it.

Slocum's column had preceded mine, and was west of Averasboro. Our wing resumed its march from Fayetteville the 16th of March. Sherman's mind, fully determined, was to pass from Cape Fear to the Neuse river, making Goldsboro his objective point. He greatly desired to make connection with Schofield and Terry coming from the sea, at or near Goldsboro, before fighting a general battle. Slocum went by the way of Kyles' Landing, aiming for Bentonville. Kilpatrick's cavalry was clearing the way on Slocum's left and front. The day we started, the 16th of March, Slocum found a large Confederate force, still under Hardee and not Johnston, thrown across his way. Slocum says: 'Kilpatrick came upon the enemy behind a line of intrenchments. He moved his cavalry to the right while Jackson's and Ward's two divisions (Infantry) of the 20th Corps were employed in front of the enemy's line.' Slocum continues: 'General Sherman, who had just joined me at that time, directed me to send a brigade to the left in order to get in rear of the intrenchments, which was done, and resulted in the defeat of the enemy, and in the capture of McBeth's. Charleston battery and 217 of Rhett's men.'

A little later, Hardee's men made a firm stand covering themselves with strong breastworks a short distance in the rear of the first intrenchments encountered.

Slocum carefully skirmished up to the new position and went into camp in front of the Confederate line. In these operations there had been severe skirmishing and several sharp encounters between regiments and brigades of the opposing forces. Slocum's closing words concerning this battle are: 'During the night, Hardee retreated, leaving 108 dead for us to bury, and 68 wounded. We lost 12 officers and 65 killed and 477 men wounded. Such is the brief record of the battle of Averasboro. The Confederate commander, General Johnston, says concerning this battle that Hardee was informed by Hampton, his cavalry commander, that our Army of the Tennessee had already crossed the Black river, so that his left was substantially turned. This made him abandon his position in the night and march back toward Smithfield as far as the place name Elevation. The work of our wing in pressing forward so as to pass beyond Averasboro was all the part we, of the Army of the Tennessee, bore in that sharp conflict.

Now follow the preliminaries of the approaching engagement, namely, the battle of Bentonville. A glance at my four-sided terrain suggest the simplicity of what we call strategy. Just north of Burlington, Vt., the city where I live, is a field fenced in where a ferocious bull is usually found feeding or in a surly way watching for an opportunity to vent his fierce spleen upon some man or animal that may venture in his way. One day, toward evening, as he stood on the north side bellowing and pawing the dirt, he caught sight of a workman who had cleared the fence on the south side and was innocently crossing the field. There are some few trees midway. The bull made a rush for the man who had just time to escape his horns and clambered up a tree. Here the bull continued to hold the man a prisoner till another man, coming from the east, was crossing the field. He saw the bull and made towards his flank. As the animal turned to face his new enemy the workman dropped quickly from the tree, the two together being too much for his majesty, the bull, they soon drove him to cover. This is about the strategy of Bentonville. Johnston is represented by the bull, Slocum by the workman and Howard the other man coming into the field.

General Johnston's instructions from Richmond he received the 23d of February, 1865, at his residence in Lincolnton, N. C. They were: To concentrate all available forces and drive Sherman back. This was undertaken by General Johnston with the full consciousness that the Confederates could have no other object in continuing the war than to obtain fair terms of peace. 'For the Southern cause must have appeared hopeless to all intelligent and dispassionate Southern men.' Johnston hastened to Smithfield to gather from all quarters what fragments he could. He had with him in a short time the veteran Generals Hardee, Hampton, Cheatham, Steward, Stevenson and Stephen D. Lee. He probably had, for naturally there were no longer accurate reports, from twenty to twenty-five thousand men. His whole attention was bent upon the middle of the terrain, Bentonville, through which village Slocum would have to pass on his way to Goldsboro; therefore, while Goldsboro was so plainly Sherman's objective point, Bentonville was Johnston's.

During the 18th of March, Slocum's wing was slowly continuing its advance toward Bentonville. Our wing, on the same day was moving along a road farther south, and from the character of the country was obliged to go around some swamps and thus to separate us more and more from each other, till toward night Logan again bore to the northward to encamp about eleven miles south of Bentonville, while Blair was far back following some crooked roads in the vicinity of Troublefield's store.

Slocum's entire command was northwest of us, and straight across the country, the columns were probably not more than six to eight mile apart. We had but little resistance all day on our front, and what there was came from the habitual worrisome source, the Confederate cavalry. Our roads, during the march, fair enough before we touch them, had a bad undercrust, and were soft and springy in places, so they inevitably elongated our column.

It was near noon while I was watching the work of one of General J. E. Smith's divisions repairing the road, when I heard the roar of cannon, apparently in the direction of Bentonville. Suspecting that Slocum was attacked, Major Osborne, my chief of artillery, was hurried off to pass to my rear division, Hazen's: and ordered to cause it to counter march to Slocum's aid, by taking any convenient cross road at hand. Osborne was also to hasten on to Slocum and explain what had been done, and to call for more force if the action demanded it. Not long after this, a conflicting report came to us, namely that Slocum had met only cavalry, which he was driving back. At once the orders to Hazen were suspended by Sherman. This news made us believe that Johnston would rush to our front, and if possible hold the road at Cox's bridge over the Neuse. We were further told that Slocum had obtained possession of the Smithfield wagon-road north of Johnston, therefore Cox's bridge road was the only practicable one for the Confederates to pass over in an easterly direction. Lieutenant-Colonel Strong, our chief of staff, hastened off with Colonel Clark R. Wever of the 17th Iowa, commanding the Second Brigade of General J. E. Smith's Division and the 10th Iowa Infantry of his brigade, to secure that bridge. He found only Confederate cavalry there, drove them away, took the bridge and the cross-roads near by, and rapidly fortified the position.

Soon, however, we found that our reports were not true. Slocum had met something besides cavalry, and he was not holding the Smithfield road north of Johnston. Heavy firing northwest of us continued and increased, and we very much feared from the sound and from a report brought by Lieutenant Foraker that Slocum's column was having a hard battle indeed. This young officer, Foraker, is now the greatly honored senator from Ohio. On Foraker's arrival, General Sherman caused Hazen's division to turn back toward Slocum and to hasten its march.

Taking, now, for a moment the Confederate side; by the 18th of March Johnston was holding points between Smithfield and Bentonville with all his force. Wade Hampton, commanding his cavalry, fell back as Slocum advanced. General Joseph E. Johnston, quickened by the news from Hampton that our wings were so separated and divergent as to render a junction difficult, did just as he had done before, particularly in 1862, at the battle of Fair Oaks. He rushed forward, struck a portion of the Union army, Slocum's wing, temporarily isolated, and sought to crush it before possible help could arrive. This is how it came about. The ground chosen by Hampton, which Johnston came forward to occupy the morning of the 19th, was along the Clinton road, with high ground and good artillery positions near at hand on the west. It was position substantially at right angles to Slocum's approach. A better position for a sudden descent and attack could not have been selected. Bragg's command, Hoke's division, held the left, near Slocum's road, Hardee the center and Stuart the right, while Hampton's cavalry covered the front and flanks. Hardee, having farther to march than Johnston estimated, was replaced by part of Hampton's cavalry pending his arrival. Such was the arrangement.

Now let us pass to Slocum's front. General Carlin's division of the 14th Corps, during the morning of the 19th of March, was moving steadily toward Bentonville probably in the usual column of fours, covered on front and flank by active skirmishers. The Confederate cavalry became more stubborn than usual; so much so that Carlin sent his division into line. So far to the left did he deploy that the watchful corps commander, General Jeff. C. Davis, sent Morgan's division to the right of Carlin. All this development was intended to force back the Confederate cavalry, or uncover Confederate infantry and artillery, if they were there. It was this Union force which pressed Hampton's cavalry so hard that it hastened back, according to orders, to give space to Johnston's battle lines. Hampton very soon being out of the way a fearful Confederate fire opened at once at short range against the whole 14th Corps advance. At first Carlin's men were considerably shaken. Perceiving a growing disorder, the Confederates, those to the right of the Slocum road, suddenly took the offensive. They advanced in line against Carlin's left. We can imagine some trepidation and some breaking here and there even in the old 14th Corps; but Slocum's men were veterans, and such men rally quickly after a sudden onslaught or surprise. While the sharp fighting was going on in the outer front, the 20th Corps and those of the

14th not engaged, arranged and barricaded a new line about half a mile to the rear of the point of attack. Johnston puts it this way: 'Some distance in the (federal) rear, there was a thick wood of young pine into which the federal troops were pursued, and in which they rallied and renewed the fight.' Johnston's language would imply a partial defeat. Slocum owns up to an enforced retreat to the position already prepared, but says with praise that the retiring troops 'were handled with skill and fell back without panic or demoralization, taking places in the line established.' In a short time in front of this second position the hot engagement was renewed. But this time the opposition was too strong for Johnson's men to overcome. They charged again and again, but finally retired beyond range, doubtless hoping to renew the assault at daylight in the morning of the 20th; but during the night Johnston learned that we had re-enforced Slocum by one division, and that my entire command was approaching Bentonville form the east by Cox's road, so that a new position became necessary for the energetic Confederate, for he had to face both Slocum's column and ours. Johnston chose well the new position, and put his forces there. It was a kind of bridge-head with bended line, having Bentonville behind it, covering the crossing of Mill creek, and thus holding the Smithfield road.

Sherman compared this position of Johnston to the letter V, with the point toward our center and the sides at right angles to our converging roads. Our officers on close examination had named it a convex curve, with the convexity toward us. The curves, however, were made up of irregular and broken lines so located as to secure a thorough defense of the village and the road of retreat. During the 20th of March, our army closed up to Bentonville, driving the Southern Confederate cavalry before us. Logan went into position next to Slocum and Blair deployed his divisions to the right; thus we embraced the works of the Confederates. The whole line ran from the right to left as follows: The 17th, 15th, 14th and 20th corps, with proper reserves covering each flank. Sherman sent Kilpatrick's cavalry far to the left. Early in the morning of March 21, the 17th corps made a reconnaissance; General Mower was sent with two brigades to penetrate the thickets and search out the enemy's left. He worked his way through a swampy area where there was abundant wood and thick underbrush. With his usual eagerness, Mower pressed out beyond support, a little too far to the north, becoming with his two brigades separated from his corps. He struck, evidently some points beyond the enemy's left flank, coming upon a reserve rear guard which he had first driven before him. The Confederate commander, seeing what was upon him, made a counter attack, with a larger force, upon Mower's front and flank. He thus forced him to withdraw, and General Hampton says that that withdrawal was in great haste, in fact a complete repulse. Hampton is doubtless right; but as soon as an appeal came from Mower, Blair was ordered to support him with his whole corps, and Logan was directed to make a diversion by advancing and seizing the skirmish rifle pits along his front. All this was done and well done; but just as Mower was again confidently leading a connected column against the same Confederate flank with better prospects of a complete success, then it was that General Sherman called him back. Sherman also withdrew Blair's entire command, after which counter movement there was nothing more till evening except a little cannon firing and skirmishing between the lines. Our general's final action created much feeling at the time, and some severity of criticism. One reason he gave was that Mower was apt to be too rash and he thought he was acting of his own motion; another that he had himself over-estimated Johnston's force and still another, which was doubtless the governing reason at the time, there had been bloodshed enough, and that Johnston would surely retreat northward and leave him, leaving Sherman to go on and complete his connections and establish his new base of supplies. None of these reasons fully satisfied our officers at the time, but events were already ripening which very soon made us glad that this last battle had not been pushed to an extremity and made more bloody. During the night of the 21st, Johnston hurried away, makings his usual clean retreat. Our aggregate loss, as we gave it, was 1604. Johnston's, as he rendered it, was 2343.

General Slocum accounted for 338 prisoners captured, General Howard for 1287, making 1625 in all; whereas, General Johnston acknowledges but 653, a difference of 972 in the count.

It is easy to see that the Confederate organizations at the time were too broken and too mixed up to admit of accurate estimates or accounts. General Sherman, in speaking of this last battle, had remarked: 'With the knowledge now possessed of his (Johnston's) small force, I committed an error in not overwhelming his army on the 21st of March, 1865."(35)

The following are the losses that the 31st Missouri Infantry Regiment received from March 9th through March 22nd. The battle losses are listed above. Private John Morrison of Company A was buried at the National Cemetery at Paduka, Kentucky on March 14, 1865, cause of death unknown. Private Nathaniel Tipton of Company C from Hopewell, Missouri was transferred to the Veteran Reserve Corps on March 15, 1865.

The Battle of Bentonville, North Carolina was over, the Federal army was again on the march in the direction of Raleigh, North Carolina following the Confederate army. Lieutenant Lynch records in his diary, "Thurs. Mar. 23 - B.(attalion) marched in the direction of Goldsboro, N.C. marched about 8 miles & went into camp at 2 p.m. B.(attalion) was in advance of the Division."(1) Private Smith wrote basically the same, "Thur. 23rd. Marched about 10 miles and in the direction of Goldsboro and camped for the night."(2) The 1st Division foragers were waiting for their regiments to come to Everetsville, North Carolina. They had come into possession of plenty of salt pork but was still not sure which way the division was going to march. The 1st Division, who followed the 3rd Division on the march, did not see any Confederate cavalry during the whole day going into camp about a quarter of a mile from Falling Creek with his ambulance, ordnance train and artillery across the creek to keep them away from the enemy in case of an attack.

The 2nd Division left camp at six-thirty a.m. marching to the Hall's House which for some unexplained reason caught on fire and burned down. The 3rd Division left camp at seven-thirty a.m. and marched eleven miles on the Goldsborough Road going into camp around four p.m. camping on the road near Falling Creek Church. On the march they were following the 4th Division.

A report was issued that listed the amount of prisoners captured by the 1st Division from the January 27, 1865 through March 22, 1865.

"HDQTRS. FIRST DIVISION, FIFTEENTH ARMY CORPS,
OFFICE OF PROVOST-MARSHALL,
In the Field, N.C., March 23, 1865.
CAPTAIN: I have the honor to submit the following report of prisoners of war, captured by this division during the past campaign, commencing on the 27th day of January and ending on the 22d day of March, 1865, viz:

Colonel..	1
Captains...	3
First lieutenants..	4
Second lieutenants.......................................	4
Sergeants...	9
Corporals...	13
Privates..	331
Total...	365
Total commissioned.....................................	12
Total non-commissioned..............................	22
Total privates..	331

I have the honor to be, very respectfully,
GEO. A. HENRY
Captain and Provost-Marshal.
Capt. Fred. H. Wilson,
Actg. Asst. Adjt. Gen.,
First Division, Fifteenth Army Corps."(3)

Lieutenant Lynch records in his diary, "Fri. Mar. 24 - moved to & went into camp at Goldsboro N.C."(4) Private Smith wrote in his diary, "Fri. 24th. Marched 12 miles crossed Neuse river passed Goldsboro and camped 2 miles from town."(5) The 1st Division left their camp site at eight a.m. following behind the 3rd Division. They crossed the Neuse River over a pontoon bridge leaving the 3rd Brigade over on the other side of the river in order to become the guard for the division train. The rest of the 1st Division went into camp on the New Berne Road at Rouse's Plantation about one and one-half mile east of a town named Webbville, North Carolina. General Woods made his headquarters at the home of Mister Rouse while his men went on line near the road throwing up defensive works to protect themselves from the Confederates. Not only were they going to spend a night here, it was here that they prepared to go into camp to stay awhile. Major-General Charles R. Woods issued special orders number forty-nine, explaining that they would now be going into camp with the establishment of regimental streets, sinks (sinks- are places for the men to go to the bathroom) for the men with detailed orders not to go to the bathroom anywhere else. They were to clean their weapons, leather and other accouterments. All this was in preparation for the drills and inspections that were going to take place once the camp was fully set up. The men were all ordered to get a haircut to meet military specifications.

The 2nd Division left their camp site of the day before they marched to Goldsborough, North Carolina where they went into camp about one mile east of town. The 3rd Division left camp at seven forty-five a.m. following the 4th Division when they went into camp about one mile east of Goldsborough. The right of the division went into camp next to the 1st Division with the left flank going into camp on the North Carolina Railroad coming into contact with the 4th Division.

Lieutenant-Colonel Abraham J. Seay commanding the Consolidated Battalion 31st and 32nd Missouri Infantry in a report to Colonel Samuel P. Simpson, Adjutant-General of Missouri, dated March, 25, 1865 states:

"Many of our men are without shoes blankets, and but little clothing of any kind, but their health and morale were never better. They feel that under the leadership of 'Old Tecumseh' one more short and vigorous campaign must end this the most wicked rebellion of modern times. We have marched over a hostile country almost impassable by reason of its numerous swamps and streams, at a season of the year when the weather is most unfavorable, subsisting on the country, and have driven before us an army mad with desperation; forced the enemy to evacuate Charleston and Wilmington, and whipped Johnston's concentrated forces on his own chosen grounds; then marched into and occupied Goldsborough, to which point the railroad from Wilmington and New Berne will soon be in running order."(6)

The following diary entry by Lieutenant Lynch, "Sat. Mar. 25 thru April 9th - remained in camp & worked on R.(ifle) pits received large mail from north on March 29th - B.(attalion) were on Pickett on Apr. 4th - Did Drill."(7) The following are the entries in Private Fielding Jenkins Smith diary from March 25th till the last day of record on March 30th.

"Sat. 25th. Wrote letter to Father and lay by all day.
Sun. 26th. Got a large mail, which was the first for near two months.
Mon. 27th. On guard and got three letters from home.
Tues. 28th. On fatique in the P.M. and Dress parade.
Wed. 29th of Mar. Wrote a letter home and one to P. F. Marton and got 2 from home and one from Fielding W. Jenkins.

Thur. 30th. Dress parade in the P.M."(8)

On March 28th, General Order Number Twelve from 15th Army Corps was a repeat of the order of General Woods order on conduct around camp. While in camp there would be three roll-calls for the troops. It appears that they were somewhat afraid that the men would take advantage of the time in camp to wander off. Below is one of the paragraphs in this order.

"III. Company commanders will be held responsible for the cleanliness and soldierly bearing of their men, and should consider themselves always on duty to this end. Non-commissioned officers in charge of squads will see that the men wash their hands and faces daily; that they comb and brush their heads; that their hair is kept short; that those on duty are properly dressed, and that those absent from camp on passes are clean and present a soldierly appearance. They will report to their company officers for punishment such men as are slovenly in their habits and careless with their arms and accouterments."(9)

The 3rd Brigade, 2nd Division, 15th Army Corps arrived at Goldsborough with the forage train with whom they were guards. They saw no Confederate troops on their thirty mile march. In his report Brigadier-General John M. Oliver said he observed a large number of men from the 15th Army Corps who were mounted on horses stripping the country side of everything that could be used by the citizens. This included bedding, dishes, cooking utensils and any food. If they happened to come to a house that was unoccupied they would take what they wanted and burn it down. There is no record of anything being done about the information that was supplied.

On April 6, 1864, 1st Lieutenant Beverly A. Davis of Company D, of the Consolidated Battalion of the 31st and 32nd Missouri Volunteer Infantry wrote a letter to his niece Ellen Davis of Steelville, Mo. It is included below.

"Head Quarters Co D Con. Batt. 31st and 32nd Mo Vols Infantry

Rouses Plantation, N.C. Apr 6th/65

My Dear Niece,

I received a letter from you Several days ago. And would have answered sooner. But have been so busy getting my papers all-right that I had no time to write letters. I was glad to have a letter from you again. I havent any news to write you, only that we have it officially that Richmond is in our possession. They did not only loose the city but also lost 25,000 prisoners and 500 pieces of Artilery. So says dispatch. I think we will be on the move again soon. I hope so for I want to see this war come to and end. I think there is better prospect than ever at this time of having peace soon. Tell Billy to write to me. I would like to get letters from all of you. Don't wait for me to write for I havent much time to write. I will have to close and go on dress parade.

This leaves me in good health.

Write soon. I am as ever your Uncle,

Beverly"(10)

On April 9, 1865 General Robert E. Lee surrendered his Army of Northern Virginia to Lieutenant-General U. S. Grant at Appomattox Court House, Virginia. In the written terms given to General Lee, officers would be allowed to keep their sidearms, baggage and horses along with verbal terms that would allow the men who claimed that they owned the horses they rode could keep them. At four-thirty p.m on April 9th General Grant telegraphed Secretary of War E. M. Stanton that General Lee had surrendered to the terms proposed by himself.

The following order was issued that dealt with the 15th Army Corps flags.

"GENERAL ORDER: HDQTRS. 15TH ARMY CORPS.

  # 21   GOLDSBOROUGH, N.C.   APRIL 9,1865

I. The flags hereinafter described will be used to designate corps, division, and brigade headquarters, and will accompany the several commanding officers on the march, and in action will designate the position to the troops and to the commanding officers.

II. Headquarters of the corps: Flag, silk or bunting, five feet six inches fly, five feet, hoist; field quartered with division colors-red, white, blue, and yellow fringe; in center of field, corps badge, and cartridge-box, regulation size, with the inscription over the box in gilt letters, "Forty rounds."

III. First. Headquarters First Division: Silk or bunting, same size as corps flag; field red, fringe yellow; with corps badge, the cartridge-box, in center of field, with motto above the box. Second. Headquarters Second Division: Silk or bunting, same size as corps flag; field white, fringe yellow; with corps badge, the cartridge-box, in center of field, with motto above the box. Fourth. Headquarters Fourth Division: Silk or bunting, same size as corps flag; field yellow fringe lighter shade same color; with corps badge, the cartridge-box, in center of field, with motto above.

IV. Brigade flags to be swallow-tailed, five feet from the peak to the end of swallow tail, and three feet to the fork, four feet five inches on pike. The field of the flag will be of the division color, and besides fringe, it will have a border of one of the corps colors other than the particular division color in the order of the brigade, for instance: First. First Brigade, First Division, field red, border white, fringe yellow, cartridge-box equidistant between pike and fork of swallow tail, motto above box. Second. Second Brigade, First Division, field division color, border blue, fringe yellow, corps badge as in First Brigade flag. Third. Third Brigade, First Division, same as First Brigade flag, border yellow.

V. The corps badge remains as announced in General Orders, Numbers 10, current series, from these headquarters, and will be worn by all the officers and men of this command. Division commanders will see that it is procured for the troops, and it is made the duty of the inspectors-general of the corps to report all cases of disobedience of this paragraph coming under their notice.

VI. All wagons and ambulances will be marked with their divisional badge, and corps headquarters supply train with headquarters badge.

By command of Major General John A. Logan:

MAX. WOODHULL,

Assistant Adjutant-General."(11)

Lieutenant Lynch records in his diary, "Mon. April 10th- B.(attalion) left Camp at 5 a.m. with command in direction of Raleigh, N.C. 1st Brigade was in the advance. Skirmished with the Rebs. We marched about 17 miles & camped at sunset."(12) The 1st Division marched on the road directly leading to Pikeville, North Carolina which was a railroad station on the Weldon Railroad. Once they arrived to within three miles of Pikeville they turned on a road that caused them to almost immediately cross Nahunta Creek. It was here that they met some resistance from a small force of Confederate cavalry.

Marching about three more miles they came to the road that led to Beulah and Folk's Bridge which crossed the Little River. It was here that they met the main force of Confederate cavalry which showed fight but once they figured the size of the Federal unit that they were facing they decided to evacuate the area. 1st Brigade went into their camp, that was estimated to have contained approximately fifteen hundred men, with the fires still burning. The 1st Division went into camp at five p.m. at a cross-roads which was the road that they had been traveling and a road that led to the towns of Beulah and Wilson, North Carolina. There were no casualties reported for the day.

Lieutenant Lynch records in his diary, "Tues. Apr. 11-B. (attalion) moved at 6 1/2 a.m. - Roads Bad - Skirmishing in our front all day. The Rebel Cavalry destroyed the bridges in our front."(13)   At six a.m the 1st Division moved out on the road toward Beulah, North Carolina and were in constant contact with the Confederate cavalry keeping up constant skirmishing throughout the march. After marching six miles they came to a bridge across a stream called the Great Swamp where the Confederate cavalry had tried to make a stand while they burned the bridge. Colonel Gage's 29th Missouri Infantry (Mounted) engaged the Confederates at the bridge, driving them off and saved the bridge from burning. The 1st Division reached Folk's Bridge at eleven a.m. when they came to the bridge it had been torn up by the Confederate cavalry, which consisted of a force of about fifteen hundred men, the bridge was repaired at about four p.m. The 1st Division continued to march for about another hour arriving about two miles from the Little River. They went into camp at a place on the road where it forked which was called Smithfield and Pineville roads. With the amount of skirmishing that had gone during the day it was amazing that the 1st Division reported no casualties for the days march.

The 2nd Division did not move very far on this date waiting for the wagon train carrying supplies to come up which was expected to arrive the next day. The 4th Division, after marching eleven miles on April 10th, marched twelve miles having to corduroy about four of these miles on April 11th. Part of the division went into camp in front of a swamp being separated three miles from the rest of the division which was ordered to go into camp where they were and prepare to leave early the next morning.

Lieutenant Lynch records in his diary, "Wed. Apr. 12 - B.(attalion) moved at 6 a.m. in direction of Raleigh. Roads Bad. Glorious news from Grant. Lee entire army surrendered on the 9th April at Appomattox C. H."(14) The joy in the whole army must have been hard to describe. It is hard to figure if the men knew that the war was over for them or did they expect to have to continue to fight until General Johnston surrendered. With the war almost over who wanted to fight and maybe end up being the last one killed. Did those who were still alive think about those who had died and who were buried throughout the south without ever seeing their loved ones again. I think they probably did. Even though the news was good it still meant that the Confederate army to their front still was prepared to fight. What was the possibility of those who had surrendered with General Lee come south and join up with General Johnston to continue the fight. These were thoughts that could have been going through the men. They could have also been thinking that it won't be long till they get home and see their loved ones which for some had been almost three years since they left them.

The following entries in the diary of Lieutenant Lynch for the time from April 13th through April 28th.

"Thurs. Apri. 13 - B.(attalion) moved to near Raleigh & went into camp. Marched about 15 miles. Raleigh evacuated. Rebels made but slight resistance. The 14th A. C. were first troops to enter Raleigh.

Fri. Apr. 14 - B.(attalion) moved at 8 a.m. passed through Raleigh in review and marched beyond 2 miles & went into camp.

Sat. Apr. 15 through 20 remained in camp. Mon. Apri. 17 learned of Presidents L. assination.

Thurs. Apr. 20 through April 28th - remained in camp. Moved camp to the east side of Raleigh. - Sat. Apr. 22 - B.(attalion) escorted the 1st Div. grain into country to obtain forge for animals.

Tues. April 25th - Troops reviewedby Gen'l Grant.

Thurs. Apr. 27th Johnston Surrenders."(15)

The reason that there was some doubts about the surrender is because of bad timing. General Lee had surrendered to General Grant on April 9th which was before the death of President Lincoln. General Sherman had made terms of surrender to General Johnston that were similar to what General

Grant had offered General Lee but had offered a few more items based upon what he believed President Lincoln had implied to him when he had been at City Point. The surrender negotiations happened after the death of President Lincoln. President Johnson and Secretary of War Stanton were not so sympathetic to the conquered army and refused to accept the terms offered by General Sherman. They sent General Grant to Raleigh to replace General Sherman. This and an article in the New York Times that the Secretary of War released caused General Sherman to blow up because he believed that the Secretary of War had slandered him and called him insubordinate by assuming to much authority in the surrender negotiations. This caused a rift in the relationship between Mr. Stanton and General Sherman that was never repaired. At the reviewing stand in Washington D. C. General Sherman snubbed Mr. Stanton by not shaking his proffered hand. General Sherman had to go back and tell General Johnston that the Federal government did not accept the terms and that he would have to accept the same terms as General Lee or there would be a resumption of hostilities. General Johnston did accept the terms which was good because General Sherman had ordered his army to be prepared to march at a moments notice. Can you imagine the men in the army and thinking that the surrender of the army facing them was a fact and then told to prepare to go fight again and with the possibility of being killed or wounded.

Major George W. Nichols wrote the following in his book, "The History of the Great March."

"April 13th.--In the order of march described yesterday the army has moved upon Raleigh. The central column and left wing crossed the river at Smithfield, the right wing going over at Battle's Bridge, fifteen miles farther up. The information we have received seems to indicate that Johnston will not fight until he reaches the Danville and Charlotte Road.

This morning news of the surrender of Lee reached us. Our army went wild with excitement when this glorious result was announced, and blessings were showered upon the grand old Army of the Potomac, which, after so many mortifying failures, is thus crowned by Grant's genius with magnificent laurels. Our troops gave cheer after cheer to express their joy, and then, when cheers became too feeble an expression, uttered yell upon yell until they waked the echoes for miles around. Then the bands burst forth in swelling strains of patriotic melody, which the soldiers caught up and re-echoed with their voices. Every body was proud and glad. In the language of our noble General, 'Glory to God and our glorious country!"(16)

The 1st Division went into camp on April 13th after crossing the Neuse River about one mile and one half beyond the river. They camped near the main road into Raleigh, North Carolina camping at the Wilder's Plantation. They had to spend some time corduroying the road that was pretty well tore up by the 3rd Division and 4th Division passing in front of them. On April 14th the 1st Division moved out in the late morning hours and marched through Raleigh following the 3rd Division again. They marched on the Hillsborough Road and going into camp some three miles beyond town on the west bank of Beaver Dam Creek on the right side of the road. General Logan was concerned about the continued problem of stragglers and some men who were using the surgeons to give them permission to travel in front of the army. Both groups of these men were using their freedom to raid the residences of the citizens. On April 26th the 3rd Division of the 15th Army Corps was disbanded and the regiments assigned to the three other divisions in the corps.

On April 27th General Howard issued an order to General Logan informing him that they would probably be heading toward Richmond and since they were no longer at war, they were to turn in all ammunition both artillery and infantry. The infantrymen were allowed to keep the customary forty rounds in their cartridge boxes. General Howard was also concerned about the reputation of the army while on the march. For the past two years the Federal army of the Western Theater had been foraging liberally from the country that they been marching through. Now to show the states that had once been their enemies that they were no longer at war. It was important that they march through the states of North Carolina and Virginia without destroying the property and robbing the citizens. It was so important that they sent guards in front of the army to guard civilian houses and public property. Those who might have been tempted to rob from the citizens was warned that if they were caught that punishment would be severe and immediate.

Lieutenant Lynch recorded in his diary, "Sat. Apr. 29 - B.(attalion) moved at 7 a.m. marched 12 miles went into camp at 2 p.m."(17) There was a whole new aspect to this march that was unlike any march that the 31st Missouri Infantry Regiment had ever taken before. They were on their way home. They were no longer chasing General Johnston and his Confederate Army, there was not the major fear of encountering a strong force of soldiers drawn up in a line of battle ready to kill them. They were still in a position that they might have to defend themselves in case they would come into contact with some renegades who were not quite willing to admit the war was over. It should be an easy walk in the park for the army.

Lieutenant Lynch recorded in his diary, "Sun. Apr. 30 - B.(attalion) remained in camp - Mustered by Lt. Col. Seay for the months of March & April 65 went to church in 27th Mo."(18) Throughout the war the privilege to observe a worship service on a Sunday was almost unheard of. They were either marching or fighting on the Lord's day.

Lieutenant Lynch records in his diary the following for May 1st through May 22nd with anything in parenthesis I have put in to give the place where they camped taken from reports from the Official Records. In his diary "B." is one way that he abbreviates Battalion.

"Mon. May 1 - B. moved at 6 a.m. marched 23 miles during the entire day.

Tues. May 2 - B. moved at 5 a.m. moved about 20 miles and camped. (Fishing Creek on the Shady Grove Road)

Wed. May 3 - B. moved at 5 a.m. marched to Roanoke River & camped.

Thurs. May 4 - B. moved in the afternoon crossing Roanoke River at Robinson Ferry marched about 12 miles & went into camp.

Fri. May 5 - B. moved at 5 a.m. marched 20 miles & camped. (Spencer's Plantation not far from Wyatt's crossing on the Nottoway River)

Sat. May 6 - B. moved at 5 a.m. marched about 18 miles and camped at a small creek called "Stony Creek".

Sun. May 7 - B. moved at 6 a.m. marched to & went into camp near Petersburg, Va.

Mon. May 8 - Remained in camp.

Tues. May 9 - Batt left camp at 7 a.m. for Richmond,

VA. marched about 10 miles & camped (crossed the Appomattox River).

Wed. May 10 - B. moved to & went into camp at Manchester, VA. Pinkney Mayberry - SGT Co "B" Cons. Batt. died very suddenly of conjestive he was a good man & an excellent soldier. He was buried with honors of war; near Manchester, VA.

Thurs. May 11 - B. remained in camp thru Fri. May 12th.

Sat. May 13 - B. left camp enroute for Washington D. C. passed thru Richmond at 8 a.m. marched to the Chickamauga River & camped.

Sun. May 14 - B. moved at 5 a.m. marched to Hanover C. H. & camped.

Mon. May 15 - B. moved at 5 a. m. marched about 20 miles.

Tues. May 16 - B. moved at 5 a.m. marched to near Fredericksburg, VA. & went into camp.

Wed. May 17 - B. moved to & crossed the Raphiden at Fredericksburg passed Stafford C. H. & went into camp.

Thursday May 18 - B. moved at 4 a.m. (Camped at Occoquan, Virginia)

Fri. May 19 - B. moved to within 3 miles of town & went into camp.

Sat. May 20 - B. remained in camp.

Sun. May 21 - B. moved to & went into camp at Alexandria.

Mon. May 22 - B. remained in camp - roads very muddy."(19)

In his diary Lieutenant Lynch records some of the most important things that happened to them on the march which was the loss of Sergeant Pinkney Mayberry and how far they marched especially on days when they marched twenty miles or more. They passed through some of the famous battlefields of earlier in the war such as Fredericksburg and Petersburg. On May 11th, the army remained in camp and severe heavy thunderstorms began with four soldiers being killed near General Logan's headquarters.

Lieutenant Lynch records in his diary, " Tues. May 23 - B.(attalion) moved across the Potomac & camped in Washington D.C."(20) Orders came for the 15th Army Corps with directions on who was to pass the reviewing stand first. They would pass in this order with the corps headquarters and its escorts with the divisions following in order. 1st, 2nd, 4th Divisions followed by the Artillery Brigade of the 15th Army Corps. They marched with two days cooked rations in their haversacks, no knapsacks. They marched with column of companies in closed mass. There was a small space between regiments, brigades and divisions. The route they took was the starting point from the Treasury Department to Seventeenth Street then proceeded down Pennsylvania Avenue with their weapons carried at shoulder arms with bayonets fixed. The infantry divisions were to follow the Pioneer troops, made of mostly ex-slaves who had enlisted into the Pioneers, of its division who marched with axes and spades at right-shoulder shift. Some of the commanders had also allowed ex-slave women with their children to accompany the march with goats, cows and pack mules loaded down with poultry and ham to represent the following of so large a group of ex-slaves on the march not only through the Carolinas but also Georgia. Six ambulances were to follow behind each brigade with the ambulances traveling three across, these represented the baggage trains.

Lieutenant Lynch recorded in his diary, "Wed. May 24th - B.(attalion) went on Review. I saw the President."(21) Lieutenant-Colonel Abraham J. Seay in his report to Missouri Adjutant-General Colonel Samuel P. Simpson, dated May 30, 1865, "On the 24th day of May 1865, we were reviewed at the White House by President Johnson and Lieutenant-General Grant. My battalion marched so well that it elicited much admiration and praise. After the review we marched to Crystal Springs our present camp."(22) At nine a.m. the review started with General Sherman leading the way accompanied by General Howard and all of his staff. Once General Sherman had passed the reviewing stand he went on it and there shook hands with all but Secretary of War Stanton with whom he did not shake hands because he was still upset about the controversy of the terms of peace he had offered to General Johnston. They were followed by General Logan, who finally received command of the Army of the Tennessee. I'm sure that the 15th Army Corps got to lead the way because it was General Shermans old corps. He was followed by Major General W. B. Hazen, who was in command of the 15th Army Corps. He was followed by the 1st Division led by Major General Charles R. Woods and staff with the 29th Missouri Infantry led by its commander, Colonel Gage.

The 29th Missouri had served the latter part of the war as mounted infantry. Following them was the 1st Brigade, led by Brigadier Genreal William B. Woods leading the 76th Ohio, 27th Missouri, 93rd Indiana, 31st and 32nd Consolidated Battalion of Missouri Volunteer Infantry, 4th Minnesota and 15th Indiana. The 2nd Brigade followed with Colonel Catterson commanding leading the 93rd Illinois, 40th Ohio, 46th Ohio, 26th Illinois, 100th Indiana and 103rd Illinois. They were followed by the 3rd Brigade with Colonel George A. Stone commanding, leading the 4th, 5th, 25th, 30th, 26th and 31st Iowa Volunteer Infantry Regiments. They were followed by the remaining divisions of the 15th Army Corps and the artillery brigade of the 15th Army Corps. They were followed by the 17th Army Corps who along with the 15th Army Corps made up the Right Wing on the march through the Carolina's. The 20th Army Corps followed them closely followed by the 14th Army Corps who together made the Left Wing of the march through the Carolinas. This review lasted six and one-half hours.

It was a review of contrasts. On May 23rd the Army of the Potomac had marched in their brand new uniforms and starched collars. They wore their knapsacks and looked every bit the well dressed soldier of the United States. The Army of the West was, by reputation a bunch of roughs who seemed never to be in the proper uniform. They were rough in dress and it was believed that they could not march as well as the Army of the Potomac and thus were not expected to put on the performance of the previous day. But when you had marched over all parts of the United States east of the Mississippi and south of the Mason Dixon line they were as able to march as their counterparts from the east.

The following is an article that was printed in the "Daily Missouri Democrat," a Saint Louis, Missouri daily paper, that described the review, of what was referred to as the western army. It was printed on Tuesday morning, May 30, 1865.

"THE REVIEW.
ARMIES OF THE WEST.
APPEARANCE OF THE TROOPS.
THE POPULAR DEMONSTRATION.
(Correspondence of the Cincinnati Commercial.)
Washington, May 24.—The card here is the 'Western Army,' as the four corps, under Sherman, who have arrived here, are constantly called. The Army of the

Potomac is familiar here. It has several times passed through the city. The boys in blue from the far West, are what the crowd comes to see—the boys who have marched from the Ohio to the ocean; from Atlanta to the Atlantic; from the Tennessee to the Savannah; from the Savannah to the Potomac. These are the men who broke the egg-shell of the Southern Confederacy, and came upon Lee's communications in North Carolina before the Army of the Potomac had made conquest of the territory between the James and the Potomac.

There is the most vivid curiosity here to see the victors at Fort Donelson and Vicksburg, Stone River, Lookout Mountain, and Jonesboro, the heroes of the historic fields of the West.

SHERMAN AND HIS GENERALS.

At daylight the stir commenced on the street, and in a little while the sidewalks were full. The morning was beautiful, not a cloud in the sky. At nine o'clock precisely, General Sherman, with General Howard and staff, rode up Pennsylvania avenue. Sherman sat erect, and his bearing was, it seemed, slightly haughty. He barely acknowledged the cheering on the sidewalk, giving a slight, jerky nod, that one could hardly tell was a nod. Howard rode quietly along, his empty right sleeve noted by all observers. He lost an arm when serving as a Colonel, at the head of a regiment from Maine, at the battle of Fair Oaks. Next Came Major General John A. Logan, black haired and swarthy, with a long mustache, black as ink. His appearance has greatly changed since he was here as a Congressman, and greatly improved.

As he rode up the avenue he was vociferously cheered, and bowed his acknowledgments repeatedly. A negro woman ran out to hand him a bouquet, which he accepted and carried. Arriving at the President's stand, Generals Sherman and Howard took their places upon it. The group on the stand was very interesting. In the center was President Johnson, looking very well; on his right was the Lieutenant General, and next to him the Secretary of War. On the left was General Sherman, and something like a dozen Major Generals. The old Army of the Tennessee was delighted to see the familiar features of their old commander, Grant, with whom they had fought and conquered from Donelson to Vicksburg, and under whose eye they advanced to the assault of Mission Ridge.

DIFFERENCES IN THE ARMIES.

There was a decided difference in the Armies of the Potomac and the West, apparent to all spectators. The Western boys looked hard. They were dingy, as if the smoke of many battles had dyed their garments, and the dirt and mud of the sacred soil of a dozen insurrectionary States had adhered to them. Their wool hats, well worn and dirty gave them a most somber covering. The weather-beaten style of the whole army was only the more apparent in the splendor of the unclouded sun.

THE NEGRO ENGINEERS.

One of the most noticed features of Sherman's army was the negro regiments of engineers, all black as death, dingy in their old plantation clothes, and carrying spades, picks and axes. They marched well and were received with immense applause. But they looked neither to the right nor to the left, but moved on with a grim, moody silence, each a specimen of a Sphynx. Every man of them had been recruited with liberty for bounty in the fields of the far South. It was about as good an advertisement of the abolition of slavery as one could wish to see. The ragged standards, with such words as 'Vicksburg' and 'Atlanta' on them, were the exclamation points in the page of history that this triumphal march illuminates. Wherever displayed they were greeted with enthusiastic acclamations, and feelings that were too deep and grateful for loud applause, suggesting tears of thanksgiving rather than the cheering that is too common on light occasions, to be most appropriate in the festivals in which are celebrated a nation's deliverance.

The boys carried their guns a little carelessly (as compared with the Army of the Potomac), and marched with that long, steady, slashing step, in which alone they would have made their immortal tour of the continent. They had not such a number of fine brass bands as discoursed such eloquent music for the Army of the Potomac, but the deep roll of their drums was eloquent enough. Those drums had been heard on the banks of the Ohio and all the way of Sherman's march down to the sea, and up again to the Potomac; and they would be at marches of victory around the globe, if there were orders to so.

THE STERN AND MARTIAL BEARING OF THE ARMY.

The fixed, stern bearing of General Sherman, his style—which a profane person might denominate his 'don't care a damnativeness'—characterized his whole army. There was a look almost fierce and sullen on nearly every face. There was a rigidity of jaw and straight forward scornfulness of eye in every rank, that no observer could fail to mark. The great, grim, dingy, gloomy masses, marched as if in solemn contempt of all such displays; marched with a bitter, business-like scowl, as if they might be going to battle. Evidently, no part of the American people have been converted into soldiers so thoroughly, as these gaunt veterans of Sherman's army.

It is the army of the desolation of the South, that has made its mark of blood and ashes for two thousand miles, littering the whole line of its tremendous march with graves and the ruins of the habitations of its enemies. These are the men who brought the first wail of despair from the enemies of American nationality; and you can read something of this grand and terrible history in the dark faces of the heroes.

The ambulances were worn, and had many marks of hard service and long journeying. The old stretchers, upon which the wounded had been carried to the rear, from the battle-fields of the far West, were carried along as if for immediate use. The absence of all the ornament, all the fuss and feathers, and the presence of all the utilities of war, was seen from one end to the other of the massive column. The army was at its best fighting weight and condition. If there had been such an army as this four years ago, the war would have been over in Mr. Seward's first ninety days. But of course it would take four years to make such an army, in a country where the arts of peace had been so exclusively cultivated as in ours.

Sherman's artillery passed by batteries, six guns abreast, and the heavy jar and sullen rattle of the ponderous carriages made the pavements tremble. The horses, after all their hard work dragging the black muzzled dogs of war through the swamps of the Carolinas and the quicksands of Virginia, though thin, were in fair serviceable condition, and the harness, although plainly it had stood the tug and fret of many a weary pull, was good for hard work yet.

Sherman's men did not look upon themselves as favored by the opportunity of displaying themselves, but regarded the performance as a bore of large proportions, and some of the line officers were not in line, having embraced a chance to avoid a march of nearly fifteen miles through the heat and dust.

A PICTURESQUE TRAIN.

The most picturesque and remarkable feature of the day was the train of pack-animals that followed Geary's division of the 20th corps. It gave a better idea of campaigning than anything ever before seen north of the Potomac. All sorts of jackasses were gathered together, some wonderfully small, mounted by juvenile darkies, who rode along in the most every-day manner imaginable. Others were gigantic, big and uncouth as camels, and bearing wonderful loads of blankets and camp equipments. On some of them the packs were monstrous, and it was a puzzle how the patient things contrived to tramp along. One fellow had a beautiful white goat on a pack. Mr. Goat seemed to take the world very easily. The soldier leading the ass was asked, 'Where did you get your goat, Mister?' 'In Atlanta,' was the reply; no words wasted. On several packs were seen fine specimens of game chickens; and, from their complacent attitude, one would suppose the scene was by no means novel or interesting to them.

COMPARISON.

Comparisons between armies may be invidious, but it is impossible not to make them. At least, there is no man, woman or child in Washington who has not compared and thought of the difference between the army that marched up Pennsylvania avenue yesterday, and the one that marched to-day; and it is not because I am a Western man that I write that the verdict is universally and cordially given that the Army of the West was most like an army! The marching of our Western boys was magnificent. But adjectives fail to tell what all it

590

was. It was glorious to see. Lord bless you, the boys had done it before. They had marched two thousand miles in an enemy's country-why shouldn't they have made a display 'grand, gloomy and peculiar,' in the capital of their country? They did it. It was triumph for them, to-day, such as has rarely been witnessed upon the earth. The great, solid masses of boys in blue, bristling with steel, moved up Pennsylvania avenue, and before the President of the United States, conquerors and the heroes of the day. And there was not an eye, loyal to the flag of the Nation, that did not kindle, to see how compact, how splendid, and how admirable they were.

I looked from the front of the Treasury Building, upon the 14th corps-the boys, of the West, who were a wall of steel and fire at Chickamauga-and saw them fill the whole avenue, from the Capitol to the marble columns of the Treasury, and Europe never saw a grander sight, not a braver one. It was like a mighty serpent, winding in the majesty of power, on its way, each bristle a spike of steel, shining in the full splendor of the sun, that all day looked down upon this memorable pageant, from a sky that had not a speck of cloud to dim the brilliance of its blue-blue, the color of the boys who marched so grandly to-day under the flag, and keeping step to the music of the Union."(23)

After the grand review they went into camp at Crystal Springs they remained there until May 31st when they boarded the railroad cars for the trip to Louisville, Kentucky. Nothing much happened while they were in camp of note except that Lieutenant Lynch was promoted to Captain of Company D, Consolidated Battalion and Private McGill of Company D shot Syl. Young in the breast causing a serious wound. Private McGill was intoxicated at the time. The good news for the 31st and 32nd Missouri Infantry Regiments was that they were to be mustered out. Any regiment who would have three years in by October 1, 1865 were to be mustered out. Most of the men in the 31st Missouri Infantry met this requirement and were mustered out on June 13, 1865 in Washington D.C.

At the twenty-first meeting of the Army of the Tennessee at Toledo, Ohio, General Leggett was asked to make a speech and he gave his speech on what he saw at the review stand.

His speech is listed as follows.

"I was on the platform in Washington during the two days of that review at the close of the war. The first day the Army of the Potomac marched in review, and the second day General Sherman's army marched in review. During the whole of the first day I sat and saw the troops march by. During the second day my division was near the head of the column, and as soon as its head had passed, I took my place upon the platform, and remained there during the rest of the day. And I was interested in the conversation of the generals of the eastern army, while our troops were marching by. They would turn, and look at each other, and say, 'Why, they march as if they were well drilled, and they march as if they understood tactics as well as our army!' Perfectly astonished that we could march well, and that we could keep an alignment, and that we could be real soldiers. If they had seen the men running out from the lines, and catch a chicken on the side of the street somewhere, why, it would have met their expectation; but the idea that they could move right forward in a solid body, and keep step to the music, and not drop out, and every man minding his own business, was astonishing. I don't suppose that there was a better drilled army in the country than the Army of the Tennessee."(24)

Most of the 31st Missouri Infantry Regiment along with most of the 27th and 29th Missouri Infantry Regiments went home to Missouri being mustered out in Washington, D.C. They soon arrived in East Saint Louis, Illinois where the following article from the "Daily Missouri Democrat" will describe the reception they received.

"RETURN OF THE 27TH, 29TH AND 31ST MISSOURI.

Grand Reception of the Veterans.

Banquet at Turners' Hall.

Eloquent Speech of Gov. Fletcher.

As soon as it became known in the city that the Missouri soldiers, who accompanied Sherman in his grand march to the sea, had arrived at Washington, and would shortly come home, a committee of citizens was extemporized, and preparations were made to give the heroes a grand reception.

About ten o'clock yesterday morning it was ascertained

that the 27th, 29th and 31st Missouri infantry had arrived at East St. Louis. The committee, with a band of music, proceeded across the river to escort the veterans to the shores of Missouri. Governor Fletcher, who was the first colonel of the 31st, had come down from Jefferson City to meet his old companions in arms, and Adjutant General Simpson, originally lieutenant colonel of the same regiment, accompanied him, and both went over to see the boys on their arrival. The men at once recognized their old officer, and the meeting was joyous one. Several other gentlemen, formerly connected with one of the regiments, went over to meet them, among whom we may mention General D. C. Coleman, Colonel James Peckham, Colonel Lalhold, Lieutenant Colonel Phil. H. Murphy, Lieutenant Colonel Thos. McVicker, Colonel Jno. S. Cavender, Captain W. H. Judd, Captain Geo. A. Maguire, Captain Ed. Allen, Captain Ed. Stevens, Quartermaster Bryan Foley, and others. Mayor Thomas and several members of the old Veteran Reception Committee formed a part of the committee.

When the committee and the accompanying citizens arrived on the other side of the river they were vociferously cheered by the veterans, drawn up in line, and returned the compliment in the same style.

THE VETERANS
presented a fine appearance. There were 445 of them, of which 106 belonged to the 27th, 166 to the 29th, and 173 to the 31st. They had been mustered out at Washington City, but owing to some informality, are to be mustered out again at Benton barracks. They are all fine, healthy looking men, and a true type of the American volunteer soldier. Among them were a few who exhibited a devil-may-care recklessness, and we set them down as belonging to General Sherman's 'bummers.' The great majority, however, were quiet, orderly, intelligent looking men, who will beat their swords into pruning hooks, and step gracefully form the business of war into the pastures of peace.

ROSTER OF OFFICERS.
27th Regiment—Colonel Thomas Curly; Major, Denis O'Conner; Adjutant, Robert G. Reilly; Captain Thomas C. Ryan; Lieutenants, John C. Johnson, B. K. Nelson,

Albert C. Haney.

29th Regiment—Colonel, Joseph S. Gage; Major Christian Burkhart; Adjutant William Goodwin; Quartermaster, Moses Osborn; Assistant Surgeon Moses B. Carr; Captains, Thomas L. Morgan, Wm. Haney, Henry A. Simbert and David Allen, Jr. Lieutenants Joseph H. Russell, Berhurt Uhrig, Edwart Argast, Frank N. Taylor and Gus. Slicker. This Regiment was lately mounted as cavalry.

31st Regiment—Captain Mathias Minor; Lieutenants David H. Mittendorf, John Sweeney and Wm. J. Wilson.

THE BADGE OF THE 15TH ARMY CORPS.

The officers and men of this remnants of regiments wore the badge of the 15th army corps-a cartridge box on a red ground, with the figure '40' on it. When the corps went from Vicksburg to Chattanooga they had no such thing as a badge, and the incident which led them to adopt the present and is thus related by a letter-writer at Chattanooga, where they joined the Army of the Cumberland:

The troops which came here from the Army of the Potomac brought with them various ornamental habits and customs that were new to the Western soldiers. Among them was the corps badge which designated the corps to which officers and men were attached. For instance the badge of the 11th corps is a crescent; that of the 12th a star. The badge is made of any material-gold, silver, or red flannel-and is worn conspicuously on some part of the clothing. The Western corps have no such badge. How an Irishman explained the matter is thus told. A soldier came by the headquarters of General Butterfield, a tired, weather-beaten straggler. He was one of those who made Sherman's march from Memphis to Chattanooga, thence to Knoxville, and was now returning in the terrible cold of that returning march, thinly clad, one foot covered with a badly worn army shoe, the other with a piece of raw hide bound with strings about a sockless foot-both feet cut and bleeding. 'Arms at will,' he trudged past the headquarters guard, intent only upon overtaking his regiment. 'Halt,' said a sentinel with a bright piece, clean uniform and white gloves.

What do you belong to? '8ᵗʰ Missoory, sure.

What division?

Morgan L. Smith's, av course.

What brigade?

Giles Smith's 2d brigade of the 3d division, Col. Dave Coleman's regiment.

But what army corps?

The 15ᵗʰ, you d—d fool. I am one of the heroes of Vicksburg. Anything more, Mr. Sentinel?

Where is your badge?

My badge, is it. What is that?

Do you see this star on my cap? That is the badge of the 12ᵗʰ corps. That crescent on my partner's cap is the badge of the 11ᵗʰ corps.

I see now. That's how yez Potomick fellers gits home by dark nights. Ye takes the moon and shtars with ye.

But what is the badge of your corps?

Making a round-about, and slapping cartridge-box, our soldier replied: D' ye see that? A cartridge box-with a U.S. on a brash plate, and forty rounds in the cartridge-box—and sixty rounds in our pockets. That's the badge f the 15ᵗʰ, that came from Vicksburg to help ye fight Chattanoogy.'

THE RECEPTION.

After marching through the streets, and paying their respects to Generals Dodge and Pope, the veterans proceeded to Turner's Hall, where Governor Fletcher and other friends awaited them, and where the committee had prepared a magnificent banquet.

AT TURNER'S HALL.

On arriving at Turners' Hall, the soldiers stacked their arms and after hearty congratulations from their friends and relations, who had assembled to welcome their return. Judge T. J. Dailey as Chariman of the Committee on Reception, called the assemblage to order. He said their arrival had taken them by surprise; the committee had expected twenty-four hours notice of their arrival, in order that the citizens of St. Louis might give them a reception worth of the name of St. Louis. They had, however, done the best they could. A little delay would be necessary before the dinner hour, which he hoped would be borne with patience; in the meantime they would hear from his Excellency, Governor Fletcher, Colonel of the 31st, now Governor of this great State. Mr. Dailey concluded by calling General McNeil to the Chair.

General McNeil said,

Officers and Soldiers of the 1st Brigade, 1st Division, 15th Army Corps:

I feel proud in having the duty assigned me to preside over the ceremonies that attend your reception in St. Louis. It is unnecessary for me to make any remarks upon the occasion. I will merely do my duty in presenting to you his Excellency Governor Thomas C. Fletcher, now Governor of your proud State. Governor Fletcher was received with loud and prolonged cheering. (I have omitted his long speech)

RESPONSE OF COLONEL CURLEY.

As the representative of this little band which stands before you, I return you our sincere thanks for the kind reception which we have received at your hands to-day. Our worthy Governor and myself were associated in command of two of these regiments that stand before you. He is well acquainted with the history of these small regiments, as we and myself, and it is useless for me to go into a detail of what you are all well acquainted with. Suffice it to say, sir, that the little band which stand before you cannot be excelled for good soldiers and brave men in the army of General Sherman. But, sir, the little band that stands before you is but a small representation of the old Light Brigade, know in Missouri and in St. Louis as the Blair Light Brigade, [Cheers.] That brigade, sir, the part that is here to-day, has gone through many trials, and we have seen many bloody fields in the last three years. We left St. Louis three years ago with full regiments and we have traveled through every State in the Southern Confederacy since that time, with two exceptions—Texas and Florida. And now we have returned here, we find that we have not been doing all the work, and we do not take all the credit to ourselves. The people whom we have left behind have been doing their share, and we find on coming back to the free State of Missouri, and that the stain of slavery is wiped out from the Constitution as long as the State

596

of Missouri shall exist. In conclusion I wish to present to Governor Fletcher, in behalf of the 27th Missouri, which I have had the honor to command for the last three years, the flag which we have borne with us through all our career.

At the conclusion of Colonel Curley's remarks Colonel Peckham requested all the officers to sign the muster roll of the Turner Hall association, after which Governor Fletcher received the flag of the 27th and responded as follows.

RESPONSE BY GOVERNOR FLETCHER.

These old flags will be held very dear by the people of Missouri and will be preserved as testimonials of the glorious part which you have borne in this war. The Secretary of War has informed me that the chief mustering officer is directed to turn over to the Governors of the States the flags of all the regiments. We will preserve and cherish them in time to come so that posterity may look upon them with pride. And now just one word in conclusion. You are to give up these flags and stack forever the arms which you have borne so proudly and with such honor to yourselves, and in laying down these flags and in stacking these arms I trust you will bear away with you the sentiment announced by President Lincoln in his last inaugural message, and that you will treasure it in your hearts, because you are done with war and you go back to peaceful pursuits with malice towards none., with charity for all; with firmness in the Right as God enables you to see the Right. To work and bind up the nation's wounds, and care for him who shall have borne the battle and for his widow and orphans and I trust that the golden links of friendship which should unite the people who have agreed to live again under one government may grow lighter and brighter in the coming time, sot that they may gleam forth distinctive in the darkest and most trying hours which we shall know in the future, and that through all coming time we may live a united, happy and prosperous people.[Cheers]

A SOCIAL REUNION.

At the conclusion of the speaking in the hall, the veterans made a fray upon sundry kegs of lager, on tap in different parts of the room, while the officers retired to another apartment to take a social glass with quite a number of their former comrades who were not so fortunate as to be with them at the breaking of the backbone of the rebellion. Numerous bottles of champagne were uncorked, and brief speeches, pithy toasts and patriotic songs were the order of the day. Gen. Sherman, known as 'the Old Tycoon,' Gen. Grant, Gen. Logan, Gen. Blair, Gov. Fletcher and others were toasted and cheered and the memory of Gen. Lyon and Gen. McPherson was revived. Capt. W. M. Wilson, 4ht U. S. cavalry, a splendid looking officer, sang the spirited war song, 'Tramp, tramp' and Dick Johnson, Ed. Stevens, Col. Lalbold, Capt. Ehlert, Col. Peckham, Judge Daily, Mayor Thomas, General Coleman, Governor Fletcher, and a number of others mingle freely with the veterans, and made them feel 'at home.'

The banquet came off at last, and was highly relished. Although prepared on short notice, it was not unworthy of the heroes of Sherman's army.

To-day the boys will go out to Benton Barracks and in a short time will be paid off and mustered out, and return to the duties of citizenship."(25)

Those soldiers who were left in the Battalion had almost another month to spend in the military. Captain William H. Lynch of Company D Consolidated Battalion of 31st and 32nd Missouri Infantry Regiments in his diary describes what the rest of the battalion did that remaining night.

"June 4 - Sunday - The B.(attalion) arrived & went into camp at Louisville, KY at dark.

Mon. June 5 - The B.(attalion) drew 5 days rations the saltmeat was ham.

Tues. June 6 - B.(attalion) remained in camp till Monday July 17.

June 11 - Governor of Mo. visited the Batt. made speech - Samuel P. Simpson Adj. Gen. & commander of Mo. State troops with him.

Tues. July 4, 1865 - Gen. Sherman gave short speech after which we bid him farewell & the troops returned to camp.

Tues. July 18 - Batt. were mustered out of the service of the USA by Capt. Alexander & left Louisville, KY for

St. Louis, Mo. on the cars arrived at St. Louis, Mo. in morning of the 20th & went to Benton Bks. Day cloudy & Wet.

Fri. July 21 - Batt. remained in camp.

Sat. July 22 - Batt.. remained in Barracks till 2 o'clock when they left for the paymaster in St. Louis were paid & discharged. The Batt. broke ranks for the last time. May each & everyone live to enjoy the government he so nobly defended.

Thursday Aug. 10 - I arrived at my house."(26)

This ended the long hard struggle that the 31st Missouri Infanty Regiment had to endure for almost three years. They had traveled one thousand two hundred miles by railroad, two thousand five hundred miles by water and marched over three thousand miles on foot. This gave them a total distance traveled by all means of over six thousand seven hundred miles. They had marched and fought in seven Confederate states, marched through eleven states in rebellion and was engaged in twenty-nine battles, skirmishes and sieges making an aggregate of 166 days under fire. The total casualties in the regiment were: Killed - officers, two; men twenty: Died of wounds - officers, two; men, twenty-six: Died of disease - officers, three; men, two hundred and twelve: Deserted - men, one hundred and forty: Honorably Discharged - officers, nineteen; men, two hundred and sixty-five: Discharged for Disability - officers, one; men, one hundred and thirty-four: Dismissed - officers, three: Resigned - twenty-five: Missing in battle - men, fifty-two: Dishonorably Discharged - men, four: Killed by Sunstroke - men, one.

EPILOGUE

In trying to figure what to write for an epilogue, or if I even needed one, I have decided to do what I have done so much in this book is to quote someone who was there. I would have liked to have said this but I didn't. It is a quote from "The Story of the Great March" by Brevet Major George Ward Nichols printed in 1865. It is taken from pages 320 and 321, and is as follows.

"April 28th.--The orders are issued for the return of the army home. The 23d and 10th Corps, with Kilpatrick's gallant troopers, remain here to garrison the country. The rest--the faithful, patient 14th: the swift, tireless, heroic 15th; the tried veterans of the 17th; the noble, war-worn heroes of the 20th--companions of many a wearisome march and hasty bivouac--comrades upon many a battle-field--never defeated, always victorious, brothers always--are going to their homes, to be welcomed by the loving embrace of wife, mother, and sister--to meet the warm grasp of a brother's hand--to receive from the Nation the high honors she gladly and proudly pays to her gallant defenders.

Yet, in these hours of parting, let us not forget the brave and noble Dead! The companions of our journey who sleep in obscure but honorable graves, merit the meed of our profound and earnest homage. The memory of our dead is their noblest monument. Thousands of gallant spirits, whose remains are lying in the valley of the Tennessee, on the banks of the Oostanaula, by the Allatoona Pass, at Atlanta, and in the swamps of the Carolinas, live with us to-day. They shall never be forgotten while our hearts beat or the nation lives. The army pays them that tribute of respect which can only be given truly by the soldier who has stood side by side with the departed, hour by hour, day by day, year after year, in storm and sunshine, on the march or in the cloud of battle, in the bivouac or at the moment of sudden death. Peace to their ashes! May their memory be green, and our thought of them in coming years be that of love and pride!"

Amen and Amen!

ABBREVIATIONS;
The following abbreviations are used throughout the reference notes. This information is repeated where first used. They are listed here for easy reference.

C.M.S.M. – Chisholm Trail Museum – Governor Seay Mansion
c/o Ms. Renee' Mitchell
605 Zellers Avenue
Kingfisher, Oklahoma 73750

M.H.S. – Missouri Historical Society Library and Collections
P. O. Box 11940, Saint Louis, MO 63112-0040
314-746-4599

O. R. – The War of the Rebellion: A Compilation of the Official Records of the Union and Confederate Armies.

R.S.A.T.-Reunions of the Society of The Army of the Tennessee

W.H.M.C. – Western Historical Manuscript Collections.
These are collections at the University of Missouri campus'. The collections can be found on the internet. Go to a search and type in Missouri.

CHAPTER 1: BIRTH OF REGIMENT

1. DAILY MISSOURI DEMOCRAT OF SAINT LOUIS, MO.; JULY 11,1862
2. Ibid.
3. Ibid.
4. REPORT OF THE ADJUTANT GENERAL OF MISSOURI 1863, MISSOURI HISTORICAL SOCIETY, PRINTED 1863. MISSSOURI HISTORICAL SOCIETY LIBRARY, ST. LOUIS, MO (HEREAFTER REFERRED TO AS M.H.S.)
5. THE WAR OF THE REBELLION: A COMPILATION OF THE OFFICIAL RECORDS OF THE UNION AND CONFEDERATE ARMIES; SERIES 1, VOLUME 13, PAGE 693 (HEREAFTER REFERRED TO AS O. R. FOR OFFICAL RECORDS)
6. MESSAGES AND PROCLAMATIONS OF THE GOVERNORS OF THE STATE OF MISSOURI; VOLUME IV, PAGE 46 & 47. PUBLISHED BY THE STATE HISTORICAL SOCIETY OF MISSOURI, COLUMBIA MISSOURI; 1924
7. REUNIONS OF THE SOCIETY OF THE ARMY OF THE TEN-

NESSEE; CLEVELAND, OHIO; 16TH MEETING; OCTOBER,17&18, 1883; PAGES 501 THROUGH 503 (HEREAFTER REFERRED TO AS R.S.A.T.)

8. DAILY MISSOURI DEMOCRAT OF SAINT LOUIS, MO.

9. MORNING REPORT COMPANY C; RG 94: REGIMENTAL BOOKS, 31MO INF.;NATIONAL ARCHIVES, WASHINGTON D.C.

10. KUCK, HENRY, PAPERS, 1861-1865; (SL242) WESTERN HISTORICAL MANUSCRIPT COLLECTION, UNIVERSITY OF MO- ST. LOUIS, MO. (HEREAFTER REFERRED TO AS W.H.M.C.)

11. REGIMENTAL ORDER # 3; NOVEMBER 6, 1862; 31st MISSOURI REGIMENT ORDERS BOOK; RG 94: REGIMENTAL BOOKS, 31 MO. INF; NATIONAL ARCHIVES, WASHINGTON, D.C.

CHAPTER 2: VALLEY OF DEATH

1. KUCK, HENRY, PAPERS, 1861-1865 (SL242); W. H. M. C., UNIVERSITY OF MO-ST. LOUIS, MO.

2. KUCK, HENRY, PAPERS, 1861-1865 (SL242); W.H.M.C., UNIVERSITY OF MO-ST. LOUIS, MO

3. Ibid

4. HISTORY OF THE FORTY-EIGHTH OHIO VETERAN VOLUNTEER INFANTRY: BY JOHN A. BERING — LATE MAJOR 48TH OHIO AND THOMAS MONTGOMERY LATE CAPTAIN 48TH OHIO; 1880; PAGE 62 (HEREAFTER REFERRED TO AS 48TH OHIO VETERAN VOLUNTEER INFANTRY)

5. CIVIL WAR DIARY OF COLONEL ABRAHAM JEFFERSON SEAY; 32ND MISSOURI VOLUNTEER INFANTRY REGIMENT; PAGE 14; TYPESCRIPT COPY OF DIARY AT CHISHOLM TRAIL MUSEUM–GOVERNOR SEAY MANSION ;KINGFISHER, OKLAHOMA.(HEREAFTER REFERRED TO AS C.M.S.M.)

6. Ibid., PAGE 15

7. Ibid.

8. Ibid

9. Ibid, PAGE 15 & 16

10. O. R., VOLUME 17, CHAPTER 29, PAGE 654

11. O. R., VOLUME 17, CHAPTER 29, PAGE 655

12. R.S.A.T.;36TH MEETING AT COUNCIL BLUFFS, IOWA NOVEMBER 8-9, 1906; PAGE 95 - A LEAF FROM THE DIARY OF CAPTAIN LYMAN RICHARDSON

13. HISTORY OF THE THIRTEENTH ILLINOIS VOLUNTEER INFANTRY REGIMENT;PAGE 244; M.H.S., ST. LOUIS, MO

14. Ibid; PAGE 246

15. CIVIL WAR DIARY OF COLONEL ABRAHAM JEFFERSON SEAY; 32ND MISSOURI VOLUNTEER INFANTRY REGIMENT; PAGE 16; TYPESCRIPT COPY OF DIARY AT C.M.S.M.; KINGFISHER, OKLAHOMA.

16. R.S.A.T.;16TH MEETING AT COUNCIL BLUFFS, IOWA OCTOBER 17-18, 1883; PAGE 465

17. DAILY MISSOURI DEMOCRAT; SAINT LOUIS MISSOURI; WEDNESDAY MAY 20TH, 1863

18. GENERAL SHERMAN'S MEMOIRS, PAGE 443

19. Ibid., PAGE 471

20. HISTORY OF THE THIRTEENTH ILLINOIS VOLUNTEER INFANTRY REGIMENT; PAGE 282 & 283; M.H.S., ST. LOUIS, MO

21. CONFEDERATE VETERAN - APRIL 1894 - DECEMBER 1895 - VOLUME 2 #10 PAGE 295: EXTRACT FROM LETTER OF CAPT. S. J. RIDLEY, OF WHITER'S ARTILLERY, WHO WAS KILLED AT BAKER'S CREEK, MISSISSIPPI; GEORGIA STATE ARCHIVES; ATLANTA, GA.

22. CIVIL WAR DIARY OF COLONEL ABRAHAM JEFFERSON SEAY;32ND MISSOURI VOLUNTEER INFANTRY REGIMENT; PAGE 16 – 18; TYPESCRIPT COPY OF DIARY AT C.M.S.M.; KINGFISHER, OKLAHOMA.

23. DAILY MISSOURI DEMOCRAT; MONDAY JANUARY 1863

24. KUCK, HENRY, PAPERS, 1861-1865 (SL242); W.H.M.C., UNIVERSITY OF MO-SAINT LOUIS

25. Ibid

26. HISTORY OF THE 48TH OHIO VETERAN VOLUNTEER INFANTRY; PAGE 100

27. REESE, A.W. (C3627) RECOLLECTIONS OF THE CIVIL WAR 1870; W.H.M.C.- UNIVERSITY OF MO-COLUMBIA

CHAPTER 3: ARKANSAS POST, ARKANSAS

1. DAILY MISSOURI DEMOCRAT; SAINT LOUIS, MISSOURI; APRIL 11, 1863

2. PERSONAL MEMOIRS OF U. S. GRANT: VOLUME 1, PAGE

439 & 440; NEW YORK; CHARLES L. WEBSTER & COM-PANY 1885-COPYRIGHT 1885 BY ULYSSES S. GRANT

3. EIGHT MONTHS CAMPAIGN IN DIXIE; DIARY OF LIEUTENANT WILLIAM H. LYNCH, COMPANY I, 32ND MISSOURI INFANTRY; W.H.M.C. UNIVERSITY OF MO-ROLLA

4. BATTLE OF ARKANSAS POST - OFFICAL REPORT OF MAJOR-GENERAL JOHN A. McCLERNAND; DATED JANUARY 20, 1863 - DAILY MISSOURI DEMOCRAT; SAINT LOUIS, MISSOURI; FEBRUARY 20, 1863

5. MEMOIRS OF GENERAL WILLIAM T. SHERMAN, PAGE 321, LIBRARY OF AMERICA

6. CIVIL WAR DIARY OF COLONEL ABRAHAM JEFFERSON SEAY; 32ND MISSOURI VOLUNTEER INFANTRY REGIMENT; PAGE 18 & 19; TYPESCRIPT COPY OF DIARY AT C.M.S.M.; KINGFISHER, OKLAHOMA.

7. KUCK, HENRY, PAPERS, 1861-1865 (SL252) W.H.M.C.; UNIVERISTY OF MO-SAINT LOUIS

8. RG 94: REGIMENTAL BOOKS 31 MISSOURI INFANTRY - NATIONAL ARCHIVES, WASHINGTON, D.C.

9. Ibid.

CHAPTER 4: YOUNG'S POINT, LOUISIANA

1. CIVIL WAR DIARY OF COLONEL ABRAHAM JEFFERSON SEAY; 32ND MISSOURI VOLUNTEER INFANTRY REGIMENT; PAGES 18 & 19; TYPESCRIPT COPY OF DIARY AT C.M.S.M.; KINGFISHER, OKLAHOMA.

2. EIGHT MONTHS CAMPAIGN IN DIXIE; DIARY OF LIEUTENANT WILLIAM H. LYNCH CO I, 32ND MISSOURI INFANTRY; W.H.M.C.; UNIVERSITY OF MO-ROLLA

3. KUCK, HENRY PAPERS, 1861- 1865 (SL242); W.H.M.C.; UNIVERSITY OF MO-SAINT LOUIS

4. PERSONAL MEMOIRS OF U. S. GRANT: VOLUME 1 PAGE 446 - NEW YORK; CHARLES L. WEBSTER & COMPANY 1885; COPYRIGHT 1885 BY ULYSSES S. GRANT

5. CIVIL WAR DIARY OF COLONEL ABRAHAM JEFFERSON SEAY; 32ND MISSOURI VOLUNTEER INFANTRY REGIMENT; PAGES 22-27; TYPESCRIPT COPY OF DIARY AT C.M.S.M.; KINGFISHER, OKLAHOMA.

6. KUCK, HENRY PAPERS, 1861-1865 (SL242) W.H.M.C.; UNI VERSITY OF MO- SAINT LOUIS

CHAPTER 5: ROAD TO JACKSON, MISSISSIPPI

1. PERSONAL MEMOIRS OF U.S. GRANT; VOLUME 1, PAGE 482; NEW YORK CHARLES L. WEBSTER & COMPANY 1885-COPYRIGHT 1885 BY ULYSSES S. GRANT
2. EIGHT MONTHS CAMPAIGN IN DIXIE, DIARY OF LIEUTENANT WILLIAM H. LYNCH COMPANY I, 32ND MISSOURI INFANTRY REGIMENT – W.H.M.C.; UNIVERSITY OF MO-ROLLA
3. CIVIL WAR DIARY OF COLONEL ABRAHAM JEFFERSON SEAY; 32ND MISSOURI VOLUNTEER INFANTRY REGIMENT; PAGES 32-37; TYPESCRIPT COPY OF DIARY AT C.M.S.M.; KINGFISHER, OKLAHOMA
4. KUCK, HENRY, PAPERS, 1861 – 1865 (SL242); W.H.M.C. UNIVERSITY OF MO-SAINT LOUIS
5. MEMOIRS OF GENERAL WILLIAM T. SHERMAN; LIBRARY OF AMERICA   PAGE 345
6. EIGHT MONTHS CAMPAIGN IN DIXIE, DIARY OF LIEUTENANT WILLIAM H. LYNCH COMPANY I, 32ND MISSOURI INFANTRY REGIMENT (R202) W.H.M.C.-UNIVERSITY OF MISSOURI - ROLLA
7. PERSONAL MEMOIRS OF U.S. GRANT; VOLUME 1, PAGE 483; NEW YORK CHARLES L. WEBSTER & COMPANY 1885-COPYRIGHT 1885 BY ULYSSES S. GRANT
8. CIVIL WAR DIARY OF COLONEL ABRAHAM JEFFERSON SEAY; 32ND MISSOURI VOLUNTEER INFANTRY REGIMENT; PAGES 38-40; TYPESCRIPT COPY OF DIARY AT C.M.S.M.; KINGFISHER, OKLAHOMA
9. Ibid. PAGES 40 & 41
10. Ibid. PAGE 40
11. Ibid. PAGE 41
12. Ibid. PAGES 41 & 42
13. Ibid. PAGE 42
14. EIGHT MONTHS CAMPAIGN IN DIXIE, DIARY OF LIEUTENANT WILLIAM H. LYNCH; COMPANY I, 32ND MISSOURI INFANTRY REGIMENT (R202) W.H.M.C.; UNIVERSITY OF MISSOURI – ROLLA
15. CIVIL WAR DIARY OF COLONEL ABRAHAM JEFFERSON SEAY; 32ND MISSOURI VOLUNTEER INFANTRY REGIMENT; PAGES 42-44; TYPESCRIPT COPY OF DIARY

AT C.M.S.M.; KINGFISHER, OKLAHOMA

16. EIGHT MONTHS CAMPAIGN IN DIXIE, DIARY OF LIEUTEN-
ANT WILLIAM H. LYNCEH; COMPANY I, 32ND MISSOURI
INFANTRY REGIMENT (R202) W.H.M.C.; UNIVERSITY OF
MISSOURI – ROLLA

17. MORNING REPORTS COMPANY C, RG 94: REGIMENTAL
BOOKS, 31 MO. INF.; NATIONAL ARCHIVES,
WASHINGTON, D.C.

CHAPTER 6: ON TO VICKSBURG

1. PERSONAL MEMOIRS OF U.S. GRANT: VOLUME 1, PAGE
508 & 509; NEW YORK; CHARLES L. WEBSTER & COM-
PANY 1885 – COPYRIGHT 1885 BY ULYSSES S. GRANT

2. CIVIL WAR DIARY OF COLONEL ABRAHAM JEFFERSON
SEAY; 32ND MISSOURI VOLUNTEER INFANTRY REGIMENT,
PAGES 44 & 45; TYPESCRIPT COPY OF DIARY AT C.M.S.M.;
KINGFISHER OKLAHOMA

3. Ibid. PAGE 45

4. Ibid. PAGE 46

5. EIGHT MONTHS CAMPAIGN IN DIXIE, DIARY OF LIEUTEN-
ANT WILLIAM H. LYNCH COMPANY I, 32ND MISSOURI IN-
FANTRY REGIMENT (R202) W.H.M.C.; UNIVERSITY OF
MISSOURI – ROLLA.

6. Ibid.

7. CIVIL WAR DIARY OF COLONEL ABRAHAM JEFFERSON
SEAY; 32ND MISSOURI VOLUNTEER INFANTRY REGIMENT;
PAGE 46; TYPESCRIPT COPY OF DIARY AT C.M.S.M.; KING-
FISHER, OKLAHOMA.

8. PERSONAL MEMOIRS OF U.S. GRANT: VOLUME 1, PAGE
529; NEW YORK; CHARLES L. WEBSTER & COMPANY
1885 – COPYRIGHT 1885 BY ULYSSES S. GRANT

9. CIVIL WAR DIARY OF COLONEL ABRAHAM JEFFERSON
SEAY; 32ND MISSOURI VOLUNTEER INFANTRY REGIMENT;
PAGE 47; TYPESCRIPT COPY OF DIARY AT C.M.S.M.; KING-
FISHER, OKLAHOMA.

10. PERSONAL MEMOIRS OF U.S. GRANT: VOLUME 1 PAGE
530; NEW YORK; CHARLES L. WEBSTER & COMPANY 1885
– COPYRIGHT 1885 BY ULYSSES S. GRANT

11. EIGHT MONTHS CAMPAIGN IN DIXIE, DIARY OF LIEUTEN-
ANT WILLIAM H. LYNCH COMPANY I, 32ND MISSOURI IN-
FANTRY REGIMENT (R202) W.H.M.C.; UNIVERSITY OF MIS-

SOURI-ROLLA

12. CIVIL WAR DIARY OF COLONEL ABRAHAM JEFFERSON SEAY; 32ND MISSOURI VOLUNTEER INFANTRY REGIMENT; PAGE 47; TYPESCRIPT COPY OF DIARY AT C.M.S.M.; KINGFISHER, OKLAHOMA.

13. Ibid. PAGE 48

14. PERSONAL MEMOIRS OF U.S. GRANT: VOLUME 1, PAGE 535 & 536; NEW YORK; CHARLES L. WEBSTER & COMPANY 1885 – COPYRIGHT 1885 BY ULYSSES S. GRANT

15. EIGHT MONTHS CAMPAIGN IN DIXIE, DIARY OF LIEUTENANT WILLIAM H. LYNCH COMPANY I,   32[ND]MISSOURI INFANTRY REGIMENT (R202) W.H.M.C.; UNIVERSITY OF MISSOURI - ROLLA.

16. CIVIL WAR DIARY OF COLONEL ABRAHAM JEFFERSON SEAY; 32ND MISSOURI VOLUNTEER INFANTRY REGIMENT; PAGE 51; TYPESCRIPT COPY OF DIARY AT C.M.S.M.; KINGFISHER, OKLAHOMA

17. EIGHT MONTHS CAMPAIGN IN DIXIE, DIARY OF LIEUTENANT WILLIAM H. LYNCH, COMPANY I, 32ND MISSOURI INFANTRY REGIMENT (R202) W.H.M.C.; UNIVERSITY OF MISSOURI-ROLLA

18. KUCK, HENRY, PAPERS, 1861-1865 (SL242) W.H.M.C., UNIVERSITY OF MO–SAINT LOUIS

19. EIGHT MONTHS CAMPAIGN IN DIXIE, DIARY OF LIEUTENANT WILLIAM H. LYNCH COMPANY I, 32ND MISSOURI INFANTRY REGIMENT (R202) W.H.M.C.; UNIVERSITY OF MISSOURI — ROLLA.

20. FLETCHER, THOMAS C., JAMES O. BROADHEAD PAPERS; A. C. LETTER: ARCHIVES AT M. H. S. ; ST LOUIS, MO.

21. PERSONAL MEMOIRS OF U. S. GRANT: VOLUME 1, PAGE 551 & 552; NEW YORK; CHARLES L. WEBSTER & COMPANY 1885- COPYRIGHT 1885 BY ULYSSES S. GRANT

22. EIGHT MONTHS CAMPAIGN IN DIXIE, DIARY OF LIEUTENANT WILLIAM H. LYNCH COMPANY I, 32ND MISSOURI INFANTRY REGIMENT (R202) W.H.M.C.; UNIVERSITY OF MISSOURI- ROLLA

23. KUCK, HENRY, PAPERS, 1861-1865 (SL242) W.H.M.C., UNIVERSITY OF MO–SAINT LOUIS

24. Ibid.

25. EIGHT MONTHS CAMPAIGN IN DIXIE, DIARY OF LIEUTENANT WILLIAM H. LYNCH COMPANY I, 32ND MISSOURI INFANTRY REGIMENT (R202) W.H.M.C.; UNIVERSITY OF MIS-

SOURI – ROLLA

26. HISTORY OF THE THIRTEENTH ILLINOIS VOLUNTEER IN-
FANTRY REGIMENT: PREPARED BY A COMMITTEE OF THE
REGIMENT, 1891; PAGE 332 : 1892; M.S.H.L.. – SAINT
LOUIS, MISSOURI
27. Ibid.
28. Ibid.
29. Ibid. – PAGE 332 & 333
30. Ibid. – PAGE 333
31. KUCK, HENRY, PAPERS, 1861-1865 (SL242) W.H.M.C.,
UNIVERSITY OF MO.–SAINT LOUIS
32. HISTORY OF THE THIRTEENTH ILLINOIS VOLUNTEER IN-
FANTRY REGIMENT: PREPARED BY A COMMITTEE OF THE
REGIMENT, 1891; PAGES 333 & 334:1892: M.S.H.L. SAINT
LOUIS, MISSOURI
33. Ibid. PAGES 335 & 336
34. Ibid. PAGE 336
35. KUCK, HENRY, PAPERS, 1861-1865 (SL242) W.H.M.C.,
UNIVERSITY OF MO–SAINT LOUIS
36. PERSONAL MEMOIRS OF U. S. GRANT: VOLUME 1, PAGE
508 & 509; NEW YORK; CHARLES L. WEBSTER & COM-
PANY 1885 – COPYRIGHT BY ULYSSES S. GRANT.
37. DAILY MISSOURI DEMOCRAT; TUESDAY MORNING, AU-
GUST 11,1863:
38. Ibid. – WEDNESDAY MORNING, JULY 8, 1863

CHAPTER 7: ON TO CHATTANOOGA

1. O.R., SERIES 1, VOLUME 33, CHAPTER 52, PAGES 747 &
748
2. Ibid
3. DAILY MISSOURI DEMOCRAT, WEDNESDAY MORNING –
OCTOBER 7, 1863
4. PERSONAL MEMOIRS OF U.S. GRANT; VOLUME 2, PAGE
17; NEW YORK; CHARLES L. WEBSTER & COMPANY
1886 – COPYRIGHT, 1885, BY ULYSSES S. GRANT.
5. Ibid, PAGE 18
6. EIGHT MONTHS CAMPAIGN IN DIXIE, DIARY OF LIEUTEN-
ANT WILLIAM H. LYNCH, COMPANY I, 32ND MISSOURI IN-
FANTRY (R202) W.H.M.C.– UNIVERSITY OF MO – ROLLA
7. MEMOIRS OF GENERAL W. T. SHERMAN, PAGE 373 ; LI-
BRARY OF AMERICA, 1990

8. EIGHT MONTHS CAMPAIGN IN DIXIE, DIARY OF LIEUTEN-ANT WILLIAM H. LYNCH, COMPANY I, 32ND MISSOURI IN-FANTRY (R202) W.H.M.C.– UNIVERSITY OF MO – ROLLA

9. HISTORY OF THE THIRTEENTH ILLINOIS VOLUNTEER REGIMENT, PREPARED BY A COMMITTEE OF THE REGI-MENT, 1891- PAGE 374 & 378; 1892; M.H.S.L.. SAINT LOUIS, MISSOURI

10. Ibid., PAGE 348 & 349

11. Ibid., PAGE 348

12. EIGHT MONTHS CAMPAIGN IN DIXIE, DIARY OF LIEUTEN-ANT WILLIAM H. LYNCH, COMPANY I, 32ND MISSOURI IN-FANTRY (R202) W.H.M.C. – UNIVERSITY OF MO – ROLLA

13. HISTORY OF THE THIRTEENTH ILLINOIS VOLUNTEER REGIMENT, PREPARED BY A COMMITTEE OF THE REGI-MENT, 1891 – PAGE 349 1892; M.H.S.L., ST. LOUIS, MIS-SOURI

14. KUCK, HENRY, PAPERS, 1861 – 1865)SL242) W.H.M. C. UNIVERSITY OF MO–ST. LOUIS, OCTOBER 11, 1863

15. Ibid., OCTOBER 18TH, 1863

16. EIGHT MONTHS CAMPAIGN IN DIXIE, DIARY OF LIEUTEN-ANT WILLIAM H. LYNCH, CO I, 32ND MISSOURI INFANTRY (R202) W.H.M.C.; UNIVERSITY OF MO–ROLLA

17. HISTORY OF THE THIRTEENTH ILLINOIS VOLUNTEER REGIMENT, PREPARED BY A COMMITTEE OF THE REGI-MENT, 1891 – PAGE 351 & 352; 1892; M.H.S., ST. LOUIS, MO

18. Ibid., PAGE 352

19. EIGHT MONTHS CAMPAIGN IN DIXIE, DIARY OF LIEUTEN-ANT WILLIAM H. LYNCH, CO I, 32ND MISSOURI INFANTRY (R202) W.H.M.C.; UNIVERSITY OF MO–ROLLA

20. Ibid.

21. HISTORY OF THE THIRTEENTH ILLINOIS VOLUNTEER REGIMENT, PREPARED BY A COMMITTEE OF THE REGI-MENT, 1891;PAGE 352; 1892; M.H.S. ST. LOUIS,MO

22. EIGHT MONTHS CAMPAIGN IN DIXIE, DIARY OF LIEUTEN-ANT WILLIAM H. LYNCH, CO I, 32ND MISSOURI INFANTRY (R202) W.H.M.C.; UNIVERSITY OF MO–ROLLA

23. HISTORY OF THE THIRTEENTH ILLINOIS VOLUNTEER REGIMENT, PREPARED BY A COMMITTEE OF THE REGI-MENT, 1891–PAGE 352;1892;M.H.S.L.,ST LOUIS,MO

24. Ibid., PAGES 352 – 354

25. O.R., SERIES 1 – VOLUME XXXI – PART 1 , CHAPTER 54

PAGES 22 & 23

26. HISTORY OF THE THIRTEENTH ILLINOIS VOLUNTEER REGIMENT, PREPARED BY A COMMITTEE OF THE REGIMENT,1891;PAGE 387;1892;M.H.S.L.,ST. LOUIS,MO

27. MORNING REPORT, COMPANY D; RG 94: REGIMENTAL BOOKS 31 MISSOURI INFANTRY. NATIONAL ARCHIVES WASHINGTON, D.C.

28. CIVIL WAR DIARY OF COLONEL ABRAHAM JEFFERSON SEAY; 32ND MISSOURI VOLUNTEER INFANTRY REGIMENT; PAGES 57-60; TYPESCRIPT COPY OF DIARY AT C.M.S.M.; KINGFISER, OKLAHOMA

29. HISTORY OF THE THIRTEENTH ILLINOIS VOLUNTEER REGIMENT, PREPARED BY A COMMITTEE OF THE REGIMENT, 1891-PAGES 364-365-1892; M.H.S.L., ST LOUIS, MO

30. CIVIL WAR DIARY OF COLONEL ABRAHAM JEFFERSON SEAY; 32ND MISSOURI VOLUNTEER INFANTRY REGIMENT; PAGES 61 & 62; TYPESCRIPT COPY OF DIARY AT C.M.S.M.; KINGFISHER, OKLAHOMA

31. KUCK , HENRY, PAPERS, 1861 – 1865 (SL242) W.H.M.C.; UNIVERSITY OF MO – ST LOUIS

32. MEMOIRS OF GENERAL W.T. SHERMAN, PAGE 389 – LIBRARY OF AMERICA, 1990

33. KUCK, HENRY, PAPERS, 1861-1865 (SL242) W.H.M.C.; UNIVERSITY OF MO–ST LOUIS

CHAPTER 8: LOOKOUT MOUNTAIN THROUGH RINGGOLD GAP

1. O.R., SERIES 1, VOLUME 31, PART 2, PAGE 315 – REPORT #89 – REPORT OF MAJ. GEN. JOSEPH HOOKER

2. Ibid

3. Ibid, PAGES 600 & 601

4. Ibid, PAGES 471 &472

5. CIVIL WAR DIARY OF COLONEL ABRAHAM JEFFERSON SEAY; 32ND MISSOURI VOLUNTEER INFANTRY REGIMENT; PAGES 62 & 63; TYPESCRIPT COPY OF DIARY AT C.M.S.M.; KINGFISHER, OKLAHOMA

6. KUCK, HENRY, PAPERS, 1861-1865 (SL242) W.H.M.C.; UNIVERSITY OF MO – ST LOUIS; NOVEMBER 30, 1863

7. HISTORY OF THE THIRTEENTH ILLINOIS VOLUNTEER IN-

FANTRY REGIMENT, PREPARED BY A COMMITTEE OF THE REGIMENT, 1891; PAGE 378; 1892; M.H.S.L.; ST LOUIS, MO

8. Ibid

9. Ibid

10. KUCK, HENRY, PAPERS, 1861-1865 (SL242) W.H.M.C.; UNIVERSITY OF MO–ST LOUIS; NOVEMBER 30, 1863

11. HISTORY OF THE THIRTEENTH ILLINOIS VOLUNTEER INFANTRY REGIMENT PREPARED BY A COMMITTEE OF THE REGIMENT, 1891; PAGE 378 & 379; 1892; M.H.S.L.; ST LOUIS, MO

12. TAKEN FROM CAST IRON TABLET IN THE BRAGG RESERVATION, ON MISSIONARY RIDGE IN NEAR CHATTANOOGA, TENNESSEE

13. R.S.A.T.; 26TH MEETING – COUNCIL BLUFFS, IOWA; OCTOBER 3 & 4, 1894 – PRINTED 1895 – PAGES 75 & 76

14. CIVIL WAR DIARY OF COLONEL ABRAHAM JEFFERSON SEAY; 32ND MISSOURI VOLUNTEER INFANTRY REGIMENT; PAGE63; TYPESCRIPT COPY OF DIARY AT C.M.S.M.; KINGFISHER, OKLAHOMA.

15. CONFEDERATE VETERAN – VOLUME 40, NUMBER 2, FEBRUARY 1932, PAGES 50 & 52

16. R.S.A.T.; 27TH MEETING AT CINCINNATI, OHIO & CHATTANOOGA, TENNESSEE – SEPTEMBER 16-21, 1895 – PRINTED 1896 – PAGE 226

17. HISTORY OF THE THIRTEENTH ILLINOIS VOLUNTEER INFANTRY REGIMENT, PREPARED BY A COMMITTEE OF THE REGIMENT, 1891; PAGE 378; 1892; M.H.S.L.; ST LOUIS, MISSOURI

18. O.R., SERIES 1, VOLUME 31, PART 2, PAGE 471 – 472

19. HISTORY OF THE THIRTEENTH ILLINOIS VOLUNTEER INFANTRY REGIMENT, PREPARED BY A COMMITTEE OF THE REGIMENT, 1891; PAGE 344; 1892; M.H.S.L.; ST LOUIS, MO

20. R.S.A.T.; 27TH MEETING AT CINCINNATI, OHIO & CHATTANOOGA, TENNESSEE – SEPTEMBER 16-21, 1895 –PRINTED 1896 – PAGES 227 & 228

21. KUCK, HENRY, PAPERS, 1861-1865 (SL242) W.H.M.C.; UNIVERSITY OF MO–ST LOUIS –NOVEMBER 30, 1863

22. DAILY MISSOURI DEMOCRAT; TUESDAY MORNING, DECEMBER 7, 1863

23. O.R., SERIES 1, VOLUME 31, PART 2, PAGES 606 – 609;

REPORT #192 REPORT OF BRIG-GEN CHARLES R. WOODS
24. HISTORY OF THE THIRTEENTH ILLINOIS VOLUNTEER INFANTRY REGIMENT, PREPARED BY A COMMITTEE OF THE REGIMENT, 1891; PAGE 400; 1892 – M.H.S.L.; ST LOUIS, MO
25. Ibid
26. Ibid
27. REPORT OF THE ADJUTANT GENERAL OF MISSOURI – 1863, PAGE 312; M.H.S.L.; SAINT LOUIS MISSOURI

CHAPTER 9: WINTER CAMP

1. O.R., SERIES 1, VOLUME 31, PART 3, PAGE 306
2. KUCK, HENRY, PAPERS, 1861—1865 (SL242) W.H.M.C.; UNIVERSITY OF MO–ST LOUIS;
3. HISTORY OF THE THIRTEENTH ILLINOIS VOLUNTEER REGIMENT, PREPARED BY A COMMITTEE OF THE REGIMENT, 1891; PAGES 400 & 401; 1892; M.H.S.L. ST LOUIS, MO
4. Ibid, PAGE 401
5. Ibid
6. KUCK, HENRY, PAPERS, 1861—1865 (SL242) W.H.M.C., UNIVERSITY OF MISSOURI – ST LOUIS
7. CIVIL WAR DIARY OF COLONEL ABRAHAM JEFFERSON SEAY; 32ND MISSOURI VOLUNTEER INFANTRY REGIMENT; PAGES 65—69; TYPESCRIPT COPY OF DIARY AT C.M.S.M.; KINGFISHER, OKLAHOMA.
8. CIVIL WAR HISTORY OF 31ST MISSOURI VOLUNTEER INFANTRY REGIMENT, COMPANY "F" AND PRIVATE WILLIAM CARROLL; BY CLARENCE M. CARROLL & ROBERT E. PARKIN. 1990; PAGE 29
9. KUCK, HENRY, PAPERS, 1861 – 1865 (SL242) W.H.M.C., UNIVERSITY OF MO–ST LOUIS
10. Ibid, LETTER 2-25-1864
11. CIVIL WAR DIARY OF COLONEL ABRAHAM JEFFERSON SEAY; 32ND MISSOURI VOLUNTEER INFANTRY REGIMENT; PAGES 69-74; TYPESCRIPT COPY OF DIARY AT C.M.S.M.; KINGFISHER, OKLAHOMA.
12. REGIMENTAL ORDER BOOK, 31ST MISSOURI INFANTRY; RG 94: REGIMENTAL BOOKS 31 MO INF, ORDER # 139 NATIONAL ARCHIVES, WASHINGTON, D.C.
13. CIVIL WAR DIARY OF COLONEL ABRAHAM JEFFERSON

SEAY; 32ND MISSOURI VOLUNTEER INFANTRY REGIMENT; PAGE 75; TYPESCRIPT COPY OF DIARY AT C.M.S.M.; KING-FISHER, OKLAHOMA.

14. Ibid, PAGE 77

15. OSTERHAUS PAPERS–DIARY OF PETER J. OSTERHAUS, MAJOR—GENERAL 1864 – MAY 27TH, IN ARCHIVES AT M.H.S.L., ST LOUIS, MO

16. REGIMENTAL ORDER BOOK, 31ST MISSOURI INFANTRY; RG 94: REGIMENTAL BOOKS 31 MO INF, ORDER # 62 NATIONAL ARCHIVES, WASHINGTON, D.C.

17. OSTERHAUS PAPERS– DIARY OF PETER J. OSTERHAUS, MAJOR – GENERAL 1864 – APRIL 1ST, IN ARCHIVES AT M.H.S.L., ST LOUIS, MO

18. CIVIL WAR DIARY OF COLONEL ABRAHAM JEFFERSON SEAY; 32ND MISSOURI VOLUNTEER INFANTRY REGIMENT; PAGE 78; TYPESCRIPT COPY OF DIARY AT C.M.S.M.; KING-FISHER, OKLAHOMA.

19. OSTERHAUS PAPERS-DIARY OF PETER J. OSTERHAUS, MAJOR – GENERAL 1864 - APRIL 11TH, IN ARCHIVES AT M.H.S.L., SAINT LOUIS MISSOURI

20. Ibid., APRIL 21ST

21. Ibid., APRIL 26TH

22. Ibid., APRIL 29TH

CHAPTER 10: THE BATTLE AT RESACA

1. MEMOIRS OF GENERAL WILLIAM T. SHERMAN; PAGE 487; LIBRARY OF AMERICA, 1990.

2. OSTERHAUS PAPERS, DIARY OF PETER J. OSTERHAUS MAJ-GEN 1864-MAY 1; IN ARCHIVES AT M.H.S.L., ST. LOUIS, MO

3. THE DIARY OF A CIVIL WAR SOLDIER, WITH SHERMAN IN GEORGIA, JOHN T. CLARK. MISSOURI HISTORICAL SOCIETY REVIEW, M.H.S.L., ST. LOUIS, MO.

4. OSTERHAUS PAPERS, DIARY OF PETER J. OSTERHAUS MAJ-GEN. 1864-MAY 2; IN ARCHIVES AT M.H.S.L., ST. LOUIS, MO

5. Ibid. — MAY 4

6. Ibid. — MAY 5

7. O. R. , SERIES 1, VOLUME 38, CHAPTER 50, PAGE 53

8. OSTERHAUS PAPERS, DIARY OF PETER J. OSTERHAUS MAJ-GEN 1864-MAY 6; IN ARCHIVES AT M.H.S.L., ST. LOUIS, MO

9. THE DIARY OF A CIVIL WAR SOLDIER, WITH SHERMAN IN GEORGIA, JOHN T. CLARKE, MAY 6TH, M.H.S.L., ST. LOUIS, MO

10. OSTERHAUS PAPERS, DIARY OF PETER J. OSTERHAUS MAJ-GEN 1864—MAY 7; IN ARCHIVES AT M.H.S.L. , ST. LOUIS, MO

11. Ibid. — MAY 8

12. O.R. SERIES 1, VOLUME 38, CHAPTER 50 , PAGE 133

13. OSTERHAUS PAPERS, DIARY OF PETER J. OSTERHAUS MAJ-GEN 1864-MAY 10 & 11; IN ARCHIVES AT M.H.S.L., ST. LOUIS, MO.

14. O.R., SERIES 1, VOLUME 38, CHAPTER 50, PAGE 150

15. Ibid. PAGE 160

16. KUCK, HENRY, PAPERS, 1861-1865 (SL242) W.H.M.C.; UNIVERSITY OF MO – ST. LOUIS

17. OSTERHAUS PAPERS, DIARY OF PETER J. OSTERHAUS MAJ-GEN 1864—MAY 16; IN ARCHIVES AT M.H.S.L., ST. LOUIS, MO

18. O.R., SERIES 1, VOLUME 38, CHAPTER 50, PAGE 218 & 219

19. KUCK, HENRY, PAPERS, 1861 – 1865 (SL242) W.H.M.C.; UNIVERSITY OF MO–SAINT LOUIS

CHAPTER 11: FROM DALLAS TO BIG SHANTY

1. OSTERHAUS PAPERS - DIARY OF PETER J. OSTERHAUS MAJ-GEN 1864 - MAY 17; IN ARCHIVES AT M.H.S.L., ST LOUIS, MO

2. Ibid. — MAY 19

3. THE DIARY OF A CIVIL WAR SOLDIER - WITH SHERMAN IN GEORGIA - JOHN T. CLARKE MAY 20 ; M.H.S.L., ST LOUIS, MO

4. OSTERHAUS PAPERS - DIARY OF PETER J. OSTERHAUS MAJ-GEN. 1864 -MAY 20; IN ARCHIVES AT M.H.S.L., SAINT LOUIS, MISSOURI

5. O. R., SERIES 1, VOLUME 38, CHAPTER 50, PAGE 272

6. KUCK, HENRY, PAPERS, 1861-1865 (SL242) W.H.M.C.; UNIVERSITY OF MO—ST LOUIS, MO

7. THE DIARY OF A CIVIL WAR SOLDIER - WITH SHERMAN IN GEORGIA - JOHN T. CLARKE; MAY 21 ; M.H.S.L., ST LOUIS, MO
8. CIVIL WAR DIARY OF COLONEL ABRAHAM JEFFERSON SEAY; 32ND MISSOURI VOLUNTEER INFANTRY REGIMENT; PAGE 86; TYPESCRIPT COPY OF DIARY AT C.M.S.M.; KINGFISHER, OKLAHOMA
9. OSTERHAUS PAPERS - DIARY OF PETER J. OSTERHAUS MAJ-GEN 1864-MAY 23; IN ARCHIVES AT M.H.S.L., ST LOUIS, MISSOURI
10. Ibid. , MAY 24
11. O.R., SERIES 1, VOLUME 38, CHAPTER 50, PAGE 313
12. CIVIL WAR DIARY OF COLONEL ABRAHAM JEFFERSON SEAY; 32ND MISSOURI VOLUNTEER INFANTRY REGIMENT; PAGE 86; TYPESCRIPT COPY OF DIARY AT C.M.S.M.; KINGFISHER, OKLAHOMA
13. OSTERHAUS PAPERS -DIARY OF PETER J. OSTERHAUS MAJ-GEN 1864 - MAY 26; IN ARCHIVES AT M.H.S.L.; ST LOUIS, MO
14. CIVIL WAR DIARY OF COLONEL ABRAHAM JEFFERSON SEAY; 32ND MISSOURI VOLUNTEER INFANTRY REGIMENT; PAGE 87; TYPESCRIPT COPY OF DIARY AT C.M.S.M.; KINGFISHER, OKLAHOMA
15. OSTERHUAS PAPERS – DIARY OF PETER J. OSTERHAUS MAJ–GEN 1864 -MAY 27; IN ARCHIVES AT M.H.S.L., ST LOUIS, MO
16. CIVIL WAR DIARY OF COLONEL ABRAHAM JEFFERSON SEAY; 32ND MISSOURI VOLUNTEER INFANTRY REGIMENT; PAGE 87; TYPESCRIPT COPY OF DIARY AT CHISHOLM TRAIL MUSEUM-GOVERNOR SEAY MANSION, KING-FISHER, OKLAHOMA
17. OSTERHAUS PAPERS–DIARY OF PETER J. OSTERHAUS, MAJ-GEN. 1864, MAY 28; IN ARCHIVES AT M.H.S.L.; ST LOUIS, MO
18. THE DIARY OF A CIVIL WAR SOLDIER - WITH SHERMAN IN GEORGIA - JOHN T. CLARKE; MAY 28 ; M.H.S.L., ST LOUIS, MO
19. CIVIL WAR DIARY OF COLONEL ABRAHAM JEFFERSON SEAY; 32ND MISSOURI VOLUNTEER INFANTRY REGIMENT; PAGE 87; TYPESCRIPT COPY OF DIARY AT C.M.S.M.; KINGFISHER, OKLAHOMA
20. Ibid.

21. KUCK HENRY, PAPERS, 1861-1865 (SL242) W.H.M.C., UNIVERSITY OF MO—ST LOUIS
22. R.S.A.T.; 1881-1891; VOLUMES XXI-XXIII; XXII MEETING-CINCINNATI, OHIO SEPTEMBER 25TH & 26TH 1889; PAGES 330 – 332.
23. OSTERHAUS PAPERS- DIARY OF PETER J. OSTERHAUS MAJ-GEN 1864-MAY 28; IN ARCHIVES AT M.H.S.L., ST LOUIS, MO
24. THE DIARY OF A CIVIL WAR SOLDIER - WITH SHERMAN IN GEORGIA - JOHN T. CLARKE; JUNE 3, M.H.S.L., ST LOUIS, MO
25. OSTERHAUS PAPERS-DIARY OF PETER J. OSTERHAUS MAJ-GEN 1864-JUNE 5; IN ARCHIVES AT M.H.S.L., ST LOUIS, MO
26. O.R., SERIES 1, VOLUME 38, CHAPTER 50, PAGE 416
27. OSTERHAUS PAPERS- DIARY OF PETER J. OSTERHAUS MAJ-GEN 1864-JUNE 6; IN ARCHIVES AT M.H.S.L., ST LOUIS, MO
28. CIVIL WAR DIARY OF COLONEL ABRAHAM JEFFERSON SEAY; 32ND MISSOURI VOLUNTEER INFANTRY REGIMENT; PAGE 86; TYPESCRIPT COPY OF DIARY AT C.M.S.M.; KINGFISHER, OKLAHOMA.
29. KUCK, HENRY, PAPERS, 1861-1865 (SL242) W.H.M.C.; UNIVERSITY OF MO—ST LOUIS

CHAPTER 12: KENNESAW MOUNTAIN

1. OSTERHAUS PAPERS - DIARY OF PETER J. OSTERHAUS MAJ-GEN 1864-JUNE 10; IN ARCHIVES AT M.H.S. ST LOUIS, MO
2. CIVIL WAR DIARY OF COLONEL ABRAHAM JEFFERSON SEAY; 32ND MISSOURI VOLUNTEER INFANTRY REGIMENT; PAGE 86; TYPESCRIPT COPY OF DIARY AT C.M.S.M.; KINGFISHER, OKLAHOMA.
3. OSTERHAUS PAPERS- DIARY OF PETER J. OSTERHAUS, MAJ-GEN 1864 – JUNE 11; IN ARCHIVES AT M.H.S., ST LOUIS, MO
4. REESE, A.W.; (C3627) RECOLLECTIONS OF THE CIVIL WAR, 1870; W.H.M.C. UNIVERSITY OF MO-COLUMBIA VOLUME II, PAGES 14 &15.
5. OSTERHAUS PAPERS-DIARY OF PETER J OSTHERHAUS, MAJ-GEN. 1864 – JUNE 13; IN ARCHIVES AT M.H.S.,

ST LOUIS, MO
6. THE DIARY OF A CIVIL WAR SOLDIER- WITH SHERMAN IN GEORGIA - JOHN T. CLARKE; JUNE 18;   M.H.S., ST LOUIS, MO
7. CIVIL WAR DIARY OF COLONEL ABRAHAM JEFFERSON SEAY; 32ND MISSOURI VOLUNTEER INFANTRY REGIMENT; PAGE 90; TYPESCRIPT COPY OF DIARY AT C.M.S.M.; KINGFISHER, OKLAHOMA.
8. OSTERHAUS PAPERS- DIARY OF PETER J. OSTERHAUS MAJ-GEN 1864-JUNE 18; IN ARCHIVES AT M.H.S., ST LOUIS, MO
9. Ibid., JUNE 19, 20 & 21
10. CIVIL WAR DIARY OF COLONEL ABRAHAM JEFFERSON SEAY; 32ND MISSOURI VOLUNTEER INFANTRY REGIMENT; PAGE 90; TYPESCRIPT COPY OF DIARY AT C.M.S.M.; KING-FISHER, OKLAHOMA.
11. O.R., SERIES 1, VOLUME 38, REPORT OF GENERAL LO-GAN CHAPTER 50, PAGE 85
12. CIVIL WAR DIARY OF COLONEL ABRAHAM JEFFERSON SEAY; 32ND MISSOURI VOLUNTEER INFANTRY REGIMENT; PAGE 91; TYPESCRIPT COPY OF DIARY AT C.M.S.M.; KINGFISHER, OKLAHOMA.
13. THE DIARY OF A CIVIL WAR SOLDIER - WITH SHERMAN IN GEORGIA - JOHN T. CLARKE; JUNE 27; M.H.S.L., ST LOUIS, MO
14. CIVIL WAR DIARY OF COLONEL ABRAHAM JEFFERSON SEAY; 32ND MISSOURI VOLUNTEER INFANTRY REGIMENT; PAGE 92; TYPESCRIPT COPY OF DIARY AT C.M.S.M.; KINGFISHER, OKLAHOMA
15. R.S.A.T.; 1888-1891—VOLUMES XXI-XXIII. PUBLISHED BY THE SOCIETY, 1893, CINCINNATI. PAGES 333 & 334 AT THE TWENTY-SECOND MEETING HELD AT CINCINNATI, OHIO ON SEPTEMBER 25T^H & 26TH, 1889.
16. THE DIARY OF A CIVIL WAR SOLDIER – WITH SHERMAN IN GEORGIA – JOHN T. CLARKE; JUNE 28; M.H.S.L., SAINT LOUIS, MISSOURI
17. CIVIL WAR DIARY OF COLONEL ABRAHAM JEFFERSON SEAY; 32ND MISSOURI VOLUNTEER INFANTRY REGIMENT; PAGE 92; TYPESCRIPT COPY OF DIARY AT C.M.S.M.; KINGFISHER, OKLAHOMA.
18. Ibid. PAGE 93
19. O.R., SERIES 1, VOLUME 38, CHAPTER 50, PAGE 47

20. OSTERHAUS PAPERS-DIARY OF PETER J. OSTERHAUS MAJ-GEN 1864 - JULY 4; IN ARCHIVES AT M.H.S.L., ST LOUIS, MO
21. DAILY MISSOURI DEMOCRAT; SAINT LOUIS, MISSOURI; THURSDAY MORNING, JULY 21,1864
22. THE DIARY OF A CIVIL WAR SOLDIER - WITH SHERMAN IN GEORGIA - JOHN T. CLARKE ;JULY 5; M.H.S.L., ST LOUIS, MO
23. CIVIL WAR DIARY OF COLONEL ABRAHAM JEFFERSON SEAY; 32ND MISSOURI VOLUNTEER INFANTRY REGIMENT; PAGE 92; TYPESCRIPT COPY OF DIARY AT C.M.S.M.; KINGFISHER, OKLAHOMA.
24. KUCK, HENRY PAPERS, 1861-1865 (SL242) W.H.M.C.; UNIVERSITY OF MO—ST LOUIS
25. CIVIL WAR DIARY OF COLONEL ABRAHAM JEFFERSON SEAY; 32ND MISSOURI VOLUNTEER INFANTRY REGIMENT; PAGE 94; TYPESCRIPT COPY OF DIARY AT C.M.S.M.; KINGFISHER, OKLAHOMA.
26. OSTERHAUS PAPERS–DIARY OF PETER J. OSTERHAUS, MAJ-GEN; 1864-JULY 13; IN ARCHIVES AT M.H.S.L., ST LOUIS, MO
27. DAILY MISSOURI DEMOCRAT; SAINT LOUIS, MISSOURI; THURSDAY MORNING, JULY 21,1864
28. OSTERHAUS PAPERS–DIARY OF PETER J. OSTERHAUS, MAJ-GEN; 1864-JULY 14; IN ARCHIVES AT M.H.S.L., ST LOUIS, MO

CHAPTER 13: ON TO ATLANTA

1. O.R. ,SERIES 1, VOLUME 38, CHAPTER 50, PAGE 168
2. Ibid.,
3. CIVIL WAR DIARY OF COLONEL ABRAHAM JEFFERSON SEAY; 32ND MISSOURI VOLUNTEER INFANTRY REGIMENT; PAGE 94 & 95; TYPESCRIPT COPY AT C.M.S.M.; KINGFISHER, OKLAHOMA
4. Ibid. PAGE 95
5. Ibid
6. THE DIARY OF A CIVIL WAR SOLDIER - WITH SHERMAN IN GEORGIA - JOHN T. CLARKE-JULY 20: M.H.S.L., ST LOUIS, MO
7. CIVIL WAR DIARY OF COLONEL ABRAHAM JEFFERSON SEAY; 32ND MISSOURI VOLUNTEER INFANTRY

REGIMENT; PAGE 95; TYPESCRIPT COPY AT C.M.S.M;
KINGFISHER, OKLAHOMA

8. MEMOIRS OF GENERAL WILLIAM T. SHERMAN ; PAGE 555;
LIBRARY OF AMERICA—1990

9. THE DIARY OF A CIVIL WAR SOLDIER - WITH SHERMAN
IN GEORGIA - JOHN T. CLARKE-JULY 22 ; M.H.S.L.,
ST LOUIS, MO

10. KUCK, HENRY, PAPERS, 1861-1865 (SL242) W.H.M.C.,
UNIVERSITY OF MO-ST LOUIS

11. O. R., SERIES 1, VOLUME 38, CHAPTER 50, PAGE 164,
165 & 166

12. R.S.A.T.; AT CLEVELAND, OHIO; 16TH MEETING ON OC-
TOBER 17-18, 1883. VOLUME 16, PAGES 477 – 493.

13. CIVIL WAR DIARY OF COLONEL ABRAHAM JEFFERSON
SEAY; 32ND MISSOURI VOLUNTEER INFANTRY REGIMENT;
PAGE 95; TYPESCRIPT COPY OF DIARY AT C.M.S.M.;
KINGFISHER, OKLAHOMA.

14. THE DIARY OF A CIVIL WAR SOLDIER - WITH SHERMAN
IN GEORGIA - JOHN T. CLARKE-JULY 24, M.H.S.L.,
ST LOUIS, MO

15. CIVIL WAR DIARY OF COLONEL ABRAHAM JEFFERSON
SEAY; 32ND MISSOURI VOLUNTEER INFANTRY
REGIMENT; PAGE 96; TYPESCRIPT COPY OF DIARY AT
C.M.S.M.; KINGFISHER, OKLAHOMA.

16. REESE, A.W.; (C3627) REFLECTIONS OF THE CIVIL WAR,
1870; VOLUME 2, PAGE 73; W.H.M.C. UNIVERSITY OF
MO-COLUMBIA

17. R.S.A.T.; TWENTIETH MEETING HELD AT DETROIT,
MICHIGAN - SEPT 14 & 15 1887 - PAGE 472

18. R.S.A.T.; WASHINGTON, D.C.; 34TH MEETING ON
OCTOBER 15-16, 1903. VOLUME 34, PAGES 110 &
111. PRINTED 1906.

19. CIVIL WAR DIARY OF COLONEL ABRAHAM JEFFERSON
SEAY; 32ND MISSOURI VOLUNTEER INFANTRY
REGIMENT; PAGE 96; TYPESCRIPT COPY OF DIARY AT
C.M.S.M.; KINGFISHER, OKLAHOMA.

20. THE DIARY OF A CIVIL WAR SOLDIER- WITH SHERMAN
IN GEORGIA - JOHN T. CLARKE-JULY 26, M.H.S.L.,
ST LOUIS, MO

21. CIVIL WAR DIARY OF COLONEL ABRAHAM JEFFERSON
SEAY; 32ND MISSOURI VOLUNTEER INFANTRY
REGIMENT; PAGE 96; TYPESCRIPT COPY OF DIARY AT

C.M.S.M.; KINGFISHER, OKLAHOMA.
22. Ibid.
23. Ibid.
24. KUCK, HENRY, PAPERS, 1861-1865 (SL242) W.H.M.C.; UNIVERSITY OF MO-ST LOUIS
25. O.R. , SERIES 1, VOLUME 38, CHAPTER 50, PAGE 168 & 169
26. R.S.A.T.; COUNCIL BLUFFS, IOWA; 26TH MEETING, OCTOBER 3RD&4TH, 1894;VOLUME 26, PAGES 135–139.
27. CIVIL WAR DIARY OF COLONEL ABRAHAM JEFFERSON SEAY; 32ND MISSOURI VOLUNTEER INFANTRY REGIMENT; PAGE 97; TYPESCRIPT COPY OF DIARY AT C.M.S.M.; KINGFISHER, OKLAHOMA.
28. THE DIARY OF A CIVIL WAR SOLDIER - WITH SHERMAN IN GEORGIA - JOHN T. CLARKE-JULY 30 & 31, M.H.S.L., SAINT LOUIS, MISSOURI
29. DAILY MISSOURI DEMOCRAT, ST LOUIS, MO. MONDAY MORNING, AUGUST 8, 1864.
30. O.R., SERIES 1, VOLUME 38, CHAPTER 50, PAGE 169
31. Ibid., - PAGE 171
32. CIVIL WAR DIARY OF COLONEL ABRAHAM JEFFERSON SEAY; 32ND MISSOURI VOLUNTEER INFANTRY REGIMENT; PAGE 98; TYPESCRIPT COPY OF DIARY AT C.M.S.M.; KINGFISHER, OKLAHOMA.
33. Ibid.
34. O.R., SERIES 1, VOLUME 38, CHAPTER 50, PAGE 365
35. THE DIARY OF A CIVIL WAR SOLDIER - WITH SHERMAN IN GEORGIA - JOHN T. CLARKE-   AUGUST 21. M.H.S.L., ST LOUIS, MO
36. O. R. SERIES 1, VOLUME 38, CHAPTER 50, PAGE 586
37. R.S.A.T.; 32ND MEETING AT DETROIT, MICHIGAN, NOVEMBER 14 – 15, 1900. VOLUME 32, PAGE 38.
38. O. R. SERIES 1, VOLUME 38, CHAPTER 50, PAGE 586
39. DAILY MISSOURI DEMOCRAT; ST LOUIS, MO; TUESDAY AUGUST 30, 1864
40. OSTERHAUS PAPERS - DIARY OF PETER J. OSTERHAUS MAJ-GEN 1864; AUGUST 25; IN ARCHIVES AT M.H.S.L., SAINT LOUIS
41. Ibid., AUGUST 26
42. CIVIL WAR DIARY OF COLONEL ABRAHAM JEFFERSON SEAY; 32ND MISSOURI VOLUNTEER INFANTRY REGIMENT; PAGE 101; TYPESCRIPT COPY OF DIARY

AT C.M.S.M.; KINGFISHER, OKLAHOMA.

43. OSTERHAUS PAPERS– DIARY OF PETER J. OSTERHAUS, MAJ-GEN 1864; AUGUST 27; IN ARCHIVES AT M.H.S.L., ST LOUIS, MO

44. MEMOIRS OF GENERAL WILLIAM T. SHERMAN, PAGE 578 & 579; LIBRARY OF AMERICA-1990

45. O.R., SERIES 1, VOLUME 38, CHAPTER 50, PAGE 686 & 687

46. OSTERHAUS PAPERS - DIARY OF PETER J. OSTERHAUS MAJ- GEN 1864- AUG. 28; IN ARCHIVES AT M.H.S.L., ST LOUIS, MO

47. CIVIL WAR DIARY OF COLONEL ABRAHAM JEFFERSON SEAY; 32ND MISSOURI VOLUNTEER REGIMENT; PAGE 101; TYPESCRIPT COPY OF DIARY AT C.M.S.M.; KINGFISHER, OKLAHOMA.

48. Ibid.

49. OSTERHAUS PAPERS—DIARY OF PETER J. OSTERHAUS, MAJ-GEN 1864; AUGUST 30; IN ARCHIVES AT M.H.S.L., ST LOUIS, MO

50. CIVIL WAR DIARY OF COLONEL ABRAHAM JEFFERSON SEAY; 32ND MISSOURI VOLUNTEER INFANTRY REGIMENT; PAGE 102; TYPESCRIPT COPY OF DIARY AT C.M.S.M.; KINGFISHER, OKLAHOMA

51. O.R., SERIES 1, VOLUME 38, CHAPTER 50, PAGE 728 & 729

52. OSTERHAUS PAPERS - DIARY OF PETER J. OSTERHAUS MAJ-GEN 1864; SEPTEMBER 1; IN ARCHIVES AT M.H.S.L., ST LOUIS, MO

53. CIVIL WAR DIARY OF COLONEL ABRAHAM JEFFERSON SEAY; 32ND MISSOURI VOLUNTEER INFANTRY REGIMENT; PAGE 102; TYPESCRIPT COPY OF DIARY AT C.M.S.M.; KINGFISHER, OKLAHOMA.

54. MEMOIRS OF GENERAL WILLIAM T. SHERMAN, PAGE 581 & 582; LIBRARY OF AMERICA-1990

55. PERSONAL MEMOIRS OF U.S. GRANT, PAGE 583

56. OSTERHAUS PAPERS - DIARY OF PETER J. OSTERHAUS MAJ-GEN. 1864; SEPTEMBER 2; IN ARCHIVES AT M.H.S.L., ST LOUIS, MO

57. CIVIL WAR DIARY OF COLONEL ABRAHAM JEFFERSON SEAY; 32ND MISSOURI VOLUNTEER INFANTRY REGIMENT; PAGE 102; TYPESCRIPT COPY OF DIARY AT C.M.S.M.; KINGFISHER, OKLAHOMA.

58. O.R., SERIES 1, VOLUME 38, CHAPTER 50, PAGE 771
59. AUTOBIOGRAPHY OF OLIVER OTIS HOWARD MAJOR-GENERAL U. S. ARMY; VOLUME 2, PAGES 42 & 43; NEW YORK, THE BAKER & TAYLOR COMPANY 1908; THE TROW PRESS, NEW YORK; M.H.S.L., B-H835
60. CIVIL WAR DIARY OF COLONEL ABRAHAM JEFFERSON SEAY; 32ND MISSOURI VOLUNTEER INFANTRY REGIMENT; PAGE 102; TYPESCRIPT COPY OF DIARY AT C.M.S.M.; KINGFISHER, OKLAHOMA.
61. Ibid. PAGE 103
62. Ibid.
63. Ibid., PAGE 171 & 172
64. Ibid., PAGE 114
65. DAILY MISSOURI DEMOCRAT; SAINT LOUIS, MO. TUESDAY MORNING, SEPTEMBER 27, 1864.
66. Ibid. PAGE 170
67. O.R., SERIES 3, VOLUME 3

CHAPTER 14: CHASING GENERAL HOOD AND THE CONFEDERATE ARMY

1. MEMOIRS OF GENERAL WILLILAM T. SHERMAN ; PAGE 593; LIBRARY OF AMERICA-1990
2. CIVIL WAR DIARY OF COLONEL ABRAHAM JEFFERSON SEAY; 32ND MISSOURI VOLUNTEER INFANTRY; PAGE 104; TYPESCRIPT COPY OF DIARY AT C.M.S.M.; KINGFISHER, OKLAHOMA.
3. OSTERHAUS PAPERS - DIARY OF PETER J. OSTERHAUS MAJ. - GEN. 1864; SEPTEMBER 25; IN ARCHIVES AT M.H.S., ST LOUIS, MO
4. CIVIL WAR DIARY OF COLONEL ABRAHAM JEFFERSON SEAY; 32ND MISSOURI VOLUNTEER INFANTRY; PAGE 105; TYPESCRIPT COPY OF DIARY AT C.M.S.M.; KINGFISHER, OKLAHOMA.
5. MEMOIRS OF GENERAL WILLIAM T. SHERMAN ; PAGE 620; LIBRARY OF AMERICA - 1990
6. OSTERHAUS PAPERS - DIARY OF PETER J. OSTERHAUS MAJ. - GEN. 1864 - OCTOBER 4; IN ARCHIVES AT   M.H.S., ST LOUIS, MO
7. REESE, A.W.; (C3627) RECOLLECTIONS OF THE CIVIL WAR; 1870; VOLUME 2 PAGES 1 & 2. W.H.M.C., UNIVERSITY OF MO-COLUMBIA.

8. OSTERHAUS PAPERS - DIARY OF PETER J. OSTERHAUS MAJ-GEN 1864 - OCTOBER 5; IN ARCHIVES AT M.H.S., ST LOUIS, MO.

9. REESE, A.W.; (C3627) RECOLLECTIONS OF THE CIVIL WAR; 1870; VOLUME 2 PAGES 4-9. W.H.M.C.; UNIVERSITY OF MO- COLUMBIA.

10. Ibid., PAGES 10-12.

11. OSTERHAUS PAPERS - DIARY OF PETER J. OSTERHAUS MAJ. - GEN. 1864 - OCTOBER 8; IN ARCHIVES AT M.H.S., ST LOUIS, MO

12. REESE, A.W.; (C3627) RECOLLECTIONS OF THE CIVIL WAR; 1870; VOLUME 2 PAGES 13 & 14. W.H.M.C.; UNIVERSITY OF MO- COLUMBIA.

13. MEMOIRS OF GENERAL WILLIAM T. SHERMAN ; PAGE 627; LIBRARY OF AMERICA-1990

14. OSTERHAUS PAPERS- DIARY OF PETER J. OSTERHAUS MAJ-GEN 1864 -OCTOBER 10; IN ARCHIVES AT M.H.S.L., ST LOUIS, MO

15. REESE, A.W.; (C3627) RECOLLECTIONS OF THE CIVIL WAR; 1870; VOLUME 2 PAGES 18-22. W.H.M.C.; UNIVERSITY OF MO- COLUMBIA.

16. Ibid. PAGES 22 & 24-25

17. OSTERHAUS PAPERS - DIARY OF PETER J. OSTERHAUS MAJ-GEN 1864-OCTOBER 11; IN ARCHIVES AT M.H.S.L., ST. LOUIS, MO.

18. REESE, A.W.; (C3627) RECOLLECTIONS OF THE CIVIL WAR; 1870; VOLUME 2 PAGES 27-29 W.H.M.C.; UNIVERSITY OF MO- COLUMBIA.

19. MEMOIRS OF GENERAL WILLIAM T. SHERMAN; PAGE 630; LIBRARY OF AMERICA-1990

20. OSTERHAUS PAPERS -DIARY OF PETER J. OSTERHAUS MAJ-GEN 1864-OCTOBER 13; IN ARCHIVES AT M.H.S.L., ST. LOUIS, MO

21. Ibid., OCTOBER 15

22. REESE, A.W.; (C3627) RECOLLECTIONS OF THE CIVIL WAR; 1870; VOLUME 2 PAGES 27-29 W.H.M.C.; UNIVERSITY OF MO- COLUMBIA.

23. OSTERHAUS PAPERS -DIARY OF PETER J. OSTERHAUS MAJ-GEN 1864-OCTOBER 16-M.H.S.L., ST. LOUIS, MO

24. REESE, A.W.; (C3627) RECOLLECTIONS OF THE CIVIL WAR; 1870; VOLUME 2 PAGES 46-52 W.H.M.C.; UNIVERSITY OF MO- COLUMBIA.

25. OSTERHAUS PAPERS -DIARY OF PETER J. OSTERHAUS
MAJ-GEN 1864-OCTOBER 17 - M.H.S.L., ST. LOUIS, MO.
26. REESE, A.W.; (C3627) RECOLLECTIONS OF THE CIVIL
WAR; 1870; VOLUME 2 PAGE 30 W.H.M.C.; UNIVERSITY
OF MO- COLUMBIA.
27. Ibid. PAGE 31.
28. Ibid
29. OSTERHAUS PAPERS -DIARY OF PETER J. OSTERHAUS
MAJ-GEN 1864-OCTOBER 20; IN ARCHIVES AT M.H.S.L.,
ST. LOUIS, MO
30. REESE, A.W.; (C3627) RECOLLECTIONS OF THE CIVIL
WAR; 1870; VOLUME 2 PAGE 60 W.H.M.C.; UNIVERSITY
OF MO- COLUMBIA.
31. MEMOIRS OF GENERAL WILLIAM T. SHERMAN,
PAGE 636; LIBRARY OF AMERICA - 1990
32. OSTERHAUS PAPERS - DIARY OF PETER J. OSTERHAUS
MAJ-GEN1864; OCTOBER21; IN ARCHIVES AT M.H.S.L.,
ST.LOUIS, MO
33. KUCK, HENRY, PAPERS 1861-1865 (SL242) W.H.M.C.,
UNIVERSITY OF MO-ST. LOUIS
34. OSTERHAUS PAPERS - DIARY OF PETER J. OSTERHAUS
MAJ-GEN 1864-OCTOBER 24; IN ARCHIVES AT M.H.S.L.,
ST. LOUIS, MO
35. Ibid.,   OCTOBER 25
36. Ibid.,   OCTOBER 26
37. Ibid.,   OCTOBER 29
38. REESE, A.W.; (C3627) RECOLLECTIONS OF THE CIVIL
WAR; 1870; VOLUME 2 PAGES 73-75; W.H.M.C.;
UNIVERSITY OF MO- COLUMBIA.
39. Ibid. PAGES 76-79.
40. OSTERHAUS PAPERS - DIARY OF PETER J. OSTERHAUS
MAJ-GEN 1864-OCTOBER 31; IN ARCHIVES AT M.H.S.L.,
ST. LOUIS, MO
41. MUSTER SHEET, 31st MISSOURI INFANTRY REGIMENT
OCTOBER 31, 1864-MISSOURI STATE ARCHIVES
42. OSTERHAUS PAPERS-DIARY OF PETER J. OSTERHAUS
MAJ-GEN 1864-NOVEMBER 1; IN ARCHIVES AT
M.H.S.L., ST. LOUIS, M0
43. REESE, A.W.; (C3627) RECOLLECTIONS OF THE CIVIL
WAR; 1870; VOLUME 2 PAGES 83-85; W.H.M.C.;
UNIVERSITY OF MO- COLUMBIA.
44. OSTERHAUS PAPERS-DIARY OF PETER J. OSTERHAUS

MAJ-GEN 1864-NOVEMBER 2; IN ARCHIVES AT
M.H.S.L., ST. LOUIS, MO
45. REESE, A.W.; (C3627) RECOLLECTIONS OF THE CIVIL
WAR; 1870; VOLUME 2 PAGES 86-88; W.H.M.C.;
UNIVERSITY OF MO- COLUMBIA.
46. OSTERHAUS PAPERS-DIARY OF PETER J. OSTERHAUS
MAJ-GEN 1864; NOVEMBER 3; IN ARCHIVES AT
M.H.S.L., ST. LOUIS, MO
47. Ibid., NOVEMBER 4, 5, & 6
48. REESE, A.W.; (C3627) RECOLLECTIONS OF THE CIVIL
WAR; 1870; VOLUME 2 PAGES 89; W.H.M.C.;
UNIVERSITY OF MO- COLUMBIA.
49. WILLIAM H. LYNCH, DIARY 1864 (C1153); NOVEMBER 6
W.H.M.C.- UNIVERSITY OF MO-COLUMBIA
50. CIVIL WAR DIARY OF COLONEL ABRAHAM JEFFERSON
SEAY; 32ND MISSOURI VOLUNTEER INFANTRY; PAGE
108; TYPESCRIPT COPY OF DIARY AT C.M.S.M.;
KINGFISHER, OKLAHOMA.
51. OSTERHAUS PAPERS-DIARY OF PETER J. OSTERHAUS
MAJ-GEN 1864; NOVEMBER 8; IN ARCHIVES AT
M.H.S.L., ST. LOUIS, MO
52. REESE, A.W.; (C3627) RECOLLECTIONS OF THE CIVIL
WAR; 1870; VOLUME 2 PAGES 98 & 99; W.H.M.C.;
UNIVERSITY OF MO- COLUMBIA.
53. Ibid. PAGES 101-104
54. Ibid. PAGES 104 & 105
55. OSTERHAUS PAPERS - DIARY OF PETER J. OSTERHAUS
MAJ-GEN 1864; NOVEMBER 9; IN ARCHIVES AT M.H.S.L.,
ST. LOUIS, MO
56. Ibid., NOVEMBER 10
57. WILLIAM H. LYNCH DIARY 1864 (C1153)-NOVEMBER 10
W.H.M.C.; UNIVERSITY OF MO-COLUMBIA
58. Ibid. NOVEMBER 11
59. REESE, A.W.; (C3627) RECOLLECTIONS OF THE CIVIL
WAR; 1870; VOLUME 2 PAGES 110-112; W.H.M.C.;
UNIVERSITY OF MO- COLUMBIA.
60. OSTERHAUS PAPERS-DIARY OF PETER J. OSTERHAUS
MAJ-GEN 1864; NOVEMBER 12; IN ARCHIVES AT
M.H.S.L., ST. LOUIS, MO
61. CIVIL WAR DIARY OF COLONEL ABRAHAM JEFFERSON
SEAY; 32ND MISSOURI VOLUNTEER INFANTRY; PAGE
108; TYPESCRIPT COPY OF DIARY AT C.M.S.M.;

KINGFISHER, OKLAHOMA
62. OSTERHAUS PAPERS-DIARY OF PETER J. OSTERHAUS
MAJ-GEN 1864; NOVEMBER 13 & 14; IN ARCHIVES AT
M.H.S.L., ST. LOUIS, MO.

CHAPTER 15: ON TO SAVANNAH

1. CIVIL WAR DIARY OF COLONEL ABRAHAM JEFFERSON
SEAY; 32ND MISSOURI VOLUNTEER INFANTRY
REGIMENT: PAGE 109; TYPESCRIPT COPY AT C.M.S.M.
KINGFISHER, OKLAHOMA.
2. OSTERHAUS PAPERS - DIARY OF PETER J. OSTERHAUS
MAJ-GEN 1864; NOVEMBER 15; IN ARCHIVES AT
M.H.S., ST LOUIS, MO
3. MEMOIRS OF GENERAL WILLIAM T. SHERMAN ; PAGE
657; LIBRARY OF AMERICA-1990
4. OSTERHAUS PAPERS - DIARY OF PETER J. OSTERHAUS
MAJ-GEN 1864; NOVEMBER 16; IN ARCHIVES AT
M.H.S.L., ST LOUIS, MO
5. CIVIL WAR DIARY OF COLONEL ABRAHAM JEFFERSON
SEAY; 32ND MISSOURI VOLUNTEER INFANTRY
REGIMENT: PAGE 109; TYPESCRIPT COPY AT
C.M.S.M.; KINGFISHER, OKLAHOMA.
6. LIZZIE'S LETTER; ATLANTA GEORGIA, SUNDAY MORN-
ING APRIL 23, 1944, PAGES 3 & 10. ATLANTA
HISTORY MUSEUM. ATLANTA, GEORGIA
7. WILLLIAM H. LYNCH DIARY 1864 (C1153) W.H.M.C.; NO-
VEMBER 17; UNIVERSITY OF MO-COLUMBIA
8. OSTERHAUS PAPERS - DIARY OF PETER J. OSTERHAUS
MAJ-GEN 1864; NOVEMBER 17; IN ARCHIVES AT
M.H.S., ST LOUIS, MO
9. Ibid., - NOVEMBER 18
10. CIVIL WAR DIARY OF COLONEL ABRAHAM JEFFERSON
SEAY; 32ND MISSOURI VOLUNTEER INFANTRY
REGIMENT: PAGE 109; TYPESCRIPT COPY AT C.M.S.M.;
KINGFISHER, OKLAHOMA.
11. OSTERHAUS PAPERS - DIARY OF PETER J. OSTERHAUS
MAJ-GEN 1864; NOVEMBER 19; IN ARCHIVES AT
M.H.S., ST LOUIS, MO
12. CIVIL WAR DIARY OF COLONEL ABRAHAM JEFFERSON
SEAY; 32ND MISSOURI VOLUNTEER INFANTRY

REGIMENT: PAGE 109; TYPESCRIPT COPY AT C.M.S.M.
KINGFISHER, OKLAHOMA.

13. OSTERHAUS PAPERS - DIARY OF PETER J. OSTERHAUS
MAJ-GEN 1864; NOVEMBER 20; IN ARCHIVES AT
M.H.S., ST LOUIS, MO

14. CIVIL WAR DIARY OF COLONEL ABRAHAM JEFFERSON
SEAY; 32ND MISSOURI VOLUNTEER INFANTRY
REGIMENT: PAGE 109; TYPESCRIPT COPY AT C.M.S.M.;
KINGFISHER, OKLAHOMA.

15. Ibid. PAGE 110

16. OSTERHAUS PAPERS - DIARY OF PETER J. OSTERHAUS
MAJ-GEN 1864; NOVEMBER 21; IN ARCHIVES AT
M.H.S., ST LOUIS, MO

17. WILLIAM H. LYNCH DIARY 1864 (C1153); NOVEMBER 22
W.H.M.C.; UNIVERSITY OF MO - COLUMBIA

18. OSTERHAUS PAPERS - DIARY OF PETER J. OSTERHAUS
MAJ-GEN 1864; NOVEMBER 22; IN ARCHIVES AT
M.H.S., ST LOUIS, MO

19. CIVIL WAR DIARY OF COLONEL ABRAHAM JEFFERSON
SEAY; 32ND MISSOURI VOLUNTEER INFANTRY
REGIMENT: PAGE 110; TYPESCRIPT COPY AT C.M.S.M.
KINGFISHER, OKLAHOMA.

20. WILLIAM H. LYNCH DIARY 1864 (C1153); NOVEMBER 23
W.H.M.C.; UNIVERSITY OF MO - COLUMBIA

21. OSTERHAUS PAPERS-DIARY OF PETER J. OSTERHAUS
MAJ-GEN 1864; NOVEMBER 23; IN ARCHIVES AT
M.H.S., ST LOUIS, MO

22. CIVIL WAR DIARY OF COLONEL ABRAHAM JEFFERSON
SEAY; 32ND MISSOURI VOLUNTEER INFANTRY
REGIMENT: PAGE 110; TYPESCRIPT COPY AT C.M.S.M.
KINGFISHER, OKLAHOMA.

23. MEMOIRS OF GENERAL WILLIAM T. SHERMAN ; PAGE
665; LIBRARY OF AMERICA- 1990

24. OSTERHAUS PAPERS -DIARY OF PETER J. OSTERHAUS
MAJ-GEN 1864; NOVEMBER 24; IN ARCHIVES AT
M.H.S., ST LOUIS, MO

25. WILLIAM H. LYNCH DIARY 1864 (C1153);NOVEMBER 25
W.H.M.C.; UNIVERSITY OF MO-COLUMBIA

26. OSTERHAUS PAPERS-DIARY OF PETER J. OSTERHAUS
MAJ-GEN 1864; NOVEMBER 25; IN ARCHIVES AT
M.H.S., ST LOUIS, MO

27. CIVIL WAR DIARY OF COLONEL ABRAHAM JEFFERSON

SEAY; 32ND MISSOURI VOLUNTEER INFANTRY
REGIMENT: PAGE 110; TYPESCRIPT COPY AT C.M.S.M.
KINGFISHER, OKLAHOMA.

28. WILLIAM H. LYNCH DIARY 1864 (C1153); NOVEMBER 26
    W.H.M.C.; UNIVERSITY OF MO-COLUMBIA

29. OSTERHAUS PAPERS - DIARY OF PETER J. OSTERHAUS
    MAJ-GEN 1864; NOVEMBER 26; IN ARCHIVES AT
    M.H.S., ST LOUIS, MO

30. Ibid., NOVEMBER 27

31. CIVIL WAR DIARY OF COLONEL ABRAHAM JEFFERSON
    SEAY; 32ND MISSOURI VOLUNTEER INFANTRY
    REGIMENT: PAGE 110; TYPESCRIPT COPY AT C.M.S.M.
    KINGFISHER, OKLAHOMA.

32. WILLIAM H. LYNCH DIARY 1864 (C1153); NOVEMBER 29
    W.H.M.C.; UNIVERSITY OF MO, COLUMBIA

33. CIVIL WAR DIARY OF COLONEL ABRAHAM JEFFERSON
    SEAY; 32ND MISSOURI VOLUNTEER INFANTRY
    REGIMENT: PAGE 111; TYPESCRIPT COPY AT C.M.S.M.
    KINGFISHER, OKLAHOMA.

34. OSTERHAUS PAPERS - DIARY OF PETER J. OSTERHAUS
    MAJ.-GEN. 1864; NOVEMBER 30; IN ARCHIVES AT
    M.H.S., ST LOUIS, MO

35. Ibid., NOVEMBER 31

36. Ibid., DECEMBER 1

37. CIVIL WAR DIARY OF COLONEL ABRAHAM JEFFERSON
    SEAY; 32ND MISSOURI VOLUNTEER INFANTRY
    REGIMENT: PAGE 111; TYPESCRIPT COPY AT C.M.S.M.;
    KINGFISHER, OKLAHOMA.

38. Ibid.

39. OSTERHAUS PAPERS - DIARY OF PETER J. OSTERHAUS
    MAJ-GEN 1864; DECEMBER 2; IN ARCHIVES AT
    M.H.S., ST LOUIS, MO

40. Ibid., DECEMBER 3

41. CIVIL WAR DIARY OF COLONEL ABRAHAM JEFFERSON
    SEAY; 32ND MISSOURI VOLUNTEER INFANTRY
    REGIMENT: PAGE 111; TYPESCRIPT COPY AT C.M.S.M.;
    KINGFISHER, OKLAHOMA.

42. MEMOIRS OF GENERAL WILLIAM T. SHERMAN ; PAGES
    668 & 669; LIBRARY OF AMERICA-1990

43. OSTERHAUS PAPERS - DIARY OF PETER J. OSTERHAUS
    MAJ-GEN 1864; DECEMBER 4; IN ARCHIVES AT
    M.H.S., ST LOUIS, MO

44. CIVIL WAR DIARY OF COLONEL ABRAHAM JEFFERSON SEAY; 32ND MISSOURI VOLUNTEER INFANTRY REGIMENT: PAGE 111; TYPESCRIPT COPY AT C.M.S.M.; KINGFISHER, OKLAHOMA

45. OSTERHAUS PAPERS - DIARY OF PETER J. OSTERHAUS MAJ-GEN 1864; DECEMBER 5; IN ARCHIVES AT M.H.S., ST LOUIS, MO

46. CIVIL WAR DIARY OF COLONEL ABRAHAM JEFFERSON SEAY; 32ND MISSOURI VOLUNTEER INFANTRY REGIMENT: PAGE 111; TYPESCRIPT COPY AT C.M.S.M.; KINGFISHER, OKLAHOMA

47. WILLIAM H. LYNCH DIARY 1864 (C1153); DECEMBER 6; W.H.M.C.; UNIVERSITY OF MO-COLUMBIA

48. CIVIL WAR DIARY OF COLONEL ABRAHAM JEFFERSON SEAY; 32ND MISSOURI VOLUNTEER INFANTRY REGIMENT: PAGE 112; TYPESCRIPT COPY AT C.M.S.M.; KINGFISHER, OKLAHOMA

49. O.R., SERIES 1, VOLUME 44, CHAPTER 56, PAGE 85

50. OSTERHAUS PAPERS - DIARY OF PETER J. OSTERHAUS MAJ.-GEN. 1864; DECEMBER 6; IN ARCHIVES AT M.H.S., ST LOUIS, MO

51. Ibid., DECEMBER 7

52. Ibid., DECEMBER 8

53. CIVIL WAR DIARY OF COLONEL ABRAHAM JEFFERSON SEAY; 32ND MISSOURI VOLUNTEER INFANTRY REGIMENT: PAGE 112; TYPESCRIPT COPY AT C.M.S.M.; KINGFISHER, OKLAHOMA

54. O.R., SERIES 1, VOLUME 44, CHAPTER 56, PAGE 86

55. OSTERHAUS PAPERS - DIARY OF PETER J. OSTERHAUS MAJ.-GEN. 1864; DECEMBER 9; IN ARCHIVES AT M.H.S., ST LOUIS, MO

56. CIVIL WAR DIARY OF COLONEL ABRAHAM JEFFERSON SEAY; 32ND MISSOURI VOLUNTEER INFANTRY REGIMENT: PAGE 112; TYPESCRIPT COPY AT C.M.S.M.; KINGFISHER, OKLAHOMA

57. Ibid., DECEMBER 10

58. WILLIAM H. LYNCH DIARY 1864 (C1153); DECEMBER 10 W.H.M.C.; UNIVERSITY OF MO - COLUMBIA

59. CIVIL WAR DIARY OF COLONEL ABRAHAM JEFFERSON SEAY; 32ND MISSOURI VOLUNTEER INFANTRY REGIMENT: PAGE 112; TYPESCRIPT COPY AT C.M.S.M.; KINGFISHER, OKLAHOMA

60. WILLIAM H. LYNCH DIARY 1864 (C1153); DECEMBER 11
    W.H.M.C.; UNIVERSITY OF MO-COLUMBIA
61. OSTERHAUS PAPERS - DIARY OF PETER J. OSTERHAUS
    MAJ-GEN 1864; DECEMBER 11; IN ARCHIVES AT
    M.H.S.L., SAINT LOUIS, MISSOURI
62. CIVIL WAR DIARY OF COLONEL ABRAHAM JEFFERSON
    SEAY; 32ND MISSOURI VOLUNTEER INFANTRY
    REGIMENT: PAGE 112; TYPESCRIPT COPY AT C.M.S.M.;
    KINGFISHER, OKLAHOMA
63. OSTERHAUS PAPERS - DIARY OF PETER J. OSTERHAUS
    MAJ-GEN 1864; DECEMBER 12; IN ARCHIVES AT
    M.H.S.L., ST LOUIS, MO
64. WILLIAM H. LYNCH DIARY 1864 (C1153); DECEMBER 13
    W.H.M.C.; UNIVERSITY OF MO-COLUMBIA
65. OSTERHAUS PAPERS -DIARY OF PETER J. OSTERHAUS
    MAJ-GEN 1864; DECEMBER 13; IN ARCHIVES AT
    M.H.S.L., ST LOUIS, MO
66. WILLIAM H. LYNCH DIARY 1864 (C1153); DECEMBER 14
    W.H.M.C.; UNIVERSITY OF MO.-COLUMBIA
67. OSTERHAUS PAPERS - DIARY OF PETER J. OSTERHAUS
    MAJ-GEN 1864; DECEMBER 14; IN ARCHIVES AT
    M.H.S.L., SAINT LOUIS, MISSOURI
68. JOHN SHERMAN'S RECOLLECTIONS OF FORTY YEARS
    IN THE HOUSE, SENATE AND CABINET. AN
    AUTOBIOGRAPHY. VOLUME I. 1895
69. CIVIL WAR DIARY OF COLONEL ABRAHAM JEFFERSON
    SEAY; 32ND MISSOURI VOLUNTEER INFANTRY
    REGIMENT: PAGE 113 & 114; TYPESCRIPT COPY AT
    C.M.S.M.; KINGFISHER, OKLAHOMA
70. WILLIAM H. LYNCH DIARY 1864 (C1153) DECEMBER 18
    W.H.M.C.; UNIVERSITY OF MISSOURI-COLUMBIA
71. Ibid., DECEMBER 20
72. Ibid., DECEMBER 21
73. CIVIL WAR DIARY OF COLONEL ABRAHAM JEFFERSON
    SEAY; 32ND MISSOURI VOLUNTEER INFANTRY
    REGIMENT: PAGE 114; TYPESCRIPT COPY AT C.M.S.M.;
    KINGFISHER, OKLAHOMA
74. MEMOIRS OF GENERAL WILLIAM T. SHERMAN ; PAGE
    711; LIBRARY OF AMERICA-1990
75. O.R., SERIES 1, VOLUME 44, CHAPTER 56,
    PAGES 89 & 90
76. WILLIAM H. LYNCH DIARY 1864 (C1153); DECEMBER 24

W.H.M.C.; UNIVERSITY OF MO-COLUMBIA
77. CIVIL WAR DIARY OF COLONEL ABRAHAM JEFFERSON SEAY; 32ND MISSOURI VOLUNTEER INFANTRY REGIMENT: PAGE 114; TYPESCRIPT COPY AT C.M.S.M.; KINGFISHER, OKLAHOMA
78. O.R. SERIES 1, VOLUME 44, CHAPTER 56, PAGES 101 THROUGH 103
79. CIVIL WAR DIARY OF COLONEL ABRAHAM JEFFERSON SEAY; 32ND MISSOURI VOLUNTEER INFANTRY REGIMENT: PAGE 114 & 115; TYPESCRIPT COPY AT C.M.S.M.; KINGFISHER, OKLAHOMA

CHAPTER 16: COLUMBIA, SOUTH CAROLINA IS BURNING

1. O.R. , SERIES 1, VOLUME 47, PAGE 191, REPORT # 9
2. WILLIAM H. LYNCH DIARY 1864 (C1153) JANUARY 1 THRU 9 – W.H.M.C.; UNIVERSITY OF MO-COLUMBIA
3. DIARY OF FIELDING JENKINS SMITH - PRIVATE, COMPANY F, 31ST MISSOURI INFANTRY REGIMENT; JANUARY 1- TYPED COPY
4. Ibid.
5. Ibid., JANUARY 2 THROUGH 9
6. R.S.A.T.; EIGHTEENTH MEETING, CHICAGO, IL. SEPTEMBER 9TH & 10TH, 1885; PUBLISHED BY THE SOCIETY IN 1893.
7. DIARY OF FIELDING JENKINS SMITH - PRIVATE, COMPANY F, 31ST MISSOURI INFANTRY REGIMENT JANUARY 10- TYPED COPY
8. WILLIAM H. LYNCH DIARY 1864 (C1153); JANUARY 10 – W.H.M.C.; UNIVERSITY OF MO-COLUMBIA
9. DIARY OF FIELDING JENKINS SMITH - PRIVATE, COMPANY F, 31ST MISSOURI INFANTRY REGIMENT JANUARY 11- TYPED COPY
10. WILLIAM H. LYNCH DIARY 1864 (C1153); JANUARY 11 W.H.M.C.; UNIVERSITY OF MO-COLUMBIA
11. DIARY OF FIELDING JENKINS SMITH - PRIVATE, COMPANY F, 31ST MISSOURI INFANTRY REGIMENT JANUARY 12 - TYPED COPY
12. WILLIAM H. LYNCH DIARY 1864 (C1153); JANUARY 12 W.H.M.C.; UNIVERSITY OF MO-COLUMBIA,
13. DIARY OF FIELDING JENKINS SMITH - PRIVATE, COMPANY F, 31ST MISSOURI INFANTRY REGIMENT

JANUARY 13 - TYPED COPY

14. WILLIAM H. LYNCH DIARY 1864 (C1153); JANUARY 13; W.H.M.C.; UNIVERSITY OF MO-COLUMBIA

15. DIARY OF FIELDING JENKINS SMITH - PRIVATE, COMPANY F, 31ST MISSOURI INFANTRY REGIMENT JANUARY 14 - TYPED COPY

16. Ibid., JANUARY 15

17. Ibid., JANUARY 16

18. Ibid., JANUARY 17

19. Ibid., JANUARY 18

20. WILLIAM H. LYNCH DIARY 1864 (C1153); JANUARY 18 W.H.M.C.; UNIVERSITY OF MO-COLUMBIA

21. O.R., SERIES 1, VOLUME 47, PART 1, PGE 221, REPORT #11

22. WILLIAM H. LYNCH DIARY 1864 (C1153); JANUARY 19 W.H.M.C.; UNIVERSITY OF MO-COLUMBIA

23. DIARY OF FIELDING JENKINS SMITH - PRIVATE, COMPANY F, 31ST MISSOURI INFANTRY REGIMENT JANUARY 29 - TYPED COPY

24. WILLIAM H. LYNCH DIARY 1864 (C1153); JANUARY 19 THRU 29; W.H.M.C.; UNIVERSITY OF MO-COLUMBIA

25. Ibid., JANUARY 21

26. DIARY OF FIELDING JENKINS SMITH - PRIVATE, COMPANY F, 31ST MISSOURI INFANTRY REGIMENT JANUARY 20 THROUGH 29 - TYPED COPY

27. O.R., SERIES 1, VOLUME 47, PART 1, PAGE 256

28. THE STORY OF THE GREAT MARCH:BY BREVET MAJOR GEORGE WARD NICOLS, AIDE-DE-CAMP TO GENERAL SHERMAN; NEW YORK: 1865; PAGES 128-130

29. O.R., SERIES 1, VOLUME 47, PART 1, PAGE 1079

30. DIARY OF FIELDING JENKINS SMITH - PRIVATE, COMPANY F, 31ST MISSOURI INFANTRY REGIMENT JANUARY 30 - TYPED COPY

31. WILLIAM H. LYNCH DIARY 1864 (C1153); JANUARY 30 W.H.M.C.; UNIVERSITY OF MO-COLUMBIA

32. DIARY OF FIELDING JENKINS SMITH - PRIVATE, COMPANY F, 31ST MISSOURI INFANTRY REGIMENT JANUARY 31 - TYPED COPY

33. Ibid., FEBRUARY 1

34. WILLIAM H. LYNCH DIARY 1864 (C1153); FEBRUARY 1 W.H.M.C.; UNIVERSITY OF MO-COLUMBIA

35. O.R., SERIES 1, VOLUME 47, PART 1, PAGE 252

36. DIARY OF FIELDING JENKINS SMITH - PRIVATE, COMPANY F, 31ST MISSOURI INFANTRY REGIMENT FEBRUARY 2 - TYPED COPY

37. WILLIAM H. LYNCH DIARY 1864 (C1153); FEBRUARY 2 W.H.M.C.; UNIVERSITY OF MO-COLUMBIA

38. DIARY OF FIELDING JENKINS SMITH - PRIVATE, COMPANY F, 31ST MISSOURI INFANTRY REGIMENT FEBRUARY 3 - TYPED COPY

39. WILLIAM H. LYNCH DIARY 1864 (C1153); FEBRUARY 3 W.H.M.C.; UNIVERSITY OF MO-COLUMBIA

40. Ibid., FEBRUARY 4

41. DIARY OF FIELDING JENKINS SMITH - PRIVATE, COMPANY F, 31ST MISSOURI INFANTRY REGIMENT FEBRUARY 4 - TYPED COPY

42. Ibid., FEBRUARY 5

43. WILLIAM H. LYNCH DIARY 1864 (C1153); FEBRUARY 5 W.H.M.C.; UNIVERSITY OF MO-COLUMBIA

44. Ibid., FEBRUARY 6

45. DIARY OF FIELDING JENKINS SMITH - PRIVATE, COMPANY F, 31ST MISSOURI INFANTRY REGIMENT FEBRUARY 6 - TYPED COPY

46. WILLIAM H. LYNCH DIARY 1864 (C1153); FEBRUARY 7 W.H.M.C.; UNIVERSITY OF MO-COLUMBIA

47. DIARY OF FIELDING JENKINS SMITH - PRIVATE, COMPANY F, 31ST MISSOURI INFANTRY REGIMENT FEBRUARY 7 - TYPED COPY

48. WILLIAM H. LYNCH DIARY 1864 (C1153); FEBRUARY 8 W.H.M.C.; UNIVERSITY OF MO-COLUMBIA

49. DIARY OF FIELDING JENKINS SMITH - PRIVATE, COMPANY F, 31ST MISSOURI INFANTRY REGIMENT FEBRUARY 8 - TYPED COPY

50. Ibid., FEBRUARY 9

51. WILLIAM H. LYNCH DIARY 1864 (C1153); FEBRUARY 9 W.H.M.C.; UNIVERSITY OF MO-COLUMBIA

52. Ibid., FEBRUARY 10

53. DIARY OF FIELDING JENKINS SMITH - PRIVATE, COMPANY F, 31ST MISSOURI INFANTRY REGIMENT FEBRUARY 10 - TYPED COPY

54. WILLIAM H. LYNCH DIARY 1864 (C1153) FEBRUARY 11 W.H.M.C.; UNIVERSITY OF MO-COLUMBIA

55. DIARY OF FIELDING JENKINS SMITH - PRIVATE, COMPANY F, 31ST MISSOURI INFANTRY REGIMENT

FEBRUARY 11 - TYPED COPY
56. Ibid., FEBRUARY 12
57. O.R., SERIES 1, VOLUME 47, PART 1, PAGE 225
58. WILLIAM H. LYNCH DIARY 1864 (C1153); FEBRUARY 12
    W.H.M.C.; UNIVERSITY OF MO-COLUMBIA
59. Ibid., FEBRUARY 13
60. DIARY OF FIELDING JENKINS SMITH - PRIVATE
    COMPANY F, 31ST MISSOURI INFANTRY REGIMENT
    FEBRUARY 13 - TYPED COPY
61. WILLIAM H. LYNCH DIARY 1864 (C1153); FEBRUARY 14
    W.H.M.C.; UNIVERSITY OF MO-COLUMBIA
62. DIARY OF FIELDING JENKINS SMITH - PRIVATE,
    COMPANY F, 31ST MISSOURI INFANTRY REGIMENT
    FEBRUARY 14 - TYPED COPY
63. O.R., SERIES 1, VOLUME 47, PART 1, PAGE 242
64. O. R., SERIES 1, VOLUME 47, PART 2, PAGE 419
65. THE STORY OF THE GREAT MARCH: BY BREVET MAJOR
    GEORGE WARD NICHOLS; AID-DE-CAMP TO GENERAL
    SHERMAN; NEW YORK: 1865; PAGES 153 AND 154
66. DIARY OF FIELDING JENKINS SMITH - PRIVATE,
    COMPANY F, 31ST MISSOURI INFANTRY REGIMENT
    FEBRUARY 15 - TYPED COPY
67. WILLIAM H. LYNCH DIARY 1864 (C1153); FEBRUARY 15
    W.H.M.C.; UNIVERSITY OF MO-COLUMBIA
68. Ibid. FEBRUARY 16
69. DIARY OF FIELDING JENKINS SMITH - PRIVATE,
    COMPANY F, 31ST MISSOURI INFANTRY REGIMENT
    FEBRUARY 16 - TYPED COPY
70. Ibid. FEBRUARY 17
71. WILLIAM H. LYNCH DIARY 1864 (C1153); FEBRUARY 17
    W.H.M.C.; UNIVERSITY OF MO-COLUMBIA
72. THE STORY OF THE GREAT MARCH: BY BREVET MAJOR
    GEORGE WARD NICHOLS: AID-DE-CAMP TO GENERAL
    SHERMAN; NEW YORK: 1865; PAGE 166
73. Ibid. FEBRUARY 18
74. DIARY OF FIELDING JENKINS SMITH - PRIVATE,
    COMPANY F, 31ST MISSOURI INFANTRY REGIMENT
    FEBRUARY 18 - TYPED COPY
75. WILLIAM H. LYNCH DIARY 1864 (C1153); FEBRUARY 19
    W.H.M.C.; UNIVERSITY OF MO-COLUMBIA
76. DIARY OF FIELDING JENKINS SMITH - PRIVATE,
    COMPANY F, 31ST MISSOURI INFANTRY REGIMENT

CHAPTER 17: THE MARCH FROM COLUMBIA TO NORTH CAROLINA

1. WILLIAM H. LYNCH DIARY 1864 (C1153); FEBRUARY 20
    W.H.M.C.; UNIVERSITY OF MO-COLUMBIA
2. Ibid., FEBRUARY 21
3. DIARY OF FIELDING JENKINS SMITH - PRIVATE,
    COMPANY F, 31ST MISSOURI INFANTRY REGIMENT FEB-
    RUARY 21 - TYPED COPY
4. Ibid., FEBRUARY 22
5. WILLIAM H. LYNCH DIARY 1864 (C1153); FEBRUARY 22
    W.H.M.C.; UNIVERSITY OF MO-COLUMBIA
6. Ibid. FEBRUARY 23
7. DIARY OF FIELDING JENKINS SMITH - PRIVATE,
    COMPANY F, 31ST MISSOURI INFANTRY REGIMENT
    FEBRUARY 23 - TYPED COPY
8. Ibid., FEBRUARY 24
9. WILLIAM H. LYNCH DIARY 1864 (C1153); FEBRUARY 24
    W.H.M.C.; UNIVERSITY OF MO-COLUMBIA
10. Ibid., FEBRUARY 25
11. DIARY OF FIELDING JENKINS SMITH - PRIVATE,
    COMPANY F, 31ST MISSOURI INFANTRY REGIMENT
    FEBRUARY 25 - TYPED COPY
12. O.R., SERIES 1, VOLUME 47, PART 2, PAGE 568
13. Ibid., PAGE 571
14. DIARY OF FIELDING JENKINS SMITH - PRIVATE,
    COMPANY F, 31ST MISSOURI INFANTRY REGIMENT
    FEBRUARY 26 - TYPED COPY
15. WILLIAM H. LYNCH DIARY 1864 (C1153); FEBRUARY 26
    W.H.M.C.; UNIVERSITY OF MO-COLUMBIA
16. Ibid., FEBRUARY 27
17. DIARY OF FIELDING JENKINS SMITH - PRIVATE,
    COMPANY F, 31ST MISSOURI INFANTRY REGIMENT
    FEBRUARY 27 - TYPED COPY
18. Ibid., MARCH 1
19. Ibid., MARCH 2
20. WILLIAM H. LYNCH DIARY 1864 (C1153); MARCH 2
    W.H.M.C.; UNIVERSITY OF MO-COLUMBIA
21. Ibid., MARCH 3
22. DIARY OF FIELDING JENKINS SMITH - PRIVATE,
    COMPANY F, 31ST MISSOURI INFANTRY REGIMENT

MARCH 4 - TYPED COPY
23. WILLIAM H. LYNCH DIARY 1864 (C1153); MARCH 4
W.H.M.C.; UNIVERSITY OF MO-COLUMBIA
24. DIARY OF FIELDING JENKINS SMITH - PRIVATE,
COMPANY F, 31ST MISSOURI INFANTRY REGIMENT
MARCH 4 - TYPED COPY
25. Ibid., MARCH 5
26. WILLIAM H. LYNCH DIARY 1864 (C1153); MARCH 5
W.H.M.C.; UNIVERSITY OF MO-COLUMBIA
27. DIARY OF FIELDING JENKINS SMITH - PRIVATE,
COMPANY F, 31ST MISSOURI INFANTRY REGIMENT
MARCH 6 - TYPED COPY
28. WILLIAM H. LYNCH DIARY 1864 (C1153); MARCH 6
W.H.M.C.; UNIVERSITY OF MO-COLUMBIA
29. O.R., SERIES 1, VOLUME 47, PART 2, PAGE 701
30. WILLIAM H. LYNCH DIARY 1864 (C1153); MARCH 7
W.H.M.C.; UNIVERSITY OF MO-COLUMBIA
31. DIARY OF FIELDING JENKINS SMITH - PRIVATE,
COMPANY F, 31ST MISSOURI INFANTRY REGIMENT
MARCH 7 - TYPED COPY
32. Ibid., MARCH 8
33. WILLIAM H. LYNCH DIARY 1864 (C1153); MARCH 8
W.H.M.C.; UNIVERSITY OF MO-COLUMBIA

CHAPTER 18: BATTLE OF BENTONVILLE, NORTH CAROLINA

1. THE STORY OF THE GREAT MARCH: BY BREVET MAJOR
GEORGE WARD NICHOLS; AID-DE-CAMP TO GENERAL
SHERMAN; NEW YORK: 1865; PAGES 221-223
2. WILLIAM H. LYNCH DIARY 1864 (C1153); MARCH 9
W.H.M.C.; UNIVERSITY OF MO-COLUMBIA
3. DIARY OF FIELDING JENKINS SMITH - PRIVATE,
COMPANY F, 31ST MISSOURI INFANTRY REGIMENT
MARCH 9 - TYPED COPY
4. WILLIAM H. LYNCH DIARY 1864 (C1153); MARCH 10
W.H.M.C.; UNIVERSITY OF MO-COLUMBIA
5. DIARY OF FIELDING JENKINS SMITH - PRIVATE,
COMPANY F, 31ST MISSOURI INFANTRY REGIMENT -
MARCH 10 - TYPED COPY
6. Ibid., MARCH 11
7. WILLIAM H. LYNCH DIARY 1864 (C1153) MARCH 11

W.H.M.C.; UNIVERSITY OF MO-COLUMBIA
8. Ibid., MARCH 12
9. DIARY OF FIELDING JENKINS SMITH - PRIVATE, COM-
    PANY F, 31ST MISSOURI INFANTRY REGIMENT MARCH
    12 - TYPED COPY
10. Ibid., MARCH 13
11. WILLIAM H. LYNCH DIARY 1864 (C1153) MARCH 13
    W.H.M.C.; UNIVERSITY OF MO-COLUMBIA
12. Ibid., MARCH 14
13. DIARY OF FIELDING JENKINS SMITH - PRIVATE,
    COMPANY F, 31ST MISSOURI INFANTRY REGIMENT –
    MARCH 14 - TYPED COPY
14. Ibid., MARCH 15
15. WILLIAM H. LYNCH DIARY 1864 (C1153); MARCH 15
    W.H.M.C.; UNIVERSITY OF MO-COLUMBIA
16. DIARY OF FIELDING JENKINS SMITH - PRIVATE,
    COMPANY F, 31ST MISSOURI INFANTRY REGIMENT
    MARCH 16 - TYPED COPY
17. WILLIAM H. LYNCH DIARY 1864 (C1153); MARCH 16
    W.H.M.C.; UNIVERSITY OF MO-COLUMBIA
18. Ibid., MARCH 17
19. DIARY OF FIELDING JENKINS SMITH - PRIVATE, COM-
    PANY F, 31ST MISSOURI INFANTRY REGIMENT MARCH
    17 - TYPED COPY
20. WILLIAM H. LYNCH DIARY 1864 (C1153); MARCH 18
    W.H.M.C.; UNIVERSITY OF MO-COLUMBIA
21. O.R., SERIES 1, VOLUME 47, PART 2, PAGE 887 & 888
22. WILLIAM H. LYNCH DIARY 1864 (C1153); MARCH 19
    W.H.M.C.; UNIVERSITY OF MO-COLUMBIA
23. DIARY OF FIELDING JENKINS SMITH - PRIVATE,
    COMPANY F, 31ST MISSOURI INFANTRY REGIMENT
    MARCH 19 - TYPED COPY
24. O.R., SERIES 1, VOLUME 47, PART 2, PAGE 900
25. WILLIAM H. LYNCH DIARY 1864 (C1153); MARCH 20
    W.H.M.C.; UNIVERSITY OF MO-COLUMBIA
26. DIARY OF FIELDING JENKINS SMITH - PRIVATE,
    COMPANY F, 31ST MISSOURI INFANTRY REGIMENT -
    MARCH 20 - TYPED COPY
27. O.R., CHAPTER 59, PAGE 246, REPORT # 12
28. WILLIAM H. LYNCH DIARY 1864 (C1153); MARCH 21
    W.H.M.C.; UNIVERSITY OF MO-COLUMBIA
29. DIARY OF FIELDING JENKINS SMITH - PRIVATE,

COMPANY F, 31ST MISSOURI INFANTRY REGIMENT –
MARCH 21 - TYPED COPY
30. O.R., SERIES 1, VOLUME 47, PART 2, PAGE 253 & 254
31. Ibid., PAGE 259 & 260
32. Ibid., PAGE 267 & 268
33. WILLIAM H. LYNCH DIARY 1864 (C1153) MARCH 22
W.H.M.C.; UNIVERSITY OF MO-COLUMBIA
34. DIARY OF FIELDING JENKINS SMITH - PRIVATE,
COMPANY F, 31ST MISSOURI INFANTRY REGIMENT -
MARCH 22 - TYPED COPY
35. R.S.A.T.; 18TH MEETING IN ST LOUIS, MO, NOVEMBER 18
– 19, 1896; PAGES 67-76

CHAPTER 19: THE MARCH TO WASHINGTON, D.C. AND HOME

1. WILLIAM H. LYNCH DIARY 1864 (C1153); MARCH 23
W.H.M.C.; UNIVERSITY OF MO-COLUMBIA
2. DIARY OF FIELDING JENKINS SMITH - PRIVATE,
COMPANY F, 31ST MISSOURI INFANTRY REGIMENT
MARCH 23 - TYPED COPY
3. O.R., SERIES 1, VOLUME 47, PART 1, PAGE 248
4. WILLIAM H. LYNCH DIARY 1864 (C1153); MARCH 24
W.H.M.C.; UNIVERSITY OF MO-COLUMBIA
5. DIARY OF FIELDING JENKINS SMITH - PRIVATE,
COMPANY F, 31ST MISSOURI INFANTRY REGIMENT
MARCH 24 - TYPED COPY
6. O.R., SERIES 1, VOLUME 47, PART 1, PAGE 257
7. WILLIAM H. LYNCH DIARY 1864 (C1153); MARCH 25
THRU APRIL 9;W.H.M.C.;UNIVERSITY OF MO-COLUMBIA
8. DIARY OF FIELDING JENKINS SMITH - PRIVATE,
COMPANY F, 31ST MISSOURI INFANTRY REGIMENT
MARCH 25 THROUGH 30 - TYPED COPY
9. O.R., SERIES 1, VOLUME 47, PART 3, PAGE 45
10. LETTER BY BEVERLY DAVIS (R204); W.H.M.C.;
UNIVERSITY OF MO-ROLLA
11. O.R., SERIES 1, VOLUME 47, PART 3, PAGE 142
12. WILLIAM H. LYNCH DIARY 1864 (C1153); APRIL 10
W.H.M.C.; UNIVERSITY OF M0-COLUMBIA
13. Ibid. APRIL 11
14. Ibid. APRIL 12
15. Ibid. APRIL 13

16. THE STORY OF THE GREAT MARCH; BY BREVET MAJOR GEORGE WARD NICHOLS: AID-DE-CAMP TO GENERAL SHERMAN; NEW YORK: 1865; PAGE 293
17. WILLIAM H. LYNCH DIARY 1864 (C 1153); APRIL 29 W.H.M.C.; UNIVERSITY OF MO-COLUMBIA
18. Ibid. APRIL 30
19. Ibid., MAY 1 THROUGH MAY 22
20. Ibid., MAY 23
21. Ibid., MAY 24
22. O.R., VOLUME 47, PART 1, CHAPTER 59, PAGE 257
23. DAILY MISSOURI DEMOCRAT; TUESDAY MORNING MAY 30, 1865
24. R.S.A.T.; 21ST MEETING AT TOLEDO, OHIO. SEPTEMBER 5TH AND 6TH, 1888; PAGES 95 & 96.
25. DAILY MISSOURI DEMOCRAT; TUESDAY MORNING JUNE 20, 1865
26. WILLIAM H. LYNCH DIARY 1864 (C 1153); JUNE 4-AUGUST 10: W.H.M.C.; UNIVERSITY OF MO-COLUMBIA

APPENDIX B: NAMES IN THE 31ST MISSOURI VOLUNTEER INFANTRY REGIMENT

The following is a list of men who were mustered into 31st Missouri Infantry Regiment. There are approximately 1,020 men and officers on this list that at one time or another served with the regiment. Unless otherwise stated all names of towns or counties are in Missouri. The names of the towns or counties may not be the place they lived but where they enlisted or went into camp. In the case of the town named Canaan. There are fifty-eight names listed from that town. There was a camp at Canaan where the soldiers went after they had enlisted. At that time Canaan was not that large or I doubt if it has ever been large enough to supply that many men.

Ranks are the rank that the men held at the time of their muster into service and were subject to change due to promotions, reductions and transfers.

I listed the places of burial that I could find of the men who died during the war. The names listed as buried at the National Cemeteries were found mostly in a set of books listed as the "Honor Roll" of Federal Soldiers who died in the war. As I found to be the case at Jefferson Barracks National Cemetery they are buried in that section but may have a different grave number. For example, Private John P. Hicknaugh, buried at Jefferson Barracks, is listed in the "Honor Roll" as being buried in Section 25, Grave # 6. When checking the grave locator at the main building they didn't even have his name listed. I then went to Section 25 and walked down the rows and found his grave. It was Grave #5490. Almost all the grave numbers in the cemetery were different than what was listed in the "Honor Roll" book.

Almost all the names on this list were taken from a roll of microfilm purchase from the Missouri State Archives in Jefferson City, Mo. which is run by the Secretary of State. This roll of film is now in possession of the Scenic Library in Pacific, Missouri. Additional names were taken from the "Report of the Hospital at Jefferson Barracks, Mo." Jefferson Barracks Historical Site is in possesion of the microfilm.

NAME	RANK	COMPANY	PLACE ENLISTED
ABERNATHY, Marcus	Private	D	Carondelet
ALBERTY, Nathan	Private	K	Patterson
ADAMS, James W.	Private	D	Greenville
ADAMS, John G.	Corporal	K	Irondale
ADAMS, Joseph	Corporal	A	Victoria
ADAMS, William	Private	A	Victoria
ADEU, Alexander	Sergeant	A	Victoria
AGEE, Claib D.	Private	D	Greenville
AHERNS, Henry	Private	G	St Louis
AINLEY, Joseph	Private	B	St Louis
AKE, Jacob G.	Private	B	St Louis
AKE, William	Private	B	St. Louis
AKERS, William H.	Private	K	Caledonia
ALEXANDER, William	Corporal	I	St. Louis
ALFORD, Lewis H.	Corporal	A	Victoria
ALFORD, William	Private	A	Victoria
ALLEN, Edward E.	Captain	B	

Wounded at Battle of Chickasaw Bayou, MS

NAME	RANK	COMPANY	PLACE ENLISTED
ALMON, James A.	Private	D	Greenville
ALMON, John	Private	B	St. Louis
ANDERSON, Andrew	Private	E	Moselle
ANDERSON, Edward	Private	C	Hopewell
ARNOLD, John W.	Private	E	Moselle
ARNOLD, Reuben	Corporal	D	Greenville

Buried at Jefferson Barracks, Mo. National
Cemetery Section 26 Grave # 5854 Died 10-2-1862

NAME	RANK	COMPANY	PLACE ENLISTED
ASH, Henry	Private	I	St. Louis
ASHIN, Thomas	Private	H	Wayne Co.
ASHIN, Samuel	Private	H	Wayne Co.
ATCHINSON, Willis	Private	C	Hopewell
AUBUCHON, John C.	1st Sergeant	E	Moselle
AUSTIN, Henry	Private	D	Greenville
AUSTIN, O.		A	

Buried at Chattanooga, Tn. National Cemetery
Section L Grave #757

NAME	RANK	COMPANY	PLACE ENLISTED
AUSTIN, William	Private	A	Victoria
BAADE, Charles	Private	B	St. Louis
BAIRD, Columbus	Sergeant	H	Wayne Co.
BAIRD, James C.	Sergeant	C	Hopewell

BAIRD, Timothy P.   Sergeant   H   Wayne Co.
          Wounded Twice once at the Battle of Lookout
          Mountain, TN and Wounded in Neck slight at
          Battle of Ezra Church, GA.
BALDT, Henry   Private   E
          Buried at Jefferson Barracks, Mo. National
          Cemetery. Section 6 Grave #8   4-26-1863
BALLDRIDGE, Urias   Private   B Washington Co.
BANNON, Filder C.   Private   G Washington Co.
          Killed at Battle of Chickasaw Bayou,MS.
BARBER, Zike   Private   H   Wayne Co.
BARGER, David S.   Corporal   K   Caledonia
BARGER, Jacob   Private   K   Caledonia
BARKLEY, David   Private   C   Hopewell
BARLOW, William H.   1st Lieutenant   St. Louis
BARNEY, Herman   Private   K   Moselle
BARNS, James   Private   D   Greenville
BARRETT, Alexander   Private   H   Wayne Co.
BAUMAN, Rudolph   Private   G Washington
BAYCE, Elijah   Private   K   Ironton
BEARS, Lewis   Private   K   Caledonia
BEATY, Franklin   Private   H   Wayne Co.
          Killed at Battle of Dallas,GA
BECK, Paul   Musician   G   St. Louis
BECKETT, Henry C.   2nd Lieutenant   C
BELEU, William H.   Corporal   B Washington Co.
BELLFIELD, John G.   Private   C   Hopewell
BEUTNAGLE, Hartiveck   Private   G Camp Fletcher
BILES, John J.   Private   F   Cannan
          Missing at Battle of Chickasaw Bayou, MS.
BLAKE, James A.   Sergeant   A   Victoria
BLAKE, John W.   Wagoner   A   Victoria
BLACKENSHIP, Vincent Private   B Washington Co.
BOAS, William H.   Private   B Washington Co.
BOEDEKER, Henry A.   Private   A   Victoria
          Severely in arm at Battle of Lookout Mountain, Tn.
BOLLT, Henry   Private   G Camp Fletcher
BONE, Charles   Private   I   Mineral Point
BONE, Frank   Private   C   Hopewell
BONE, Joseph   Private   C   Hopewell
          Buried at Mississippi River National Cemetery
          Memphis, Tn. Section 1 Grave #73   3-4-1863

BONE, John	Private	C	Hopewell

Wounded in bowels, Died of wounds received at
Battle of Resaca, Georgia

BONE, Lewis	Private	I	Mineral Point
BORNING, John	Private	I	Mineral Point
BOUCHARD, Matthew	Private	B	St. Louis
BOY, Henderson	Private	I	Patterson
BOYD, Robert	Private	D	Greenville
BOYER, Felix	Private	K	Washington Co.
BOYER, Frederick	Private	B	Washington Co.
BOYER, Lewis	Private	K	Washington Co.
BOZARTH, William M.	Private	K	Ironton
BRANSON, Tell E.	Corporal	F	Canaan
BRANSON, Thomas J.	Private	F	Canaan
BRANSON, William W.	Private	F	Canaan
BRECKINRIDGE, John C.	Corporal	B	Washington Co.

Wounded in hand, slight, July 28, 1864 at
Battle of Ezra Church.

BRECKINRIDGE, Marian	Wagoner	B	Washington Co.
BREWER, Allen	Private	E	Moselle
BREWER, George W.	Private	D	Greenville
BREWER, William	Private	E	Moselle
BREWER, Wiley	Private	D	Greenville
BREWSTER, Edward	Musician	B	St. Louis
BRIDGET, Frederick G.	Private	B	Ironton
BRIENE, William	Private	D	Ardius
BRIGGS, Augustus 2nd Lieutenant		D	Moselle
BRONCON, Thos.	Private	F	

Buried at Jefferson Barracks, Mo. National Cemetery
Died 7-29-1863

BROOKS, David	Private	D	Greenville

Died of wounds received at Battle of Chickasaw Bayou , MS

BROOKS, John	Private	A	Victoria
BROOKS, Josiah J.	Private	A	Victoria
BROOKS, Ransome	Private	D	Greenville
BROWN, George W.	Corporal	I	Benton Barracks

Wounded at the Battle of Chickasaw Bayou, MS

BROWN, Jacob H.	Private	E	Moselle
BROWN, James	Private	D	Patterson
BROWN, Martin	Private	F	Canaan
BROWN, Thomas H.	Private	E	Moselle
BROWN, William	Private	E	Moselle

BROWN, William D.	Private	K	Benton Barracks
BROWN, William R.	Private	F	Cannan
BRUCE, Andrus	Private	D	Greenville
BRUCE, Isaac	Private	D	Greenville

Killed at Battle of Arkansas Post, Ark.

BRUCE, John A.	Private	D	Greenville
BRUNCE, Harmon	Private	I	Danville
BRUNK, James E. F.	Private	C	Hopewell
BRYAN, Boone	Private	A	Victoria

Captured at Ruggels, GA

| BRYAN, Philip G. | Private | K | Potosi, Mo |
| BUCHHOLZ, William | Private | G | Herman |

Killed at Battle of Chickasaw Bayou, MS

| BUDWELL, Willam H. | Private | E | Leesburg |
| BULLARD, Isaac | Private | D | Greenville |

Died of wounds received at Chickasaw Bayou,MS

| BURCH, William H. | 1st Lieutenant | E | Moselle |

Wounded at Battle of Bentonville, NC

| BURGESS, Jackson W. | 2nd Lieutenant | I | St. Louis |
| BURROWS, John | Sergeant | I | St. Louis |

Wounded at Battle of Pigeon Mountain, GA
Wounded severly at Battle of Griswold Station, GA

BURTON, William F.	Private	C	Hopewell
BUSHMEIER, Frederck	Private	G	Dutzow
CAIN, Alfred (Alpin)	Private	D	Hopewell

Buried at Jefferson Barracks Mo. National Cemetery
Section 26 Grave # 236 Died 2-6-1863

CAIN, Henry H.	Private	E	Moselle
CAIN, John G.	Private	E	Moselle
CALBRONIE, Johnie	Private		Murphysboro Tn

Enlisted 4-27-64 at Woodville, Ala

CALDWELL, Rodney	Sergeant	C	Hopewell
CALVIN, John	Cook	D	Woodville, Ala
CAMPBELL, Joseph	Private	C	Hopewell
CAMPBELL, Thomas	Private	K	Caledonia
CANTRELL, William R.	Private	A	St Louis
CARDIFF, George W.	Private	E	Cuba
CARLOCK, Ranson M.	Private	H	Wayne Co.
CARLOCK, William N.	Private	H	Wayne Co.

Buried at Vicksburg Ms. National Cemetery
Section E Grave #104   4-16-1863

| CARLON, Francis | Private | B | Jefferson Co. |

Died of wounds received at Battle of Chickasaw
Bayou,MS

CARMAN, Augustus	Private	F	Canaan
CARMAN, Barney	Private	E	Moselle

Captured at Clayrick, Ala

CARROLL, John J.	Private	F	Canaan

Died in hospital at Memphis, Tn between
March 28 to April 3,1863

CARROLL, William	Private	F	Cannan
CARVER, George W.	Private	C	Hopewell
CASEY, George W.	Private	H	Wayne Co.

Wounded at Battle of Chickasaw Bayou, MS

CAVENAUGH, David S.	Private	E	Moselle
CHANDLER, George W.	Private	E	

Buried at Jefferson Barracks, Mo. National Cemetery
Section 6 Grave # 90   8-5-1863

CHAUBONEAW, Eugene	Private	E	Moselle
CHARZELLE, Charles	Private	C	Hopewell
CHATMAN, Jasper H.	Corporal	H	Wayne Co.

Wounded in face slight, July 28, 1864
At Battle of Ezra Church, GA.

CHILDRESS, Major L.	Private	D	Harrison
CHRISTY, James S.	Private	I	Montgomey Co.
CIMBREL, John	Private	D	Greenville,
CLARK, Robert	Private	K	Ironton
CLARKE, John T.	Private	I	Mineral Point
CLAY, Charles	Private	E	Moselle
CLEMENS, Benjamin	Private	I	Montgomery Co.
CLEMENS, Gustave	2nd Lieutenant	A	St. Louis
CLEMENS, William	Private	H	Washington Co.
CLEMENTS, Augustine	Private	H	Wayne
CLEMENTS, William R.	Private	G	Danville

Wounded at the Battle of Arkansas Post, Ark. Died of
wounds 4-20-1863 Buried at Jefferson Barracks Mo.
National Cemetery, Setion 2 Grave # 72

CLUB, Antoine W.	Private	E	Moselle
CLUBB, Daniel	Private	H	Stoddard
COB, Madison	Private	D	Patterson
COBB, John	Private	C	Hopewell
COBB, Madison	Private	K	Ironton
COBB, Reuben	Private	D	Greenville
COFFMAN, Benjamin	Private	K	Caledonia

COLE, William S.	Corporal	C	Hopewell
COLEMAN, John H.	Private	C	Hopewell

Killed at the Battle of Chickasaw Bayou, MS

COLLIER, William R.	Private	F	Cannan
COLLINS, Lewis J.	Private	E	Moselle
COLOWAY, Samuel P.	Private	B	Ironton
COLTON, James	Private	I	

Buried at Jefferson Barracks, Mo. National Cemetery
Section 1 Grave # 63   4-19-1863

COMBALL, Charles	Private	E	Cuba
COMPTON, John H.	Corporal	E	Moselle

Buried at Jefferson Barracks, Mo. National Cemetery
Died 6-18-1863

CONGER. James	Private	I	St. Louis
CONWAY, Thomas H.	Private	C	Hopewell
CONNELLY, James	Private	B	St. Louis

Wounded at Battle of Chickasaw Bayou, MS

COOPER, Benjamin F.	Corporal	F	Cannan
COPE, Alexander	Private	D	Greenville
COPELAND, Dale	Private	D	Greenville
CORNWALL, Charles N.	Musician	E	Cuba
COSGRIFF, James	Private	B	St. Louis

Wounded in head, slight, May 27, 1864

COSTILE, Philip	Private	I	St. Louis
COWAN, David B.	Corporal	I	Danville
COWAN, William H.	Private	I	Montgomery Co.
COWELY, Michael	Private	E	Moselle
COX, Charles E.	Private	E	
COX, John	Private	D	Patterson
COX, Robert	Private	K	Patterson
COZART, Chesley	Sergeant	H	Wayne Co.
COZART, James H.	Private	H	Wayne Co.

Killed at Battle of Dallas, GA, May 29, 1864

CRAFT, John F.	Private	I	
CRAIG, Robert	Private	B	St. Louis
CRAMER, Arnold	Private	F	Cannan

Died of Wounds received at the Siege of Vicksburg, MS

CRINNION, Patrick	Private	I	St. Louis
CROMER, Harrison	Private	F	Cannan
CROMER, Joseph A.	Private	F	Cannan

Buried atJefferson Barracks, Mo. National Cemetery
Section 1 Grave #15   Died 4-3-1863

CROSS, Edward P.	Private	A	Victoria
CRUMB, Benjamin	Private	C	Hopewell
CRUTCHFIELD, Hiram	Private	H	Wayne Co.
CRUTCHFIELD, John	Private	H	Wayne Co.
CULTON, George	Private	I	Mineral Point
CULTON, Hart	Private	I	Mineral Point
CULTON, James	Private	I	Mineral Point
CUNNINGHAM, George S.	Sergeant	C	Hopewell
CUSTER, Isaac N.	Private	B	St. Louis
CUTHLERTION, Shereck	Private	F	Cannan
CZSECHENE, Ferdinand	Private	F	Cannan

Wounded at Battle of Chickasaw Bayou, MS

DALE, John M.	Private	D	Carter Co,

Wounded in right arm, severe, June 14, 1864

DALE, Wiley	Private	D	Patterson

Buried at Jefferson Barracks, Mo. National Cemetery
Section 39 Grave # 120   12-27-1862

DANIELS, Kibble	Private	D	
DANIELS, William	Private	D	Carter Co.
DAVIDSON, Isaac M.	1st Lieutenant	D	
DAVIDSON, Thomas J.	Private	H	Wayne Co.
DAVIS, Andrew J.	Private	F	Cannan
DAVIS, Daniel S.	Private	F	Cannan
DAVIS, Francis M.	Private	H	Wayne Co.
DAVIS, Francis M.	Private	K	Ironton
DAVIS, George W.	Private	A	Victoria
DAVIS, John A.	5th Corporal	H	Patterson
DAVIS, John W.	Private	A	Victoria
DAVIS, Thomas R.	Private	H	Patterson
DAVIS, William J.	Private	F	Cannan
DEAL, Marcus M.	Private	D	Greenville
DEARING, William Jr.	Private	B	St. Louis
DEARING, William Jr.	Private	B	Jefferson City
DECLAUS, Artwine	Private	D	Moselle
DeCLUE, Antoine	Private	E	
DEGEL, Christian	Private	G	Washington
DEFFENBACHER, Frederick	Private	D	

Buried at Mississippi River National Cemetery
Memphis, Tn. Section 1 Grave #71   2-26-1863

DEIRSTEIN, Carl	Private	I	St. Louis
DENNISON, Francis M.	Private	D	Greenville

Buried at Jefferson Barracks, Mo. National Cemetery.

GRAND ARMY OF THE REPUBLIC; SOLDIERS HOME, SAINT JAMES, MISSOURI APPROXIMATELY 1912; PRIVATE DANIEL DAVIS LIVED THERE OFF AND ON IN HIS LATER YEARS. BURIED THERE.

SOLDIERS HOME AT SAINT JAMES, MISSOURI as it looked when Private Daniel Davis lived there.

Section 39 Grave #253 1-31-1863

DEVINE, Leander	Private	K	Carondelet
DEVANCE, B.		K	

Buried at Jefferson Barracks, Mo. National Cemetery.
Section 39 Grave #16

DICKERMAN, Joseph	Private	A	Victoria
DICKMAN, B		K	

Buried at Jefferson Barracks, Mo. National Cemetery.
Section 39 Grave #239

DICUS, Samuel C.	Private	B	Jefferson Co.

Wounded at Battle of Chickasaw Bayou, MS

DIZMANG, James W. 2nd Lieutenant		D	Carondelet

Died of Wounds in arm received at Battle of
Chickasaw Bayou, MS

DODGE, George W.	Private	B	Washington
DODSON, Foreman	Private	C	Hopewell
DODSON, George W.	Private	A	Victoria
DODSON, William J.	Private	E	Moselle
DOGGET, William H.	Private	C	Hopewell
DOHERTY, Francis	Captain	K	Ironton

Missing and Captured at Battle of Chickasaw Bayou,
MS; Returned to Regiment in May 1863
Died of Wounds received at Battle of Ringgold, GA.

DOHERTY, Roderick O.	Captain	B	Ironton

Killed at Battle of Jonesboro, Ga

DONNELLY, Micheal	Private	B	Carondelet
DOVER, Oscar	Captain	A	St. Louis
DOWNEY, James	Private	D	Greenville
DOWINE, Charles	Private	C	Hopewell
DRENING, James	Private	E	Moselle
DRENING, John	Private	E	Moselle

(Drenning)

Wounded in thigh, severe, at the Battle of Resaca
And wounded again at Battle of Atlanta, GA

DRINCKCORN, Henry	Private	A	

Wounded in back, very slight, June 14, 1864.

DRINNIN, John E.	Private	E	
DRUS, John	Private	G	St. Louis

?(DRUESE)

Wounded at Battle of Jonesboro, GA and also
Wounded at Battle of Ringgold Gap, GA

DUCLOS, Francis	Private	B	Washington Co.

Killed at Battle of Chickasaw Bayou, MS

DUCLOS, Leon A.	Private	B	Washington Co.
DUBBERT, Frederick	Private	G	Greenville
DUFFENBACHER, Benjamin	Private	D	Greenville
DULEY, James	Private	K	Carondelet

Killed at Battle of Chickasaw Bayou, MS

DULTON, James M.	Private	I	Carondelet
DUMPHREY, Paul	Private	B	Washington Co.
DUCKHOM, Henry	Private	A	Victoria
DUNN, Peter	Private	I	Desoto
DURBIN, Christopher L.	Private	F	Canaan

Wounded at Battle of Chickasaw Bayou, MS

DUVALT, Thomas	Private	C	Hopewell

Killed at Battle of Dallas GA, May 27, 1864

EASLEYS, Nathaniel	Private	I	Monroe Co.
EAST, Anderson A.	Private	H	Wayne Co.

Wounded at Battle of Chickasaw Bayou, MS

EAST, Charles	Private	C	St. Francis Co.
EAST, Ezekial	Private	H	Wayne Co.
EATON, James D.	Private	K	Patterson
EATON, Jermiah	Private	D	Carter Co.
EATON, Jesse L.	Private	K	Washington Co.
EATON, John	Private	C	St. Francis Co.

Buried at Jefferson Barracks, Mo. National Cemetery.
Section 1 Grave #98 Died 5-3-1863

ECKERT, Philip	Private	G	St. Louis
EDWARDS, David F.	Private	D	Wayne Co.

Wounded at Battle of Chickasaw Bayou, MS

EGAN, John	Sergeant	B	St. Louis
ELICIS, Hert	Private	G	

enlisted 3-19-1864

ELLIOT, Joseph		D	

Buried at Jefferson Barracks, Mo. National Cemetery
Section 25 Grave #2 2-6-1863

ELLIOTT, Joseph	Private	C	Washington Co.
ELLIS, Thomas C.	Private	C	Washington Co.
ELSTON, Addison	Assistant Surgeon		
ENGELAGE, Charles	Private	G	Dutzow

Wounded at Battle of Chickasaw Bayou, MS
Died of Gunshot Wounds in Hospital at Jefferson
Barracks, MO

EPLEY, Jesse W.	Private	?	Wayne Co.

ESTES, Asa N.	Private	H	Wayne Co.
ESTES, Jesse E.	Private	H	Wayne Co.
ESTIS, Noel H.	Private	H	
EVANS, Marion	Corporal	B	Washington Co.
EVANS, William M.	Sergeant	I	Caledonia
EVANS, William H.	Captain	C	Washington Co.

Wounded at Battle of Chickasaw Bayou, MS

EVENDEN, Jonathan W.	Captain	F	St. Louis
EVERT, Earnest	Commisary Sergeant		St. Louis
FALLET, John H.	Private	E	Franklin Co.
FARLEY, Thomas F.	Private	A	Hillsboro
FARMER, Isaac	Corporal	K	Caledonia
FARR, John T.	Private	K	Patterson
FARREL, Thomas O.	Private	B	Washington Co.
FATCHETT, Thomas	Private	C	Washington Co.
FAIDTE, Adolph	Private	C	Carondelet
FEAR, Frederick	Private	C	Potosi
FERGUSON, Robert F.	Private	B	St. Louis
FIELDER, Barron C.	Private	G	Washington

Killed at Battle of Chickasaw Bayou, Mo

| FINGADE, Charles F. | Private | D | Ripley Co. |
| FINKE, Henry | Corporal | G | Washington |

Severely Wounded at Battle near Chattanooga, TN

FISHER, George W.	Private	C	Carondelet
FISHER, George W.	Private	F	Middleton
FISHER, James H.	Private	E	Franklin Co.
FISHER, William P.	Private	E	Franklin Co.
FLETCHER, Carrol	Private		
FLETCHER, Thomas C.	COLONEL		Ironton

Wounded and Prisoner at Battle of Chickasaw Bayou,
MS; Returned to duty May 1863

FLETCHER, William	Private		
FLYNN, James	Private	B	Washington Co.
FOCTDMAN, Wm.	Sergeant	G	

Wounded in jaw, slight, July 28, 1864 At Battle of
Ezra Church, GA

| FOLEY, Michael | Private | E | Ironton |
| FORRESTER, Alber W. | Corporal | K | Caledonia |

Captured at Battle of Haines Bluff, MS

| FORRESTER, Francis M. | Private | H | Wayne Co. |

Wounded at Battle of Chickasaw Bayou, MS

| FORRESTER, Jefferson C. | Private | K | Caledonia |

FORRESTER, John H.	Private	H	Wayne Co.
FORRESTER, William D.	Corporal	K	Caledonia
FORRESTER, William	Sergeant	K	Caledonia

Killed at Battle of Chickasaw Bayou, MS

FORSHA, Francis W.	Private	C	Washington Co.
FORSHA, John H.	Private	C	Washington Co.
FORSHA, Valentine	Private	C	Washington Co.
FORSHEE, Joseph F.	Private	C	Washington Co.
FORST, Michael	Private	A	Hillsboro

Wounded in head at Battle of Chickasaw Bayou, MS

FOUCH, James	Private	I	St. Louis
FRANKLIN, John W.	Private	E	Franklin Co.
FRANKLIN, Samuel M.	Private	E	Franklin Co.

Buried at Jefferson Barracks, Mo. National Cemetery.
Section 25 Grave #48 12-18-1862

FRAZIER, James	Private	E	Franklin Co.
FRENCH, William	Private	E	Franklin Co.
FREYBERG, Ernest	Private	G	St. Louis
FRICK, Adolph	2nd Lieutenant	G	Washington
FRICKE, Henry C	Private		
FRITZ, George	Private	G	Carondelet
FRY, Jacob	Private	K	Caledonia

Killed at Battle of Chickasaw Bayou, MS

FRYER, John R.	Private	E	St. Clair
FUTEN, Gustavus K.	Sergeant	H	Potosi

Wounded in leg at Battle of Chickasaw Bayou, MS

GARDALL, John	Private	G	
GARIN, James	Private	K	St. Louis
GARITY, Thomas	Private	H	St. Charles
GARRETT, John D.	Private	B	Washington Co.
GARRISON, Levi	Private	H	Wayne Co.
GARRISON, Samuel A.	Private	D	Randolph Co.

Killed at Siege of Vicksburg,MS

GERDEL, Henry	Private	G	St. Louis
GERDEL, Nicholas	Private	G	St. Louis

Severely wounded in neck, at Battle of Resaca, GA

GERNA, James W.	Corporal	H	Carondelet
GETHINGS, Jeremiah	Private	D	Greenville
GETTINGS, John		C	

Buried at Jefferson Barracks, Mo. National Cemetery.
Section 26 Grave #183 11-17-1862

GIBBONS, Michael	Private	K	Potosi, Mo

GIBBONS, William	Private	F	Gasconade Co.

Wounded at Battle of Arkansas Post, Arkansas

GIBSON, Lewis S.	Private	B	St. Louis

Wounded at Battle of Chickasaw Bayou, MS

GILLISPY, Thomas	Private	K	St. Louis
GLEASON, Michael	Private	K	St. Louis
GLECKLER, Jacob	Private	K	Maries Co.

Killed at Battle of Chickasaw Bayou, MS

GLORE, Jesse M.	Corporal	C	Washington Co.
GOFF, Andrew	Private	?	
GOFF, William M.	Private	?	Washington Co.
GOFORTH, Allen M.	Private	K	Caledonia
GOFORTH, Lafayette T	1st Sergeant	E	Moselle
GOLDEN, Amos	Sergeant	H	Moura, Ill
GOODMAN, Benedict	Private	B	St. Louis
GRAHAM, John	Private	A	Hillsboro
GRAVES, James H.	Private	H	Desoto
GREEN, Joseph M.	Corporal	D	Wayne Co.
GREEN, Lewellyn	Private	B	Dundee
GREEN, Uriah	Private	B	Ironton
GREENE, William M.	Corporal	H	Wayne Co.
GREENSTREET, Alfred	Private	B	Franklin Co.
GREENSTREET, David	Private	B	Franklin Co.
GREENWALD, Joseph	Private	A	Hillsboro
GREGORY, Robert M.	Private	H	Van Buren, Ark
GRIER, W.	Private	K	

Buried at Mound City, Illinois National Cemetery

GRIFFIN, Jefferson	Private	K	Potosi, Mo
HAMPTON, Wesley	Corporal	B	St. Louis
HACKWORTH, William	Private	E	St. Louis
HAGGATT, James H.	Private	H	Wayne Co.
HAIN, Fritz	Private	F	Cannan

Wounded in head at Battle of Chickasaw Bayou, MS.
Died aboard Hospital Ship - John J. Roe

HAINES, Eli	Private	F	Cannan
HAINES, Richard	Private	F	Gasconade Co.
HALE, Edward Jr.	Captain	I	
HALL, John H.	Private	F	Gasconade Co.

Buried at Mound City, Illinois National Cemetery
died 2-20-1863

HAMILTON, James	Private	?	Travis
HAMILTON, William	Private	E	Hillsboro

Taken Prisoner at Ringgold, Ga; Died of Diarrhea at
Andersonville Prison,September 17,1864 Buried there
Section H, Grave #9042

HAMM, Peter   Private   G   Washington
Buried at Jefferson Barracks, Mo. National Cemetery
Section 39 Grave #210   4-14-1863

HANNONG, Charles   Private   A

HARDY, Richard S.   Private   A   Hillsboro
Wounded at Battle of Chickasaw Bayou, MS

HARKEE, Richard   Private   H   Wayne Co.
Buried at Vicksburg, MS. National Cemetery
Section H   Grave #73   5-21-1863

HARMONY, Charles W.   Private   A   Jefferson City
Wounded in shoulder, Battle of Chickasaw Bayou, MS

HARRIS, Joshua   Private   I   Desoto

HARRISON, Andrew A.   Captain   D   Leesburg

HASSEL, Jesse D.   Private   D   Carter Co.

HAUSE, James   Private   H   Wayne Co.

HAUSE, Lewis   Private   H   Wayne Co.

HAUSNER, Paul   Private   G   St. Louis

HAVERSTICK, Philip R.   Private   A   Victoria
Severly Wounded at Battle near Chattanooga, Tn.

HAWALEY, Lorenzo D.   Private   ?   Monroe Co.

HEATON, Franklin D.   1st Lieutenant   C   Ellville, Ill

HELM, Alexander   Private   H   Wayne Co.

HELM, Meredith   Private   I   Calloway Co.

HELMS, Thomas B.   Private   H   Wayne Co.

HENDERSON, Joseph G.   Private   H   Wayne Co.

HENDERSON, William   Private   I   Moura, Illinois

HENDRICKS, Joseph   Private   H   Wayne Co.

HENDRICKSON, George W.   Private   A   Hillsboro

HENDRICKSON, William   Chaplain   Hillsboro

HENRY, Alexander G.   Private   K   Potosi

HENRY, Michael   Private   K   St. Louis

HENSLEY, Applebery B.   Private   A   Hillsboro

HESSER, James P.   Corporal   A   Jefferson City

HIBLER, William R.   Private   F   Cannan

HICKNAUGH, John B,   Private   A   Hillsboro
Buried at Jefferson Barracks, Mo. National Cemetery.
Section 25 Grave #6   2-3-1863

HILL, Benjamin G.   Private   C   Washington Co.

HILL, Egbert Oswell   Captain   F

Wounded at Siege of Vicksburg, MS

HILL, James W.	Private	E	Hillsboro
HILL, William L.	Private	C	Washington Co.

Wounded Slightly at Battle of Ringgold Gap, GA

HINSON, William R.	Private	F	Gasconade Co.
HOARD, Horace (HOOD?)	Sergeant	A	Hillsboro

Wounded Slightly at Battle of Ringgold Gap, GA

HOCKWORTH, John	Private	D	Carter Co.
HOFFMAN, E.H.	Assistant Surgeon		
HOFFMAN, William	Private	F	Gasconade Co.
HOGAN, Joseph	Corporal	B	Washington Co.
HOLERMESS, Herman	Private	?	Enlisted 3-22,1864
HOLLANDSWORTH,Elisha G,Private		F	Gasconade Co.
HOLLANDSWORTH, J. V.	Private	F	Gasconade Co.
HOLLANDSWORTH, Jonathon	Corporal	E	GasconadeCo.
HOLLANDSWORTH, W. W.	Private	F	Carondelet
HOLMAN, Thomas	Private	A	Hillsboro
HOLT, John H.	Private	F	Gasconade Co.
HOLT, William R.	Private	F	Cannan
HOLTHAUS, Henry	Private	G	Washington
HOMFIELD, Diedrich	Private	G	Warren Co.
HOPKINS, William W.	Private	K	Caledonia
HOPPER, Adam	Private	D	Popular Bluff
HORINE, Thomas T.	1st Lieutenant	D	Desoto
HORTON, Absalom	Private	H	Washington Co.
HORTON, John M.	Wagoner	H	Washington Co.
HOTAWA, John	Private	B	Ironton
HOUNE, Thomas	Private	A	Hillsboro
HOUNDREMENT, Michael	Private	G	St. Louis
HOUSEMAN, James A.	Private	F	Gasconade Co.
HUCKEY, John	Private	A	Hillsboro
HUCKY, William M.	Private	A	Hillsboro
HUGHES, Ambrose	Private	I	Monroe Co.
HUGHES, George	Sergeant	C	Belleview

Wounded at Battle of Chickasaw Bayou, MS

HUGHSON, William J.	Private	D	Ripley Co.
HUGHES, Thomas	Sergeant	I	Montgomery Co.
HUGHES, Victor H.	Private	I	Monroe Co.
HULSEY, James	Private	E	St. Clair
HUMPHREY, William N.	Private	H	Wayne Co.

Buried at Marietta & Atlanta National Cemetery, GA

Section G Grave #1516, Marietta, Georgia 7-20-1864

HUNTER, Frank	Private	G	St. Louis
HUSKEY, James	Private	A	Hillsboro
HUSKEY, John	Corporal	A	Hillsboro
HUTCHINSON, Bennet	Corporal	H	Washington Co.

Killed at Battle of Chickasaw Bayou, MS

IRVIN, Aquilla	Private	B	Washington Co.
IRVIN, William S.	Private	I	Washington Co.
ISERMANN, Frederick A	Private	G	Warren Co.
JACKO, Joseph	Private	E	St. Louis
JACKSON, James H.	Private	D	Butler Co.
JACKSON, Lafayette	Private	B	Washington Co.

Buried at Vicksburg, MS National Cemetery
Section H Grave #83 5-26-1863

JACKSON, Lewis M.	Private	C	Washington Co.
JACKSON, Richard B.	Private	B	Washington Co.

Missing at Battle of Chickasaw Bayou, MS

JACKSON, Thomas N.	Private	B	Washington Co.
JACKSON, William B.	Private	D	Butler Co.
JAENSCH, Frederick	Major		St. Louis

Wounded & Prisoner at Battle of Chickasaw Bayou,MS

JAMES, Ephraim	Private	D	Butler Co.
JAMESON, Thomas	Private	E	St. Louis
JAMISON, George	Private	?	Cuba
JARVIS, Eugennus	Private	F	Cannan
JARVIS, John	Private	F	Cannan
JASPER, Bernard	Wagoner	F	Warren Co.
JASPER, Charles	Musician	E	St. Louis
JEMISON, S. R.	Private	A	
JENKINS, Andrew J.	Corporal	F	Gasconade Co.
JENNISON, Robert J.	Private	E	Cuba
JOHNSON, George M.	Private	B	Washington Co.
JOHNSON, Wiley W.	Private	B	Washington Co.

Wounded in arm at Battle of Chickasaw Bayou, MS

JOLLEY, John	Private	B	Washington Co.
JOLLY, Francis	Sergeant	C	Washington Co.
JOLLY, John	Private	C	Washington Co.

Wounded in arm and side, severe, later died.
Near Atlanta, Ga on 8-6-1864 Buried at
Marietta & Atlanta National Cemetery, GA
Section G   Grave #1231

JONES, Charles	Corporal	D	Butler Co.

JONES, Henry H. Jr.	Private	A	Desoto
JONES, Thomas S. G.	Sergeant	E	Saint Clair
JOPLIN, Thomas H.	Private	A	Desoto
JORDAN, Zenos	Private	H	Wayne Co.
JUDD, William H.	Captain	C	

Wounded at Battles of Chickasaw Bayou,MS
and at Battle of Pigeon Mountain, GA

JULIET, James	Private	B	Washington Co.
JUNGER, Marion	Private	G	St. Louis
KAIN, Harvey H.	Private	E	St. Louis
KAIN, Patrick	Private	B	Carondelet
KALLERHALS, Joseph	Private	I	Montgomery Co.

?(KELLERHAND)

Wounded Slightly at Battle of Ringgold Gap, GA

KASEL, Herman	Private	G	Warren Co.
KEARNEY, Marvin	Private	A	Valley Mines

Died of Wounds While Prisoner of War

KEEN, Peter	Private	I	St. Louis
KEENEY, Robert E.	Sergeant	A	Hillsboro

Missing in Action near Battle at Chattanooga, TN

KELLER, Francis	Private	I	Monroe County, IL
KERNON, Burney	Private	E	St. Clair
KING, Samuel G.	Private	H	Wayne Co.
KIRKPATRICK, Samuel	Sergeant	H	Wayne Co.

Killed at Battle of Chickasaw Bayou, MS

KIRKPATRICK, Wallis	Private	H	Wayne Co.

Wounded at Battle of Chickasaw Bayou, MS

KLEIN, John	Private	G	St. Louis
KLINGE, ?	?	G	Hermann

Died of Wounds at Vicksburg, MS

KLINGE, Justus	2nd Sergeant	G	St. Louis
KLINGMAN, Fred	Private	G	Carondelet

Wounded Slightly at Battle of Ringgold Gap, GA

KLINGLEHOFER, Louis	Private	G	Montgomery Co
KLINGLEHOEFER, Martin	Private	I	Montgomery Co.
KLIPSTINE, John	Private	A	Hillsboro

Buried at Mississippi River National Cemetery
Memphis, Tn. Section 1 Grave # 46 8-6-1864

KNIP, Joseph	Private	G	St. Louis
KOEDING, John	Private	G	Warren Co.
KOPP, Charles	Private	G	Washington
KOUNCE, James C.	Private	A	Morse Mills

Buried at Marietta & Atlanta National Cemetery Ga.
Section G   Grave #487   10-26-1864

KRAFT, John	Private	I	Montgomery Co.
KUCK, Henry	Private	G	St. Louis

Wounded in leg at Battle of Chickasaw Bayou, MS

KUEN, Daniel	Private	G	
KUHNER, Albert	Private	G	St. Louis
KUNTZ, William	Private	G	Warren Co.

Wounded in bowels, slightly, August 8, 1864

LACHANCE, John	Private	G	Washington
LACY, Henry A.	Private	H	Wayne Co.
LANE, Jesse	Private	D	Carter Co.
LANHAM, Benjamin	Private	A	Hillsboro
LANHAM, Berry H.	Private	A	Hillsboro
(LANDHAM?)			

Wounded Slightly at Battle of Ringgold, Gap, GA

LANHAM, James M.	1st Sergeant	A	Victoria
(LANAHAN?)			

Severly Wounded at Battle of Ringgold Gap, GA

LANHAM, John	Private	A	Hillsboro
LAROSE, Lewis Roy B.	Private	I	
LATHAM, George W.	Private	A	Desoto
LAVELLE, Patrick	Private	B	St. Louis
LAWRENCE, Andrew	Corporal	H	Wayne Co.

Killed at Battle of Jonesboro, GA   9-1-1864

LEACH, James	Private	D	Carter Co.
LEMONS, Thomas J.	Private	F	Cannan
LINNCHAM, Thomas	Private	B	St. Louis
LOESCHMANN, Erhart	Private	G	St. Louis
LOGEM, William	Private	D	Wayne Co.
LONG, William C.	Private	H	Wayne Co.
LOVEINGS, Lawernce	Private	D	Wayne Co.
LOWE, Lewis E.	Private	C	Washington Co.
LUFFEY, Levi	Private	H	Wayne Co.
LUPING, Louis	Private	G	St. Louis

Killed at Battle of Jonesboro, GA Buried at
Marietta & Atlanta National Cemetery, Georgia
Section F Grave #435   9-1-1864

LYNCH, William	Private	I	St. Louis
LYONS, Peter H.	Private	C	Washington Co.
McCALLISTER, James	Private	H	Wayne Co.
McCLAY, Charles	1st Lieutenant	B	Washington Co.

McCLAY, Samuel R.   2nd Lieutenant   B Washington Co.
McCONNEL, Alexander   Corporal   F Washington Co.
    Died in hands of enemy 3-1-64 At Jackson, MS
McCONNEL, William   Private   F   Cannan
McCONNELL, Joseph N.   Private   H   Stoddard Co.
McCOOL, Hall   Private   G   Washington
  Died of Wounds received at Battle of Chickasaw Bayou, MS
McCOOL, Joseph   Private   G   Washington
McCORMICK, James I.   Private   A   Desoto
McCREERY, William   Private   E   Calvey
McCROSSIN, George   Private   ?   St. Louis
McCLUE, George   Sergeant   B   St. Louis
McCUNE, John   Musician   C   St. Louis
McDANIEL, James J.   Private   F Gasconade Co.
    Missing at Battle of Chickasaw Bayou, MS
McDANIEL, James   1st Lieutenant   F
McFRY, Peter   Private   A   Morse Mill
    Killed at Battle of Chickasaw Bayou, MS
McGRUDER, Daniel   Private   K   St. Louis
    Enlisted 2-16-1865
McGUIRE, George A. 1st Lieutenant   K   St. Louis
McJIRNEY, William   Private   C   Carter Co.
McKANNA, Patrick   Private   B   St. Louis
McKEAN, William J.   Private   F   Cannan
McKEEN, Robert M.   Private   A   Hillsboro
    Died of Wounds while a prisoner of war.
McKEE, John E.   Corporal   I   Jefferson Co.
    Missing at Battle near Chattanooga, TN
McKEE, William S.   Corporal   I   Jefferson Co.
McKowan, Ross H.   Commisary Sergeant
    Non-commissioned staff.
McLANE, Jackson   Private   C   Carondelet
McMAYBRY, H.G.   1st Lieutenant   G
McMICKEN, Hamilton   Sergeant   E   Cuba
    Killed at Battle of Chickasaw Bayou, MS
McMINN, Thomas   Private   C   Butler Co.
    Killed at Battle of Chickasaw Bayou, MS
McMULLIN, Richard   Private   I   Desoto
McMULLIN, Thomas J.   Private   I   Desoto
    Killed at Battle of Chickasaw Bayou, MS
McMURTRY, James S.   Captain   H   Patterson
    Missing in Action at Battle of Chickasaw Bayou, MS.

Returned to Regiment in May 1863

McNAIR, Fred A. E.	Private	I	Carondelet
McNULTY, Charles	Private	A	Victoria
McVAY, Willis	Private	C	Washington Co.

Wounded in the arm at Chickasaw Bayou, MS

MABREY, Henry Y.	1st Lieutenant	H	Wayne Co.
MABREY, James R.	Private	H	Wayne Co.
MABREY, Philip P.	Corporal	H	Wayne Co.
MACLAY, Charles	1st Lieutenant	B	
MACLAY, Samuel R.	Captain	E	White Cloud

(See McClay)

MAGUIRE, George A.	Captain	A	
MAHLER, Charles K.	Private	C	Washington Co.
MALLOW, James H.	Private	H	Wayne Co.

Buried at National Cemetery Nashville, Tn.
Section E Grave#1105

MANSKER, Matthew E.	Private	D	Randolph Co.

Wounded in Battle of Chickasaw Bayou, MS

MANSKER, William J.	Private	D	Randolph Co.

Buried at Jefferson Barracks, Mo. National Cemetery.
Section 224 Grave #36   2-23-1863

MANION, Joseph	Private	G	
MARLER, Charles K.	Private	C	Washington Co.
MARLER, George	Private	C	Washington Co.
MARLER, James K.	Private	C	Washington Co.
MARLER, Joseph H.	Private	C	Washington Co.
MARLER, Joseph M.	Private	C	Washington Co.
MARLER, John J.	Private	C	Washington Co.
MARLES, J. N.	Private	D	

Buried at Jefferson Barracks, Mo. National Cemetery.
Section 2   Grave #55 4-17-1863

MARTIN, James H.	Private	A	Victoria
MARTIN, Leander	Private	C	Butler Co

Buried at Jefferson Barracks, Mo. National Cemetery.
Section 5 Grave #20 4-8-1863

MARTYWEILER, Fritz	Private	G	St. Louis

Killed at Battle of Chickasaw Bayou, MS

MATTLOCK, Samuel H.	Sergeant	F	Canaan
MAXWELL, Campbell	Private	I	Montgomery Co.
MEDLOCK, Henry	Private	A	Victoria
MEGEL, Nathan W.	Private	H	

Buried at Jefferson Barracks, Mo. National Cemetery.

Section 25 Grave #153   3-2-1863

| MENDENHALL, Jacob K. | Private | D | Butler Co. |

Killed at Battle of Chickasaw Bayou, MS

MEREDITH, John J.	Corporal	F	Canaan
MEREDITH, Thomas	Private	F	Canaan
MEYER, Bernard	Private	G	Washington
MEYERS, Henry	Private	G	St. Louis

Wounded on November 26, 1863

MEYER, Henry	Private	A	Morse Mill
MEYER, Thomas	Sergeant	G	Herman
METZ, Jacob	Private	A	Desoto
MIDDENDORF, D. H.	1st Sergeant	B	St. Louis
MIDGET, Nathan W.	Private	H	Wayne Co.
MILLER, Benjamin M.	Private	I	Carondelet

Wounded at Battle of Chickasaw Bayou, MS
Died of Wounds at Paducah, KY May 2, 1863

MILLER, George W.	Private	H	Wayne Co.
MILLER, James	Private	B	Washington Co.
MILLER, Lewis H.	Corporal	A	Herculaneum

Wounded in head at Battle of Chickasaw Bayou, MS

| MILLER, Samuel | Private | E | Leesburg |

Killed at Battle of Chickasaw Bayou, MS

| MITCHELL, William H. | 1st Sergeant | C | Irondale |

Wounded Slightly at Ringgold Gap, GA

| MITCHELL, William F. | Private | B | Ironton |
| MOFFAT, Joseph G. | Private | I | Danville |

Wounded at Battle of Chickasaw Bayou, MS

| MOFFAT, James | Corporal | I | Jefferson Co. |

Buried at Vicksburg, Ms. National Cemetery
Section E   Grave #154   4-30-1863

| MOFFET, Warren | Private | I | Danville |

Buried at Mississippi River National Cemetery
Memphis, Tn. Section 1 Grave #42   5-30-1863

MOFFRY, Christiam	Corporal	G	Warren Co.
MOLLEY, John G.	Private	C	Carter Co.
MONROE, James	Private	I	St. Louis
MOONEY, Samuel M.	Private	A	Herculaneum
MOORE, Eli B.	Private	K	Caledonia
MOORE, Francis M.	Private	K	Caledonia
MOORE, John	Private	H	Wayne Co.

Killed June 30, 1864 at Kennesaw Mountain, GA

| MOORE, Joseph | Private | E | Franklin Co. |

662

Killed at Battle of Chickasaw Bayou, MS

MORRIS, James	Private	A	Valley Mines
MORRISON. John	Private	A	
MORSE, Frank	Private	H	

Killed at Battle of Resaca, GA

MURPHY, Michael	Private	K	St. Louis
MURPHY, William A.	Sergeant	E	Moselle

Wounded and captured Chickasaw Bayou, MS

MUSGROVES, Charles B.	Private	E	Stanton
NEIDERHOLTMEYER, Frank	Private	G	Washington
NETHERINGTON, Henry W.	Private	B	Washington Co.
NEUNER, Mathias	Sergeant	G	St. Louis
NEUNOBLE, John	Private	G	Dutzow
NEWTON, Joseph J.	Private	D	Greenville
NICOLS, Joseph A.	Corporal	B	Washington Co.
NIELAUER, George H.	Private	G	St. Louis
NOBLE, John Nio	Private	G	Lincoln Co.
NOLAN, Peter (NOLEN?)	Private	B	Washington Co.
NOLTE, Christian	Private	G	St. Louis
NORRIS, Wesley E.	Private	I	Sulpher Springs

Wounded at Battle of Chickasaw Bayou, MS

NORTHCUT, George	Private	B	Washington Co.
NOW, Henry	Private	G	St. Louis

Killed at Battle of Dallas, GA- May 27, 1864

OESKER, Robert	Private	G	Carondelet
OGLE, Elbert	Sergeant	A	Victoria
OGLE, Landon	Private	A	Victoria

Died of Wounds at Battle of Chickasaw Bayou, MS

ORME, Andrew	Private	C	Hopewell
ORR, William J.	Private	K	Ironton
OSBURNE, William F.	Private	D	Greenville
OSTERHORN, William	Captain	G	Carondelet

Wounded slightly in Skirmish near Vicksburg, MS

OWSLY, George S.	Private	K	Caledonia
PAGE, Moses M.	Private	E	Moselle
PAGE, Peter C.	Corporal	E	Moselle
PAGE, William S.	Corporal	E	Moselle
PALMER, Elisha	Private	I	Potosi

Wounded at Battle of Chickasaw Bayou, MS

PALMER, James	Private	F	Canaan

Wounded slightly in breast near Vicksburg, MS

Name	Rank	Co.	Location
PALMER, Joseph	Private	F	Canaan
PALMER, Montgomery	Private	I	Potosi
PALMERSTON, Valentine	Private	E	Moselle
PARKINS, Richard	Wagoner	F	Mineral Point
PARMLEY, Robert	Private	I	Potosi, Mo
PATTERSON, George G.	Private	D	Randolph Co. AK
PATTON, Alfred	Private	E	Moselle
PATTON, John D.	Private	E	Moselle
PAUL, Thomas	Private	B	Washington Co.
PENN, Joseph	Private	K	Danville
PENNELL, William	Private	B	St. Louis
PENNINGTON, Willas	Private	F	Gasconade Co.
PERCY, Isaiah	Private	K	Danville
PERKINS, Adolphus E.	Private	H	Wayne Co.
PERKINS, James	Private	H	Wayne Co.

Buried at Jefferson Barracks, Mo. National Cemetery.
Section 24 Grave #28   11-14-1862

Name	Rank	Co.	Location
PEYTON, Baylie	Corporal	D	Greenville
PHILLIPS, Jesse	Private	E	Moselle
PHILLIPS, Patrick	Private	E	Moselle

Missing in Action 11-27-1863; Died of Dysentery
at Andersonville Prison 4-26-1864, Buried there
Section K Grave #10755

Name	Rank	Co.	Location
PIERSON, Orson	Corporal	C	Hopewell
POLITE, Jule Narcice (POLIET?)	Private	B	Washington Co.

Buried at Jefferson Barracks, MO National Cemetery.
Section 25 Grave #46, Died 12-14-1862

Name	Rank	Co.	Location
POLITE, Yenno	Private	B	Washington Co.
PORCH, Joseph	Private	H	Butler Co.
PORTER, Thomas L.	Private	I	Victoria
PORTELL, Cyprian (PORTAL?)	Private	B	Washington Co.

Wounded shot in the head at Battle of Ringgold, GA

Name	Rank	Co.	Location
POUNDS, Falkland H. W.	Private	F	Hillsboro
POUNDS, Isaac E.	Private	F	Cannan
POWERS, John C.	Private	I	St. Louis
PRATT, William B.	1st Lieutenant		St. Louis
PREWITT, John W.	Private	A	St. Louis
PRIESTER, George	Private	A	St. Louis
PRICE, Pleasant F.	Corporal	F	Canaan
PRUETT, Obediah	Private	K	Ironton

PRUITT, Austin	Private	E	Moselle
PRYOR, Francis M.	Private	F	Canaan
PUTNAM, Spencer	Private		St. Louis
PUNCH, Thomas A.	Sergeant	D	Greenville
RAGLIN, Joseph H.	Private	H	Wayne Co.

Wounded at Battle of Chickasaw Bayou, MS

RAHE, Herman H.	Private	K	St. Louis
RAINER, Barney	Private	K	St. Louis
RAMSEY, Hiram S.	Private	H	Caledonia

Missing at Battle of Ringgold GA
Died at Andersonville Prison, GA in April 1864

RAMSEY, Joseph T.	Private	H	Caledonia

Killed at Battle of Chickasaw Bayou, MS

RAMSEY, Jasper N.	Private	K	Washington Co.
RAMSEY, William B.	2nd Lieutenant	K	Ironton
RAUSCH, Hugo	Private	G	Dutzow
READER, Frederick	Corporal	G	Montgomery Co

Killed at Battle of Chickasaw Bayou, MS

REED, John	Captain	I	Victoria
REED, Letcher	Private	F	Gasconade Co.

Died of wounds received at Chickasaw Bayou, MS

REED, Manuel	Private	F	Canaan

Buried Mississippi River National Cemetery
Memphis, Tn. Section 1 Grave # 384   12-26-1862

REED, Matthias	Private	F	Canaan

Buried at Jefferson Barracks, Mo. National Cemetery.
Section 7 Grave #184   12-23-1863

REED, Thomas H.	Private	I	Montgomery Co.

Wounded in Left Leg

REED, Solomon	Private	F	Canaan

Wounded in hand, slight, June 27, 1864 at the
Battle of Kennesaw Mountain, GA.

REESE, Alexander	Surgeon		Saline Co.
REEVES, Joseph	Wagoner	C	Hopewell
REINSCHMIDT, William	Private	K	St. Louis
RESLEY, John	Private	C	
REYNOLDS, John B.	Private	A	Victoria
REYNOLDS, William J.	Private	A	Victoria
REYNOR, Barnard	Musician	A	St. Louis
RHEVIS, George	Private	A	Steelville
RHODES, Jarvis	Private		Patterson
RICHARDS, Daniel F.	Private		

RICHARDSON, Andrew J.   Private   B Washington Co.
    Missing/ Died as prisoner of war at
    Battle of Chickasaw Bayou, MS
RICHARDSON, Elisha   Private   H   Wayne Co.
RICHARDSON, Jacob F.   Private   K   Potosi
RICHARDSON, James   Private   H Washington Co.
RICHARDSON, Robert   Private   A   Victoria
    Wounded in hand, slight at Battle of Resaca
RICHARDSON, William   Private   B Washington Co.
RICHIE, Walter D.   Private   K   Ironton
RICHTER, Herman H.   Private   A   Victoria
RICTER, Lewis   Private   K   Desoto
RIDER, Jacob   Private   E
    Killed at Battle of Resaca, GA
RIPLEY, John   Private   D   Greenville
ROBERTSON, John   Private   A   Victoria
    Killed at Battle of Chickasaw Bayou, MS
ROBERTSON, Marshall B.   Private   D   Greenville
    Died of wounds received at Battle of Ringgold, Ga
ROBINSON, William   1st Lieutenant   I   Danville
    Killed at the Battle of Vicksburg, MS 5-22-1863
    Buried at Vicksburg, Ms. National Cemetery
    Section O, Grave #51
RODENBERG, Frederick   Private   G   St. Louis
RODERIGNE, John J.   Private   B Washington Co.
RODGERS, Francis M.   Private   D   Greenville
RODGERS, William C.   Private   F   Canaan
RODGERS, William W.   Corporal   C   Hopewell
ROESENER, Jacob   Sergeant   G   Washington
ROLAND, James H.   Private   D   Greenville
RONGEY, William L.   Private   I   Mineral Point
ROTH, Charles   Private   G   Dutzow
ROY, Henderson   Private   D   Carter Co.
ROYAL, Andrew   Captain   I   Louisville, KY
RUBLE, Lorenzo D.   Private   H   Wayne Co.
RUDD, Abraham W.   Corporal   I   Desoto
RUDERSHAUSEN, Frederick 1st Lieutenant G   St. Louis
RUGE, Charles E.   1st Lieutenant   G   Carondelet
RUGE, Julius A.   Assistant Surgeon   St. Louis
RUIDICILE, Ephraim C.   Corporal   D   Greenville
RUSSELL, Harry E.   Musician   I   St. Louis
    Killed at Battle of Dallas, GA,   May 28, 1864

RUTHERFORD, Nathaniel W Private   A   Victoria
RYAN, Dennis   Private   B   St. Louis
SABINE, Michael   Musician   B   St. Louis
SAGO, Samuel A.   Corporal   C   Hopewell
     Missing at Battle of Chickasaw Bayou, MS
SANDILIO, H.   K
     Buried at Jefferson Barracks, Mo. National Cemetery.
     Section 30 Grave # 82   11-1-1862
SANLIN, Hardy   Private   H   Wayne Co.
SCAGGS, John   Private   A   Victoria
SCANTLIN, John   Private   F   Canaan
     Wounded in thigh at Battle of Chickasaw Bayou, MS
SCHAUB, Frank(Francis L)   Private   I   St. Louis
     Wounded slightly in arm, Battle of Ringgold Gap, GA
SCHIERDING, John H.   Private   G   Warren Co.
SCHINDLER, Allice   Private   I   St. Louis
     Wounded slightly at Battle of Ringgold Gap, GA
     Died while Prisoner of War
SCHMIDT, Edward   Private   G   St. Louis
SCHOFIELD, William H.   Private   B   Ironton
SCHRIVER, Henry   Private   I   St. Louis
     Wounded in shoulder, Battle of Chickasaw Bayou, MS
SCHULER, Jerome B.   Private   H   Wayne Co.
SCHWALBE, Angus   Private   A   Victoria
SCHWARTZE, William   Private   G   Dutzow
     Wounded slightly at Battle of Ringgold Gap, GA
     Wounded severly 4-4-1864
SCOTT, John W.   Private   C   Hopewell
SEATON, James C.   Private   F   Canaan
     Buried at Mississippi River National Cemetery
     Memphis, Tn. Section 1 Grave #44   5-26-1863
SEATON, Philip E.   Private   F   Canaan
SECREASE, Andrew J.   Private   A   Victoria
SELF, Thomas B.   Private   C   Hopewell
Wounded in thigh, slight, at Battle of Dallas,GA. May 28,1864
SESSLER, John   Private   G   Dutzow
SHANNAN, Thomas   Private   B   St. Louis
SHAW, Samuel E.   Private   K   Caledonia
SHEETS, Griffin   Private   K   Potosi
     Killed at Battle of Chickasaw Bayou, MS 12-29-1862
SHELTON, Daniel K.   Private   K   Caledonia
SHELTON, William   Private   K   Caledonia

SHERMAN, W. T.   C
    Buried at National Cemetery at Beaufort, S.C.
    Section 20   Grave #64
SHIMSON, Aaron   Private   St. Louis
SHINDLER, A.   Private   D
    Buried at Mississippi River National Cemetery
    Memphis, Tn. Section 1 Grave #64
SHINDLER, Ollis   Private   F   Cannan
    Buried at Belle Island, Virginia National Cemetery
    Died 12-13-1863
SHIRLEY, Andrew J.   Corporal   C   Hopewell
    Wounded in Shoulder, Battle of Chickasaw Bayou, MS
SHIRLEY, Thomas J   Private   C   Hopewell
SHIERDIENG, Herman   Private   G   Dutzow
SHOCKLEY, William L.   Corporal   F   Canaan
    (SCHOCKLEY?)
        Died on Hospital Boat- John J. Roe from wounds
        received at Battle of Chickasaw Bayou, MS
        Buried at Jefferson Barracks, Mo. National Cemetery
        Section 6 Grave #24   5-13-1863
SHOEMAKER, Daniel   Private   F   Canaan
SHOOKMAN, William M.   Private   B   Ironton
    Missing/Died while Prisoner at Battle of
    Chickasaw Bayou, MS
SHUTZ, John   Private   A   Victoria
SIMMERMAN, Henry L.   Private   B   Pilot Knob
SIMMERMAN, Henry L.   Private   K   Ironton
SIMON, Emil   Corporal   G   Dutzow
SIMPSON, Edward   Private   C   Hopewell
SIMPSON, George   Private   B Washington Co.
SIMPSON, Samuel P.   Lieutenant Colonel
    Wounded in left side at Battle of Chickasaw Bayou, MS
SINGER, William P.   2nd Lieutenant   K   Potosi
SILES, Elijah   Private   E   Moselle
SITTON, Nicholas B.   Corporal   F   Canaan
SKAGGS, Joham   Private   E   Moselle
SKEGGS, I. E.   Private   E   Moselle
SKINNER, James   Private   I Montgomery Co.
SLOAN, Thomas   Private   I Sulpher Springs
SMALL, George W.   Private   C   Hopewell
SMELSER, Rueben W.   Private   D   Greenville
SMITH, Benjamin F.   Private   B Washington Co.

SMITH, Daniel W.	Private	C	Hopewell
SMITH, Fielding Jenkins	Private	F	Canaan
SMITH, Harland M.	Private	F	Canaan
SMITH, Hiriam T.	Private	C	Hopewell
SMITH, Isaac A.	Private	D	Greenville
SMITH, Jacob	Private	A	Victoria
SMITH, James	Private	B	Ironton

Wounded in shoulder, Battle of Chickasaw Bayou, MS

SMITH, Johiel B.	2nd Lieutenant		
SMITH, John E.	Private	F	Canaan
SMITH, John W.	Corporal	D	Greenville
SMITH, Michael	Private	C	Hopewell
SMITH, William	Private	I	St. Louis
SNYDER, Theodore M.	3rd Sergeant	F	Franklin Co.

Wounded in right hip at Vicksburg, MS

SPAIN, George W.	Private	F	Canaan
SPARKS, Aquila V.	Private	B	Ironton
SPARKS, William	Private	E	Moselle
SPAULDING, William	Private	F	Canaan
SPEAKS, Robert	Private	E	Moselle
SPEAR, Elijah H.	Private	F	Canaan
SPENCER, James	Private	K	Patterson
SPENCER, James A.	Private	B	St. Louis
SPENCER, Putnam	Private		St. Louis
STACKWELL, Thomas	Private	B	St. Louis
STAGGS, Hiram T.	Private	C	Greenville

Buried at Jefferson Barracks, Mo. National Cemetery
Section 25 Grave #17, 12-23-1862

STAPLES, Benjamin F.	Private	B Washington Co.
STAPLES, George W.	Private	B Washington Co.
STAPLES, James D.	Private	B Washington Co.

Buried at Jefferson Barracks, MO National Cemetery
Section 39 Grave #250, Died 3-26-1863

STAPLES, James M.	Private	B
	Carondelet	

Buried at Mississippi River National Cemetery
Memphis, Tn. Section 1 Grave #39 4-3-1863

STAPLES, Samuel O.	Corporal	Bwashington Co.
STAPP, Henry H.	Corporal	C	Hopewell
STARTZEL, George	Private	A	Victoria

Wounded at Battle of Chickasaw Bayou, MS

STATLER, Aaron	Private	D	St. Louis

STATON, William N.	Private	I	St. Louis
STEPHENS, Elijah	Private		St. Louis
STEPHENS, George B.	Private	E	Cuba
STEPHENS, Joseph L.	Sergeant		Potosi

Died in 1863 while in Hands of the Enemy

STEPHENS, William	Private		St. Louis
STERLING, Austin W.	Private	E	Moselle
STEVENS, James W.	Private	B	Washington,Co.
STEVENS, Milton	Private		St. Louis
STEWART, Jesse	Private	D	Greenville

Missing at Battle of Chickasaw Bayou, MS

| STEWART, Nathan | Private | D | Greenville |
| STITES, John | Sergeant | F | Canaan |

Killed at Battle of Chickasaw Bayou, MS   12-29-1862
Buried Vicksburg Ms. National Cemetery
Section G Grave #1084

| STILL, John | Private | F | Canaan |
| STILL, William | Private | K | Willsburg |

Wounded in Back   Jefferson Barracks Mo.
National Cemetery, Section 34 Grave #242
Died 11-4-1864

STINSON, Oran H.	Private		St. Louis
STIRZEL, Richard	Private	K	Desoto
STOCK, John C. S.	Private	B	St. Louis
STOCKTON, Samuel K.	Private	D	Greenville
STODART, M.	Private	E	

Mississippi River National Cemetery Memphis, Tn.
Section 1 Grave #73   3-4-1863

STODDARD, Sylvester B.	Private	I	St. Louis
STONE, Oliver H. P.	Assistant Surgeon		
STONE, Walter R.	Sergeant	B	St. Louis
STONEY, Joseph	Private	C	Hopewell
STRAIN, George W.	Private	F	Canaan

Wounded in Arm at Battle of Chickasaw Bayou, MS

STRAIN, Tipton B.	Private	F	Canaan
STROTHER, Churchill G.	Surgeon		Warrenton
STROUP, Louis	Private	A	Victoria
STROUP, Washington	Private	D	Greenville
STUDDARD, James W.	Private	E	Hillsboroo
STUDER, John	Private	G	St. Louis
STUMP, Gideon	Private	K	Canaan

Died of Wounds at Battle of Arkansas Post, Ark

STUTZMAN, John   Private G Dutzow
  Buried at Vicksburg Ms. National Cemetery
  Section C Grave #312 3-26-1863
SULLIVAN, John B.   Private D Greenville
  Mississippi River National Cemetery Memphis, Tn.
  Section 1 Grave #30 4-19-1863
SULLIVAN, Patrick K. Private E St. Louis
  Severly Wounded at the Battle of Ringgold Gap, GA
SULLIVAN, ZENOS F. Private H Wayne County
SUTHERLIN, Charles Corporal D Greenville
SUTHERLIN, William H. Private D Greenville
SUTTON, Jesse   Private A Victoria
SWANDER, R. M. Regimental Adjutant St. Louis
SWEENEY, John   Private K St. Louis
SWEENEY, John   Private I St. Louis
SWINNEY, George W. Corporal D Greenville
SWINNEY, John W. Private D Greenville
TARWATER, Adam   Private H Wayne County
TATE, George M.   Private E Moselle
TAYLOR, B.F. 2nd Lieutenant G
TAYLOR, John W.   Private I Sulpher Spring
TAYLOR, Preston J. Corporal E Moselle
TENNYSON, Solomon R. Sergeant K Caledonia
  Died of Wounds received at Battle of Chickasaw Bayou, MS
TESSON, William   Private K Danville
TEYTON, Bailey   Corporal D Greenville
THEODUSKY, Benon W. Private A Victoria
THOMAS, Emile F. 2nd Lieutenant St. Louis
THOMAS, James C. Sergeant D Greenville
  Killed at the Battle of Dallas, GA May 28, 1864
THOMAS, Pleasant V. Corporal D Greenville
THOMAS, William   Private K
THOMPSON, John   Private F Canaan
THOMPSON, Larkin Sergeant I Danville
  Wounded, Shot in Abdomen.
THORNHILL, William J. Private A St. Louis
THURMAN, Alfred   Private E Moselle
THURMAN, James   Private K Caledonia
TILLEY, Martin   Private E Moselle
  Buried at Jefferson Barracks, Mo. National Cemetery
  Section 24 Grave #27 11-9-1862
TILLEY, Richard   Private H Caledonia

TINKER, Thomas	Private	K	Potosi
TIPSON, W. B.	Private	H	
TIPTON, Nathaniel	Private	C	Hopewell
TOBIN, Michael	Musician	B	St. Louis
TOETTMAN, William	Corporal	G	Carondelet
TOFT, Jans	Private	G	Dutzow
TRIMBEL, Henry C.	Corporal	B	St. Louis
TUCKER, David W.	Private	A	Victoria
TULLEY, Ferl	Private	B	Montgomery
TURNER, Daniel W.	Private	F	Canaan
TURNER, Richard T.	Private	K	Potosi
TWEEHAUS, Henry	Private	G	Washington
TYLER, Burgen F.	2nd Lieutenant	H	Wayne County
UCKERMAN, Adolph	Private	G	Dutzow

Prisoner in Jackson, MS, Retaken May 17, 1863

VALLEY, Peter	Private	B	Washington Co.
VAUGHN, Elijah	Private	D	Greenville

Buried atJefferson Barracks Mo. National Cemetery.
Section 32 Grave # 79   10-3-1863

VAUGHN, James A.	Private	F	Canaan

Wounded at Battle of Chickasaw Bayou, MS

VAUGHN, Jeremiah	Private	D	Greenville
VAUGHN, Richard T.	Private	C	Hopewell
VAUGHN, Samuel	Private	C	Hopewell
VAUGHN, William R.	2nd Lieutenant	F	Canaan
VEACH, Richard	Private	B	Washington Co.
VEST, Joshua	Private	E	Moselle
VILLIAMIER, Charles H.	Private	C	Hopewell

Wounded at Battle of Chickasaw Bayou, MS

VINYARD, Alexander	Private	B	Washington Co.
WAHL, Henry	Private	G	St. Louis
WALKER, Benjamin C.	Private	H	Wayne County
WALKER, John J.	Private	H	Wayne County

Jefferson Barracks Mo. National Cemetery.
Section 5 Grave # 29   4-28-1863

WALLACE, Benjamin R.	Private	A	Victoria
WALLACE, James W.	Private	A	Victoria
WALLER, Thomas J.	Private	D	Patterson
WALLS, George Spencer	Private	E	Moselle
WALTER, Aaron	Private		St. Louis
WALTER, August	Drummer	G	St. Louis
WALTHER, Frederick	Private	I	Hillsboro

WALTERS, Thomas J.   Private   D   Greenville
WARD, Adam S.   Private   G   Montgomery
WARD, Charles D.   Private   E   Moselle
    Buried at Vicksburg Ms. National Cemetery
      Section G   Grave #1284   7-18-1863
WARD, Michael   Private   B   St.Louis
WARD, Rainey   Private   H   Wayne County
    Died at Jackson,MS in Hands of Enemy
WARDEN, Charles   Private   F   Canaan
    Wounded in hand & hip, Battle Chickasaw Bayou, MS
WARE, Henry B.   Private   A
WARMACK, George   Private   D   Patterson
WARMACK, Matthew   Private   D   Patterson
WASHBURNE, Samuel   Private   A   Victoria
    Wounded slightly at Battle of Jonesboro, GA
WEBBER, John F.   1st Lieutenant   A   Victoria
WEILER, George   Private   G   St. Louis
WEIMAN, Fred   Private   G
WEISBROD, Francis   Private   A   Victoria
    Died of Disease While a Prisoner
WELLENKAMP, Conrad   Private   G   Washington
WELLER, Joseph   Private   I   Adams County
WESTOVER, John D.   Private   D   Patterson
WELTER, Nicholas   Private   G   Camp Fletcher
WHALEY, Adolphus   Private   C   Hopewell
WHEAT, Martin   Private   F   CanaanMo
WHEELER, John B. W.   Private   D   Greenville
    Mississippi River National Cemetery Memphis, Tn.
      Section 1 Grave #63
WHITE, Alexander   Private   H   Wayne County
WHITE, Andrew   Private   C   Hopewell
WHITE, Henry   Corporal   H   Wayne County
WHITE, Luke   Private   H   Wayne County
WHITE, James A.   Private   A   Victoria
    Wounded in neck at Battle of Chickasaw Bayou, MS
WHITE, John   Private   B   St. Louis
WHITE, John   Private   K   Caledonia
    Killed at the Battle of Haynes Bluff, MS
WHITE, William P.   Private   H   Wayne County
WHITMIRE, Jacob F.   Private   E   Moselle
WHITMIRE, William A. W.   Corporal   E   Moselle
WIDEMAN, Jacob   Private   E   Hillsboro

WIDEMAN, James A.	Private	A	Victoria
WIDEMAN, Mark	Private	A	Victoria

Killed in Action near Atlanta,GA buried at
Marietta & Atlanta National Cemetery, Ga.
Section H Grave #810   8-6-1864

WIEDEY, William	Private	I	St. Charles
WIEMAN, George F.	Private	G	Washington
WIGGER, Sidney	Private	C	Hopewell
WILEY, Sampson	Private	A	
WILEY, William W.	Corporal	C	Hopewell
WILLCHECK, Franklin	Private	F	Canaan
WILLIAMS, Andrew I.	Private	D	Greenville
WILLIAMS, Austin	Private	A	Victoria
WILLIAMS, Ezekial	Private	B	St Louis
WILLIAMS, Forklin	Private	A	Carondelet
WILLIAMS, Hiram	Private	A	Victoria
WILLIAMS, Jacob N.	Private	D	Greenville
WILLIAMS, John	Private	A	Victoria
WILLIAMS, John	2nd Lieutenant	A	Victoria

Wounded at Battle of Chickasaw Bayou, MS

WILLIAMS, John N.	Private	A	Victoria

Missing in Action 11-27-1863 Died while P.O.W.

WILLIAMS, Jonathon C.	Private	D	Greenville
WILLIAMS, Landon S.	Private	A	Victoria

Wounded at Battle of Chickasaw Bayou, MS

WILLIAMS, Peter H.	Private	A	Victoria
WILLIAMS, Thomas L.	Private	K	Ironton
WILLIAMS, Thomas L.	Private	A	Victoria
WILLIAMS, Washington	Private	A	Victoria
WILLIAMS, William H.	Private	D	Greenvill

Marietta & Atlanta National Cemetery in Ga.
Section G Grave #1513   7-26-1864

WILLMORE, Simpson	Private	H	Wayne County
WILLS, David	Private	H	Wayne County
WILSON, Andrew J.	Private	E	Moselle
WILSON, James	Private	D	Greenville
WILSON, John	Private	F	Canaan
WILSON, John B.	Private	E	Moselle
WILSON, W. I.(J)	Corporal	E	Cuba

Wounded in the face at Chickasaw Bayou, MS

WILSON, William	Private	B	Patterson
WINTERBERG, Hermann	Private	G	Washington

WITHROW, Charles	Private	C	Hopewell

Wounded in brow, slight, June 28, 1864

WITT, Joshua	Private	E	Moselle
WITT, William	Private	E	Moselle
WOOD, George C.	Private	D	Greenville
WOOD, William C.	Private	D	Greenville
WOOD, William H.	Private	D	Greenville
WOODS, Andrew J.	Private	C	Hopewell
WOODS, William H.	Private	K	Ironton
WOOLARD, John A.	Private	H	Wayne County

Wounded at Battle of Chickasaw Bayou,MS

WORTHAM, David S.	Private	C	Hopewell
WORTHAM, Jame R.	Private	C	Hopewell
WORTHAM, Robert A.	Private	C	Hopewell
WRANA, Pascal Pavlid	Private	I	St. Charles
WRIGHT, Christopher C.	Private	D	Greenville
WRIGHT, Harvey C.	Private	I	Carondelet
WRIGHT, John W.	Private	E	Moselle
WRIGHT, Samuel H.	1st Lieutenant	H	Charleston
WRIGHT, Smith C.	Private	H	Wayne County

Mississippi River National Cemetery Memphis, Tn
Section 1 Grave #322   6-27-1863

WRIGHT, T.H.	Commisary Sergeant	
WUNDERLICH, F.W.	Assistant Surgeon	
YATES, Elias	Private	K	Potosi
YAWBACH, Henry	Private	G	Dutzow
YOUNG, Benjamin F.	3rd Corporal	A	Wounded

At Chickasaw Bayou,MS never heard from again
Was on way home on Hospital Ship John J. Roe

YOUNG, Esquire	Private	E	Moselle
YOUNG, Francis M.	Private	D	Victoria
YOUNG, Jesse	Private	E	Moselle
YOUNG, Samuel	Private	E	Moselle
YOUNGER, Maurice	Private	G	Carondelet
YOUNT, David	Private	C	Hopewell
ZALE. R. G.	Private	G	
ZERMAN, Augustus	2nd Lieutenant		St. Louis
ZGOZALI, Bartch	Private	G	Marthasville

APPENDIX C: ROLL OF THE CONSOLIDATED BATTALION

CONSOLIDATED BATTALION OF THE 31ST AND 32ND REGIMENTS MISSOURI INFANTRY VOLUNTEERS NOVEMBER 9,1864.

The 31st Missouri Infantry was divided up into three companies. They made up Company A, B and C.

The following were the officers in these companies.

COMPANY A: Captain W. H. Judd;
    1st Lieutenant David H. Middendorf
COMPANY B: Captain William Burch;
    1st Lieutenant John W. Wilson
COMPANY C: Captain Matthias Neuner;
    1st Lieutenant John Burrows

The 32nd Missouri Infantry was divided up into three companies. They made up Company D, E and F.

The following were the officers in these companies.

COMPANY D: Captain John A. McArthur;
    1st Lieutenant William H. Lynch
COMPANY E: Captain Robert M. Askin;
    1st Lieutenant Beverly A. Davis
COMPANY F: Captain Andy B. Freece;
    1st Lieutenant Charles G. Warner

The Field and Staff for this Battalion are:
Lieutenant Colonel Samuel P. Simpson (31st Missouri)
Major Abraham J. Seay (32nd Missouri)
Surgeon Thomas J. Watson (32nd Missouri)
Assistant Surgeon Addison Elston (31st Missouri)
Regimental Quartermaster 1st Lieutenant William H.
    Barlow(31st Missouri)

COMPANY A

ADAMS, James	Private, Regimental Teamster
CALVIN, John	Private, Regimental Forager
CHAZELL, Charles	Private, Ambulance Driver
CLARK, Robert	Private, Teamster 15th Army Corps Hdqtrs.

FOLEY, Michael	Private, Teamster 15th Army Corps Hdqtrs.
GARRIN, James	Private, Pioneer 15th Army Corps Hdqtrs.
HAMILTON, James	Private, Detached Service Hdqtrs 1st Div.
MOORE, William R.	Private, Detached Service Pioneer Corps 1st Div.
MURPHEY, William H.	1st Sergeant, Detached Service 15th Army Corps
OSBORN, William T.	Private, Regimental Forager
ADAMS, James	Private
ADAMS, John J.	Private
AIMLY, Joseph	Private
ANDERSON, Andrew C.	Private
ARNOLD, John W.	Private
AUSTIN, Hari	Private
BARGER, Jacob S.	Private
BOYD, Robert	Private
BROWN, Jacob H.	Corporal
CAIN, John J. G.	Private
CARROLL, William	Private
CIMBREL, John	Private
CUTHBERTSON, ? J.	Private
DAVIS, Andrew J.	Private
DALE, John M.	Private, Absent at Jeffersonville, Ind. WIA
DAVIS, Daniel S.	Private
DAVIS, William J.	Private
DEVINE, Leander L.	Private
DODSON, William I.	Private
DRINNING, James	Private
EVANS, William M.	Sergeant
FINCADE, Charles F.	Private
FISHER, William P.	Private
FRANKLIN, John W.	Private
GREEN, Joseph M.	2nd Corporal
GRIFFIN, Jefferson	Sergeant
HAINS, Richard	Private
HENSON, William R.	Private
HIBLER, William J.	2nd Sergeant
HICKS, Thomas	Corporal

HOLLANDSWORTH, E. G.	Private
HOLLANDSWORTH, J. V.	Private
HOLLANDSWORTH, W. W.	Private
HOPPER, Adam	Private
HOSSELL, Jesse	Private
JACKSON, James H.	Private
JAMISON, George	Private
JASPER, Charles	Private
JARVIS, Eugenus	Private
JARVIS, John	Private
LANHAM, James M.	Private
LEACH, James	Private
LUTHERLIN, Charles	3rd Sergeant
McCROSSIN, George	Private
MALLOY, John T.	2nd Sergeant
MEREDITH, John J.	Private
MURPHEY, William A.	Private
ORR, William J.	Private
OSBORNE, William H.	Private
PALMER, Joseph	Private
PALMERSTON, Voluntine T.	Private
PATTON, John D.	Private
PENN, Joseph	Private
PERCY, Isaiah	Private, In Hospital Nashville, TN WIA
PEYTON, Bailie	1st Sergeant
PUTNAM, Spencer	Private
REED, Solomon	Private
RIVERSMITH,William	Private
ROWLAND, James	1st Corporal
SITTON, Nicholas B.	Private
SMELSER, Paulser W.	Private
SMITH, Fielding Jenkins	Private
SPAIN, George W.	Private
STEPHENS, George B.	Private
STEPHENS, Milton	Private
STILL, William	Private
STITZEL, Richard	Private
SULLIVAN, Patrick	Private
TAYLOR, Presley I.	Corporal
THURMON, James	Private
TILLEY, Richard	Private

WALLS, George I.	Private
WHEAT, Martin	Private
WHEELER, John B. W.	Private
WILLIAMS, Jonathon C.	Private
WILSON, John	Private
WITT, William	Private
WOOD, George	Private
WOOLCHECK, Frank	Private
YOUNG, Benjamin F.	3rd Corporal

COMPANY B

ATCHINSON, Willis	Private, Detached Service 1st Division Train
BROWN, Jacob H.	Private, Regimental Forager
CUSTER, Isaac N.	Private, Detached Service 15th Corps Hdqtrs
DODGE, George	Private, Teamster 1st Division 15th Army Corps
HORINE, Thomas T.	Sergeant, Regimental Colorbearer (31st Mo)
LYON, Peter H.	Private, Detached Service 1st Division Train
REEVES, Joseph	Wagoneer, Detached Service 15th Army Corps Hdqtrs
SIMMERMAN, Henry L.	Private, Detached Service 15th Army Corps Hdqtrs
SMITH, Benjamin F.	Private, Detached Service Hospital Marietta, GA
SMITH, Michael	Private, Detached Service 1st Division Train
McKENNA, Paddy	Private, Company Cook
AKE, Jacob F.	Private
BELEW, Frederick G.	Private
BOAS, William H.	Private
BONE, Frank	Private
BOYER, Firman	Private
BRECKENRIDGE, John C	1st Corporal
BREWSTER, Edward	Drummer
BRIDGER, Frederick G.	Private

BRUNK, James F.	3rd Sergeant
CAMPBELL, Joseph B.	Private
CHATMAN, Jasper, N.	Corporal
CHAYELL, Charles	Private
CLEMENTS, William	Private
CONNELLY, James	Private
CONWAY, Thomas H.	Private
COSGRIFF, James	Private
CRAIGG, Robbert	Private
DAVIS, John A.	Corporal
DEARING, William	Private
DODSON, Herman M.	Private
ELLIS, Thomas C.	Private
ESTES, Jesse E.	Private
FORSHEE, Valentine	Private
GLOONE, Jesse M.	Private
GREEN, Lewellyn	Private
GREEN, Uriah	5th Sergeant
GREENSTREET, Alfred	Private
GREENSTREET, David	Private
HAUPTMAN, Wesley	Private
HILL, Benjamin F.	Private
HILL, William L.	Private
HOGGETT, James H.	Private
HORINE, Thomas T.	4th Sergeant
IRVIN, Aquila J.	1st Sergeant
JACKSON, Allen J.	Private
JACKSON, Richard H.	Private
JACKSON, Thomas N.	Private
JOLIET, James	Private
KAIN, Patrick	Private
LACHANE, John	Private
McALLISTER, James	Private
McLANE, Jackson	Private
McKENNA, Patrick	Private
MABRY, James R.	2nd Sergeant
MABRY, Phillipp P.	1st Sergeant
MILLER, James	Private
MITCHELL,William H.	1st Sergeant Absent at Irondale, Mo WIA
NICHOLS, Joseph A.	3rd Sergeant
NOLEN, Peter	Private

NOTHINGTON, Henry K.	Private
PAUL, Thomas	Private
PENNELL, William	3rd Corporal
PORCH, Joseph	Private
RICHARDSON,William	2nd Corporal
RODRIQUE, John J.	Private
SEACRESE, Andrew I.	Private
SCOTT, John W.	Private
SELF, Thomas B.	Private
SMITH, James	Private
SPARKS, Aquila	Private
STAPLES, Benjamin F.	Private
SULLIVAN, Zenas F.	Private
VILLIAMIER, Charle H.	Private
WILLMORE, Simpson	Private
WILLS, David	Private
WITHROW, Charles	Private
WORTHEM, David S.	Private
WORTHEM, James K.	Private
WORTHEM, Robert A.	Private

COMPANY C

ALEXANDER, William	1st Corporal, Detached Service 1st Division 15th A.C.
BRUNS, Herman	Private, Nurse in Hospital
CLARK, John T.	Private, Detached Service Saint Louis, Mo.
CROSS, E. R.	Private, Regimental Forager
CULTON, George	Private , Regimental Wagon Master
HARDY, Richard S.	Private, Detached Service Hdqtrs 1st Division
HESSER, James P.	Corporal, Detached Service 15th Army Corps Hdqtrs
HUSKEY, William M.	Private, Detached Service at Headquarters
KLINGELHOPER, Louis	Private, Detached Service 1st Division

WEILEY, George	Private, Colonels Orderly
BECK, Paul	Fifer
BERNHARD, Jasper	Private
BLAKE, Joseph E.	Private
BOEDEKER, Henry A.	Private
BONE, Charles	Private
BONES, Lewis D.	Private
BORRING, John	Private
BROOKS, John W.	Private
BROWN, George	Private
BRUNCE, Herman	Private
BUSHMEYER, Freid	Private
CONGER, James	2nd Sergeant
COWAN, William W.	Private
CRINNIAN, Patrick	Private
CROSS, Edward P.	Private
CROTTO, Philip	Private
CULTON, George	Wagoneer
CULTON, Hart	Private
DEGEL, Christian	Private
DRUS, John	Private
FAITH, Adolph	Private
FINKE, Henry	2nd Sergeant
FISHER, George W.	Private
FRITZE, George	4th Sergeant
GERDEL, John	Private
GERDEL, Nicolaus	Private
GINN, James W.	3rd Corporal
GOWAN, Reason	Private
GREENWALD, Joseph	Private
HAUSNER, Paul	Private
HAVERSTICK, Philip R.	Corporal
HILL, James W.	Private
HIRT, Elias	Private
HOARD, Horace	3rd Sergeant
HOLTHAUS, Henry	Private
HOMFELD, Diedrich	Private
HUGHES, Thomas	Private
HUSKEY, John S.	Private
IRVIN, William S.	Private
JUNGER, Marion	Private
KEADING, John	Private

KELLER, Francis	Private
KELLERHALE, Joseph	Private
KLIEN, John N.	Corporal
KLINGEMANN, Fred	Private
KOPP, Charles	Private
KUCK, Henry	Corporal
KUEN, Daniel	Private
KUHNER, Albert	Private
KUNTZE, William	Corporal
LANHAM, Berry H.	Private
LANHAM, John	Private
LOESHMANN, Ehrhardt	Private
McKEE, William S.	2nd Corporal
MAXWELL, Gambell	Private
MEDLOCK, Henry	Private
METZ, Jacob	Private
MEYER, Berhard	Private
MEYER, Henry	Private
MEYER, Henry	Private
MEYER, Thomas	Private
MILLER, Benjamin N.	Private
MILLER, Louis H.	2nd Sergeant
MOFFREY, Christian	Corporal
NEILOUR, George Henry	Private
NEUNOBEL, John	Private
NIEDERHOLTMEYER, Frank	Private
PARMLEY, Robert	Private
POWERS, John C.	Private
PREWITT, John W.	Private
PRIESTER, George	Private
RAUSS, Hugo	3rd Sergeant
REYNOLDS, John B.	Corporal
REED, Thomas H.	Private
RICHARDSON, Robert	Corporal
RODENBERG, Frederick	Private
SCHAUB, Francis	Private
SCHWARTZE, Elias	Private
SESSLER, John	Private
SHULTZ, John	Private
SIMON, Emiel	Corporal
SMITH, Jacob	Private
SKAGGS, John	Private

STATZEL, George	Private
STUDER, John	Corporal
SWEENEY, John	1st Sergeant
TAYLOR, John W.	Private
THORNHILL, William	Private
TWIEHAUS, Henry	Private
WALECE, James W.	Private
WALTHER, Frederick	Private
WEIDEY, William	Private
WEILER, George	Private
WELLENKAMP, Conrad	Corporal
WELLER, Joseph	Private
WILLIAMS, Peter	Private
WILLIAMS, Washington	Private

COMPANY D

ANGUS, Andrew I.	Private
BEER, James	Private
BOYAN, Stephen	Private
BRITTON, Ashley	Private
BYRON, John M.	Private
CAMPBELL, Richard	Private ,Company Cook
CLARK, William	Private, Regimental Teamster
COLE, William	Private
COURT, Wiliam	Private
DENNIS, John	Private
DOLL, Mathias	Private
DOTY, Edward	Private
FARRAR, Thomas F.	Private
GILMORE, John	Private, Ambulance Corps
GRAVENS, Andrew J.	Private
GRIFFIN, Patrick	Private
GUINON, Thomas	Private
HAINES, John	Private
HALL, Eaton	Private
HOLDCROM, Jordon	Private
LEACH, Edwin	Private
LUNSFORD, Hyrum	Private
McCLELLEN, James	Private

McINTIRE, John	Private
MILLER, Luke	Private
MORTON, Charles	Private
MURRAY, Bennett	Private
POUNDS, Basil	Private
POUNDS, Isaac	Private
RICHARDSON, John W.	Private
SERGEANT, Widon	Private
SPENCER, James	Private
STOUT, Solomon	Private
SUMFORD, Hiram	Private
SUTHERLAND, Benjamin	Private
TERRY, Thomas F.	Private
TOLTON, John I.	Private
WHITE, Joseph	Private
WOLF, Fred	Private
WHITEHEAD, Joseph	Private

COMPANY E

JONES, Woodford	Private Company Cook
OGLE, Perry	Sergeant Regimental Colorbearer (32nd Mo)
ARNOLD, Henry M.	Private
ARTHURS, John	Private
BARR, Jacob	Private
BLUM, David	Private
BRINSON, Thomas	Private
BRISTORY, Ashley	Private
BROWN, William	Private
COFFMAN, John B.	Private
COOK, Israel B.	Private
COOK, William	Private
COPENHAVEN, Martin S	Private
DAVIS, Thomas R.	Private
DUMBACH, John	Private
EBELER, Casper	Private
ELSEY, James H.	Private
FALTERS, Hoarce	Private
FRANKLIN, Isaac	Private

GASSLICK, Harmon	Private
GIBBON, James B.	Private
GIBSON, James R.	Private
GILES, MARK	Private
GRINNELL, William	Private
GUFFY, John	Private WIAat Bentonville, N.C.
HANKEY, Simon	Private
HENKY, Solomon	Private
HOBBS, Thomas H.	Private
HUMPHRIES, John D.	Private
KINSLOW, Isaac	Private
LEACH, Edwin	Private
LEEK, James	Private
LEGGETT, Robert	2nd Sergeant
LEVA, Chris T.	Private
McBEE, William P.	Private
McDONALD, John	Private
McINTYRE, James	Private
MARQUESS, James	Captain
MAY, James	Private
MAYBRY, ROBERT G.	Private
MAYFIELD, James	Private
MYERS, James	Private
OGLE, Benjamin	Private
PARKER, Samuel E.	Private
PERCY, George	Private
PERRON, Kent	2nd Corporal
POTT, William	Private
POWELL, George	2nd Lieutenant
PRUETT, William	Private
RICHARD, Henry	Private
ROMINS, Thomas J.	Private
RONEY, Thomas	Private
ROONEY, William	Private
SACHES, Charles	Private
SALYA, August	Private
SHELTON, James	Private
SHOEMATE, William	Private
SIMPSON, Napoleon B.	Private
WATERMAN, August	Private
WILLIAMS, Benjamin	Private
WILSON, Thomas	Private

WORKMAN, Henderson   Private

COMPANY F

LEONARD, Abner H.	Private Company Cook
ALDIN, Willard	Private
BANCHEE, Ambrose	Private
BERNARD, Louistian	Private
BROWNING, Joseph N.	Private
BURGHARDT, Henry J.	Sergeant
CARVER, Thomas J.	Private
CISSNOW, Charles A.	Sergeant
CLIFT, James	Private
CLOUNTS, Elb	Private (WIA)
CONNELLY, William	1st Lieutenant
DODD, Ennis	Private
ELLIOTT, David	Private
ELLIS, William	Private
FRANKLIN, Henry	Private
GALLOWAY, Jesse F.	Private
GORTNER, James	Private
HACKWORTH, George W.	Private
HAMILTON, James	Private
HANEY, Albert	Sergeant
HARDIN, James	Private
HARLY, Greenberry	Private
HAYWARD, Thomas E.	Private
HEFNER, Daniel	Private
HENSON, William L.	Private
HOGAN, George V.	Private
HOLT, David	Private
HUMPHREYS, John D.	Private(Shot in leg and Crippled)
ISBELL, Henderson	Private
JENKINS, William	Private
KELLY, Joseph	Private
KINWORTHY, George	Private
KIRTLEY, James	Private
LANE, Richard R.	Private
LEPP, Henry A.	Private
LIVINGSTON, Wesley	Private

McALLISTER, William	Private
McMULLLIN, Samuel E.	Private
MARTIN, Dabner	Private
MORRIS, James	Private
MURRAY, James S.	Private
PARRISH, Meredith L.	1st Sergeant
PATRICK, Daniel	Corporal
PATRICK, Levi	Private
PEASE, John A.	Wagoner
PELTS, William	Private
PELTS, Joseph P.	Private
PIGG,Mitchell	Private
PIRTLE, George W.	Private
PIRTLE, Lemon	Private
PITTS, Thomas	Private
PORTTE, John T.	Sergeant
PREMAN, Louis	Private
RANDAL, U. G.	1st Sergeant
REMFELDT, Henry	Private
RICE, John W.	Private
ROBERTSON, William W.	Private
ROBINSON, John C.	Private
ROGERS, Hiram C.	Corporal
ROYAL, Andrew	2nd Lieutenant
SHAW, George S.	Private
SITTON, Benjamin C.	Private
SMITH, Burton J.	Private
STEPHENS, Willis A.	Private
STONE, William W.	Sergeant
STRINGER, Alexander C.	Private
WINNEHAM, John	Private
VINCENT, John	Private
VINSON, Benjamin	Private

I'm placing the following men of the old companies of the 32nd Mo Infantry Regiment in the new companies of the Consolidated Battalion

31st and 32nd Mo Infantry Regiment.
Old Company G into the New Company E
Old Company I into the New Company F
Old Company K into the New Company F.

JANUARY 1,1864 REGISTER OF COMMISSIONED OFFICERS
ACTUALLY IN SERVICE OF

THE 31ST MISSOURI INFANTRY REGIMENT

TAKEN FROM THE DESCRIPTIVE ROLL OF JANUARY 1864

NAME	RANK	ACTIONS
FLETCHER, Thomas C.	COLONEL	Chickasaw Bayou
		WIA/POW
		Lookout Mountain
SIMPSON, Samuel Parsons	LT.COLONEL	Chickasaw Bayou
		WIA/Left side of head
Arkansas Post		Vicksburg
Lookout Mountain		Missionary Ridge
Pidgeon Mountain		
JAENSCH, Fredrick	MAJOR	Pea Ridge
		Chickasaw Bayou
		POW
		Vicksburg
STROTHER, Churchill G.	SURGEON	Chickasaw Bayou
HENDRICKSON, William	CHAPLAIN	
ALLEN, Edward E.	CAPTAIN	Chickasaw Bayou
		WIA/ Neck
		Vicksburg
HARRISON, Andrew Ashely	CAPTAIN	Mexican War
		Pea Ridge
		Chickasaw Bayou
		Vicksburg
HILL, Egbert Oswell	CAPTAIN	Vera Cruz
		City of Mexico
Chickasaw Bayou		Vicksburg
		WIA /Right Thigh
OSTERHORN, William	CAPTAIN	Carthridge
		Wilson Creek
Chickasaw Bayou		Vicksburg
		WIA/Left Shoulder
Lookout Mountain		Missionary Ridge
Pidgeon Mountain		

MAGUIRE, George A.   CAPTAIN   ADC to General Blair
                                       since Muster in
REED, John   CAPTAIN   Chickasaw Bayou
         Vicksburg   Lookout Mountain
         Missionary Ridge   Pidgeon Mountain
JUDD,William Henry   CAPTAIN   Chickasaw Bayou
                                       Vicksburg
                                       WIA/Right Arm
         Lookout Mountain   Pidgeon Mountain
         Missionary Ridge
         WIA/Right Thigh
BURCH, William   CAPTAIN   Chickasaw Bayou
         Arkansas Post   Vicksburg
         Lookout Mountain   Missionary Ridge
         Pidgeon Mountain
BARLOW,William Henry 1st LIEUTENANT   Quarter Master
MACLAY, Charles   1st LIEUTENANT   Chickasaw Bayou
                                       Arkansas Post
                                       Vicksburg
RENDERSHAUSEN,Frederick 1st LIEUTENANT Carthage
                                       Wilson Creek
         Chickasaw Bayou   Vicksburg
         Missionary Ridge   Pigeon Mountain
EVENDEN,Jonathon Wilson 1st LIEUTENANT
                                       Chickasaw Bayou
                                       Vicksburg
PRATT,William B. 1st LIEUTENANT ADJUTANT
                                       Chickasaw Bayou
                                       Arkansas Post
                                       Vicksburg
HENDRICKSON, James Franklin 1st LIEUTENANT
                                       Chickasaw Bayou
                                       Arkansas Post
DOHERTY, Roderick O. 1st LIEUTENANT   Vicksburg
                                       Lookout Mountain
                                       Missionary Ridge
                                       Pigeon Mountain
BURROWS,John   1st LIEUTENANT   Chickasaw Bayou
                                       Arkansas Post
                                       WIA/Left Arm
         Vicksburg   Lookout Mountain
         Pidgeon Mountain

HENTON, Franklin Davenport 1st LIEUTENANT
      Chickasaw Bayou   Arkansas Post
      Vicksburg   Lookout Mountain
      Pidgeon Mountain
MIDDENDORF,David Henry 1st LIEUTENANT Carthage
                         Arkansas Post
                         Vicksburg
MACLAY,Samuel Ralph   1st LIEUTENANT Chickasaw Bayou
      Vicksburg   Lookout Mountain
      Missionary Ridge   Pidgeon Mountain
SINGER, William F.   2nd LIEUTENANT Lookout Mountain
                         Missionary Ridge
                         Pidgeon Mountain

CASUALTIES OF COMMISSIONED OFFICERS
FROM SEPTEMBER 1862 THROUGH JANUARY 1 1864
TAKEN FROM DESCRIPTIVE ROLLS

NAME	RANK	DATE
	REASON	

RUGE, Julius   Assistant Surgeon   8-11-1863
      Resigned Special Order #8 Department of Tennessee
STONE, O.H.P.   Assistant Surgeon   4-4-1863
      Dismissed Special Order #103 War Department
      Dismissal to date 9-5-62
DOVER, Oscar   Captain Co. A   2-20-1863
      Resigned Special Order #51 Department of Tennessee
EVANS, William H.   Captain Co. C   8-10-1863
      Resigned Special Order #217 Department of Tennessee
McCREERY,George L   Captain Co. E   12-16-1863
      Resigned Special Order #81Headquarters
      Department of Missouri
McMARTY, James S.   Captain Co. H   8-8-1863
      Resigned Special Order #215 Department of Tennessee
HALE, Edward Jr.   Captain Co. I   1-25-1863
      Resigned Special Order #17 Department of Tennessee
DOHERTY, Francis   Captain Co. K   12-1-1863
      Died of wounds received at Pidgeon Mountain
      November 27,1863
SWANDER, Robert M. Captain Co. E
      Dismissed Sentence of Court Martial

Department of Missouri

DAVIDSON, Isaac M.   1st Lieutenant Co. D   12-11-1862
    Resigned Special Order #389 War Department
McDANIEL, James   1st Lieutenant Co. F   4-25-1863
    Dismissed Special Order #139 War Department
RUGE, Charles E.   1st Lieutenant Co.G   4-12-1863
    Resigned Special Order #71 Department of Tennessee
MABREY, Henry Y.   1st Lieutenant Co. H   8-10-1863
    Resigned Special Order #271 Department of Tennessee
ROBINSON, William   1st Lieutenant Co. I   5-22-1863
    Killed in Action at Siege of Vicksburg
WILLIAMS, John   2nd Lieutenant Co. A   6-19-1863
    Resigned Special Order #165 Department of Tennessee
BECKET, Henry C.   2nd Lieutenant Co. C   4-28-1863
    Resigned Special Order Department of Tennessee
DISMANG, James W.   2nd Lieutenant Co. D   1-15-1863
    Died of wounds received at Chickasaw Bayou,MS
BRIGGS, Augustus   2nd Lieutenant Co. E   2-10-1863
    Resigned Special Order #41 Department of Tennessee
VAUGHAN, William Riley 2nd Lieutenant Co. F   8-21-1863
    Resigned Special Order Department of Tennessee
FORCKE, Charles Adolph 2nd Lieutenant Co. G   8-10-1863
    Resigned Special Order #217 Department of Tennessee
TYLER, Burgen F.   2nd Lieutenant Co. H   7-8-1863
    Discharged Special Order #203 War Department
BURGESS, Jackson W   2nd Lieutenant Co. I   8-10-1863
    Resigned Special Order Department of Tennessee

APPENDIX E: FROM DIARY OF CAPTAIN WILLIAM H. LYNCH

NOVEMBER

	RECEIVED		PAID
1	Coffee Pot		2.50
7	To Washing		.15
8	To Washing		.20
10	Traife		6.15
11	Pants		2.00
10	1 Brush		1.00
10	1 pr. gloves		2.50
10	1 shirt		5.00
10	5 ?		4.00
10	4 Pr. socks		1.40
12	Trade		1.80
16	1 Knife		3.00
16	Trade		1.00
16	Vest		3.00
16	Trade		6.50
18	Tobacco		28.00
30		Amt.	47.45
			22.75
	Pct. Pvt. Lick		10.00
		amt.	32.75

THE VICKSBURG CAMPAYNE.
By J. W. Matthews, Private of Co., H.   32nd Mo. Vol. (Western
Historical Manuscript Collection at University of Missouri-Rolla)

In August Eighteen, and Sixty-two,
I volunteer'd as freeman do,
The Constitution to defend
Against the Rebel, Foe of Friend.

To Benton Barracks we did go,
And there remained, till it did snow.
'Twas in December –(Sixteenth day)
We Marched for Vicksburg far away.

On Sucker State we did embark,
And sailed South as would the Lark.
Down Mississippi, to Yazoo,
Where we found the Great Buggerboo.

We fought four days, and went away;
The Rebels say they gain'd the day.
Up the River, the Boatsman steer'd
With all the host volunteer'd.

Up Arkansas unto the Post,
Did Sherman lead this valent host.
'Twas here we pent the Rebels up,
And made them sip the bitter cup.

In January – Sixty Three,
Eleventh day as you may see,
We run them into rifle pits,
And there we give those Rebels fits.

Having filled our mission here,
We turn'd our course, and down did steer.
In sight of Vicksburg we did land;

All on Youngs Point to make a stand.

Here we remain'd the Winter through;
'Mid rain, and mud, and sickness too;
Of seven hundred men, we had
Two hundred left, as poor as shad.

'Twas on the second day of May,
From Millikens Bend we marched away.
Toward Grand Gulf, we made our pitch
They fought, and tried to hold their ditch;

But all in vain – they tried to run
And leave behind their heaviest Gun.
Here we remained about one day,
We left there on the Eight of May.

We steer'd our course for Johnson's band;
To whip, and drive them from our land.
'Twas on the Fourteenth day of May,
We fought them nearly all that day.

The muskets crak'd, and cannons roar'd,
While rain from Heaven in torrents roar'd,
Yet undismaye'd we proved the fight,
That we might enter town that night.

The Rebels ran, and we went in —-
Drank Rum and Brandy, Wine and Gin,
Some got Milk, and some got Honey.
Some got Clothes and some got Money.

The next fight was at Champion Hill,
Which was to Rebs a bitter pill.
They could not go to Vicksburg then,
For loss of Guns, and loss of men.

Old Pemberton, was left alone,
To hold Vicksburg while Johnson's gone.
'Twas on the eighteenth day of May;
In sight of Rebel works we lay.

Unflinching still we pressed them hard,
In talking distance of their Guard.
Our guns threw, thirteen inch shell;
Which made some sign, where e'er it fell.

They fixed their dens, and tried to hide;
Though shells flew thick from every side.
But after all, they had to eat;
In place of beef, they eat mule meat.

'Twas on the Fourth of July,
The celebration drawing nigh,
They stacked their arms, and Vicksburg fell,
And now at Vicksburg all is well.
              July, 1863

THE BIOGRAPHICAL SKETCHES ARE TAKEN FROM "GOODSPEED'S HISTORY OF FRANKLIN, JEFFERSON, WASHINGTON, CRAWFORD & GASCONADE COUNTIES, MISSOURI." Printed in 1888.

FRANKLIN COUNTY

ROBERT CRAIG, farmer and stock dealer of Township 45, is the son of John and Margaret W. (Barkley) Craig. The father came to the United States from Ireland about 1847 or 1848, and died here in 1851. The mother and children did not come until 1853. Mrs. Craig is still living, and is over eighty years of age. She furnished three sons for the Union army, and now draws a pension for the eldest, who died while in service. The second son was a lawyer, and at one time was assistant United States district attorney, at Memphis Tenn. He died about 1872. Robert was born in Ireland in 1840, and received but very meager educational advantages. In 1862 he enlisted in Company B, Thirty-first Missouri Infantry, was at Vicksburg and all through the Georgia and Atlanta campaigns, etc. He was in active service for nearly three years, and was discharged at St. Louis in 1865. December, 1871, he married Miss Caroline Custer, who died in 1883, leaving four children: Anna, William, Henry and Mary. In 1884 Mr. Craig married Mrs. Mary D. Schulte, who bore him one child, Maggie. She had four children by her first husband. Mr. Craig has made his home in Franklin County since 1853, and on his present farm since 1867. He owns about 325 acres, all the result of his own labor. He is a self-made man in every sense of the word, as he was obliged to make his own living in early childhood. He is a member of the G.A.R., and he and wife are members of the Methodist Episcopal Church.

THEODORE M. SNYDER, notary public, justice of the peace and land agent at Sullivan, Mo., was born in Allegany County, N.Y., May 31, 1834, and is the seventh of eleven children of Daniel and Catherine (Bowers) Snyder, who immigrated to Ohio when our subject was but nine years of age, and settled on a farm in Perry County. Theodore M. Snyder had limited educational advantages, and was reared to the occupation of farming. When seventeen years of age he began serving an apprenticeship to the carpenter's trade under his brother in Nelsonville, Ohio, and has worked more or less at his trade through life. January 21, 1856, he was married to Sophia J., daughter of John C. Hiles, a prominent farmer of Hocking County, Ohio. Of the seven children born to this union two are deceased. Those living are: Flora E. (wife of Joseph Pitts), Mary L. wife of Bennett W. Doyle), Dora J. (Wife of Ira Claspell), Anna V. (wife of John Junkerman), all living in Franklin County, Mo., following agricultural pursuits; a son, Ulysses T., is living with his father. Mr. Snyder owns his residence in Sullivan, and makes a good living out of his agency, notary and justice business. he is a Republican, and cast his first presidental vote for Fremont. During the late war he seved in the Union army, Thirty-first Missouri Infantry, as third sergeant; was wounded in the right hip at Vicksburg; was discharged for a time, but was again drafted in 1864, and served until after the close of the war. he is a member and commander of G.A.R. Post, No. 324, at Sullivan, and, with his wife, is a worthy member of the Methodist Episcopal Church South. Mr. Snyder immigrated to Missouri in 1859, followed farming and carpentering until 1882, when he engaged in his present business. He is also local land agent for the St. Louis & San Francisco Railroad Company at Sullivan, Mo.

C. THOMAS HORINE, of the firm of Thomas & Horine, attorney-at-law, at Hillsboro, is a native of that place, born in 1844. He was educated in the public schools, and at the age of fourteen received a position in the circuit clerk's office, which position he filled until about the age of eighteen, when he enlisted in Company A, Thirty-first Missouri Volunteer Infantry, under Col. (afterward Gov.) Fletcher, and took part in every engagement in which his command participated. He enlisted as a private, and was mustered out as lieutenant after twenty-eight months' service; participated in the siege of Vicksburg, Arkansas Post, Lookout Mountain, Missionary Ridge and the entire Georgia and Atlanta campaign. At Jonesboro, Ga., it was decided that a portion of the officers of the Thirty-first and Thirty-second Missouri Infantry, by reason of consolidation of the two regiments, should retire, and Mr. Horine was one of the three commisioners who were appointed by Gen. Howard to designate the officers who should or could retire. Our subject being one, returned home, and soon resumed his old position in the circuit clerk's office. In 1865 he was appointed by Gov. Fletcher to a position in the office of secretary of State. In the fall of 1866 he returned to the circuit clerk's office, but two years later retired, to give place to a cousin of the chief. He afterward served four years as deputy circuit clerk, under W.S. Boyce, and in 1874 was elected to the position of circuit clerk, which office he held for twelve years. In January, 1887, he entered as a partner with W.H.H. Thomas, in the law business, having been admitted to the bar about sixteen years previous to this. He was married July 6, 1865, to Miss Cerinda Shelton, a native of Jefferson County, Mo., and the daughter of John Shelton. Four children were the result of this union. Mr. Horine is a Democrat, and has frequently been a delegate to congressional and State conventions. He is a member of the Masonic fraternity, of the I.O.O.F., of the A.O.U.W., and he and his wife are members of the Baptist Church.

MAJOR JOHN T. CLARKE, well known for the past fourteen years as an efficient, capable and obliging book-keeper in the State Auditor's office, and for the past six and a half years chief clerk in that office, was born in Culpeper County, Va., at Stevensburg, March 20, 1843. James Clarke, his father, a native of Orange County, Va., was a soldier in the War of 1812, and died in 1854, leaving three children, of whom John T. is the eldest. A brother, James W., is a postmaster at De Soto, and a sister, Mary A., is now Mrs. A.J. Norwine. Mrs Clarke, whose maiden name was Elizabeth T. Murphy, was married a second time to Rev. James Keen (deceased). She is still a resident of Washington County. John T. received his education in the schools of Virginia and Missouri, attending during the sessions of 1858-59 and 1860-61 the State University, at Columbia. In July, 1861, he commenced to teach school, but soon discontinued it on account of the turbulent condition of the country. In August, 1862, convinced that the preservation of the Union was paramount to all other considerations, he enlisted as a private in the Thirty-first Regiment, Missouri Volunteer Infantry, under command of Thomas C. Fletcher, was attached to Frank P. Blair's brigade, and later came under command of Maj.-Gen. John A. Logan, being assigned to duty on the adjutant-general's staff. In September, 1864, he was transferred to Gen. Rosecrans' headquarters at St. Louis, where he served until honorably discharged July1, 1865. Upon returning home he was engaged in the drug business at Irondale for a time, and from the fall of 1866 until November 1870, served faithfully as deputy sheriff and collector of Wahington County; was then elected sheriff and collector, and among other duties performed during his official career was the execution of Jolly and Armstrong, elsewhere mentioned in this work. In 1873, upon expiration of his term, he entered the office of State auditor, as referred to above, where his subsequent career is too well known to need any additional words of empty comment. In the State campaign of 1884 he warmly supported the candidacy of Gov. John S. Marmaduke, who after his election, tendered him the office of commissioner of labor statistics. This offer was declined. Maj. Clarke belongs to that class of stalwart Union Democrats, who, passing through the dark days of war and reconstruction, never faltered or weakened in the faith. He was married December 10,1874 to Miss Sadie Bolton, a daughter of Dr. Bolton, of Cole County, Mo. They have two children, Bessie and Fletcher.

GASCONADE COUNTY

JUDGE WILLIAM TOEDTMANN, another sucessful farmer and stock-raiser of Richland Township, was born inLippe-Detmold, Germany, in 1831, and is the third of seven children born to Gottlieb and Mry (Siker) Toedtmann, who came to the United States about 1843, settling in Boulware Township, where the father took up a claim on Gasconade River, but one year later moved back to the valley, where he improved a good farm. He was a farmer and carpenter by occupation, and died in 1869, at the age of sixty-eight. The mother is still living on the old farm, and is about seventy-eight years old. William attended school in his native country until he came to the United States, when he attended the English schools for about four months. he assisted in improving the farm until August, 1862, when he enlisted in Company C, Thirty-first Missouri Volunteer Infantry, served in the Fifteenth Army Corps, operated in Missouri, Arkansas, Mississippi, Tennessee, Alabama, Kentucky and South Carolina, was in fourteen engagements, Chickasaw Bayou, Arkansas Post, through the siege of Vicksburg, Lookout Mountain, Missionary Ridge, Ringgold's Point, Resaca, and through the Georgia and Atlanta campaigns without being wounded or captured. He was mustered out of service at Nashville, Tenn., about May, 1865. He enlisted first as a private, but was immediately made corporal, and afterward sergeant. He then returned home, purchased his present farm of 160 acres, situated fifteen miles west of Hermann, and in 1867 married Miss Katie, daughter of George Meyer, a native of Pennsylvania, but one of the first settlers of

Gasconade County, where Mrs. Toedtmann was born. She died in 1868, and in 1870 our subject took for his second wife Miss Louisa Meyer, a native of Gasconade County, and the daughter of William Meyer. Of the nine children born to Judge Toedtmann and wife, only three are now living: Charlie, Lizzie and Hulda. Judge Toedtmann is extensively engaged in the breeding of short-horn cattle, and Berkshire and Suffolk hogs. The Judge is a prominent man in the conty. In 1878 he was elected county judge for the Ninth District, re-elected in 1880, and served four years with satisfaction. He was formerly a member of the school board, and is a public-spirited man. He was formerly a Republican in his political views, and his first presidential vote was for J.C. Fremont, in 1856. He is now a Democrat and a member of the Reformed Church.

THE FOLLOWING INFORMATION IS TAKEN FROM THE BRECKENRIDGE, CLARENCE EDWARD PAPERS 1897, 1960. THESE PAPERS ARE PART OF THE COLLECTION AT THE WESTERN HISTORICAL MANUSCRIPT COLLECTION AT THE UNIVERSITY OF MISSOURI-COLUMBIA, COLUMBIA, MISSOURI.

JOHN C. BRECKENRIDGE

In 1862 he enlisted in Company B, 31st Missouri Volunteers, Union Army. His first battle being December 29, 1862 at Vicksburg, known as Chickasaw Bayou. There he was taken prisoner, and was in jail at Vicksburg and Jackson Mississippi for about three months, then he was paroled and sent inside the Union lines at New Orleans, thence to St. Louis to await exchange. He rejoined his regiment in time to participate in the battles of Lookout Mountain, Missionary Ridge and Ringgold. He was also in the battles of Buzzards Roost, Resaca, Snake Creek Gap, Marietta, Peachtree Creek, Atlanta, July 22nd and 28th. On July 28th he was wounded at Atlanta. he was with Sherman on his "March to the Sea" and in all the battles around Savannah. He was in the battle at Columbia, South Carolina and Raleigh, North Carolina and marched through Richmond to Washington D.C. where he ws discharged in June 1865 and returned home. At Savannah, he received a commission as Lieutenant which may have been the coALmmission as Second Lieutenant of Company B, 31st and 32nd Regiment Consolidated Battalion, Missouri Volunteer Infantry U.S.A. effective date November 12, 1864 issued by Thomas C. Fletcher, Governor of Missouri.

THE FOLLOWING IS TAKEN FROM THE MISSOURI HISTORICAL SOCIETY IN SAINT LOUIS, MISSOURI. IT IS FOUND IN THEIR COLLECTIONS UNDER; SCHENK, JOHN, CAPTAIN: QUARTERMASTER LETTER-BOOK; RE. LETTER & ORDER BOOKS 1864 DECEMBER-1866 MAY. BOX 2 O2 2

1st Division,	Quartermaster Letter Book
15th Army Corps	RE Back Papers
Army of the Tennessee	1864 Mar 31-1870 Mar 9

On the 24th of May our division the leading Division of Maj. Gen. W. T. Shermans Army passed in Review before the President of the U.S. It was the last act in the rapid and wonderful drama of our Army. With Banners proudly flying: some of which were in 1862 unfurled at Pea Ridge in the far Southwest, Chickasaw Bayou, Arkansas Post, Port Gibson, Champion Hill, Black River Bridge, Vicksburg, etc. etc.

Ranks in close and magnificient array under the eye of our beloved chief, and amid the thundering plaudits of countless thousands of enthusiastic spectators. The noble army of 10,000 Veterans paid their marching salute to the President of the Nation they had helped to preserve in its integrity.

After the review was over our Division took up camp at Chrystal Springs, the following morning early I crossed my trains over the long bridge across the Potomac and parked my trains near our Division.

FOUND IN BOX 1 0F 2 IN THE SAME COLLECTION IS THE FOLLOWING

Page 9
21 Oct. 1863- In possesion of 31st Mo.

1 saddle Horse, 2 saddle Mules, 4 work horses, 46 work mules
7 government wagons, 1 2 horse wagon, 3 2 horse ambulances
2 Hospital tents, 14 wall tents & 50 common tents
                          Camp Cherokee, Al Oct 22/63
31st Mo. turned into Gen. Osterhaus
        1 government wagon and 6 mules

Page 50
31st Mo. received Invoice of Clothing, camp & gear equipage
Date of Transfer
Woodville, Ala Mar 27,64 Lt. W. H. Barlow, R.Q.M.